OKA HOLISSO

CHICKASAW & CHOCTAW WATER RESOURCE PLANNING GUIDE

Oka Holisso Hardcover ISBN: 978-1-952397-72-1
Oka Holisso Paperback ISBN: 978-1-952397-73-8

Principal Writer/Editor, Layout & Graphics
Brian R. Vance, Duane Smith & Associates

Editing/Writing/Research
Pennie Embry, Duane Smith & Associates

Mapping & Data
Frank Schalla & Justin Baker, Aqua Strategies, Inc.
Michael P. Sughru, Duane Smith & Associates

Developmental support for the Oka Holisso provided by the following members of the Chickasaw-Choctaw Regional Water Planning Team:

Aqua Strategies, Inc.
Barney Austin & Angela Kennedy

Chickasaw Nation
Kristopher Patton, Kara Berst, Stephen Greetham, Wayne Kellogg, Newakis Weber
Jennifer Bryant, Chaylum Hogue & Shane Jemison

Choctaw Nation of Oklahoma
Tye Baker, Ethan Schuth & Ahndria Duran-Ablett

Duane Smith & Associates
Duane A. Smith

Special thanks to the legal, cultural and historic preservation staff of the Chickasaw and Choctaw Nations for their thoughtful review and input.

Photographs courtesy of Flycatcher Photography, unless otherwise noted.

Cover Design: Gentry Chapman
Book Design: Hannah Simpson

Humankind has not woven the web of life.

We are but one thread within it.

Whatever we do to the web, we do to ourselves.

All things are bound together.

All things connect.

— Chief Seattle, 1854

Let us put our minds together and see

what life we can make for our children.

— Sitting Bull

Anyone who traveled up the Mississippi in 1100 CE would have seen it looming in the distance: a four-level earthen mound bigger than the Great Pyramid of Giza. Around it like echoes were as many as 120 smaller mounds, some topped by wooden palisades, which were in turn ringed by a network of irrigation and transportation canals; carefully located fields of maize; and hundreds of wooden homes with mud-and-straw plastered floors and high-peaked, deeply thatched roofs like those on traditional Japanese farms.

Located near the confluence of the Missouri, Illinois, and Mississippi Rivers, the Indian city of Cahokia was a busy port. Canoes flitted like humming birds across its waterfront: traders bringing copper and mother-of-pearl from faraway places; hunting parties bringing such rare treats as buffalo and elk; emissaries and soldiers in long vessels bristling with weaponry; workers ferrying wood from upstream for the ever hungry cookfires; the ubiquitous fishers with their nets and clubs.

— **Charles C. Mann**
1491: New Revelations of the Americas Before Columbus

Contents

Introduction

Before the Chickasaw and Choctaw were forcefully removed to Indian Territory, today known as Oklahoma, both tribal groups built homes and communities along rich bottomlands and ridges in the southeastern reaches of North America. There, our Chickasaw and Choctaw ancestors thrived.

Housing at least 15,000 people near present-day St. Louis, the Cahokia community was the biggest known concentration of people. Cahokia was the major city of the Mississippian culture, which some believe gave rise to several tribal nations, including Chickasaw and Choctaw.[1] Direct kinship between the Chickasaws and Choctaws goes back thousands of years, according to oral tradition and archaeology. Our language and culture are so similar that we today share a common heritage and cultural identity, which includes a fundamental connection to the land and its waters.

Water has always been an integral element of the Chickasaw and Choctaw identity. Both tribal nations share a migration story centering on the leadership of two siblings, Chiksa and Chahta. According to oral stories, the brothers and numerous followers traveled out of the west in search of a suitable and peaceful home provided by Aba Binili (the Creator). In a central turning point of the narrative, Chiksa and Chahta came to a great body of water, which we have interpreted today to be the Mississippi River. After crossing this prodigious threshold, the brothers parted ways, thus forming two distinct tribal nations that, while forever kin, would travel separate paths to an independent future.

Along with other prominent Indigenous nations in this historic homeland—including the Alabama, Biloxi, Cherokee, Chitimacha, Coushatta, Miccosukee, Muscogee, Seminole and Tunica—the early Chickasaws and Choctaws inhabited some of the most fertile land in North America. Later, in present-day Oklahoma, the Chickasaw and Choctaw Nations leveraged available land and water resources to establish agriculture, which supported both early communities and their burgeoning economies and trade. Sustainable practices, borne out of essential reverence for these resources, ensured a fruitful bounty each year and for subsequent generations.

Pursuant to a series of federal-tribal treaties, federal statutes and Supreme Court decisions that span more than 200 years and document their specific relationship with the United States, the Chickasaw Nation and Choctaw Nation of Oklahoma today occupy an area in Oklahoma containing a relative abundance of water resources that support diverse communities, cultures, economies and habitats. As sovereigns with rights and responsibilities relating to their citizenry and their territory, the Nations exercise their legal, cultural and moral position to sustainably manage the treaty homeland's water resources. This position was reinforced, and its future execution detailed, through the historic state-tribal water agreement reached in August 2016.

By rendering an accurate, science-based picture of water use and availability, this publication—the Nations' *Oka Holisso* (or "Book of Water")—serves as an initial decision-making tool in facilitating sensible implementation of the water agreement. While formal technical analyses may be required, *Oka Holisso* data provide valuable first-stage guidance on water use proposals, potential permits, or related water management projects within the settlement area, including the Nations' territories. Importantly, the *Oka Holisso* also assists in focusing current and future tribal initiatives, many of which will require the existence of readily available water sources and supplies. And it espouses the water planning doctrine of the two Nations, applied through ongoing development of the Nations' joint Chickasaw–Choctaw Regional Water Plan (CCRWP), initiated in 2011.

Guided by essential water-centric priorities for the region, the CCRWP underpins sound resource and practice assessments and the development of management strategies to support the ecological, cultural and economic health of the contemporary homeland. A commitment to supporting such health is the foundation for all planning activities. The Nations accordingly engage with governmental partners and other stakeholders in studies designed to address local and regional concerns and integrate a sustainability-based value system in the management of integral water resources, both today and long into the future.

While the *Oka Holisso* further shapes a process for the two Nations' engagement on water issues, it also serves as a valuable reference publication that provides detailed information on water use and availability. Furthermore, the *Oka Holisso* illustrates how sound management of the Nations' waters provides multi-value benefits surrounding economic development, ecological health and the very basic preservation of tribal cultural heritage. Sites and areas of significant economic value, especially those of cultural and historical significance or ecological importance, are also featured as are facilities that serve recreation, the region's third-largest industry that is a staple of local economies.

In addition to a regional overview, the *Oka Holisso* includes local assessments of water resources, supplies, and management in the Settlement Area based upon the thirty planning basins delineated in the agreement. In some instances, these basins—largely consistent with those utilized by the state in the *2012 Update of the Oklahoma Comprehensive Water Plan (OCWP)*—are grouped into more homogenous watershed units. The resulting nineteen basin/watershed summaries highlight both the

diversity and utility of natural resources throughout the Nations' Oklahoma homelands. Each summary includes extensive data on important rivers and streams, major lakes, aquifers, water quality and related land uses, and each focuses on how basin water is currently utilized through state-permitted rights for municipalities, industries, agriculture and other consumptive users as well as to support non-consumptive water requirements. Data on water supply system providers and associated infrastructure is included.

The Chickasaw Nation

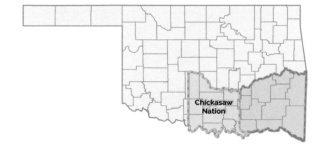

The Choctaw Nation

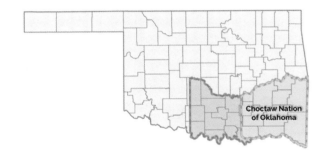

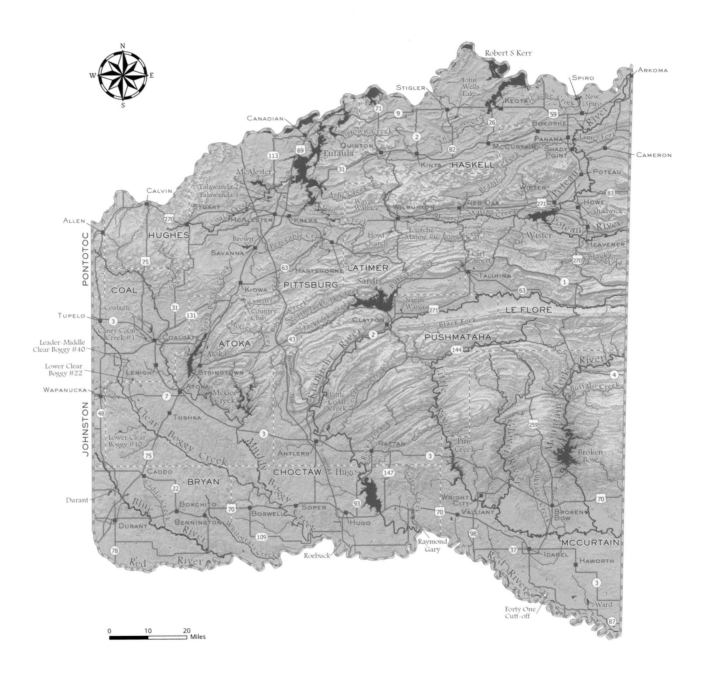

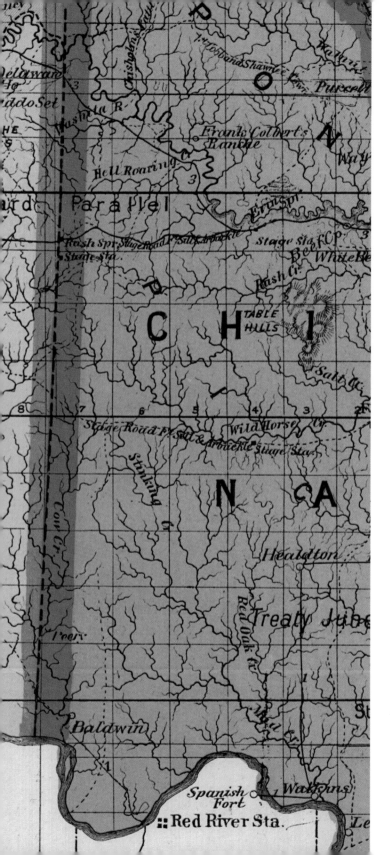

A Historical and Cultural Journey

The aboriginal Homeland of the Chickasaw Nation and Choctaw Nation of Oklahoma (more informally referred to as simply the Choctaw Nation) includes thousands of square miles of what today constitutes the southeastern United States. This bountiful area is rich in water and related environmental resources, which has been central to Chickasaw and Choctaw life for more than 600 generations. Water supported families and communities, established a foundation for extensive trade, transportation and communication routes, supported agricultural endeavors, fostered indispensable fish and wildlife resources, and played a direct role in Chickasaw and Choctaw language and culture. And while today it has assumed a more conventional role in support of tribal economic initiatives, water continues to nurture multi-generational beliefs and practices.

For centuries, Chickasaw and Choctaw ancestors built and maintained a complex political system that was supported by a kinship system as well as deep spiritual beliefs. As a living culture, throughout the colonial era and first decades of the United States' existence the Chickasaw and Choctaw incorporated new materials and methods introduced by Europeans and American settlers to reshape and strengthen their political and social institutions to carry on their traditional ways. Water, in particular, empowered the Chickasaws and Choctaws both economically and militarily, as witnessed by other Southeastern Indian tribes and later documented by Europeans.

The Nations' military dominance of key waterways spawned economic power as trade long before the arrival of Europeans. As new settlers infiltrated Homeland communities, they soon joined in the economic bounty. Organically, social interactions became increasingly complex. Indeed, historians credit the Nations for their contributions during the Revolutionary War, specifically for enabling the young United States' victory against the British in the Pensacola Campaign and the defense of New Orleans during the War of 1812. Extensive annual export of foods, spices, pottery, baskets, leather, and furs laid the foundations of today's cities of Mobile and New Orleans. The Chickasaws and Choctaws truly had a profound impact on early American history, and vice versa.

Close relations and interests notwithstanding, the United States shifted its policies in the 1820s to escalate the forced removal of tribal nations, including the Chickasaw and Choctaw, from their lands east of the Mississippi River. The Choctaw, a numerous tribe with a population exceeding 22,000, was the first to be removed. Under threats of violence, the U.S. forced Choctaws to cede their aboriginal homeland and its abundant resources to burgeoning numbers of white settlers in exchange for lands west of the Mississippi, the new Indian Territory. Pursuant to the 1830 Treaty of Dancing Rabbit Creek, the Choctaw Nation was to hold their new homelands forever, in fee simple, and exclusive of any future state government.[2] For the greater good and safety of their people, the Chickasaw conceded to removal seven years later in 1837, becoming a retroactive party of the 1830 Treaty. By signing a treaty with the Choctaw Nation in 1837, the Chickasaw Nation established itself as a district within the Choctaw

Nation's treaty homeland — recrossing the Mississippi and rejoining the Choctaws.

A new treaty with the United States in 1855, however, re-established separate government-to-government relationships between the Chickasaw and Choctaw Nations, respectively, and the United States. The Chickasaw Nation resumed its distinct sovereign status within the federal legal system while retaining undivided interests in the sovereign estate with the Choctaw Nation, as vested under the Treaty of Dancing Rabbit Creek. Following the post-Civil War Treaty of 1866, the United States reduced the Nations' shared sovereign estate by forcing the cession of all original treaty lands that lay west of the 98th meridian, which runs north to south near an approximate center-line of present-day Oklahoma.

Figure 2. Painting of an early Choctaw village by Francois Bernard, 1869. The women appear to be coloring strips of cane. (Credit: Wikimedia Commons)

Following removal, the Nations set about rebuilding their communities, many near streams, springs and other vital, treasured water sources in the new territory. In addition to various hardships incidental to wholesale removal — especially disturbance of centuries-old tribal clan systems and governance — this land was unfamiliar and lacked many traditional resources. However, bolstered by a drive to balance subsistence with sustainability, these significant challenges, which could have consumed the lives and culture of others, were well met due to the resourcefulness of tribal leaders and the people. Settlements grew and the experience further strengthened the Chickasaw and Choctaw people and influences the Nations' practices and decision-making even today.

The Chickasaw and Choctaw Nations established robust, independent governments within their new home north of the Red River. Operating a government in accord with its own constitution, each Nation exercised a distinct degree of autonomy and control throughout

Figure 1. The signing of the Treaty of Dancing Rabbit Creek on September 27, 1830, as depicted by artist Douglass Crockwell (1941). The mural hangs in the Macon, Mississippi post office not far from the original site of the event, which set the stage for removal of the Choctaw people (and later, the Chickasaw) from their ancestral homelands to Indian Territory. (Credit: Keith Parish and the United States Postal Service)

its respective territory—a system the United States Supreme Court has recognized as essentially unparalleled within Indian Country. Under new governance systems, the Chickasaw and Choctaw Nations provided for their people by building school systems and communities, authorizing infrastructure, and developing legal codes to support economic productivity and tribal continuance for a new era.

The Nations and their citizens built successful businesses in present-day Oklahoma that capitalized on the region's water and other natural resources—moving goods up and down the Red, Kiamichi and other river systems, operating ferries and toll bridges that enabled overland movement of commodities, as well as constructing and operating mills that harnessed the power of moving water to grind grain. In these ways,

the resilient Chickasaws and Choctaws worked vigorously, overcoming numerous obstacles to rebuild and establish commerce in the new land.

Tribal ancestors in the southeastern United States developed agriculture independently, one of only ten places in the world where this has occurred throughout human history. The Chickasaws and Choctaws applied this ancient drive and skill to fuel a new form of agriculture in present-day Oklahoma, expanding ancestral crop cultivation and subsistence practices into profitable, market-oriented operations.

While many areas of the new lands were poorly suited for crop production, they were well-adapted to grazing; tallgrass prairies in the east gave way to lush mixed grasslands for prime spring and summer grazing, while stretches of buffalo grass served as excellent

winter forage for cattle and horses. Prior to the forced removal, the Chickasaw and Choctaw Nations were already known for their large cattle herds as well as other livestock. An 1884 report by the Commissioner of Indian Affairs showed that the two Nations combined owned 270,000 head of cattle, 320,000 swine and 38,000 horses, and large numbers of sheep and mules.[3]

The perfect year-round grazing lands, so indispensable to the stock-producing business, were a magnet to cattle drovers moving herds from the Texas plains to Kansas stockyards. While the Nations initially leased grazing parcels to Texas cattlemen, the sheer numbers of cattle moving north through Chickasaw and Choctaw country threatened the sustainability of their pastures and prairies. Two earlier droughts had devastated vast expanses of the shared territory, drying up creeks and other sources of water and damaging available forage. In an early example of natural resource management and drought preparedness, tribal council members drafted and passed laws to protect their lands from over-grazing.[4]

While cattle production was a primary economic driver in the new territory, not all areas of the Chickasaw and Choctaw Nations were unsuitable to crop production. Lands in the bottoms, along rivers and streams, were fertile and productive, as was a good portion of the land belonging to the Chickasaw Nation. Extensive cotton operations, some thousands of acres in size, lined the north banks of the Red River; these continued well into the twentieth century. Prosperous farms with large cornfields and orchards stretched along the Arkansas, Canadian and Washita Rivers. The

Figure 3.   Choctaw men shooting fish with bow and arrow at unknown location in southeast Oklahoma, 1902. (Credit: Oklahoma Historical Society)

Nation and its citizens traded with Texas and other nearby states; corn, pecans, cotton and additional crops were commonly exported from the area in exchange for manufactured goods.

Beyond the obvious sustenance and economic benefits, these aquatic areas also satisfied a host of fundamental social and cultural needs. Flowing water and springs were valued sites for meetings and ceremonies; water provided the key element of practices surrounding the physical and spiritual cleansing of both body and soul. And water propagated countless resources essential to everyday life. Choctaws estimate that more than 300 plants used by their early people — for medicine, food, tools, clothing and other purposes — occur in and along rivers, streams, wetlands and floodplains. Mussel shells, river cane and clay are but a few examples. And where the quality was somewhat suspect, Chickasaw and Choctaw citizens mined brine waters for salt and other minerals.

As tribal agriculture (including a profitable timber industry) flourished, so did a brisk shipping business along the Arkansas and Red Rivers, and even up the Kiamichi and Washita Rivers. Soon steamboats and keelboats on these watercourses, rather than the sparse and poorly maintained system of roads, moved most freight in and out of Indian Territory.

Rivers and streams in the shared treaty area also supported many types and sizes of mills. Most prominent were grain mills that processed wheat, cornmeal, crushed apple seed and bois d'arc seeds as well as all-important lumber. Mills were integral to the tribes' once-thriving timber industry that tapped the dense

Figure 4. The Chickasaw National Capitol building under construction, 1898. (Credit: Chickasaw Nation)

forests in Choctaw country, timber regions essentially co-extensive with the current national forest lands in what is now southeastern and south-central Oklahoma. As the territory's population increased, so did demand for timber. Tribal councils and tribal legislatures created laws to responsibly manage their vast timberlands.[5]

These laws not only safeguarded the timber industry for a time, but also protected watersheds, setting an early precedent for future implementation of tribal natural resource management practices throughout the Nations' Oklahoma lands. Still, threats to Chickasaw and Choctaw natural resources accelerated. Powerful railroad interests sought to benefit not only from timber, but specifically from the valuable Chickasaw–Choctaw coal seam, first documented by Thomas Nuttall in his 1819 journey through the region and later by railroad

surveyors who, in the 1850s, witnessed the Nations making commercial and domestic use of coal. Congress soon bowed to pressure from those interests, authorizing the building of two railroads through the new tribal homelands.

That introduction of the railroad to Indian Territory in 1872 and the rapid influx of outsiders pushed the Choctaw General Council to pass laws further regulating the usage of natural resources. Choctaw leaders like Coleman Cole called for the development of a mining industry to create revenue to invest and further expand their intricate school system.[6] By taking control over their natural resources, the Choctaw Nation demonstrated capability to manage their own lands and astute foresight for navigating the new capitalist economy. Despite this, U.S. government challenges to Choctaw

Cultural Resources: RIVER CANE

Prior to European colonization, river cane, a bamboo-like plant once common in river lowlands, was essential to the Chickasaws and Choctaws in their ancestral homelands as it provided an essential ingredient for homes, weapons (arrows, for example), baskets, fishing equipment, jewelry, musical instruments, furniture, boats and medicines. It was even used for fuel, and occasionally food, while constituting excellent wildlife habitat. Miles-long swaths of river cane no longer frequent Oklahoma streambanks due to clearing, farming and fire suppression; only about 2 percent of its original ecosystem base remains. But the plant's importance endures as the Nations and their citizens cultivate renewed strands in their homelands for various culture-based materials and goods.[66]

sovereignty persisted as did the undermining of lands secured through treaty, unleashing a dispossession of the Nations' timber, coal and land in what author Angie Debo stated "exploitation that is almost beyond belief." More than 1.3 million acres of valuable timberlands which, by law, were to be held in trust for the Chickasaw and Choctaw tribes, were sold off, with most of the proceeds being diverted to wealthy industrialists. After years of protracted litigation, in 2015, the Chickasaw and Choctaw Nations won a historic $186 million settlement against the Departments of Interior and Treasury for the mismanagement of trust funds and trust assets stretching back to the early 1900s.

As the nineteenth century drew to a close, Congress renewed its push to acquire Indigenous nation lands. In the decades following the Civil War, Congress embraced yet another set of policies targeting Chickasaw and Choctaw lands. Originally exempted from the 1887 Dawes Act that allotted First American lands, the Five Tribes faced increasing pressure to individualize land ownership rather than owning the land collectively as the Nations had done since 1830 and 1855. The U.S. government aimed to open treaty boundaries of the two Nations, as well as other Indian Territory tribes, to non-tribal settlement and ownership. Using its considerable power over federal-tribal affairs, Congress enacted a series of laws and otherwise acted to coerce a new set of agreements that paved the way for Indian Territory to become a state.[7] Ultimately, these efforts resulted in the new state of Oklahoma — translating to "red people" in both the Chickasaw and Choctaw languages.

The statehood movement in neighboring Oklahoma Territory ushered in dark days for the tribal nations of Indian Territory. Statehood meant the imposition of new legal system and federal takeover of tribal property and governing systems. This culminated in the United States overseeing near-complete dismantlement of the estate vested in 1830. During this period, the U.S. government passed laws to restrict tribal courts and legislatures, and it suspended tribal elections, leading to the direct appointment of the Chickasaw Governor and Choctaw Principal Chief, subject only to White House approval.[8] The entire apparatus of the federal government was turned toward dismantling tribal systems and, yet again, forcing the assimilation of Chickasaws and Choctaws, as well as members and citizens of other tribal nations, into non-tribal legal, economic and cultural systems. However, despite these incongruous federal policies and powers, Chickasaws and Choctaws continued to gather in homes and churches, keeping language and cultural identity alive.

Fighting for autonomy on the local level as their shared boundaries became a target for non-tribal settlement, at the close of the nineteenth century the Nations took action to protect important mineral springs in and around the Sulphur area. Long before removal, the Chickasaws and Choctaws had learned of this region of their future homeland—near the current site of the Chickasaw National Recreation Area (CNRA). Some hold that tribal people had previously traveled from their homelands east of the Mississippi to hunt deer, panther, wild turkey and other game in the area.

While there, they likely took advantage of the waters' perceived therapeutic and healing power.

Shortly after the arrival to Indian Territory, the Chickasaw Nation began making commercial use of the unique mineral springs, which we know today are supported by the prolific Arbuckle-Simpson aquifer. Chickasaw legislators passed statutes granting tribal members the rights to develop land surrounding the springs, an allowance that quickly resulted in the establishment of summer resorts for travelers from as far away as Arkansas and Texas who sought the waters to assuage various ailments. Lawmakers also established measures to protect the area's land.

Uncontrolled commercial interests—hotel and bath house owners and others—were gradually overtaking many access points to the springs. Establishing a plan that has become one of the tribes' earliest and greatest water management accomplishments, the Governor of the Chickasaw Nation and Principal Chief of the Choctaw Nation sold most of the springs and 640 acres surrounding them to the Department of Interior in 1902.[9] The new Sulphur Springs Reservation—later renamed Platt National Park—established federal protection and ensured liberal public access to the springs. In 1976, the park was combined with the nearby Arbuckle Recreation Area to create the CNRA, which today spreads across nearly 10,000 acres and draws

Figure 5. In its early days, as now, the natural waters of Platt National Park (e.g., Chickasaw National Recreation Area) attracted visitors from throughout the region and country. (Credit: Oklahoma Historical Society)

more than three million visitors each year. Admission to CNRA remains free.

In the 1960s, as the civil rights movement swept the country, Chickasaw and Choctaw community leaders organized to press the federal government to relinquish its control of the Nations and step aside in favor of restored tribal self-government and self-determination. Choctaw members, in particular, helped put a stop to congressional legislation that would have terminated the Choctaw Nation's legal status.[10] The steadfast commitment of these contemporary, energetic leaders led to Congress's passage of the Principal Chiefs Act of 1970, which restored power to tribal citizens to elect their own leadership and led, ultimately, to reformation of original tribal constitutions as well as legal and government systems. Since that time, the Chickasaw and Choctaw Nations have led a resurgence and revitalization of tribal

Figure 7.   The Artesian Hotel Casino and Spa, in Sulphur, was completed by the Chickasaw Nation in 2013. The building is a faithful reconstruction of the original structure, a luxury hotel built in 1906 but destroyed by fire in 1962. The Chickasaw Motor Inn, which had occupied this site in the interim, was purchased by the Nation in 1972, making it the first business owned and operated solely by the tribe. The new Artesian honors both local and tribal heritage.

Figure 6.   Joseph Oklahombi, a Choctaw citizen and World War I code talker, and Mary Frances "Te Ata" Thompson Fisher, famed Chickasaw story-teller, applied ancient tribal language in unique ways, yet each helped preserve valued cultural traditions. (Credit: Oklahoma Historical Society)

cultural and economic health that is transforming their shared treaty lands. As Chickasaw Nation citizen (and U.S. Representative) Tom Cole frequently emphasizes, this success creates long-term benefits for the region and state as neither Nation will ever shift its headquarters out of state or overseas. This is the eternal home of the Nations and its people.

In total, the Chickasaw Nation and Choctaw Nation of Oklahoma span twenty-three counties in Oklahoma. The modern-day Chickasaw Nation occupies all or part of thirteen counties encompassing some 7,648 square miles in south central Oklahoma. The adjacent Choctaw Nation, the third largest federally-recognized tribe in the United States, similarly occupies all or part of ten and half counties in the southeast.

The Nations are exemplary leaders in economic development within their boundaries. Building on federal self-determination policies, the Nations have leveraged success in gaming and entertainment into an expanding and diverse portfolio of tribal enterprise—from destination resorts to health care to construction, manufacturing and technological innovation. Each dollar earned is directly invested in support of economic stability and in providing much-needed government programs and services to Chickasaw and Choctaw citizens and their cities and towns.

And as the Nations' enterprises grow, so too do area communities through the creation of thousands of jobs and investments in water and wastewater infrastructure, roads, schools and other vital elements of a healthy region. According to a 2012 study, the Chickasaw and Choctaw Nations annually produce 30,610 jobs, $785 million in state income and $4.33 billion in the production of goods and services in Oklahoma.[11] Increasingly, the Chickasaw and Choctaw Nations apply their core cultural values and past to Oklahoma's future, and as they do so, they forever commit to the health and success of their citizens and communities, large and small.

As a primary driver of their revitalized economies, the Chickasaw and Choctaw Nations maintain a keen interest in the management and use of vital water resources throughout southeastern and south-central Oklahoma. On the one hand, continued economic growth increases the demand for water; on the other hand, continued economic success is dependent on ecological health and sustainability. The Nations, accordingly, have committed to working toward the long-term health of both the region's economy and its natural water systems.

Fortunately, the Nations — as tribal sovereigns and land stewards enjoying a burgeoning economic capacity — are well-positioned to comprehensively assess resource and infrastructure needs while working with federal, state and local parties to develop and implement water resource strategies and programs that support long-term economic and ecological health. The Nations' primary initiative focused on this target is the CCRWP, which leverages governmental and stakeholder partnerships to improve understanding of water resource

Cultural Resources: MUSSELS

Centuries ago, as today, the Chickasaw and Choctaw people used freshwater mussel shells to fabricate pottery and fashion tools and ornaments.[67] And the mussel itself was a frequent source of food.[68] Mussels are also valued for their vital ecological benefits, and they are key indicators of aquatic health. While the high-quality waters of the Kiamichi River, which hosts more than half of Oklahoma's mussel fauna, continue to support healthy mussel communities, three of the river's 31 mussel species are now federally listed.[69] Regionally, mussels are imperiled by pollution, soil erosion, drought, changes in streamflow hydrology, and invasive species. Of the original 297 North American species, 35 are now extinct and 180 are critically impaired. The Nations remain diligent stewards of riverine environments through stream monitoring and related water quality improvement programs, reflecting both respect for natural resources and preservation of age-old tribal values.

needs and address drought and other challenges to water security.

Many challenges lie ahead, but water remains essential — to the Nations, their citizens, our shared region, and the State of Oklahoma. It is essential to who we are as a people. It is essential to our economy. And it is essential to the health of our natural systems. Accordingly, it is work to which we are committed and in which we will do our best.

⬦ SIGNIFICANT HISTORICAL
⬦ & CULTURAL RESOURCES

The contemporary homelands contain numerous areas of significant economic value, including sites of cultural and historical importance to the Nations and their people as well as other tribal nations that lived here before Chickasaw and Choctaw removals. Many of these resources and facilities, which routinely influence water management decisions, are included on the National Park Service's Register of Historic Places, which is the official list of the Nation's historic places worthy of preservation. Authorized by the National Historic Preservation Act of 1966, the National Register is part of a federal program to coordinate and support public and private efforts to identify, evaluate and protect America's historic and archeological resources.[12]

Also important to the tribes are nature preserves, wildlife refuges and management areas; state and federal parks; educational institutions, including colleges, universities and research facilities; public hunting and game management areas; national forests and recreational areas; and state and federal lakes and their associated lands. The following pages summarize these sites, the locations of which are indicated on the included map; some locations are approximate as evidence of their existence is no longer apparent. Also worth mentioning are churches and the many largely forgotten First American towns, cemeteries, and other historic and archaeological sites submerged in the waters of Lakes Texoma, Wister, Sardis, Broken Bow and other man-made reservoirs in the Settlement Area.

Forts and Military Encampments

While the marker for the **Camp Leavenworth** (Basin 21) sits on the west side of Kingston on U.S. Highway 70, the site itself is two miles south, under the waters of Lake Texoma. This temporary camp was named for Gen. Henry Leavenworth, who died nearby in 1834 from injuries sustained during a buffalo hunt. Leavenworth was en route from Fort Gibson to the western Indian Territory, leading a large expeditionary force for the U.S. Army whose mission was to make peace with the Plains Indian tribes.[13]

Established by the U.S. government in 1851 as one of two initial military posts in Indian Territory, **Fort Arbuckle** (Basin 14) was built on the slopes of the Arbuckle Mountains near Wild Horse Creek in Garvin County. It served primarily Chickasaw and Choctaw citizens to counter raids and attacks from the Kiowa and Comanche and to safeguard emigrants making their

Figure 8. The Choctaw Nation's new Durant headquarters consolidates employees and functions from thirty-two locations across the city, fostering productivity and synergy among tribal staff. While the building and its surrounding satellite offices reflect the Nation's contemporary direction and ethic, the new construction also incorporates important historical and cultural aspects of the Choctaw Nation.

way west. Both the fort and surrounding mountains were named after Brigadier General Matthew Arbuckle, the commander of the Military Department of Missouri, who died of cholera on April 11, 1851.[14] Fort Arbuckle was preceded by **Camp Arbuckle** (Basin 15), just south of the Canadian River, one mile northwest of present-day Byars in McClain County. The site was chosen by Captain R.B. Marcy while escorting gold-seekers to California in 1849. Marcy's troops erected tents and a few cabin-style buildings before abandoning Camp Arbuckle in 1851 for Fort Arbuckle further south. After its abandonment, members of the Delaware tribe, led by the famous Black Beaver—who was also credited with establishing the California and Chisholm trails—made the site their home until their migration to the Anadarko area during the Civil War.[15] Fort Arbuckle was abandoned in 1870, and its cavalry moved west to Fort Sill. Today, all that remains of the fort are a few stones. No trace exists of Camp Arbuckle. However, following abandonment of Fort Arbuckle, men surveying lands for the Chickasaw and Choctaw Nations, as described in the Treaty with U.S., Choctaw and Chickasaw of 1855, used Fort Arbuckle's flagstaff to reference **Initial Point** (Basin 14) as the intersection of a north-south line called the Indian Meridian and an east-west line called the Indian Base Line. According to the 1871 Report of the Commissioner of the General Land Office, this arbitrary point was subsequently used to survey all land in Oklahoma, other than "No Man's Land" in the Panhandle. Today, a sandstone marker identifies this location.[16]

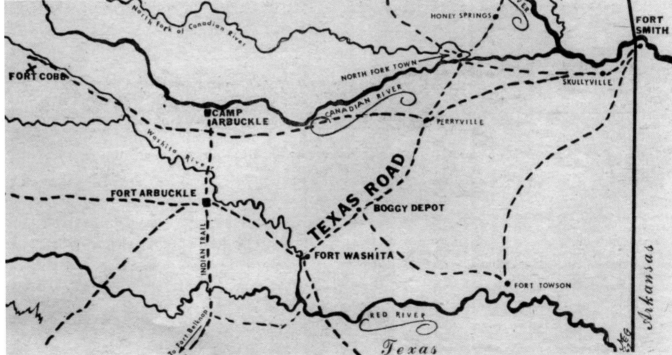

Figure 9. Above is a portion of an 1853 sketch of the original Camp Arbuckle by Heinrich B. Mollhausen. Below is a map of a portion of pre-Civil War Indian Territory indicating forts and military roads established primarily to protect First Americans from "hostiles"; the Camp Arbuckle location was temporary and later moved. (Map courtesy Tulsa World, March 17, 1968. Sketch from Mark of Heritage, Oklahoma Historical Society)

Figure 10. Passengers on Colbert's Ferry, date unknown. (Credit: Oklahoma Historical Society)

One of the oldest communities in Oklahoma, the LeFlore County settlement of **Fort Coffee** (Basin 46) has pre-contact roots tied to the nearby Spiro Mounds. In 1832, Choctaw families newly removed from Eastern homelands, many traveling by steamboat, settled in this area south of the Arkansas River. In 1834 the federal government built the fort on Swallow Rock, a high bluff overlooking the river. Soldiers garrisoned there constructed roads that later formed the foundation for the Butterfield stage line and mail routes. Fort Coffee was abandoned in 1838, later becoming a Choctaw boarding school.[17]

The **Fort McCulloch** site (Basin 12), listed on the National Register of Historic Places, exists today on private property about three miles southwest of Kenefic in Bryan County.[18] Established in 1862 by Gen. Albert Pike, this earthen fortification served as the main Chickasaw–Choctaw stronghold in southern Indian Territory during the Civil War. The fort was strategically located on a bluff above the south bank of the Blue River along routes leading to Forts Gibson and Washita. Although no permanent structures were part of the fort, outlines of the extensive breastworks are partially visible today.[19]

Built in 1824 near the confluence of the Kiamichi and Red Rivers in Choctaw County, the **Fort Towson** (Basin 5) cantonment initially served as an outpost on the border between the United States and Mexico. It was closed in 1829, then reopened in 1832 and designated as a fort to deliver supplies to members of the Choctaw Nation arriving by military trail to their new homelands. It was one of four arrival stations for the thousands of Choctaws settling in Indian Territory after removal.[20]

Located in present Bryan County on the banks of Lake Texoma, **Fort Washita** (Basin 21) was constructed in 1842 to maintain peace and security for the Chickasaw and Choctaw Nations within their new lands, pursuant to treaty obligations. The site, just east of the Washita River and 18 miles north of the Red River, was approved by Gen. Zachary Taylor. The fort was abandoned in 1865 and first granted to the Chickasaw Nation, then later allotted to Chickasaw citizens. In 1962, the Oklahoma Historical Society acquired Fort Washita and restored it; the historic site and a museum are now open to the public. In 2017, the Chickasaw Nation partnered with the Oklahoma Historical Society to assume responsibility and management of the fort. Fort Washita is designated as a National Historic Landmark and is listed on the National Register of Historic Places.[21]

Settlements and Towns

The Chickasaw and Choctaw town of **Boggy Depot** (Basin 7) grew from a single First American log cabin built in 1837 to a thriving trade center at the junction of travel on the Texas and California roads. It was also a principal station for the Butterfield Overland Mail and temporarily served as the Choctaw capitol in 1858. In 1872, when the railroad bypassed the site, Boggy Depot began to decline. Choctaw Chief Allen Wright, who named the state "Oklahoma," is buried in the cemetery, which is all that is left of the old town.[22]

In the 1850s, the Chickasaw Legislature authorized Chickasaw citizen B.F. Colbert to operate a ferry across the Red River at his residence near the Texas border in present-day Bryan County. **Colbert's Ferry/Stage Stand** (Basin 21) became a popular accommodation for travelers, emigrants and drovers traversing the Texas Road, and later Colbert's residence became the territory's last stage stand for the north-south run of the Butterfield Overland Mail, providing food and rest for stage travelers. After the Civil War, the prosperous ferry transported up to 200 wagons per day across the river.[23]

Doaksville (Basin 5) began as a small trading center west of Fort Towson around 1824, but it soon grew into a town. In the 1830s, many Choctaw citizens coming to their new territory through the fort settled in or near Doaksville, quickly turning it into one of the most important towns in the new Choctaw Nation. It was also a key political center where Chickasaw and Choctaw leaders signed agreements with each other and with the United States through which Chickasaws acquired lands in the Choctaw territory. From 1850 to 1863, Doaksville served as the second capitol of the Choctaw Nation. The area where the town once stood has been designated a National Historic Site.[24]

Good Spring (Basin 21), known for its pure, sweet groundwater flowing into lower Pennington Creek, marked a new beginning as forced removal of the Chickasaw

Nation lasted into the 1890s. After separating from the Choctaw Nation in 1855 and reforming their own government, the Chickasaws established a new capital at Good Spring (Kulli Chokma), an area between Fort Washita and Fort Arbuckle used for camping and gathering. There, a log cabin with an adjacent brush arbor served as the Chickasaw Council House until 1858. As permanent homes replaced the temporary camps, Good Spring's name was changed to Tishomingo in honor of one of their last leaders who served in their historic Homeland.[25]

The Chickasaw community of **Kullihoma** (or Red Springs, Basin 8) was first settled around 1856 near a once plentiful spring. The settlement thrived until statehood, with a school where the Chickasaw language was kept alive. In 1936, more than 146 acres were put into trust by the U.S. government for the Chickasaw Nation. By 1975, almost 628 acres were in trust. In 1991, another 850 acres were added to Kullihoma and there were an additional 483 acres added in 2011. Today, Kullihoma covers more than 1,961 acres. The area is set aside for community tribal use such as camping, fishing, and Chickasaw celebrations. Structures onsite include a council house, a raised corn crib, a winter house, and a summer house.[26]

Nail's Station (Basin 12) was also a stage stop on the old Butterfield Mail route, the first transcontinental link between the Atlantic seaboard and Pacific coast. Travelers of the Texas Road also forded the Blue River at Nail's Station (or Crossing), located on the east side of the Blue River in what is now Bryan County, across from Fort McCulloch. One of twelve Butterfield stations in Chickasaw–Choctaw Territory, Nail's Station was operated by Joel H. Nail, a member of a prominent Choctaw family.[27]

Figure 11. People traversing Nails Bridge, eight miles west of Caddo at Kenefic, Indian Territory; date unknown. (Credit: Oklahoma Historical Society)

The names and locations (including existing markers) of the remaining ten **Butterfield Overland Mail and Stage stations** in the Chickasaw-Choctaw Territory are: Walker's, about one and a half miles northeast of Spiro; Trahern's, at Latham, eight miles west of Shady Point; Holloway's, three miles northeast of Red Oak; Riddle's, east of Wilburton off U.S. 270; Pusley's, south of Gaines Creek, three miles southwest of Higgins; Blackburn's, north of Pine Top School; Waddell's, on County Road three miles west of Wesley; Geary's, one and a half miles southwest of Stringtown, now under Lake Atoka; Boggy Depot, four miles south of the State Highway 7 bridge, in Boggy Depot Park; and Fisher's, two miles south of U.S. 70, four miles west of Durant.[28]

Nanih Waiya (Basin 6) was the first capitol of the Choctaw Nation in Indian Territory, and it was here in 1834 that the oldest legislative body ever to assemble in Oklahoma met to write and adopt the first Choctaw constitution. In the Choctaw language, Nanih Waiya means "sloping/leaning hill," representing the giver of life and the

Figure 13. A home and family near the Choctaw Agency house in Skullyville, circa 1880s. (Credit: Oklahoma Historical Society)

Figure 12. Public Council House at Nanih Waiya, date unknown. (Credit: Oklahoma Historical Society)

actual ancient earthwork in central Mississippi constructed during the Middle Woodland period (about 1-300 CE), which the Choctaw people venerate as the sacred location of their origin. According to Choctaw oral history, their citizens brought soils from Nanih Waiya to Indian Territory, depositing them in a new mound near the capitol.[29] The site is in close proximity to **Lake Nanih Waiya**, just southeast of Sardis Lake in Pushmataha County, which is owned by the ODWC but managed through a cooperative agreement between that agency and the Choctaw Nation.

Named for its founder, Chickasaw–Choctaw citizen John Perry, **Perryville** (Basin 48) was an important commercial center and Butterfield stage stop situated on

military roads serving Forts Washita, Arbuckle, Smith and Gibson, as well as along the Texas and California trails. Initially in the Chickasaw Nation, treaty boundaries established in 1855 placed Perryville in the adjacent Choctaw Nation. During the Civil War, the town was an important supply depot, but was burned down near the end of the conflict.[30]

Skullyville (Basin 46), located near several perennial springs, was a Choctaw political, commerce and education center that served as a gateway west for many Choctaw and Chickasaw citizens on their way to new homelands. The name is derived from the Choctaw word "iskuli" (money) as annuities due Choctaws were paid here. Two Choctaw schools were located nearby, and the town housed the first Butterfield Overland stage stop out of Fort Smith. The Skullyville Constitution, which united different factions of the Choctaw Nation, was signed at the town's 1857 convention.[31]

Schools

In their new territory, both Chickasaw and Choctaw people brought with them a long-standing educational system model founded on the understanding that education is vital to the tribes' survival and future relevance. In the Treaty of Dancing Rabbit Creek, the Choctaws had stipulated that the United States would help pay for the construction of replacement schools in the new territory, including funding teachers and scholarships. By 1836, Choctaws had established eleven neighborhood schools with 228 Choctaw children enrolled. These schools were soon supported by council appropriations.[32] The Chickasaw Nation also maintained an organized education system carried out in neighborhood schools.[33] In partnership with Protestant and other denomination missionaries, these early schools served, collectively, as a cornerstone of the Nation's revival in Indian Territory, and they also facilitated an important sovereign-to-sovereign relationship with the United States government. By the middle of the nineteenth century, the Chickasaws and Choctaws founded numerous boarding academies for tribal youth in south-central Oklahoma.

The Nations' leaders recognized that their future hinged on properly educating their youth, exemplified by Choctaw Principal Chief Isaac Garvin (1878–80), who declared, "I say educate! Educate! Or we perish!" In 1842, the Choctaw General Council enacted a law that established six boarding schools.[34] While general control of the Chickasaw and Choctaw schools was ceded to the new government upon statehood, the tribal educational structure heavily influenced development of the state system.

Opened in 1845, **Armstrong Academy** (Basin 5) began classes with thirty-three boys near Doaksville in Pushmataha District (near what is now Bokchito, Bryan County). In addition to taking agricultural, mechanical, geography and classical literature classes, boys cleared land and cultivated a farm to sustain the boarding school. From 1863 to 1883, the school served as the Choctaw Nation capital and was given the name "Chahta Tamaha." During the Civil War, it also served as a hospital camp for Confederate forces in the area, and more than 250 of the war's dead are buried just west of where school buildings once existed. Armstrong continued as an academy for Choctaw boys until it was destroyed by fire in 1920.[35]

The **Bloomfield Academy** (Basin 13) for Chickasaw Females opened in 1852, near what is now Achille, Oklahoma. Rivaling the best non-native eastern boarding schools, with academic, textbook and entrance standards established by Chickasaw law, Bloomfield graduates became the ancestors of many of today's prominent Chickasaws. Bloomfield was relocated in 1914 to Ardmore; later named Carter Seminary, it continued as a boarding school for girls until 1949, when it began admitting boys. It

Figure 14. Burney Institute students. A portion of the Institute is visible on the right; the dormitory is on the left. (Credit: Chickasaw Times, 2006)

Figure 15. Students at the Harley Institute (later renamed the Chickasaw Manual Labor Academy for Boys). The Institute was located two miles southeast of Tishomingo. (Credit: Oklahoma Historical Society)

remained an academy preparing Chickasaw children to be leaders until 1953.[36]

Established in 1854, the **Burney Institute** (Basin 21) opened as a boarding school for Chickasaw high school girls in 1859 near the town of Lebanon. The school was named for a local Chickasaw whose infant son, Benjamin Crooks Burney, would one day become Governor of the Chickasaw Nation. Like other Chickasaw boarding schools, it closed at the onset of the Civil War. After the

Civil War it reopened; it housed Chickasaw Civil War orphans and was known as the Lebanon Orphan Institute and soon began teaching both boys and girls. In 1887 the institute became the Chickasaw Orphan Home and Manual Labor School as it continued to care for Chickasaw orphans and instruct Chickasaw youth until 1906, when the school closed. In 2006, the Chickasaw Nation purchased the old Burney Institute and its 176 acres near the Red River. In 2015, Chickasaw Nation officials funded a complete restoration of the historic landmark.[37]

The first Chickasaw school, **Chickasaw Manual Labor Academy** (Basin 21), created exclusively for boys, opened in 1851. The original two-story schoolhouse and accompanying farm were funded almost entirely by the Chickasaw people. Students learned agricultural and mechanical skills, along with Latin, logic, music and sacred studies. The original 200 acres that comprised that self-sustaining farm are now part of the Tishomingo National Wildlife Refuge.[38] Today, a historical marker guides the park's visitors to the site of the school.

Originally a manual labor boarding school for Chickasaw boys, the **Collins Institute** (Basin 9 and referred to as Colbert Institute) opened in 1854 located in Perryville, Indian Territory within the Choctaw Nation. In 1856 it was moved to the Chickasaw District at the headwaters of the Boggy Creek near Stonewall in Pontotoc County. The school operated until 1906 when it was placed under the control of the Government Indian School Service. The school was named was after Judson D. Collins, a distinguished member of the Chickasaw Senate who piloted the act creating the school through the Chickasaw legislature.[39]

Wapanucka Institute (i.e., **Chickasaw Rock Academy**, Basin 21), a tribal boarding school, opened in 1852. The school site, which included a spring, was located two miles east of Bromide; the limestone used in the building was quarried a short distance from the site. The school opened with forty female students who studied domestic skills, and it stayed open until the beginning of the Civil War. Wapanucka Institute reopened in 1876, and despite being in a state of disrepair due to the war, once again became prosperous under tribal management. In 1890 it became a school for boys; its female students were moved to the Collins Institute.[40]

The **Wheelock Academy Historic Site** (Basin 3), located in present day McCurtain County, includes the remaining buildings and grounds of Wheelock Academy, a boarding school for native girls that operated from 1832 to 1955. The Academy, a National Historic Landmark, is currently on the National Register of Historic Places and has been on America's Most Endangered Places list. The campus site includes three buildings: the former teachers' dormitory, which now houses the museum and gift shop; superintendent's cottage; and superintendent's office, which may be used for small meetings. The museum utilizes informative panels, historic photographs, personal

Figure 16. Authentic re-creation of the Chikasha Inchokka Traditional Chickasaw Village from the 1750s era on the grounds of the Chickasaw Cultural Center in Sulphur. (Credit: Chickasaw Cultural Center)

items and artifacts to tell the story of the school and lives of its former students. Available to visitors are tours of the museum and campus, a variety of cultural classes, Heritage Mondays and quarterly Movie Nights. The site also hosts a reunion for alumni each year. Staff also work in conjunction with area schools, Choctaw Nation programs and other local organizations.[41]

Other boarding schools established by the Choctaw Public School Act of 1842 include, but not limited to, **Spencer Academy** (Basin 6) for boys, some of whom became renowned Choctaw leaders including Chief Allen Wright, Chief Jackson McCurtain, Chief B.F. Smallwood and Chief Jefferson Gardner, and in the Mushulatubbee District, **Fort Coffee Choctaw Boys Academy** (Basin 46), located at the abandoned Fort Coffee site, as well as **New Hope Seminary** (Basin 46) for girls, located five miles from Fort Coffee, near Skullyville.[42] The intent of these boarding schools was to teach boys agricultural and mechanical arts and to teach girls how to do household chores, including sewing and making clothing. The Civil War closed down Choctaw boarding schools and a large majority never reopened. Many that were reestablished operated as boarding schools for orphan boys and girls. In 1898, the Curtis Act placed all Choctaw schools under U.S. government control.

Two of the three so-called "normal" schools created in Oklahoma after statehood in 1907: East Central (now **East Central University**, Basin 9) in Ada and Southeastern State Normal School (now **Southeastern Oklahoma State University**, Basin 11) in Durant. This more advanced school model, which provided

Figure 17. The Chickasaw White House. (Credit: Chickasaw Nation)

six years of instruction consisting of four years of high school courses and two years of college work, exposed the larger statewide populace, including tribal citizens, to higher education.[43] **Murray State College**, named after Oklahoma Governor Alfalfa "Bill" Murray, was established as the Murray State School of Agriculture by the first Oklahoma Legislature in 1908. Its initial class included about one hundred students, primarily Chickasaw and Choctaw. The school's alumni include Bill Anoatubby, Governor of the Chickasaw Nation.[44]

Other Tribal Historical and Cultural Sites

Located in Sulphur, the **Chickasaw Cultural Center** (Basin 14) is a 184-acre world-class destination that showcases and promotes the culture and traditions of the Chickasaw Nation and its people. The unique, sprawling campus features a welcome center, art gallery, gardens, a gift shop, café and movie theater as well as a forty-foot-high "sky pavilion" that allows visitors to get a bird's-eye view of a replicated traditional Chickasaw village. The facility also enhances community outreach and education through Holisso: The Center for Study of Chickasaw History and Culture. The Cultural Center also features rotating, interactive exhibits and numerous cultural activities.[45]

Construction on the **Chickasaw National Capitol** building (Basin 21), in Tishomingo, began in April 1898. The stately Victorian structure, consisting of red granite quarried and hauled to the site from nearby Pennington Creek, served as the Chickasaw National Capitol until 1906. The Capitol was turned over to Johnston County in 1910. After decades of negotiations initiated by Governor Overton James in the 1960s, tribal ownership was reclaimed by Governor Bill Anoatubby in 1992. Today, the building serves as a museum and reminder of how the Chickasaw people have persevered and remained united.[46]

The **Chickasaw White House** (Basin 12), south of Milburn, is the 1895 Victorian style home of Chickasaw Governor Douglas H. Johnston. Importantly, it served as a social and political hub for the Chickasaw Nation as the nineteenth and twentieth centuries converged, and Indian Territory transitioned into statehood. From here, Governor Johnston negotiated with President Theodore Roosevelt to maintain tribal control over Chickasaw schools and strove to protect tribal government by insisting the U.S. live up to its treaty obligations. The house, located on the north edge of Emet, west of the Tishomingo National Wildlife Refuge, is now a museum open to the public and it's on the National Register of Historic Places.[47]

In 1883, the Choctaw General Council appropriated funds for the construction of a new red-brick council house in what would be the final location of the Choctaw capitol. Completed in 1884, the **Choctaw Council**

Figure 18. Shell gorget with spider motif, which was recovered at Spiro Mounds, on display at Woolaroc Museum, near Bartlesville. (Credit: Marc Carlson)

House (Basin 6), near Tuskahoma, housed the Choctaw Nation government until 1907.[48] The Choctaw Nation Tribal Court is still held here, and the building, which is listed on the National Register of Historic Places, is now a museum displaying articles of Choctaw history.

The **Choctaw Nation Cultural Center** (Basin 13), a world-class facility that serves to share the Choctaw story, encompasses approximately 98,000 square feet in Durant. It houses two exhibit halls, an art gallery, auditorium, children's area, classrooms, offices, gift shop and café. The surrounding site includes a stickball field, living village and a traditional mound. The primary exhibit hall focuses on the history of the Choctaw tribe from ancestral times (circa 1250) to current day in Oklahoma.

Opened in 1970, **Heavener Runestone Park** (Basin 45) features a Swedish-inscribed sandstone slab rediscovered in the 1920s. Choctaw oral history mentions that the runestone was first encountered in the 1830s by a Choctaw hunting party. Some claim that the stone's mysterious inscriptions document Viking exploration of southeastern Oklahoma in about 1000 CE, while others suggest the runes were carved in the early 1700s. The fifty-five acre park includes group shelters for picnics, picnic tables, outdoor grills, comfort stations, an amphitheater, playground, campsites and hiking as well as an interpretative center with educational information about the runestone.[49]

Located along a bend of the Arkansas River northeast of Spiro, the **Spiro Mounds Archaeological Center** (Basin 46) preserves 150 acres of one of North America's most important First American sites. The mounds were created by the Spiro people who exhibited a sophisticated

Figure 19. Heavener Runestone Park. (Credit: MARELBU/Panoramio)

culture that influenced the nation's entire southeast region. Much of the Spiro culture is still a mystery, as well as the reasons for the decline and abandonment of the area. The site includes twelve mounds, the elite village area and part of the support city. The location became a permanent settlement around 800 CE and was used until about 1450 CE. During this period (the Mississippian), Spiro leaders were developing political, religious and economic ties with people from the Gulf of California to the Gulf of Mexico and from the coast of Virginia to the Great Lakes. While the Choctaw cleared the mound site for farming late in the 1800s, they did not allow any major disturbance of the site until the Great Depression when excavations revealed the tremendous significance of the prehistoric civilization. The Oklahoma Historical Society, which owns and operates the site, offers interpretive exhibits, an introductory slide program and a small gift shop. There are nearly two miles of interpreted trails, including a one-half-mile nature trail. A staff archaeologist is available to answer questions and lead tours.[50]

Parks and Recreational/Wildlife Areas

The Settlement Area contains numerous parks and lands that contribute significantly to tribal and local economies as well as reflect the cultural, environmental and natural resource values of the Chickasaw and Choctaw people. Among these are Oklahoma's Wildlife Management Areas (WMAs), tracks of land managed and operated by the Oklahoma Department of Wildlife Conservation specifically for hunting, fishing and outdoor recreation. In these areas, the ODWC employs various land use practices—such as prescribed burning, plowing, controlled grazing, brush hogging and plantings—to maintain, improve and expand habitat diversity. Dozens of WMAs on territorial lands provide extensive hunting, fishing, bird and wildlife watching and hiking opportunities. Additionally, tribal lands include many public fishing and hunting areas (although most aren't specifically mentioned in the following summaries).[51]

Opened in October 2017, **Arbuckle Springs WMA** (Basin 12) is located just west of Bromide in far northeastern Johnston County. This new protected hunting destination, which includes 3,869 acres in the Arbuckle Uplift, is comprised of shallow limestone soils covered in native grasses and shrubs, interspersed with small patches of oak and other hardwood timber. The mix of small springs, rocky areas and gently sloping terrain is home to various game animals, predominately deer and turkey.

Located on a peninsula of Lake Eufaula, **Arrowhead State Park** (Basin 48) includes 2,200 acres featuring 100 tent and ninety-one recreational vehicle (RV) sites. The park also offers fishing, picnic shelters, a marina, playgrounds, trails, miniature golf, a swimming area, mountain biking, an equestrian campground, stables, twenty-five miles of equestrian trails and an eighteen hole golf course. Group camps with a kitchen and bunkhouses are available and can sleep up to 144 people. The marina, including a restaurant, is located in the Echo Ridge area.[52]

Atoka WMA (Basin 8) covers 6,440 acres in Atoka County. Terrain within the WMA ranges from steep to moderately steep. Vegetation consists mainly of oak-hickory association with scattered openings. One designated primitive camping area is offered in the area. Additional camping and cabin rental can be obtained at McGee Creek State Park. Fishing opportunities consist of numerous ponds and Atoka and Bluestem Lakes.

Once part of a Choctaw settlement, **Beavers Bend State Park** (Basin 4) is the second most visited state park in Oklahoma. Its 3,500 wooded acres along the Mountain Fork River and around 14,000-acre Broken Bow Lake are in the Ouachita National Forest. The wide variety of available activities include boating, canoeing, kayaking, swimming, scuba diving, trout and fly-fishing, astronomy and geology outings, hiking and camping.

Figure 20. Beavers Bend State Park. (Credit: Carolyn Fletcher)

Its nature center hosts numerous educational programs and activities throughout the year.

Encompassing 3,367 acres of prime wildlife habitat along and around six and a half river miles, the **Blue River WMA** (Basin 12) is located about eleven miles northeast of Tishomingo. Also known as Blue River Public Fishing and Hunting Area, such formalized activities in the area date back to the 1890s when a Chickasaw couple, Austin Britt Hughes and Mamie Cravatt, set up one of Oklahoma's first fishing/hunting camps on their land. The ODWC established the WMA in 1967 and today facilitates opportunities to fish for native sunfish, catfish and bass, as well as trout, which are stocked by the agency throughout the winter months.[53]

Boggy Depot Park (Basin 9), formerly a state park in Atoka County, is today managed by the Chickasaw Nation as it was one of the first sites Chickasaws settled after the forced removal from their original homelands.[54] The site was also part of the Butterfield Stage route, a Confederate outpost during the Civil War, and Choctaw

Figure 21. Broken Bow Lake.

Chief Allen Wright is buried in the cemetery there. Its thirty-five acres feature a fishing lake, nature trails, and camping and picnic grounds. Boggy Depot was added to the National Register of Historic Places in 1972.[55]

Located adjacent to Broken Bow Lake and the Ouachita National Forest, **Broken Bow WMA** (Basin 4) covers 5,420 acres in northern McCurtain County. Among Oklahoma's most scenic locations, the area is a mixture of hardwood, pine and riparian forests, the latter of which consists primarily of hardwoods, such as sweet and black gums, red maple and elms. Only a small portion of the WMA is accessible by road, and no camping or related facilities are available, aside from the adjacent Holly Creek Primitive Camping Area. Fishing opportunities abound on the lake and in the Mountain Fork River. Primary river species include smallmouth bass and sunfish. Broken Bow Lake is known for its black bass fishing, but largemouth, smallmouth and spotted bass are all present. The lower Mountain Fork River designated trout area, below Broken Bow dam, offers year-round fishing for both rainbow and brown trout. Bald eagles routinely winter on the reservoir and river.

The hugely popular **Chickasaw National Recreation Area** (Basin 14) is steeped in history. Shortly after removal treaties were initiated, the Chickasaw Nation began making commercial use of local groundwaters and freshwater and mineral springs deriving from the Arbuckle-Simpson aquifer. They established summer resorts for regional travelers visiting the area to sample the reportedly therapeutic waters. By the end of the nineteenth century, as their shared homeland became a target for non-tribal settlement, the Nations feared

Figure 22. Boat dock at Veterans Lake in the Chickasaw National Recreation Area.

losing the springs, along with the prairie oasis that protected them, to unchecked commercial interests. Working in concert with the federal government, a mutual plan was developed that led to one of the tribes' earliest and greatest water management accomplishments.

In 1902, the Governor of the Chickasaw Nation and the Chief of the Choctaw Nation sold most of the springs—along with 640 acres surrounding them—to the Department of Interior. This resulted in creation of Sulphur Springs Reservation, and protection for the springs in it. The park was later renamed Platt National Park, one of the country's first. In 1976, the Park and Arbuckle Recreation Area were combined to create the CNRA, which today spreads across nearly 10,000 acres and draws more than 3 million visitors each year. Veterans Lake, located in the western portion of park, offers excellent opportunities for small boat use, fishing, hiking, and picnicking. Built in 1933, the sixty-seven-acre lake was named in honor of American war veterans.[56]

South of Sardis Lake and the Kiamichi River in the Choctaw Nation is the 500-acre **Clayton Lake State**

Park (Basin 6). Its eighty-acre lake and surrounding area features fishing, boating, hiking, swimming and other recreation in the Kiamichi Mountains.

Cross Timbers WMA (Basins 22, 21 and 23) extends over 10,300 acres in Love County. The habitat, which includes some improved pastures, is a mix of oak, hickory and mid-tall native prairie grasses. While there are many stock ponds in the area, none are reliable water sources. There is limited access to the area.

The **Durant State Fish Hatchery** (Basin 12) is situated in the lower end of the Blue River watershed. It is the largest of four state fish hatcheries in Oklahoma that together produce millions of stocking fish each year. The facility was constructed in 1917 in response to over-fishing of waters in Indian Territory, despite Chickasaw and Choctaw legal provisions created to protect the area's natural resources. Its establishment was the result of a series of Territorial game and fish laws bridging tribal law in the new Oklahoma legislature. The hatchery, which is fed by the high-quality waters of

Figure 23. The Durant hatchery is integral to Oklahoma's Florida largemouth bass populations. (Credit: Noble Research Institute)

Figure 24. Gary Sherrer Wildlife Management Area. (Credit: Oklahoma Department of Wildlife Conservation)

the Blue River, is an integral part of the ODWC's successful Florida largemouth bass production program.[57]

Eufaula WMA (Basin 48) located just east of Henryetta, includes 48,614 acres within three distinct units of land along Lake Eufaula. The Gaines Creek Unit and a portion of the South Canadian Unit are located within the Choctaw Nation. Hunting species include bobcat, White-tailed deer, dove, duck, quail, rabbit, squirrel and wild turkey.

Fobb Bottom WMA (Basin 21) is located in southern Marshall County along the shores of Lake Texoma. The 2,205-acre area consists primarily of floodplain, river bottom and cropland.

Gary Sherrer WMA (Basin 6) covers 1,280 acres northwest of Sardis Lake in Pittsburg County. The area is comprised of a mixture of oak/pine forest with steep slopes, shallow soils and rocky terrain. Native tree spe-

cies include shortleaf pine, post oak, red oak, black oak, water oak, sycamore, hackberry, hickory, elm, blackgum, sweetgum, rusty blackhaw, flowering dogwood and hawthorn. There is a designated camping area at the entrance. Fishing opportunities exist along Bolen Creek, which runs through the area.

Grady County WMA (Basins 14 and 15) encompasses 1,036 acres east of Rush Springs in Grady County. It consists primarily of two non-contiguous tracts with an additional 33-acre tract located between them. The area is characterized by open uplands bisected by wooded draws and creeks typical of the interspersed postoak-blackjack oak and tall grass prairie habitat. Only limited fishing opportunities are available.

Grassy Slough WMA (Basin 1) covers 1,016 acres in McCurtain County. Habitat consists of a 120-acre Moist Soil Unit divided into three compartments. The

Figure 25. Frog at Hickory Creek WMA. (Credit: ODWC)

area is mostly old farm fields with some areas replanted to hardwoods. Tree varieties include six species of oak as well as ash, hickory, pine, river birch, willow, sand plum, holly, sumac and numerous grasses and legumes. The many water sources in the area help support game and non-game species. However, no camping is available and there is no fishing at Grassy Slough.

Hickory Creek WMA (Basin 21) covers 7,363 acres of eastern Love County near Marietta. Post oak-blackjack timber dominates the uplands with bottom-land hardwoods occurring in low-lying areas. Native grasslands comprised of little bluestem and Indian grass dominate the upland openings. Bald eagles winter at Hickory Creek near the Lake Texoma portion of the area. Several undesignated primitive camping areas are offered at the WMA. A shooting range can be found on the north side.

Honobia Creek WMA (Basins 3, 4 and 6), in LeFlore, Pushmataha and McCurtain Counties, covers 91,721 acres. It consists of a mixture of pine and hardwood forests, primarily loblolly pine plantations of various age classes interspersed with hardwood benches and streamside management zones dominated by oaks and hickories. An annual land access permit and fee is required of all who hunt or fish on the WMA. No designated camping areas exist, but primitive camping is allowed everywhere. Fishing opportunities exist for sunfish species, flathead catfish, channel catfish and smallmouth, largemouth and spotted bass in the Little River. Small ponds in the area host bass, sunfish and channel catfish.

The 8,300 acres comprising **Hugo Lake State Park** (Basin 5) and the adjacent USACE management area provide a host of recreational opportunities for the more than 100,000 annual visitors to this lake at the confluence of the Kiamichi and Red Rivers. The park includes wooded campgrounds, a marina, boat ramps, sandy beaches, playgrounds, hiking, horseback riding and cycling trails, and hunting opportunities. Bass and catfish tournaments are held regularly on Hugo Lake.

Hugo WMA (Basin 5,) located along the Kiamichi River and lake shore primarily in Choctaw County, covers 19,227 acres. The area includes public camping, fishing and hunting areas.

James Collins WMA (Basins 46 and 48) covers 21,353 acres in northern Pittsburg and Latimer Counties. The area provides a wide variety of upland habitats, starting with pine covered ridges in the east and changing to oak/hickory forests with many openings in the western portion. Native grasslands are interspersed throughout. Camping is offered at the entrance to the area. A primitive restroom as well as water is available in the campground. The WMA includes a rifle range, and numerous fishing opportunities exist on area ponds and creeks; most of the ponds are walk-in only.

Lake Murray State Park (Basin 21), Oklahoma's oldest and largest, consists of 12,500 acres of forested, rolling hills around the lake. The park's diverse terrain, exceptional trails and historic sites make it a favorite destination among outdoor, water sport and all-terrain vehicle (ATV) enthusiasts. Visitors can choose between RV and tent campgrounds, while fifty-six cabins dot the park, which includes a modern lodge. Many of the cabins are historic structures built in the 1930s by the Civilian Conservation Corps. Three seasonal group camps are also located within the park. Other outdoor activities include golf, picnicking, camping, trail riding, hayrides, hiking, swimming, miniature golf and paddle boating. Sports facilities include a golf course, tennis courts, and softball and baseball fields. There are almost 1,000 acres of trails for ATVs, motorcycles and dirt bikes. The park also features an extensive trail system for hikers and mountain bikers.[58]

Besides premier fishing (including advanced guide services) and a myriad of watersports, **Lake Texoma State Park** (Basin 21) offers swimming, camping, picnic areas, wildlife viewing opportunities and hiking. The park features comfort stations with showers, boat ramps and a small hiking trail. A privately operated, full-service marina is also available. Park facilities include RV sites (with full hook-ups) and tent campgrounds.[59]

Serving as a gateway to the beautiful Ouachita National Forest, **Lake Wister State Park** (Basin 45) offers five camping areas around the 115 miles of scenic shoreline. Available recreational activities include hiking, camping, biking, boating and water skiing as well as a water spray park. Nestled in a ring of pine- and oak-covered mountains—the Sans Bois, Jackforks, Kiamichis and Ouachitas—lodging facilities include fifteen cabins, RV sites (full hook-ups or some with water and electric only) and tent sites. Visitors can also enjoy playgrounds, a swimming beach and miniature golf. Hiking trails include a self-guided nature trail and 6.4-mile trail into the surrounding wilderness. During the winter, the park and lake host Golden and Bald eagles. Mountain streams provide ideal water for fishing for northern bluegill, channel catfish, flathead catfish, and white, smallmouth and largemouth bass. The park also offers a fully equipped group camp that can accommodate up to one hundred visitors.[60]

Figure 26. Buncombe Creek Marina at Lake Texoma.

The **Little River National Wildlife Refuge** (Basin 2) shelters some of the only remaining fragments of the river floodplain's once vast bottomland hardwood forest ecosystem. The 15,000 swampy acres include limestone cliffs, oxbow lakes, creeks, marshes and hardwood forests that provide critical habitat for numerous migratory birds and local wildlife species, including alligators. Hunting, fishing, hiking, wildlife watching, and photography are permitted in many areas of the refuge.

Love Valley WMA (Basin 21) covers 7,746 acres of south-central and eastern Love County just east of Interstate 35. Post oak-blackjack timber dominates the uplands with bottomland hardwoods occurring next to the Red River. Native grasslands comprised of little bluestem and Indian grass dominate the upland openings. Large agricultural fields are present throughout

the WMA. Extensive mudflats along the Red River arm of Lake Texoma are seeded annually to enhance waterfowl habitat. Area lands offer several undesignated primitive camping areas.

Set aside by the Oklahoma Legislature in 1918, the **McCurtain County Wilderness Area** (Basin 4) is the oldest ODWC area in the state and the largest untouched shortleaf pine/hardwood forest remaining in the nation. Located adjacent to Broken Bow reservoir, the area's 14,000 acres has limited public access with some controlled hunting.

The 2,600 pristine wilderness acres comprising **McGee Creek State Park** (Basins 8 and 6) are located on the southwest edge of the Ouachita Mountain range in Atoka County. Featuring the 3,350-acre McGee Creek Reservoir, one of Oklahoma's top trophy bass lakes, the park abounds with recreational opportunities, such as fishing, water-skiing, boating, camping, and equestrian and hiking trails.

Adjacent to McGee Creek State Park, hunters frequent the 10,000-acre **McGee Creek WMA** (Basin 8), which is stocked with deer, dove, turkey and waterfowl. One designated primitive camping area is offered on the area. In addition to bass, McGee Creek Reservoir is known for catfish and crappie fishing.

Oka Yanahli Preserve (Basin 12) is a cooperative venture of the Nature Conservancy, Chickasaw Nation and other conservation-minded organizations to protect and expand the riparian corridor along a two-mile stretch of the Blue River south of Connerville. The Preserve—which protects almost 3,600 acres of native prairie, as well as area springs and land providing es-

Figure 27. McCurtain County Wilderness Area is ODWC's oldest management area and home to Oklahoma's last remaining population of the federally endangered Red-cockaded woodpecker. (Credit: ODWC)

Figure 28. Oka Yanahli Preserve. (Credit: The Nature Conservancy)

sential recharge for the Arbuckle-Simpson aquifer—is considered a model of collaborative land and water conservation and restoration. The Preserve derives its name from the Chickasaw phrase, "flowing water."[61]

The oldest national forest in the southern U.S., the **Ouachita National Forest** (Basins 4, 3 and 2) consists of 1.78 million acres stretching across much of western Arkansas and part of southeast Oklahoma. About 363,000 acres of the forest are in Oklahoma.

Adjacent to and north of the forest in LeFlore and McCurtain Counties, the **Ouachita WMA** (Basins 45, 6, 4 and 3) covers an enormous area (232,000 acres) managed cooperatively between the ODWC and U.S. Forest Service. The area's primary species is deer and turkey for which more than 400 acres of food plots are planted annually. With breathtaking vistas along the top of Winding Stair Mountain from Highway 271 to the Arkansas line, the **Talimena National Scenic Byway** cuts through the Ouachita WMA. The road is known far and wide for its spectacular fall and spring foliage. Camping is available along the route and at Cedar Lake Campground. There are three larger bodies of water (Cedar Lake, Crooked Branch and Boney Ridge) managed for fishing, primarily bass, catfish and sunfish. Many primitive camping sites exist in the area while two sites at Cedar Lake and Winding Stair Vista contain modern facilities; there are two shooting ranges in the area. Also included in the WMA is **Winding Stair Mountain National Recreation Area** with 23 campsites and numerous amenities.[62]

Adjacent to the Little River and Pine Creek Lake, **Pine Creek WMA** (Basin 3) extends over 10,280 acres

Figure 29. Camping at Cedar Lake in the Ouachita National Forest.

in McCurtain and Pushmataha Counties. Habitat consists of mature stands of hardwoods in the bottomland areas; elsewhere are hardwood/pine tree mixes as well as large stands of mostly pine. Some of the area is old farm field habitat that is maintained through intensive management practices. Soil types vary from deep sand to rocky as the area is part of the Kiamichi Uplift. Camping is allowed at primitive sites, with more modern facilities available on Corps lands. At Pine Creek Lake, black bass, catfish, crappie, and smallmouth are in abundance. The Little River provides quality fishing for smallmouth bass and sunfish, and it is floatable via canoe during the spring.

Located in the upper end of the Blue River watershed overlying the Arbuckle-Simpson aquifer, the **Pontotoc Ridge Preserve** (Basin 12) is distinguished by 2,906 acres of bottomland forests, oak savannas (essential for migratory birds), mixed-grass and tallgrass prairies, springs and streams that support a diversity of plant and animal species. Originally a gift from the Buddy Smith family, the Preserve is protected and maintained by the Nature Conservancy.

Pushmataha WMA (Basin 6), with 19,247 acres on the western fringe of the Ouachita mountain range, is comprised of a mixture of oak/pine forest and oak/pine savannahs with steep slopes, shallow soils and rocky terrain. The WMA dates back to 1947 when it was first established as a deer preserve. On the site in 1982, one of the longest running research projects focusing on vegetation response to fire frequency was initiated and continues on the area today. Tours of the research area are available by appointment. The WMA is home to numerous species of flora and fauna, with many excellent fishing opportunities available at nearby lakes and streams.

Red Slough WMA (Basin 1) is one of the largest, most biologically diverse wetland reserves in the nation. This former rice farm is home to 320 species of birds, 171 species of butterflies and damsel/dragonflies, and 57 species of amphibians and reptiles. Its 5,814 acres, located in the Ouachita National Forest, shelter a variety of habitats that include lakes, riparian zones, marshes, wet prairies and bottomland hardwoods. Red Slough offers numerous unique wildlife viewing opportunities, including ten observation platforms and 25 miles of levees.

Located in the scenic woodlands of the Sans Bois Mountains, **Robbers Cave State Park** (Basin 45) is a favorite destination of rappellers, equestrians, hikers and outdoor lovers. Others come for the hunting, seasonal trout fishing and many miles of hiking and equestrian trails. Centered around a famous outlaw cave hidden in sandstone hills and cliffs that served as a hideout for

Figure 30. Roseate spoonbills at Red Slough WMA. (Credit: PBase)

outlaws Jesse James and Belle Starr, the park contains 8,246 acres, including 189 acres of water occupied by Lake Carlton, Lake Wayne Wallace and Coon Creek. Campground facilities include RV sites with either full hookups or water/electric hookups, and primitive camping areas along secluded trails. Other accommodations include a lodge, 26 cabins, lake hut and two large group camp facilities. Equestrian campsites are also available. The park's nature center offers naturalist programs and exhibits.[63]

Adjacent to the park is **Robbers Cave WMA** (Basins 45 and 46), which covers 6,180 acres of Latimer County, including 3,800 acres of forested hunting ground. The area consists mostly of hills covered with pine timber, with scattered oaks and hickory and very few openings. Limited fishing opportunities exist on the management area, however, one of Oklahoma's most popular winter-time trout fisheries is located in the park below Lake Carlton.

Stringtown WMA (Basin 8) covers 2,260 acres of south-central Atoka County. Terrain within the WMA ranges from steep to moderately steep while vegetation consists of oak-pine association. One designated primitive camping area is available. Fishing opportunities are somewhat limited.

Talimena State Park (Basin 6) serves as Oklahoma's entrance to the Talimena National Scenic Byway. The 20-acre state park offers opportunities for hiking, camping, biking and wildlife watching.

Three Rivers WMA (Basins 3 and 4) covers 216,503 acres and a significant portion of McCurtain and Pushmataha Counties where it abuts the Ouachita National Forest and Ouachita WMA. The area is a mixture of pine and hardwood forests. Loblolly pine plantations of various age classes dominate the WMA. Interspersed within the pine plantations are hardwood benches and streamside management zones dominated by oaks and hickories. The land encompassed within the Three Rivers WMA is privately owned by the Weyerhaeuser Company; however, the land is available to hunters and other recreationists through purchase of a land access fee. No designated camping areas exist, but primitive camping is allowed everywhere on the WMA. Fishing opportunities exist for sunfish, bass and channel catfish on some small ponds throughout the WMA. The Glover River, which bisects the WMA, offers smallmouth bass, sunfish and other species.

Tishomingo National Fish Hatchery (Basin 21) was established in 1928 on 312 acres acquired through First

Figure 31. Robbers Cave Nature Trail. (Credit: Arklahoma Hiker)

Figure 32. Tishomingo National Wildlife Refuge at Lake Texoma.

Americans heirs. The site of this hatchery was chosen due to the high-quality water particular to Pennington Creek, which originates from the Arbuckle-Simpson aquifer. Original land acquisition included one of the oldest water rights in the state—the right to divert 10 cubic feet per second from the creek for fish culture. While the hatchery's basic mission is to produce warm-water fish for distribution to federal waters throughout the western United States, it also conserves imperiled aquatic species found in the Arkansas and Red River Basins. These important captive breeding and rearing programs uncover vital information beneficial to the protection and management of threatened species like the Arkansas River shiner, alligator gar and alligator snapping turtle.[64]

The **Tishomingo National Wildlife Refuge** (Basin 21), which encompasses the Cumberland Pool in the Washita River arm of Lake Texoma, has deep, historic ties to the Chickasaw Nation. Named for Chickasaw leader Tishominko, the refuge is on the original 200-acre site of the first Chickasaw boarding school for tribal youth called the Chickasaw Manual Labor Academy. Established in 1946, the refuge contains 16,464 acres of protected land managed by the Fish and Wildlife Service.[65] While hunting is the primary recreational use of the refuge, it is also popular with hikers, wildlife watchers and anglers.

Turner Falls Park (Basin 14) is the oldest park in Oklahoma. Located in the Arbuckle Mountains, its natural caves, hiking trails, fishing streams and iconic Turner Falls, which drops 77 feet into a natural swimming pool, attract thousands of visitors each year. The park is owned and operated by the City of Davis.

Whitegrass Flats WMA (Basin 1) covers 391 acres in McCurtain County. Habitat consists of a 90-acre Moist Soil Unit divided into three compartments. The area is mostly old farm fields with some areas replanted to hardwoods. Trees in the area include six species of oak, ash, hickory, pine, river birch and willow as well as sand plum, holly, sumac, and a large variety of grasses and legumes. Soil types vary from deep sand to sandy loam. Neither camping nor fishing is available at the WMA, although opportunities exist nearby.

Near Lake Wister State Park in central LeFlore and eastern Latimer Counties, **Wister WMA** (Basin 45) covers 35,500 acres of river bottoms, upland and foothills. Bottomland consists primarily of oaks and other hardwood species. Upland sites are a mixture of small fields of native grass, greenbrier and sumac; foothills consist of post oak, hickory and pine. The Poteau and Fourche Maline Rivers run through the eastern and western portions of the area. Primitive camping sites are offered throughout the WMA while two concrete boat ramps are available on the Poteau River portion.

Yourman WMA (Basin 48) covers 2,860 acres of central Latimer County where the terrain is comprised of a mixture of oak/pine forest with steep slopes, shallow soils and rocky ground. Native tree species include shortleaf pine, post oak, red oak, black oak, water oak, sycamore, hackberry, hickory, elm, blackgum, sweetgum, rusty blackhaw, flowering dogwood and hawthorn. Because the area is relatively small, it has been designated only for walk-in access. There is a pavilion on the northern entrance of the area where camping is allowed. Fishing opportunities exist at several area lakes and streams.

The Chickasaw Nation: SIGNIFICANT SITES

Figure 33. Significant cultural and historical sites, Chickasaw Nation.

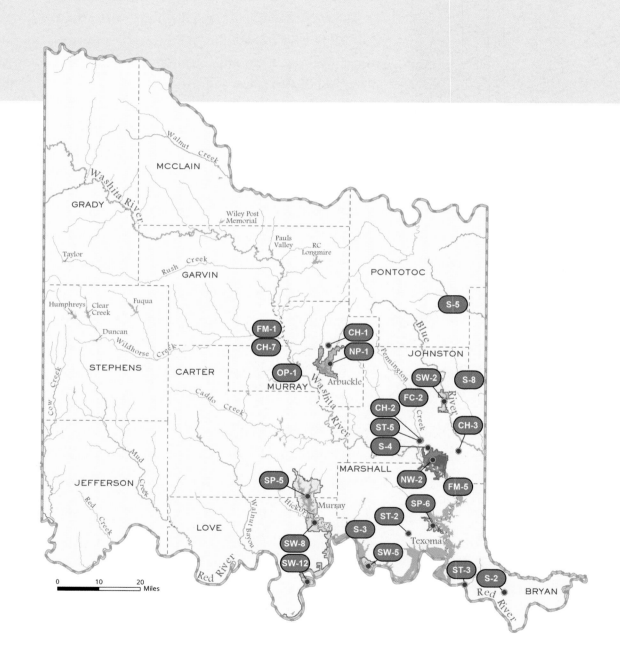

Site Codes:

CH: Cultural/Historical Site
FC: Fish Culture
FM: Fort/Military Site
NF: National Forest
NP: National Park
NW: National Wildlife Refuge

OP: Other Park
S: School
ST: Settlement/Town
SP: State Park
SW: State Wildlife Management
     or Wilderness Area

CH-1:	Chickasaw Cultural Center	S-5:	Collins Institute
CH-2:	Chickasaw National Capitol	S-8:	Wapanucka Institute
CH-3:	Chickasaw White House	SP-5:	Lake Murray State Park
CH-7:	Initial Point	SP-6:	Lake Texoma State Park
FC-2:	Tishomingo National Fish Hatchery	ST-2:	Camp Leavenworth
FM-1:	Fort Arbuckle	ST-3:	Colbert's Ferry Site
FM-5:	Fort Washita	ST-5:	Good Spring
NP-1:	Chickasaw National Recreation Area	SW-2:	Blue River Public Fishing & Hunting Area
NW-2:	Tishomingo NWR	SW-5:	Fobb Bottom WMA
OP-1:	Turner Falls Park	SW-8:	Hickory Creek WMA
S-2:	Bloomfield Academy Site	SW-12:	Love Valley WMA
S-3:	Burney Institute		
S-4:	Chickasaw Manual Labor Academy		

The Choctaw Nation: SIGNIFICANT SITES

Figure 34. Significant cultural and historical sites, Choctaw Nation.

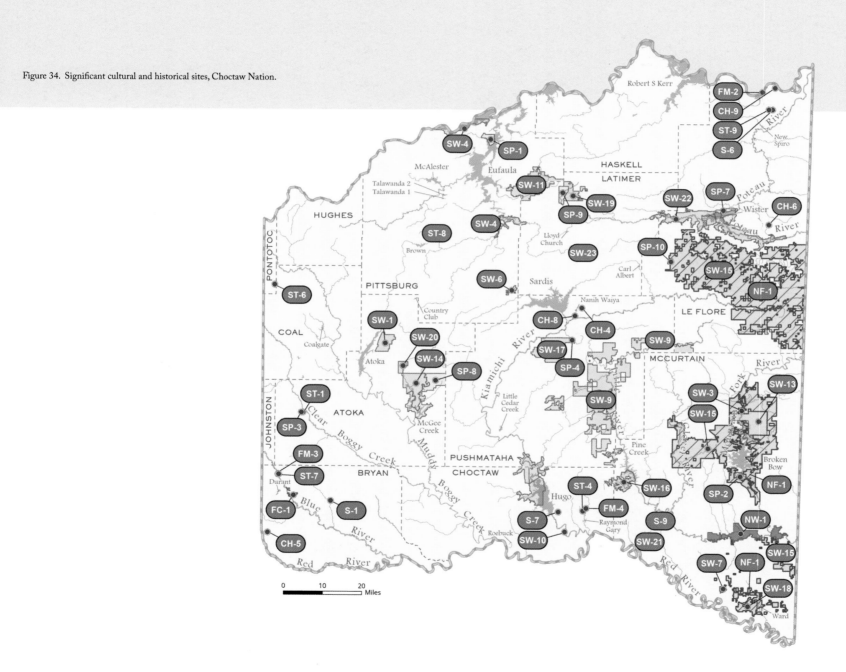

Site Codes:

CH:	Cultural/Historical Site		OP:	Other Park
FC:	Fish Culture		S:	School
FM:	Fort/Military Site		ST:	Settlement/Town
NF:	National Forest		SP:	State Park
NP:	National Park		SW:	State Wildlife Management
NW:	National Wildlife Refuge			or Wilderness Area

CH-4:	Choctaw Council House	SP-2:	Beavers Bend State Park	SW-6:	Gary Sherrer WMA
SCH-5:	Choctaw Cultural Center	SP-3:	Boggy Depot State Park	SW-7:	Grassy Slough WMA
CH-6:	Heavener Runestone Park	SP-4:	Clayton Lake State Park	SW-9:	Honobia Creek WMA
CH-8:	Nanih Waiya	SP-7:	Lake Wister State Park	SW-10:	Hugo WMA
CH-9:	Spiro Mounds Arch. Center	SP-8:	McGee Creek State Park	SW-11:	James Collins WMA
FC-1:	Durant State Fish Hatchery	SP-9:	Robbers Cave State Park	SW-13:	McCurtain County Wilderness Area
FM-2:	Fort Coffee & Choctaw Boys Acad.	SP-10:	Talimena State Park	SW-14:	McGee Creek WMA
FM-3:	Fort McCulloch	ST-1:	Boggy Depot	SW-15:	Ouachita WMA
FM-4:	Fort Towson	ST-4:	Doaksville	SW-16:	Pine Creek WMA
NF-1:	Ouachita National Forest	ST-6:	Kullihoma	SW-17:	Pushmataha WMA
NW-1:	Little River NWR	ST-7:	Nail's Station	SW-18:	Red Slough WMA
S-1:	Armstrong Academy Site	ST-8:	Perryville	SW-19:	Robbers Cave WMA
S-6:	New Hope Seminary	ST-9:	Skullyville	SW-20:	Stringtown WMA
S-7:	Spencer Academy	SW-1:	Atoka WMA	SW-21:	Whitegrass Flats WMA
S-9:	Wheelock Academy Historic Site	SW-3:	Broken Bow WMA	SW-22:	Wister WMA
SP-1:	Arrowhead State Park	SW-4:	Eufaula WMA	SW-23:	Yourman WMA

Historical and Cultural Works Cited

1. "Moundville Archaeological Park – Ancient Site." *Moundville Archaeological Park*, University of Alabama. moundville. museums.ua.edu/ancient-site/.

2. "Indians at the Post Office, Native Themes in New Deal-Era Murals, Signing of the Treaty of Dancing Rabbit Creek." Smithsonian National Postal Museum. postalmuseum. si.edu/indiansatthepostoffice/mural22.html.

3. U.S. Office of Indian Affairs. "Annual Report of the Commissioner of Indian Affairs for the Year 1884." Government Publishing Office (1884).

4. Chickasaw Nation Legislature: Session Laws October 1876, October 1896, and April 1889; *and* Debo, Angie. *The Rise and Fall of the Choctaw Republic*. University of Oklahoma Press (1961) (pp. 143–145).

5. Acts of the Choctaw Nation: October and November 1883, October 1892, October 1893, and October 1894; *and* Chickasaw Nation Legislature: Session Laws October 1876 and October 1884; *and* Debo at p. 145.

6. "Coleman Cole Collection." Western History Collection, Choctaw Nation Manuscript Collections at the University of Oklahoma Libraries.

7. Leeds, Stacy L. "Defeat or Mixed Blessing: Tribal Sovereignty and the State of Sequoyah." *Tulsa Law Review* 43, No. 1: 5-16 (2007).

8. Debo at pp. 260–263, 269, 277–285, and 289.

9. Parent, Laurence. *Chickasaw National Recreation Area*. Western National Parks Association (1993) (pp. 8–10).

10. Lambert, Valerie. "Political Protest, Conflict, and Tribal Nationalism: The Oklahoma Choctaws and the Termination Crisis of 1959–1970." *American Indian Quarterly* 31, No. 2: 283-309 (2007).

11. Dean, Kyle D. "Estimating the Oklahoma Economic Impact of the Chickasaw Nation." Steven C. Agee Economic Research & Policy Institute; *see also* Dean, Kyle D. "The Statewide Impacts of Oklahoma Tribes." Steven C. Agee ERPI (2012).

12. "National Register of Historic Places – Index." *U.S. National Park Service* (updated 14 September 2020). nps.gov/subjects/ nationalregister/index.htm.

13. Wright, Muriel H., George H. Shirk, and Kenny A. Franks. *Mark of Heritage*. Oklahoma Historical Society (1976) (p. 29).

14. Wright et al. at pp. 64–65.

15. May, Jon D. "Black Beaver." *The Encyclopedia of Oklahoma History and Culture* (accessed 3 July 2020). okhistory.org/ publications/enc/entry.php?entry=BL001.

16. Wright. "Initial Point and Fort Arbuckle." Oklahoma Club Woman. Oklahoma State Archives, Vertical Files (originally published March 1937); *and* Wright et al. at 27.

17. Faulk, Odie B., Kenny A. Franks, and Paul F. Lambert, eds. *Early Military Forts and Posts in Oklahoma*. Oklahoma Historical Society (1978) (pp. 42–50); *and* Wright et al. at p. 67.

18. Weiser-Alexander, Kathy. "Fort McCulloch, Oklahoma." *Legends of America* (February 2020). legendsofamerica.com/ fort-mcculloch-oklahoma/.

19. Faulk et al. at pp. 65–77; *and* Wright et al. at p. 71.

20. Faulk et al. at pp. 9–25.

21. Wright et al. at p. 76; *and* "Fort Washita." *The Chickasaw Nation* (accessed 17 August 2019). chickasaw.net/FortWashita.

22. Morris, John W. *Ghost Towns of Oklahoma*. University of Oklahoma Press (1978); *and* Culbertson, Charline M. *Interview with William T. Culbertson*. University of Oklahoma: Western History Collections—Indian Pioneer Collection (30 April 1937).

23. Ruth, Kent. "Ferry on Red River Served State's Pioneering Traffic." *The Oklahoman* (5 January 1986); *and* Wright et al. at p. 46.

24. Morris at p 67.

25. Bamburg, Maxine. "Tishomingo." *The Encyclopedia of Oklahoma History and Culture*; *and* Wright et al. at p. 198.

26. Chickasaw.TV. "Kullihoma: A Traditional Community." *The Chickasaw Nation*, Chickasaw TV: Video Network (accessed 19 January 2019). chickasaw.tv/videos/kulliho-ma-a-traditional-community; *and* "Kullihoma Grounds." *Chickasaw Country*. chickasawcountry.com/history-culture/kullihoma-grounds.

27. Wright, Muriel H. "The Butterfield Overland Mail One Hundred Years Ago." *The Chronicles of Oklahoma* 35(1), 71 (January 1957).

28. Wright et al. at pp. 185–186.

29. Lewis, Anna. "Nunih Waiya." *The Chronicles of Oklahoma*, 16(2), 214-21 (June 1938).

30. Workers of the Writers' Program of the Work Projects Administration in the State of Oklahoma. *Oklahoma: A Guide to the Sooner State*. University of Oklahoma Press (1941).

31. Morris at pp. 177–178.

32. Debo. *The Rise and Fall of the Choctaw Republic* at pp. 60–63.

33. Debo, Angie. *And Still the Waters Run: The Betrayal of the Five Civilized Tribes*. Princeton University Press (1973) (pp. 7–8).

34. Acts of the Choctaw Nation: November 1842.

35. Miles, Dennis B. "Educate or We Perish: The Armstrong Academy's History as Part of the Choctaw Educational System." *The Chronicles of Oklahoma* 89(3): 312-37 (Fall 2011); *and* Wright et al. at p. 35.

36. Cobb-Greetham, Amanda J. *Listening to Our Grandmothers' Stories: The Bloomfield Academy for Chickasaw Females, 1852–1949*. University of Nebraska Press (2007) (Kindle ed. at pp. 89, 136, 647, 900).

37. "Chickasaw Emphasis on Education Inspired Burney Institute." *The Chickasaw Times*, Vol. XXXXI No. 1 (January 2006); *and* Davis, Kendall. "A Tribute and Educational Reminder: The Burney Institute." *Lake Texoma* (accessed 23 September 2018). laketexoma.com/entertainment--a-trib-ute-and-educational-reminder-the-burney-institute/5159.

38. "Wildlife Sanctuary Offers Unique View of the Chickasaw Nation." *The Chickasaw Nation* (accessed 10 October 2018). chickasaw.net/News/Press-Releases/Release/Wildlife-sanctuary-offers-unique-view-of-the-Chick-1503.aspx.

39. Burris, George W. "Reminiscences of Old Stonewall." *The Chronicles of Oklahoma* 20 (June 1942) (pp. 152–158).

40. "Wapanucka Institute – Chickasaw Rock Academy." *The Gateway to Oklahoma History* – The Oklahoma Historical Society (12 November 2013); *and* "Wapanucka Academy." Binders, Local Histories, Narratives and Articles. Holisso Research Center at the Chickasaw Cultural Center, Sulphur, Oklahoma.

41. "Wheelock Academy Historic Site." *Choctaw Nation of Oklahoma Cultural Services* (accessed 27 March 2020). choctawnationculture.com/wheelock/wheelock-academy-historic-site.aspx.

42. Wright et al. at p. 149; *and* Morrison, James D., and ed. Joy Culbreath and Kathy Carpenter. *Schools for the Choctaws*. Durant, Oklahoma: Ameba Publishing (2016) (pp. 66, 70).

43. Norris, L. David. "Colleges and Universities, Normal." *The Encyclopedia of Oklahoma History and Culture*. okhistory.org/publications/enc/entry.php?entry=CO027.

44. Rodden, Kirk A. "Murray State College." *The Encyclopedia of Oklahoma History and Culture* (accessed 20 November 2020). okhistory.org/publications/enc/entry.php?entry=MU012.

45. "Chickasaw Cultural Center – The Heartbeat of a Nation." *Chickasaw Cultural Center*. chickasawculturalcenter.com/about-us.

46. "Chickasaw National Capitol." *The Chickasaw Nation*. chickasaw.net/Capitol.

47. "Chickasaw White House." *The Chickasaw Nation* (accessed 3 November 2019). chickasaw.net/WhiteHouse.

48. Debo. *The Rise and Fall of the Choctaw Republic* at p. 159.

49. "Heavener Runestone Park." *Travel Oklahoma* – Oklahoma Tourism and Recreation Department. travelok.com/listings/view.profile/id.3398.

50. Peterson, Dennis A. "Spiro Mounds." *The Encyclopedia of Oklahoma History and Culture*. okhistory.org/publications/enc/entry.php?entry=SP012.

51. Oklahoma Department of Wildlife Conservation. "Wildlife Management Areas: Alphabetical List." *Oklahoma Department of Wildlife Conservation*. (See: Atoka, Arbuckle Springs, Broken Bow, Cross Timbers, Fobb Bottom, Gary Sherrer, Grady County, Grassy Slough, Hickory Creek, Honobia Creek, Hugo, James Collins, Love Valley, McCurtain County Wilderness Area, McGee Creek, Ouachita Leflore Unit, Ouachita McCurtain Unit, Pine Creek, Pushmataha, Robbers Cave, Stringtown, Three Rivers, Whitegrass Flats, Wister, Yourman) (access dates: April 2020). wildlifedepartment.com/hunting/wma/all; *and* "Oklahoma State Parks." *Oklahoma State Parks*. stateparks.com/oklahoma_parks_and_recreation_destinations.html; *and* "TravelOK.Com – Oklahoma's Official Travel & Tourism Site." *Travel Oklahoma* – Oklahoma's Official Travel & Tourism Site. travelok.com/listings/search/4%7C9.

52. "Arrowhead State Park." *Oklahoma State Parks*. stateparks.com/arrowhead_state_park_in_oklahoma.html.

53. Burge, Steve. "Blue River Public Hunting and Fishing Area." *Outdoor Oklahoma* (January/February 2007).

54. Manandhar, Sharmina. "Boggy Depot State Park operations unchanged under Chickasaw Nation management." The Chickasaw Nation. https://www.chickasaw.net/News/Press-Releases/Release/Boggy-Depot-State-Park-operations-unchanged-under-1187.aspx. (September 12, 2011).

55. Layden, Logan. "Tribes Save Boggy Depot Park After State Spending Cuts." *StateImpact Oklahoma* (29 September 2011). stateimpact.npr.org/oklahoma/2011/09/29/tribes-save-boggy-depot-park-after-state-spending-cuts/.

56. Parent at pp. 8–10.

57. "Durant State Fish Hatchery – Durant, Oklahoma." *Waymarking* (18 August 2009). waymarking.com/waymarks/WM71H7_Durant_State_Fish_Hatchery_Durant_Oklahoma.

58. "Lake Murray State Park." *Travel Oklahoma* – Oklahoma Tourism and Recreation Department. travelok.com/state-parks/4358?gclid=Cj0KCQjwoub3BRC6ARIsABGhny am5sqFtFg-rJ8sEzaD2AqZjb_Fb1zYpD30u4NNzyu-HInw36blPw4aAjZQEALw_wcB.

59. "Lake Texoma State Park." *Travel Oklahoma* – Oklahoma Tourism and Recreation Department. travelok.com/state-parks/4383?gclid=Cj0KCQjwoub3BRC6ARIsABGhnyYzhXHW9RoK8vXfVErhjQDdsmaeWoAM9szD1DkkLg-wuEXLM6WPTSKoaApcNEALw_wcB.

60. "Lake Wister State Park." *Travel Oklahoma* – Oklahoma Tourism and Recreation Department. travelok.com/state-parks/4390.

61. "Oka Yanahli Preserve – Places We Protect." *The Nature Conservancy* (accessed 18 April 2018). nature.org/en-us/get-involved/how-to-help/places-we-protect/okayanahli-preserve.

62. "Winding Stair Recreation Area." *Travel Oklahoma* – Oklahoma Tourism and Recreation Department. travelok.com/listings/view.profile/id.8580.

63. "Robbers Cave State Park." *Travel Oklahoma* – Oklahoma Tourism and Recreation Department. travelok.com/state-parks/robbers-cave-state-park.

64. Tishomingo National Fish Hatchery. *U.S. Fish and Wildlife Service* (accessed 13 November 2018). fws.gov/southwest/fisheries/tishomingo/.

65. O'Dell, Larry. "Tishomingo National Wildlife Refuge." *The Encyclopedia of Oklahoma History and Culture*. okhistory.org/publications/enc/entry.php?entry=TI009.

66. "Searching for the Wild River Cane." The Creative-Native Project (28 May 2011). creativenativeproject.blogspot.com/2011/05/searching-for-wild-river-cane.html.

67. Moss, Bret. "OU Students Learn How Water Has Shaped Choctaw Culture, Past and Present." *The Choctaw Nation*, News and Events. choctawnation.com/news-events/press-media/ou-students-learn-how-water-has-shaped-choctaw-culture-past-and-present.

68. Choctaw Nation Historic Preservation Department. "Traditional Uses of Freshwater Mussels." *The Biskinik* (February 2013). choctawnation.com/sites/default/files/2015/10/14/2013.2_Traditional_uses_of_freshwater_mussels.pdf.

69. Vaughn, Caryn C., Jason P. Julian, Carla L. Atkinson, and Kiza Gates. "Environmental Flow Considerations for Freshwater Mussels: Droughts, Dams, Timing, and Temperature" (presentation). U.S. Fish and Wildlife Service (unpublished).

Tribal-State Water Settlement

From our origin and migration stories to our lived experiences, water has always been fundamental to Chickasaw and Choctaw identity. The Nations' aboriginal homelands are dominated by major waterways and riparian bottomlands, including those known today as the Mississippi, the Tombigbee, and the Tennessee Rivers. These storied waterways and their myriad tributaries imbued the Nations' culture and language with concepts of place and relation, while also providing the means for life and the infrastructure for transportation, trade, and military strength. Fundamental notions of what it means to *be* Chickasaw and Choctaw were formed in these water-rich lands.

Throughout early European colonization of our homelands and the emergence of a young United States, the Chickasaw and Choctaw people persevered against a steadily growing tide of non-First American incursion on our homelands. When confronted with the United States and its forced removal policy in the 1820s and 1830s, our leaders made difficult choices to ensure our survival as sovereign nations. Accordingly, those leaders worked to secure crucial intergovernmental treaties, which implemented homeland-for-homeland exchanges and guaranteed our continued existence as self-governing peoples. The treaties entitled each Nation to select lands west of the Mississippi best suited to its needs, and both Nations selected lands in what is now southeastern and south-central Oklahoma. The Chickasaw and Choctaw remain neighbors today in our new treaty homelands, connected as ever by the land and its water.

Water sustained the Nations' lifeways and economies during the early Chickasaw and Choctaw Republics in Indian Territory. The fertile waters of the new treaty homelands served as vital corridors for Chickasaw and Choctaw culture, trade, and transportation. As federal policy shifted again, and the promises made in earlier treaties were broken, the new State of Oklahoma began to encourage its citizens to utilize the waters belonging to the Nations for their own benefit. Today, as we continue to rebuild our governing systems after generations of federal and state control, these waters support Chickasaw and Choctaw survival, sustainability, and health, and provide the foundation for a shared economy and our region's unique character.

Settlement Area Hydrologic Basins:

Figure 35. Current boundaries of the Chickasaw Nation and Choctaw Nation of Oklahoma. (Right)
Figure 36. Settlement Area Hydrologic Basins delineated in the Settlement agreement. (Below)

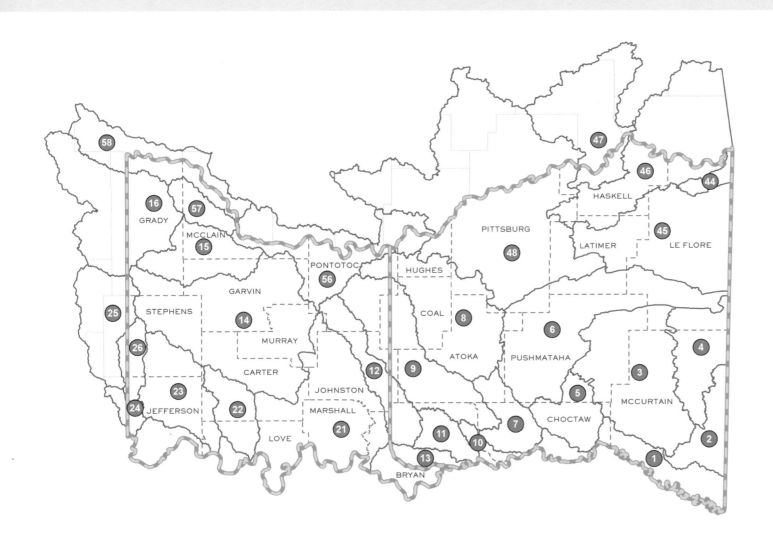

BASIN #	WATERSHED
1, 10, 13, 21:	Red
2:	Little
3:	Upper Little
4:	Mountain Fork
5, 6:	Kiamichi
7, 8:	Muddy Boggy
9:	Clear Boggy
11, 12:	Blue
14:	Lower Washita
15:	Middle Washita (Class A)
16:	Middle Washita (Class C)
22:	Walnut Bayou
23:	Mud Creek
24, 25, 26:	Beaver Creek
44, 45:	Poteau
46, 47:	Lower Arkansas
48, 56:	Lower Canadian (Class C)
57:	Lower Canadian (Class A)
58:	Middle Canadian

WATERSHEDS (HYDROLOGIC BASINS)

A watershed (or hydrologic/drainage basin) is an area of land that shares a common outlet for precipitation runoff and streamflow, with flow (commonly measured in cubic feet per second) generally increasing from headwaters at their source to the lowest elevation at the basin's outlet. The bed of a major river or stream at the basin outlet typically represents the lowest elevation in that contiguous land area. The thirty planning basins subject to the Settlement agreement (which, for the purposes of the *Oka Holisso* have been aggregated into nineteen watershed units exhibiting similar attributes) are part of either the larger Red or Arkansas River Basins. In turn, the Red and Arkansas Basins are important components of the even larger Mississippi River watershed, which drains much of the central U.S. and terminates at the Gulf of Mexico. Consistently, most basin streams in the Nations' lands flow in a generally southerly or southeasterly direction.

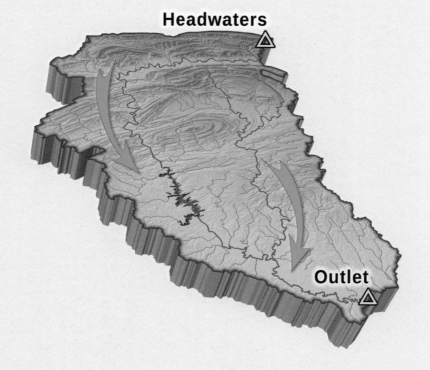

Headwaters

Outlet

EMERGENCE OF TRIBAL & STATE WATER CONFLICT IN THE TREATY TERRITORIES

In the 1980s, Chickasaw and Choctaw representatives asserted general rights to our treaty homelands' waters. During the two subsequent decades, efforts to secure tribal-state agreements premised on the marketing of water resources failed, but nevertheless provided tangible recognition of the centrality of tribal interests in treaty territory waters. Learning from these experiences, we continued to work to ensure the recognition and protection of these rights. Much progress was accomplished in partnership with non-tribal partners as we strived to ensure adequate supplies of clean water throughout our region and to restore riparian habitats for key plant and animal species. Throughout our work, we confirmed our commitment to long-term sustainability as an overarching principle of resource management.

In 2009, the simmering conflict erupted over the state's proposed plan to make more than 100,000 acre-feet per year (AFY) of Kiamichi River water available for Oklahoma City. The controversial proposal also called for the state to transfer its rights to the water storage capacity in Sardis Lake to the city. Sardis Lake is a water development project in the Kiamichi River basin that was designed and constructed by the U.S. Army Corps of Engineers (USACE). The state planned to convey its storage rights in exchange for the city assuming responsibility for repayment of the state's federal Sardis Lake construction debt.

After initial tribal-state negotiations failed to gain traction, the Chickasaw and Choctaw filed suit in federal court challenging the city's pending water right permit application as well as the state-city water storage transfer agreement. Relying on our removal-era treaties and the homeland-for-homeland exchange negotiated with the United States, we asserted treaty-protected rights to waters sufficient to support a *permanent and sustainable* homeland. We further alleged our treaty rights preempted Oklahoma from proceeding with its plan, which we argued would be inconsistent with the long-term health and welfare of the Nations' homelands. After two years of complex litigation and much controversy, the Nations, state and city began meaningful negotiations to discover mutually acceptable resolutions.

⧂ THE WATER SETTLEMENT

Successful negotiations required the parties to navigate through many complex and conflicting goals. The Nations emphasized sovereignty and sustainability, arguing generally for a voice in the handling of major water rights actions and meaningful protections for the treaty territories' consumptive and non-consumptive use needs. The state emphasized protecting existing regulatory structures and predictability in administration of governing rules, and the city emphasized its goal of obtaining access to additional water for its citizens. Finally, the United States—acting both as fiduciary for tribal interests as well as a sovereign with

its own governing and proprietary rights—monitored the parties' progress throughout our discussions while highlighting its various policy priorities.

In August 2016, the parties announced that settlement terms were successfully reached, and four months later the president of the United States signed federal legislation ratifying the terms and directing the secretary of the U.S. Department of the Interior to sign the agreement on the federal government's behalf. Since then, the settlement parties have worked diligently to satisfy preconditions necessary to enforce the agreement, working in partnership to finalize and implement our broad Settlement agreement.

In broad terms, finalized tribal and state water settlements typically include the following three elements: (1) a full and final waiver of tribal claims, which is generally a federal prerequisite; (2) a quantification of tribal rights to use water; and (3) rules for the administration of water rights or for addressing intergovernmental conflicts. Frequently, water settlements also make federal financial and other material support available to the tribes, and occasionally to other settlement parties. Each settlement is unique, but generally include these elements, or variations of them.

The Chickasaw and Choctaw Nations' settlement uniquely focuses on scientifically assessing water use proposals at the regulatory stage, i.e., *before* property rights attach. Nevertheless, this emphasis on *regulatory* standards and procedures, as opposed to *property rights*, covers each of the three standard water settlement elements. For example, in lieu of authorizing a new water development project, our settlement establishes new

allocations and limits on an existing federal project, i.e., Sardis Lake. The congressionally approved allocation of Sardis water storage capacity emphasizes the use of Sardis Lake by and for the benefit of local water uses through the following means:

- Permanently dedicating almost half of Sardis storage to maintain and bolster fish, wildlife, and related recreation purposes and needs, and
- Allocating 13 percent of Sardis storage capacity for water users delivering water to a ten-county area of southeastern Oklahoma comprised of Le-Flore, McCurtain, Pushmataha, Latimer, Haskell, Choctaw, Pittsburg, Coal, Atoka, and Bryan Counties. Furthermore, this "set aside" storage will be made available on favorable terms.

A copy of the fully conformed and executed Settlement agreement is included in the *Oka Holisso* appendix, but the following offers a high-level, section-by-section summary:

- **Preamble:** Providing context and essential settlement objective;
- **Section 1:** Defining key and operative settlement terms and phrases, each of which controls interpretation of the Settlement's substantive provisions;
- **Section 2:** Setting forth the Chickasaw and Choctaw Nations' waivers of claims, including certain exceptions thereto;
- **Section 3:** Providing for waivers of federal, tribal, and state sovereign immunity for purposes of enforcing the terms of the agreement;

Tribal/State Water Settlement:

Oklahoma City Requirements Related to the Use of Sardis Lake Water Storage

Sardis Lake

Kiamichi River

Local use set-aside and implementation of the Sardis Lake Level Management Plan to reserve at least 20,000 AFY of reservoir supply.

Implementation of municipal water conservation measures during drought conditions.

A bypass flow stipulation of at least 50 cubic feet per second in the Kiamichi River at the Moyers diversion point to protect downstream needs, including non-consumptive water demands for recreation, fish and wildlife and endangered species.

The Agreement also establishes a $10 million fund to enhance recreation, fish and wildlife habitat, and environmental protections at both Sardis Lake and Lake Atoka.

MOYERS

Figure 37. Section 6 of the Water Settlement agreement includes requirements that Oklahoma City must follow to ensure protection for the many uses and users of basin waters.

- **Section 4:** Providing for settlement's enforceability date, i.e., setting forth the conditions that must be satisfied for the parties' legal rights and obligations to vest (note, that by written agreement and as authorized by both the settlement and federal legislation, the parties have extended the deadline for satisfying these conditions to March 31, 2022);

- **Section 5:** Establishing terms for future Oklahoma Water Resource Board (OWRB) rulemaking and permitting decisions (including delineation and definitions of Class A, B and C Settlement Area Hydrologic Basins), providing critical mechanisms relating to tribal-state engagement on development of hydrologic models, state conformance with uniform pre-permitting regulatory inquiries, and administration of the groundwaters of the particularly sensitive Arbuckle-Simpson aquifer;

- **Section 6:** Establishing terms and conditions to resolve the Nations' jurisdictional objections to OWRB's permitting Oklahoma City to divert and use waters of the Kiamichi Basin, providing critical mechanisms for protecting Sardis Reservoir lake levels, diversion point bypass flows, allocations of waters stored in Sardis, funds for mitigation and conservation projects, and other protective measures;

- **Section 7:** Recognizing, identifying, and providing for the protection of existing tribal water use rights and establishing rules for development of future tribal rights, providing generally for management of intergovernmental interests in competing water uses;

- **Section 8:** Recognizing, identifying, and providing for both the protection of tribal allottee water use rights, providing critically the opportunity for individual allottee's to litigate for additional rights, at his or her own option;
- **Section 9:** Declaring tribal-state common interest in long-term water sustainability, providing importantly for intergovernmental communication and collaboration on water planning;
- **Section 10:** Setting forth general commitments among the parties to ensure sound implementation of the settlement;
- **Section 11:** Setting forth addresses and points of contact for notice purposes;
- **Section 12:** Setting forth a disclaimer as to what the settlement does not do or mean;
- **Section 13:** Setting forth a plain statement of the settlement's legal effect; and
- **Section 14:** Authorizing the parties to execute the agreement in counterparts.

With respect to water planning, rights, permitting and use, the settlement's primary provisions can be found in Sections 5 through 9. Tribal settlement implementation efforts will focus predominantly on the intergovernmental framework these sections establish. In terms of legal structure, these sections also form the analytical spine around which we have developed the *Oka Holisso*.

Also included in the *appendix* are the Chickasaw general resolution and Choctaw council bill relating to each Nation's sign-on to the agreement, and a copy of the 2016 Water Infrastructure Improvements for the Nation Act (Section 3608), which lays out provisions relevant to the settlement.

Mean Available Flow

Rather than utilizing the State of Oklahoma's methodology to assess the potential impact of proposed water use permits, during negotiations the Nations proposed an alternate, more protective, mechanism under provisions of the Settlement agreement. As a result, the final agreement introduced a more expansive concept of assessing available streamflow as an integral component of permit review to recognize and protect water quality, ecological, recreational and related non-consumptive needs within each of the Settlement Area's 31 delineated hydrologic basins.

Section 1.39 of the Tribal-State Water Settlement agreement defines "mean available flow" at a proposed specific point of diversion as that remaining after subtracting flows necessary to satisfy:

- permitted appropriative uses;
- any surface water right developed by either Nation pursuant to Section 7.7, which relates to future surface water development within Settlement Area basins;
- domestic use set-aside (i.e., six acre-feet/year per 160 acres within the basin);
- prior vested rights;
- any surface water right recognized pursuant to Section 8 (to the extent not already subtracted);
- pending applications;
- reservoir yields; and
- other designated purposes in basin, including apportionment provisions of applicable interstate stream compacts.

Mean available flow in a particular basin is a key variable of conferral threshold determinations and bipartisan technical review and modeling of proposed water use permit applications. Applications for the use of water outside of the basin of origin or Settlement Area that trigger the agreement's conferral process must ensure a quantity of flow sufficient to satisfy water quality, ecological and recreational needs within that basin or area. This new and innovative strategy to ensure the availability of water specifically for non-consumptive needs directly reflects the Nations' foundational sustainability ethic, and it recognizes the true value of water to key economic sectors within the Chickasaw and Choctaw territories.

THE SETTLEMENT AND
THE OKA HOLISSO

As noted, tribal and state water rights settlements rarely include mechanisms for tribes to influence state water rights permitting decisions. Our settlement, however, dedicates three sections to provide the Nations with a "seat at the table" when it comes to major permitting decisions as well as in setting long-term policy and planning work: Sections 5 and 6 address non-tribal water use, with Section 6 laying out conditions to Oklahoma City's future use of Kiamichi Basin waters and Section 5 modifying the OWRB's permitting protocols and inquiries to meet tribal objectives; and Section 9 makes unique provision for a declaration of common tribal-state sustainability policies and cooperation on future water planning work. Additionally, Section 7 recognizes, identifies, and protects existing tribal water uses while providing also for predictable yet flexible mechanisms for future tribal development of water resources, all while preserving tribal rights to self-government while we interface in a more stable intergovernmental framework with Oklahoma. Collectively, these sections inform our work to support the long-term sustainability of both the water resources of the treaty territories and the communities on which our quality of life and economic health depend.

No agreement solves every issue, and unforeseeable situations are inevitable, presenting unanticipated consequences. We approached the negotiation and implementation of this settlement, though, with the clear goal of establishing new governing principles and a new intergovernmental relationship. We have worked hard to build a new set of rule-based expectations as to *how water would be managed*.

To use this new structure effectively, it is critical that we work with good data that we have collected and analyzed, being mindful of *how it will be used in future permitting and planning processes*. Accordingly, in developing the *Oka Holisso* we have paid particular and special heed to the operative provisions of, for example, Section 5 — e.g., the conferral thresholds, modeling requirements, and regulatory inquiries that will control future permitting decisions — to ensure we are collecting and analyzing data in a manner that provides us with the tools required to protect our water resource-related interests in future proceedings. Likewise, we have developed our *Oka Holisso* to help identify areas of critical or emerging need, including communities that need additional water supplies or stream systems that may require additional restoration or protection, so we can best focus our planning efforts. Our Settlement and the *Oka Holisso* are best understood as *living documents*, with the Settlement setting forth enforceable and agreed-upon terms and the *Oka Holisso* providing a threshold means for our marshalling the facts and informing our understanding of the resource and our ecological and economic needs for it. Water work is never completed; like the resource itself, it is dynamic and changing. The Settlement and *Oka Holisso* are part of the Nations' ongoing efforts to engage in this critical work and to constantly strengthen our capacities to provide for our peoples' and our homelands' continuance and health.

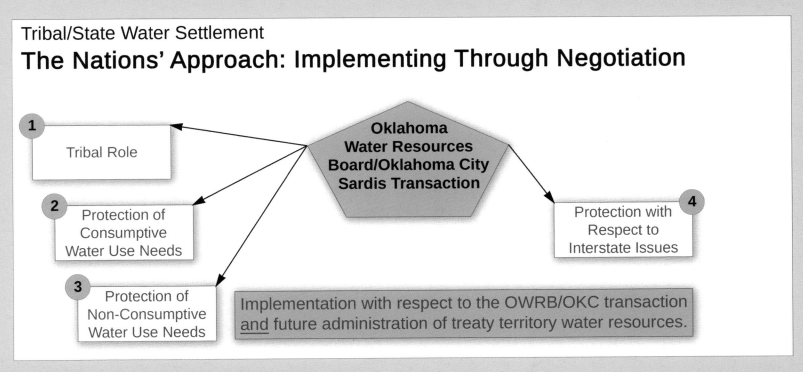

Figure 38. The Nations' approach to implementing the Water Settlement agreement.

The Nations' Water Resources

omprehensive data—utilized through the application of sound science and long-term planning—is a foundational element of tribal water management. It is essential to effective implementation of the Tribal-State Water Settlement as tribal leadership endeavors to ensure that sufficient supplies of water are available for current and future generations of citizens residing in the Nations' homelands. The water-related data and information presented in this section have been assembled largely to align decision-making with principles of the Settlement agreement. Moreover, it serves to establish reliable water supply for varied uses and users within the Settlement Area's delineated hydrologic basins and watersheds. However, concerning official actions in response to future water use proposals and potential permit applications in the region, this information is intended to provide only an initial, cursory guide in determining if more detailed evaluation or study is warranted.

⌗ CLIMATE

The availability, use and management of Oklahoma's water resources, including the flow regime of rivers and streams, is heavily influenced by climate as well as geography. This is especially true in the southeast quadrant of Oklahoma, which generally encompasses the Chickasaw and Choctaw Nations. This region is characterized by a warm, temperate climate characterized by hot, humid summers and mild winters. Warm, moist air moving northward from the Gulf of Mexico exerts considerable influence over the Nations' territories, contributing to generous precipitation—quite the opposite of mostly arid western Oklahoma, which is influenced by dry northern arctic air. This results in a relative abundance of surface water throughout the region, especially in the east. Both temperature and precipitation are discussed in more detail in the following sections.

- Evaporation has a significant effect on water availability. Statewide average annual evaporation (Figure 39) exceeds rainfall in some parts of the Tribal region.

- The growing season, or freeze-free period (Figure 40), gets progressively longer from the northwest to southeast portion of the region, although this trend is interrupted in the Ouachita Mountains, where the active growing period is three to four weeks shorter than the surrounding area. The growing season ranges between 225 and 230 days in the southern tier of counties.
- Flooding in the region is a relatively common occurrence, especially in the spring, resulting in significant property damage and occasional loss of life. Occasionally, hurricanes or tropical storms spawned in the Gulf or Atlantic Ocean will impact southeast Oklahoma, stalling over the area and contributing heavy rainfall over an extended period.

While regular Gulf moisture reduces the frequency of drought events, episodes are still common and often severe, impacting municipal and rural surface water supplies, farms and ranches, recreational facilities, and other economic interests. Ecological drought has also become a concern here as extended dry periods can alter the delicate balance of natural ecosystems and associated fish and wildlife species.

Temperature

Temperatures in the Chickasaw-Choctaw Tribal region are relatively moderate compared to western Oklahoma. However, in the far southeast portion of the region, high

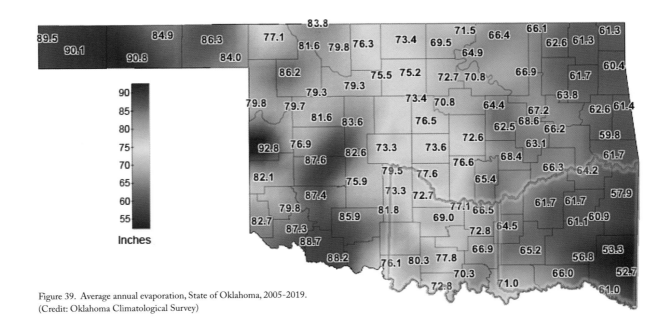

Figure 39. Average annual evaporation, State of Oklahoma, 2005-2019.
(Credit: Oklahoma Climatological Survey)

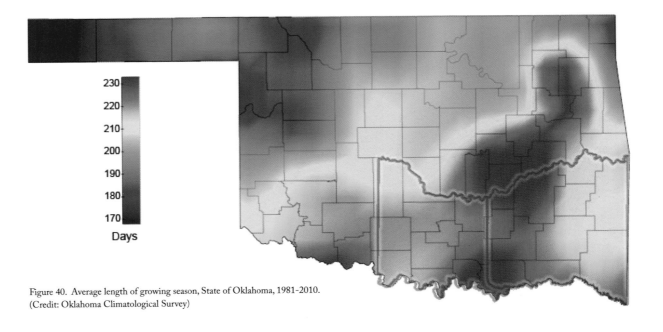

Figure 40. Average length of growing season, State of Oklahoma, 1981-2010.
(Credit: Oklahoma Climatological Survey)

humidity generates heat index values of 105 degrees or more, on average, at least 40 times each year, as reported by the Oklahoma Climatological Survey (OCS). The hottest temperature ever recorded in the region is 120° Fahrenheit (F) at Poteau in 1936, which also ties the statewide record. Temperatures of 32°F or less occur about 60 days per year in this area.

Figure 41 displays the average minimum temperature variation across the region that ranges from 48°F to 53 °F. The average maximum temperature ranges from 70 °F to 75 °F (Figure 42). The far eastern portion of the region exhibits a particularly wide range of average minimum and maximum temperatures.

Six Mesonet sites (Figure 43) were selected to compare the average temperature for each month of the year across the region. Figure 44 displays the range of average monthly temperatures from west (Minco) to east (Broken Bow). July–August is the hottest period of the year while January is generally the coolest month.

The variation in temperature each month between the six stations ranges from 1.75°F to 5.4°F. The larger variation between stations occurs during the winter months. Minco is the coolest station during the winter months and Wister and Broken Bow are the coolest during the summer months. Durant exhibits the warmest monthly temperatures year-round relative to the other five stations.

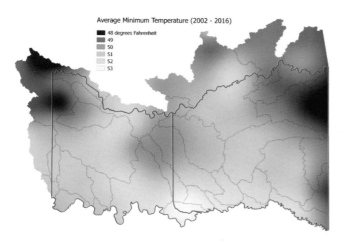

Figure 41. Average minimum temperature, southeast Oklahoma (2002–2016).

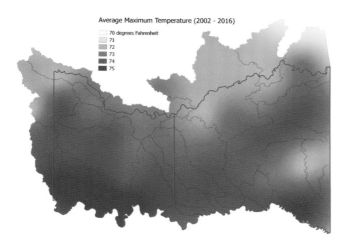

Figure 42. Average maximum temperature, southeast Oklahoma (2002-2016).

Precipitation

Annual precipitation, as with temperature, is variable across the Tribal region (as demonstrated in Figure 45, a summary of average annual precipitation from the Mesonet). Average precipitation ranges from 32 inches in the extreme west to a high of 54 inches in the southeast. The most annual precipitation recorded at an official reporting station in both the region and state was 84.47 inches at Kiamichi Tower, a former reporting station in LeFlore County, in 1957.

Figure 46 compares average monthly precipitation at the six selected Mesonet stations in the Tribal region. The driest period generally occurs during January–February, but August is also quite dry; May is the wettest month. The most pronounced precipitation variability between the six sites occurs in the winter months. In general, Wister and Broken Bow receive the highest monthly precipitation relative to the other sites, with the exception of Idabel in December. Minco and Sulphur receive the lowest monthly precipitation in three of four seasons, not including during the summer months.

Figure 47 and Figure 48 present a time series of precipitation from 1895 to 2017 and plots of 60-month average precipitation relative to long-term average precipitation in the South Central (8) and Southeast (9) Climate Divisions. Average annual precipitation in CD8 and CD9 during this 122-year period is 37.78 inches and 47.61 inches, respectively.

Climate Variability

The precipitation time series graphs also illustrate that the climate in the Tribal region, as elsewhere in Oklahoma, experiences considerable variability characterized by significant flooding events — usually resulting from intense, concentrated rainfall in areas — and more

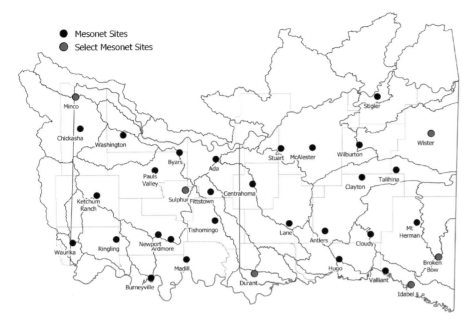

Figure 43. Active Mesonet stations and selected sites in the Tribal region.

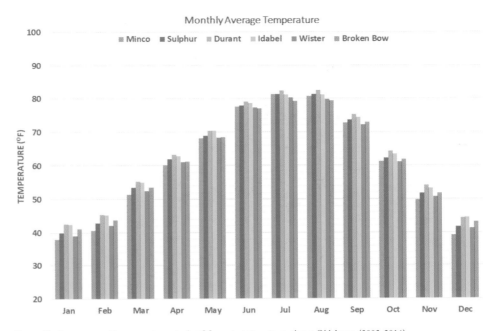

Figure 45. Average monthly temperature at select Mesonet stations in southeast Oklahoma (2002-2016).

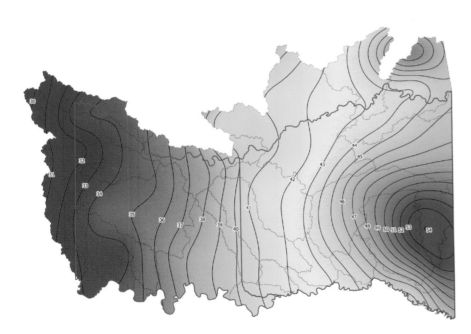

Figure 44. Annual average precipitation (inches), southeast Oklahoma.

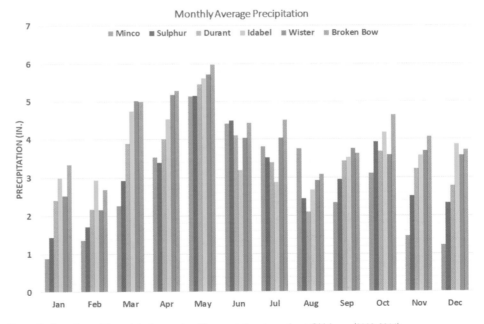

Figure 46. Annual monthly precipitation at select Mesonet stations in southeast Oklahoma (2002-2016).

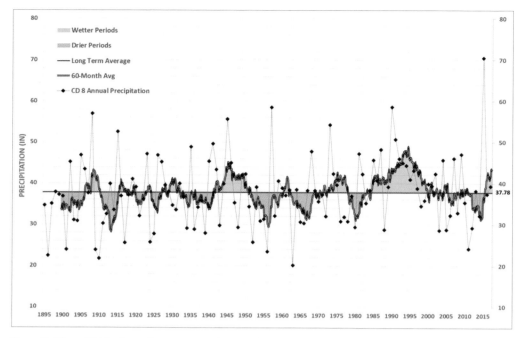

Figure 47. Climate Division 8 annual precipitation with 60-month averages, 1895 to 2017.

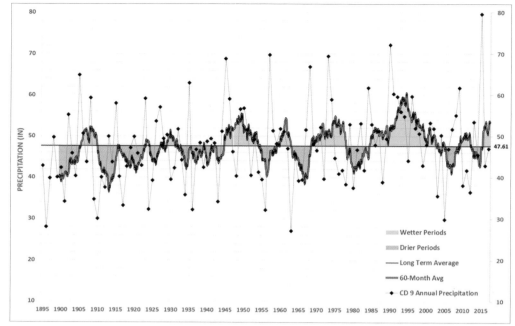

Figure 48. Climate Division 9 annual precipitation with 60-month averages, 1895 to 2017.

widespread drought episodes, such as the devastating statewide drought in 2010–15. While longer and more severe drought episodes typically occur in western Oklahoma, wherever droughts occur they are often punctuated by heavy precipitation events and flooding.

Data also indicate that, since at least the 1980s and through onset of the recent severe drought, the Tribal region and Oklahoma in general have experienced a very favorable annual precipitation pattern. This is further exemplified by Figure 49, a time series of the Palmer Drought Severity Index (PDSI) in the central Great Plains region, which was assembled from tree-ring data dating back to 1000 CE (The PDSI utilizes available temperature and precipitation data to estimate relative dryness. It's particularly useful in determining long-

term drought.) Both the general trend and extremes indicate the possibility that the 2010–15 drought was less an abnormal event and more an indicator that climate in the Great Plains region may be returning to a drier "normal."

A recent study sponsored by the South Central Climate Adaptation Science Center (SCCASC)—housed at the University of Oklahoma (OU) as part of a federal network of eight regional centers in the nation—sought to determine the long-term climate outlook for the Red River Basin, which includes much of the Tribal region. The study's particular focus was potential climate impacts on future water availability throughout the region. Using publicly available climate model results and a range of plausible carbon emission

scenarios, the climate data were downscaled and applied to rainfall-runoff and water availability models.

Results showed that while the western area of the Red River Basin will likely get drier, eastern-most reaches will probably experience overall wetter conditions. In the Chickasaw and Choctaw Nations, under modest emission scenarios, projections indicate that the region will get warmer but not much drier over the next seventy-five years. However, precipitation events will become more concentrated—and rainfall patterns generally more erratic—while higher temperatures will increase evaporation from lakes, soils and plants, stressing agricultural and natural systems. Scientists also speculate that future droughts in this region may

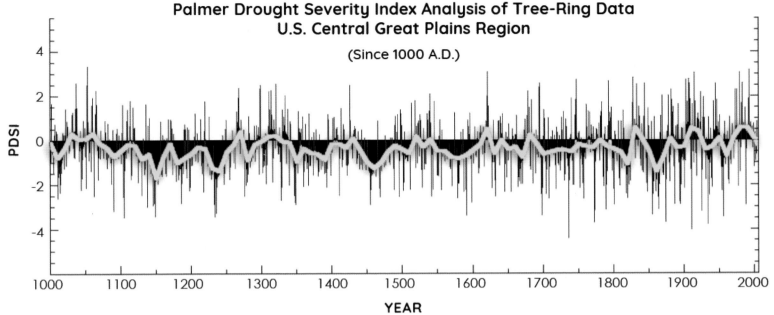

Figure 49. Tree-ring analysis of the Palmer Drought Severity Index, Central Great Plains.

be longer and more severe while flooding events may become more extreme.

Such a scenario will pose unique challenges to economic, social and natural resource sectors, including municipal and rural drinking water supply systems; agriculture, including winter wheat and sorghum; energy infrastructure, including oil, natural gas, and wind; navigation infrastructure and waterborne commerce; fish and wildlife habitat; and recreational interests, especially visitation to state and national parks and related facilities.

Facing the potential of a warmer and drier water future, it will be imperative to identify and implement appropriate adaptation measures for both the Nations and citizens in south-central and southeast Oklahoma.

TRIBAL ECOREGIONS

The state of Oklahoma contains 12 Level III ecoregions—that is, ecosystem areas containing generally similar environmental resources, including physiography, geology, climate, soils, land use, wildlife, fish, hydrology and natural vegetation. Ecoregion delineations, most recently defined by the U.S. Environmental Protection Agency (EPA) in 2005, serve as a spatial framework facilitating the research, assessment and monitoring of ecosystems and their components. Most importantly, ecoregion data is useful in defining and implementing targeted management strategies to conserve and restore natural resources while meeting the economic and cultural needs of local communities.

Relevant EPA ecoregion assessments provide an excellent broad representation of lands, waters and related resources within the Chickasaw and Choctaw Nations. Local stream channel morphology and substrate characteristics that are unique to ecoregions are especially significant as they typically have a significant influence on water quality, habitat variability and fish species composition.

The Chickasaw and Choctaw Nations are comprised of six principal (Level III) ecoregions. The Central Great Plains and Cross Timbers dominate Chickasaw lands while Choctaw lands are primarily comprised of the Arkansas Valley, Ouachita Mountains and South Central Plains. The much smaller East Central Texas Plains ecoregion roughly occupies both tribal territories along and near the Red River in the south. Level III ecoregions are further subdivided into more detailed Level IV regions.

Cross Timbers

Separating the forests of eastern ecoregions from the prairies of drier, western ecoregions, the Cross Timbers is a mix of savanna, woodland and prairie occurring across low hills, cuestas, ridges and plains. The boundary between the Cross Timbers — occupying about 5,000 square miles of the Chickasaw and Choctaw Nations — and the almost treeless Central Great Plains coincides with the western limit of many mammals and insects. Post oak–blackjack oak woodland and savanna are native on porous, course-textured soils derived from sandstone; the percentage of blackjack oak increases westward. Tall grasses are native on fine-textured, moisture-deficient soils derived from limestone, shale or marl. However, recent fire suppression has increased forest density and allowed eastern red cedar to invade many areas. Abandoned, depleted farmland is common in the region. The remaining cropland is largely restricted to valleys near channelized streams whose degraded habitat supports poor assemblages of aquatic fauna. Two types of streams are common. The first is characterized by a mixture of shaded riffles, runs and pools with gravel or cobble substrates. The second stream type, commonly found downstream, is characterized by lower gradients and wide, shallow, sand-choked channels. In the summer,

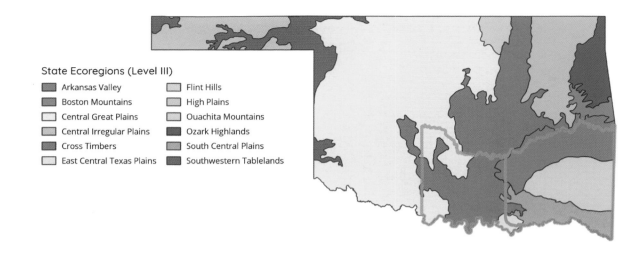

State Ecoregions (Level III)
- Arkansas Valley
- Boston Mountains
- Central Great Plains
- Central Irregular Plains
- Cross Timbers
- East Central Texas Plains
- Flint Hills
- High Plains
- Ouachita Mountains
- Ozark Highlands
- South Central Plains
- Southwestern Tablelands

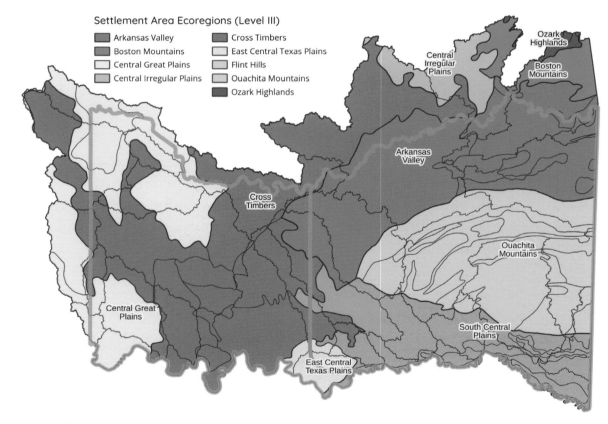

Settlement Area Ecoregions (Level III)
- Arkansas Valley
- Boston Mountains
- Central Great Plains
- Central Irregular Plains
- Ozark Highlands
- Cross Timbers
- East Central Texas Plains
- Flint Hills
- Ouachita Mountains

Figure 50. Above, Oklahoma's Level III ecoregions. Below, Level III ecoregions, including Level IV delineations (not referenced) within the Settlement Area hydrologic basins.

surficial flow is often absent from lower reaches. Erratic streamflow has led to the construction of many reservoirs in the region. Generally, stream conditions in the Cross Timbers are more stressful for fish than in far eastern Oklahoma. As a result, many sensitive eastern fish species are absent from the region. Common minnows include the red, sand, and redfin shiners and the suckermouth minnow. The redfin and orangethroat darters, smallmouth buffalo, river carpsucker, black and golden redhorses, and channel and flathead catfishes occur in many streams.

Within the Nations' lands, the Cross Timbers includes the following Level IV ecoregions: Arbuckle Mountains, Arbuckle Uplift, Eastern Cross Timbers, Grand Prairie, Northern Cross Timbers, Northwestern Cross Timbers and Western Cross Timbers.

Arkansas Valley

Characteristically transitional, diverse and distinct, the Arkansas Valley separates the Ouachita Mountains region to the south from the Ozark Plateau north of the homelands. Plains, hills, floodplains, terraces and scattered mountains all occur. A mix of oak savanna, prairie, oak–hickory–pine forest, and oak–hickory forest is native on uplands; bottomland forest is native on floodplains and low terraces. Today, steep slopes are wooded and used for timber and woodland grazing. Gently sloping uplands are used as pastureland or hayland. Cropland and pastureland occur on bottomlands. Other primary/

CLIMATE MONITORING & ASSESSMENT

Climate assessment in Oklahoma is greatly enhanced by the Oklahoma Mesonet, a world-class network of 120 automated climate monitoring stations, including thirty-three active sites in the Chickasaw and Choctaw Nations. Established collaboratively by researchers at Oklahoma University and Oklahoma State University in the early 1990s, the Mesonet includes at least one site in every state county, enabling the comprehensive collection of real-time temperature, precipitation, relative humidity, wind speed, air pressure and related data in five-minute intervals.

Facilitating the assessment of this climate data are Oklahoma's nine climate divisions (CD), which are aligned to county boundaries and used by the National Climatic Data Center (NCDC) to assess general climatic variations. Most of the Nations' territories includes CD8 and CD9.

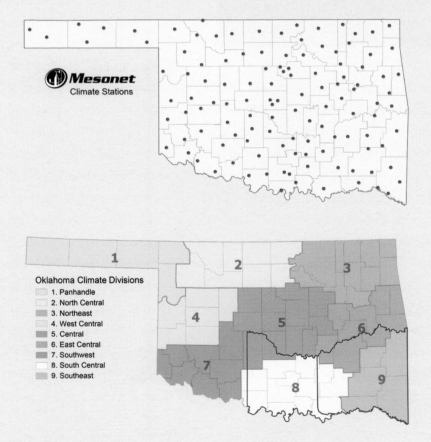

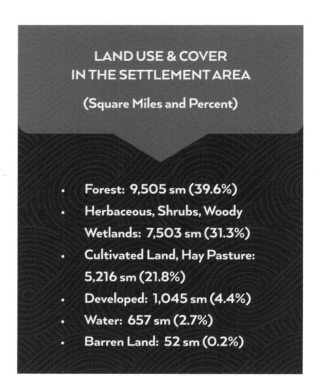

LAND USE & COVER IN THE SETTLEMENT AREA

(Square Miles and Percent)

- Forest: 9,505 sm (39.6%)
- Herbaceous, Shrubs, Woody Wetlands: 7,503 sm (31.3%)
- Cultivated Land, Hay Pasture: 5,216 sm (21.8%)
- Developed: 1,045 sm (4.4%)
- Water: 657 sm (2.7%)
- Barren Land: 52 sm (0.2%)

specific land uses include poultry farming, coal mining and natural gas production. Land use throughout the ecoregion tends to be the primary factor influencing stream water quality. Turbidity, total suspended solids, total organic carbon, total phosphorus and biochemical oxygen demand values are higher than in surrounding ecoregions, but mean stream gradients and dissolved oxygen levels are lower. Summer flow in small streams is often limited or nonexistent. However, the Arkansas Valley ecoregion contains the richest fish fauna in Oklahoma, including many sensitive species; a sunfish- and minnow-dominated community exists along with large numbers of darters and catfishes. Common fishes include the bigeye, steelcolor and redfin shiners; orangethroat and redfin darters; and suckers, including the creek chubsucker, golden and black redhorses, river carpsucker, spotted sucker and smallmouth buffalo.

Within the Nations' lands, the Arkansas Valley includes the following Level IV ecoregions: Arkansas River Floodplain, Arkansas Valley Plains, Lower Canadian Hills, and Scattered High Ridges and Mountains.

Ouachita Mountains

Similar in size to the adjacent Arkansas Valley region in the tribal territories, the Ouachita Mountains ecoregion is characterized by forested low mountains underlain by folded, sedimentary rocks of Paleozoic age. In Oklahoma, mean annual rainfall in this humid area ranges up to 57 inches, making it the wettest region in Oklahoma. Oak–hickory/shortleaf pine forest is native on uplands, contrasting with the oak–hickory forest of the Boston Mountains and Ozark Highlands ecoregions and the oak savanna or prairie of drier regions to the west. The Ouachita Mountains region remains mostly forested, but pastureland and hayland occur in wider valleys. Logging and recreation are major land uses. Most streams have gravel, cobble, boulder or bedrock substrates; a few have sandy bottoms. Stream gradients are naturally steeper than those closer to the Red River. Turbidity, total phosphorus, total suspended solids and biological oxygen demand values are lower, and dissolved oxygen levels higher, than in the streams of adjacent north and south ecoregions. Common fishes include the longear and green sunfishes, yellow bullhead, brook silverside, blackstripe and blackspotted topminnows, largemouth bass, smallmouth bass, redfin darter, suckers, and the bigeye, Ouachita Mountain and ribbon shiners. Orangebelly darters, grass pickerels and tadpole madtoms—which are absent from adjacent regions—are also found here.

Within the Nations' lands, the Ouachita Mountains includes the following Level IV ecoregions: Athens Plateau, Central Mountain Ranges, Fourche Mountains, Western Ouachita Valleys and Western Ouachitas.

South Central Plains

The South Central Plains ecoregion is an irregular, forested plain cut by shallow valleys and underlain by poorly-consolidated deposits; it is lithologically and physiographically distinct from the Ouachita Mountains region. This humid ecoregion, featuring a mean annual rainfall from 45 to 55 inches, occupies the edge of the southern coniferous forest belt; farther west, scrubby oak savanna and prairies occur. Natural vegetation is oak–hickory–pine forest on uplands and southern floodplain forest on bottomlands. Prairies once occurred on soils derived from limestone, marl and calcareous shale. Today, uplands are largely pastureland or forest dominated by shortleaf pine, loblolly pine, oaks and hickories. Poorly drained floodplains support bottomland forests and wetlands. Cropland is extensive along the Red River.

Streams in forested watersheds typically exhibit low concentrations of suspended solids; however, the Red River is continuously turbid. Summer flow in many small streams is limited or nonexistent, but enduring, deep pools usually occur here. Species richness markedly increases towards the east as fauna from the Mississippi Valley are encountered. In addition, downstream influences of the Ouachita Mountains on aquatic flora and fauna occur far into South Central Plains. Sunfishes, catfishes, gars, crappies, grass pickerels, orangebelly darters and bigeye, ribbon, striped and redfin shiners are common. Redhorses and creek chubsuckers are numerous in small and medium size streams. Smallmouth bass is an important game species. In Oklahoma, the dollar sunfish naturally occurs only in the South Central Plains whereas the pirate perch is limited to the ecoregion's ponds, swamps, oxbows and slowly moving streams. The lower Red River and its tributaries, Muddy Boggy Creek and the Blue River, are the only uncontrolled rivers in Oklahoma that flow to the Gulf of Mexico; estuarine fish and the American eel reside in these waters.

Within the Nations' lands, the South Central Plains includes these Level IV ecoregions: Blackland Prairie, Cretaceous Dissected Uplands, Floodplains and Low Terraces, Pleistocene Fluvial Terraces and Red River Bottomlands.

Central Great Plains

Dominating most of western Oklahoma and far western portions of the Chickasaw Nation, the Central Great Plains are largely underlain by red, Permian-age sedimentary rocks and include scattered hills, breaks, salt plains, low mountains, gypsum karst, sandy flats and sand dunes. Landform diversity is greater and elevations are lower than in the High Plains. Mean annual rainfall greatly increases eastward, reaching about 38 inches in the tribal region. The upland natural vegetation in this dry-subhumid area is mostly mixed grass prairie, but buffalo grass and shinnery oak are native, respectively, to

10 LARGEST CITIES IN THE SETTLEMENT AREA

(Population)

- Ardmore: 23,079
- Duncan: 21,732
- McAlester: 16,370
- Ada: 15,820
- Chickasha: 14,988
- Durant: 12,823
- Poteau: 7,210
- Idabel: 6,957
- Pauls Valley: 6,150
- Hugo: 5,978

the south and to sandy areas; potential natural vegetation is distinct from the shortgrass prairie of the semiarid High Plains as well as tall grass prairies to the north of the Nations' boundaries and the oak savanna of the Cross Timbers. Riparian corridors can be wooded. The eastern boundary of the ecoregion, including the Chickasaw Nation, coincides with the eastern limit of America's winter wheat belt. Cropland is extensive with wheat, alfalfa and grain sorghum representing primary crops. In addition, soybeans are grown in the east, where rainfall is greatest, and cotton occurs, especially on irrigated flat land in the south.

Rangeland and grassland, commonly found in more rugged areas, are being invaded by eastern redcedar. Streams are laden with suspended sediment when flows are high. Streams draining rangeland carry less sediment load than those that are downstream of cropland. Flow greatly decreases during the summer, but scattered pools endure and serve as summer refuges for aquatic fauna. Salt or gypsum deposits and leaching produce high mineral concentrations in many streams and rivers. Numerous streams have been channelized and/or impounded, resulting in the loss of riparian forest, unnatural flow regimes, entrenchment, bank erosion, substrate alteration and fauna modification. In some streams of the Central Great Plains, the plains killifish exists in large numbers. The most common minnows include the red shiner, sand shiner, suckermouth minnow and plains minnow; the endemic (and threatened) Arkansas River shiner also occurs here. Slenderhead darters are widespread in the ecoregion. Freckled madtoms and isolated pockets of orangethroat and dusky darters also appear. The Red River pupfish is found in pools and backwaters of sandy-bottomed streams and rivers where temperature, salinity and alkalinity are high.

Within the Nations' lands, the Central Great Plains includes the following Level IV ecoregions: Broken Red Plains, Cross Timbers Transition and Prairie Tableland.

East Central Texas Plains

The East Central Texas Plains ecoregion, occupying about 380 square miles of the Nations' territories, is composed of plains with fine-textured soils and claypans. Substrates of large streams are typically composed of mud and very fine sand. Mean annual rainfall in this moist-subhumid region ranges from 42 to 45 inches.

The Northern Post Oak Savanna sub-region of the tribal territories is characterized by level to rolling plains, extensive clay flats and slowly permeable soils that were derived from Cretaceous-age plastic shale, marl, limestone, sand and gravel. Tallgrass prairie and oak savanna are native and contrast with the oak–hickory–pine forest of the neighboring South Central Plains ecoregion to the north and east. Cropland and pastureland are now common here. Primary crops are peanuts, soybeans, grain sorghum, small grains, hay and cotton.

Within the Nations' lands, the East Central Texas Plains includes the Northern Post Oak Savanna Level IV ecoregion.

⧈ POPULATION

In addition to being a useful economic indicator, population growth is an integral factor in estimating future water demands. According to the U.S. Census Bureau (July 2019), the current estimated population of the state of Oklahoma is 3,956,971. Recent census figures indicate that Oklahoma is home to the second-highest number and percentage of First Americans among all states in the country. This is especially true within the Nations' territories.

State-level projections of growth through 2075, developed by the Oklahoma Department of Commerce using population counts from the 2010 Decennial Census, estimate that Oklahoma's population will top 5 million by the mid-2050s: an average annual growth rate of 0.73 percent. Most of this growth is forecasted to occur in and around the cities of Tulsa and Oklahoma City, which should remain the most populous areas in the state. The fourteen counties included in the Tulsa and Oklahoma City metropolitan areas are forecasted to represent 64.2 percent of the state's total population in 2075.

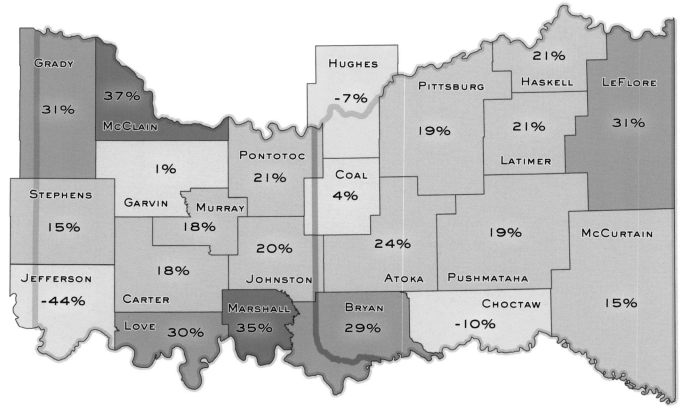

Figure 51. Projected county population change, by percent, within the Chickasaw and Choctaw Nations (2020-2075).

The projected 2075 population of the twenty-two-county area included within the Chickasaw and Choctaw Nations is 756,557, a net increase of 169,834 (22 percent) from 2020 estimates. These projections indicate that Grady County will be the most populous in 2075, followed closely by LeFlore County. McClain County is expected to experience the largest annual growth percentage (1.21 percent) through the period.

Three counties—Jefferson, Choctaw and Hughes—are projected to undergo net decreases in population, however, Choctaw County is the only one of these contained entirely within the Settlement Area. Growth in Garvin County is expected to remain generally flat.

⚇ GROUNDWATER RESOURCES

Groundwater provides significant water supply benefits to both the Chickasaw and Choctaw Nations, their citizens and other residents and businesses in south-central and southeast Oklahoma. Some aquifers, such as the Arbuckle-Simpson, also provide life-sustaining baseflow for rivers and streams and thus contribute, in numerous ways, to the region's economic welfare as well as its considerable environmental diversity.

Due to its general availability, surface water is the primary source of supply for much of the Nations' homelands. However, public water suppliers and other users who have been hard hit by increasingly frequent and severe drought episodes in the region are now

integrating groundwater into their supply portfolios to enhance reliability.

Thirty-one major and minor aquifers, as defined by the Oklahoma Water Resources Board (OWRB), underlie surface water basins comprising the Settlement Area (Figure 52). Relevant data on aquifers within the Nations' jurisdictions is presented on the following pages. Comprehensive data is currently unavailable for those groundwater basins on which hydrologic studies have yet to be completed. The default equal proportionate share (EPS) of 2.0 acre-feet/acre has been established on these aquifers until a study has been conducted and subsequent EPS approved by the OWRB. As of May 2020, studies have been completed on the Arbuckle-Simpson, Garber-Wellington, Gerty Sand, North Canadian River Alluvium, Canadian River Alluvium and Rush Springs aquifers. Studies are underway on the Washita River (Reaches 3 and 4), Boone-Roubidoux and Ada-Vamoosa.

Information on major and minor bedrock and alluvium/terrace aquifers underlying the confines of Settlement Area basins and corresponding watersheds is also presented in the Basin Summaries section.

Groundwater Quality

Groundwater, like surface water, is vulnerable to contamination and certain aquifers and areas receive protection under criteria established in Oklahoma's Water

Projected Tribal County Populations 2020 through 2075
(Oklahoma Department of Commerce)

County	2020	2075	Increase/ Decrease	Percent Growth
Atoka	14,910	19,527	4,617	0.58
Bryan	45,741	64,574	18,833	0.80
Carter	50,065	60,858	10,793	0.43
Choctaw	14,993	13,627	-1,366	-0.16
Coal	6,030	6,300	270	0.10
Garvin	27,322	27,487	165	0.01
Grady	56,561	82,549	25,988	0.88
Haskell	13,130	16,711	3,581	0.47
Hughes	13,405	12,570	-835	-0.16
Jefferson	6,153	4,265	-1,888	-0.52
Johnston	11,601	14,509	2,908	0.50
Latimer	11,764	14,889	3,125	0.52
LeFlore	54,597	79,488	24,891	0.89
Love	10,372	14,746	4,374	0.87
Marshall	16,693	25,880	9,187	1.04
McClain	38,671	61,698	23,027	1.21
McCurtain	34,744	40,989	6,245	0.36
Murray	13,796	16,778	2,982	0.38
Pittsburg	47,757	58,648	10,891	0.43
Pontotoc	39,526	50,247	10,721	0.52
Pushmataha	12,190	15,093	2,903	0.47
Stephens	46,702	55,124	8,422	0.34
TOTAL	586,723	756,557	169,834	

Quality Standards (OWQS). Protected areas are summarized below.

Wellhead Protection Areas are established to protect drinking water supplies. The designation limits potential pollution-related activities on land surrounding public groundwater supplies.

Oil and Gas Production Special Requirement Areas include such features as specially lined drilling mud pits (to prevent leaks and spills) or tanks whose contents are removed upon completion of drilling activities; well set-back distances from streams and lakes; restrictions on fluids and chemicals; or other related protective measures.

Nutrient-Vulnerable Groundwater is a designation afforded to hydrogeologic basins considered as having high or very high vulnerability to contamination from surface pollution sources. This designation can impact land application of manure for regulated agriculture facilities.

Class 1 Special Source Groundwaters are those of exceptional quality and particularly vulnerable to contamination. This classification includes groundwaters located underneath watersheds of Scenic Rivers, within OWQS Appendix B areas or below wellhead or source water protection areas.

Appendix H Limited Areas of Groundwater are localized areas where water quality is unsuitable for default beneficial uses due to natural conditions or irreversible human-induced pollution.

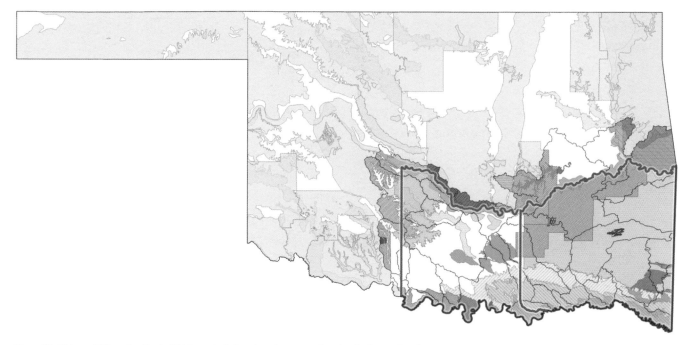

Figure 52. Major and Minor Aquifers in Oklahoma, including those (accentuated) within Settlement Area basins.

Aquifer Summaries

Major Aquifers

Thirteen major aquifers—defined by the OWRB and State of Oklahoma as those from which wells yield at least 50 gallons per minute (gpm) on the average basin-wide if from a bedrock aquifer, and at least 150 gpm if from an alluvium and terrace aquifer—exist in the tribal region: the Antlers, Arbuckle-Simpson, Arkansas River Alluvium, Canadian River Alluvium, Gerty Sand, Red River Alluvium, Rush Springs and Washita River Alluvium.

Ada-Vamoosa
- Area Underlying Settlement Region: 175 square miles (sq. mi.)
- EPS: 2.0 acre-feet per acre (af/ac)
- Hydraulic Conductivity: 3.0 feet/day
- Recharge Rate: 1.52 in/yr

Rocks in the younger Ada and older Vamoosa Groups are of Pennsylvanian age deposited in a near-shore environment ranging from marine on the west to non-marine on the east. The aquifer consists of layers of fine- to coarse-grained sandstone irregularly interbedded with shale and limestone. Exhibiting a maximum thickness of about 900 feet, the aquifer stretches north from Pontotoc County to beyond the Oklahoma-Kansas border. It serves as the primary source of potable water for Cushing, Stroud and Seminole. The aquifer outcrops on the east and dips to the west where it becomes confined. The water turns brackish downdip from the recharge zone. Generally, the water is of a sodium-potassium chloride-sulfate type with total dissolved solids (TDS) of less than 500 mg/L. Yields are commonly 25 to 150 gpm, but can reach 300 gpm.

Antlers
- Area Underlying Settlement Region: 4,276 sq. mi.
- EPS: 2.1 af/ac
- Hydraulic Conductivity: 0.10 to 12.97 feet/day
- Transmissivity: 112 to 19,149 gallons per day (gpd)/foot
- Storage Coefficient: 0.0004 to 0.0010 dimensionless
- Specific Capacity: 3.2 to 11.1 gallons per minute (gpm)/foot
- Recharge Rate: 0.3 to 1.7 inches/year

Cretaceous seas covering the southern portion of the Arbuckle and Ouachita Mountains deposited the Antlers aquifer. This enormous bedrock formation consists of sandstone and sands that are white to reddish-yellow, orange-brown and gray. Materials are fine- to coarse-grained quartzose cross-bedded and interbedded with varicolored clays and conglomerates. The formation, which contains fossilized wood and dinosaur remains, also includes fluvial deposits associated with rivers and streams. The thickness ranges from zero feet on the northern end to 900 feet in the subsurface along the Red River. Well yields range from 100 to 500 gpm. Water from the aquifer contains low TDS in the recharge area—less than 500 milligrams per liter (mg/L)—but concentrations generally increase to more than 1,000 mg/L to the south in confined areas toward the Red River.

Arbuckle-Simpson
- Area Underlying Settlement Region: 530 sq. mi.
- EPS: 0.2 af/ac
- Hydraulic Conductivity: 0.39 ft/day (Simpson) and 3.3 ft/day (Arbuckle)
- Transmissivity: 1,324 gpd/ft (Simpson) and 83,028 gpd/ft (Arbuckle)
- Recharge Rate: 5.58 in/yr

The Arbuckle-Simpson bedrock aquifer consists of sandstone and shale in the Simpson formation and limestone and dolomite in the Arbuckle formation. Saturated thickness of the aquifer is estimated to be from 2,500 to 3,500 feet. Yields typically range from about 25 to 600 gpm with deeper wells yielding in excess of 1,000 gpm. The aquifer's EPS was reduced to 10 percent of its default number (2.0 acre-feet per acre) in 2011 following study and a related legislative initiative requiring protection of springs and streams in the region. Water in the Arbuckle-Simpson exhibits good quality with TDS of less than 500 mg/L. The Arbuckle-Simpson is Oklahoma's only "sole source aquifer," a designation by EPA that provides enhanced protection for certain groundwater basins that serve as the principal source of local drinking water supply.

Arbuckle-Timbered Hills
- Area Underlying Settlement Region: 23 sq. mi.
- EPS: 2.0 af/ac
- Hydraulic Conductivity: 0.5 ft/day
- Recharge Rate: < 0.6 in/yr
- Storage Coefficient: 1.2 x 10-5
- Specific Capacity: 0.25 to 0.88 gpm/ft
- Transmissivity: 1,720 gpd/ft

The freshwater Arbuckle Timbered Hills aquifer, which outcrops north of the Wichita Mountains, is two formations consisting of limestone and dolomite with some interbedded sandstone and shale that are intensely folded and faulted. The aquifer is also present south of the mountains where it is overlain by younger sediments. TDS concentrations in the south range from 500 to 10,000 mg/L. There are groundwater wells within the boundaries of the aquifer, including in Basin 25, but some of these likely produce from the younger Post Oak Conglomerate and/or Garber Sandstone aquifers.

Arkansas River Alluvium
- Area Underlying Settlement Region: 270 sq. mi.
- EPS: 2.0 af/ac
- Transmissivity: 50,000 to 109,000 gpd/ft
- Storage Coefficient: 0.004 to 0.2
- Recharge Rate: 9 in/yr

The Arkansas River Alluvium is one to three miles wide. Grain sizes range from gravel and coarse sand near the base to silt or clay near the surface. The total and saturated thicknesses average 42 and 25 feet, respectively. Terrace deposits, composed primarily of sand and small amounts of sand and gravel near the base, yield small to moderate supplies of water for domestic use and to stock wells. Water well yields range from 130 to 860 gpm. The water is considered hard and is predominantly

MAJOR AQUIFERS

Aquifer delineations represent the official boundaries of groundwater basins recognized by the OWRB. In some cases, these boundaries align directly with county lines or related political borders due to varying well production rates (and related aquifer classifications), the intersection of two or more water-bearing geologic formations, water quality factors, and associated management considerations.

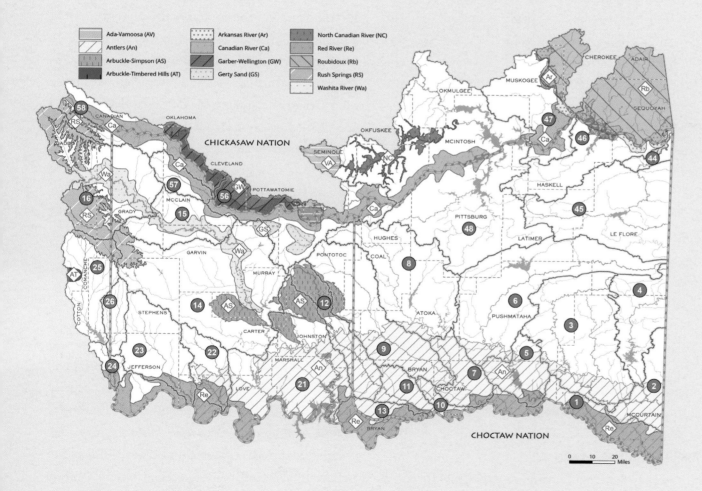

Figure 53. Major aquifers within Settlement Area basins.

of a calcium, magnesium bicarbonate type with variable dissolved solids content of 148 to 702 mg/L.

Canadian River Alluvium

- Area Underlying Settlement Region: 1,254 sq. mi.
- EPS: 2.0 af/ac
- Hydraulic Conductivity: 0.1 to 100 ft/day (39 ft/day average)
- Recharge Rate: 2.0 in/yr

The Canadian River alluvial aquifer consists of clay and silt coarsening downward to fine- to coarse-grained sand with lenses of basal gravel. The aquifer has a thickness ranging from 20 to 40 feet; the terrace deposits have a maximum thickness of 50 feet. Yields range from 100 to 400 gpm in the alluvium and 50 to 100 gpm in the terrace deposits. Water in the formation is of a very hard calcium bicarbonate type with TDS concentrations of approximately 1,000 mg/L.

Garber-Wellington

- Area Underlying Settlement Region: 343 sq. mi.
- EPS: 2.0 af/ac
- Hydraulic Conductivity: 3.3 ft/day (fine sandstone) and 0.33 ft/day (silty claystone)
- Storage Coefficient: 0.0013
- Recharge Rate: 1.84 in/yr

The Garber-Wellington aquifer, also known as the Central Oklahoma aquifer, is a sandstone formation that supplies water to many municipalities in the region, including Edmond, Norman, Yukon, Mustang, Moore and Nichols Hills. The aquifer is comprised of the Garber sandstone, Wellington shale and sandstone as well as members of the Oscar Group. The sand was deposited in a shallow sea during Permian times from rivers that flowed from east to west. The greatest concentration of sand is found in central Oklahoma and its thickness decreases in both directions to the north and south. Wells completed in the aquifer, some 1,000 feet deep, commonly yield 100 to 300 gpm and locally yield more than 500 gpm. The saturated thickness of the aquifer ranges from 150 to 650 feet. In some areas, water exceeds the EPA drinking water standard for arsenic.

Gerty Sand
- Area Underlying Settlement Region: 110 sq. mi.
- EPS: 0.65 af/ac
- Transmissivity: 12,000 to 27,000 gpd/ft
- Recharge Rate: 0.9 to 1.0 in/yr

The Gerty Sand alluvial aquifer consists of gravel, sand, silt, clay and volcanic ash. The saturated thickness averages 28 feet, but varies from 5 to 75 feet. Depth to water ranges from 10 to 110 feet. Typical yields range from 100 to 450 gpm. Water quality is fair to good and moderately hard with TDS values usually less than 1,000 mg/L.

North Canadian River Terrace
- Area Underlying Settlement Region: 159 sq. mi.
- EPS: 0.8 (Phase 3a) and 1.3 af/ac (Phase 3b)
- Hydraulic Conductivity: 310 ft/day
- Storage Coefficient: 0.15
- Recharge Rate: 3.3 in/yr

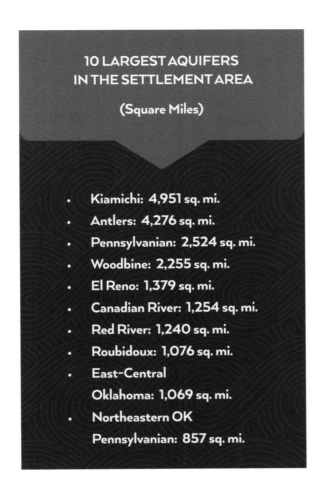

10 LARGEST AQUIFERS IN THE SETTLEMENT AREA

(Square Miles)

- Kiamichi: 4,951 sq. mi.
- Antlers: 4,276 sq. mi.
- Pennsylvanian: 2,524 sq. mi.
- Woodbine: 2,255 sq. mi.
- El Reno: 1,379 sq. mi.
- Canadian River: 1,254 sq. mi.
- Red River: 1,240 sq. mi.
- Roubidoux: 1,076 sq. mi.
- East-Central Oklahoma: 1,069 sq. mi.
- Northeastern OK Pennsylvanian: 857 sq. mi.

The North Canadian River Terrace deposits, which were originally deposited by the migration of the ancestral river, stretch from the Oklahoma Panhandle to Lake Eufaula in eastern Oklahoma. The deposits consist of inter-fingered lenses of clay, sandy clay, and cross-bedded, poorly sorted sand and gravel. The average thickness is 75 feet with an average saturated thickness of 27 feet. Yields can be as much as 600 gpm, but average 200 gpm. The deposits are partially recharged by irrigation return flow. The amount of water stored in the alluvium and terrace deposits of the North Canadian

River averages about 3,000 acre-feet per square mile. It flows over the recharge areas of two major aquifers (Garber-Wellington and Ada-Vamoosa) and two minor ones (East Central and El Reno) before it drains into Lake Eufaula. Modeling indicates that as development is increased to 20 percent (about 500 wells), the river will essentially cease to flow within three years of pumping.

Red River Alluvium
- Area Underlying Settlement Region: 1,240 sq. mi.
- EPS: 2.0 af/ac
- Recharge Rate: 2.5 to 5 in/yr

The Red River Alluvium consists of both alluvial and terrace deposits with the formation containing sand, silt, clay and gravel. The deposits overlie the Cretaceous-age Woodbine and Antlers aquifers. The average saturated thickness is thought to be around 20 to 30 feet.

Roubidoux
- Area Underlying Settlement Region: 1,076 sq. mi.
- EPS: 2.0 af/ac
- Hydraulic Conductivity: 2.3 to 4.0 ft/day
- Transmissivity: 2,992 to 5,236 gpd/ft
- Specific Capacity: 0.29 to 18.50 gpm/ft
- Storage Coefficient: 1×10^{-6}

The Roubidoux formation is a light-colored, cherty dolomite with sandstone layers 15 to 20 feet thick. The formation, with average thickness of 175 feet, is confined in Oklahoma; the recharge zone is in Missouri. Many of the wells completed in the Roubidoux are also open in the overlying Cotter and Jefferson City dolomites; a few wells are also open in the underlying Gasconade dolomite. Large concentrations of sodium and chloride make groundwater in the Roubidoux unsuitable as a water supply. Chloride concentrations in the eastern portion exceed 250 mg/L at depths of 1200 to 1500 feet. TDS is generally less than 200 mg/L in the eastern portion, but increases to more than 800 mg/L in the west. Large concentrations of gross-alpha radioactivity (radium 226) occur in groundwater on the western edge of the transition zone.

Rush Springs

- Area Underlying Settlement Region: 687 sq. mi.
- EPS: 2.0 af/ac
- Transmissivity: 5,012 to 13,988 gpd/ft
- Specific Yield: 0.13 to 0.34
- Recharge Rate: 1.8 in/yr

The Rush Springs aquifer, comprised of the Permian-age Rush Springs and Marlow Formations, is a fine-grained sandstone with some shale, dolomite and gypsum. Thickness ranges from 200 to 300 feet. Water is not produced from the Marlow Formation as it acts as a confining unit that retards downward movement of the groundwater. The aquifer is used primarily for irrigation but is also used for municipal and industrial purposes; yields range from 25 to 400 gpm. The OWRB and U.S. Geological Survey (USGS) are currently conducting a comprehensive study of the aquifer to establish a new EPS. Water in the Rush Springs tends to be very hard, requiring some softening. Levels of dissolved solids are generally less than 500 mg/L. In some areas, nitrate and sulfate concentrations exceed drinking water standards.

Washita River Alluvium

- Area Underlying Settlement Region: 515 sq. mi.
- EPS: 1.5 af/ac (Reach 3) and 1.0 af/ac (Reach 4)
- Recharge Rate: 2.65 to 4.41 in/yr

The Washita River alluvium consists of silt and clays coarsening downward into fine and coarse sands. The alluvial valley averages about two miles in width with a maximum width of three miles. The average thickness of the aquifer is 64 feet with a maximum thickness of 120 feet. Maximum thickness of the alluvial terrace deposits is 50 feet. Depth to water in the alluvium is generally less than 20 feet while wells are commonly drilled between 50 and 100 feet deep. Recharge to the older alluvial terraces is primarily from local precipitation and runoff from adjacent uplands; generally, the older terraces are not hydraulically continuous with the younger terraces and alluvium. Discharge from the alluvium contributes to the base flow of the Washita River. During high river stages, the normal hydraulic gradient is sometimes reversed with river water entering the alluvium. Yields are typically between 100 and 300 gpm in the alluvium and 20 to 100 gpm in the terrace deposits. Water is generally of a calcium-magnesium bicarbonate type with dissolved solids concentrations usually less than 1,000 mg/L.

Eighteen minor aquifers — defined as those not meeting "major" aquifer average well yield parameters — exist in the Tribal region: the Ashland Isolated Terrace, Beaver Creek Alluvium, Boone, Broken Bow, East-Central Oklahoma, El Reno, Haworth Isolated Terrace (Region 2), Hennessey-Garber, Holly Creek, Kiamichi, Little River Terrace/Alluvium, Marietta, Northeastern Oklahoma Pennsylvanian, Pennsylvanian, Pine Mountain, Potato Hills, Texoma and Woodbine.

Ashland Isolated Terrace

- Area Underlying Settlement Region: 24 sq. mi.
- EPS: 2.0 af/ac
- Hydraulic Conductivity: 104 to 125 ft/day
- Transmissivity: 19,488 gpd/ft
- Specific Yield: 0.2
- Recharge Rate: 3.9 in/yr

The Ashland Isolated Terrace is comprised of terrace deposits that occur as unconsolidated clay, silt, sand and gravel. The deposits have an average thickness of 50 feet and an average saturated thickness of around 21 feet. The average yield of wells in the formation is about 135 gpm. Water quality is limited, but wells typically have low pH and alkalinity, which makes the water highly corrosive. The water's high iron content is also problematic.

Beaver Creek Alluvium

- Area Underlying Settlement Region: 56 sq. mi.
- EPS: 1.0 af/ac

- Hydraulic Conductivity: 132 ft/day
- Transmissivity: 15,840 gpd/ft
- Specific Yield: 0.17
- Recharge Rate: 3.45 in/yr

The alluvial aquifer of Beaver Creek is unconfined with thickness averaging 33 feet and ranging from 10 to 65 feet. The average saturated thickness is 16 feet and wells typically yield around 77 gpm with a range of 5 to 500 gpm. In addition to precipitation, the aquifer recharges through infiltration from losing streams and through groundwater from the underlying Hennessey-Garber aquifer. TDS ranges from 500 to 1,000 mg/L.

Boone
- Area Underlying Settlement Region: 255 sq. mi.
- EPS: 2.0 af/ac
- Hydraulic Conductivity: 22 ft/day
- Transmissivity: 32,912 gpd/ft
- Specific Yield: 0.07
- Recharge Rate: 10 in/yr

The Boone Formation is Mississippian in age along with overlying Quarternary-age alluvium and terrace deposits not associated with the Neosho River groundwater basin. The Boone aquifer, which overlies the Roubidoux, consists of highly fractured, fine-grained limestone and massive gray chert. Well yields average 10 gpm, but can exceed 100 gpm if fractures or caverns are encountered in drilling. The average saturated thickness is 200 feet. TDS increases abruptly to more than 500 mg/L in the confined portion of the aquifer where chloride concentrations exceed 100 mg/L and sulfate concentrations are 50 mg/L or more. Radon levels exceed

MINOR AQUIFERS

Aquifer delineations represent the official boundaries of groundwater basins recognized by the OWRB. In some cases, these boundaries align directly with county lines or related political borders due to varying well production rates (and related aquifer classifications), the intersection of two or more water-bearing geologic formations, water quality factors, and associated management considerations.

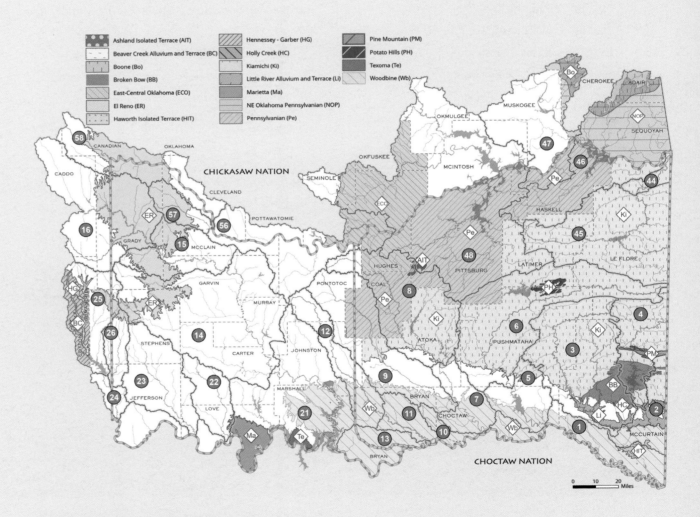

Figure 54. Minor aquifers within Settlement Area basins.

proposed microliters (mcL) of 300 picocuries per liter (pCi/L) in almost one-half of samples.

Broken Bow
- Area Underlying Settlement Region: 234 sq. mi.
- EPS: 2.0 af/ac
- Hydraulic Conductivity: 0.5 ft/day
- Transmissivity: 1,047 gpd/ft
- Specific Yield: 0.005
- Storage Coefficient: 10-3 to 10-5
- Recharge Rate: 1.2 in/yr

Lithology of the Broken Bow aquifer includes shale, sandstone, chert and minor layers of limestone and coal that are typically tilted at the surface. The openings on bedding planes along with joints and fractures are the principal conduits for water movement. The primary water-bearing formations are the Bigfork Chert and Arkansas Novaculite, which consists of novaculite and chert with some interbedded shale and sandstone. The highly broken and fractured rocks can potentially yield moderate to large amounts of water with wells averaging 14 gpm and reaching as high as 100 gpm in localized areas. Water quality is considered generally good.

East-Central Oklahoma
- Area Underlying Settlement Region: 1,069 sq. mi.
- EPS: 2.0 af/ac
- Hydraulic Conductivity: 1.25 ft/day
- Transmissivity: 252 gpd/ft
- Specific Yield: 0.005 (shales) and 0.125 (sands)
- Recharge Rate: 2.8 in/yr

The Pennsylvanian age bedrock of the East-Central Oklahoma aquifer consists primarily of alternating thick shales and fine to medium-grained sandstones with a few thin limestones and conglomerates. Minor alluvium and terrace deposits consisting of floodplain sediments and terrace sands, high-level gravels and eolian sands that are linked hydrologically with the underlying sediments are not distinguished as a separate unit. Fresh water has been found in wells at depths ranging from 300 to 400 feet. The average depth to water is 50

Figure 55. The Arbuckle Mountains east of the Turner Falls lookout.

feet. Yields are generally less than 15 gpm, but reach 30 gpm in some areas. Water quality is highly variable and ranges from poor to excellent. Hardness typically exceeds 120 mg/L and TDS ranges from 100 to 900 mg/L. Relatively high levels of iron and manganese also pose issues.

El Reno

- Area Underlying Settlement Region: 1,379 sq. mi.
- EPS: 2.0 af/ac
- Hydraulic Conductivity: 1.0 ft/day
- Transmissivity: 1,571 gpd/ft
- Specific Yield: 0.01 (shale) and 0.05 (sandstone)
- Recharge Rate: 0.75 in/yr

The El Reno Group is a Permian age formation consisting of reddish-brown shales, siltstones and sandstones interbedded with thin persistent beds of gypsum, dolomite and thick-bedded evaporate units interbedded with shale. Overlying parts of the bedrock are thin unconsolidated deposits of clay, silt, sand and gravel of Quaternary age deposited by rivers and streams. The El Reno Group consists of the Cedar Hills Sandstone, which grades to siltstone toward the south; Duncan Formation consisting of sandstone with minor amounts of interbedded shales and siltstone conglomerates; Chickasha Formation, a deltaic formation of sandstone, shales, siltstone and siltstone conglomerate; Flowerpot Shale, reddish-brown shale with several salt and gypsum beds; and Blaine Formation, a series of interbedded gypsum, shale and dolomite. Higher production areas in McClain, Grady and Stephens Counties produce from the Duncan and Chickasha Formations near their outcrops. Water quality is variable. Lower concentrations of TDS and sulfate correspond to the Chickasha and Duncan formations in the south and Cedar Hills formation in the east.

Haworth Isolated Terrace

- Area Underlying Settlement Region: 25 sq. mi.
- EPS: 1.0 af/ac
- Hydraulic Conductivity: 50 ft/day
- Transmissivity: 6,358 gpd/ft
- Specific Yield: 0.15
- Recharge Rate: 4.8 in/yr

These deposits consist of variable proportions of sand, silt and clay with fine-grained sand near the surface and medium-grained sand at the base. The average yield is 25 gpm with 100 gpm possible in localized areas. The groundwater is typically a calcium-magnesium bicarbonate type and can be classified as hard. The TDS is low to moderate and well below 500 mg/L. Sulfate and chlorides are also low to moderate.

Hennessey-Garber

Area Underlying Settlement Region: 216 sq. mi.
EPS: 1.6 af/ac
Hydraulic Conductivity: 28 to 107 ft/day
Transmissivity: 16,000 gpd/ft
Specific Yield: 0.02
Recharge Rate: 4.1 in/yr

The Hennessey-Garber aquifer exists on the flanks of the Wichita Mountains and is both a confined and unconfined aquifer. The aquifer is comprised of sandstone, shale and conglomerates with well yields averaging 110 gpm with a range of 0.3 to 800 gpm. The average thickness is 50 feet with a saturated thickness averaging 20 feet. A portion of the aquifer outcrops at the surface. Elsewhere it is overlain by the Beaver Creek and Tillman Alluvial aquifers and Post Oak aquifer, and a portion sits atop the Arbuckle Timbered-Hills aquifer. The Hennessey-Garber is hydraulically connected to all four aquifers.

Holly Creek

- Area Underlying Settlement Region: 30 sq. mi.
- EPS: 2.0 af/ac
- Hydraulic Conductivity: 10 ft/day
- Transmissivity: 2,244 gpd/ft
- Specific Yield: 0.1
- Recharge Rate: 1.2 in/yr

The lithology is composed of lenticular beds of gravel, silt clay and sand. About half of the pebbles in the gravel are quartz; the remainder is novaculite generally interbedded with silt and clay. Yields are typically low and sufficient only for domestic or livestock use. However, some localized areas can yield as much as 50 to 75 gpm. Information is limited, but the quality appears to be good with no parameters in exceedance of water quality standards.

Kiamichi

- Area Underlying Settlement Region: 4,951 sq. mi.
- EPS: 2.0 af/ac
- Hydraulic Conductivity: 0.055 ft/day

- Transmissivity: 94 gpd/ft
- Specific Yield: 0.005
- Recharge Rate: 1.1 in/yr

The Kiamichi aquifer, which is the largest in the Nation's territory, is composed primarily of Pennsylvanian and Mississippian age rocks that occur as shale, sandstone, siltstone, coal, marl, limestone, clay, silt and sand units. The storage and movement of water are largely controlled by the lateral and vertical distribution of rock units, geologic structures and physical characteristics of the rock. The formations are tilted at the surface exposing bedding planes that serve as avenues for water entry and movement. Other openings for water movement are fractures and joints formed during flooding of the brittle rock. Yields average about 5 gpm with thicker zones yielding 50 to 100 gpm. Water quality is highly variable.

Little River Terrace & Alluvium
- Area Underlying Settlement Region: 144 sq. mi.
- EPS: 1.0 af/ac
- Hydraulic Conductivity: 40 ft/day
- Transmissivity: 4,488 gpd/ft
- Specific Yield: 0.15
- Recharge Rate: 4.8 in/yr

Formed by deposition of sediment from the Little River, the lithology consists of gravel, sand, clay and silt with fine-grained sand in the upper portions and gravel in the lower portions. The average well yield is 15 gpm, but can be as much as 100 gpm in localized areas. Average analytical results obtained from two wells indicate that groundwater exceeds maximum contaminate levels for pH, turbidity and iron. Sulfate and chlorides are typically low.

Marietta
- Area Underlying Settlement Region: 156 sq. mi.
- EPS: 2.0 af/ac
- Transmissivity: 374 gpd/ft
- Specific Yield: 0.05
- Recharge Rate: 1.6 in/yr

The lithology of the Marietta aquifer consists of Cretaceous and Quaternary deposits that occur as shales, sandstones, siltstones, coal, marl, limestone, clay and sand units. Water is derived in small quantities from thin sandstone units and cracks and solution channels in the limestone. Yields average 14 gpm with local areas capable of yielding 40 to 60 gpm. The groundwater is typically a sodium-potassium-bicarbonate. TDS ranges from 76 to 1900 mg/L and hardness ranges from hard to very hard.

Northeastern Oklahoma Pennsylvanian
- Area Underlying Settlement Region: 857 sq. mi.
- EPS: 2.0 af/ac
- Hydraulic Conductivity: 0.003 ft/day
- Transmissivity: 3.74 gpd/ft
- Specific Yield: 0.01
- Recharge Rate: 2.1 in/yr

The Northeastern Oklahoma Pennsylvanian groundwater basin is comprised of Pennsylvanian and Mississippian deposits that occur as shale, siltstone, coal, thin limestone and widely separated sandstone. The groundwater in the upper portion is generally unconfined whereas water in the deeper portion is confined. Groundwater is generally encountered within 50 feet of the surface. The average saturated thickness is estimated at 200 feet and wells typically yield about four gpm. TDS ranges from 71 to 3700 mg/L and the pH from 6 to 8. The water quality of the aquifer is generally suitable for most uses.

Pennsylvanian
- Area Underlying Settlement Region: 2,524 sq. mi.
- EPS: 2.0 af/ac
- Hydraulic Conductivity: 1.25 ft/day (sandstone) and 0.0001 ft/day (fractured shale or siltstone)
- Transmissivity: 980 gpd/ft (sandstone) and 2 gpd/ft (shale)
- Specific Yield: 0.125 (sandstone) and 0.005 (shale) for unconfined portion
- Storage Coefficient: 0.001 for confined portion
- Recharge Rate: 1.1 in/yr

Typical deposits range from coarse-grained sandstone to siltstone and shale with some fracturing. Sandstone comprises about 30 percent of the formation's thickness. Groundwater is generally encountered at 50 feet under confining conditions and it typically rises to within 25 feet of the surface. The average base of fresh water is about 400 feet. Yields are generally low (less than 5 gpm), but some wells penetrating thick units of fractured sandstone can make 80 gpm. Water quality is extremely variable and typically of a sodium bicarbonate type. The TDS ranges from 300 to 2,000 mg/L and pH ranges from 6 to 8. Water is mostly very hard (more than 120 mg/L).

Pine Mountain
- Area Underlying Settlement Region: 30 sq. mi.
- EPS: 2.0 af/ac
- Hydraulic Conductivity: 0.5 ft/day
- Transmissivity: 1,047 gpd/ft
- Specific Yield: 0.005
- Storage Coefficient: 10-3 to 10-5
- Recharge Rate: 1.2 in/yr

The lithology is typically shale, sandstone, chert and minor layers of limestone and coal often tilted at the surface. The openings on bedding planes and along joints and fractures are the major conduits for water movement. The primary water-yielding formations are the Bigfork Chert and Arkansas Novaculite, which consists of novaculite and chert with some interbedded shale and sandstone. The highly broken and fractured rocks can yield moderate to large amounts of water averaging 14 gpm and reaching as high as 60 to 100 gpm in areas. Water quality is generally good.

Potato Hills
- Area Underlying Settlement Region: 32 sq. mi.
- EPS: 0.65 af/ac
- Transmissivity: 1,403 gpd/ft
- Specific Yield: 0.005
- Recharge Rate: 1.15 in/yr

The aquifer is comprised of Mississippian, Silurian and Ordovician age deposits with shale, sandstone, chert, and minor limestone and coal seams. Its brittle rocks have been subjected to low-grade metamorphism. Primary water-yielding formations include the Big Fork Chert and Arkansas Novaculite (a primarily fractured chert). Three divisions of the Novaculite are recognized (except in the north). The Lower division is white massive-bedded novaculite with some interbedded gray shales near the base, the Middle is greenish to dark gray shales interbedded with thin beds of dark novaculite, and the Upper white, thick-bedded, often calcareous novaculite. Conodonts and other microfos-

Figure 56. Farmland in Garvin County.

BRACKISH GROUNDWATER— AUGMENTING SUPPLIES

Future drought episodes and related reliability concerns have spawned the search for numerous solutions to improve water reliability throughout the Chickasaw and Choctaw Nations. Brackish groundwater, typically found deep underground, is a particularly promising option that can substantially diversify municipal and industrial water supply portfolios. While this relatively common resource is high in salts/chlorides, it is more than suitable for uses — such as the irrigation of certain plants, cooling water for power generation, aquaculture, and oil and gas industry uses (drilling, enhanced recovery and hydraulic fracturing) — that require water of only marginal quality. This alternative supply results in the conservation of freshwater for drinking and other higher priority needs.

Brackish water is commonly defined as having a dissolved mineral content of 1,000 to 10,000 milligrams per liter (mg/L). In comparison, saline (sea) and brine water contain more than 30,000 mg/L. While some brackish sources can be utilized for drinking water, advanced treatment, including desalination or reverse osmosis, is required.

Little data exists on the availability of brackish groundwater in Oklahoma, although the USGS recently concluded its first national brackish groundwater assessment in more than 50 years. Known brackish aquifers in Oklahoma and the treaty homelands are now being studied to determine their water supply potential. These include the Arbuckle-Timbered Hills, Arbuckle-Simpson, Ada-Vamoosa, Garber-Wellington, Red River alluvium, Duncan Sandstone, Roubidoux, Boone and Antlers (Trinity) in the far southeastern tip of McCurtain County and northeastern Texas.

DISSOLVED SOLIDS CONCENTRATIONS OF WATER (MG/L)

Brine	> 35,000
Saline	30,000 to 35,000
Slightly Saline	10,000 to 30,000
Very Brackish	3,000 to 10,000
Brackish	1,000 to 3,000
Slightly Brackish	500 to 1,000
Freshwater	< 500

sils are common. The formation is up to 900 feet thick in its southern outcrops, but thins rapidly to 60 feet in the north. The Arkansas Novaculite outcrops in the Ouachita Mountains in the Potato Hills and Broken Bow uplifts. The area is remote and contains very few wells, so very little water quality data is available. The Choctaw Nation's Office of Environmental Health and Engineering provided analytical data from two wells in the study area which revealed that water exceeds recommended maximum contaminant levels for TDS, chloride, and alkalinity. TDS ranges from 428 to 1,303 mg/L with a median value of 866 mg/L.

Texoma

- Area Underlying Settlement Region: 25 sq. mi.
- EPS: 2.0 af/ac
- Transmissivity: 374 gpd/ft
- Specific Yield: 0.05
- Recharge Rate: 1.8 in/yr

The Texoma lithology is Cretaceous and Quaternary deposits that occur as shales, sandstones, siltstones, coal, marl, limestone, clay and sand units. Water is derived in small quantities from thin sandstone units and cracks and solution channels in the limestone. Yields average 14 gpm with local areas capable of yielding 40 to 60 gpm. The groundwater is typically a sodium-potassium-bicarbonate. TDS ranges from 76 to 1,900 mg/L and hardness generally ranges from hard to very hard.

Woodbine

- Area Underlying Settlement Region: 2,255 sq. mi.
- EPS: 2.0 af/ac
- Hydraulic Conductivity: 0.5 ft/day
- Transmissivity: 935 to 1,219 gpd/ft
- Specific Yield: 0.06 (loose unconsolidated sandstone) and 0.02 (clay and limestone)
- Storage Coefficient: 0.001 (confined sandstone) and 0.00001 (confined clay and limestone)
- Recharge Rate: 2.28 in/yr

The Woodbine Formation is younger than the underlying Antlers Formation, which is separated by approximately 10 million years. The formation contains four unique members — the Dexter, Red Branch, Lewisville, and Templeton — which are comprised of fine- to coarse-grained sandstones, shales, varicolored clays, coals, and localize tuffaceous deposits. The Woodbine includes some gravels, but little to no quartz. Localized plant and dinosaur fossils can occur. The thickness increases eastward, ranging from 325 feet to 455 feet. The Woodbine produces small amounts of poor to good water quality. The mean yield is 14 gpm with local areas yielding 40 to 60 gpm.

⋈ SURFACE WATER RESOURCES

The water resources in and around the Nations' territories in south-central and southeast Oklahoma exhibit many similarities. Yet the quantity and quality of these waters — as well as other characteristics impacting their availability for various uses — vary considerably from west to east. In most cases, water flows in a generally southeast direction, consistent with stream gradients and basin slope, before confluence with the two predominant state rivers: the Arkansas and Red. Basin elevations range from approximately 2,665 feet in Basin 45 (Poteau River) to 272 feet in Basin 2 where the Little River leaves the state in McCurtain County and enters Arkansas.

The characteristics — such as stream morphology, substrate and slope — of each watershed, or basin, have a profound effect on local water quantity and quality, species and habitat, and land use. Many river basins in the Nations' territories include man-made reservoirs utilized for water supply, flood control, hydropower, industrial needs and other important purposes integral to local and regional economies. In general, the only natural lakes both in Oklahoma and the tribal region are small oxbows formed where orphaned stream channels have been cut off from major river channels. Some twenty-six oxbow lakes occur along and near the widely meandering Red River in McCurtain County.

More specific data on the Nations' surface waters, including water quality information, is presented in the Basin Summaries section of *Oka Holisso*.

Streamflow and Surface Water Characteristics

Aside from storage in lakes and reservoirs — as well as groundwater storage, especially in aquifers where pumpage rates roughly equal recharge — streamflow is among the most important determinants of water supply availability for various purposes.

The USGS' network of streamgages (Figure 58) — currently funded in partnership with about 850 federal, state, tribal, regional, and local agencies nationwide, including the Chickasaw and Choctaw Nations — has provided essential hydrologic data nationwide for more than a century. The first USGS gauge was established in 1889 on the Rio Grande River near Embudo, New Mexico. Specifically, this data is used for water availability assessments, reservoir engineering and daily operations, flood forecasting, drought monitoring, water quality management, support of fish and other aquatic species, and numerous other purposes. Currently, 121 Oklahoma gauging stations yield historic and/or real-time data to assist in various aspects of Settlement agreement implementation.

Average annual flows, typically measured in cubic feet per second (cfs) or acre-feet per year (AFY), are largely determined by precipitation, runoff, evaporation, diversions and other factors, and they vary widely according to time and place. Streamflow data provides a general representation of the ability of a river and its associated tributaries to provide surface water supply on an annual basis. The utilization of such data on this timescale is often the cornerstone of assessments conducted by state and federal water agencies in determining water available for appropriation from stream systems. To fully capture a watershed's full productivity, estimates utilize period of record data at a river's furthest downstream USGS streamgage.

GROUNDWATER— A VITAL SOURCE OF WATER SUPPLY

An aquifer, or groundwater basin, is an underground water-bearing formation. The upper extent of saturated rocks, sand and pores is referred to as the water table. While aquifers may consist of a variety of material, there are generally two types. Alluvial and (older) terrace aquifers are deposited by rivers and streams and commonly consist of gravel, silt, sand and/or clay. Bedrock aquifers are usually comprised of more consolidated material; water settles in fractures and joints in the rock.

Groundwater occurs at all depths, a few feet in shallow formations or thousands of feet below the surface in deeper, older rock. Deep, confined water can be thousands of years old. Underground water isn't stationary, but it usually moves very slowly. However, in some cases, groundwater moves freely between the ground and surface, such as in limestone/karst formations.

Aquifers are typically recharged through precipitation and surface runoff. Water infiltrates the ground until it reaches a less porous layer of rock. When such layers exist both above and below, an aquifer is considered confined. In such cases, the internal pressure might be sufficient to yield water in a well without the need of a pump. The hydrological connection between surface and groundwater is complex. Commonly, alluvial formations are recharged by overlying, intersecting streams, but aquifers can also support streamflow.

AQUIFER CHARACTERISTICS

Both major and minor aquifers in Oklahoma are assigned an **equal proportionate share (EPS)**, which is the portion of the maximum annual yield of water from a groundwater basin that is allocated to each acre of land overlying the basin or subbasin.

Hydraulic conductivity measures an aquifer's capacity to transmit water. It can be expressed in either feet per day or gallons per day per square foot.

Recharge rates, typically expressed in inches per year, account for replenishment of water to the aquifer through rainfall and surface runoff. Many aquifers recharge very slowly.

Specific capacity is the short-term sustainable discharge of water from an aquifer divided by the drawdown yielding the discharge, usually in gallons per minute per foot.

Specific yield describes the amount of water that can be drained by gravity from one cubic unit of aquifer material in unconfined aquifers as a percent of the total volume of aquifer material being drained. Some water is retained in the pore space. Typical specific yields range from 0.01 to 0.03.

Storage coefficient depicts the amount of water that can be released from storage by compression of the aquifer and expansion of water during pumping. Typical storage coefficients range from 10-3 to 10-5 (i.e., 0.003 to 0.00005).

Transmissivity is the rate of flow through an aquifer based on a one-foot-wide section extending an aquifer's full saturated height under a hydraulic gradient of 1.

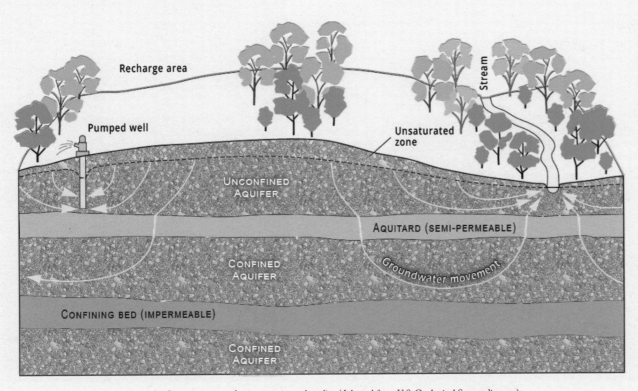

Figure 57. Aquifer characteristics and influences on groundwater quantity and quality. (Adapted from U.S. Geological Survey diagram)

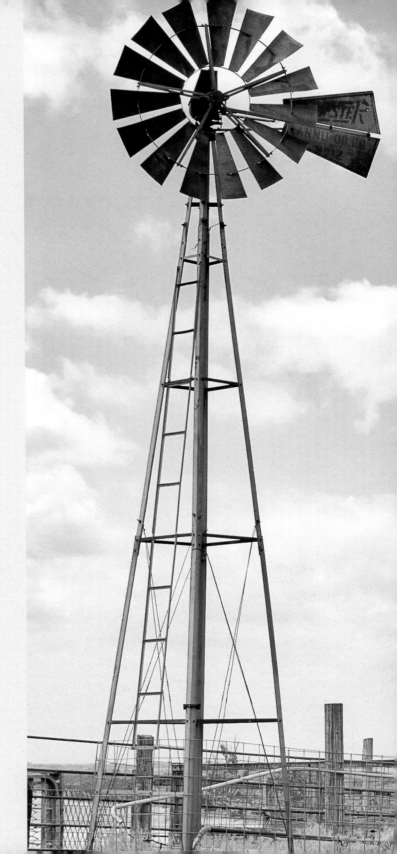

CHARACTERISTICS OF SETTLEMENT AREA BASINS

- Largest Area: Basin 48/ Washita River (3,223 sm)
- Maximum Mean Slope: Basin 4/Mountain Fork River (15.3%)
- Minimum Elevation: Basin 2/Little River (272 ft)
- Maximum Elevation: Basin 45/Poteau River (2,665 ft) & Basin 6/Kiamichi River (2,662 ft)

However, streamflows routinely fluctuate during seasons or as a result of flooding events, and they can be highly variable from month to month, or even day to day. Thus, while annual flows may reflect a considerable quantity of water, that amount is rarely available at any given point in time. For example, average flows occur 50 percent of the time while more robust flows occur less frequently. As a result, while variable flows that are part of a stream's natural regime can benefit many aquatic species and their habitats, streamflow alone is usually considered an unreliable source for municipal and rural drinking water and many other uses.

The Settlement Area is home to hundreds of important lakes and reservoirs, including a number of large federal and state projects. As elsewhere in Oklahoma, most of these were constructed between the 1930s and 1980s, generally culminating with the impoundment of McGee Creek Reservoir in 1987. In large projects constructed by the USACE and Bureau of Reclamation (BOR), storage is reserved expressly for municipal (i.e., drinking water) and industrial needs. Flood control is also a vital function of these impoundments, preventing many millions of dollars in flood damages each year throughout the Nations' lands. Other recognized benefits for which reservoir storage is commonly set aside include hydroelectric power generation, irrigation, water quality, (industrial) cooling water, conservation, navigation, low flow regulation, recreation, and fish and wildlife propagation.

Permits and Water Use

Surface and groundwater permits prescribe allowances on the relative amounts of water that can be diverted from lakes and reservoirs or withdrawn (pumped) from wells. In some cases, water from these points is utilized in an adjacent basin. There are 2,452 surface water (Figure 60) and groundwater (Figure 61) permits allocating 1,624,292 AFY (Figure 59) currently active within Settlement Area basins. While surface water use far outpaces that of groundwater, permits from groundwater sources are more plentiful.

Permit applications, developed in compliance with Oklahoma water law, are granted by the OWRB. In Oklahoma, surface water is considered to be publicly-owned and laws are designed to prevent speculation and to preserve water for future needs. If studies determine that water is indeed available from a stream system, the appropriation must be used for a beneficial purpose and not wasted. Various beneficial uses include — though are not limited to — agriculture, irrigation, public water supply, mining, commercial, industrial, and recreation, fish and wildlife. Associated water rights are considered "first in time, first in right" with priority given to senior holders. The use of water from a federal reservoir

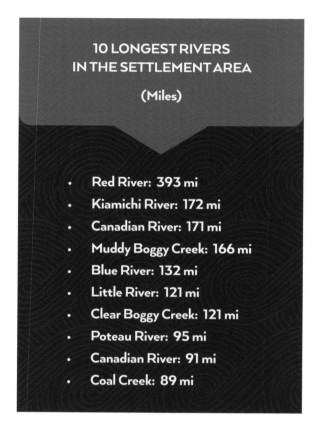

10 LONGEST RIVERS IN THE SETTLEMENT AREA

(Miles)

- Red River: 393 mi
- Kiamichi River: 172 mi
- Canadian River: 171 mi
- Muddy Boggy Creek: 166 mi
- Blue River: 132 mi
- Little River: 121 mi
- Clear Boggy Creek: 121 mi
- Poteau River: 95 mi
- Canadian River: 91 mi
- Coal Creek: 89 mi

Streamgages

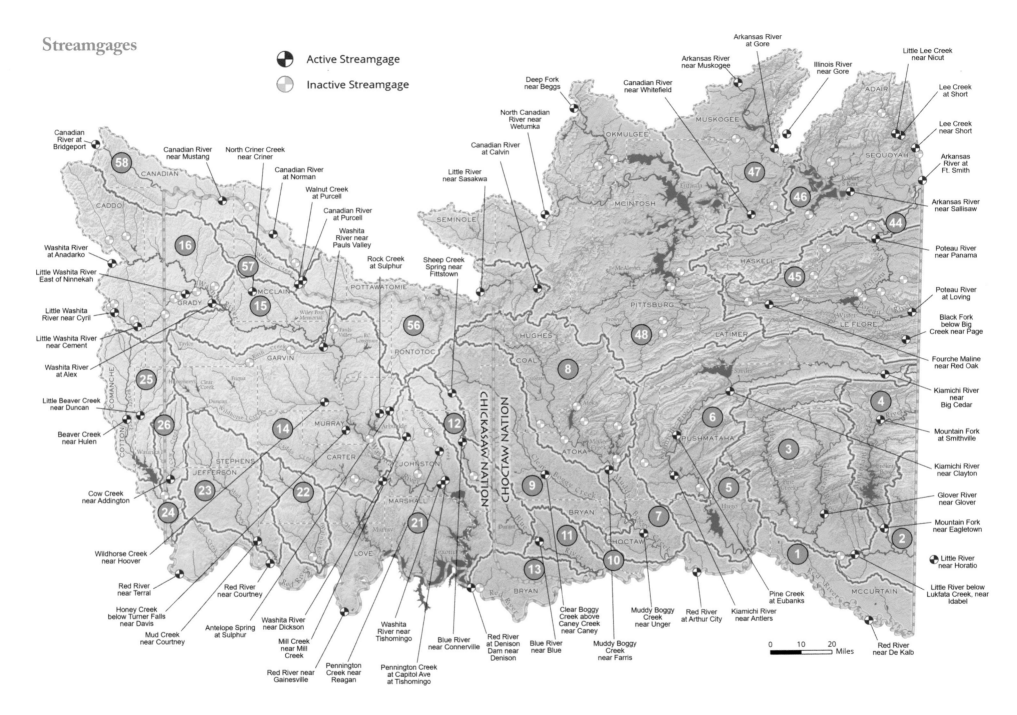

Figure 58. USGS streamgages utilized for Settlement agreement implementation. While only active gages are labeled, historical information from inactive gages is also important to hydrologic and related water resource studies. These stations could also be reactivated in the future. Numbered areas denote Settlement Area basins. (September 2017 data)

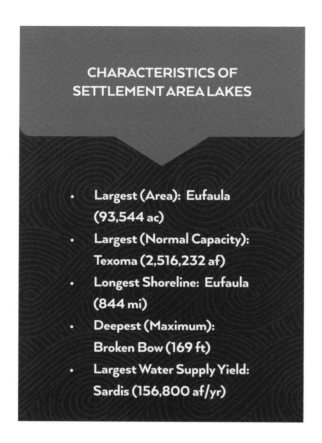

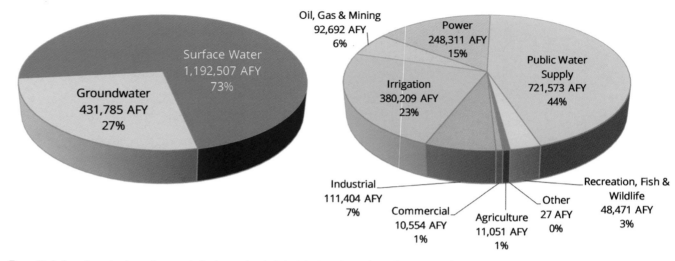

Figure 59. Left, total permitted water by source in Settlement Area hydrologic basins indicates that surface water use far exceeds that of groundwater in the region. Right, the distribution of permitted water uses within those basins, which provides a general indication of economic activity in the region. (September 2019 data)

requires both a permit and a contract for the associated storage with the federal government. Protection is also afforded to domestic uses, such as water required by a rural household or for limited farming purposes.

In addition to regular appropriation permits that authorize year-round use, the OWRB issues seasonal permits facilitating the use of water during a specific period each year as well as term permits that authorize use for a finite period of time. Seasonal and term permits may be issued even if the OWRB finds no unappropriated water available. "Provisional temporary" (PT) permits may be administratively issued without notice and hearing, but authorize use for no more than ninety days. These permits are frequently utilized by oil and gas companies for water required in the drilling of wells.

In stark contrast to surface water, groundwater in Oklahoma is considered private property that belongs to the overlying surface owner. Although its use is subject to "reasonable" regulation, apportioned water is based upon the amount of land owned and applied to the EPS. "Temporary" groundwater permits refer to allocations in aquifers for which a formal hydrologic study and determination of the MAY is still pending. These permits are assigned a temporary/default EPS of two acre-feet annually for each acre of land owned or leased by the applicant.

It is important to note that the utilization of state groundwaters is based upon "mining" concepts that largely ignore the finite nature of the resource. Extending to surface waters, current Oklahoma water law generally fails to account for non-consumptive water use and the many benefits of instream flows. Nor do these laws recognize the potential for long-term climate change or the intrinsic hydrologic connection between surface and groundwater resources. However, momentum to integrate these factors in state water management and conservation programs is growing. In addition, recreation and environmental protection are receiving greater relevance as state and local decision-makers now acknowledge the potential impacts of a future drier climate in both Oklahoma and the surrounding region.

Conferral Threshold

As mentioned, the Settlement agreement establishes, as a precondition to the OWRB's consideration of proposals contemplating water use outside of the basin of origin or Settlement Area, a threshold that triggers bipartisan technical conferral and associated modeling of water use permit applications. The threshold amount,

Surface Water Diversions

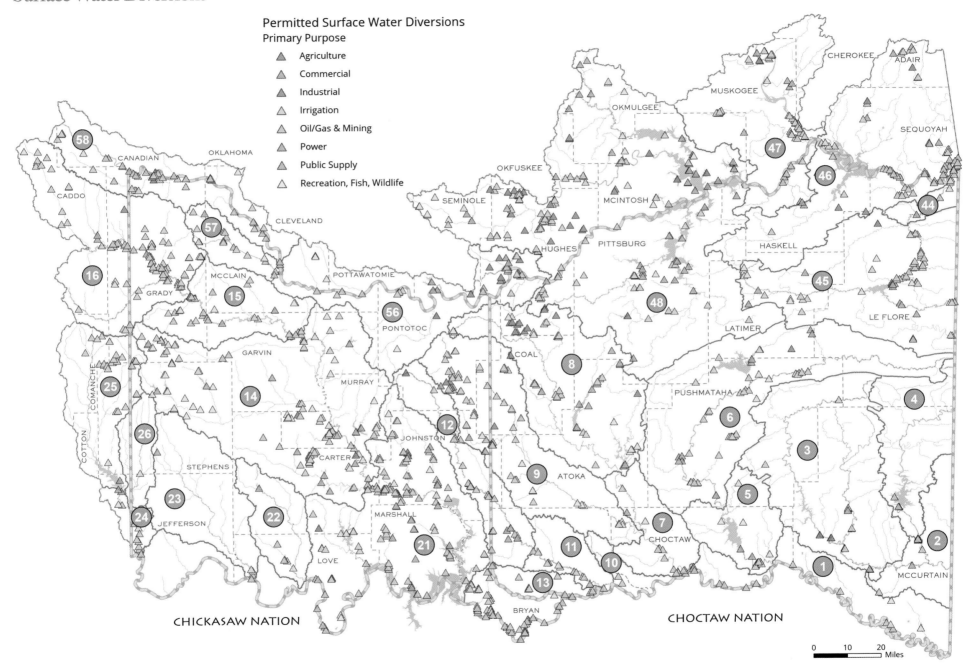

Figure 60. Diversion points and uses associated with surface water permits in Settlement Area basins as of September 2019.

Groundwater Wells

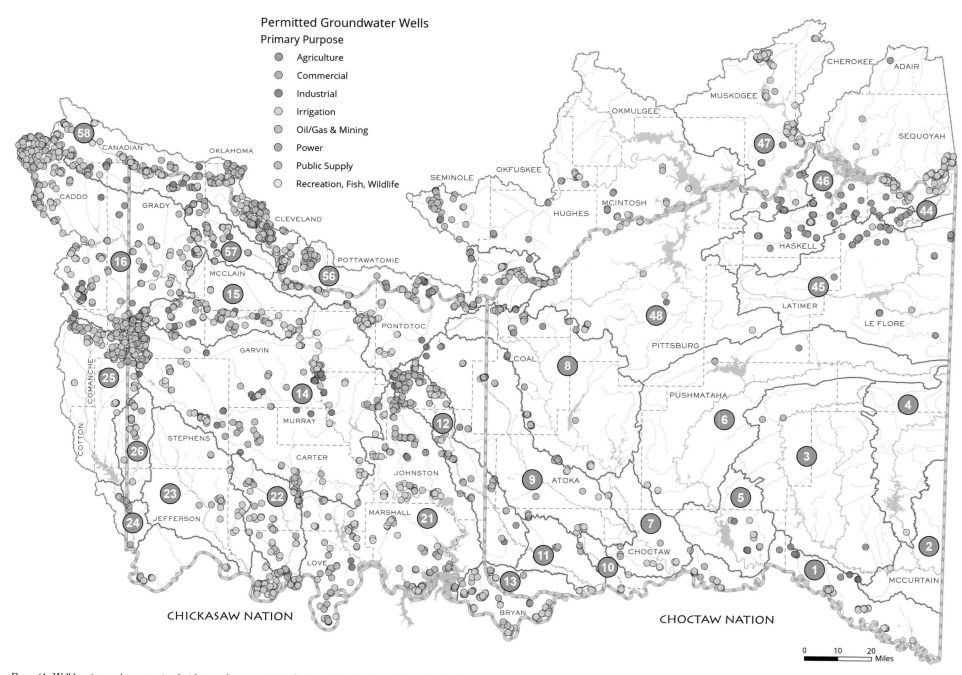

Permitted Groundwater Wells
Primary Purpose
- Agriculture
- Commercial
- Industrial
- Irrigation
- Oil/Gas & Mining
- Power
- Public Supply
- Recreation, Fish, Wildlife

Figure 61. Well locations and uses associated with groundwater permits in Settlement Area basins as of September 2019.

which is included in each of the basin summaries, varies according to a calculated percentge of each basin's mean available streamflow and/or a specified amount of water.

Water Quality

Both surface and groundwaters assume the characteristics of the particular rocks and substrate with which they come into contact, but water is also influenced by naturally-occurring organisms. The wide-ranging quality of the Nations' groundwaters is described in the groundwater section and, for surface water, throughout the various Basin Summaries.

Constant among all waters is the importance of intelligent water quality (in addition to quantity) management, which is essential to the continued social and economic welfare of the Nations and their citizens. In Oklahoma, specific beneficial uses—in addition to those pertaining to the appropriation and allocation of water supplies—are designated for all waters. These delineated uses are protected through numerical water quality standards as well as associated narrative criteria that prevent the degradation of existing water quality. More specifically, standards establish limits associated with the development of point source discharge permits and guide various programs designed to regulate contributions of nonpoint sources. Water quality beneficial uses designated for waterbodies in Oklahoma include: emergency water supply, public and private water supply,

fish and wildlife propagation, agriculture, recreation, navigation and aesthetics.

Oklahoma's water quality standards afford additional protection to special or particularly sensitive waters through five specific designations:

Outstanding Resource Waters (ORW) or *Scenic Rivers*: Waters that constitute an outstanding resource or have exceptional recreational and/or ecological significance. These may include waters located within national and state parks, forests, wilderness areas, wildlife management areas, and wildlife refuges or waters that contain species listed pursuant to the federal Endangered Species Act. This designation prohibits any new point source discharges or additional loading of pollutants. An Appendix B designation is applicable to some waters located within areas similar to those mentioned, but Appendix B areas allow for additional point source discharges or additional loading with limits ensuring maintenance of the waterbody's recreational and ecological features.

High Quality Waters (HQW): Waters possessing water quality that exceeds levels required to support propagation of fish, shellfish, wildlife and recreation in and on the water. This designation prohibits new point source discharges or additional loading of pollutants.

Sensitive Water Supplies (SWS): Waters particularly susceptible to pollution events. This designation restricts point source discharges in the watershed and institutes additional measures to address potential taste and odor problems and reduce water treatment costs.

Nutrient Limited Watersheds (NLW): A watershed of a waterbody assigned a designated beneficial use that

10 LARGEST SURFACE WATER PERMITS & USES IN THE SETTLEMENT AREA

(Acre-Feet/Year)

- City of Oklahoma City: 115,000 AFY (Public Supply; Basin 6)
- Oklahoma Gas & Electric Company: 98,598 AFY (Power; Basin 47)
- City of Oklahoma City: 60,300 AFY (Public Supply; Basin 8)
- Waurika Master Conservancy District: 44,022 AFY (Public Supply; Basin 25)
- City of Oklahoma City: 40,000 AFY (Public Supply; Basin 8)
- International Paper Company: 33,605 AFY (Industrial; Basin 3)
- City of Oklahoma City: 31,367 AFY (Public Supply; Basin 8)
- Western Farmers Electric Coop: 30,669 AFY (Power; Basin 5)
- Oklahoma Gas & Electric Company: 30,000 AFY (Power; Basin 47)
- Hugo Municipal Authority: 28,800 AFY (Public Supply; Basin 5)

is adversely affected by excess nutrients as determined by trophic status using chlorophyll-a as the indicator.

Source Water Protection (SWP) Areas: This designation applies to areas containing public water supply sources that are particularly sensitive to ongoing activities in the vicinity.

Section 303(d) of the Clean Water Act requires states to determine which waterbodies fail to meet defined water quality standards and submit updated lists of those waters to the U.S. Environmental Protection Agency (EPA) every two years. For waterbodies on the 303(d) list, the Clean Water Act requires development of a pollutant load reduction plan or Total Maximum Daily Load (TMDL) to correct each cause of impairment (such as low dissolved oxygen, turbidity, oil and grease, bacteria—specifically E. coli and Enterococci—and phosphorus). TMDLs must document the nature of the water quality impairment, determine the maximum amount of a pollutant that can be discharged consistent with standards, and identify allowable loads from the contributing sources.

Public Water Supply Systems

Public water systems (PWS) in the Settlement Area region (Figure 64) utilize a variety of surface and groundwater sources. While requirements vary based upon characteristics of the natural source water, treatment methods typically involve coagulating particles and pre-cipitates, settling out solids, and filtering the very small particles. Water is then disinfected prior to distribution.

The disinfection process can be significantly influenced by natural constituents of source waters. Excepting the Lower Arkansas region, many systems in the region that rely on surface water have difficulty meeting disinfection by-product (DBP) regulations, as set forth by the EPA Stage 2 Disinfectants and Disinfection Byproducts Rule (DBPR). The Stage 1 DBPR was implemented in 1998 for the purpose of reducing drinking water exposure to potentially harmful byproducts of the water disinfection process, especially involving the use of chlorine and its undesired reaction with naturally present organic compounds in water. The rule applies to community water systems and non-transient, non-community systems, including those serving fewer than 10,000 customers that add a disinfectant during any phase of the treatment process. The Stage 2 DBPR, which went into effect in 2006, is more stringent with increased compliance monitoring requirements.

System operations as well as the particular chemical and physical properties comprising a water source determine the presence and levels of DBPs, including potential violations, in treated water. The primary cause of DBP exceedance is elevated total organic carbon (TOC) concentrations. Seasonal variability of water demand and TOC in the source water can lead to both overuse of disinfectant and long residence times in the distribution system, resulting in DBP violations. Bromide and pH levels in source water are contributing factors.

Many PWSs in the region with DBP violations purchase treated water from regional sources. The only control these systems have in managing DBPs is in their own distribution systems. A regional approach to managing DBPs would be most effective for these systems — for example, the implementation of a coordinated disinfection booster system to maintain residuals in each respective PWS distribution system and reduce the disinfectant dose required at the treatment plant.

Water and wastewater treatment plants, distribution systems and related infrastructure are too often an overlooked determinant of water reliability. At the same time, especially in the Settlement Area, this infrastructure is fraught with numerous vulnerabilities that impact the effective delivery of safe public water supply to users, including insufficient and/or unreliable supply sources; distribution, treatment and storage deficiencies; insufficient secondary/emergency supply; and growth and/or demand issues. The substantial cost associated with maintaining infrastructure is yet another persistent problem facing rural and municipal water suppliers. And those who rely upon the Arbuckle-Simpson aquifer are challenged by new regulatory measures established to preserve this important groundwater source.

In a study conducted for the most recent update of the OCWP, estimates identified roughly a $6 billion need for drinking water infrastructure in the Nations' reservations through 2060 (Figure 65). A similar obligation is associated with projected wastewater infrastructure costs. In general, small providers are anticipated to assume the most significant portion of expenditures required for upgrades and improvements. As a result, a major initiative of the Nations is to promote sustainable practices among south-central and southeast Oklahoma water providers, including proactive support for maintenance and replacement of infrastructure as well as sound management and regionalization of facilities.

Figure 62. The City of Wynnewood, which purchases water from Arbuckle Master Conservancy District (MCD). While not a traditional water supply system, the MCD is a vital supplier as it sells and delivers approximately 12,000 acre-feet per year of raw water from the Lake of the Arbuckles to Wynnewood, Davis and Ardmore, as well as the Wynnewood oil refinery and rural districts.

Water Providers

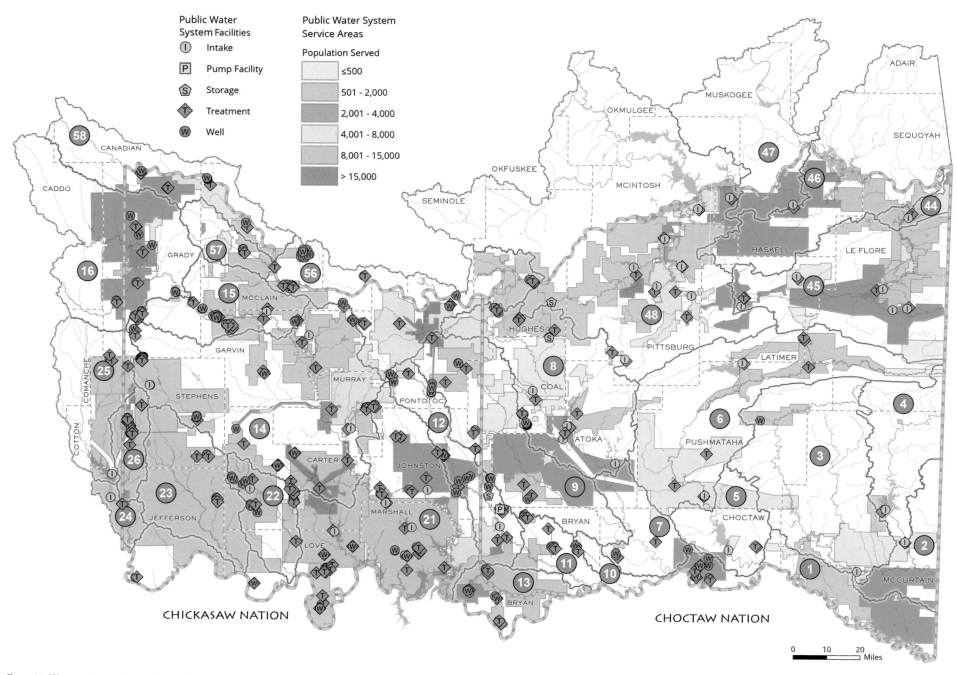

Figure 63. Water supply providers serving the Settlement Area.

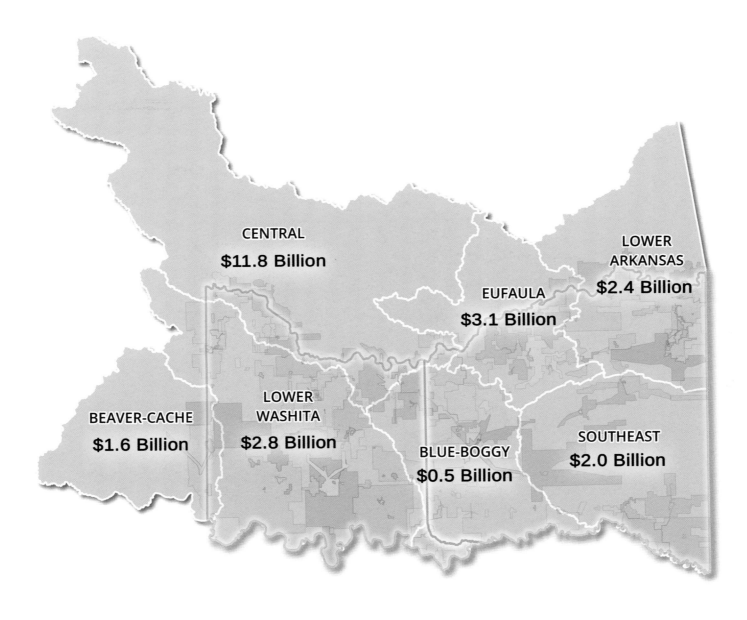

Figure 64. Projected 2060 drinking water infrastructure costs for each of the OCWP Watershed Planning Regions intersecting the Nations' territories (2007 dollars). The approximate service areas of water supply systems serving residents of the Chickasaw and Choctaw Nations are also displayed. It is important to note that figures for the Lower Arkansas, Eufaula and, especially, the Beaver-Cache and Central regions are inflated relative to the costs within the corresponding portions of the Nations' territories. However, current infrastructure costs and needs could be significantly higher than those projected for the OCWP. (Data from OCWP 2012 Update)

LAKES AND RESERVOIRS—
ESSENTIAL TO TRIBAL ECONOMIES

Lakes contribute in myriad ways to tribal, state and local economies in the Settlement Area. Major federal projects, in particular, are vital sources of municipal drinking water and fuel local industry. Large reservoirs are the centerpieces of outdoor recreation, such as swimming, boating, fishing and various downstream activities. Surrounding lands provide camping, hiking, wildlife watching and hunting opportunities. They provide beneficial habitat for fish and wildlife.

Larger projects here, including most of the seventeen lakes comprising more than 1,000 surface acres, have been designed to meet specific local and regional needs. This is central to the federal government's multipurpose concept, which seeks to allocate appropriate storage and/or reservoir operations to maximize particular uses identified during each project's design phase.

Of particular importance from a water supply perspective is the yield, or the maximum amount of water a reservoir can dependably supply from storage during a drought of record. Yield estimates, typically presented in millions of gallons per day (mgd), are calculated from detailed analyses of current and historical hydrologic data, reservoir characteristics and related information. The resulting figure is utilized by contracted water providers as an essential economic planning tool to ensure that enough supply remains available for both current and future customers. It is important to note that current standard yield calculations

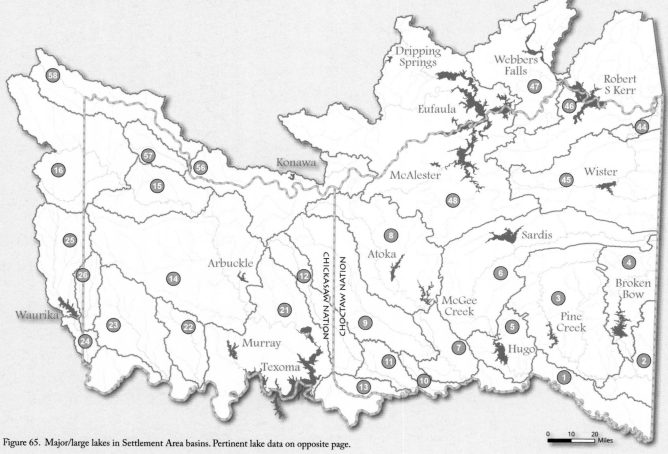

Figure 65. Major/large lakes in Settlement Area basins. Pertinent lake data on opposite page.

don't incorporate natural, variable streamflow regimes and fail to address impacts from upstream water rights.

The distinct uses of multipurpose projects constructed by the USACE, BOR and others are delineated in laws initially authorizing construction — or relevant laws passed later — as well as more general enablements arising from the Flood Control Act (1944), Water Supply Act (1958), Endangered Species Act (1973) and related legislation.

The authorized purposes and amount of storage space assigned to each influence how impounded water is managed through individual balanced and well-vetted water control plans. Sometimes purposes conflict with each other, thus complicating management decisions.

While reservoir purposes aren't typically prioritized by need, flood control and water supply would generally be considered the most consequential. Among large lakes in the Settlement Area, all of the projects built by the USACE or BOR — except Robert S. Kerr and Webbers Falls, two of the three reservoirs supporting the McClellan-Kerr Navigation System — include these stated purposes.

Five of the ten Corps reservoirs in this region are authorized for hydropower. The water quality purpose, which is typically fulfilled through the release of lake waters to augment downstream flows, is included in four reservoirs in

the Settlement Area. Waurika Lake is the sole project with irrigation as a stated purpose. All but Lake Konawa, as well as Webbers Falls and Wister, are managed to benefit recreation; seven were designed to support fish and wildlife conservation and protection, also an essential priority of the Chickasaw and Choctaw Nations.

Many reservoir projects engender incidental benefits, such as when the augmentation of low flows for fish and

wildlife propagation enhances a river's downstream water quality. Lake Murray's official sole purpose is recreation, yet it contains 1,008 AFY of water supply yield, of which the Southern Oklahoma Water Corporation utilizes more than half for its residential customers. Lake Konawa, which was built specifically to supply cooling water for a power generation facility, has become one of Oklahoma's most productive fishing lakes.

Tribal Water Planning Initiatives

As stewards of the land and water, the Chickasaw and Choctaw Nations consider it their ethical duty to protect and sustainably manage these resources on behalf of future generations. Emboldened by this responsibility, in 2011 the tribes initiated development of Oklahoma's first sustainability-based water plan. Today, the Chickasaw–Choctaw Regional Water Plan (CCRWP) is responsible for dozens of projects and programs collectively designed to secure a robust future economy, not only for tribal citizens, but all Oklahomans in south-central and southeast Oklahoma. The CCRWP is a comprehensive, long-term initiative to guide the use, protection and development of the Nations' shared waters. It also serves as the primary tool to ensure fair and justifiable implementation of the Tribal-State Water Settlement agreement.

Water is recognized as the most powerful economic development tool in the region, and it possesses significant, largely untapped potential to create jobs and related opportunities. At the same time, there are many existing water-related challenges, such as providing citizens with safe drinking water and industries with reliable supplies, that must be addressed. Waters supporting recreation, the region's third largest industry, require similar atten-

tion. The Chickasaw National Recreation Area, Turner Falls Park, Lake Eufaula, Broken Bow Lake, Beavers Bend State Park, and other popular destinations provide enormous benefits to their local economies. The Nations' ethical and cultural responsibilities also extend to the environment and preservation of habitat required for local fish and wildlife resources. Without question, these non-consumptive values of water will increasingly factor into tribal water management decisions, especially as demand grows and, along with it, competition for limited supplies.

As water itself is essential, tribal leadership have also established seven "Essential" principles to guide water management and protection throughout the Nations' jurisdictional lands in south-central and southeast Oklahoma. These value points—with Unity and Sustainability serving as the foundation for Urban Needs, Town and Rural Needs, Tourism, Agriculture and Drought Defense—and their specific goals form the basis of a policy and process framework that directs the Nations' planning initiatives.

Building upon available water resource data and prioritizing science-based assessment of resource availability and best management practices, the CCRWP planning team—working in a broad intertribal coalition of staff from the environmental science and natural resource branches of the two Nations, assisted by experienced water consultant professionals—is developing multiple evaluative and community-engaged planning projects. For each initiative, the planning team carefully balances water resource needs with social, ecological and economic priorities throughout the Nations, an approach that facilitates the development of sensible and effective water management policies, action plans and resource management institutions. The CCRWP not only establishes a detailed and progressive strategy to guide the use of available water supplies and resources, it also provides a mechanism to improve reliability, including assurances for water quality, region-wide.

Strengthening the effectiveness and efficiency of water supply systems in the Chickasaw and Choctaw Nation territories is imperative, especially as climate variability and drought threaten water security and complicate plans for development. Even large communities—such as Ardmore, McAlester, Ada and Durant—struggle to establish supplies sufficient to address growth. Although a significant financial commitment is often required, the infrastructure and delivery mechanisms of public water providers, especially those serving rural customers, must be maintained, improved and expanded as needs require.

In light of this, tribal leaders have instituted an over-arching initiative integral to effective implementation of the Settlement agreement: i.e., "sustainable communities." This foundational strategy to ensure the long-term reliability of local water supply, quality and

infrastructure accentuates good planning and practices that maximize the value of capital investments as well as associated operation and maintenance costs.

But sustainability is more than a goal. Indeed it has long been an inherent *value* of the Nations since time immemorial. Likewise, a truly sustainable community is founded not only upon a commitment to the long-range water needs of its citizens, but also fundamental respect for the resource itself.

The planning team seeks to provide utility managers

> **A truly sustainable community is founded not only upon a commitment to the long-range water needs of its citizens, but also fundamental respect for the resource itself.**

and operators throughout the Nations with the resources and direct assistance they require to independently maintain, repair, and replace assets as needed. In addition to asset management, water management personnel in the region are encouraged to enact sensible water pricing and rate structures, develop conservation and drought plans, educate and involve customers, and pursue related

strategies that ensure both supply reliability and robust local economies.

At the same time, the Nations and their planning team leverage state and federal funding programs to assist with implementation of sustainability-based projects. Additionally, they will work with regulatory and financial agencies to ensure that good system management is rewarded while responsible water providers are provided the help they need when experiencing inevitable problems or complications in delivering supply to customers.

CCRWP water management strategies include both structural and non-structural measures. Structural components might include a new pipeline, stormwater retention basin or additional water treatment capacity. In some areas, regionalization of provider systems and infrastructure can enhance water treatment and delivery as well as reduce costs. Maintenance of infrastructure is also imperative; it is not uncommon for municipal and rural systems to lose up to 60 percent or more of their supply due to leakage. And the reuse of reclaimed water, as well as brackish and other marginal quality waters, can significantly reduce the usage and increase the availability of invaluable potable water supplies.

Non-structural solutions include demand management (conservation or drought contingency planning), changes in water policy or the allocation of water rights, reallocating water storage in existing reservoirs from one use to another, or simply identifying new data needs or policies that will help improve the quantity and quality of water supplies and resources. Responsible manage-

The Nations' Essential Water Planning Principles

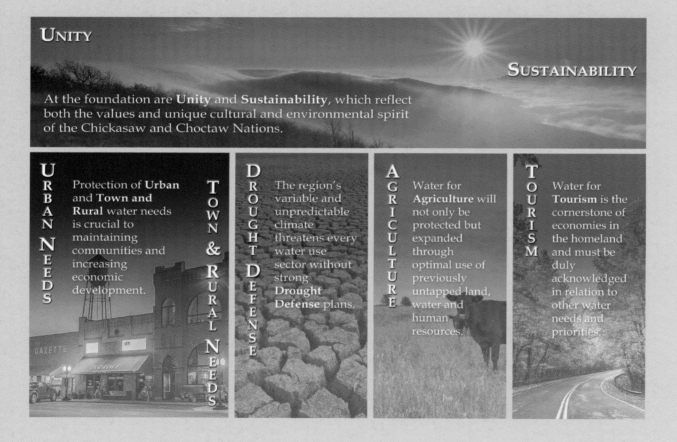

UNITY

SUSTAINABILITY

At the foundation are **Unity** and **Sustainability**, which reflect both the values and unique cultural and environmental spirit of the Chickasaw and Choctaw Nations.

URBAN NEEDS / **TOWN & RURAL NEEDS**

Protection of **Urban** and **Town and Rural** water needs is crucial to maintaining communities and increasing economic development.

DROUGHT DEFENSE

The region's variable and unpredictable climate threatens every water use sector without strong **Drought Defense** plans.

AGRICULTURE

Water for **Agriculture** will not only be protected but expanded through optimal use of previously untapped land, water and human resources.

TOURISM

Water for **Tourism** is the cornerstone of economies in the homeland and must be duly acknowledged in relation to other water needs and priorities.

ment of assets, along with requisite training, can greatly enhance treatment and distribution efficiency.

As a sovereign entity, the Nations and their planning team cooperate with the USACE, BOR, USGS, Bureau of Indian Affairs (BIA) and other federal partners to implement the CCRWP. The Corps' Planning Assistance to States and Tribes (PAST) program and BOR's Native American Affairs Technical Assistance Program (TAP) have become particularly reliable sources of funding. Recognizing the considerable costs often associated with the resolution of water issues, the Nations routinely leverage tribal resources with available federal assistance to shape and execute water-related planning initiatives. While TAP funding is contributed entirely by the BOR, PAST studies are cost-shared, 50/50 federal/non-federal. The Nations and other study sponsors have the option of providing in-kind services of up to 100 percent of their share of PAST project costs. Occasionally, tribal grants are provided directly to communities to resolve isolated or emergency water problems. Providing expert technical support to the planning team are staff from the Oka Institute at East Central University. Through financial support provided by the Chickasaw Nation and City of Ada, the Institute was founded in 2016 to facilitate regional water sustainability and management research and advocate for sound water policy.

To date, through the CCRWP and its many invaluable cooperators, the Chickasaw and Choctaw Nations have implemented dozens of initiatives to sustainably manage area water resources while ensuring that citizens continue to have access to reliable water supplies for a variety of purposes. The following is an overview of past, present and future projects and the inventive solutions being applied to the Nations' numerous water-related challenges. (Refer to the maps on the following pages for project locations within the respective Nations.)

WATER SUPPLY & INFRASTRUCTURE

Perhaps the most common problem faced by the Nations' communities and rural citizens alike is insufficient quantities of high-quality water to meet near-term or projected needs. Whether it's providing guidance to communities facing water supply challenges — including inadequate infrastructure — or implementing wider initiatives, the planning team, first and foremost, seeks to maximize water reliability. While many strategies can be utilized to enhance the supply needs of cities, towns and rural areas, a combination of measures are normally required to fully resolve reliability concerns. Therefore, the Nation's water professionals work cooperatively with communities and other partners to implement a variety of solutions that improve water system integrity, increase efficiency, reduce water demand and prepare the Nations' citizens for inevitable drought episodes.

Community Water Supply Planning and Assistance

In **Ada** [WS-1], the planning team has proposed an evaluation to determine the feasibility of connecting the city to Oklahoma City's Atoka pipeline, which runs northeast of the city, as well as constructing a new water treatment plant to meet the community's future needs and those of rural citizens in the area. The City's water supply has been significantly decreased as a result of Senate Bill 288, which mandated a hydrologic study that led to a ten-fold reduction in allowable groundwater withdrawals from the Arbuckle-Simpson aquifer. The Nations are partnering with Ada to fund a second study of the aquifer that would employ an expanded computer model, originally developed by the USGS, to help understand the sustainability of water supplies for Ada and the surrounding area in light of the new state regulations.

Another important CCRWP initiative is to diversify water supply utilized by the City of **Durant** [WS-2]. The city is reliant upon a single source of raw water, the Blue River, whose baseflow, in turn, is largely dependent upon its hydrologic connection with the Arbuckle-Simpson. Secondary sources of supply, including a new well, are under investigation. The Choctaw Nation has also assisted city officials in securing BOR funds to help finance the installation of smart meters to assist in the detection of leaks and increase conservation efforts. Decreasing the amount of treated water lost due to distribution line leakage can increase the resiliency of a community's overall water supply as well as decrease treatment costs.

Exacerbated by municipal and regional growth, water supply for the City of **Lone Grove** [WS-3] has become severely limited. While surrounding economies are expanding, supply issues for Lone Grove have led to enactment of a moratorium on new home construction since 2009. As a result, the Chickasaw Nation is working with the community to establish a reliable source of additional water supply. Two new groundwater wells are envisioned to expand supply sources. The ongoing project is funding the drilling of test wells to evaluate the productivity and water quality of potential well sites.

Groundwater supply wells currently utilized by the City of **Sulphur** [WS-4] are insufficient to address anticipated growth. Sulphur currently possesses a contract to draw supply from nearby Lake of the Arbuckles, but lacks the infrastructure and funding necessary to deliver and treat the water. In March 2013, the BOR evaluated the feasibility of constructing a water pipeline from the lake to the town. While the expense of this project currently represents a major obstacle to its implementation, the Chickasaw Nation has expressed a willingness to assist in the mandatory environmental assessment should the next phase of the study be pursued. Another potentially promising option for Sulphur is to obtain water from the City of Davis. A pipeline, up to eight miles long, would be required to connect Sulphur with Davis' new water treatment plant, which is modular in design and could be easily expanded for this purpose.

Tishomingo [WS-5], whose sole source of water supply from Pennington Creek is considered largely unreliable, faces similar issues with unprecedented growth. The city's current demand already far exceeds the 2060 estimate projected by the 2012 OCWP and the community's infrastructure requires significant upgrades. Direct assistance is being provided by the planning team to develop a feasible strategy to study and finance major upgrades of its water treatment plant, including the installation of smart meters to enhance water accounting and efficiency. Exploring the potential to augment the city's supply with groundwater, several test wells have been drilled into the Arbuckle-Simpson aquifer. The planning team is researching opportunities through the BOR's TAP and Corps' PAST Program to fund a formal investigation of alternative water supplies for the city. In a related study, the team is also looking into mining and related industrial activities in the Tishomingo area to determine potential detrimental impacts to Pennington Creek.

In a cooperative effort with the cities of Tishomingo and Mill Creek and Johnston County RWD #3, the Chickasaw Nation is evaluating the potential of wells at Mill Creek to establish a regional source of supply for those communities. The **Johnston County Water Supply Project** [WS-6] is being funded through BOR TAP funds secured in fiscal year 2018.

As part of a direct assistance project, the Choctaw Nation continues to seek funding to construct a new groundwater well at **Tvshka Homma** [WS-7], the Nation's tribal capitol north of Tuskahoma. This well would serve as a backup for the current supply from a small rural water district, enhancing resiliency and alleviating increased pressure on the water system, especially during the Choctaw Nation's annual Labor Day Festival, which draws upwards of 100,000 visitors each year.

Hydrographic Surveys

The planning team is awaiting funding from the USACE to conduct hydrographic surveys of **McAlester Lake** [WS-9] and an important branch of **Lake Eufaula** [WS-8]. These lakes provide the entire supply for the City of McAlester, one of the largest municipalities in the homelands. Utilizing the latest technology, the lake bottoms will be surveyed, mapped and compared with historic data to determine rates of sedimentation. Updated yield analyses will then be conducted to determine the current and future water supply potential of these important surface sources, which in the future might include nearby Lakes Talawanda 1 & 2. Under a separate study, the Choctaw Nation has completed bathymetric surveys and yield analyses on three important water supply lakes within their territory: New Spiro, Carl Albert and Wister.

Flood Control Dam Rehabilitation

The Natural Resources Conservation Service (NRCS) has identified sixty-eight flood control dams within the Chickasaw Nation that require rehabilitation to fulfill their original purposes, including water supply.

To address the issue, the Nations are currently evaluating participation in the federal Silver Jackets Program, which promotes collaboration between federal/state/tribal agencies — including the USACE, Federal Emergency Management Agency, National Weather Service and USGS — and their programs to reduce the risk of flooding and other natural disasters in a state or tribal jurisdiction. In addition, the Choctaw Nation has submitted 18 high hazard dams and more than 400 low hazard dams to the Bureau of Indian Affairs (BIA) for consideration of funding to address deferred maintenance as well as to increase dam safety and integrity.

Aquifer Studies

Funded through the BIA, the **Antlers aquifer** [WS-10] study was completed in 2013. Occupying the largest areal extent of any aquifer within the Nations' jurisdictions and extending along the Red River into north Texas, the Antlers (named the Trinity in Texas) supplies water to the town of Marietta and Southern Oklahoma Water Corporation as well as the Chickasaw Nation's WinStar Casino complex. In addition, Tishomingo and Durant are considering the aquifer as a future backup supply. Study results provide essential information related to the groundwater basin's potential expanded use in the region. The planning team has also conducted a modeling study on impacts of the aquifer's shared usage in Oklahoma and Texas.

THE GOAL— WATER RELIABILITY

The water required for a particular community, industry, agricultural operation, power facility, recreational area, environmental interest or other user must be sufficient for its relevant purpose. Above all though, the supply must be reliable — that is, it must be available in sufficient amounts and of adequate quality wherever and whenever it is required.

Needs change over time and water systems can become vulnerable to a wide range of factors. Responsible water managers must ensure that supply keeps pace with demand on the source. When a gap develops between the two, both water use and the economic benefits it provides are limited until additional supply is secured. That is why it is imperative, especially for drinking water providers, to not only possess knowledge of current needs, but also develop estimates of water demand at least fifty years into the future. Such long-term projections are often closely aligned with local population growth.

More frequently today, including within the Chickasaw and Choctaw homelands, non-consumptive uses of water (i.e,, those required for fish and wildlife and their habitats, associated environmental needs and a variety of recreational activities) are being valued and officially recognized through set-asides for instream flows and related regulatory schemes.

While quantity and both raw and treated quality are essential criteria in assessing water reliability for various entities and users, a third factor is also uniquely important: infrastructure. The water treatment and distribution systems utilized by water providers must be sufficient, including during times of drought when intense pressure is applied to these facilities and their components. It is imperative that municipalities and self-served industries — as well as irrigators and other relevant users — possess both the commitment and financial ability to maintain and replace or expand crucial infrastructure when required.

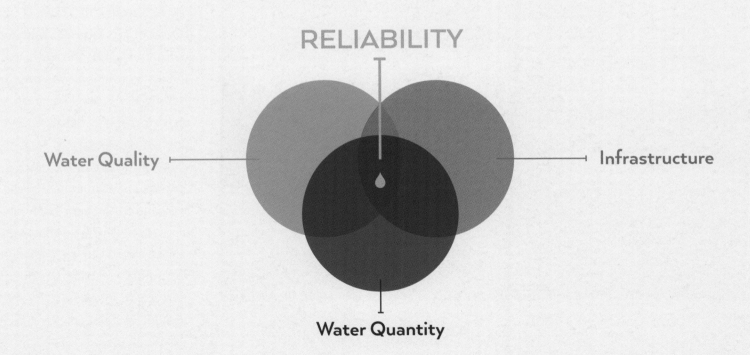

Expanding upon the USGS's original study that led to establishment of a new maximum annual yield for the aquifer, the second phase of the **Arbuckle-Simpson aquifer** [WS-11] study will include a more detailed analysis of the groundwater basin's complex hydrologic system. The planning team is currently researching funding opportunities for the study, which will also focus on establishment of an expanded, long-term monitoring program for the aquifer's springs, streams and wells.

The Antlers aquifer model will also be used as the basis for a planned study of the **Woodbine aquifer** [WS-12], which overlies the Antlers/Trinity formation. Consistent with this renewed initiative to develop available sources of groundwater, the planning team is also investigating the **availability and potential use of brackish water** throughout the region. While these sources are plentiful, many would require desalination and other advanced treatment methods to facilitate use.

Enhanced Aquifer Recharge Study

Also focusing on the Arbuckle-Simpson aquifer is the ongoing **Enhanced Aquifer Recharge Study**. Funded by the BIA and Chickasaw Nation and complementing a statewide aquifer recharge site analysis conducted for the 2012 OCWP, the study is evaluating potential locations to implement enhanced aquifer recharge in the Arbuckle-Simpson aquifer region. The technology, implemented with success throughout the U.S., involves the restoration and conservation of stored underground water to enhance local water supply availability. Its karst geology—exhibiting fractures and solution channels that allow water to infiltrate the subsurface—makes the Arbuckle-Simpson a prime candidate. Thermal imagery from drones and water level/flow data collected from local wells, sinkholes and springs will be utilized to identify the most suitable locations for enhanced recharge facilities. Researchers from the Oka Institute are also assisting in the study.

Fracking Water Usage Evaluation

Completed in 2014 through BIA financial assistance, the **Evaluation of Water Usage for Hydraulic Fracturing of Horizontal Wells** focuses primarily on the prolific SCOOP oil and gas field in the Woodford (Shale) Formation, which encompasses much of the Nations' territories. Fracturing (i.e., "fracking") involves the injection of pressurized water or other fluids (often through horizontal wells) into subterranean formations to extract oil or gas. The process utilizes large quantities of water and, while some of the produced fluid can be reused in subsequent frack jobs, the remaining waste (containing hydrocarbons, treatment chemicals and saline water) is often disposed of in deep injection wells. Recent evidence suggests these wells can be the cause of increased seismic activity and localized earthquakes. To address these concerns, including potential water

Figure 66. A rural pond and cattle in Garvin County.

supply impacts, the study identified active drilling areas and quantified amounts of water utilized for the drilling and fracking.

Ranchland Water Assessment

Cattle ranching is a prevalent industry in both south-central and southeastern Oklahoma as well as a prosperous enterprise practiced by both Nations. And like many economic activities, ranching requires a dependable supply of water. In partnership with the BOR, the planning team is conducting the **Tribal Ranchland Water Assessment** [WS-13] to inventory and evaluate existing and undeveloped water sources that could supply the Nations' widespread cattle operations. The study will also investigate the suitability of such supplies and associated lands for other sustainability-based agricultural ventures, including new or unconventional crops and those more resistant to drought. Cotton, once extensively cultivated in the Nations' Oklahoma lands but then decimated by the boll weevil, is a crop of particular interest. Concurrently, the Nations are incorporating conservation practices—such as drip and other more efficient irrigation methods—and responsible land management strategies aimed at reducing agricultural runoff containing sediment, nutrients and pesticides that contribute to water quality degradation. In addition, historical and culturally significant legume species are being cultivated at the Choctaw Nation greenhouse in Tuskahoma with plans to reintroduce these plants back

Figure 67. Wheat crop in bottomland along the Washita River.

into the diets of the Choctaw people. The propagation and proliferation of these ancient crops are particularly dependent upon reliable water supplies.

Water Infrastructure Evaluation

Employing a **water infrastructure evaluation** methodology developed in 2012 with assistance from the USACE, the planning team interviewed more than 50 water providers and wastewater treatment plant operators within the tribal territories. Results provided a generalized inventory of the Nations' water/wastewater infrastructure as well as a snapshot of current system needs. While the most urgent infrastructure problems are already being addressed, the team is currently prioritizing needs and identifying opportunities to maximize water reliability, reduce associated treatment and distribution costs, and improve drought preparedness. Consolidation and regionalization, facilitated through information that will be collected through a future region-wide water system infrastructure mapping program, is also being considered where appropriate. The Nations continue to explore establishing an assistance program to help communities upgrade and maintain their water and wastewater facilities and provide guidance related to project funding, engineering, asset management and system operator training.

WATER QUALITY & TREATMENT

In addition to adequate supply and infrastructure, the quality of both raw and treated water is an essential component of water reliability for most uses, especially within Nation lands where vulnerable surface supplies are the predominant source of water. Degraded water quality not only poses a health threat to citizens, it can also impair recreational uses that are so important to local economies. Protection of quality and remediation of impairments and related degradation issues in the watershed — especially through comprehensive assessment, modification of land uses, adequate monitoring and education — is often the most effective way to address complex water quality problems. Concerning treatment, disinfection by-products (DBPs), particularly trihalomethanes (THMs), have recently been identified as a threat. THMs are carcinogenic chemicals formed when chlorine or other disinfectants used to control microbial contaminants in drinking water react with naturally occurring organic and inorganic matter.

Blue River and Arbuckle Lake Watershed Reserved Treaty Rights Lands Project

In association with an ongoing BIA program to retain ancestral rights to tribal lands for religious and cultural use, hunting, fishing, gathering and related uses, the **Chickasaw Nation RTRL project** [WQ-1] seeks to implement a systematic approach to ecosystem restoration and sustained water quality within both the Blue River and Arbuckle Lake watersheds. Increasingly, these vital watersheds are suffering from water quality impairments which require the development of best management practices (BMPs) to restore associated uses and benefits. Prescribed fire and mechanical removal of eastern red cedar are being utilized as preferred BMPs to improve water quality. A comprehensive strategy will be developed to achieve long-term resilience to wildfire and establish fire adaptive communities throughout each watershed.

Regional Water Quality Assessment

Through its ongoing **Regional Water Quality Assessment**, the planning team is prioritizing watersheds exhibiting the most pressing water quality problems within the Chickasaw and Choctaw Nations. Potential best management practices (BMPs) will also be developed to mitigate those issues.

Impaired Waters Strategy

Through an associated study, the Team is developing a strategy to accelerate the removal of waters from the federal 303(d) list of **impaired waters**. Some of these impaired surface resources occur in "Basins of Heightened Interest (BHIs)," or those priority watersheds identified in the Water Quality Assessment. Other watersheds in the Planning Region are impacted by priority pollutants, which pose a significant human health risk. In addition to development and implementation of individual BMPs, solutions range from educational workshops to the development of state-approved Watershed Based Plans (WBPs). A variety of potential funding sources have already been identified.

Disinfection By-products Mitigation

During its water infrastructure evaluation, the planning team discovered that many of the Nations' water providers are having difficulty meeting the EPA's new standards related to DBPs. While the new federal regulations should eventually reduce or eliminate this threat, many water systems are now required to alter their current treatment processes and/or find entirely new supply sources. To address **mitigation of DBPs**, the planning team cooperated with the BOR to study mitigation of DBPs at **Antlers** [WQ-2], **Sardis Lake Water Authority** [WQ-3] and **Talihina** [WQ-4]. In May 2016, the Team completed a booklet, which was later disseminated to water plant operators throughout the region, designed to guide corrective measures and general compliance with federal regulations.

Through the USACE (PAST), $100,000 was utilized to investigate actual solutions to DBPs at **Wilburton** [WQ-9], **Poteau Valley Improvement Authority** [WQ-10] and Talihina. Further studies, enabled through

Figure 68. The train depot in Davis, Oklahoma.

BOR, will be conducted at **Atoka County RWD #4** [WQ-11], **Pushmataha County RWD #3** [WQ-12], and **Idabel** [WQ-13] to develop recommendations and address preliminary engineering needs that will allow these providers to more readily access federal funds to implement DBP solutions.

Coal Mine Stormwater Impacts Evaluation

Mining for coal and other elements has taken place in the Arkoma Basin, a major geologic province in the region, since the late 1800s. As new technology provides renewed interest and profitability in mining, both underground and on the surface, so does the attendant threat to water quality. The **Evaluation of Stormwater Impacts from Coal Mines**, which was funded through the BIA and completed by the planning team in 2014, focused on contamination of relevant streams due to runoff from tailing piles and surface mines. The primary surface water threat is from sulfides, metals and abnormally high or low pH. The study, which utilized the EPA's 303d list of impaired waters, identified the locations of suspected contributing mining sites.

New Spiro Lake Watershed Protection Project

New Spiro Lake [WQ-5], which serves as the primary drinking water source for local residents, has experienced significant water quality problems that threaten its viability. Elevated levels of nutrients (phosphorus and nitrogen) from a variety of sources in the watershed spawn extensive algal blooms during summer months. In turn, this results in poor fish habitat, increased drinking water treatment costs and potential regulatory violations related to nitrates and DBPs. Recreational benefits are also impacted. New Spiro Lake is currently included on Oklahoma's 303d list of impaired water bodies. In response, the Choctaw Nation has worked closely with local officials to restore the lake. In addition to sponsoring workshops to foster education on sedimentation and erosion concerns, the Nation funded initial water monitoring (and data collection) of the lake and its tributary streams. The planning team is currently assisting municipal leaders in identifying the best and most effective measures to improve and maintain lake water quality. Success at New Spiro Lake will be leveraged to address water quality issues and implement appropriate watershed protection strategies at other problem lakes in the region.

Kiamichi River Watershed Water Quality Program

The Choctaw Nation has obtained EPA funding to monitor and improve water quality throughout the **Kiamichi River watershed** [WQ-6]. Staff are conducting monthly sampling of nutrients, streamflow and other parameters to augment existing baseline data and identify impairments that can be addressed through BMPs.

Lake of the Arbuckles Watershed Restoration Plan

Supported by the Chickasaw Nation, Oka Institute and planning team, Sulphur-area landowners and other local citizens have united to implement an ambitious plan aimed at improving the quality of water in the **Lake of the Arbuckles** [WQ-7]. The Lake of the Arbuckles Watershed Restoration Plan, completed in April 2018 through a BOR WaterSMART Cooperative Management Program cost-share grant, recommends various strategies aimed at reducing pollutant loads from sources in the surrounding watershed and ultimately removing the lake from the state's 303d list of impaired waters. The Lake of the Arbuckles Watershed Association (LAWA), a voluntary organization of concerned stakeholders, was created to develop and implement the plan. Among various strategies, it recommends establishment of a long-term water monitoring program to evaluate the

success of BMPs and other improvements in land use. LAWA membership continues to expand as landowners aggressively pursue implementation of improved soil health practices. In addition, the organization is cooperating with a number of local organizations to establish a long-term program that utilizes prescribed fire management to restore the land. Controlled burns improve the quality and quantity of forage for livestock, reduces woody vegetation (such as invasive red cedar), removes thatch, and improves wildlife habitat.

Arbuckle Lake Watershed Economics of Prescribed Fire Study

Aligning with the ongoing Restoration Plan, this study will **estimate economic benefits resulting from prescribed fire BMP interventions** [WQ-8] that are being implemented throughout the Arbuckle Lake watershed. The study will include development of associated information and guidance for area landowners.

⚇ CONSERVATION & REUSE

Active conservation is necessary to address projected shortages and related challenges as competition increases for limited freshwater resources. Ultimately, conservation "creates" new supplies and allays the costs and difficulties often associated with the development and/or procurement of additional surface and groundwater sources. The planning team is investigating a number of strategies aimed at conserving the Nations' water supplies. Treated wastewater is a particularly promising "new" source, especially as state rules have recently been expanded to allow its usage. Nonpotable wastewater reuse, for uses other than drinking water, requires less intensive treatment. This source is also relatively abundant throughout the region. While potable reuse involves more challenges related to treatment and human health concerns, continued technological advancements will eventually facilitate this supply solution as well. The CCRWP advocates the utilization of a variety of tools to conserve supplies and reduce demand at the municipal level (and at Nation facilities), including water rate restructuring, enactment of conservation ordinances, leak detection programs, retrofitting and replacement of household water-using appliances, and citizen education. Irrigators and industries too are integrating conservation practices in their operations. Regionwide, the planning team is also working to control invasive vegetation species that consume potential water supplies. The Nations continue to promote artificial aquifer recharge, the use of marginal quality waters, and other new methods to preserve and stretch finite supplies.

Wastewater Reuse

Consistent with the tribal sustainability ethic, the Nations are assisting providers in implementing conservation strategies, including recycling and the reuse of treated effluent to reduce potable water demand.

Utilizing data provided through the 2012 infrastructure assessment and subsequent USACE funding, the planning team conducted an initial Phase I **wastewater reuse feasibility study** aimed at identifying systems with the greatest potential for this growing technology. Phase II of the study narrowed the list to six sites/systems determined to have the most promising reuse opportunities: Ada, Ardmore, Durant, McAlester, Pauls Valley and Wilburton. Preliminary engineering studies, along with obligatory community interest, will be required to determine the feasibility of each site.

Reuse could also be a potential option for **Sulphur** [CR-1], where water supply gaps are anticipated by 2030, assuming the city continues to rely solely on groundwater. A feasibility study, funded through the BOR and completed in March 2015, evaluated the direct use of Sulphur's treated wastewater for municipal irrigation, including the Chickasaw Cultural Center. A separate feasibility study to evaluate indirect use, which would involve the discharge of highly-treated effluent into the Lake of the Arbuckles, is on hold until the ODEQ implements appropriate rules to regulate this type of reuse.

Irrigation Water Conservation Project

The Nations not only assist entities in implementing water-efficient practices, they strive to ensure that tribal facilities conserve as well. The Chickasaw Nation is currently developing and implementing a number of conservation strategies aimed at reducing irrigation water requirements and use at a number of their facilities, including three casinos: **Newcastle** [CR-2], **Riverwind** in Norman [CR-3], and **WinStar** in Thackerville [CR-4]. Funds obtained through the BOR's Water and Energy Efficiency Grants (WEEG) will

Figure 69. Lower Mountain Fork River, Presbyterian Falls.

SOUTH CENTRAL CLIMATE ADAPTATION SCIENCE CENTER (SCCASC)

The SCCASC is part of a collaborative partnership among U.S. Geological Survey (USGS) scientists, resource management agencies, and a consortium of academic institutions from across the region that works to assemble scientific data and develop tools to help fish, wildlife and ecosystems adapt to the impacts of climate change. The center, which also oversees Texas, Louisiana, and New Mexico, is partially funded by the Chickasaw and Choctaw Nations.

be used to integrate automated irrigation controllers, high efficiency spray and rotor heads, weather stations and other tools into existing supply systems. Due to the significant irrigation demands at these facilities, substantial reductions in water and associated energy costs are anticipated. Expanded conservation here, as well as in large water supply systems, not only enhances overall water efficiency, but it can extend the life of regional supplies. In this region of the country, comprehensive conservation programs — including a combination of enforcement, incentives and public awareness — have resulted in more than 60-percent reductions in residential per capita demand.

Water Banking Study

Utilizing BOR funds, the planning team is also researching the potential use of **water banking** to develop strategies that promote the transfer or sale of water or water rights from one user to another. Among numerous benefits, successful banking programs can allay investments in new infrastructure. The Arbuckle-Simpson aquifer is being considered as the subject of a pilot study for this program.

SUSTAINABILITY & CLIMATE VARIABILITY

Complementing tribal water reliability initiatives are those addressing long-term climate variability and requisite adaptation measures. While preservation of conventional municipal and industrial water supplies is paramount, also important are the in situ benefits of surface and groundwater resources — those of value to recreational interests, the environment and fish and wildlife species — that historically have been neglected by state and federal planning agencies. Contributing technical and scientific support in these areas is the South Central Climate Adaptation Science Center (SCCASC), established in 2012 through a cooperative funding agreement between the Nations and USGS. The SCCASC, part of a federal network of eight such centers in the U.S., maintains full-time scientists, interns and related resources dedicated to assessing the impacts of current and future climate extremes on natural and cultural resources in the region. The Center also provides related educational opportunities.

Climate Change Assessments

The planning team recently completed its **Uncertainty and Climate Change Study**, enabled through almost $300,000 in support from the SCCASC. Results are providing information to strengthen the Nation's ability to withstand and respond to future drought and related uncertainties. Preceded by a comprehensive review of existing climate change literature, studies, models and programs, the study estimates anticipated changes in water supply and demand due to an increasingly variable climate in the region.

In 2016 the planning team, assisted by the SCCASC, completed its initial **assessment of climate change impacts on streamflows in the Red River Basin,** which extends from the New Mexico-Texas border to the Mississippi River and includes much of the Chickasaw and Choctaw territories. Through a cooperative agreement with the USACE, researchers have adapted the agency's existing RiverWare model to provide estimates of water available for all purposes (including aquatic life) basin-wide under a variety of future climate scenarios. The revised model, incorporating data from down-scaled global climate models (GCMs), includes the locations of all surface water impoundments and current water rights/diversions in the basin. This invaluable tool, which will soon be expanded to the adjacent Canadian River Basin, will help the Nations improve water management techniques in light of climate variability factors. In cooperation with the USGS, SCCASC and other partners, the planning team will also utilize the model's hydrologic data in several spin-off studies that will reevaluate important basin water issues, including supply and demand, surface/groundwater interactions, water quality, aquifer recharge, sub-basin drought planning, and endangered and invasive species. Already, the SCCASC is utilizing RiverWare to identify the most drought-vulnerable homeland communities (including individual water providers) as well as ecosystems containing fish species at particular risk from drought.

Sustainable Flows Methodology

Reflecting the integral importance of streamflow sustainability, the Nations (through financial/technical support from the USACE) defined a feasible methodology to assess and quantify base river flows required for environmental and water-based recreational benefits as well as for more traditional uses that support homeland economies. The **Sustainable Flows for Southeast Oklahoma Methodology** report — completed in 2012 with input from the OCWP Instream Flow Advisory Group and an advisory team consisting of tribal, federal, state and university experts — equips the planning team with a justifiable, science-based set of procedures to estimate and protect basin-specific streamflows required to satisfy both consumptive and non-consumptive water needs. A pilot study has been proposed for the Kiamichi River Basin to establish sustainable streamflow for the survival and proliferation of a rare and endangered mussel species that resides there.

Sector Drought Vulnerability Assessments

Utilizing resources available at the SCCASC and Oklahoma University's Division of Regional and City Planning, in 2016 the Chickasaw Nation conducted cursory **drought vulnerability assessments** associated with six relevant sectors: water supply, recreation/tourism, agriculture, public health, emergency management and green buildings. Data from the assessments, funded by the BIA, guided the format and content of drought vulnerability workshops designed to assist other tribes in the south-central U.S. region in strategies to mitigate tribal drought impacts.

⚜ MONITORING

Accurate and consistent monitoring of surface and groundwater resources, along with appropriate assessment of associated data, is imperative to effective water management. Fortunately, significant near- and real-time monitoring activities are prevalent throughout the Nations' jurisdictional boundaries: of rivers, streams and springs at USGS gages; of groundwater through well sites operated by the OWRB and USGS; of lakes by the BOR and USACE; and of climate through the Oklahoma Mesonet. Resulting data provides invaluable information related to current water availability, especially in determining the impacts of, and appropriate response to, ongoing drought episodes. This information also allows water managers and researchers to assess long-term trends and formulate reliable forecasts of water supplies. Both the Chickasaw and Choctaw Nations administer independent monitoring programs in support of various water studies and related initiatives. The Nations' ability to make informed, science-based water management decisions will rely not only upon the continuation of these monitoring programs, but also on the expansion of long-term data collection and monitoring in the region.

Cooperative Streamgaging Program

A cornerstone monitoring initiative of both Nations is a partnership with the USGS in the federal agency's **Cooperative Streamgaging Program** and network. Currently, the Chickasaw and Choctaw Nations each provide funding to support the operation and maintenance of eight (out of sixteen) USGS gaging stations within the region. These particular sites have been selected due to both locations and length of data records. Preservation of these sites through the Nations' involvement ensures additional years of data collection that will improve the accuracy of estimates of average and extreme (e.g., flooding and drought) streamflow fluctuations due to changing land use practices, surface and groundwater development, and climate change.

⚜ REGIONAL PLANNING

Past solutions to local water problems were largely prescribed by state or federal governments. Today these authorities recognize that the most effective remedies are championed at the local or regional level where impacted stakeholders are intimately familiar with local needs, priorities and challenges. Regional water planning that empowers citizens is the new standard and one that the Nations have championed with great success in addressing water supply, drought and related concerns.

Arbuckle-Simpson Aquifer Drought Contingency Plan

The statewide drought of 2011–15 took a devastating toll upon south-central Oklahoma. Flows in the spring-fed Blue River, Durant's exclusive water supply, decreased to less than 1 cfs as city leaders were forced to establish an emergency connection to a small lake nearby. Tishomingo, which relies entirely upon Pennington Creek as its source of water, saw water levels at its intake drop to within a few inches of being unusable during the worst portion of the drought. The town of Bromide was forced to drill a well after its spring dried up. Springs supplying water to Bromide and Wapanucka went dry, forcing the construction of emergency water supply wells and the hauling in of water from outside those communities. Byrd's Mill spring, Ada's typically prolific supply, also proved insufficient for the city's considerable needs. Many ranchers were forced to sell off herds at reduced prices because they could not grow enough hay in this area for feed, and it was prohibitively expensive to haul required hay in from other states. Recreation, essential to area economies, also suffered as Antelope Springs, a renowned feature of the Chickasaw National Recreation Area, went dry and the park's swimming holes were closed due to public health threats associated with the stagnant water.

A common thread running through many of these impacted supplies is the **Arbuckle-Simpson aquifer** [RP-1], the principal and, in some cases, the sole source of water for 150,000 people in the region. To help ensure the aquifer's protection, and that of its users, under future

Figure 70. Mustangs near Elmore City in Garvin County.

drought scenarios, in 2015 the Nations entered into an agreement with the BOR, through its WaterSMART Drought Response Program, to fund development of the stakeholder-driven Arbuckle-Simpson Aquifer Drought Contingency Plan (DCP). Representatives of municipalities, rural water districts, recreational and wildlife management areas, major industries, and the farming and ranching community came together for a series of meetings, facilitated by the Nations, to identify water supply vulnerabilities and develop appropriate drought mitigation and aquifer sustainability strategies. The final DCP, including a drought monitoring and early warning system to trigger response actions, was completed in late 2017.

Sardis Lake/Poteau Regional Water Supply Plan

To address water supply issues in the **Sardis Lake/Poteau region**, where groundwater resources are severely limited and surface supplies are particularly susceptible to drought, the planning team developed a regional water action plan involving relevant stakeholders. Utilizing USACE PAST cost-share funds, the team focused on the primary surface supplies— **Lake Carl Albert** [RP-2], **Lloyd Church Lake** [RP-3], **New Spiro Lake** [RP-4], **Lake Talihina** [RP-5], **Sardis Lake** [RP-6] and **Lake Wister** [RP-7]—that individually comprise the sole water source for many local cities and rural water districts. The storage in each reservoir is challenged due to sediment, water quality degradation and external water demands. A key aspect of the study included bathymetric surveys on three of the lakes to assess and update their water supply yield potential. Among several important findings, the final plan concluded that while a regional system would be infeasible at this time, interconnections between selected systems could benefit many customers in the region. Long-term implementation of the plan and its recommendations is pending.

Regional Economic Growth Potential and Water Supply Needs Assessment

Water infrastructure and supply inadequacies are plaguing the economies of several **communities in south-central Oklahoma** [RP-8]. While some of these water providers are currently able to support limited growth, the ability to meet peak demands will be severely challenged during future drought events. Water in Lake Texoma, in the southern area of the region of interest, contains salinity levels that are typically too high for potable use under conventional treatment. This project, funded through the USACE Planning Assistance Program, involves regional assessments of water supply needs and associated economic growth potential.

⚕ STEWARDSHIP & CULTURE

A broader Nation objective similarly applicable to tribal water programs is the preservation of certain resources — sites and areas — of particular cultural importance. Thousands of such sites exist throughout the region, providing not only tangible recreational and economic value to the Nations but also linking tribal citizens to their rich, shared heritage.

Blue River Watershed Economic Value of Water Study

Focusing on the often overlooked value of water, this study includes a detailed analysis and estimates of the annual economic contributions provided by water resources in **Blue River watershed** [SC-1]. The study, with particular emphasis on streamflows, is jointly funded by the State of Oklahoma and Chickasaw and Choctaw Nations.

Blue River Watershed Restoration Plan

Encouraged by LAWA's success, a similar stakeholder group has been formed to address water quality and related issues in the **Blue River watershed** [SC-2]. Completed in January 2019, the Blue River Watershed Restoration Plan is a science-based, stakeholder-centric approach to the use, management and protection of the river system's extraordinary resources that are of such unique significance to southeast Oklahoma. The Blue River Foundation, which developed the WRP in cooperation with the Chickasaw Nation and other stakeholders, seeks to foster additional study and monitoring of the watershed that will enhance future decision-making. Armed with effective tools to ensure watershed sustainability, WRP stakeholders are implementing sensible land management practices that improve soil health, reduce sediment and nutrient runoff, stabilize the riparian zone and accomplish other benefits to enhance water quality and quantity. As with the LAWA plan, the Blue River effort was funded through a BOR WaterSMART Cooperative Management Program cost-share grant.

Lake Nanih Waiya Stewardship

In an effort to preserve its cultural heritage and resources while accentuating its stewardship role, the Choctaw Nation entered into an agreement with the State of Oklahoma in 2016 to cooperatively manage **Lake**

Nanih Waiya [SC-3]. The lake area is revered by the Choctaw as the site of the Nation's original Capitol following removal. Furthermore, oral tradition recognizes the Nanih Waiya mound in the traditional Mississippi homelands as the site of the Choctaw people's creation. Through the 2016 memorandum of understanding — reflecting the Nations' desire to increase their role in the oversight, protection and promotion of recreational resources and facilities within their territories — the Oklahoma Department of Wildlife manages local fish and wildlife resources and related lake features.

Lake Talawanda Stewardship

The Choctaw Nation has established an ongoing lake monitoring program at **Lakes Talawanda 1 and Talawanda 2** [SC-4]. Choctaw tribal property surrounds both lakes, providing the impetus for the implementation of future watershed BMPs based upon monitoring results. The Choctaw Nation is committed to ensuring that both current and future generations of Oklahomans will be able to enjoy the lakes' many features and benefits.

The Chickasaw Nation: TRIBAL WATER PLANNING PROJECTS

Figure 71. CCRWP water planning projects and initiatives, Chickasaw Nation.

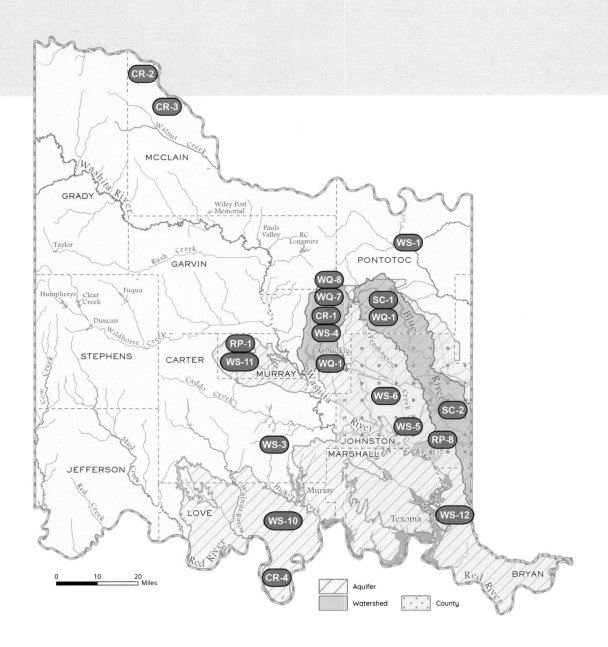

Project Categories:

WS: Water Supply & Infrastructure
WQ: Water Quality & Treatment
CR: Conservation & Reuse
RP: Regional Planning
SC: Stewardship & Culture

PLANNING PROJECTS: CHICKASAW NATION

CR-1: City of Sulphur Wastewater Reuse Study

CR-2: Irrigation Water Conservation Project (Newcastle Casino)

CR-3: Irrigation Water Conservation Project (Riverwind Casino)

CR-4: Irrigation Water Conservation Project (Winstar Casino)

RP-8: Regional Economic Growth Potential and Water Supply Needs Assessment

WQ-1: Blue River & Arbuckle Lake Watershed Reserved Treaty Rights Lands Project

WQ-7: Lake of the Arbuckles Watershed Restoration Plan

WQ-8: Lake of the Arbuckles Watershed Economics of Prescribed Fire Study

WS-1: City of Ada Water Supply Planning

WS-3: City of Lone Grove Water Supply Planning

WS-4: City of Sulphur Water Supply Planning Study

WS-5: City of Tishomingo Water Supply Planning

PLANNING PROJECTS: BOTH NATIONS

RP-1: Arbuckle-Simpson Aquifer Drought Contingency Plan

SC-1: Blue River Watershed Economic Value of Water Study

SC-2: Blue River Watershed Restoration Plan

WS-6: Johnston County Water Supply Project

WS-10: Antlers Aquifer Study

WS-11: Arbuckle-Simpson Aquifer Study (Phase 2)

WS-12: Woodbine Aquifer Study

ADDITIONAL TRIBAL PLANNING INITIATIVES

Brackish Water Study

Climate Change Streamflow Impacts Assessment

Coal Mine Stormwater Impacts Evaluation

Cooperative Streamgaging Program

Enhanced Aquifer Recharge Study

Flood Control Dam Rehabilitation

Fracking Water Usage Evaluation

Impaired Waters Strategy

The Choctaw Nation: TRIBAL WATER PLANNING PROJECTS

Figure 72. CCRWP water planning projects and initiatives, Choctaw Nation.

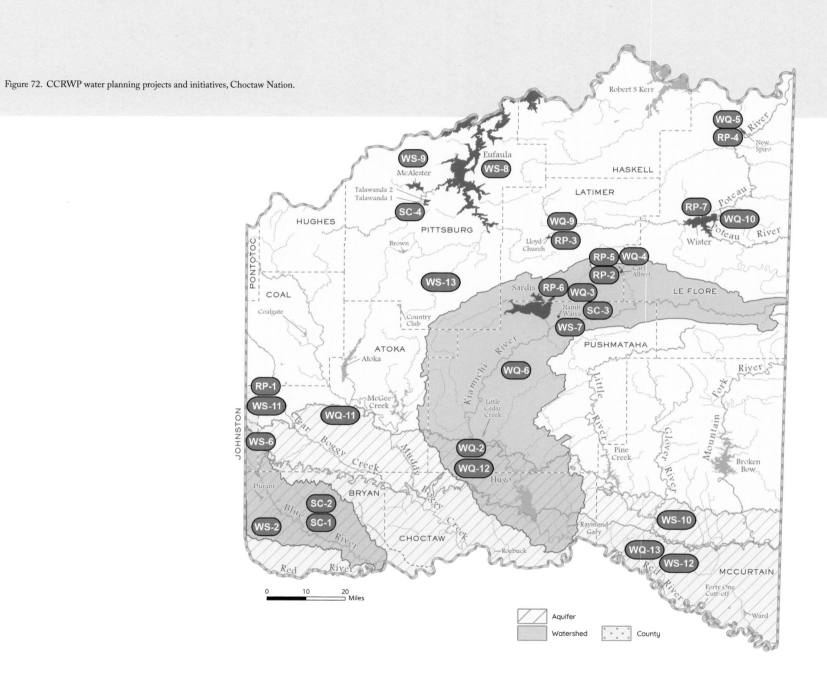

Project Categories:

WS: Water Supply & Infrastructure
WQ: Water Quality & Treatment
CR: Conservation & Reuse
RP: Regional Planning
SC: Stewardship & Culture

PLANNING PROJECTS: CHOCTAW NATION

RP-2: Lake Carl Albert Regional Supply Study

RP-3: Lloyd Church Lake Regional Supply Study

RP-4: New Spiro Lake Regional Supply Study

RP-5: Lake Talihina Regional Supply Study

RP-6: Sardis Lake Regional Supply Study

RP-7: Wister Lake Regional Supply Study

SC-3: Lake Nanih Waiya Stewardship

SC-4: Lake Talawanda Stewardship

WQ-2: City of Antlers Disinfection By-Products Mitigation

WQ-3: Sardis Lake Water Authority DBP Mitigation

WQ-4: City of Talihina DBP Mitigation

WQ-5: New Spiro Lake Watershed Protection Project

WQ-6: Kiamichi River Watershed Water Quality Program

WQ-9: City of Wilburton DBP Mitigation

WQ-10: Poteau Valley Improvement Authority DBP Mitigation

WQ-11: Atoka Co. RWD #4 DBP Mitigation

WQ-12: Pushmataha Co. RWD #3 DBP Mitigation

WQ-13: City of Idabel DBP Mitigation

WS-2: City of Durant Water Supply Assistance

WS-7: Tvshka Homma Capitol Grounds Water Supply Project

WS-8: Lake Eufaula (City of McAlester) Hydrographic Survey

WS-9: Lake McAlester (City of McAlester) Hydrographic Survey

WS-13: Tribal Ranchland (Daisy) Water Assessment

PLANNING PROJECTS: BOTH NATIONS

RP-1: Arbuckle-Simpson Aquifer Drought Contingency Plan

SC-1: Blue River Watershed Economic Value of Water Study

SC-2: Blue River Watershed Restoration Plan

WS-6: Johnston County Water Supply Project

WS-10: Antlers Aquifer Study

WS-11: Arbuckle-Simpson Aquifer Study (Phase 2)

WS-12: Woodbine Aquifer Study

ADDITIONAL TRIBAL PLANNING INITIATIVES

Regional Water Quality Assessment

Sector Drought Vulnerability Assessments

Sustainable Flows Methodology

Uncertainty & Climate Change Study

Wastewater Reuse Study

Water Banking Study

Water Infrastructure Evaluation

Basin Summaries

To assist in implementation of the Settlement agreement — and, by extension, to determine initial local and regional water supply reliability — this component of the *Oka Holisso* presents water data specifically associated with the agreement's delineated hydrologic basins through various maps, tables, charts and related products. In some cases, defined Class A, B and C hydrologic basins, which align with planning basins delineated for the latest (2012) update of the OCWP, have been combined to better illustrate watershed uniformity. Adapted from existing OWRB administrative stream systems, these planning basins, upscaled to regions for the 2012 OCWP, were drawn by subdividing the state into eighty-two surface water basins (including thirty in the Settlement Area) based on USGS twelve-digit Hydrologic Unit Code (HUC) boundaries. Where practical and to facilitate planning studies, OCWP basins were delineated to include those with a long-term USGS streamflow gage at or near the basin outlet.

WATER AND RELATED RESOURCES

Data for principal rivers/streams were supplied by the OWRB and USGS. Approximate lengths are derived from the National Hydrography Dataset (NHD). "Principal" streams included in each summary's data tables are relative to the individual watersheds, but generally include those at least ten miles in length. Reflecting the general nature of Oklahoma's typically low-gradient, meandering streams, the provided average slope (expressed as a percent) for each of the nineteen *Oka Holisso* basin/watersheds was determined through National Elevation Dataset 30-meter resolution data. The rise and run was averaged across the entire basin/watershed.

Basin summary data demonstrates all-important water variability through charts displaying annual and monthly streamflow data estimated at a hypothetical bottom-of-basin gage. Estimated baseflows, which portray a watershed's general annual "water productivity," were calculated using 1) period-of-record data from the furthest downstream gage in each basin, 2) basin drainage area from OCWP basin

Geographic Information System (GIS) shapefiles, 3) HUC 12 values, 4) data from the USGS StreamStats web application, and 5) results obtained from Purdue University's Web-based Hydrograph Analysis Tool (WHAT). The charts often demonstrate that streamflow, which is appropriated on an annual basis in Oklahoma, is frequently unavailable to users at a particular time and location. Watershed/basin maps include the locations of USGS streamgages. Inactive gages are also included as their data remains of value and these stations could be reactivated.

Similarly, streamflow exceedance estimates depict the probability of specific flow occurring at a given time and gage location, including the hypothetical streamgage at a basin/watershed's outlet. Flows vary according to the amount of upstream drainage area, precipitation and related weather/climate issues, upstream water use, land uses in the watershed, soil characteristics, the presence of upstream reservoirs, groundwater and spring contributions, and related factors. In some watersheds with multiple Settlement Area basins where major reservoir operations have a significant impact on streamflows, upstream/alternative streamgage sites were utilized to more accurately estimate primary streamflow exceedance in the watershed. These exceptions are noted.

Information on the "principal" federal, state and municipal reservoirs and lakes (i.e., defined in the *Oka Holisso* as named waterbodies with a surface area of 40 acres or more) in each basin/watershed is from the OWRB (*Lakes of Oklahoma* publication, 2012 OCWP, Oklahoma Dam Inventory and water rights data) and USACE. Additionally, named lakes of at least 20 acres in size are labeled, wherever possible, on individual surface water maps; some of these smaller bodies of water could potentially provide useful water supply to local users.

Specific purposes assigned to lakes—Water Supply (WS), Recreation (R), Hydroelectric Power (HP), Irrigation (IR), Water Quality (WQ), Fish and Wildlife (FW), Flood Control (FC), Low Flow Regulation (LF), Navigation (N), Conservation (C) and Cooling Water (CW)—are also included in accompanying tables. These are the original uses authorized by the funding entity or dam owner for the reservoir's water storage. All SCS/NRCS sites include, at a minimum, flood control. Local conservation districts are frequently the responsible authorities for these sites.

Reservoir level exceedance charts are included for the major federal and state lakes in the Settlement Area. Of particular utility from a water supply standpoint is the percentage of time that each reservoir's supply is at or near the normal pool (i.e., conservation storage) elevation. It is important to note that some reservoirs are subject to seasonal pool operation plans where the target elevation is adjusted for a period of time to accommodate a particular project objective(s), such as flood control during the rainy season or to promote the growth of beneficial fish and wildlife habitat along the shore.

Land Use

Land use data was extracted and downscaled from the National Land Cover Database (NLCD) created through the Multi-Resolution Land Characteristics (MRLC) Consortium, which consists of federal agencies who coordinate and generate consistent land cover information at the national scale for a wide variety of environmental, land management and modeling applications. In particular, this information is crucial in assessing ecosystem status and health, modeling nutrient and pesticide runoff, understanding spatial patterns of biodiversity, land use planning, deriving landscape pattern metrics, and in developing land management policies. The NLCD is derived from decadal Landsat satellite imagery and other supplementary datasets.

Specifically for the *Oka Holisso* and ease of visualization, the NLCD classification system has been sorted and consolidated into six general categories:

1. Barren Land: areas of bedrock, desert pavement, scarps, talus, slides, volcanic material, glacial debris, sand dunes, strip mines, gravel pits and other accumulations of earthen material; vegetation generally accounts for less than 15 percent of total cover.

2. Cultivated Land, Hay Pasture: areas where cultivated crops and actively tilled lands account for more than 20 percent of total vegetation; areas of grasses, legumes or grass-legume mixtures planted for livestock grazing or the production of seed or hay crops, typically on a perennial cycle.

CLASS A WATERSHEDS/BASINS

Little River: 2

Lower Canadian River: 57

Middle Washita River: 15

Mud Creek: 23

Muddy Boggy Creek: 7 & 8

Poteau River: 44 & 45

Red River: 1, 10, 13 & 21

Walnut Bayou: 22

CLASS B WATERSHEDS/BASINS

Blue River: 11 & 12

Clear Boggy Creek: 9

Kiamichi River: 5 & 6

Lower Washita River: 14

Mountain Fork River: 4

Upper Little River: 3

CLASS C WATERSHEDS/BASINS

Beaver Creek: 24, 25 & 26

Lower Arkansas River: 46 & 47

Lower Canadian River: 48 & 56

Middle Canadian River: 58

Middle Washita River: 16

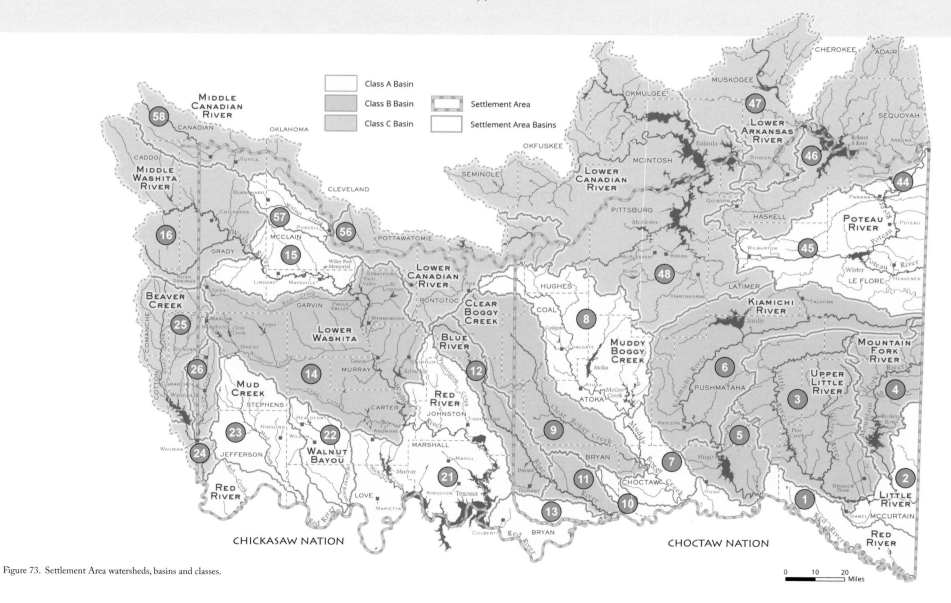

Figure 73. Settlement Area watersheds, basins and classes.

3. Developed: areas of various development intensities that include a mixture of constructed materials, but primarily vegetation in the form of lawn grasses.
4. Forest: including deciduous, evergreen and mixed.
5. Herbaceous, Shrubs, Woody Wetlands: herbaceous vegetation areas not subject to intensive management such as tilling, but can be utilized for grazing; shrubland areas dominated by shrubs less than five meters tall as well as young trees; and wetlands where the soil/substrate is periodically saturated or covered with water.
6. Water: areas of open water, generally with less than 25 percent cover of vegetation or soil.

Endangered & Threatened Species

Consistent with the environmental sustainability ethic of the Chickasaw and Choctaw Nations is the preservation of plant and animal species inhabiting treaty lands. Of special concern are officially-recognized endangered and threatened species identified through the federal Endangered Species Act (ESA), passed by Congress in 1973. Occurrences of these species, which are delineated by the U.S. Fish and Wildlife Service (USFWS), are noted throughout the basin summaries.

ESA goals are to 1) prevent the extinction of imperiled plant and animal life and 2) recover and maintain those populations by mitigating threats to their survival. The USFWS collaborates with tribes, states, private landowners, non-governmental organizations and federal partners to conserve at-risk species and their habitats.

Eleven federally endangered and six threatened species currently inhabit the thirty Settlement Area basins:

Endangered:

- Gray bat,
- Harperella (a plant belonging to the carrot family),
- Indiana bat,
- Neosho Mucket (a freshwater mussel),
- Ouachita rock pocketbook (mussel),
- Ozark big-eared bat,
- Piping Plover (a small shore bird),
- Red-cockaded woodpecker,
- Scaleshell mussel,
- Whooping crane and
- Winged Mapleleaf (mussel).

Threatened:

- American burying beetle,
- Arkansas River shiner,
- Leopard darter,
- Northern Long-Eared Bat,
- Rabbitsfoot (mussel) and
- Red knot (another migratory shore bird).

In January 2021, the USFWS announced that the least tern, a bird species that occurs throughout the Settlement Area, has fully recovered and, therefore, has been removed from the endangered species list. Although only one plant species is officially listed as occurring in the Settlement Area, many more are specified by the USFWS as "species of concern" or are under review for potentially increased protection. One additional animal species, the blackside darter, is listed as endangered by the State of Oklahoma. The darter is found in the Mountain Fork, Poteau, Kiamichi and Little River watersheds. The Nations remain committed to the protection and, where possible, recovery of imperiled species and their habitats.

Water Quality

Included in discussions of surface waters are characterizations of water quality, which is heavily influenced by the features of associated ecoregions. Information on designated beneficial uses (i.e., emergency water supply, public and private water supply, fish and wildlife propagation, agriculture, recreation, navigation and aesthetics) associated with water quality attainment and impairments, as well as the trophic status of major/principal lakes and reservoirs, is also presented.

Trophic status is essentially a measure of a lake's biological productivity, which is determined by the basin's climate and assorted lake/watershed properties (i.e., land use, soils, geology and vegetation). Generally, too much productivity can have a negative impact on overall water quality and thus limit potential attainment of assigned beneficial uses.

Trophic classifications and their characteristics include the following:

- Oligotrophic: low primary productivity and/or low nutrient levels.
- Mesotrophic: moderate primary productivity with moderate nutrient levels.
- Eutrophic: high primary productivity and nutrient-rich.
- Hypereutrophic: excessive primary productivity and excessive nutrients.

Basin summaries also attribute suspected causes of water quality impairments, which Total Maximum Daily Load (TMDL) and related studies and subsequent mitigation actions seek to remedy. These include low dissolved oxygen, turbidity, oil and grease, E. coli and Enterococci (i.e., bacteria), and total phosphorus. More specific information on state and federal water quality management is presented in the Surface Water Resources/Water Quality section.

Groundwater

Basin Summaries also present information on major and minor bedrock and alluvium/terrace aquifers underlying the confines of each basin/watershed. Aquifer boundary (i.e., the extent of outcrop areas) and related data —including each aquifer's all-important maximum annual yield (MAY, the total amount of fresh groundwater that can be withdrawn while allowing a minimum 20-year life of the basin) and equal proportionate share (EPS, the proportionate share of water allocated per acre to users) — has been provided by the OWRB. As mentioned, unstudied aquifers are assigned a default temporary EPS of 2.0 acre-feet per acre of land until a detailed hydrologic investigation is completed and the OWRB sets a final MAY and EPS. The Nations continue to advocate for a more sustainable state system to manage groundwater, as well as surface water, that sufficiently recognizes the inherent hydrologic connection between the two resources.

To assist in determinations of current water use and each basin/watershed's associated groundwater supply potential, the existing number of permitted and domestic wells is provided. This information was obtained from the OWRB's water well database, which was filtered to exclude wells used exclusively for observation/monitoring, water quality or related "non-use" purposes. Domestic wells, which typically provide relatively small amounts of water for general household and related purposes around the home, do not require a permit and are especially common in rural areas lacking access to a water provider. Where one aquifer overlaps another, usually younger overlying older formations, wells may be double-counted. More detailed analyses utilizing OWRB well logs and related information would be required to ascertain the specific groundwater source in which the well is completed. Many wells in Oklahoma draw water from less reliable, undelineated sources. Related to the Basin Summary groundwater maps, please note that significant color and shading variations may be apparent in areas where one aquifer overlies another; these relevant aquifer areas of prominent size are noted. Additional detailed information on aquifers in the Settlement Area is presented in the Groundwater Resources section.

PERMITTED WATER USE

OWRB water use permit information (initially collected in September 2019) utilized for associated maps and data tables includes the locations of streamflow diversions as well as water wells associated with various permitted users and uses. Multiple diversions or wells are often associated with a single surface or groundwater permit.

Beneficial purposes are largely self-explanatory. Some permits are assigned more than one beneficial use; in such cases, specific allowable withdrawal or diversion amounts are attributed to each. Also, it is important to note that the Recreation, Fish and Wildlife use is not directly associated with requirements to maintain or preserve instream (or environmental) flows intended to benefit plant and/or animal species and associated environmental needs. An explanation of the various types of surface and groundwater permits is presented in the Surface Water Resources section. Again, it is important to note that permitted water is primarily associated with consumptive uses and does not fully address needs associated with recreation, the environment, fish and wildlife habitat, and related resources.

The conferral threshold — i.e., the estimated minimum permit application amount that triggers the agreement's tribal-state conferral process — varies for each basin and class (A, B or C). This number is defined as either the percentage of mean available flow, which is calculated from numerous factors explained in detail in the Tribal-State Water Settlement agreement, and/or a set permit amount in acre-feet per year (AFY), whichever is smaller.

⬦ WATER SUPPLY SYSTEMS

Each summary also includes an inventory of associated public water supply systems in each basin/watershed. The most recent data from the ODEQ's Safe Drinking Water Information System (SDWIS), as well as other sources, is presented on each provider's approximate residential customers served, source(s) of supply, water sales and purchases, and essential infrastructure facilities (both active and inactive). Such facilities include intake structures to divert water from a reservoir; pump facilities to move and distribute water; water storage, such as standpipes and towers; water treatment plants, not including on-site treatment facilities, such as a chlorination station at a water well; and specific sources of groundwater, such as wells or springs. It should be pointed out that Oklahoma's water systems undergo regular changes. Therefore, obtaining the most recent data on these systems, including the Settlement Area's 196 providers, presents considerable challenges. Nevertheless, a considerable effort has been made to include the most accurate information currently available.

System boundaries, clipped to the basin's extent and often extending into adjacent watersheds, were obtained from the OWRB. Service areas are mostly unofficial and, for many municipalities, often identical to corporate limits. This information is useful to rural households desiring access to provider water service as well as to planners assessing potentially beneficial interconnections between systems as well as the sharing of infrastructure.

DATA/GIS SOURCES

Oklahoma Water Resources Board

OWRB Aquifers. https://www.owrb.ok.gov/maps/PMG/owrbdata_GW.html. November 2017.

OWRB Groundwater Wells. https://www.owrb.ok.gov/maps/PMG/owrbdata_GW.html. February 2020.

OWRB Lakes (100k). https://www.owrb.ok.gov/maps/PMG/owrbdata_SW.html. 2012.

OWRB Streams (100k). https://www.owrb.ok.gov/maps/PMG/owrbdata_SW.html. 2012.

Oklahoma Comprehensive Water Plan Basins. https://home-owrb.opendata.arcgis.com/search?tags=ocwp.2012.

Water Rights/Permitted Surface Water Diversions. https://home-owrb.opendata.arcgis.com/search?tags=rights. September 2019.

Water Rights/Permitted Groundwater Wells. https://home-owrb.opendata.arcgis.com/search?tags=rights. September 2019.

Public Water System Service Areas. https://home-owrb.opendata.arcgis.com/datasets/water-system-service-areas?geometry=-105.616%2C33.742%2C-91.048%2C36.879. 2012.

Cities. https://home-owrb.opendata.arcgis.com/datasets/cities?geometry=105.815%2C33.759%2C-91.247%2C36.895. 2020.

Oklahoma Department of Environmental Quality

Public Water Supply Systems/Safe Drinking Water Information System (SDWIS). http://sdwis.deq.state.ok.us/DWW/index.jsp. December 2019.

U.S. Geological Survey

Stream Gages. https://waterdata.usgs.gov/ok/nwis/rt. September 2017.

Elevation (Digital Elevation Models). https://www.usgs.gov/core-science-systems/ngp/tnm-delivery/gis-data-download. 2017.

Land Cover. https://www.usgs.gov/centers/eros/science/national-land-cover-database?qt-science_center_objects=0#qt-science_center_objects. 2011.

U.S. Fish and Wildlife Service

Species and Habitat/USFWS Threatened and Endangered Species Active Critical Habitat Report. https://ecos.fws.gov/ecp/report/table/critical-habitat.html. March 2021.

Oklahoma Department of Transportation

Tribal Boundaries. https://gis-okdot.opendata.arcgis.com/datasets/22acdfb12c8141ee852499cc920fe8d3_0?geometry=-104.963%2C33.742%2C92.197%2C36.879. June 2019.

University of Oklahoma Center for Spatial Analysis

Counties. https://csagis-uok.opendata.arcgis.com/. 2020.

Highways. https://csagis-uok.opendata.arcgis.com/. 2020.

State Boundary. https://csagis-uok.opendata.arcgis.com/. 2020.

Municipal Boundaries. https://csagis-uok.opendata.arcgis.com/. 2020.

Custom (Various Sources)

Sughru, Michael P., Brian R. Vance. Significant Historical and Cultural Resource Sites and Areas. December 2020.

Sughru, Michael P., Brian R. Vance. Tribal Water Planning Project Locations. January 2019.

Little River

BASIN 2

Basin 2 — The Little River at Little River Wildlife Refuge

Active Streamgage

Inactive Streamgage

Little River below
Lukfata Creek,
near Idabel

MCCURTAIN

0   5   10
Miles

Water Quality

The Little River watershed encompasses 352 square miles in far southeastern Oklahoma. The river enters Basin 2 from adjacent Basin 3, then extends eastward some twenty-five river miles across the southern extent of the watershed in McCurtain County. Along its path, the Little River encounters major portions of three federal conservation areas: the Little River National Wildlife Refuge (NWR), Ouachita Wildlife Management Area (WMA) and Ouachita National Forest. The lower Mountain Fork River, the Little River's primary tributary, enters from Basin 4 in the north and flows about seven miles prior to its confluence. The Little River then leaves Oklahoma and enters the state of Arkansas. The average annual flow of the Little River, estimated at the bottom of Basin 2, is 3,617 cubic feet per second (cfs); this flow is available about 27 percent of the time.

Basin 2 includes no major lakes, although several oxbow lakes—mostly transient bodies of water formed by abandoned stream channels—exist along the Little River's current path.

Endangered species present in the Little River watershed include the harperella, Ouachita rock pocketbook, piping plover, red-cockaded woodpecker, scaleshell mussel and winged mapleleaf. Threatened species listed by the ESA include the American burying beetle, leopard darter, northern long-eared bat, rabbitsfoot and red knot.

Basin 2 features the Ouachita Mountains and the South Central Plains ecoregions where the Little River meanders slowly with a low gradient and substrates of mud and organic matter. Salinity is extremely low in the watershed and streams are mesotrophic with low nutrient concentrations and excellent clarity. The Little River maintains exceptional habitat that supports a number of unique aquatic species. From Pine Creek Dam, in adjacent Basin 3, the river in Oklahoma is designated as High Quality Waters. A portion of the river is impaired for Fish and Wildlife Propagation due to low dissolved oxygen concentrations. In Rock Creek, in the upper portion of Basin 2, Primary Body Contact Recreation (PBCR) and fish and wildlife propagation are impaired due to elevated bacteria. In the lower watershed, fish consumption is not supported in Mud Creek due to elevated concentrations of lead.

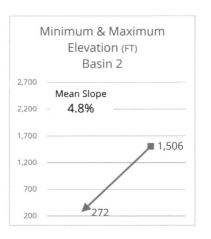

Minimum & Maximum Elevation (FT)
Basin 2

Mean Slope
4.8%

1,506

272

PRINCIPAL RIVERS & STREAMS BASIN 2	
River/Stream	**Length** MILES
Little River	27
Rock Creek	19
Mud Creek	18
Luksuklo Creek	15
Crooked Creek	13

PRINCIPAL LAKES BASIN 2
No named lakes with a surface area of 40 acres or more

LAND COVER & USES
LITTLE RIVER WATERSHED

Use	Area SQ. MI.
Forest	197
Herbaceous, Shrubs, Woody Wetlands	80
Cultivated Land, Hay/Pasture	59
Developed	15
Water	2
Barren Land	0
Total Land Area	**353**

Land Cover & Uses
Little River Watershed (A)

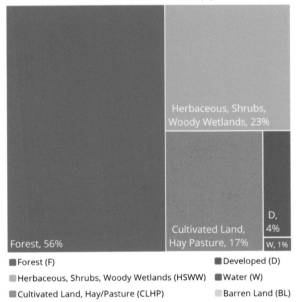

- ■ Forest (F)
- ■ Herbaceous, Shrubs, Woody Wetlands (HSWW)
- ■ Cultivated Land, Hay/Pasture (CLHP)
- ■ Developed (D)
- ■ Water (W)
- ■ Barren Land (BL)

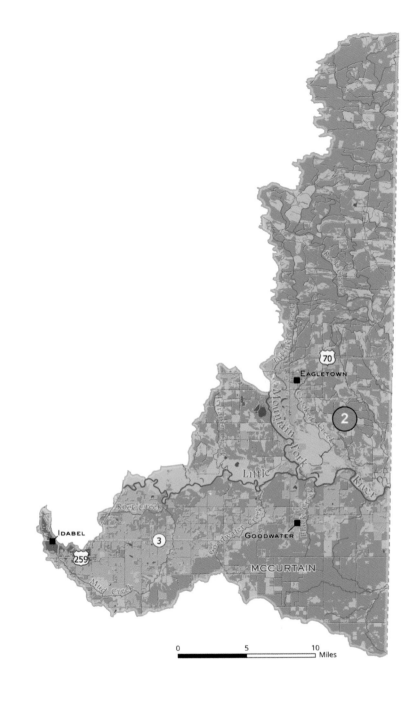

Groundwater

Much of the Little River watershed—some 225 square miles in the south—is underlain by the Antlers aquifer, a major groundwater basin that extends along the Red River across the entire extent of the Settlement Area. In Basin 2, the Antlers is the source for water wells utilized for a few permits and domestic uses. Several minor aquifers, such as the Woodbine, which overlies the older Antlers further to the south, exist in the watershed. Some 36 wells are drilled over the Antlers formation and 15 wells over the Woodbine. However, detailed well log records are required to determine depths of completion, and thus which Woodbine wells access the deeper Antlers groundwater basin. A second major aquifer, the Red River Alluvium, underlies a small area of Basin 2.

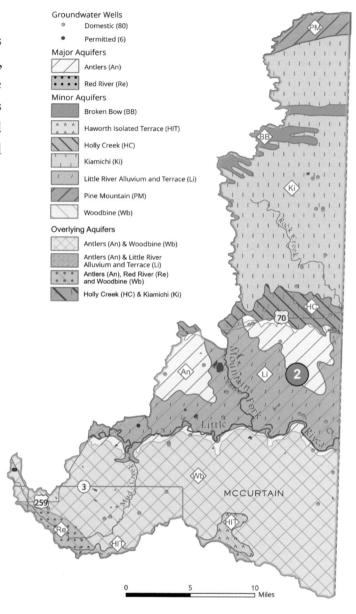

Groundwater Wells
- Domestic (80)
- Permitted (6)

Major Aquifers
- Antlers (An)
- Red River (Re)

Minor Aquifers
- Broken Bow (BB)
- Haworth Isolated Terrace (HIT)
- Holly Creek (HC)
- Kiamichi (Ki)
- Little River Alluvium and Terrace (Li)
- Pine Mountain (PM)
- Woodbine (Wb)

Overlying Aquifers
- Antlers (An) & Woodbine (Wb)
- Antlers (An) & Little River Alluvium and Terrace (Li)
- Antlers (An), Red River (Re) and Woodbine (Wb)
- Holly Creek (HC) & Kiamichi (Ki)

MAJOR & MINOR AQUIFERS- BASIN 2			
Aquifer	Area in Basin/Watershed SQUARE MILES	EPS[1] AC-FT/ACRE	Number of Permitted & Domestic Wells in Basin/Watershed[2]
Antlers	225	2.1	36
Broken Bow	9	2.0	1
Haworth	6	1.0	0
Holly Creek	14	2.0	4
Kiamichi	110	2.0	14
Little River	62	1.0	16
Pine Mountain	7	2.0	0
Red River	7	2.0	0
Woodbine	135	2.0	15
Nondelineated Source Wells			0
Total Wells			86

[1]Italic number signifies unstudied aquifers with a default temporary equal proportionate share (EPS) of 2.0 acre-feet per acre of land.
[2]Some wells are double-counted where one aquifer overlies another.

NOTE: Significant color and shading variations may be apparent in areas where one aquifer overlies another. In some cases, for state administrative purposes, aquifer boundaries align directly with county lines or related political borders rather than geologic outcrop areas.

Relative to other basins in the Settlement Area, permitted water use—especially from groundwater sources (only 4 percent)—is minimal in the Little River watershed. According to OWRB data, there are only five currently active water use permits basin-wide.

Water appropriated for public supply purposes accounts for 90 percent of all permitted water in Basin 2. Irrigation accounts for six percent. Industrial use is also minimal at three percent.

Virtually all of the permitted water in Basin 2 has been granted to McCurtain County Rural Water District (RWD) #1 via a surface water right appropriating 2,000 AFY for public supply. The next largest permit, appropriating 75 AFY also from surface water, belongs to the Idabel Public Works Authority and is used for irrigation. The sole industrial permit (63 AFY) belongs to KCS Lumber Company.

Any application to appropriate water for use at a location outside of Basin 2 could be subject to conferral, depending upon the application amount, mean available flow and other relevant factors. See conditions associated with Class A Basins in the Tribal-State Water Settlement agreement in the *Oka Holisso* appendix.

PERMITTED WATER AFY		
BASIN 2		
Groundwater	Surface Water	Total
93	2,125	**2,218**

Permitted Surface Water (AFY) Little River, Basin 2

PWS 2,000 94%

IR 125 6%

Permitted Groundwater (AFY) Little River, Basin 2

IN 63 68%

RFW 30 32%

Permitted Water Sources & Uses

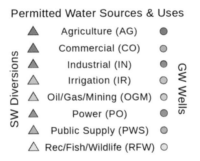

SW Diversions

- △ Agriculture (AG) ●
- △ Commercial (CO) ○
- △ Industrial (IN) ●
- △ Irrigation (IR) ○
- △ Oil/Gas/Mining (OGM) ○
- △ Power (PO) ●
- △ Public Supply (PWS) ○
- △ Rec/Fish/Wildlife (RFW) ○

GW Wells

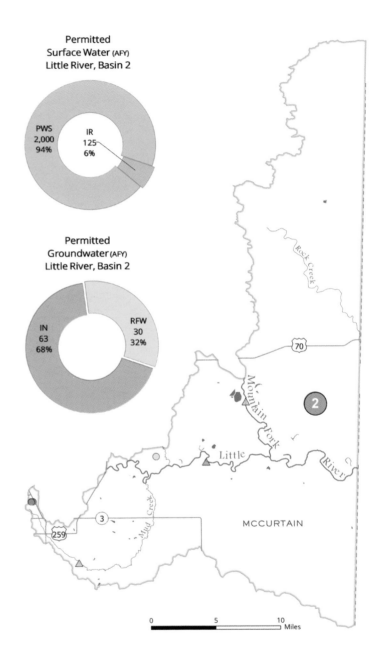

In terms of residential customers served, the Idabel Public Works Authority (PWA) operates the largest water supply system in Basin 2 with almost 7,000 users. The system receives water from a diversion on the Little River with an emergency backup provided by Broken Bow PWA. Broken Bow, with 4,320 customers of its own, treats and distributes water from Broken Bow Lake to a dozen water systems both within and outside of the Little River watershed. The lake is the sole source of water for McCurtain Co. RWDs #1 and 7 and supplements the needs of McCurtain Co. RWD #8, which utilizes the Mountain Fork River as its primary source of supply for 5,685 residential customers. There are no system facilities located within Basin 2.

PUBLIC WATER SUPPLY SYSTEMS BASIN 2									
System	Residential Customers Served[1]	Source(s) of Supply[2]	Water Sales	Water Purchases	Facilities[3]				
					Intake	Pump Facility	Storage	Treatment Plant	Well or Spring
Broken Bow PWA	4,320	SW	Garvin, Haworth PWA, Idabel PWA, McCurtain Co. #1, McCurtain Co. #2, McCurtain Co. #5, McCurtain Co. #6, McCurtain Co. #7, McCurtain Co. #8, McCurtain Co. #9, Valliant PWA, Wright City PWA	—					
Idabel PWA	6,952	SW	—	Broken Bow PWA					
McCurtain Co. RWD #1	3,842	P (SW)	Haworth PWA	Broken Bow PWA					
McCurtain Co. RWD #7	1,847	P (SW)	Garvin	Broken Bow PWA					
McCurtain Co. RWD #8 (Mt. Fork Water)	5,685	SW	—	Broken Bow PWA					

[1]Does not include wholesale customers served through water sales.

[2]GW = Groundwater; SW = Surface Water; P = Purchased.

[3]Includes both active and inactive (mostly wells) facilities in the watershed. Treatment plants include only those utilizing conventional water treatment and do not include chlorination stations associated with discrete source treatment.

Data: Oklahoma Department of Environmental Quality, Safe Drinking Water Information System, OWRB GIS and Arbuckle-Simpson Aquifer Drought Contingency Plan. Listed system facilities include those with service areas and/or facilities within relevant watershed.

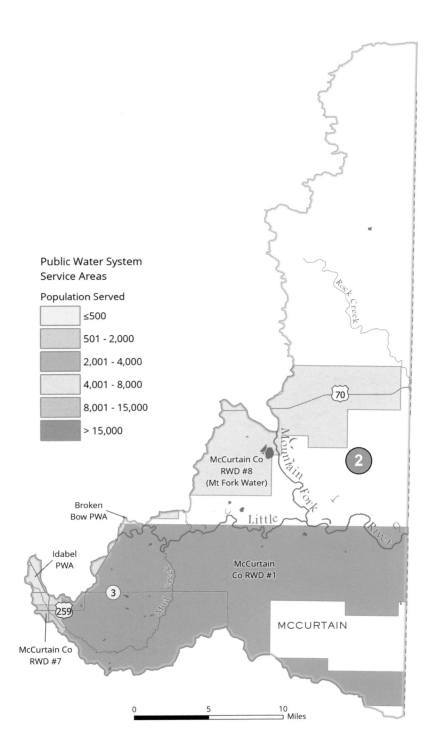

Public Water System Service Areas

Population Served

- ≤500
- 501 - 2,000
- 2,001 - 4,000
- 4,001 - 8,000
- 8,001 - 15,000
- > 15,000

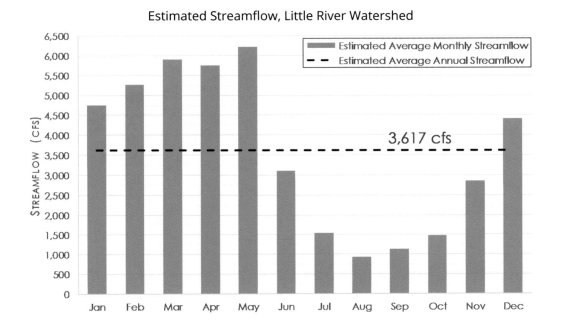

Estimated Streamflow, Little River Watershed

Legend:
- Estimated Average Monthly Streamflow
- Estimated Average Annual Streamflow

3,617 cfs

Streamflow Exceedance Probability, Little River Watershed

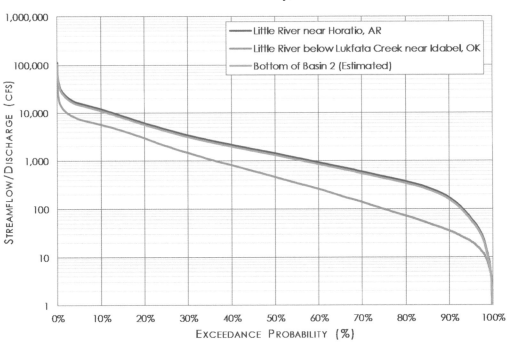

Legend:
- Little River near Horatio, AR
- Little River below Lukfata Creek near Idabel, OK
- Bottom of Basin 2 (Estimated)

Lower Canadian River

BASIN 57

Basin 57 — Purcell City Lake

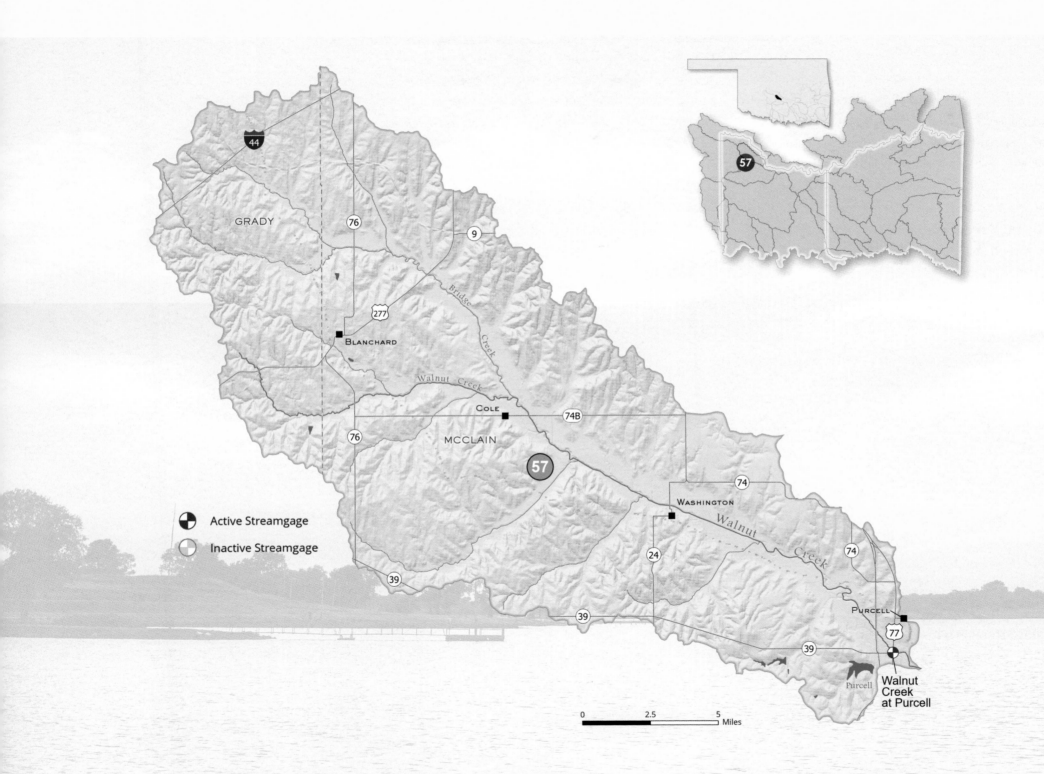

Active Streamgage

Inactive Streamgage

GRADY

44

76

9

Bridge

Creek

277

Blanchard

Walnut Creek

Cole

74B

MCCLAIN

57

76

74

Washington

Walnut

24

74

Creek

39

Purcell

39

77

39

Purcell

Walnut
Creek
at Purcell

57

0   2.5   5
                        Miles

Basin 57, which covers 203 square miles, consists of Walnut Creek, a major tributary of the Canadian River, as well as Bridge Creek, which feeds into Walnut Creek north of Cole, Oklahoma. The watershed includes only a few other minor tributaries. From the confluence of the two primary streams, Walnut Creek flows in a decidedly southeastern direction prior to leaving the basin south of Purcell. The creek immediately joins the Canadian River in Basin 56. The average annual flow of the Lower Canadian River (Walnut Creek) watershed, estimated at the bottom of Basin 57, is 82 cfs; this flow is available less than 16 percent of the time. Purcell Lake is the only reservoir of note in Basin 57.

Endangered species in Basin 57 are the piping plover and whooping crane; threatened species include the Arkansas River shiner and red knot.

Walnut Creek flows across the Central Great Plains and Cross Timbers ecoregions where streams are usually contained in shallow, sandy channels that are typically moderately to heavily incised. Average conductivity of Walnut Creek is high. Primary Body Contact Recreation is not supported due to elevated bacteria. TMDLs for bacteria have been completed in the North Fork tributary. Purcell Lake is eutrophic with good water clarity and fully supports all designated beneficial uses. It is no longer used as a source of potable water.

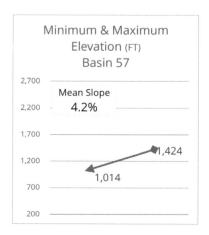

PRINCIPAL RIVERS & STREAMS BASIN 57	
River/Stream	Length MILES
Walnut Creek	28
Bridge Creek	15

PRINCIPAL LAKES BASIN 57									
Name	Stream	Authority	Normal Elevation FEET	Normal Area ACRES	Normal Capacity AC-FT	Shoreline MILES	Purpose(s)[1]	Water Supply Storage AC-FT	Water Supply Yield AC-FT/YR
Purcell	Walnut Creek Tributary (TR)	City of Purcell	1,068	144	2,600	3.1	WS, R	—	—

[1]*WS=Water Supply, R=Recreation, HP=Hydroelectric Power, IR=Irrigation, WQ=Water Quality, FW=Fish & Wildlife, FC=Flood Control, LF=Low Flow Regulation, N=Navigation, C=Conservation, CW=Cooling Water*

LAND COVER & USES
LOWER CANADIAN RIVER WATERSHED

Use	Area SQ. MI.
Forest	37
Herbaceous, Shrubs, Woody Wetlands	121
Cultivated Land, Hay/Pasture	28
Developed	16
Water	1
Barren Land	0
Total Land Area	**203**

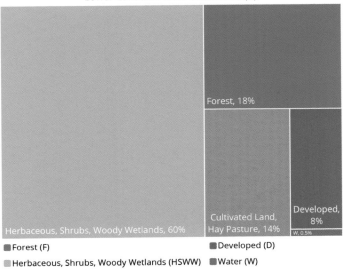

Land Cover & Uses
Lower Canadian River Watershed (A)

Forest, 18%

Cultivated Land, Hay Pasture, 14%

Developed, 8%

Herbaceous, Shrubs, Woody Wetlands, 60%

W, 0.5%

- Forest (F)
- Herbaceous, Shrubs, Woody Wetlands (HSWW)
- Cultivated Land, Hay/Pasture (CLHP)
- Developed (D)
- Water (W)
- Barren Land (BL)

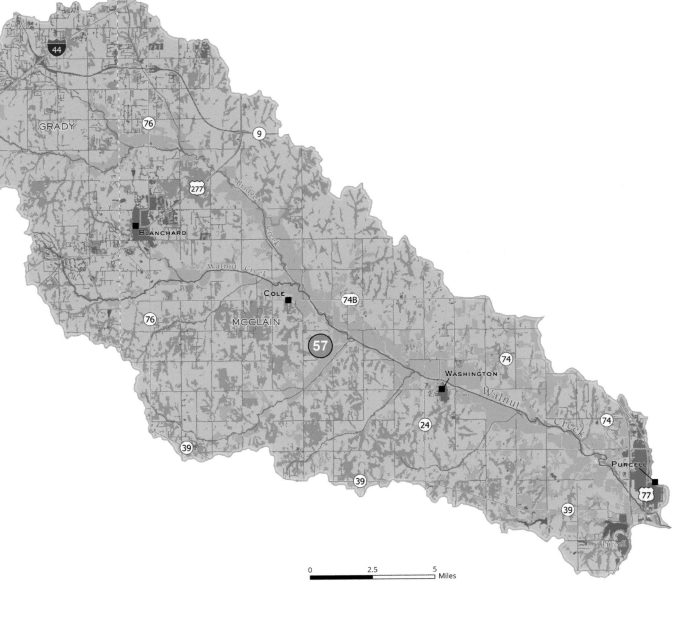

Groundwater

The Lower Canadian River watershed features one major groundwater basin, the Canadian River aquifer, which includes 192 permitted and domestic supply wells. The El Reno minor aquifer is heavily utilized with almost 1,400 identified wells. Both aquifers are currently assigned the default EPS of 2.0 acre-feet per acre.

MAJOR & MINOR AQUIFERS BASIN 57			
Aquifer	**Area in Basin/ Watershed** SQUARE MILES	**EPS[1]** AC-FT/ACRE	**Number of Permitted & Domestic Wells in Basin/ Watershed[2]**
Canadian River	71	2.0	192
El Reno	156	2.0	1,386
Nondelineated Source Wells			5
Total Wells			**1,583**

[1]*Italic number signifies unstudied aquifers with a default temporary equal proportionate share (EPS) of 2.0 acre-feet per acre of land.*

[2]*Some wells are double-counted where one aquifer overlies another.*

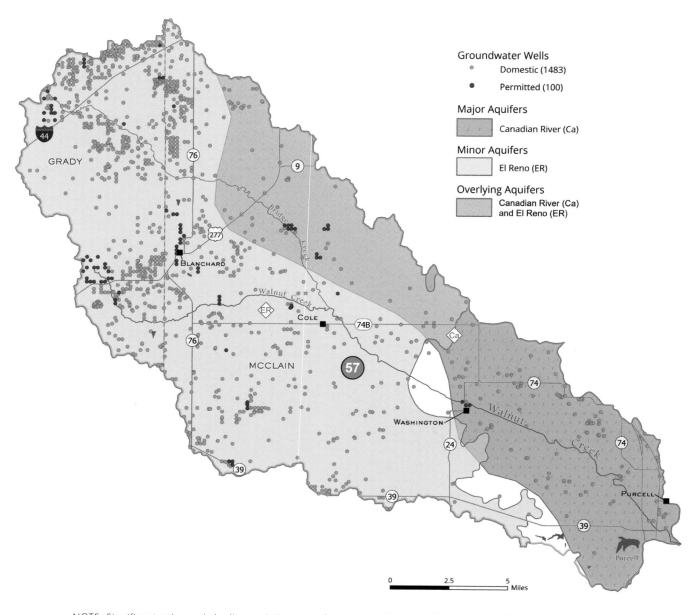

Groundwater Wells
- Domestic (1483)
- Permitted (100)

Major Aquifers
- Canadian River (Ca)

Minor Aquifers
- El Reno (ER)

Overlying Aquifers
- Canadian River (Ca) and El Reno (ER)

NOTE: Significant color and shading variations may be apparent in areas where one aquifer overlies another. In some cases, for state administrative purposes, aquifer boundaries align directly with county lines or related political borders rather than geologic outcrop areas.

The ratio of total permitted water sources in the Lower Canadian River watershed is 72 to 28 percent in favor of surface water. Total permits amount to 14,181 AFY.

At 53 percent, water permitted for oil, gas and mining purposes far exceeds all other uses, followed by irrigation (24 percent). Public water supply makes up only 17 percent of uses. Industrial uses are also minimal in Basin 57. (A number of large mining permits have been also been approved since water rights data was initially collected in 2019.)

With two surface water permits amounting to 6,187 AFY for oil, gas and mining, Bluefin Water Solutions is the largest permitted user in the watershed. Both are term permits in McClain County. The City of Blanchard (groundwater, public supply) and Purcell PWA (surface water, irrigation and fish and wildlife) possess water rights amounting to 1,650 and 1,607 AFY, respectively.

Any application to appropriate water for use at a location outside of Basin 57 could be subject to conferral, depending upon the application amount, mean available flow and other relevant factors. See conditions associated with Class A Basins in the Tribal-State Water Settlement agreement in the *Oka Holisso* appendix.

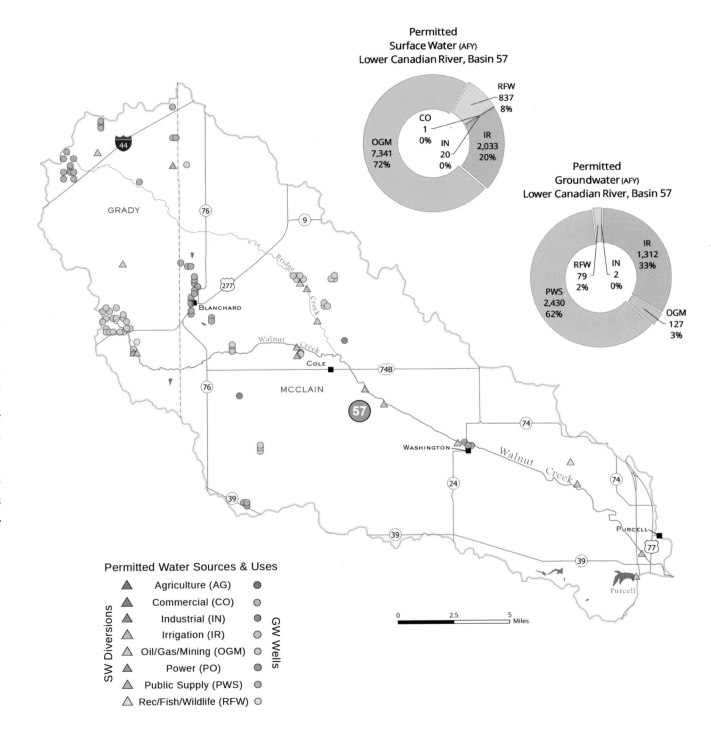

Permitted
Surface Water (AFY)
Lower Canadian River, Basin 57

RFW 837 8%
CO 1 0%
IN 20 0%
OGM 7,341 72%
IR 2,033 20%

Permitted
Groundwater (AFY)
Lower Canadian River, Basin 57

IR 1,312 33%
RFW 79 2%
IN 2 0%
PWS 2,430 62%
OGM 127 3%

Permitted Water Sources & Uses

SW Diversions / GW Wells

▲ ●	Agriculture (AG)
▲ ◔	Commercial (CO)
▲ ◕	Industrial (IN)
△ ◑	Irrigation (IR)
△ ◔	Oil/Gas/Mining (OGM)
▲ ●	Power (PO)
△ ◔	Public Supply (PWS)
△ ○	Rec/Fish/Wildlife (RFW)

PERMITTED WATER		
AFY		
BASIN 57		
Groundwater	Surface Water	Total
3,949	10,232	**14,181**

Purcell, with an estimated 8,118 customers, is the primary water supplier in the Lower Canadian watershed. The system is entirely reliant upon groundwater sources from the Garber-Wellington aquifer. While Newcastle also serves some area residents, most of its users reside in the adjacent Middle Canadian River watershed. This is also true of Goldsby Water Authority Trust. Blanchard, which sells surface water acquired from Newcastle and Tuttle to three communities in the region, is the only other large water supplier in the basin. More recent information, in addition to that provided by ODEQ, indicates that Blanchard also purchases water from the cities of Oklahoma City and Edmond.

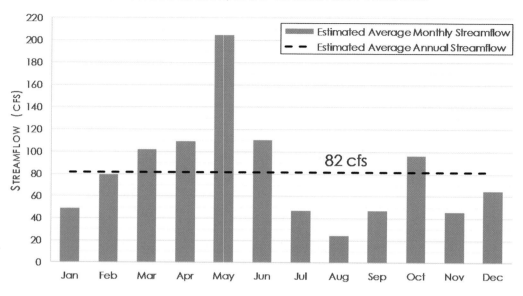

Estimated Streamflow, Lower Canadian River Watershed

	PUBLIC WATER SUPPLY SYSTEMS BASIN 57									
						Facilities[3]				
System	Residential Customers Served[1]	Source(s) of Supply[2]	Water Sales	Water Purchases	Intake	Pump Facility	Storage	Treatment Plant	Well or Spring
Blanchard	2,966	P (SW)	Cole, Dibble, Tuttle	Newcastle, Tuttle, Okla. City, Edmond					
Cole	473	P (SW)	—	Blanchard					
Dibble	550	P (SW)	—	Blanchard					
Goldsby WA Trust	2,000	GW	—	Newcastle					4
Newcastle	7,900	GW	Blanchard, Goldsby WA Trust, Tuttle	—					
Purcell	8,118	GW	—	—					
Washington	600	GW	—	—					4

[1]Does not include wholesale customers served through water sales.

[2]GW = Groundwater; SW = Surface Water; P = Purchased.

[3]Includes both active and inactive (mostly wells) facilities in the watershed. Treatment plants include only those utilizing conventional water treatment and do not include chlorination stations associated with discrete source treatment.

Data: Oklahoma Department of Environmental Quality, Safe Drinking Water Information System, OWRB GIS and Arbuckle-Simpson Aquifer Drought Contingency Plan. Listed system facilities include those with service areas and/or facilities within relevant watershed.

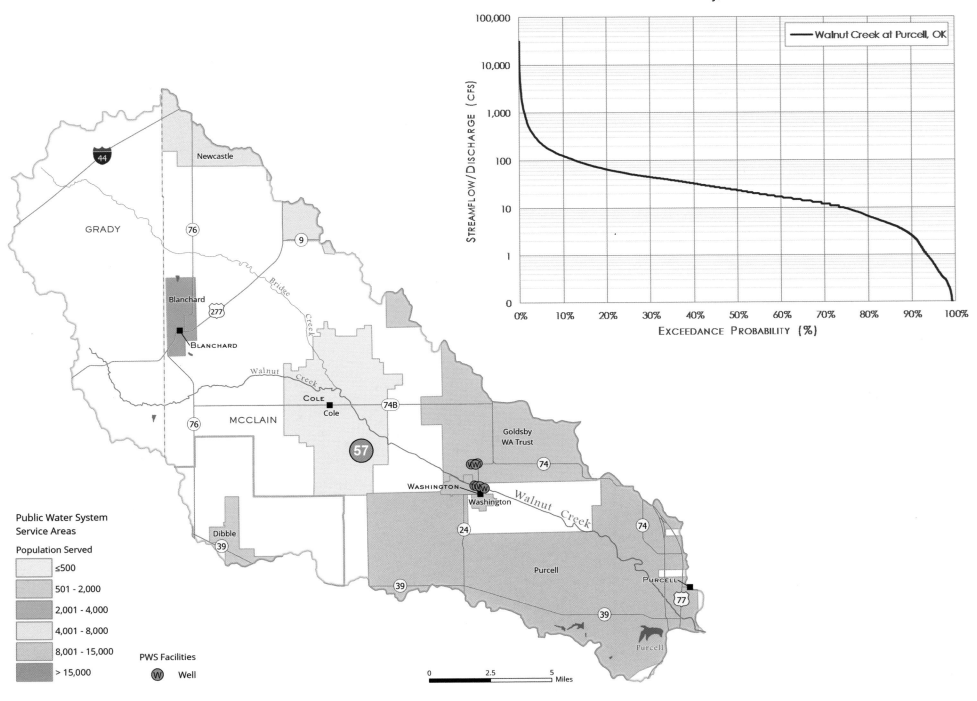

Streamflow Exceedance Probability, Lower Canadian River Watershed

Public Water System Service Areas

Population Served

- ≤500
- 501 - 2,000
- 2,001 - 4,000
- 4,001 - 8,000
- 8,001 - 15,000
- > 15,000

PWS Facilities

W Well

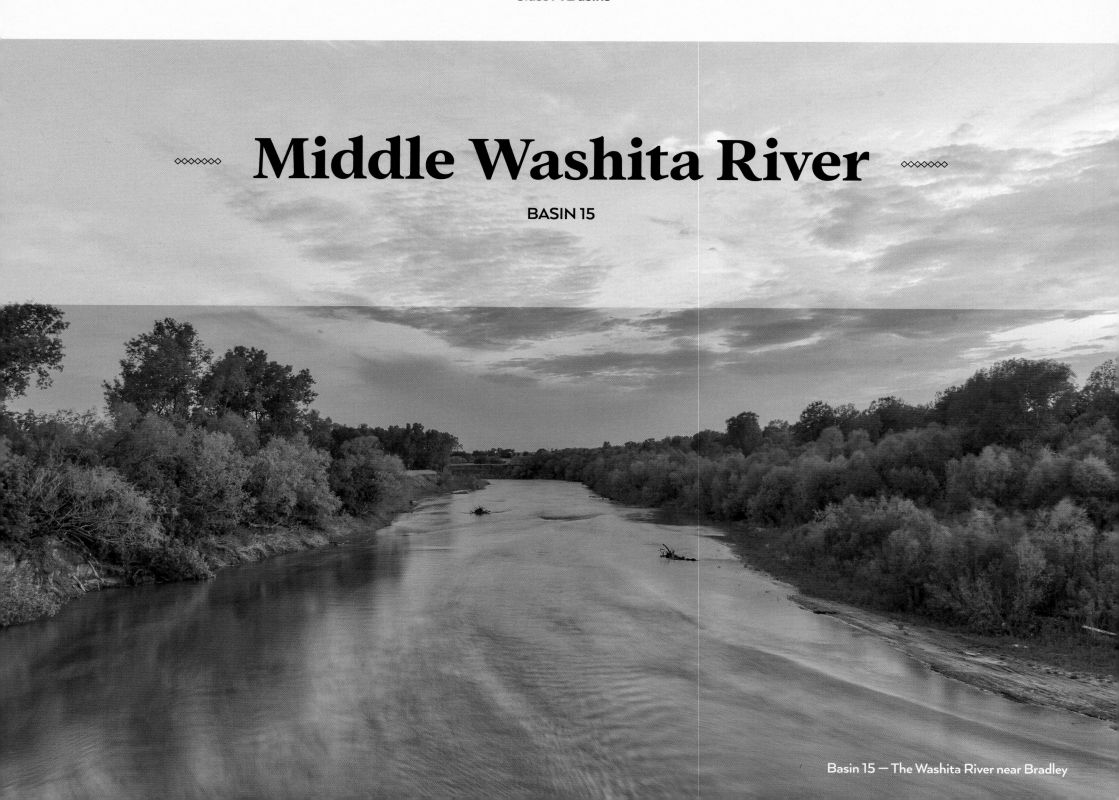

Middle Washita River

BASIN 15

Basin 15 — The Washita River near Bradley

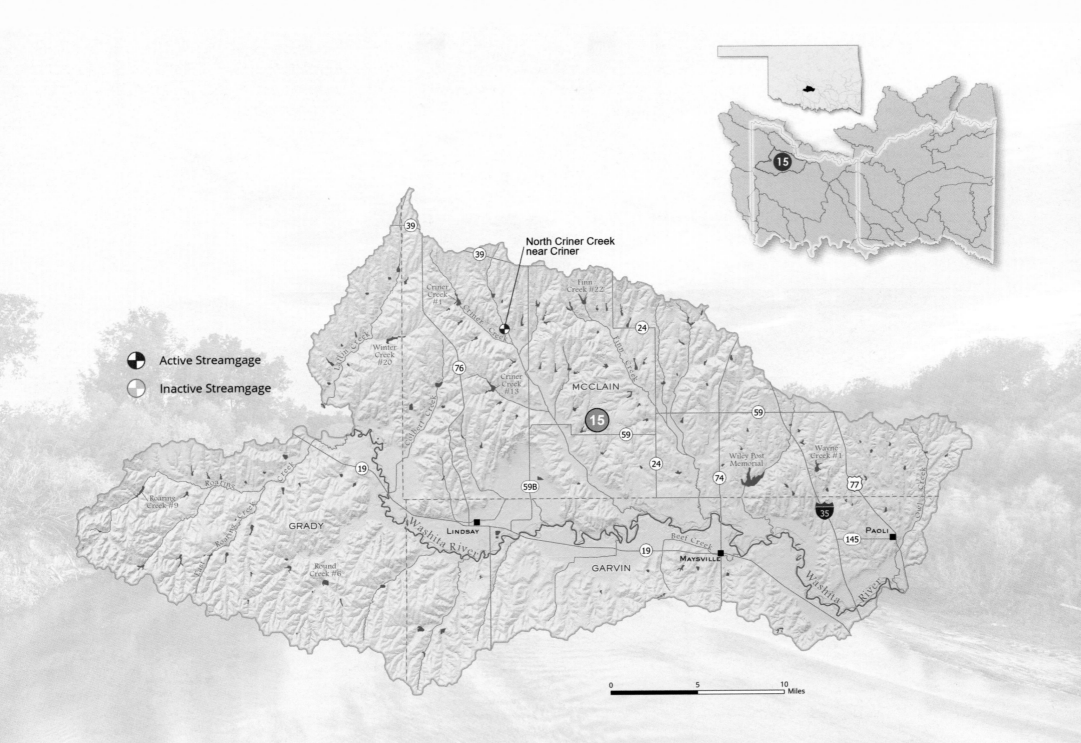

North Criner Creek
near Criner

Active Streamgage

Inactive Streamgage

39

39

Criner
Creek
#1

Finn
Creek #22

24

Winter
Creek
#20

76

Criner
Creek
#13

MCCLAIN

59

15

59

LaFlin Creek

Colbert Creek

24

74

Wiley Post
Memorial

Wayne
Creek #1

77

19

35

Roaring Creek

Roaring
Creek #9

Roaring Creek

GRADY

Washita River

LINDSAY

59B

19

Beet Creek

145

PAOLI

Flint Creek

Round
Creek #6

GARVIN

MAYSVILLE

Washita River

Owl Creek

0   5   10
                         Miles

In Basin 15, which covers 524 square miles, the Washita River enters from Basin 16 in the west then meanders through Grady and Garvin Counties in a southerly, then easterly, direction before exiting the watershed in the northern portion of Basin 14. The average annual flow of the Washita River, estimated at the bottom of Basin 15, is 880 cfs; this flow is available about 23 percent of the time.

Wiley Post Memorial Lake, the watershed's largest lake, was built by the Town of Maysville several miles north of the municipality to serve as its water supply. Hundreds of smaller lakes, including several Soil Conservation Service (SCS) sites of note, exist throughout Basin 15.

The whooping crane and piping plover are endangered species that occur within Basin 15. The Arkansas River shiner and red knot are listed as threatened.

Water Quality

The Middle Washita River watershed lies within the Central Great Plains and Cross Timbers ecoregions where streams are typically incised with rocky or muddy substrates. Stream salinity is moderate in Basin 15. The Washita River is classified as hypereutrophic. In the west, TMDLs have been completed for bacteria on Roaring and Laflin Creeks. Other TMDLs for bacteria

have been completed on Finn Creek and the Washita River. Lake clarity is poor in Wiley Post Memorial Lake where Primary Body Contact Recreation is impaired due to elevated levels of bacteria.

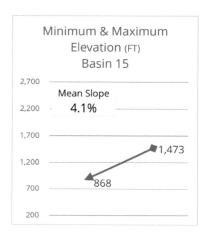

PRINCIPAL RIVERS & STREAMS BASIN 15	
River/Stream	**Length** MILES
Washita River	58
Criner Creek	18
Roaring Creek	18
Finn Creek	14
Laflin Creek	13

PRINCIPAL LAKES BASIN 15									
Name	**Stream**	**Authority**	**Normal Elevation** FEET	**Normal Area** ACRES	**Normal Capacity** AC-FT	**Shoreline** MILES	**Purpose(s)[1]**	**Water Supply Storage** AC-FT	**Water Supply Yield** AC-FT/YR
Criner Creek #1	Criner Creek	SCS/McClain Co. Conservation District	—	52	321	2.1	FC	—	—
Criner Creek #13	Criner Creek TR	SCS/McClain Co. CD	—	61	258	2.5	FC	—	—
Finn Creek #22	Finn Creek TR	SCS/McClain Co. CD	—	43	114	1.8	FC	—	—
Roaring Creek #9	Roaring Creek	SCS/Grady Co. CD	—	48	227	2.5	FC	—	—
Round Creek #6	Washita River TR	SCS/Grady Co. CD	—	42	245	1.2	FC	—	—
Wayne Creek #1	Washita River TR	SCS/McClain Co. CD	—	51	279	2.2	FC	—	—
Winter Creek #20	Laflin Creek TR	SCS/Grady Co. CD	—	61	169	2.5	FC	—	—
Wiley Post Memorial	Washita River TR	City of Maysville	965	239	2,082	4.7	WS, FC, R	0	538

[1]*WS=Water Supply, R=Recreation, HP=Hydroelectric Power, IR=Irrigation, WQ=Water Quality, FW=Fish & Wildlife, FC=Flood Control, LF=Low Flow Regulation, N=Navigation, C=Conservation, CW=Cooling Water*

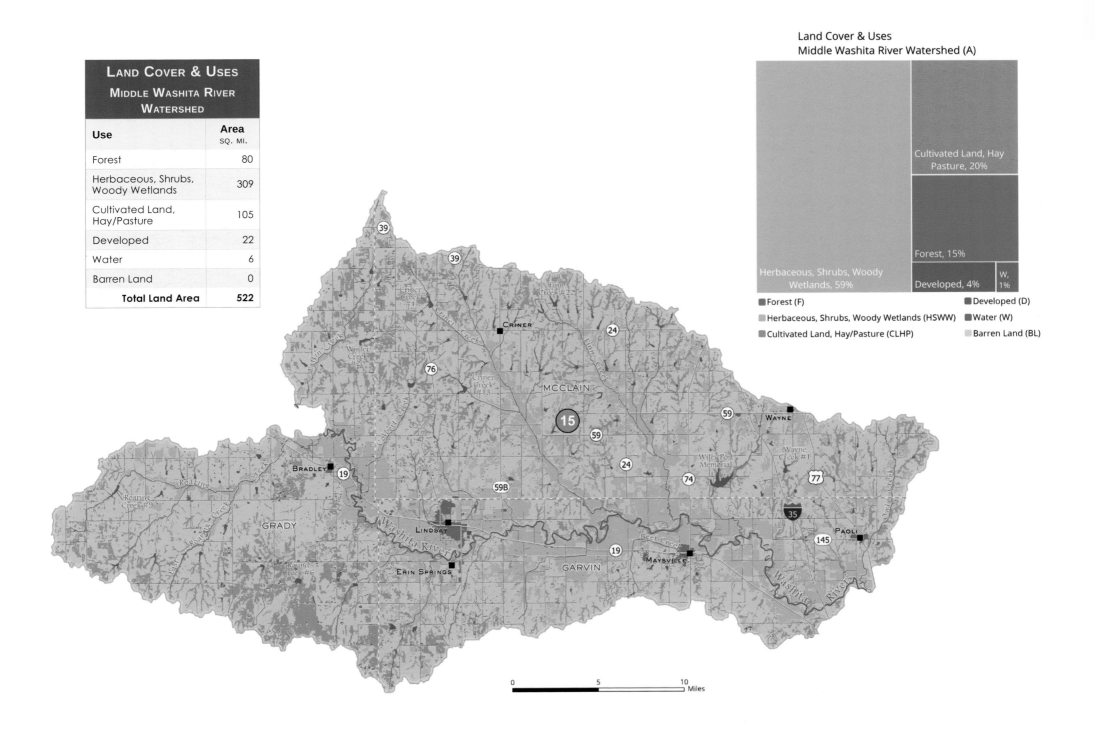

LAND COVER & USES
MIDDLE WASHITA RIVER WATERSHED

Use	Area SQ. MI.
Forest	80
Herbaceous, Shrubs, Woody Wetlands	309
Cultivated Land, Hay/Pasture	105
Developed	22
Water	6
Barren Land	0
Total Land Area	**522**

Land Cover & Uses
Middle Washita River Watershed (A)

Cultivated Land, Hay Pasture, 20%

Forest, 15%

Herbaceous, Shrubs, Woody Wetlands, 59%

Developed, 4%

W, 1%

- Forest (F)
- Herbaceous, Shrubs, Woody Wetlands (HSWW)
- Cultivated Land, Hay/Pasture (CLHP)
- Developed (D)
- Water (W)
- Barren Land (BL)

Three major aquifers underlie portions of Basin 15: the Canadian River, Rush Springs and Washita River. Of these, the Washita occupies the largest area in the subsurface: 145 square miles. The Rush Springs aquifer EPS is expected to be lowered as a result of a hydrologic investigation completed in 2018.

As in adjacent Basin 57 (Lower Canadian), the El Reno minor aquifer is a popular source of groundwater supply with 412 wells accessed over a 225-square-mile area.

MAJOR & MINOR AQUIFERS BASIN 15			
Aquifer	Area in Basin/ Watershed SQUARE MILES	EPS[1] AC-FT/ACRE	Number of Permitted & Domestic Wells in Basin/ Watershed[2]
Canadian River	16	2.0	5
El Reno	225	2.0	412
Rush Springs	10	2.0	22
Washita River	145	1.5 (Reach 3) 1 (Reach 4)	174
Nondelineated Source Wells			102
Total Wells			715

[1]Italic number signifies unstudied aquifers with a default temporary equal proportionate share (EPS) of 2.0 acre-feet per acre of land.
[2]Some wells are double-counted where one aquifer overlies another.

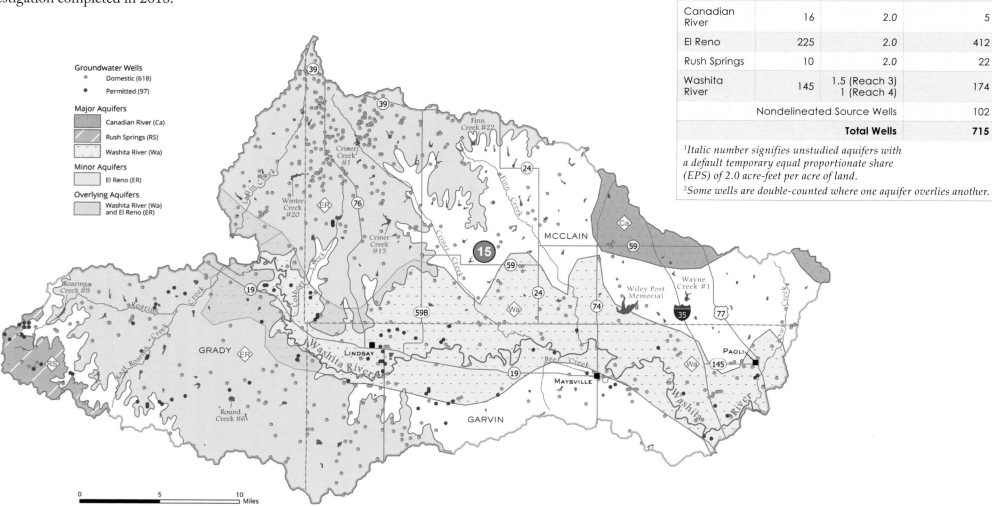

NOTE: Significant color and shading variations may be apparent in areas where one aquifer overlies another. In some cases, for state administrative purposes, aquifer boundaries align directly with county lines or related political borders rather than geologic outcrop areas.

Groundwater accounts for 60 percent of permitted water sources in the Middle Washita River watershed, making this one of the few watersheds/basins in the Settlement Area where groundwater allocations exceed surface water appropriations. Irrigation, at 42 percent, is the predominant use of permitted water in Basin 15, followed by oil, gas and mining (31 percent) and public water supply (24 percent).

Reflecting robust oil and gas production in the region, Continental Resources is the largest water rights holder via a single surface water appropriation for 1,624 AFY. Two other relatively large term permits (for 1,400 and 1,056 AFY, respectively) are held by Select Energy Services and Crescent Services LLC, both from surface sources. Basin 15 also includes several significant

irrigation permits from both surface and groundwater sources. The largest public supply rights holder is the City of Lindsay (including Lindsay PWA), which is allocated 2,168 AFY (including two prior rights), mostly from groundwater sources.

Any application to appropriate water for use at a location outside of Basin 15 could be subject to conferral, depending upon the application amount, mean available flow and other relevant factors. See conditions associated with Class A Basins in the Tribal-State Water Settlement agreement in the *Oka Holisso* appendix.

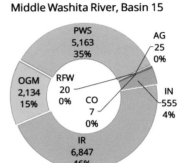

Permitted Groundwater (AFY)
Middle Washita River, Basin 15

PWS 5,163 35%
AG 25 0%
OGM 2,134 15%
RFW 20 0%
CO 7 0%
IN 555 4%
IR 6,847 46%

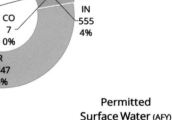

Permitted Surface Water (AFY)
Middle Washita River, Basin 15

OGM 5,529 56%
PWS 731 8%
RFW 191 2%
IR 3,362 34%

PERMITTED WATER		
AFY		
BASIN 15		
Groundwater	Surface Water	Total
14,750	9,813	24,563

Permitted Water Sources & Uses

SW Diversions			GW Wells
▲	Agriculture (AG)	●	
▲	Commercial (CO)	○	
▲	Industrial (IN)	●	
▲	Irrigation (IR)	◐	
△	Oil/Gas/Mining (OGM)	○	
▲	Power (PO)	●	
▲	Public Supply (PWS)	○	
△	Rec/Fish/Wildlife (RFW)	○	

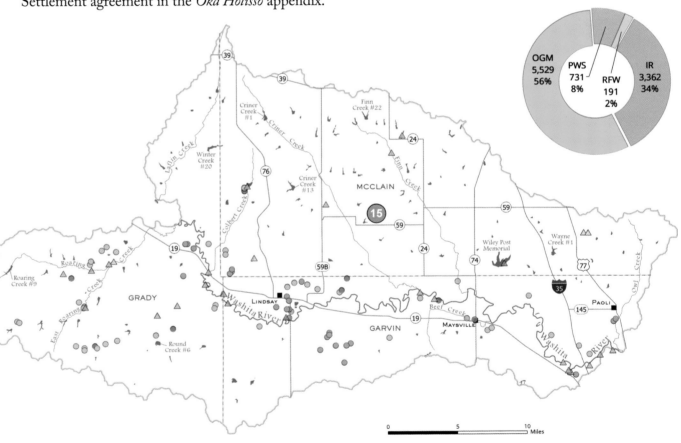

Two large water providers—Purcell in the north and Grady County RWD #7 in the west—serve the general region, but only a portion of the Middle Washita watershed. Lindsay PWA, with 2,850 customers, is the principal water system located entirely within the boundaries of Basin 15. The community utilizes three groundwater wells.

Garvin Co. RWD #2 and McClain Co. RWD #8, both groundwater users, maintain large service areas in the watershed with 1,570 and 1,897 customers, respectively. These systems and most of the other twelve providers serving Basin 15 are independent suppliers, relying upon their own water sources, primarily groundwater.

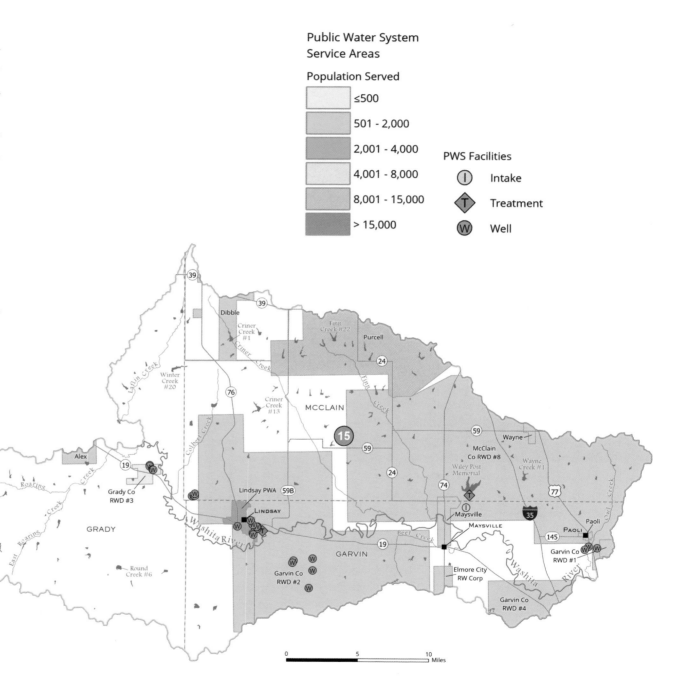

Public Water System Service Areas

Population Served

- ≤500
- 501 - 2,000
- 2,001 - 4,000
- 4,001 - 8,000
- 8,001 - 15,000
- > 15,000

PWS Facilities

- (I) Intake
- (T) Treatment
- (W) Well

Public Water Supply Systems
Basin 15

System	Residential Customers Served[1]	Source(s) of Supply[2]	Water Sales	Water Purchases	Facilities[3]				
					Intake	Pump Facility	Storage	Treatment Plant	Well or Spring
Alex	635	GW	—	—					
Dibble	550	P (SW)	—	Blanchard					
Elmore City RW Corp.	1,107	P (SW)	Elmore City	Elmore City, Pauls Valley					
Garvin Co. RWD #1	1,445	GW	—	—					
Garvin Co. RWD #2	1,570	GW	—	—					5
Garvin Co. RWD #4	1,340	P (SW)	—	Pauls Valley					
Grady Co. RWD #3	80	GW	—	—					4
Grady Co. RWD #7 (Ninnekah)	2,425	GW	—	—					2
Lindsay PWA	2,850	GW	—	—				1	13
Maysville	1,212	SW	—	—	1			1	
McClain Co. RWD #8	1,897	GW	—	—					
Paoli	610	GW	—	—					5
Purcell	8,118	GW	—	—					
Wayne	688	GW	—	—					

[1]Does not include wholesale customers served through water sales.

[2]GW = Groundwater; SW = Surface Water; P = Purchased.

[3]Includes both active and inactive (mostly wells) facilities in the watershed. Treatment plants include only those utilizing conventional water treatment and do not include chlorination stations associated with discrete source treatment.

Data: Oklahoma Department of Environmental Quality, Safe Drinking Water Information System, OWRB GIS and Arbuckle-Simpson Aquifer Drought Contingency Plan. Listed system facilities include those with service areas and/or facilities within relevant watershed.

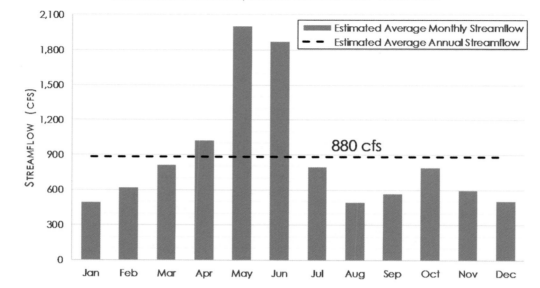

Estimated Streamflow, Middle Washita River Watershed

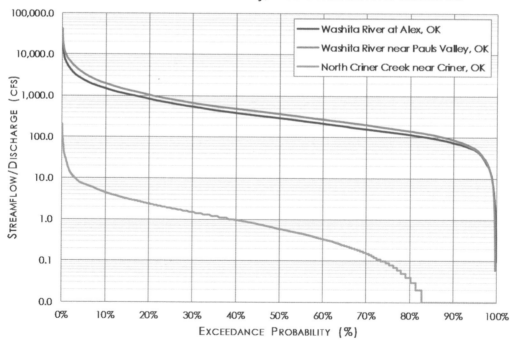

Streamflow Exceedance Probability, Middle Washita River Watershed

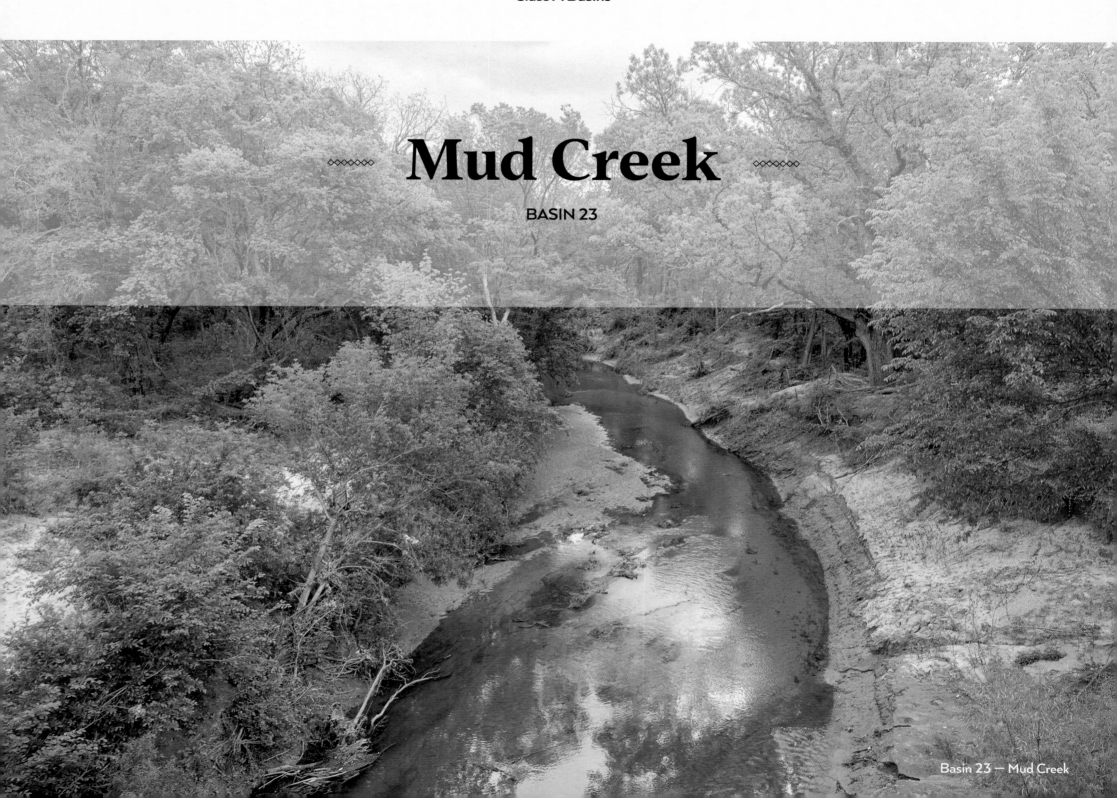

Mud Creek

BASIN 23

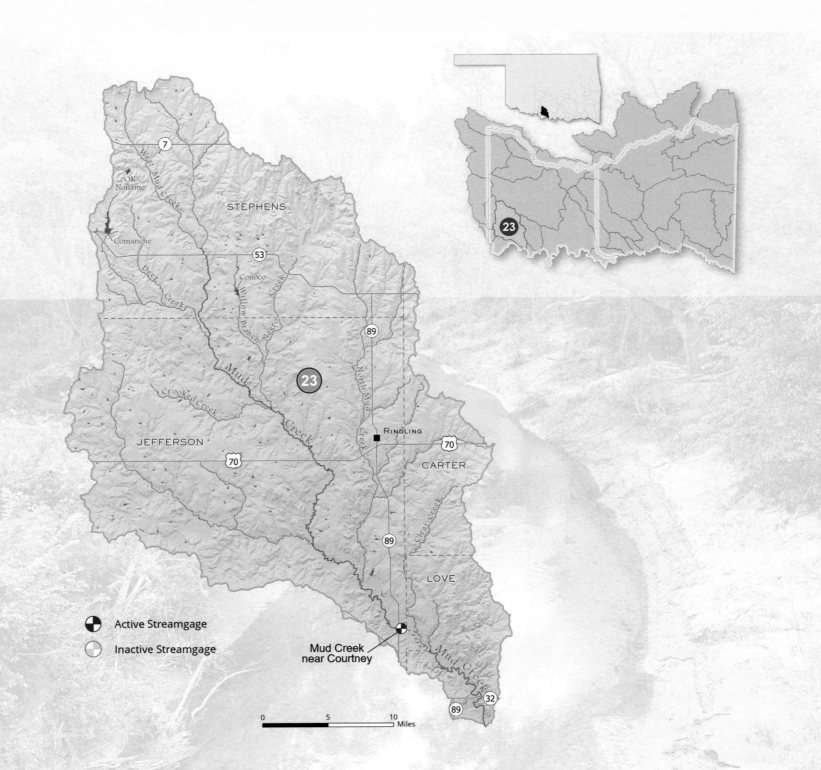

STEPHENS

7

OK Noname

West Mud Creek

Comanche

Deer Creek

53

Conoco Creek

Willow Branch Negro Creek

89

23

North Mud Creek

Crooked Creek

Mud Creek

JEFFERSON

Ringling

70

CARTER

70

Clear Creek

89

LOVE

23

Mud Creek

⬤ Active Streamgage

◯ Inactive Streamgage

Mud Creek
near Courtney

89

32

0   5   10
                         Miles

Water Quality

Basin 23 extends 649 square miles across far southern Oklahoma. Mud Creek, including its West Mud Creek tributary in the north, has its source in Stephens County. Numerous tributaries join the stream as it treks southward through Jefferson and Love counties. Mud Creek joins the Red River immediately upon leaving Basin 23. The average annual flow of Mud Creek, estimated at the bottom of Basin 23, is 208 cfs; this flow is available only about 11 percent of the time.

Comanche Lake, owned by the City of Comanche, is the largest reservoir of note in the basin; it is impounded on a tributary of Deer Creek and has a normal capacity of 2,500 acre-feet. Its designated purposes are water supply and recreation.

Within the Mud Creek watershed, the whooping crane and piping plover are considered endangered while the red knot is threatened.

Mud Creek flows across the Cross Timbers and Central Great Plains ecoregions where stream substrates typically vary between sand and firm clay, with sand more common in lower-gradient reaches. The stream is typified by high salinity and is hypereutrophic with high turbidity. Comanche Lake is phosphorus-limited and hypereutrophic with good clarity. TMDLs have been completed in the basin for turbidity, E. coli and enterococcus. Fish and Wildlife Propagation and Fish Consumption beneficial uses are not supported in the middle and lower reaches of Mud Creek due to elevated lead levels.

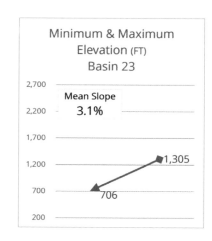

Minimum & Maximum Elevation (FT)
Basin 23

Mean Slope 3.1%

1,305
706

PRINCIPAL RIVERS & STREAMS BASIN 23	
River/Stream	**Length** MILES
Mud Creek	62
North Mud Creek	20
Clear Creek	16
West Mud Creek	14
Deer Creek	14
Negro Creek	12
Crooked Creek	11

PRINCIPAL LAKES BASIN 23									
Name	**Stream**	**Authority**	**Normal Elevation** FEET	**Normal Area** ACRES	**Normal Capacity** AC-FT	**Shoreline** MILES	**Purpose(s)**[1]	**Water Supply Storage** AC-FT	**Water Supply Yield** AC-FT/YR
Comanche	Deer Creek TR	City of Comanche	1,045	186	2,500	4.6	WS, R	—	—
Conoco	Willow Branch	Lowery Farms LLC	—	60	168	1.8	—	—	—
OK Noname	West Mud Creek TR	Berry Wendel	—	43	502	1.4	—	—	—

[1]*WS=Water Supply, R=Recreation, HP=Hydroelectric Power, IR=Irrigation, WQ=Water Quality, FW=Fish & Wildlife, FC=Flood Control, LF=Low Flow Regulation, N=Navigation, C=Conservation, CW=Cooling Water*

Land Cover & Uses
Mud Creek Watershed (A)

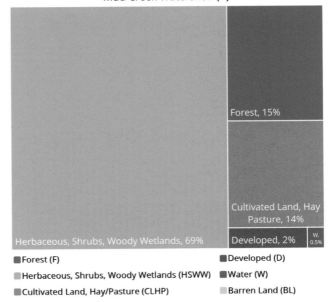

Forest, 15%

Cultivated Land, Hay Pasture, 14%

Herbaceous, Shrubs, Woody Wetlands, 69%

Developed, 2%

W. 0.5%

- ■ Forest (F)
- ■ Herbaceous, Shrubs, Woody Wetlands (HSWW)
- ■ Cultivated Land, Hay/Pasture (CLHP)
- ■ Developed (D)
- ■ Water (W)
- ■ Barren Land (BL)

LAND COVER & USES
MUD CREEK WATERSHED

Use	Area SQ. MI.
Forest	94
Herbaceous, Shrubs, Woody Wetlands	449
Cultivated Land, Hay/Pasture	88
Developed	14
Water	3
Barren Land	0
Total Land Area	**648**

Groundwater

The Red River major aquifer, in the far southern end of Basin 23, is the only groundwater source of relevance in the Mud Creek watershed. The predominant source of groundwater supply, through some 224 wells, comes from nondelineated sources.

Aquifer	Area in Basin/ Watershed SQUARE MILES	EPS[1] AC-FT/ACRE	Number of Permitted & Domestic Wells in Basin/ Watershed[2]
MAJOR & MINOR AQUIFERS **BASIN 23**			
Antlers	11	2.1	1
El Reno	1	2.0	0
Red River	75	2.0	24
Nondelineated Source Wells			224
Total Wells			**249**

[1]*Italic number signifies unstudied aquifers with a default temporary equal proportionate share (EPS) of 2.0 acre-feet per acre of land.*
[2]*Some wells are double-counted where one aquifer overlies another.*

NOTE: Significant color and shading variations may be apparent in areas where one aquifer overlies another. In some cases, for state administrative purposes, aquifer boundaries align directly with county lines or related political borders rather than geologic outcrop areas.

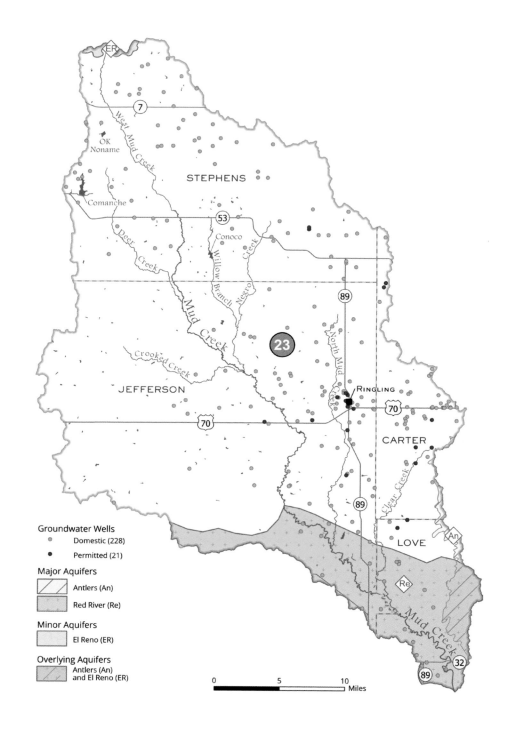

Groundwater Wells
- Domestic (228)
- Permitted (21)

Major Aquifers
- Antlers (An)
- Red River (Re)

Minor Aquifers
- El Reno (ER)

Overlying Aquifers
- Antlers (An) and El Reno (ER)

Permitted Water Use

At 93 percent, the Mud Creek watershed features the largest ratio of permitted groundwater to surface water of all Settlement Area watersheds/basins. Groundwater underlying Basin 23 is a popular source for irrigation, which accounts for 76 percent of all permitted water utilized in the watershed. Public supply, again mostly from groundwater, makes up 19 percent of total permitted uses.

The largest active water user in Basin 23, with one groundwater permit for 2,260 AFY, is a private citizen who irrigates land in Carter County. The largest public water supply rights holder in the watershed, with a groundwater allocation of approximately 716 AFY, is the City of Ringling in Jefferson County. This includes a prior right issued by the OWRB in 1985.

Any application to appropriate water for use at a location outside of Basin 23 could be subject to conferral, depending upon the application amount, mean available flow and other relevant factors. See conditions associated with Class A Basins in the Tribal-State Water Settlement agreement in the *Oka Holisso* appendix.

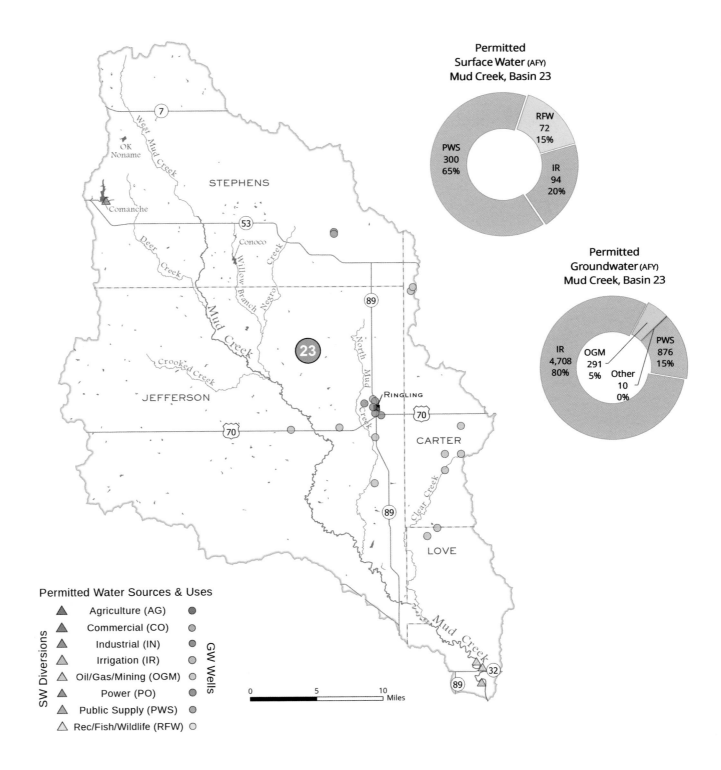

Permitted Surface Water (AFY) Mud Creek, Basin 23

- RFW 72 15%
- IR 94 20%
- PWS 300 65%

Permitted Groundwater (AFY) Mud Creek, Basin 23

- IR 4,708 80%
- OGM 291 5%
- Other 10 0%
- PWS 876 15%

Permitted Water Sources & Uses

SW Diversions:
- ▲ Agriculture (AG)
- ▲ Commercial (CO)
- ▲ Industrial (IN)
- ▲ Irrigation (IR)
- △ Oil/Gas/Mining (OGM)
- ▲ Power (PO)
- ▲ Public Supply (PWS)
- △ Rec/Fish/Wildlife (RFW)

GW Wells:
- ● Agriculture (AG)
- ● Commercial (CO)
- ● Industrial (IN)
- ● Irrigation (IR)
- ● Oil/Gas/Mining (OGM)
- ● Power (PO)
- ● Public Supply (PWS)
- ○ Rec/Fish/Wildlife (RFW)

PERMITTED WATER		
AFY		
BASIN 23		
Groundwater	Surface Water	Total
5,884	466	**6,350**

Water Supply Systems

The service area of Jefferson Co. RWD #1 extends throughout the Mud Creek watershed, providing some 8,276 residential customers with supply from local wells. During periods of high usage, this water is supplemented by purchases from Waurika PWA in the adjacent Beaver Creek watershed. ODEQ records indicate water sales to and purchases from additional providers as well. Comanche Public Works Authority (PWA), also in the Beaver Creek watershed, extends its service to a distinct portion of the western Mud Creek watershed as it sells to Jefferson County RWD #1. Some Basin 23 users could be potentially served by Stephens Co. RWD #5, a large provider that occupies a small area in the north, and the City of Healdton in the adjacent Walnut Bayou watershed.

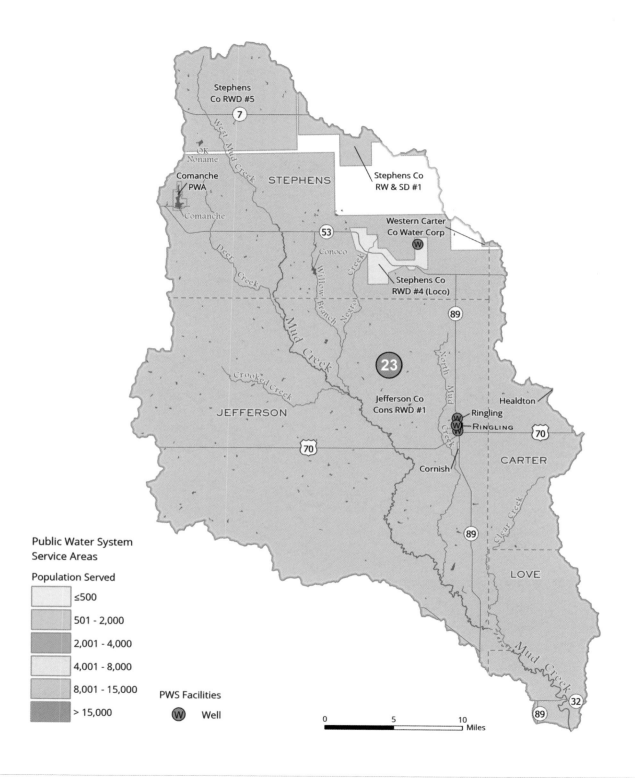

Public Water System Service Areas

Population Served

≤500

501 - 2,000

2,001 - 4,000

4,001 - 8,000

8,001 - 15,000

> 15,000

PWS Facilities

W Well

System	Residential Customers Served[1]	Source(s) of Supply[2]	Water Sales	Water Purchases	Facilities[3]				
					Intake	Pump Facility	Storage	Treatment Plant	Well or Spring
Comanche PWA	1,649	SW	Jefferson Co. #1, Stephens Co. #3	—					
Cornish	41	P (GW)	—	Ringling					
Healdton	2,785	GW/SW	—	Jefferson Co. #1					
Jefferson Co. RWD #1	8,276	GW	Healdton, Ringling, Ryan UA, Stephens Co. #4, Terral, Wilson MA	Comanche PWA, Duncan PUA, Stephens Co. #4, Waurika PWA, Wilson MA					
Ringling	1,200	GW	Cornish	Jefferson Co. #1					3
Stephens Co. RW&SD #1	960	GW	—	—					
Stephens Co. RWD #4 (Loco)	122	GW	Jefferson Co. #1	Jefferson Co. #1					2
Stephens Co. RWD #5	6,426	GW	—	Duncan PUA					
Western Carter Co. Water Corp.	658	GW	Ratliff City, West Davis RWD	Davis					

[1]Does not include wholesale customers served through water sales.

[2]GW = Groundwater; SW = Surface Water; P = Purchased.

[3]Includes both active and inactive (mostly wells) facilities in the watershed. Treatment plants include only those utilizing conventional water treatment and do not include chlorination stations associated with discrete source treatment.

Data: Oklahoma Department of Environmental Quality, Safe Drinking Water Information System, OWRB GIS and Arbuckle-Simpson Aquifer Drought Contingency Plan. Listed system facilities include those with service areas and/or facilities within relevant watershed.

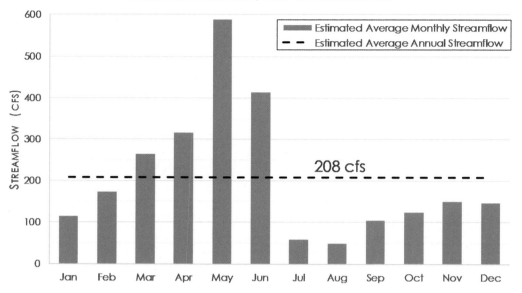

Estimated Streamflow, Mud Creek Watershed

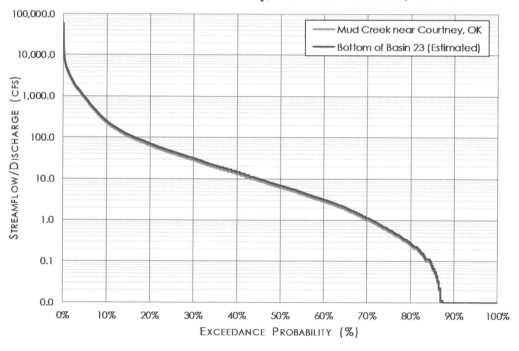

Streamflow Exceedance Probability, Mud Creek Watershed, Basin 23

Muddy Boggy Creek

BASINS 7 & 8

Basins 7 & 8 — McGee Creek Reservoir, McGee Creek State Park

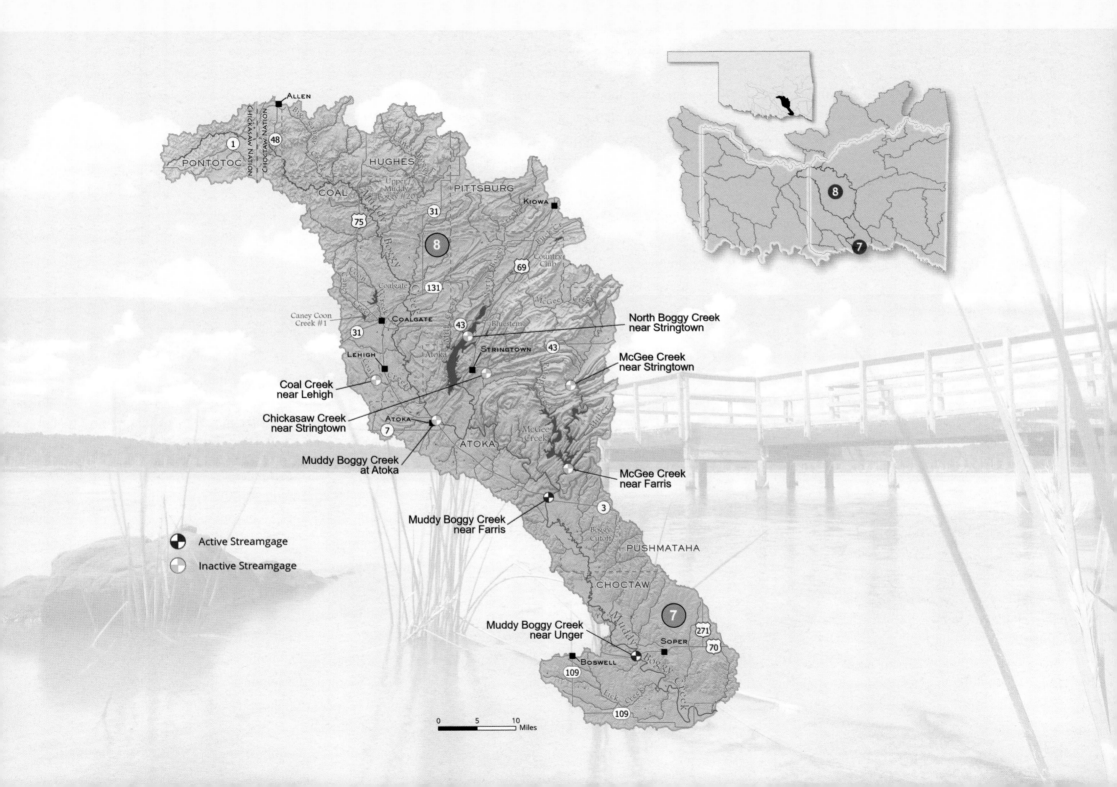

Allen

CHICKASAW NATION
CHOCTAW NATION

PONTOTOC
1

48

HUGHES

Upper
Muddy
Boggy #20

PITTSBURG

Kiowa

75

31

8

69

Country
Club

McGee Creek

131

Coalgate

Caney Coon
Creek #1

Coalgate

43

Bluestem

North Boggy Creek
near Stringtown

31

Lehigh

Stringtown

43

McGee Creek
near Stringtown

Coal Creek
near Lehigh

Atoka

McGee
Creek

Chickasaw Creek
near Stringtown

Atoka

7

ATOKA

Muddy Boggy Creek
at Atoka

McGee Creek
near Farris

3

Muddy Boggy Creek
near Farris

Boggy
Cutoff

PUSHMATAHA

CHOCTAW

Active Streamgage

Inactive Streamgage

7

Soper

271

Muddy Boggy Creek
near Unger

70

Boswell

109

Muddy Boggy Creek

Lick Creek

109

0   5   10
                          Miles

8

7

The headwaters of Muddy Boggy Creek originate in Pontotoc County, east of Ada. It then flows generally east, then decidedly south-southeast through Coal and Atoka counties. Downstream of Atoka Lake, the watercourse is joined by North Boggy Creek, and then by McGee Creek at the bottom of Basin 8. Further downstream in Choctaw County, the Muddy Boggy's flow is augmented by Clear Boggy Creek, its major tributary in Basin 9, prior to its confluence with the Red River southwest of Hugo. The average annual flow of Muddy Boggy Creek, estimated at the bottom of Basin 7, is 2,041 cfs; this flow is available about 22 percent of the time. The stream's watershed encompasses 1,435 square miles.

The Muddy Boggy watershed is home to two major reservoir projects, both in Basin 8: Atoka and McGee Creek Reservoirs. These lakes comprise the major components of Oklahoma City's southeastern water supply system, which are accessed via the City's Atoka Lake pipeline. Both reservoirs lie on tributaries of Muddy Boggy Creek. According to the OWRB, 7,192 AFY of the water supply yield (71,800 AFY) of McGee Creek Reservoir remains available for appropriation. Atoka Reservoir is fully appropriated.

Basins 7 and 8 include seven species listed as endangered: the Indiana bat, Ouachita rock pocketbook, piping plover, red-cockaded woodpecker, scaleshell mussel, whooping crane and winged mapleleaf. Threatened species are the American burying beetle, Arkansas River shiner, northern long-eared bat and red knot.

The Muddy Boggy Creek watershed spans three ecoregions with the upper reaches in the Arkansas Valley, then transitioning to the Ouachita Mountains and South Central Plains as the two basins extend to the southeast. Streams in these regions are characterized by high ecological diversity. Three sub-watersheds in the basin are designated as Sensitive Public and Private Water Supplies (SWS), including North Boggy Creek and Atoka Reservoir, McGee Creek and McGee Creek Reservoir, and Coalgate Reservoir and its watershed. These lakes are phosphorus-limited, ranging from mesotrophic (Coalgate) to eutrophic (Atoka). Metals, including mercury and lead, are elevated throughout the Muddy Boggy watershed, resulting in impairment of the beneficial use for fish consumption. TMDLs have been completed in the watershed for bacteria and turbidity.

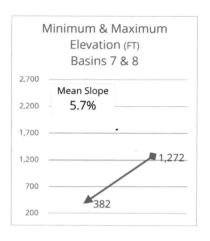

Principal Rivers & Streams Basins 7 & 8	
River/Stream	**Length** MILES
Muddy Boggy Creek	166
McGee Creek	49
North Boggy Creek	45
Caney Boggy Creek	26
Lick Creek	20
Potapo Creek	19
Mill Creek	18
Buck Creek	15
Caney Creek	14
Big Sangy Creek	14

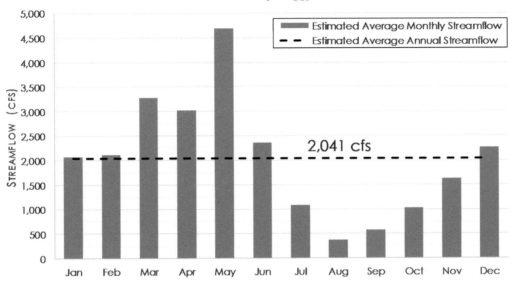

Estimated Streamflow, Muddy Boggy Creek Watershed

				PRINCIPAL LAKES						
				BASINS 7 & 8						
Name	Stream	Authority	Normal Elevation FEET	Normal Area ACRES	Normal Capacity AC-FT	Shoreline MILES	Purpose(s)[1]	Water Supply Storage AC-FT	Water Supply Yield AC-FT/YR
Atoka	North Boggy Creek	City of Okla. City	590	5,420	105,195	51.2	WS, R	123,500	92,067
Bluestem	Elm Creek	State of Oklahoma	—	97	840	2.3	—	—	—
Boggy Cutoff	Muddy Boggy Creek TR	—	—	69	—	8	—	—	—
Coalgate	Coon Creek	City of Coalgate	619	393	3,466	7.9	WS, FC, R	—	—
Country Club	Buck Creek TR	Town of Kiowa	—	133	700	2.8	—	—	—
McGee Creek	McGee Creek	BOR	577.1	5,116	113,930	94.7	WS, WQ, FC, R, FW	109,800	71,800
Caney Coon Creek #1	Caney Creek	SCS/Coal Co. CD	—	122	398	3.3	FC	—	—
Upper Muddy Boggy #20	Caney Boggy Creek TR	SCS/Coal Co. CD	—	84	644	4.2	FC	—	—

[1]WS=Water Supply, R=Recreation, HP=Hydroelectric Power, IR=Irrigation, WQ=Water Quality, FW=Fish & Wildlife, FC=Flood Control, LF=Low Flow Regulation, N=Navigation, C=Conservation, CW=Cooling Water

LAND COVER & USES
MUDDY BOGGY CREEK WATERSHED

Use	Area SQ. MI.
Forest	706
Herbaceous, Shrubs, Woody Wetlands	329
Cultivated Land, Hay/Pasture	334
Developed	43
Water	22
Barren Land	1
Total Land Area	**1,435**

Land Cover & Uses
Muddy Boggy Creek Watershed (A)

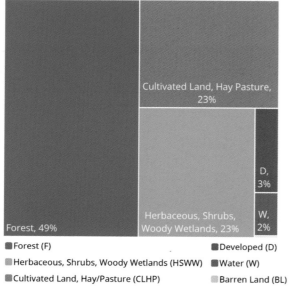

- Forest (F)
- Herbaceous, Shrubs, Woody Wetlands (HSWW)
- Cultivated Land, Hay/Pasture (CLHP)
- Developed (D)
- Water (W)
- Barren Land (BL)

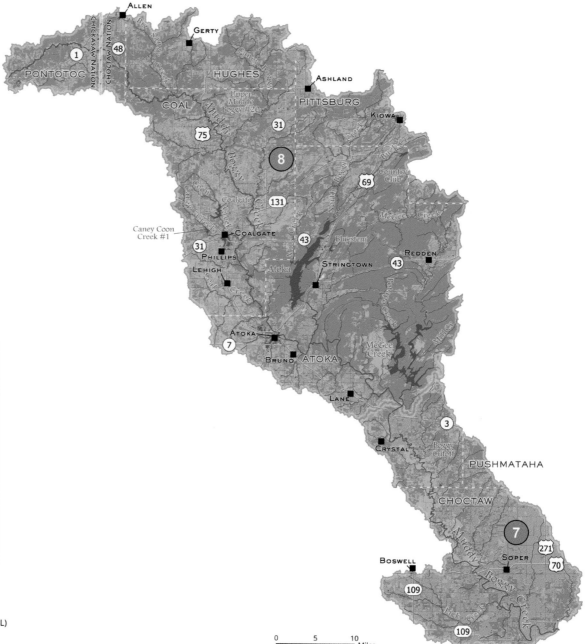

Groundwater

The major Antlers aquifer is the most notable of eight aquifers occupying the subsurface in the Muddy Boggy watershed. The Antlers supplies an estimated one-third of the region's water wells utilized for permits and domestic uses, almost exclusively in Basin 7. The younger Woodbine aquifer includes ninety-nine wells, also in Basin 7, but some of these wells might instead tap the Antlers aquifer, or vice versa.

Aquifer	Area in Basin/ Watershed SQUARE MILES	EPS[1] AC-FT/ACRE	Number of Permitted & Domestic Wells in Basin/ Watershed[2]
MAJOR & MINOR AQUIFERS BASINS 7 & 8			
Antlers	382	2.1	155
Ashland	7	2.0	5
Canadian River	4	2.0	1
East-Central Oklahoma	120	2.0	58
Kiamichi	455	2.0	29
Pennsylvanian	392	2.0	64
Red River	26	2.0	18
Woodbine	206	2.0	99
Nondelineated Source Wells			38
Total Wells			**467**

[1]*Italic number signifies unstudied aquifers with a default temporary equal proportionate share (EPS) of 2.0 acre-feet per acre of land.*
[2]*Some wells are double-counted where one aquifer overlies another.*

NOTE: Significant color and shading variations may be apparent in areas where one aquifer overlies another. In some cases, for state administrative purposes, aquifer boundaries align directly with county lines or related political borders rather than geologic outcrop areas.

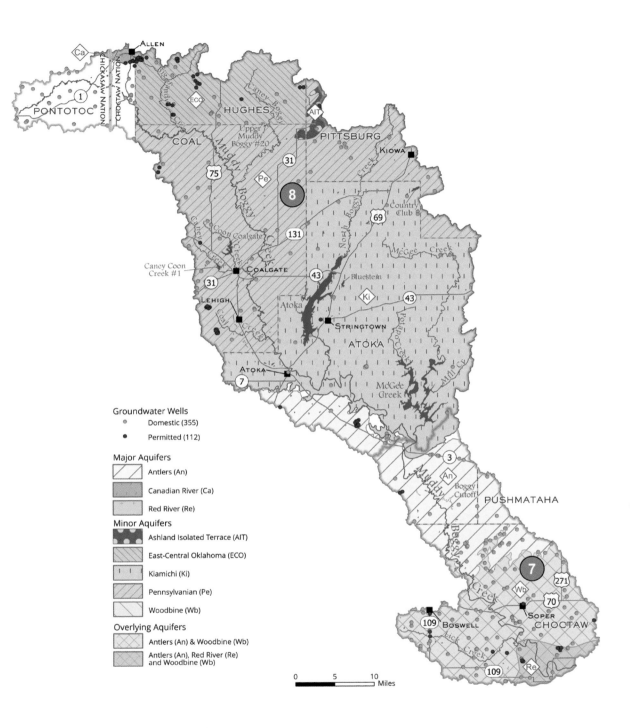

Groundwater Wells
- Domestic (355)
- Permitted (112)

Major Aquifers
- Antlers (An)
- Canadian River (Ca)
- Red River (Re)

Minor Aquifers
- Ashland Isolated Terrace (AIT)
- East-Central Oklahoma (ECO)
- Kiamichi (Ki)
- Pennsylvanian (Pe)
- Woodbine (Wb)

Overlying Aquifers
- Antlers (An) & Woodbine (Wb)
- Antlers (An), Red River (Re) and Woodbine (Wb)

0   5   10 Miles

Permitted Water Use

Users both within and outside of Basins 7 and 8 rely upon abundant water in the region's lakes and streams. About 96 percent—or 172,066 AFY—of permitted water in the Muddy Boggy Creek watershed comes from surface sources. Public water supply accounts for 86 percent of all water appropriated or allocated in the watershed, followed by industrial (7 percent) and irrigation (5 percent) uses.

Oklahoma City is far and away the largest permitted user of water in the Muddy Boggy Creek watershed as out-of-basin usage far exceeds that associated with in-basin users. The city holds three public supply permits with a cumulative total of 131,667 AFY authorizing the diversion of water from Atoka and McGee Creek Reservoirs as part of its southeastern supply system. The City of Atoka also holds a permit of 10,000 AFY to satisfy local community needs. The largest industrial permit holder in Basins 7 and 8 is the County Commissioners of Atoka County with 8,000 AFY of water rights.

Any application to appropriate water for use at a location outside of Basin 7 or 8 could be subject to conferral, depending upon the application amount, mean available flow and other relevant factors. See conditions associated with Class A Basins in the Tribal-State Water Settlement agreement in the *Oka Holisso* appendix.

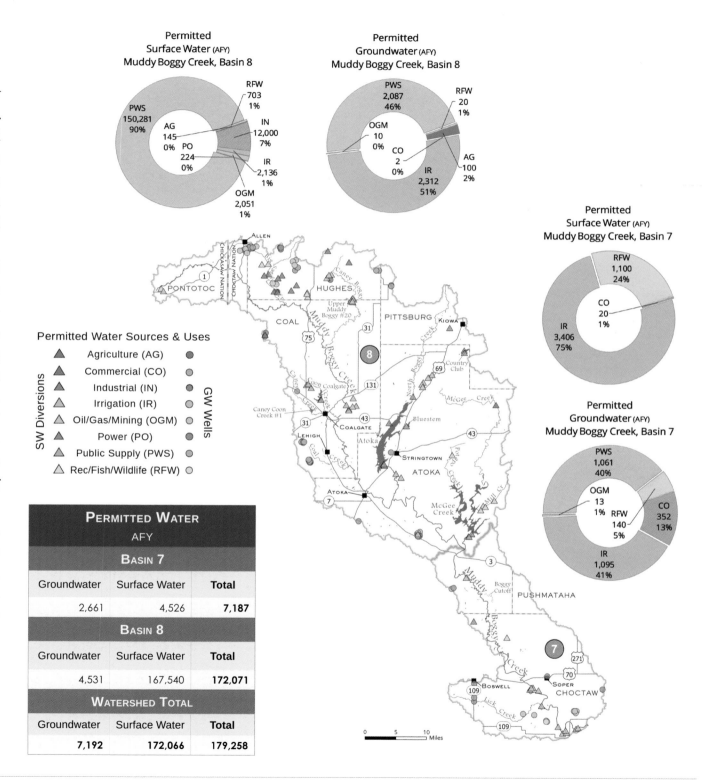

Permitted Water Sources & Uses

SW Diversions / GW Wells

- ▲ ● Agriculture (AG)
- ▲ ● Commercial (CO)
- ▲ ● Industrial (IN)
- △ ● Irrigation (IR)
- ▲ ● Oil/Gas/Mining (OGM)
- ▲ ● Power (PO)
- ▲ ● Public Supply (PWS)
- △ ● Rec/Fish/Wildlife (RFW)

Permitted Surface Water (AFY), Muddy Boggy Creek, Basin 8

- PWS 150,281 90%
- RFW 703 1%
- IN 12,000 7%
- IR 2,136 1%
- OGM 2,051 1%
- AG 145 0%
- PO 224 0%

Permitted Groundwater (AFY), Muddy Boggy Creek, Basin 8

- PWS 2,087 46%
- RFW 20 1%
- AG 100 2%
- IR 2,312 51%
- CO 2 0%
- OGM 10 0%

Permitted Surface Water (AFY), Muddy Boggy Creek, Basin 7

- RFW 1,100 24%
- CO 20 1%
- IR 3,406 75%

Permitted Groundwater (AFY), Muddy Boggy Creek, Basin 7

- PWS 1,061 40%
- CO 352 13%
- IR 1,095 41%
- RFW 140 5%
- OGM 13 1%

PERMITTED WATER		
AFY		
BASIN 7		
Groundwater	Surface Water	Total
2,661	4,526	7,187
BASIN 8		
Groundwater	Surface Water	Total
4,531	167,540	172,071
WATERSHED TOTAL		
Groundwater	Surface Water	Total
7,192	172,066	179,258

The Muddy Boggy watershed contains a substantial number of water systems, with the preponderance of these established within Basin 8. Aside from Ada, whose service area only skirts the watershed boundary (but serves Pontotoc County RWDs #1 and 7), and Pushmataha Co. RWD #3, which serves a relatively small portion of Basin 7, among the most consequential providers is Atoka Co. Rural Water Sewer and Solid Waste Management District (RWS & SWMD) #4. In addition to its 3,000 customers, Atoka Co. #4 sells water from McGee Creek Reservoir to three providers in the watershed. Other relatively large systems serving portions of the watershed include the City of Atoka, Choctaw Co. RWD #1, Coalgate PWA and Pontotoc Co. RWD #7—all with around 2,000–3,000 customers. Coalgate PWA is the most active water seller with agreements in place involving five other providers in the area.

NOTE: The corridor of land extending southeastward from near Atoka and then eastward to the Atoka County line, containing no PWS service area, denotes the general location of Oklahoma City's Atoka pipeline.

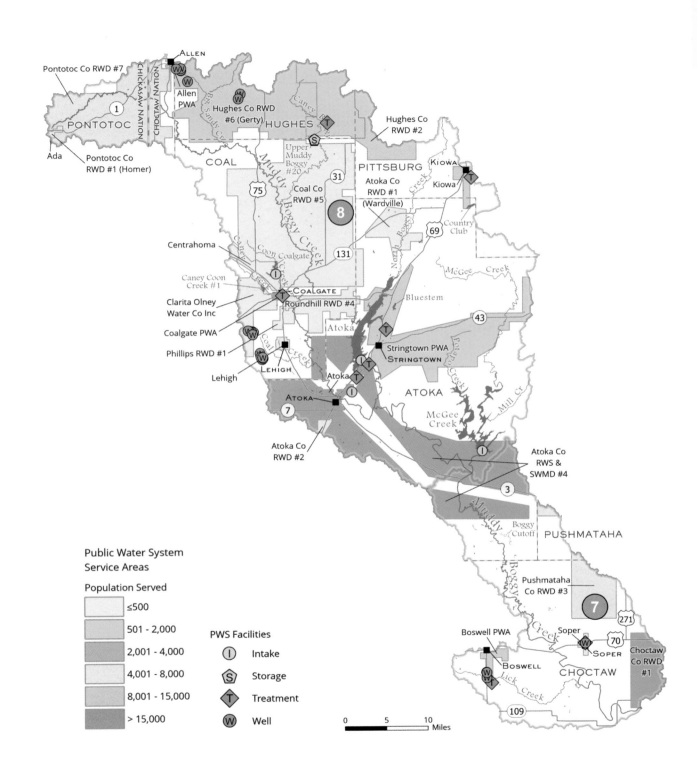

Public Water System Service Areas

Population Served

- ≤500
- 501 - 2,000
- 2,001 - 4,000
- 4,001 - 8,000
- 8,001 - 15,000
- > 15,000

PWS Facilities

- (I) Intake
- (S) Storage
- (◆) Treatment
- (W) Well

0   5   10 Miles

System	Residential Customers Served[1]	Source(s) of Supply[2]	Water Sales	Water Purchases	Facilities[3]				
					Intake	Pump Facility	Storage	Treatment Plant	Well or Spring
Ada	37,000	GW	Pontotoc Co. #1, Pontotoc Co. #6, Pontotoc Co. #7, Pontotoc Co. #9	—					
Allen PWA	937	GW	—	—					4
Atoka	2,988	SW	Atoka Co. #2	—	1			2	
Atoka Co. RWD #1 (Wardville)	125	P (SW)	—	Pittsburg Co. #11					
Atoka Co. RWD #2	500	P (SW)	—	Atoka, Atoka Co. #4					
Atoka Co. RWS & SWMD #4	3,000	SW	Atoka Co. #2, Choctaw Co. #6, Stringtown PWA	—	1			1	
Boswell PWA	932	P (SW)	—	Choctaw Co. #6				1	4
Centrahoma Water Comp.	150	P (SW)	—	Coalgate PWA					
Choctaw Co. RWD #1	2,300	GW	—	Hugo MA					
Choctaw Co. RWSG & SWMD #6	850	P (SW)	Boswell PWA	Atoka Co. #4					
Clarita-Olney Water Comp.	360	P (SW)	—	Coalgate PWA					
Coal Co. RWD #5	366	P (SW)	—	Coalgate PWA					
Coalgate PWA	2,005	GW/SW	Centrahoma Water, Clarita-Olney Water, Coal Co. #5, Phillips #1, Roundhill #4	—	1			1	6
Hughes Co. RWD #2	1,145	GW	—	—	1		2	1	
Hughes Co. RWD #6 (Gerty)	1,380	GW	Hughes Co. #4	—					4
Kiowa	731	SW	Pittsburg Co. #11	—	1			1	
Lehigh	396	GW	—	—					7
Phillips RWD #1	140	P (SW)	—	Coalgate PWA					1
Pontotoc Co. RWD #1 (Homer)	441	P (GW)	—	Ada					
Pontotoc Co. RWD #7	1,950	P (GW)	—	Ada					
Pushmataha Co. RWD #3	4,825	SW	Soper	—					
Roundhill RWD #4	219	P (SW)	—	Coalgate PWA					
Soper	300	GW	—	Pushmataha Co. #3				1	2
Stringtown PWA	1,105	P (SW)	—	Atoka Co. #4					

[1]Does not include wholesale customers served through water sales.

[2]GW = Groundwater; SW = Surface Water; P = Purchased.

[3]Includes both active and inactive (mostly wells) facilities in the watershed. Treatment plants include only those utilizing conventional water treatment and do not include chlorination stations associated with discrete source treatment.

Data: Oklahoma Department of Environmental Quality, Safe Drinking Water Information System, OWRB GIS and Arbuckle-Simpson Aquifer Drought Contingency Plan. Listed system facilities include those with service areas and/or facilities within relevant watershed.

Streamflow Exceedance Probability, Muddy Boggy Creek Watershed

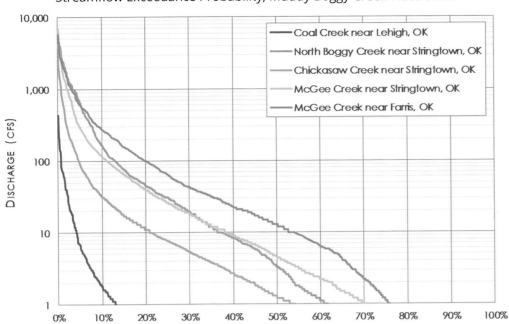

Streamflow Exceedance Probability, Muddy Boggy Creek Watershed

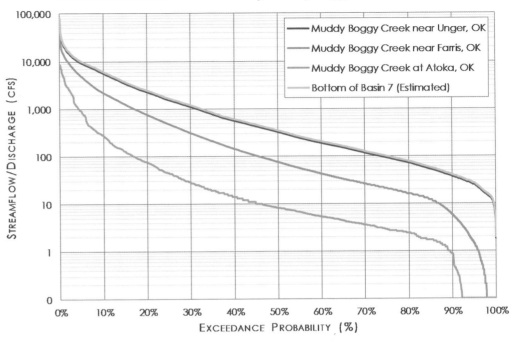

Reservoir Level Exceedance for Lake Atoka

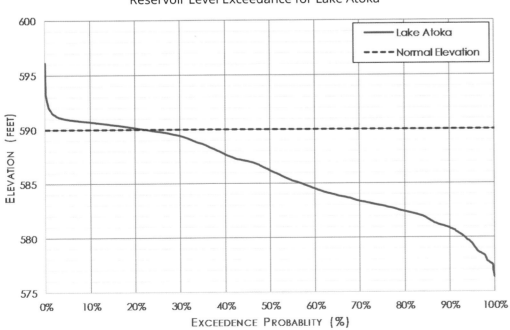

Reservoir Level Exceedance for McGee Creek Reservoir

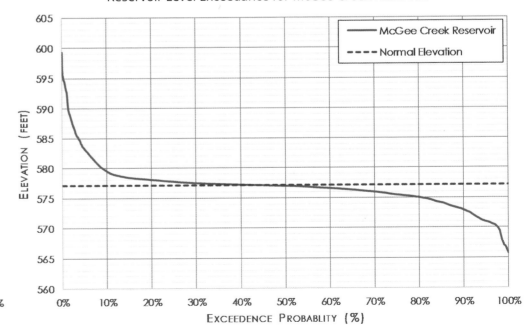

Poteau River

BASINS 44 & 45

Basins 44 & 45 — Cedar Lake, Winding Stair National Recreation Area

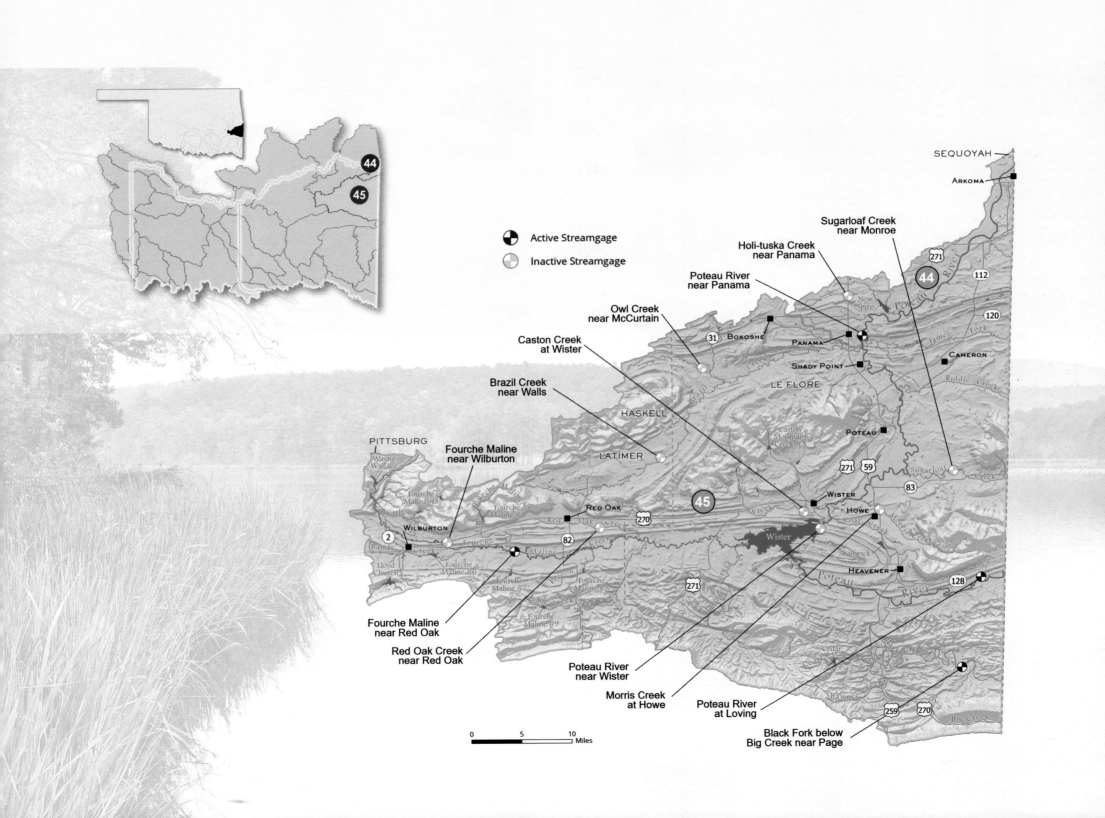

Active Streamgage

Inactive Streamgage

SEQUOYAH

ARKOMA

Sugarloaf Creek
near Monroe

Holi-tuska Creek
near Panama

Poteau River
near Panama

Owl Creek
near McCurtain

Caston Creek
at Wister

Brazil Creek
near Walls

Fourche Maline
near Wilburton

Fourche Maline
near Red Oak

Red Oak Creek
near Red Oak

Poteau River
near Wister

Morris Creek
at Howe

Poteau River
at Loving

Black Fork below
Big Creek near Page

44

45

PITTSBURG

HASKELL

LATIMER

LE FLORE

New
Spiro

BOKOSHE

PANAMA

SHADY POINT

POTEAU

WISTER

HOWE

RED OAK

WILBURTON

Carlton

Wayne
Wallace

Bandy

Lloyd
Church

HEAVENER

Shadwick

Wister

CAMERON

31

271

112

120

59

271

59

83

270

82

2

271

259

270

128

0   5   10
Miles

Water & Related Resources

The Poteau River, which heads in Scott County, Arkansas, enters eastern Oklahoma in LeFlore County and Basin 45. As the river snakes west, and extensively through Wister Wildlife Management Area (WMA), it meets Fourche Maline Creek from the east, together forming Wister Lake, a project completed by the US-ACE in 1949. Downstream of the lake, the Poteau River treks back to the east, then sharply to the north and northeast through Basin 44. The Poteau River terminates at its confluence with the Arkansas River at the Oklahoma-Arkansas border near Fort Smith. Basins 44 and 45—which are characterized by a considerable slope, relevant to other watersheds, of 9.8 percent—cover 1,349 square miles in Oklahoma. The average annual flow of the Poteau River, estimated at the bottom of Basin 44, is 2,302 cfs; this flow is available less than 31 percent of the time.

In addition to Wister, a significant regional supply, several other lakes of respectable size have been built in the Poteau River watershed in Oklahoma. New Spiro Lake, on Holi-Tuska Creek in Basin 44, and Lloyd Church Lake, on a tributary of Bandy Creek (a tributary of Fourche Maline) in the far western portion of Basin 45, provide local water supply to users in Spiro and Wilburton, respectively. According to the OWRB, none of Wister Lake's yield is currently considered available and Lloyd Church Lake contains 338 AFY of water yet to be appropriated. However, firm yield analyses conducted by the CCRWP Planning Team on those two lakes, as well as New Spiro, indicate that additional yield could be available for potential users.

PRINCIPAL RIVERS & STREAMS BASINS 44 & 45	
River/Stream	**Length** MILES
Poteau River	95
Fourche Maline Creek	65
Brazil Creek	48
Black Fork	31
Holson Creek	21
Long Creek	21
James Fork	17
Caston Creek	17
Morris Creek	13
Little Fourche Maline Creek	13
Sugarloaf Creek	13
Big Creek	13
Riddle Creek	13
Bandy Creek	13
Cedar Creek	12
Red Oak Creek	11

PRINCIPAL LAKES
BASINS 44 & 45

Name	Stream	Authority	Normal Elevation FEET	Normal Area ACRES	Normal Capacity AC-FT	Shoreline MILES	Purpose(s)[1]	Water Supply Storage AC-FT	Water Supply Yield AC-FT/YR
Cedar	Cedar Creek	USDA	718	92	1,000	2.5	R	—	—
Carlton	Fourche Maline Creek	State of Okla.	714	42	552	1.5	R	—	—
Wayne Wallace	Fourche Maline Creek	State of Okla.	797	111	1,746	3.4	R, FC	—	—
Lloyd Church[2]	Bandy Creek TR	City of Wilburton	755	171	3,025	3.5	WS, FC, R	—	1,523
New Spiro[2]	Holi-Tuska Creek	City of Spiro	426	261	2,160	5.2	WS, R	—	—
Caston Mountain Creek #3	Caston Creek TR	SCS/LeFlore Co. CD	—	51	295	1.2	FC	—	—
Fourche Maline #1	Little Fourche Maline Creek	SCS/Latimer Co. CD	—	40	239	1.9	FC	—	—
Fourche Maline #3	Fourche Maline Creek TR	SCS/Latimer Co. CD	—	41	219	1.3	FC	—	—
Fourche Maline #7	Fourche Maline Creek TR	SCS/Latimer Co. CD	—	50	397	1.6	FC	—	—
Fourche Maline #8	Pigeon Creek	SCS/Latimer Co. CD	—	42	232	1.2	FC	—	—
Fourche Maline #9	Long Creek	SCS/Latimer Co. CD	—	42	471	1	FC	—	—
Fourche Maline #6	Bandy Creek	SCS/Latimer Co. CD	—	103	430	2.1	FC	—	—
Shadwick Lake	Coal Creek	Justin Decker	—	123	330	2.4	—	—	—
Wister Lake[2]	Poteau River	USACE	478	6,078	53,359	91.3	FC, WS, LF, C	14,000	31,364

[1]WS=Water Supply, R=Recreation, HP=Hydroelectric Power, IR=Irrigation, WQ=Water Quality, FW=Fish & Wildlife, FC=Flood Control, LF=Low Flow Regulation, N=Navigation, C=Conservation, CW=Cooling Water

[2]Hydrographic surveys and associated analyses conducted by Aqua Strategies, Inc. determined firm yields of 2,395 AFY for Lloyd Church, 1,350 AFY for New Spiro, and 56,020 AFY for Wister.

Endangered species in the Poteau River watershed include the gray bat, harperella, Indiana bat, Ouachita rock pocketbook, Ozark big-eared bat, piping plover, scaleshell mussel and winged mapleleaf. The American burying beetle, leopard darter, northern long-eared bat and red knot are threatened.

Water Quality

The Poteau River flows through the Scattered High Ridges and Mountains of the Arkansas Valley. Streams here feature substrates with gravel, cobbles and boulders. Three sub-watersheds are designated as Sensitive Public and Private Water Supplies (SWS), including Holi-Tuska Creek and New Spiro Lake, Coon Creek Lake and watershed, and Lloyd Church Lake and watershed. The Wister Lake watershed is designated as a nutrient limited watershed (NLW) and the Black Fork River, upstream from Cedar Creek, is designated as High Quality Waters (HQW). Most of the streams in the Poteau River watershed are mesotrophic with low nutrient levels. However, New Spiro Lake and Wister Lake, including the Poteau River downstream of the dam, are hypereutrophic. Fish and Wildlife Propagation and Fish Consumption beneficial uses are not supported in the river downstream of Lake Wister due to high lead levels. Elevated levels of metals—including mercury, cadmium, copper, silver, selenium and lead—in other watershed streams and lakes are also impairing Fish and Wildlife Propagation. TMDLs have been completed for turbidity on the Poteau River and for bacteria on Brazil Creek and Fourche Maline Creek.

LAND COVER & USES POTEAU RIVER WATERSHED	
Use	**Area** SQ. MI.
Forest	806
Herbaceous, Shrubs, Woody Wetlands	98
Cultivated Land, Hay/Pasture	373
Developed	52
Water	18
Barren Land	2
Total Land Area	**1,349**

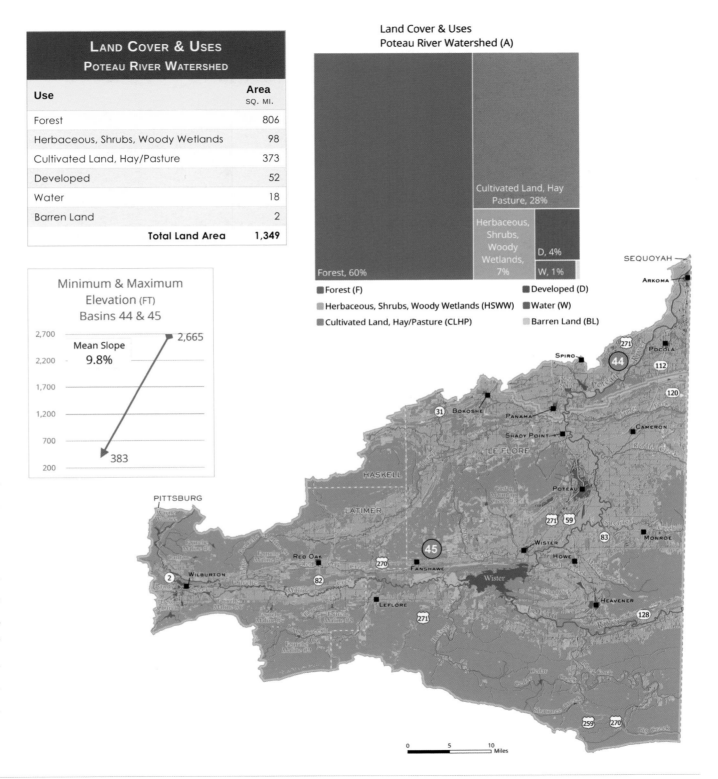

Land Cover & Uses
Poteau River Watershed (A)

Forest, 60%
Cultivated Land, Hay Pasture, 28%
Herbaceous, Shrubs, Woody Wetlands, 7%
D, 4%
W, 1%

■ Forest (F)
■ Herbaceous, Shrubs, Woody Wetlands (HSWW)
■ Cultivated Land, Hay/Pasture (CLHP)
■ Developed (D)
■ Water (W)
■ Barren Land (BL)

Minimum & Maximum Elevation (FT)
Basins 44 & 45

Mean Slope
9.8%

2,700
2,200
1,700
1,200
700
200

2,665
383

Major aquifers are a largely insignificant resource in Basins 44 and 45. However, the Kiamichi aquifer, an extensive minor bedrock groundwater basin that underlies 1,314 square miles of the watershed, supplies water required for 474 wells, almost exclusively in Basin 45. The OWRB and State of Oklahoma define "minor" aquifers as those with wells generally yielding less than 50 gallons per minute.

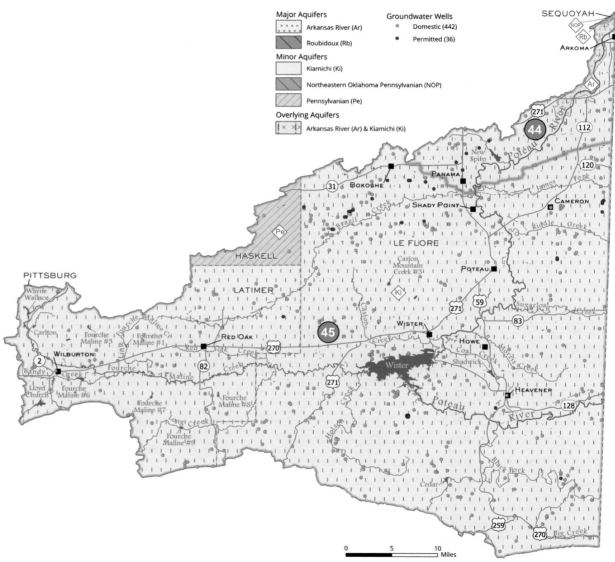

MAJOR & MINOR AQUIFERS BASINS 44 & 45			
Aquifer	**Area in Basin/ Watershed** SQUARE MILES	**EPS[1]** AC-FT/ACRE	**Number of Permitted & Domestic Wells in Basin/ Watershed[2]**
Arkansas River	11	2.0	0
Kiamichi	1,314	2.0	474
Northeastern Oklahoma Pennsylvanian	<1	2.0	0
Pennsylvanian	34	2.0	4
Roubidoux	1	2.0	0
Nondelineated Source Wells			0
		Total Wells	**478**

[1]*Italic number signifies unstudied aquifers with a default temporary equal proportionate share (EPS) of 2.0 acre-feet per acre of land.*
[2]*Some wells are double-counted where one aquifer overlies another.*

NOTE: Significant color and shading variations may be apparent in areas where one aquifer overlies another. In some cases, for state administrative purposes, aquifer boundaries align directly with county lines or related political borders rather than geologic outcrop areas.

Water use in the Poteau River watershed is characterized by the prevalent surface supplies in Basins 44 and 45; approximately 95 percent (45,957 AFY) of this region's permitted water is diverted from lakes and streams. Sixty percent of all permitted uses are utilized for public water supply purposes. Power uses (24 percent) within the watershed are also well represented as is irrigation, which accounts for 11 percent of appropriated/allocated water.

Poteau Valley Improvement Authority (PVIA), a major regional water provider, maintains 21,789 AFY in rights to support its many users. Similarly, Heavener Utilities Authority, also in LeFlore County, holds 4,426 AFY for public supply; this includes a 717 AFY groundwater right. Related to electric power generation, OG&E Energy Corporation possesses 11,600 AFY in water rights to support its power facility in LeFlore County.

Any application to appropriate water for use at a location outside of Basin 44 or 45 could be subject to conferral, depending upon the application amount, mean available flow and other relevant factors. See conditions associated with Class A Basins in the Tribal-State Water Settlement agreement in the *Oka Holisso* appendix.

PERMITTED WATER AFY		
BASIN 44		
Groundwater	Surface Water	Total
61	2,091	**2,152**
BASIN 45		
Groundwater	Surface Water	Total
2,280	43,866	**46,146**
WATERSHED TOTAL		
Groundwater	Surface Water	Total
2,341	**45,957**	**48,298**

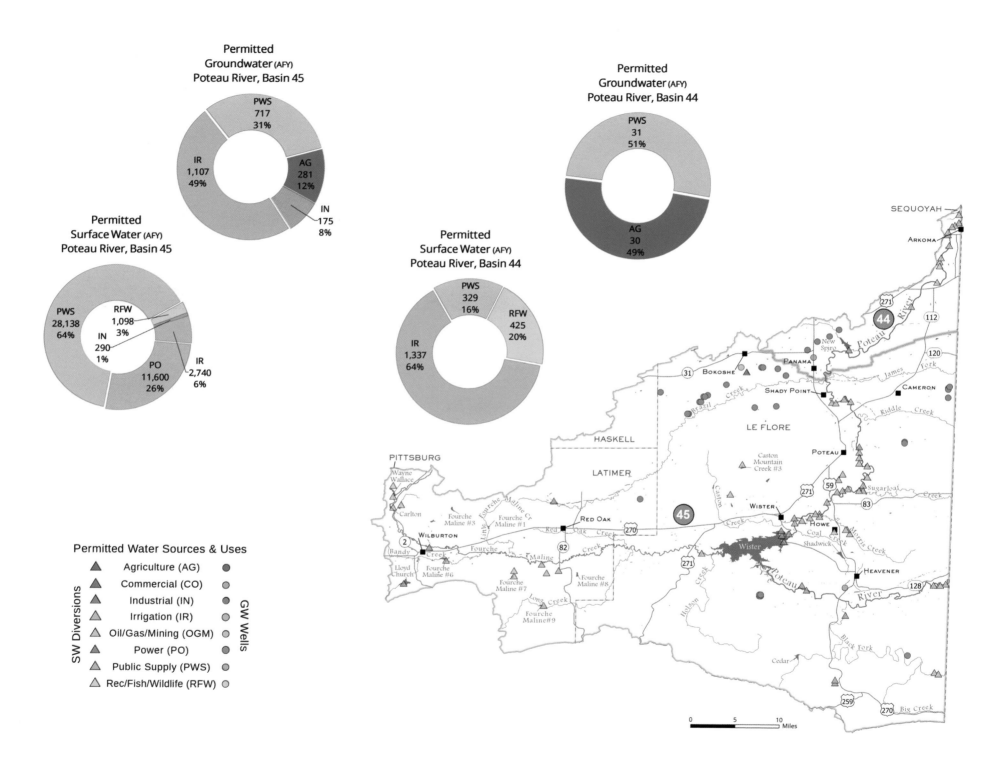

Permitted
Groundwater (AFY)
Poteau River, Basin 45

PWS
717
31%

AG
281
12%

IN
175
8%

IR
1,107
49%

Permitted
Groundwater (AFY)
Poteau River, Basin 44

PWS
31
51%

AG
30
49%

Permitted
Surface Water (AFY)
Poteau River, Basin 45

PWS
28,138
64%

RFW
1,098
3%

IN
290
1%

PO
11,600
26%

IR
2,740
6%

Permitted
Surface Water (AFY)
Poteau River, Basin 44

PWS
329
16%

RFW
425
20%

IR
1,337
64%

Permitted Water Sources & Uses

SW Diversions

▲ Agriculture (AG)
▲ Commercial (CO)
▲ Industrial (IN)
△ Irrigation (IR)
△ Oil/Gas/Mining (OGM)
▲ Power (PO)
▲ Public Supply (PWS)
△ Rec/Fish/Wildlife (RFW)

GW Wells

● Agriculture (AG)
○ Commercial (CO)
● Industrial (IN)
● Irrigation (IR)
○ Oil/Gas/Mining (OGM)
● Power (PO)
○ Public Supply (PWS)
○ Rec/Fish/Wildlife (RFW)

Water Supply Systems

The public water supply systems in the Poteau River watershed rely solely upon surface water sources and most purchase supply from the Poteau Valley Improvement Authority (PVIA). Created as a State of Oklahoma trust in 1969, PVIA provides direct supply to some 6,500 residential customers, but more than 40,000 in the region actually depend upon the authority's treatment and distribution of water from Lake Wister. Other large providers in Basins 44 and 45 include LeFlore Co. RWD #14 (9,077 customers), Poteau PWA (7,939) and LeFlore Co. RWD #2 (4,700). The latter system maintains an emergency connection with Fort Smith, Arkansas. Water Distributors, Inc. also, includes a sizable service area with some 3,875 residential customers.

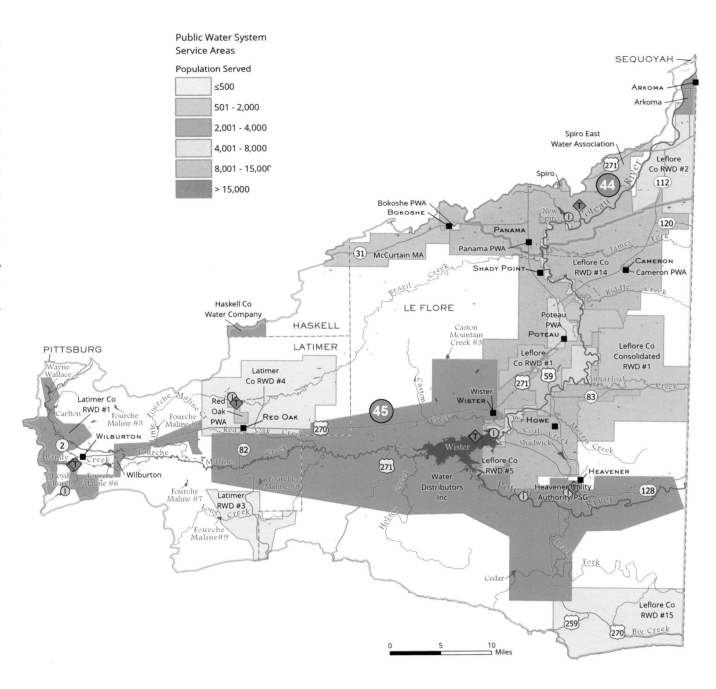

Public Water System
Service Areas

Population Served

	≤500
	501 - 2,000
	2,001 - 4,000
	4,001 - 8,000
	8,001 - 15,000
	> 15,000

PUBLIC WATER SUPPLY SYSTEMS
BASINS 44 & 45

System	Residential Customers Served[1]	Source(s) of Supply[2]	Water Sales	Water Purchases	Facilities[3] Intake	Pump Facility	Storage	Treatment Plant	Well or Spring
Arkoma	2,180	P (SW)	—	—					
Bokoshe PWA	450	P (SW)	—	PVIA					
Cameron PWA	302	P (SW)	—	PVIA					
Haskell Co. Water Comp.	3,000	SW	Keota PWA, Quinton	Stigler					
Heavener Utility Authority/PSG	3,300	SW	—	PVIA	2			1	
Latimer Co. RWD #1	2,750	P (SW)	—	Wilburton					
Latimer Co. RWD #3	175	P (SW)	—	Talihina PWA					
Latimer Co. RWD #4	412	SW	—	—	1			1	
LeFlore Co. Consolidated RWD #1	1,800	P (SW)	—	PVIA					
LeFlore Co. RWD #1	1,758	P (SW)	—	PVIA					
LeFlore Co. RWD #2	4,700	P (SW)	—	PVIA					
LeFlore Co. RWD #5	1,593	P (SW)	—	PVIA					
LeFlore Co. RWD #14	9,077	P (SW)	Spiro	PVIA					
LeFlore Co. RWD #15	425	P (SW)	—	PVIA					
McCurtain MA	560	P (SW)	—	PVIA					
Poteau Valley Improvement Authority	6,500	SW	Bokoshe PWA, Cameron PWA, Heavener UA/PSG, Keota PWA, LeFlore Co. Consolidated #1, LeFlore Co. #1, LeFlore Co. #14, LeFlore Co. #15, LeFlore Co. #2, LeFlore Co. #5, McCurtain MA, Panama PWA, Poteau PWA, Spiro, Spiro East WA, Water Distributors, Inc., Wister	—	1			1	
Panama PWA	1,400	P (SW)	—	PVIA					
Poteau PWA	7,939	P (SW)	—	PVIA					
Red Oak PWA	581	SW	Water Distributors, Inc.	—	1			1	
Spiro	2,200	SW	—	LeFlore Co. #14, PVIA	1			1	
Spiro East Water Association	1,817	P (SW)	—	PVIA					
Water Distributors, Inc.	3,875	P (SW)	—	PVIA, Red Oak PWA					
Wilburton	3,025	SW	Latimer Co. #1	—	1			2	
Wister	1,002	P (SW)	—	PVIA					

[1]Does not include wholesale customers served through water sales.

[2]GW = Groundwater; SW = Surface Water; P = Purchased.

[3]Includes both active and inactive (mostly wells) facilities in the watershed. Treatment plants include only those utilizing conventional water treatment and do not include chlorination stations associated with discrete source treatment.

Data: Oklahoma Department of Environmental Quality, Safe Drinking Water Information System, OWRB GIS and Arbuckle-Simpson Aquifer Drought Contingency Plan. Listed system facilities include those with service areas and/or facilities within relevant watershed.

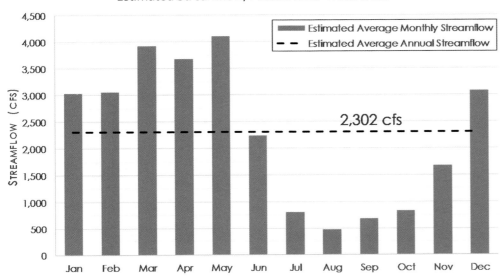

Estimated Streamflow, Poteau River Watershed

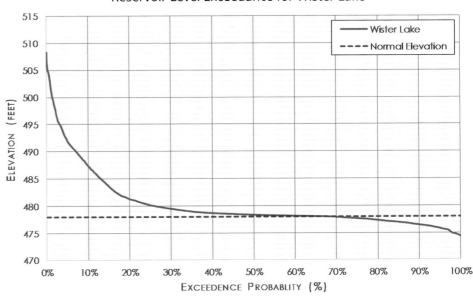

Reservoir Level Exceedance for Wister Lake

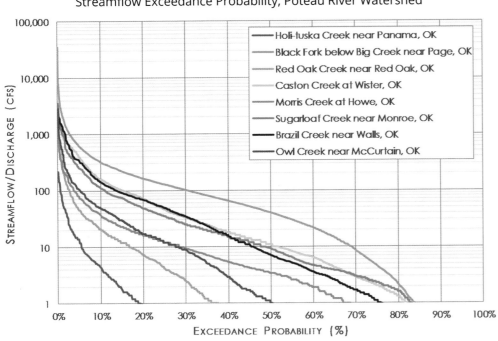

Streamflow Exceedance Probability, Poteau River Watershed

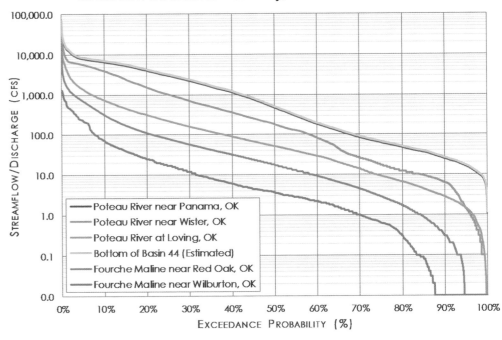

Streamflow Exceedance Probability, Poteau River Watershed

Red River

BASINS 1, 10, 13 & 21

Basins 1, 10, 13 & 21 — Lake Texoma, Tishomingo National Wildlife Refuge Area

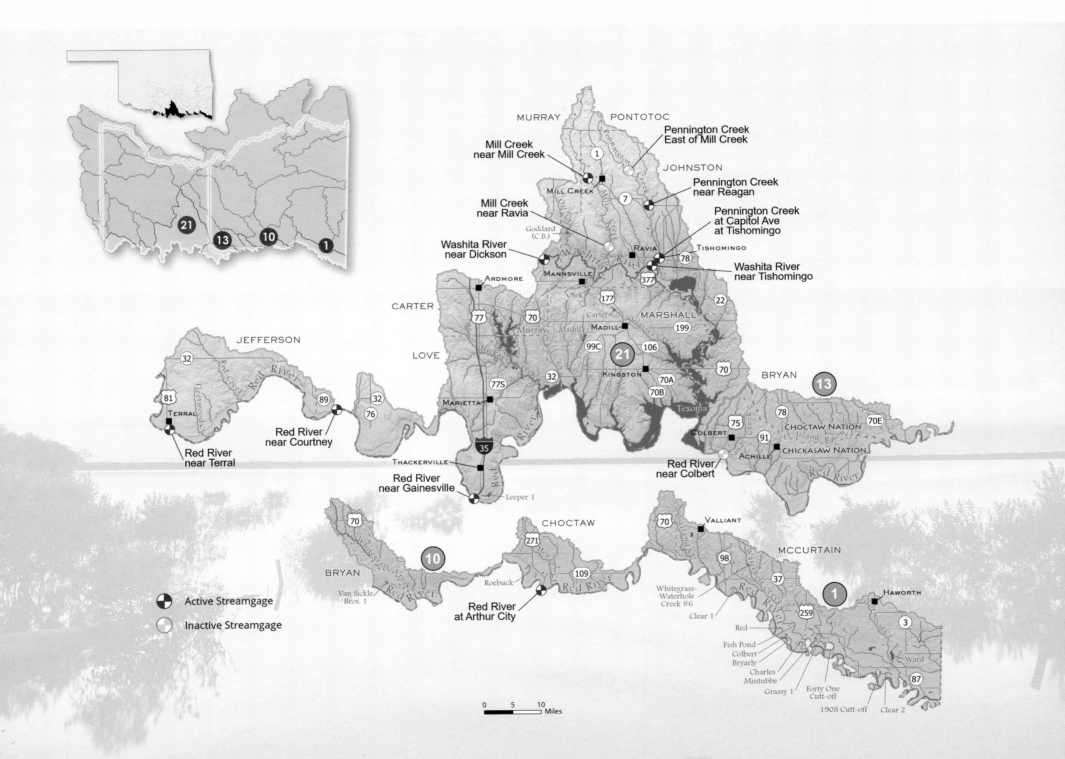

MURRAY PONTOTOC

Pennington Creek
East of Mill Creek

Mill Creek
near Mill Creek

JOHNSTON

(1)

Pennington Creek
near Reagan

MILL CREEK

(7)

Mill Creek
near Ravia

Pennington Creek
at Capitol Ave
at Tishomingo

Goddard
(C.B.)

Ravia

Tishomingo

(78)

Washita River
near Dickson

Washita River
near Tishomingo

MANNSVILLE

(377)

Olek

ARDMORE

(177)

(22)

CARTER

(77)

(70)

Carter

MARSHALL

(199)

Madill

MADILL

JEFFERSON

(32)

Red Creek

Red River

LOVE

(99C)

(106)

(70)

BRYAN

(81)

(89)

(32)

TERRAL

(32)

(76)

(77S)

MARIETTA

(32)

Kingston

(70A)

(70B)

Texoma

(78)

13

(70E)

CHOCTAW NATION

Red River
near Terral

Red River
near Courtney

(35)

THACKERVILLE

(75)

(91)

COLBERT

ACHILLE

CHICKASAW NATION

Red River
near Colbert

Red River
near Gainesville

Leeper 1

(70)

CHOCTAW

(70)

VALLIANT

MCCURTAIN

(271)

(98)

10

Roebuck

(109)

Red River

BRYAN

Van Sickle
Bros. 1

Whitegrass-
Waterhole
Creek #6

(37)

1

HAWORTH

Red River
at Arthur City

Clear 1

Red

(259)

(3)

Fish Pond
Colbert
Bryarly
Charles
Mintubbe
Grassy 1

Ward

Forty One
Cutt-off

1908 Cutt-off

Clear 2

(87)

21

13

10

1

● Active Streamgage
○ Inactive Streamgage

0   5   10
Miles

The Red River, including (from east to west) Basins 1, 10, 13 and 21, comprises the entire southern border of both the Chickasaw and Choctaw Nations. Many of the Nations' most significant rivers and streams empty into the Red River, which begins south of Amarillo, Texas, as the Prairie Dog Town Fork and eventually terminates in the Mississippi River in Louisiana. Numerous official wildlife conservation and recreation areas and parks, both in Oklahoma and Texas, exist along the river's path upstream of Texoma and around the lake in Basin 21. Many more such federal and state lands dot Basin 1 north of the Red River. In all, these four basins constitute 2,651 square miles, including 1,691 square miles in Basin 21. The average annual flow of the Red River, estimated at the bottom of Basin 1 in far southeastern Oklahoma, is 12,718 cfs; this substantial flow is available almost 28 percent of the time.

Lake Texoma, Oklahoma's largest reservoir by storage and one of the largest man-made lakes in the U.S., occupies a significant portion of the mainstem of the Red River in Bryan County. Construction of the lake and Denison Dam was completed by the USACE in 1944. Texoma's water supply storage/yield is shared evenly by the States of Oklahoma and Texas. Provisions of the Red River Compact—authorized by Congress in 1955 on behalf of member states Oklahoma, Arkansas, Louisiana and Texas—dictate how much water from the river and its tributaries each signatory state is allowed to develop or store.

Due to its high chloride content, little of Texoma Lake's supply is used in Oklahoma. However, the salty water supports a robust striper fishery. The Washita River and Pennington Creek, its tributary, combine to form the distinct northern arm of the lake, including the Cumberland Pool, which is part of the Tishomingo National Wildlife Refuge. Established in 1946, the refuge now encompasses some 16,464 acres which attract a large number and variety of waterfowl. The OWRB reports that 160,089 AFY of Texoma's yield is available for new permits in Oklahoma.

Lake Murray, which straddles the Love/Carter County line south of Ardmore on Anadarche Creek, was built by the State of Oklahoma in 1937. Like Texoma, the lake is an extremely popular tourism destination. In 1997, Lake Murray State Park became the first Oklahoma state park to be listed on the National Register of Historic Places. The entire yield of Lake Murray is currently appropriated.

Within the four basins comprising the Red River watershed of the Nations' lands, six species are listed as endangered: the piping plover, Ouachita rock pocketbook, red-cockaded woodpecker, scaleshell mussel, whooping crane and winged mapleleaf. The American burying beetle, leopard darter, northern long-eared bat, rabbitsfoot and red knot are threatened.

The Red River within the Nations' territories spans the Cross Timbers, East Central Texas Plains and South Central Plains ecoregions. Lake Murray and its watershed is designated as Sensitive Public and Private Water Supplies (SWS). The lake itself is oligotrophic with excellent clarity. In Pennington Creek, a 37-mile tributary of the Washita River in Johnston County, ecological diversity is high; the creek is designated as High Quality Waters (HQW). The Red River, including Lake Texoma, exhibits high salinity and stream clarity is poor with elevated turbidity. Many tributaries of the Red River in this watershed exhibit elevated bacteria levels. TMDLs for bacteria and turbidity have been completed for several streams, including Pennington Creek, which was recently removed from the state's impaired waters list.

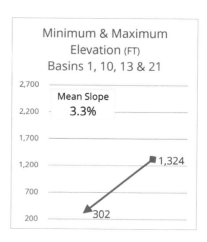

Minimum & Maximum Elevation (FT) Basins 1, 10, 13 & 21

Mean Slope 3.3%

2,700
2,200
1,700
1,200
700
200

1,324
302

PRINCIPAL RIVERS & STREAMS
BASINS 1, 10, 13 & 21

River/Stream	Length MILES
Red River	393
Washita River	71
Island Bayou	41
Hickory Creek	41
Pennington Creek	37
Mill Creek	36
Whitegrass Creek	30
Red Creek	17
Oil Creek	16
Glasses Creek	16
Waterhole Creek	16
Horse Creek	15
Norwood Creek	14
West Anadarche Creek	12
Spring Creek	11
Fleetwood Creek	11
Sandy Creek	10

PRINCIPAL LAKES
BASINS 1, 10, 13 & 21

Name	Stream	Authority	Normal Elevation FEET	Normal Area ACRES	Normal Capacity AC-FT	Shoreline MILES	Purpose(s)[1]	Water Supply Storage AC-FT	Water Supply Yield AC-FT/YR
1908 Cutt-off	Red River TR	—	—	56	—	3	—	—	—
Bryarly	Red River TR	—	—	56	—	2.6	—	—	—
Carter	Glasses Creek	City of Madill	831	108	990	3	WS, R	—	—
Charles	Red River TR	—	—	88	—	2.4	—	—	—
Clear 1	Red River TR	—	—	84	—	3.2	—	—	—
Clear 2	Red River TR	—	—	84	—	3.7	—	—	—
Colbert	Red River TR	—	—	51	—	2	—	—	—
Fish Pond	Red River TR	—	—	75	—	3.5	—	—	—
Forty One Cutt-off	Red River TR	—	—	247	—	7.9	—	—	—
Goddard (C.B.)	Oil Creek	CB Goddard	—	91	184	2.3	—	—	—
Grassy 1	Red River TR	—	—	59	—	2.2	—	—	—
Murray	Anadarche Creek	State of Okla.	750	5,458	153,250	80.8	R	111,921	1,008
Leeper 1	Red River TR	—	—	168	—	2.7	—	—	—
Madill	Red River TR	City of Madill	—	218	3,000	3.7	—	—	—
Mintubbe	Red River TR	—	—	45	—	1.8	—	—	—
Oteka	Washita River TR	Dan V & P. Little	—	54	380	2.3	—	—	—
Red	Red River TR	—	—	65	—	2.5	—	—	—
Roebuck	Red River TR	—	—	139	—	5	—	—	—
Texoma[2]	Red River	USACE	617	74,686	2,516,232	495.4	FC, WS, HP, LF, R	150,000	168,000
Whitegrass-Waterhole Creek #6	Waterhole Creek	SCS/Goolsby Ranch	—	56	302	1.5	FC	—	—
Van Sickle Bros. 1	Red River TR	JD Vansickle	—	75	247	2.9	—	—	—
Ward	Norwood Creek TR	—	—	331	—	4.3	—	—	—

[1]WS=Water Supply, R=Recreation, HP=Hydroelectric Power, IR=Irrigation, WQ=Water Quality, FW=Fish & Wildlife, FC=Flood Control, LF=Low Flow Regulation, N=Navigation, C=Conservation, CW=Cooling Water

[2]Reservoir utilizes seasonal operations plan.

LAND COVER & USES
RED RIVER WATERSHED

Use	Area SQ. MI.
Forest	721
Herbaceous, Shrubs, Woody Wetlands	960
Cultivated Land, Hay/Pasture	695
Developed	108
Water	148
Barren Land	19
Total Land Area	**2,651**

Land Cover & Uses
Red River Watershed (A)

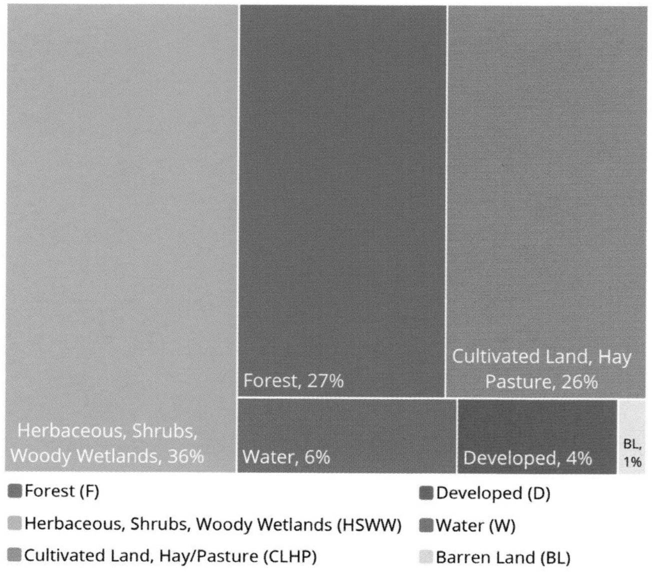

Forest, 27%

Cultivated Land, Hay Pasture, 26%

Herbaceous, Shrubs, Woody Wetlands, 36%

Water, 6%

Developed, 4%

BL, 1%

- Forest (F)
- Herbaceous, Shrubs, Woody Wetlands (HSWW)
- Cultivated Land, Hay/Pasture (CLHP)
- Developed (D)
- Water (W)
- Barren Land (BL)

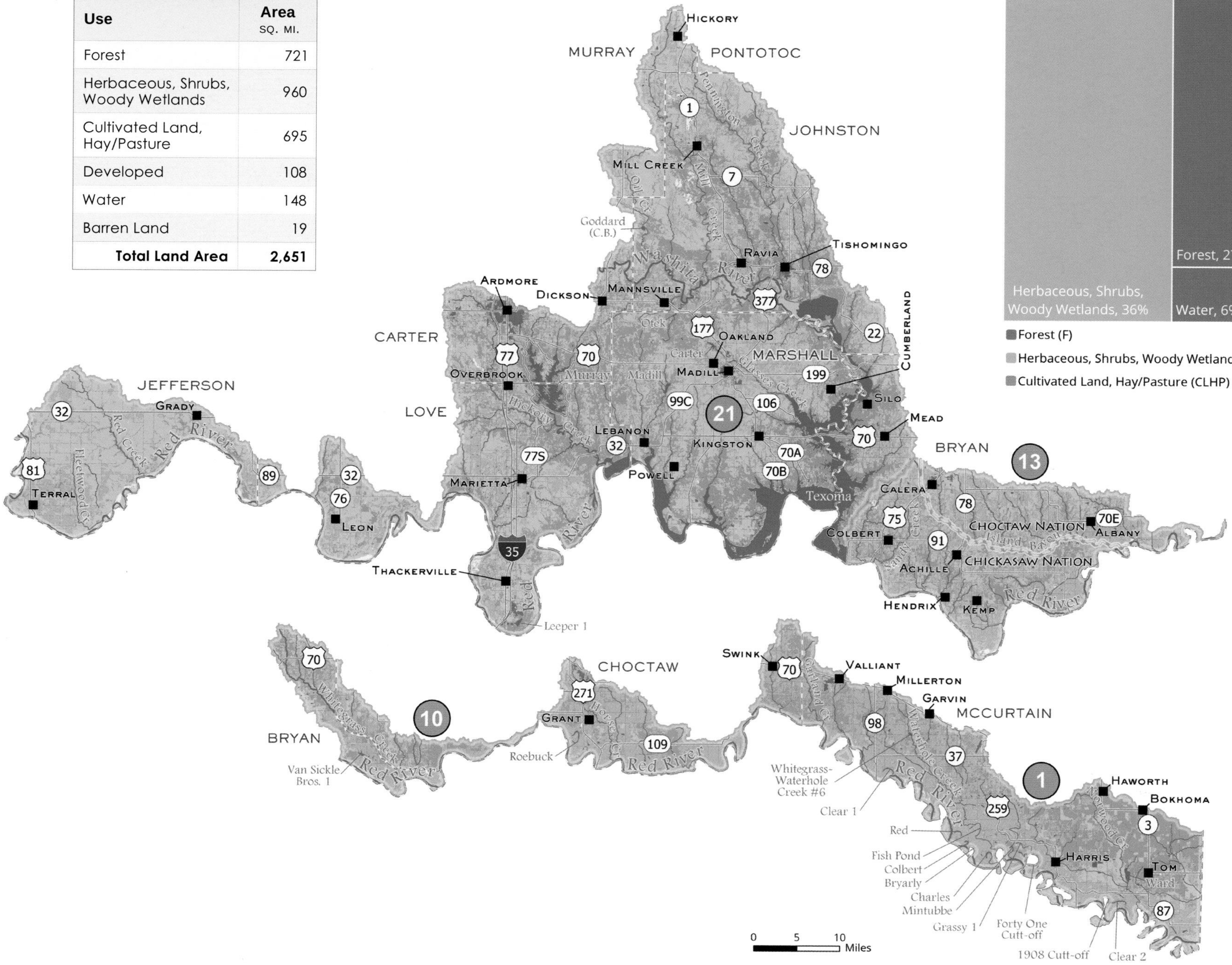

The Antlers aquifer extends beneath virtually the entire Red River watershed—almost 2,000 square miles. The aquifer supplies 1,454 permitted and domestic wells in the region. The Red River alluvium and terrace accounts for a 977-square-mile area and 627 wells. The third major aquifer in the watershed, the Arbuckle-Simpson, occupies a large portion of northern Basin 21 east and south of Sulphur. It serves as an important supply for local users. The most significant of several minor groundwater basins, the Woodbine underlies all four Red River basins and serves as the source, in conjunction with the deeper Antlers aquifer, for some 758 wells.

Groundwater Wells
- Domestic (2,359)
- Permitted (925)

Major Aquifers
- Antlers (An)
- Arbuckle-Simpson (AS)
- Red River (Re)

Overlying Aquifers
- Antlers (Ar) & Red River (Re)

NOTE: Significant color and shading variations may be apparent in areas where one aquifer overlies another. In some cases, for state administrative purposes, aquifer boundaries align directly with county lines or related political borders rather than geologic outcrop areas.

0   5   10
Miles

MAJOR & MINOR AQUIFERS
BASINS 1, 10, 13 & 21

Aquifer	Area in Basin/ Watershed SQUARE MILES	EPS[1] AC-FT/ACRE	Number of Permitted & Domestic Wells in Basin/ Watershed[2]
Antlers	1,966	2.1	1,454
Arbuckle-Simpson	186	0.2	96
Haworth	19	1.0	0
Marietta	149	2.0	91
Red River	977	2.0	627
Texoma	25	2.0	56
Woodbine	1,266	2.0	758
Nondelineated Source Wells			202
Total Wells			**3,284**

[1]Italic number signifies unstudied aquifers with a default temporary equal proportionate share (EPS) of 2.0 acre-feet per acre of land.

[2]Some wells double-counted where one aquifer overlies another.

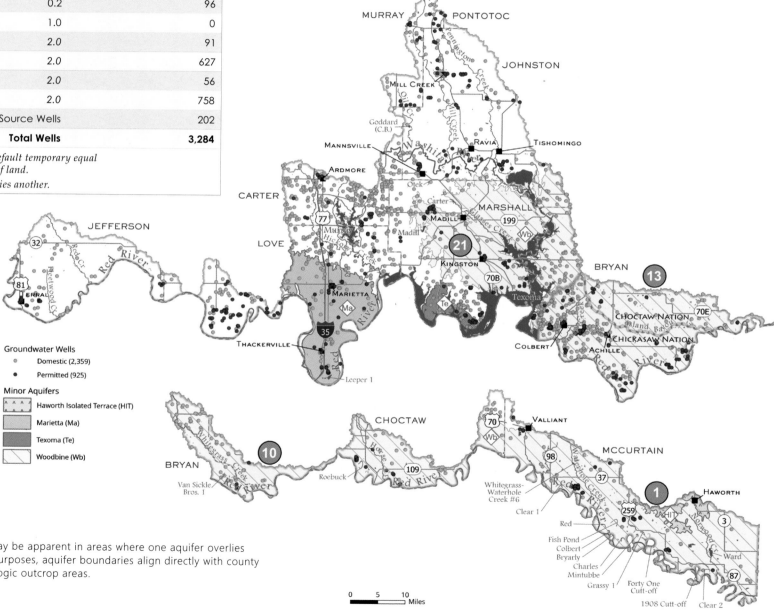

Groundwater Wells
- Domestic (2,359)
- Permitted (925)

Minor Aquifers
- Haworth Isolated Terrace (HIT)
- Marietta (Ma)
- Texoma (Te)
- Woodbine (Wb)

NOTE: Significant color and shading variations may be apparent in areas where one aquifer overlies another. In some cases, for state administrative purposes, aquifer boundaries align directly with county lines or related political borders rather than geologic outcrop areas.

0   5   10 Miles

The ratio of permitted water sources among the four basins within the Red River watershed is 61 percent (94,561 AFY) surface water to 39 percent (60,502 AFY) groundwater. Irrigation accounts for 44 percent of permitted uses, followed by public supply (21 percent) and oil, gas and mining (19 percent). A relatively large amount of this water (11 percent) is utilized for recreation, fish and wildlife uses.

The Oklahoma Department of Tourism and Recreation (ODTR) is the largest permitted water user in the Red River watershed. ODTR holds surface water rights totaling 12,938 AFY, primarily for recreation, fish & wildlife purposes in Carter County (Basin 21), but also for public water supply from Texoma (Marshall County). Among the watershed's larger water suppliers, the City of Tishomingo and Madill Public Works Authority have surface water permits amounting to 8,144 and 3,442 AFY, respectively, both in Basin 21. Three companies hold relatively substantial oil, gas and mining rights from surface sources: Ritchey Materials Company (4,839 AFY, Basin 13), Redi-Mix LLC (4,787 AFY, Basin 21) and Lattimore Materials Corporation (4,023 AFY, Basin 21). The watershed also includes a number of permitted irrigators. Chief among these is KD Holdings with three permits totaling 8,690 AFY from both surface and groundwater sources in Basin 13.

Any application to appropriate water for use at a location outside of Basin 1, 10, 13 or 21 could be subject to conferral, depending upon the application amount, mean available flow and other relevant factors. See conditions associated with Class A Basins in the Tribal-State Water Settlement agreement in the *Oka Holisso* appendix.

PERMITTED WATER AFY		
BASIN 1		
Groundwater	Surface Water	Total
7,836	3,227	**11,063**
BASIN 10		
Groundwater	Surface Water	Total
5,592	7,184	**12,776**
BASIN 13		
Groundwater	Surface Water	Total
10,264	22,889	**33,153**
BASIN 21		
Groundwater	Surface Water	Total
36,810	61,261	**98,071**
WATERSHED TOTAL		
Groundwater	Surface Water	Total
60,502	**94,561**	**155,063**

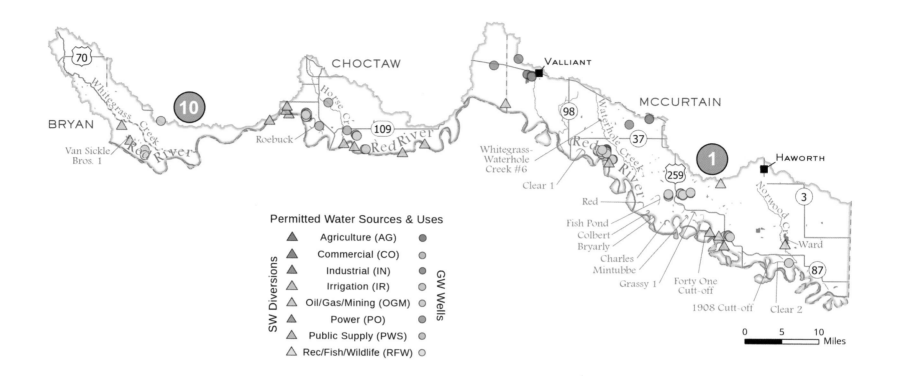

Permitted Water Sources & Uses

SW Diversions

- ▲ Agriculture (AG)
- ▲ Commercial (CO)
- ▲ Industrial (IN)
- ▲ Irrigation (IR)
- ▲ Oil/Gas/Mining (OGM)
- ▲ Power (PO)
- ▲ Public Supply (PWS)
- ▲ Rec/Fish/Wildlife (RFW)

GW Wells

- ● Agriculture (AG)
- ● Commercial (CO)
- ● Industrial (IN)
- ● Irrigation (IR)
- ● Oil/Gas/Mining (OGM)
- ● Power (PO)
- ● Public Supply (PWS)
- ○ Rec/Fish/Wildlife (RFW)

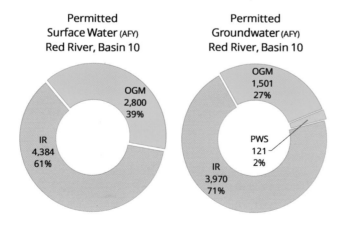

Permitted Surface Water (AFY) Red River, Basin 10

- OGM 2,800 39%
- IR 4,384 61%

Permitted Groundwater (AFY) Red River, Basin 10

- OGM 1,501 27%
- PWS 121 2%
- IR 3,970 71%

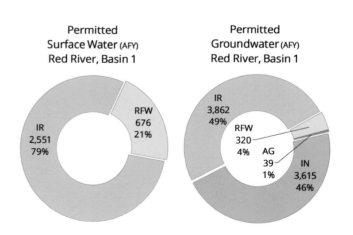

Permitted Surface Water (AFY) Red River, Basin 1

- RFW 676 21%
- IR 2,551 79%

Permitted Groundwater (AFY) Red River, Basin 1

- IR 3,862 49%
- RFW 320 4%
- AG 39 1%
- IN 3,615 46%

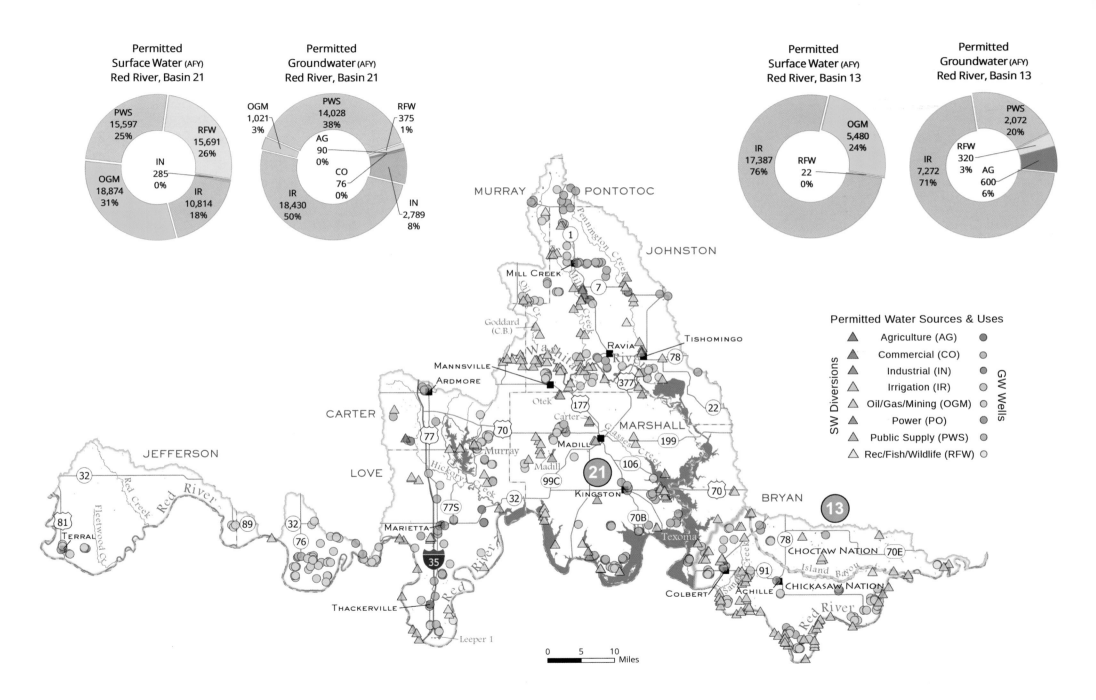

Permitted Surface Water (AFY) Red River, Basin 21
- PWS 15,597 25%
- RFW 15,691 26%
- IR 10,814 18%
- OGM 18,874 31%
- IN 285 0%

Permitted Groundwater (AFY) Red River, Basin 21
- OGM 1,021 3%
- PWS 14,028 38%
- RFW 375 1%
- AG 90 0%
- CO 76 0%
- IR 18,430 50%
- IN 2,789 8%

Permitted Surface Water (AFY) Red River, Basin 13
- OGM 5,480 24%
- IR 17,387 76%
- RFW 22 0%

Permitted Groundwater (AFY) Red River, Basin 13
- PWS 2,072 20%
- RFW 320 3%
- AG 600 6%
- IR 7,272 71%

Permitted Water Sources & Uses

SW Diversions / GW Wells
- Agriculture (AG)
- Commercial (CO)
- Industrial (IN)
- Irrigation (IR)
- Oil/Gas/Mining (OGM)
- Power (PO)
- Public Supply (PWS)
- Rec/Fish/Wildlife (RFW)

0 5 10 Miles

Users in the Red River watershed are supplied by a number of water systems with particularly large service areas. Ardmore, whose area includes a portion of Basin 21, is the most notable provider in the watershed with 25,060 residential customers, not including those served through sales to Southern Oklahoma Water Corporation (SOWC), which includes 14,000 southern Oklahoma users, and Lone Grove.

Marshall County Water Corporation serves 14,717 in Basin 21 along the Red River and a considerable distance north, including the Lake Texoma area. With a large service area of approximately 441 square miles, the corporation's supply comes from Lakes Rex Smith and Oteka. Other significant water providers serving users in the two western Red River basins include Bryan Co. Rural Water Sewer and Solid Waste Management District #2 (9,055 customers), Bryan County Rural Water and Sewer District #5 (8,250), Jefferson Co. Conservation RWD #1 (8,276) and Idabel PWA (6,952). Hugo Municipal Authority (5,536 customers) serves a portion of Basin 10. McCurtain Co. RWDs #7 and #1 are the predominant providers in Basin 1; both purchase water from Broken Bow PWA in the adjacent Upper Little River watershed.

The City of Tishomingo, which utilizes Pennington Creek as well as an emergency interconnection with Murray State College for its 3,100 customers, has been particularly impacted by recent drought. Both its sole surface water source and treatment plant are generally unreliable, especially as the community is experiencing robust growth. Johnston Co. RWD #3, whose service area surrounds Tishomingo, is also experiencing unprecedented growth as it has tripled its size in the last thirty years. The district is currently pursuing additional water rights to supplement its wells in the Arbuckle-Simpson aquifer.

System	Residential Customers Served[1]	Source(s) of Supply[2]	Water Sales	Water Purchases	Facilities[3]				
					Intake	Pump Facility	Storage	Treatment Plant	Well or Spring
Achille	506	GW	—	—					3
Ardmore	25,060	SW	Lone Grove, SOWC	Arbuckle Lake MCD, SOWC					
Bryan Co. RWS & SWMD #2	9,055	SW/GW	Bryan Co. #5	Durant UA					
Bryan Co. RW&SD #5	8,250	GW	Bokchito, Bryan Co. #7, Calera PWA, Colbert PUA	Bryan Co. RWS&SWMD #2, Durant UA					
Bryan Co. RWD #7	302	GW	—	Bryan Co. RW&SD #5					
Bryan Co. RWD #9	820	GW	—	—					3
Buckhorn RWD #2	1,260	P (GW)	—	Murray Co. #1, Sulphur					
Calera PWA	2,164	GW	—	Bryan Co. RW&SD #5					5
Choctaw Co. RWD #1	2,300	GW	—	Hugo MA					7
Choctaw Co. RWD #2	373	P (SW)	—	Valliant PWA					
Colbert PUA	2,312	GW	—	Bryan Co. RW&SD #5					9
Garvin	150	P (SW)	—	Broken Bow PWA, McCurtain Co. #7					
Haworth PWA	354	P (SW)	—	Broken Bow PWA, McCurtain Co. #1					
Hugo MA	5,536	SW	Choctaw Co. #1, Choctaw Co. RWSG & SWMD #3	—					
Idabel PWA	6,952	SW	—	Broken Bow PWA					
Jefferson Co. RWD #1	8,276	GW	Healdton, Ringling, Ryan UA, Stephens Co. #4, Terral, Wilson MA	Comanche PWA, Duncan PUA, Stephens Co. #4, Waurika PWA, Wilson MA					
Johnston Co. RWD #3	2,783	GW	Milburn PWA, Ravia	—					6
Kingston PWA	1,600	GW	—	Marshall Co. Water Corp.					4
Leon RWD #1 (Love Co.)	300	GW	—	—					2
Lone Grove	4,863	GW	—	Ardmore					

PUBLIC WATER SUPPLY SYSTEMS
BASINS 1, 10, 13 & 21

System	Residential Customers Served[1]	Source(s) of Supply[2]	Water Sales	Water Purchases	Facilities[3] Intake	Pump Facility	Storage	Treatment Plant	Well or Spring
Madill	3,410	SW	Marshall Co. Water Corp., Oakland PWA	Marshall Co. Water Corp.	1			1	
Mannsville PWA	587	GW	—	Marshall Co. Water Corp.					4
Marietta PWA	2,626	GW	—	—					5
Marshall County Water Corp.	14,717	SW/GW	Kingston PWA, Madill, Mannsville PWA	Madill	2			2	2
McCurtain Co. RWD #1	3,842	P (SW)	Haworth PWA	Broken Bow PWA					
McCurtain Co. RWD #2	755	P (SW)	—	Broken Bow PWA					
McCurtain Co. RWD #7	1,847	P (SW)	Garvin	Broken Bow PWA					
Milburn PWA	317	P (GW)	—	Johnston Co. #3					1
Mill Creek	310	GW	—	—					4
Murray Co. RWD #1	4,500	GW	Buckhorn #2, Dougherty	Sulphur					4
Oakland PWA	1,050	P (SW)	—	Madill					
Ravia	459	GW	—	Johnston Co. #3					7
Ryan UA	800	P (SW)	—	Jefferson Co. #1, Waurika PWA					
Southern Okla. Water Corp.	14,000	SW/GW	Ardmore	Ardmore	1			1	3
Terral	386	GW	—	Jefferson Co. #1					4
Thackerville	2,000	GW	—	—					5
Tishomingo MA	3,100	SW	—	—	1			1	
Valliant PWA	971	P (SW)	Choctaw Co. #2	Broken Bow PWA					

[1]Does not include wholesale customers served through water sales.

[2]GW = Groundwater; SW = Surface Water; P = Purchased.

[3]Includes both active and inactive (mostly wells) facilities in the watershed. Treatment plants include only those utilizing conventional water treatment and do not include chlorination stations associated with discrete source treatment.

Data: Oklahoma Department of Environmental Quality, Safe Drinking Water Information System, OWRB GIS and Arbuckle-Simpson Aquifer Drought Contingency Plan. Listed system facilities include those with service areas and/or facilities within relevant watershed.

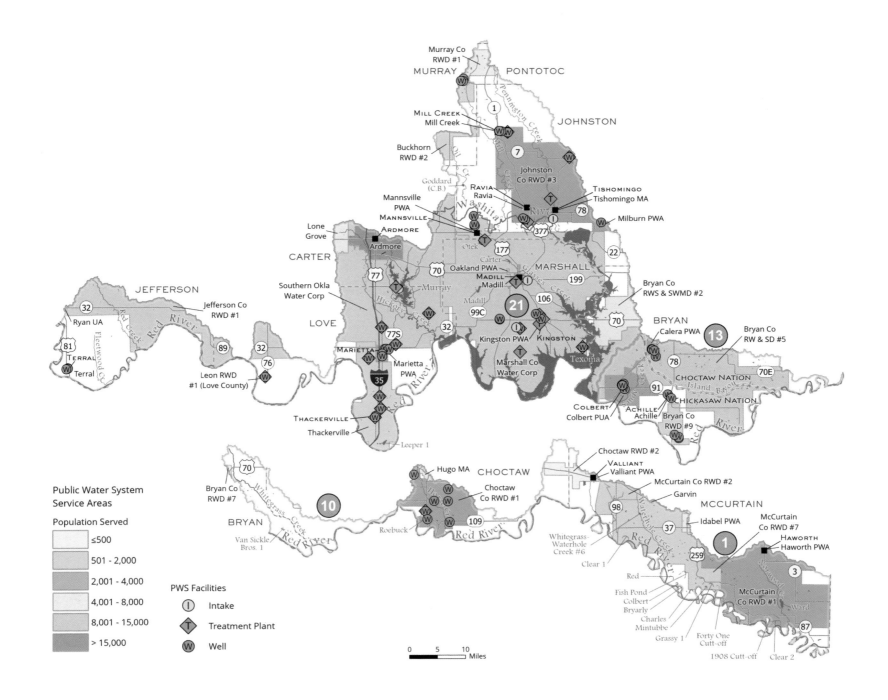

Public Water System Service Areas

Population Served

- ≤500
- 501 - 2,000
- 2,001 - 4,000
- 4,001 - 8,000
- 8,001 - 15,000
- > 15,000

PWS Facilities

- (I) Intake
- (T) Treatment Plant
- (W) Well

0 5 10 Miles

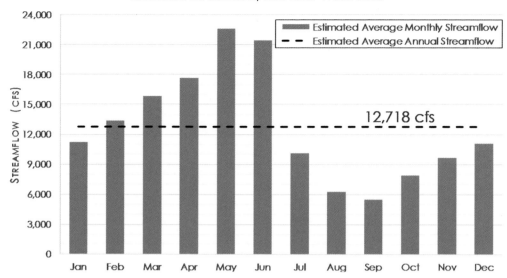

Estimated Streamflow, Red River Watershed

12,718 cfs

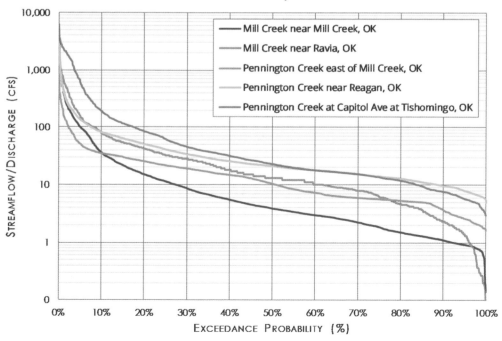

Streamflow Exceedance Probability, Red River Watershed

Reservoir Level Exceedance for Lake Texoma (Seasonal Operations)

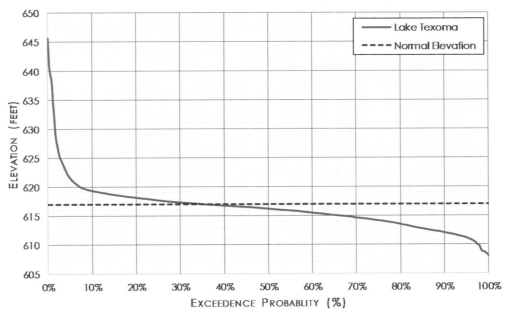

Streamflow Exceedance Probability, Red River Watershed

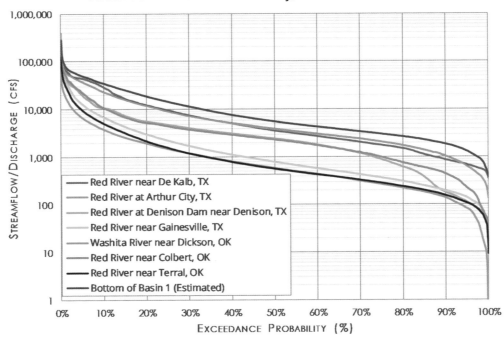

Walnut Bayou

BASIN 22

Basin 22 — Healdton City Lake

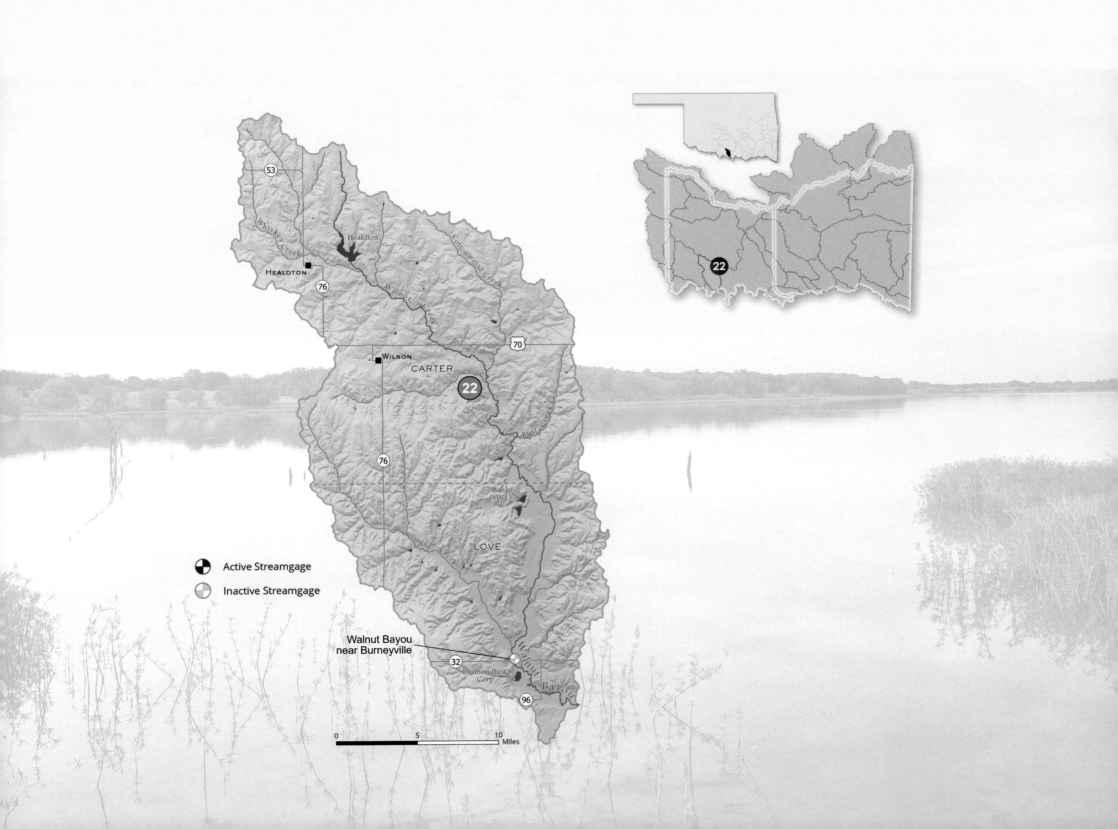

Active Streamgage

Inactive Streamgage

Walnut Bayou
near Burneyville

Whisky Creek

Healdton

HEALDTON

Cottonwood Creek

Walnut Creek

Wilson

CARTER

22

Bull Creek

Banks
(W.I.)

Simon Creek

LOVE

Diamondhead
Corp.

Walnut Bayou

53

76

70

76

32

96

22

0   5   10
                         Miles

Walnut Bayou—as well as its main tributary, Walnut Creek—has its source in Carter County. The stream flows predominantly south through Basin 22 to Walnut Bayou's confluence with the Red River in Love County. The watershed's total land area is 334 square miles. The average annual flow of Walnut Bayou, estimated at the bottom of Basin 22, is 39 cfs; this flow is available almost 11 percent of the time.

Healdton Lake, on Walnut Creek in the upper end of Basin 22, is a municipal supply for its nearby namesake city to the west of the impoundment. The lake currently contains 1,527 AFY of yield available for appropriation.

Within Basin 22, endangered species include the piping plover and whooping crane. The red knot, a shorebird, is threatened.

Water Quality

Walnut Bayou is within the Western Cross Timbers ecoregion where stream substrates typically vary between sand and firm clay, with many rocky riffles that are composed of boulders, cobbles and/or gravel. Average conductivity of the stream is high; fish and wildlife propagation and primary body contact recreation uses are impaired due to low dissolved oxygen and elevated bacteria. Sources of these impairments include riparian and rangeland grazing, wildlife and septic systems. Various drought-related issues also cause negative impacts for water users and related resources. Healdton Lake is mesotrophic with low clarity.

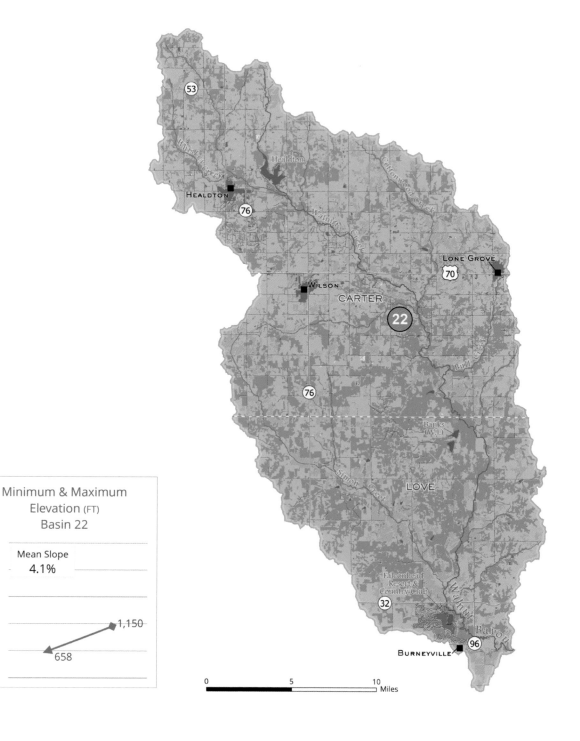

Minimum & Maximum Elevation (FT) Basin 22

Mean Slope 4.1%

2,700

2,200

1,700

1,200 — 1,150

700 — 658

200

Land Cover & Uses
Walnut Bayou Watershed (A)

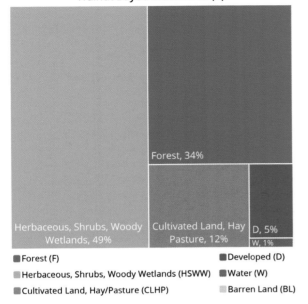

Forest, 34%

Herbaceous, Shrubs, Woody Wetlands, 49%

Cultivated Land, Hay Pasture, 12%

D, 5%

W, 1%

- Forest (F)
- Herbaceous, Shrubs, Woody Wetlands (HSWW)
- Cultivated Land, Hay/Pasture (CLHP)
- Developed (D)
- Water (W)
- Barren Land (BL)

LAND COVER & USES
WALNUT BAYOU WATERSHED

Use	Area SQ. MI.
Forest	112
Herbaceous, Shrubs, Woody Wetlands	163
Cultivated Land, Hay/Pasture	41
Developed	16
Water	2
Barren Land	0
Total Land Area	**334**

PRINCIPAL RIVERS & STREAMS
BASIN 22

River/Stream	Length MILES
Walnut Bayou	29
Walnut Creek	19
Simon Creek	16
Cottonwood Creek	11
Whiskey Creek	11

PRINCIPAL LAKES
BASIN 22

Name	Stream	Authority	Normal Elevation FEET	Normal Area ACRES	Normal Capacity AC-FT	Shoreline MILES	Purpose(s)[1]	Water Supply Storage AC-FT	Water Supply Yield AC-FT/YR
Banks (W.J.)	Walnut Bayou TR	Phillip E & Carol Green	—	66	110	1.6	—	—	—
Diamondhead Corp.	Walnut Bayou TR	Falconhead POA	—	84	40	1.5	—	—	—
Healdton	Walnut Creek	City of Healdton	889	407	3,766	7.6	WS, FC, R	—	3,000

[1]*WS=Water Supply, R=Recreation, HP=Hydroelectric Power, IR=Irrigation, WQ=Water Quality, FW=Fish & Wildlife, FC=Flood Control, LF=Low Flow Regulation, N=Navigation, C=Conservation, CW=Cooling Water*

Groundwater

The Antlers and Red River aquifers, both in the southern portion of Basin 22, are the two major groundwater basins underlying the Walnut Bayou watershed. However, users of the basin's groundwater resources are mostly reliant upon the relatively large number of wells (283) tapping nondelineated underground sources, especially in the north.

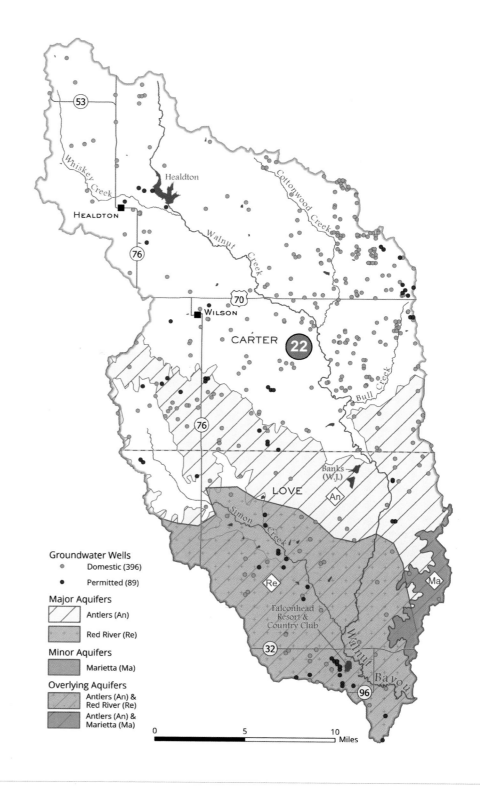

Groundwater Wells
- Domestic (396)
- Permitted (89)

Major Aquifers
- Antlers (An)
- Red River (Re)

Minor Aquifers
- Marietta (Ma)

Overlying Aquifers
- Antlers (An) & Red River (Re)
- Antlers (An) & Marietta (Ma)

MAJOR & MINOR AQUIFERS BASIN 22			
Aquifer	**Area in Basin/ Watershed** SQUARE MILES	**EPS[1]** AC-FT/ACRE	**Number of Permitted & Domestic Wells in Basin/ Watershed[2]**
Antlers	135	2.1	136
Marietta	7	2.0	2
Red River	71	2.0	64
Nondelineated Source Wells			283
Total Wells			**485**

[1]*Italic number signifies unstudied aquifers with a default temporary equal proportionate share (EPS) of 2.0 acre-feet per acre of land.*
[2]*Some wells are double-counted where one aquifer overlies another.*

NOTE: Significant color and shading variations may be apparent in areas where one aquifer overlies another. In some cases, for state administrative purposes, aquifer boundaries align directly with county lines or related political borders rather than geologic outcrop areas.

Permitted Water Use

Water permitted from groundwater sources in the Walnut Bayou watershed amounts to 15,128 AFY, about 90 percent of all water allocated and appropriated in Basin 22. Water for irrigation (10,249 AFY, or 61 percent) far outpaces all other permitted uses. Public supply accounts for 22 percent of these uses and oil, gas and mining for 12 percent.

The Noble Research Institute (NRI) is the largest water rights holder in Basin 22 with two groundwater permits for irrigation and recreation, fish and wildlife purposes in Love County totaling 3,720 AFY. NRI is a non-profit agricultural research organization that assists Oklahoma producers with soil/land management and related beneficial practices on their lands.

The City of Healdton is the largest permitted public water supplier in the watershed with 1,873 AFY of both surface and groundwater rights. The larger surface water permit allows for the diversion of water from Healdton Lake, a Soil Conservation Service (i.e., Natural Resource Conservation Service) site in the upper portion of Basin 22.

Any application to appropriate water for use at a location outside of Basin 22 could be subject to conferral, depending upon the application amount, mean available flow and other relevant factors. See conditions associated with Class A Basins in the Tribal-State Water Settlement agreement in the *Oka Holisso* appendix.

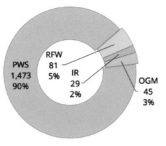

Permitted Surface Water (AFY) Walnut Bayou, Basin 22

- PWS 1,473 90%
- RFW 81 5%
- IR 29 2%
- OGM 45 3%

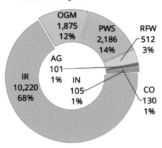

Permitted Groundwater (AFY) Walnut Bayou, Basin 22

- OGM 1,875 12%
- PWS 2,186 14%
- RFW 512 3%
- AG 101 1%
- IN 105 1%
- CO 130 1%
- IR 10,220 68%

Permitted Water Sources & Uses

SW Diversions / GW Wells

▲	Agriculture (AG)	●
▲	Commercial (CO)	●
▲	Industrial (IN)	●
▲	Irrigation (IR)	●
▲	Oil/Gas/Mining (OGM)	●
▲	Power (PO)	●
▲	Public Supply (PWS)	●
▲	Rec/Fish/Wildlife (RFW)	○

PERMITTED WATER		
AFY		
BASIN 22		
Groundwater	Surface Water	**Total**
15,128	1,628	**16,756**

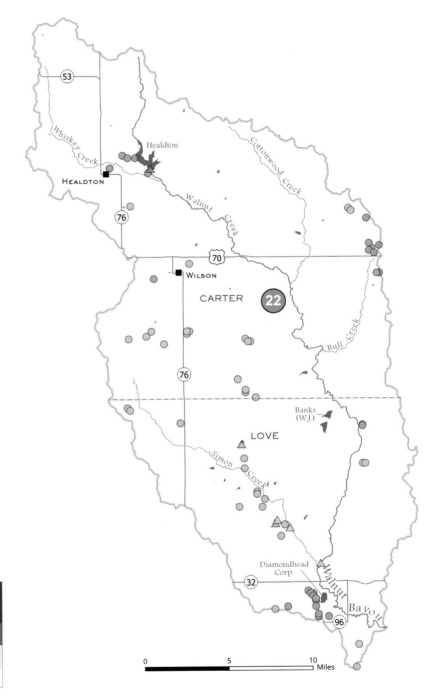

Inhabiting quite large approximated service areas, the Southern Oklahoma Water Corporation (SOWC, 14,000 residential customers) and Jefferson Co. RWD #1 (8,276 customers) are the primary suppliers in the Walnut Bayou watershed. Jefferson Co. #1, whose supply is almost exclusively derived from wells in Grady County, sells groundwater to an additional six water systems and purchases supply from several others. SOWC sells water to the City of Ardmore at their Airpark treatment plant; they also purchase water from Ardmore.

PUBLIC WATER SUPPLY SYSTEMS BASIN 22					Facilities[3]				
System	Residential Customers Served[1]	Source(s) of Supply[2]	Water Sales	Water Purchases	Intake	Pump Facility	Storage	Treatment Plant	Well or Spring
Healdton	2,785	GW/SW	—	Jefferson Co. #1	1			1	6
Jefferson Co. RWD #1	8,276	GW	Healdton, Ringling, Ryan UA, Stephens Co. #4 (Loco), Terral, Wilson MA	Comanche PWA, Duncan PUA, Stephens Co. #4 (Loco), Waurika PWA, Wilson MA					
Lone Grove	4,863	GW	—	Ardmore					7
Southern Oklahoma Water Corp.	14,000	SW/GW	Ardmore	Ardmore					
Western Carter Co. Water Corp.	658	GW	Ratliff City, West Davis RWD	Davis					
Wilson MA	1,600	GW	Jefferson Co. #1	Jefferson Co. #1					8

[1]Does not include wholesale customers served through water sales.
[2]GW = Groundwater; SW = Surface Water; P = Purchased.
[3]Includes both active and inactive (mostly wells) facilities in the watershed. Treatment plants include only those utilizing conventional water treatment and do not include chlorination stations associated with discrete source treatment.

Data: Oklahoma Department of Environmental Quality, Safe Drinking Water Information System, OWRB GIS and Arbuckle-Simpson Aquifer Drought Contingency Plan. Listed system facilities include those with service areas and/or facilities within relevant watershed.

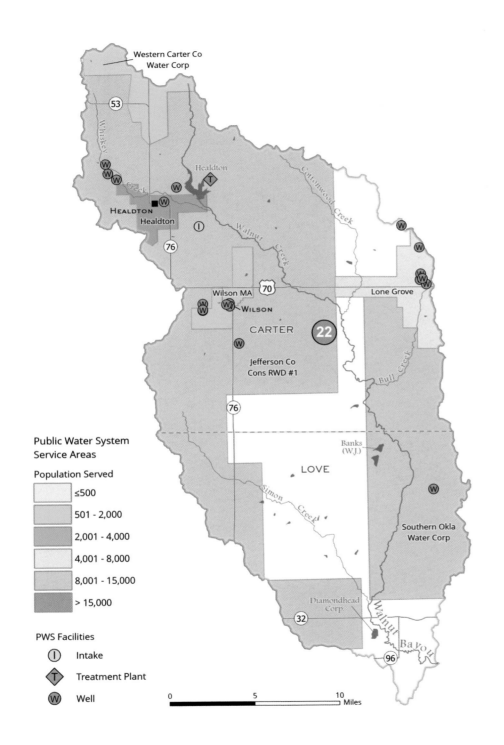

Public Water System Service Areas

Population Served

- ≤500
- 501 - 2,000
- 2,001 - 4,000
- 4,001 - 8,000
- 8,001 - 15,000
- > 15,000

PWS Facilities

- (I) Intake
- (T) Treatment Plant
- (W) Well

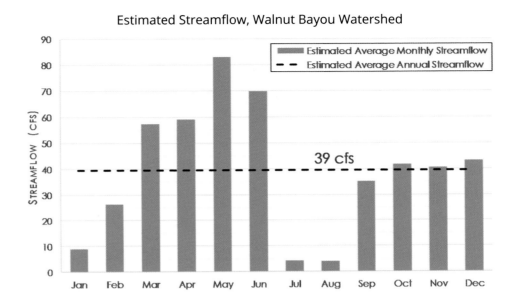

Estimated Streamflow, Walnut Bayou Watershed

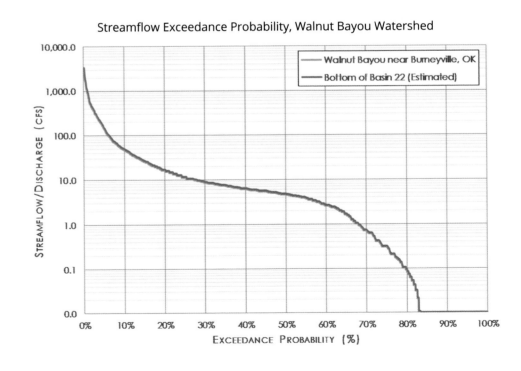

Streamflow Exceedance Probability, Walnut Bayou Watershed

Blue River

BASINS 11 & 12

Basins 11 & 12 — The Blue River, Oka Yanahli Preserve (Credit: The Nature Conservancy)

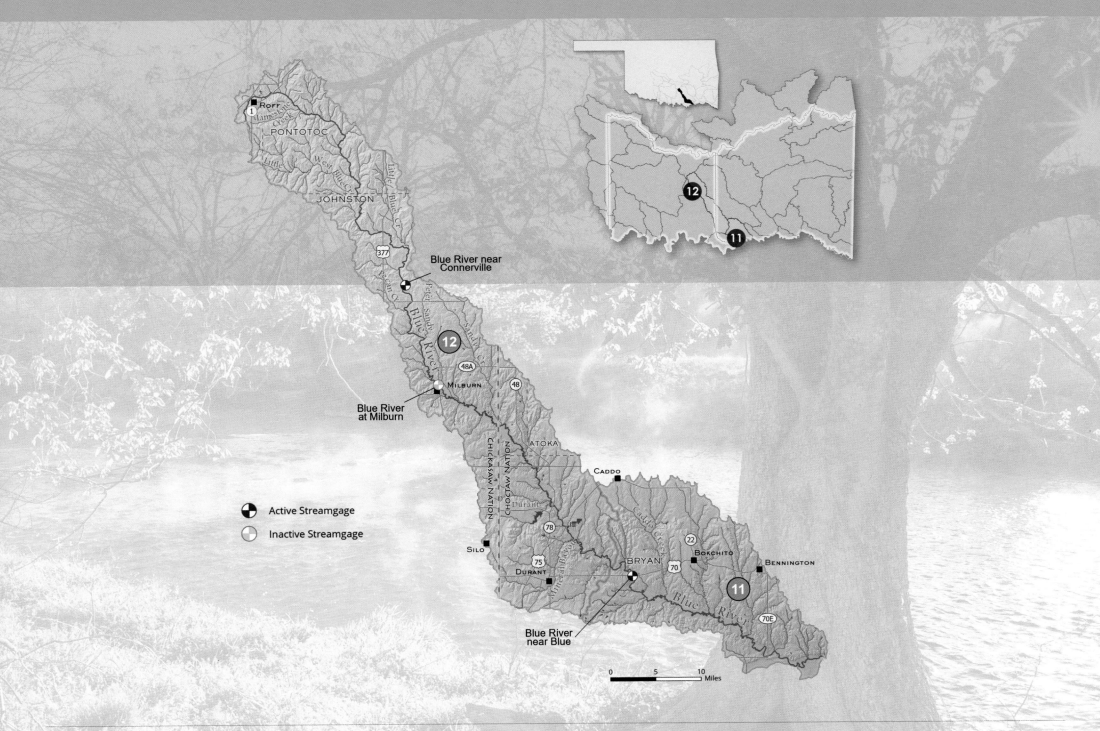

Active Streamgage

Inactive Streamgage

Blue River near
Connerville

Blue River
at Milburn

Blue River
near Blue

ROFF

PONTOTOC

JOHNSTON

Limestone Creek

Little Blue Cr

West Blue Cr

Little Blue Cr

Pecan Cr

Blue River

Peter Sandy Cr

CHICKASAW NATION

CHOCTAW NATION

ATOKA

CADDO

Durant

Caddo Creek

BOKCHITO

BENNINGTON

SILO

BRYAN

Durant

Mineral River

Blue River

377

48A

48

78

75

22

70

70E

1

12

11

12

11

0   5   10
Miles

Basins 11 and 12 collectively comprise the Blue River watershed, which spans a total land area of 687 square miles. The watershed is long and narrow with a maximum width of only fourteen miles. From its source near Roff in southwestern Pontotoc County at an elevation of 1,321 feet, the Blue River flows some 132 miles in a southeasterly direction to its confluence with the Red River in southwest Bryan County. South of Connerville, a two-mile stretch of river flows through Oka Yanahli Preserve, a cooperative conservation venture of the Nature Conservancy, Chickasaw Nation and other organizations. Further downstream in Basin 12, the Blue River encounters the Blue River Public Fishing and Hunting Area.

The Blue River is one of only two free-flowing (unregulated) rivers in the state and much of its flow is sustained and augmented by springs. The average annual flow of the river, estimated at the bottom of Basin 11, is 461 cfs; this flow is available less than 16 percent of the time.

Thirty-nine dams, which are regulated by the OWRB, have been constructed on tributaries of the Blue River; none on the mainstem. One major lake, Durant Lake, exists on the Lower Little Blue River in Bryan County (Basin 12). It provides about 10 percent of the water supply required by the City of Durant while the Blue River itself provides all other supply for city residents. Occupying 278 acres, Durant Lake serves as a supplemental source of water, but it remains largely vulnerable to drought events.

The Blue River and its exceptional ecosystem have received a great deal of attention from local, tribal, federal, and state entities in concerted efforts to protect its unique resources while enhancing water reliability for a variety of uses. Use and protection of the river is essential to local economies as it provides supply for municipal, industrial, agricultural and domestic needs. Preservation of the river's non-consumptive benefits for recreation, environmental and related needs further supplements the availability of streamflows for permits and related traditional uses of water.

Springs, which are common in the upper reaches of the Blue River and support many of the region's unique flora and fauna, are dependent upon the river's distinct hydrologic connection with the Arbuckle-Simpson aquifer. Cool waters emanating from the groundwater

PRINCIPAL RIVERS & STREAMS BASINS 11 & 12	
River/Stream	Length MILES
Blue River	132
Little West Blue Creek	19
Mineral Bayou	16
Sandy Creek	15
Caddo Creek	14
Little Blue Creek	12

PRINCIPAL LAKES BASINS 11 & 12									
Name	Stream	Authority	Normal Elevation FEET	Normal Area ACRES	Normal Capacity AC-FT	Shoreline MILES	Purpose(s)[1]	Water Supply Storage AC-FT	Water Supply Yield AC-FT/YR
Durant	Little Blue River	City of Durant	624	288	4,121	6	—	—	—

[1]WS=Water Supply, R=Recreation, HP=Hydroelectric Power, IR=Irrigation, WQ=Water Quality, FW=Fish & Wildlife, FC=Flood Control, LF=Low Flow Regulation, N=Navigation, C=Conservation, CW=Cooling Water

basin benefit numerous indigenous species, many of which are sensitive to fluctuating temperatures and streamflows. Protection of the river, its tributaries and aquifer, most notably through the recent reduction of the Arbuckle-Simpson's equal proportionate share, will help maintain the perennial nature of Blue River flows, ensure the future availability of both surface and groundwater supplies, and sustain the river's overall economic, environmental and cultural value.

Southeastern Oklahoma State University, in Durant, was founded in 1909 as Southeastern State Normal School. The city is the headquarters of the Choctaw Nation and one of Oklahoma's fastest growing communities with an estimated population of 15,856.

Two endangered species occur in the Blue watershed: the piping plover and whooping crane. Threatened species include the American burying beetle, Arkansas River shiner, northern long-eared bat and red knot.

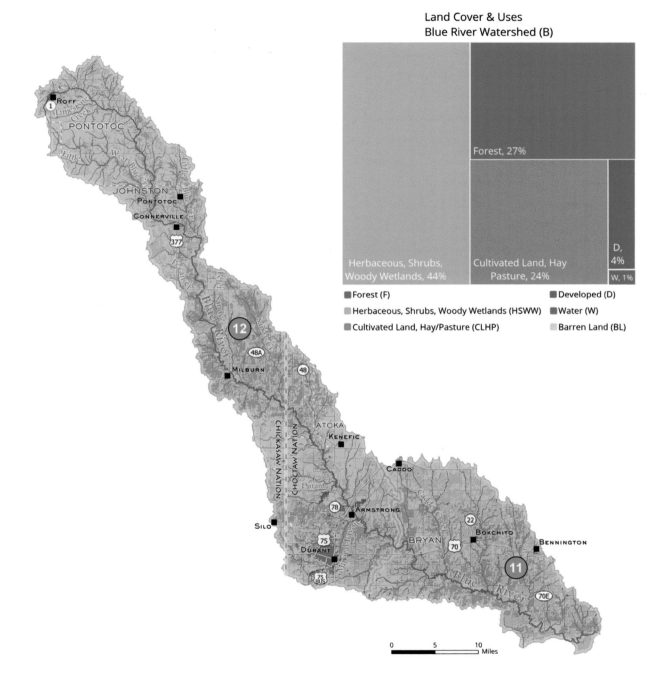

Land Cover & Uses
Blue River Watershed (B)

Forest, 27%

Herbaceous, Shrubs, Woody Wetlands, 44%

Cultivated Land, Hay Pasture, 24%

D, 4%

W, 1%

■ Forest (F)
■ Herbaceous, Shrubs, Woody Wetlands (HSWW)
■ Cultivated Land, Hay/Pasture (CLHP)
■ Developed (D)
■ Water (W)
■ Barren Land (BL)

The Blue River flows through the Cross Timbers and South Central Plains ecoregions. It alternates as a gravel/cobble/bedrock/sand system as it passes through the Arbuckle Uplift. The upper reach of the Blue River to the State Highway 7 Bridge is designated High Quality Waters (HQW). This area is considered a biodiversity hotspot containing unique habitat and a highly diverse fish community, including the orangebelly darter, which is found nowhere else in the world. In addition, the upper Blue River is home to the seaside alder, a woody plant species found only here and in coastal Maryland and Delaware.

Fishing opportunities abound in the Blue River. From November through March each year, its pristine waters support the regular stocking of rainbow trout. Only about five percent of the Blue River watershed is considered developed. Conventional agricultural land makes up about 24 percent of the total land area in Basins 11 and 12; however, the watershed's shallow, rocky soil, especially in the upper portion, has largely inhibited cultivation.

A TMDL for enterococcus has been completed for the lower reaches of the Blue River, where the substrate is dominated by silt. Tributaries to the lower Blue River—Caddo Creek, Bokchito Creek and Sulphur Creek—are also impaired for Primary Body Contact Recreation due to elevated levels of bacteria. Water clarity is good to excellent throughout the watershed.

Due to less nutrient-enrichment, much of the watershed is oligotrophic with low primary productivity and/or low nutrient levels.

A small portion of Ada's municipal limits extends into Basin 12 to provide access to city wells drilled into the Arbuckle-Simpson aquifer, but the system primarily serves the Lower Canadian and Clear Boggy watersheds in Basins 56 and 9. Pontotoc Co. RWD #8 purchases its entire supply—via Mill Spring, in the adjacent Clear Boggy Creek watershed, Basin 9—from the City of Ada. Johnston Co. RWD #3, with 2,783 total residential customers, serves a large portion of the middle Blue watershed.

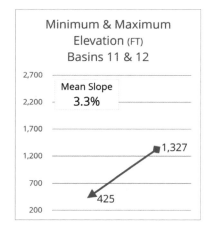

Minimum & Maximum Elevation (FT) Basins 11 & 12 — Mean Slope 3.3% — 1,327 / 425

LAND COVER & USES BLUE RIVER WATERSHED	
Use	**Area** SQ. MI.
Forest	186
Herbaceous, Shrubs, Woody Wetlands	299
Cultivated Land, Hay/Pasture	167
Developed	29
Water	4
Barren Land	0
Total Land Area	**685**

Groundwater

The Blue River watershed contains four recognized groundwater basins. About 34 percent of the total extent of the Arbuckle-Simpson aquifer, which supports much of the river's flow, underlies the northern area of the watershed in Basin 12. Extensive studies have been recently conducted on the Arbuckle-Simpson and subsequent state regulations have substantially reduced its EPS from 2.0 to 0.2 ac-ft/acre. The Chickasaw Nation continues to assist many communities who are dependent upon this vital groundwater source in adapting their water supplies and management schemes to comply with the new rules.

The Antlers and Woodbine aquifers, with outcroppings in the central and southern areas, are also important sources of water for those residing in both the watershed and region. Along with the Arbuckle-Simpson, these three sources provide both permitted water and domestic supply through more than 700 individual wells.

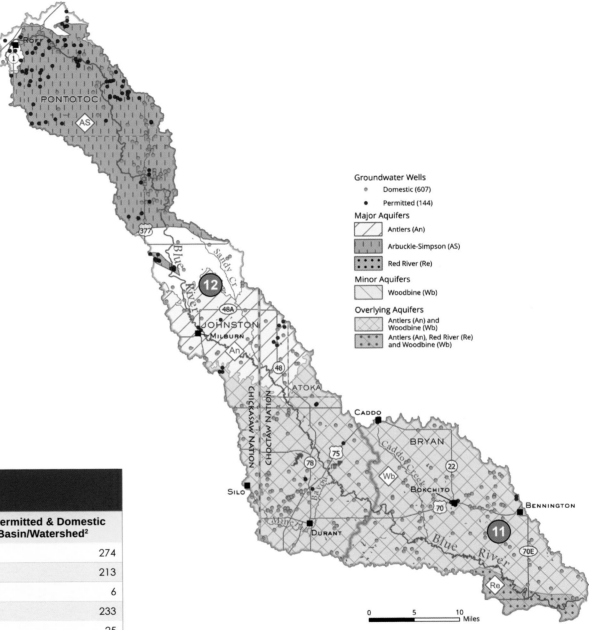

MAJOR & MINOR AQUIFERS BASINS 11 & 12			
Aquifer	**Area in Basin/Watershed** SQUARE MILES	**EPS[1]** AC-FT/ACRE	**Number of Permitted & Domestic Wells in Basin/Watershed[2]**
Antlers	474	2.1	274
Arbuckle-Simpson	158	0.2	213
Red River	19	2.0	6
Woodbine	388	2.0	233
Nondelineated Source Wells			25
Total Wells			**751**

[1]*Italic number signifies unstudied aquifers with a default temporary equal proportionate share (EPS) of 2.0 acre-feet per acre of land.*
[2]*Some wells are double-counted where one aquifer overlies another.*

NOTE: Significant color and shading variations may be apparent in areas where one aquifer overlies another. In some cases, for state administrative purposes, aquifer boundaries align directly with county lines or related political borders rather than geologic outcrop areas.

Surface sources supply 29,870 AFY, or 71 percent, of all permitted water within the Blue River watershed. Surface water permits in the watershed, entirely from the Blue River and its tributaries, appropriate almost 30,000 AFY of water, primarily for public water supply, which accounts for 53 percent of all permitted uses. However, 6,559 AFY—or 15 percent of total permitted surface water in Basins 11 and 12—is set aside expressly for recreation, fish and wildlife purposes (primarily for the Durant State Fish Hatchery). Much of the watershed's surface water, especially in Basin 11, is utilized for irrigation, which constitutes 21 percent of all uses. Six percent is associated with oil, gas and mining. Most of the groundwater allocated in the Blue watershed is assigned to public supply, including virtually all of the permitted groundwater in Basin 11.

The largest permitted surface water user in the watershed is the City of Durant, which appropriates 12,342 AFY in three permits for public water supply. The largest single permit in the watershed belongs to the ODWC authorizing 6,445 AFY of surface water for recreation, fish and wildlife uses associated with the fish hatchery. The largest permitted user of groundwater is Roos Ranch, which is allocated 2,195 AFY in three permits for public supply, oil, gas and mining, and industrial purposes. The City of Ada also holds three groundwater permits totaling 1,908 AFY, primarily for public supply.

Any application to appropriate water for use at a location outside of Basin 11 or 12 could be subject to conferral, depending upon the application amount, mean available flow and other relevant factors. See conditions associated with Class B Basins in the Tribal-State Water Settlement agreement in the *Oka Holisso* appendix.

PERMITTED WATER AFY		
BASIN 11		
Groundwater	Surface Water	Total
2,077	6,329	8,406
BASIN 12		
Groundwater	Surface Water	Total
10,364	23,541	33,905
WATERSHED TOTAL		
Groundwater	Surface Water	Total
12,441	29,870	42,311

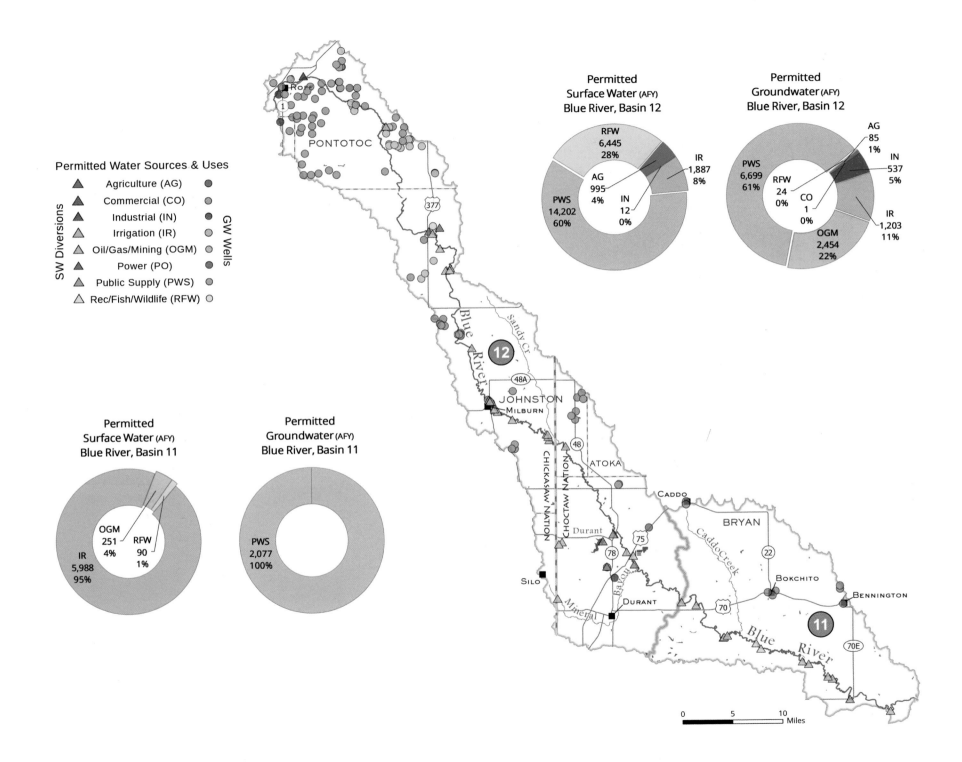

Permitted Water Sources & Uses

SW Diversions
- ▲ Agriculture (AG)
- ▲ Commercial (CO)
- ▲ Industrial (IN)
- ▲ Irrigation (IR)
- ▲ Oil/Gas/Mining (OGM)
- ▲ Power (PO)
- ▲ Public Supply (PWS)
- △ Rec/Fish/Wildlife (RFW)

GW Wells
- ● ● ● ● ● ● ● ○

Permitted
Surface Water (AFY)
Blue River, Basin 12

RFW 6,445 28%
IR 1,887 8%
AG 995 4%
IN 12 0%
PWS 14,202 60%

Permitted
Groundwater (AFY)
Blue River, Basin 12

AG 85 1%
IN 537 5%
PWS 6,699 61%
RFW 24 0%
CO 1 0%
IR 1,203 11%
OGM 2,454 22%

Permitted
Surface Water (AFY)
Blue River, Basin 11

OGM 251 4%
RFW 90 1%
IR 5,988 95%

Permitted
Groundwater (AFY)
Blue River, Basin 11

PWS 2,077 100%

The Blue River watershed includes entire or considerable portions of several large municipal and rural water supply systems, including all of Durant and its approximate 15,545 customers. The City of Durant obtains 90 percent of its water from the Blue River and 10 percent from Lake Durant.

Bryan County Rural Water and Sewer District #5, serving more than 8,000 total customers in the Blue and adjacent Red River watersheds, depends upon the City of Durant for about 95 percent of its water supply. The City also provides emergency supply for Bryan County RWS and SWMD #2, which normally depends upon the Blue River and Eagle Lake. Bryan Co. #2, serving 9,055 customers in the Blue and Red River watersheds, developed a groundwater well to address needs during the recent drought.

A small portion of Ada's municipal limits extends into Basin 12 to provide access to city wells drilled into the Arbuckle-Simpson aquifer, but the system primarily serves the Lower Canadian and Clear Boggy watersheds in Basins 56 and 9. Pontotoc Co. RWD #8 purchases its entire supply—via Mill Spring, in the adjacent Clear Boggy Creek watershed, Basin 9—from the City of Ada. Johnston Co. RWD #3, with 2,783 total residential customers, serves a large portion of the middle Blue watershed.

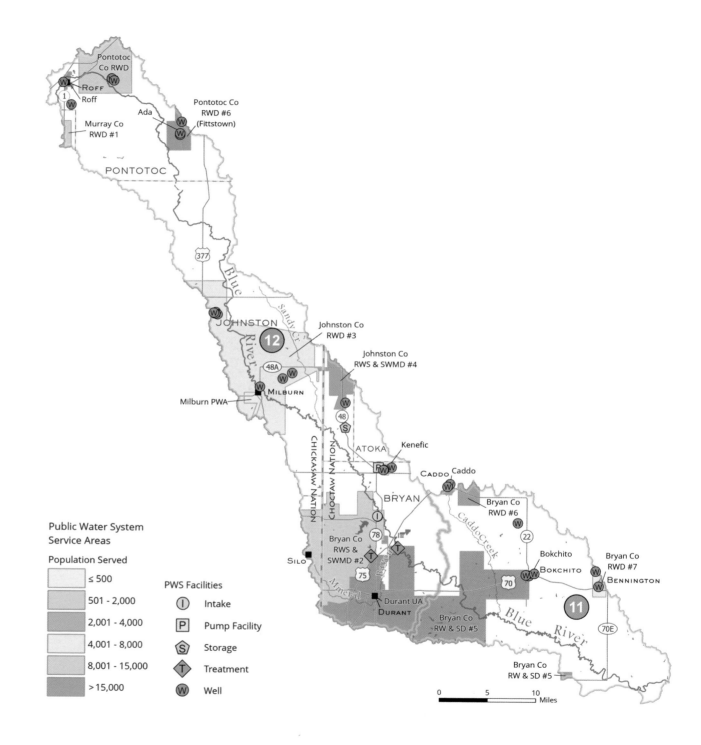

Public Water System Service Areas

Population Served

	≤ 500
	501 - 2,000
	2,001 - 4,000
	4,001 - 8,000
	8,001 - 15,000
	> 15,000

PWS Facilities

Ⓘ Intake
Ⓟ Pump Facility
Ⓢ Storage
◈ T Treatment
Ⓦ Well

System	Residential Customers Served[1]	Source(s) of Supply[2]	Water Sales	Water Purchases	Facilities[3]				
					Intake	Pump Facility	Storage	Treatment Plant	Well or Spring
Ada	37,000	GW	Pontotoc Co. RWD #1 (Homer), Pontotoc Co. #6, Pontotoc Co. #7, Pontotoc Co. #9	—					3
Bokchito	564	GW	—	Bryan Co. #5					3
Bryan Co. RWS & SWMD #2	9,055	SW/GW	Bryan Co. #5	Durant UA	1			1	
Bryan Co. RW&SD #5	8,250	GW	Bokchito, Bryan Co. #7, Calera PWA, Colbert PUA	Bryan Co. #2, Durant UA					
Bryan Co. RWD #6	990	GW	Kenefic	Caddo		1	1		1
Bryan Co. RWD #7	302	GW	—	Bryan Co. #5					3
Caddo	944	GW	Bryan Co. #6	—					2
Durant UA	15,545	SW	Bryan Co. #5, Bryan Co. #2	—	1			1	
Johnston Co. RWD #3	2,783	GW	Milburn PWA, Ravia	—					8
Johnston Co. RWS & SWMD #4	600	GW	—	—					2
Kenefic	165	GW	—	Bryan Co. #6					6
Milburn PWA	317	P (GW)	—	Johnston Co. #3					3
Murray Co. RWD #1	4,500	GW	Buckhorn #2, Dougherty	Sulphur					
Pontotoc Co. RWD #6 (Fittstown)	896	P (GW)	—	Ada					
Pontotoc Co. RWD #8	4,250	GW	Pontotoc Co. #9	Wingard Water Corp.					3
Roff	850	GW	—	—					2

[1]Does not include wholesale customers served through water sales.

[2]GW = Groundwater; SW = Surface Water; P = Purchased.

[3]Includes both active and inactive (mostly wells) facilities in the watershed. Treatment plants include only those utilizing conventional water treatment and do not include chlorination stations associated with discrete source treatment.

Data: Oklahoma Department of Environmental Quality, Safe Drinking Water Information System, OWRB GIS and Arbuckle-Simpson Aquifer Drought Contingency Plan. Listed system facilities include those with service areas and/or facilities within relevant watershed.

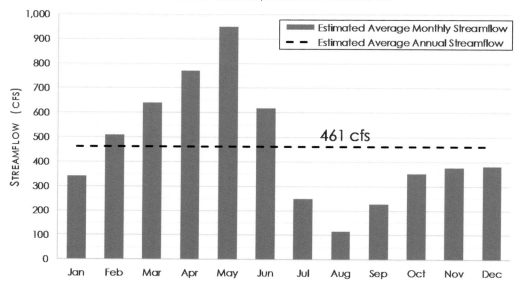

Estimated Streamflow, Blue River Watershed

461 cfs

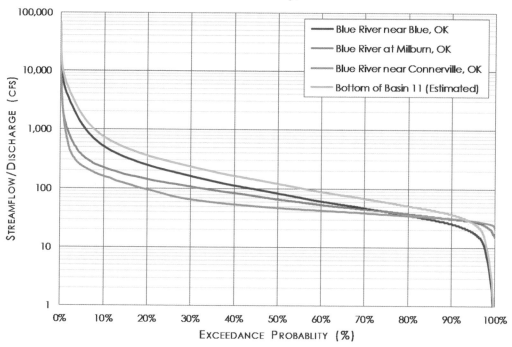

Streamflow Exceedance Probability, Blue River Watershed

Clear Boggy Creek

BASIN 9

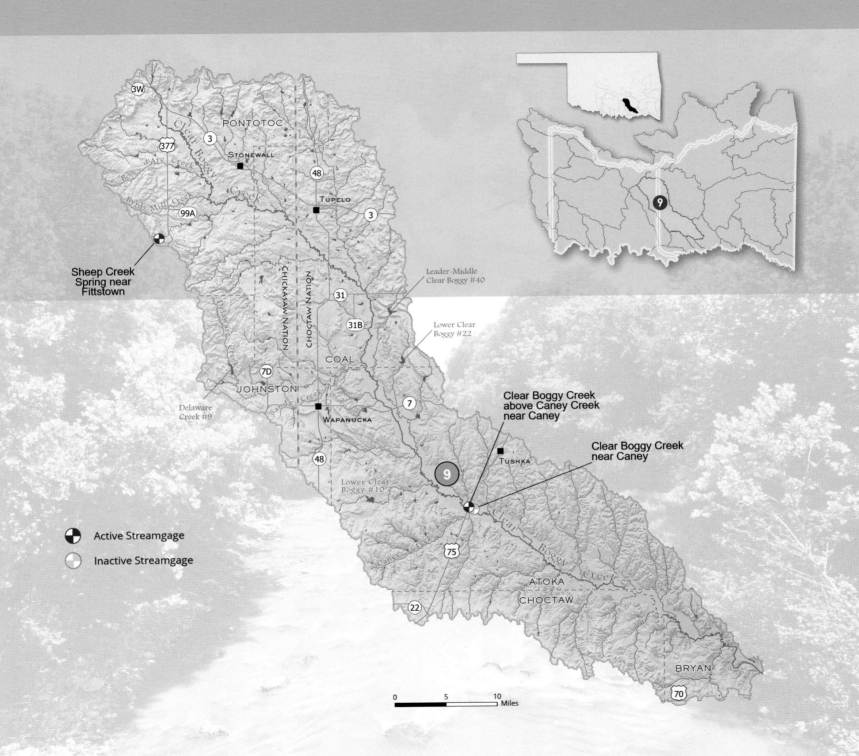

3W

PONTOTOC

377

3

Stonewall

48

Tupelo

3

99A

Byrds Mill Creek

d'Arc Creek

Clear Boggy

Creek

CHICKASAW NATION

CHOCTAW NATION

Delaware Creek

Leader-Middle
Clear Boggy #40

Lower Clear
Boggy #22

31

31B

COAL

7D

Sandy Creek

JOHNSTON

Delaware
Creek #9

WAPANUCKA

7

Sheep Creek
Spring near
Fittstown

48

Lower Clear
Boggy #10

9

Tushka

Clear Boggy Creek
above Caney Creek
near Caney

Clear Boggy Creek
near Caney

Clear Boggy Creek

75

Caney Creek

22

ATOKA

CHOCTAW

BRYAN

70

9

⊕ Active Streamgage

◒ Inactive Streamgage

0   5   10
Miles

The Clear Boggy Creek watershed, which is encompassed in Basin 9, extends over 1,003 square miles of southeastern Oklahoma. A major tributary of Muddy Boggy Creek in adjacent Basins 7 and 8 to the east, Clear Boggy has its source in central Pontotoc County, just east of Ada, where it flows predominantly to the south/southeast. At its confluence with Byrds Mill Creek about four miles southwest of Stonewall, it takes a decided turn due east as it enters Coal County before again taking a southern, then southeastern, path just east of Boggy Depot Park (formerly a state facility but now managed by the Chickasaw Nation) and through Atoka County. It eventually forms the Atoka/Bryan County line, then treks through Choctaw County before converging with Muddy Boggy Creek in Basin 7. The average annual flow of Clear Boggy Creek, estimated at the bottom of Basin 9, is 668 cfs; this flow is available about 17 percent of the time.

East Central University, located in Ada, was founded as East Central State Normal School in 1909. It houses the Oka Institute, created by the Chickasaw Nation in 2016 to facilitate regional water sustainability and management research. Ada is also the headquarters of the Chickasaw Nation.

The Clear Boggy Creek watershed contains few lakes of significant size or capacity. However, there are a number of SCS sites that control flooding in the region. Some of these could provide backup or temporary supply.

Endangered species in Basin 9 include the piping plover, scaleshell mussel, whooping crane and winged mapleleaf. Threatened species occurring in the basin are the American burying beetle, Arkansas River shiner, northern long-eared bat and red knot.

Water Quality

Clear Boggy Creek flows through the Arkansas Valley and South Central Plains ecoregions where the headwater streams are composed of a series of long pools that are interspersed with occasional, short riffle sections; larger streams are often deep and slow moving with muddy or sandy bottoms. Water clarity in the basin is average. Fish and wildlife propagation is not supported in Clear Boggy Creek due to elevated lead levels. TMDLs for bacteria have been completed for Caney Creek and for turbidity in Leader Creek.

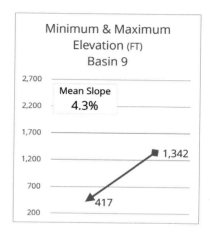

PRINCIPAL RIVERS & STREAMS BASIN 9	
River/Stream	**Length** MILES
Clear Boggy Creek	121
Delaware Creek	29
Caney Creek	13
Bois d'Arc Creek	11

| | | | PRINCIPAL LAKES | | | | | | |
| | | | BASIN 9 | | | | | | |
Name	Stream	Authority	Normal Elevation FEET	Normal Area ACRES	Normal Capacity AC-FT	Shoreline MILES	Purpose(s)[1]	Water Supply Storage AC-FT	Water Supply Yield AC-FT/YR
Caney Creek #12	Caney Creek TR	SCS/Atoka Co. CD	—	53	206	1.6	FC	—	—
Caney Creek #13	Caney Creek TR	SCS/Atoka Co. CD	—	44	77	1.6	FC	—	—
Delaware Creek #9	Delaware Creek	SCS/Johnston Co. CD	—	102	620	2.6	FC	—	—
Delaware Creek #10	Delaware Creek TR	SCS/Johnston Co. CD	—	65	143	1.7	FC	—	—
Leader-Middle Clear Boggy #23	Clear Boggy Creek TR	SCS/Pontotoc Co. CD	—	44	95	1.1	FC	—	—
Leader-Middle Clear Boggy #40	Clear Boggy Creek TR	SCS/Coal Co. CD	—	111	133	2.7	FC	—	—
Lower Clear Boggy #10	Clear Boggy Creek TR	SCS/Atoka Co. CD	—	151	281	2.7	FC	—	—
Lower Clear Boggy #14	Clear Boggy Creek TR	SCS/Atoka Co. CD	—	41	136	2.2	FC	—	—
Lower Clear Boggy #20	Clear Boggy Creek TR	SCS/Atoka Co. CD	—	57	73	1.5	FC	—	—
Lower Clear Boggy #22	Clear Boggy Creek TR	SCS/Coal Co. CD	—	109	135	2.3	FC	—	—
Lower Clear Boggy #24	Clear Boggy Creek TR	SCS/Atoka Co. CD	—	60	152	1.3	FC	—	—
Lower Clear Boggy #25	Clear Boggy Creek TR	SCS/Atoka Co. CD	—	59	179	1.5	FC	—	—
Stonewall	Clear Boggy Creek TR	M.J. & J.D. Williams	—	46	180	1.5	—	—	—
Upper Clear Boggy #7	Clear Boggy Creek TR	SCS/Coal Co. CD	—	49	92	2.4	FC	—	—
Upper Clear Boggy #9	Clear Boggy Creek TR	SCS/Coal Co. CD	—	94	172	2.7	FC	—	—
Upper Clear Boggy #23	Clear Boggy Creek TR	SCS/Pontotoc Co. CD	—	70	140	3.3	FC	—	—
Upper Clear Boggy #25	Clear Boggy Creek TR	SCS/Pontotoc Co. CD	—	42	168	1.4	FC	—	—
Upper Clear Boggy #30	Bois d'Arc Creek TR	SCS/Pontotoc Co. CD	—	52	87	1.3	FC	—	—
Upper Clear Boggy #31	Bois d'Arc Creek	SCS/Pontotoc Co. CD	—	46	190	1.3	FC	—	—
Upper Clear Boggy #32	Clear Boggy Creek TR	SCS/Pontotoc Co. CD	—	48	200	1.7	FC	—	—
Upper Clear Boggy #42	Clear Boggy Creek TR	SCS/Pontotoc Co. CD	—	58	151	1.5	FC	—	—
Upper Clear Boggy #46	Clear Boggy Creek TR	SCS/Pontotoc Co. CD	—	60	233	1.5	FC	—	—
Upper Clear Boggy #47	Clear Boggy Creek TR	SCS/Pontotoc Co. CD	—	57	145	1.5	FC	—	—
Wapanucka City	Sandy Creek TR	Johnston Co. CD	—	73	107	2.4	FC	—	—

[1]WS=Water Supply, R=Recreation, HP=Hydroelectric Power, IR=Irrigation, WQ=Water Quality, FW=Fish & Wildlife, FC=Flood Control, LF=Low Flow Regulation, N=Navigation, C=Conservation, CW=Cooling Water

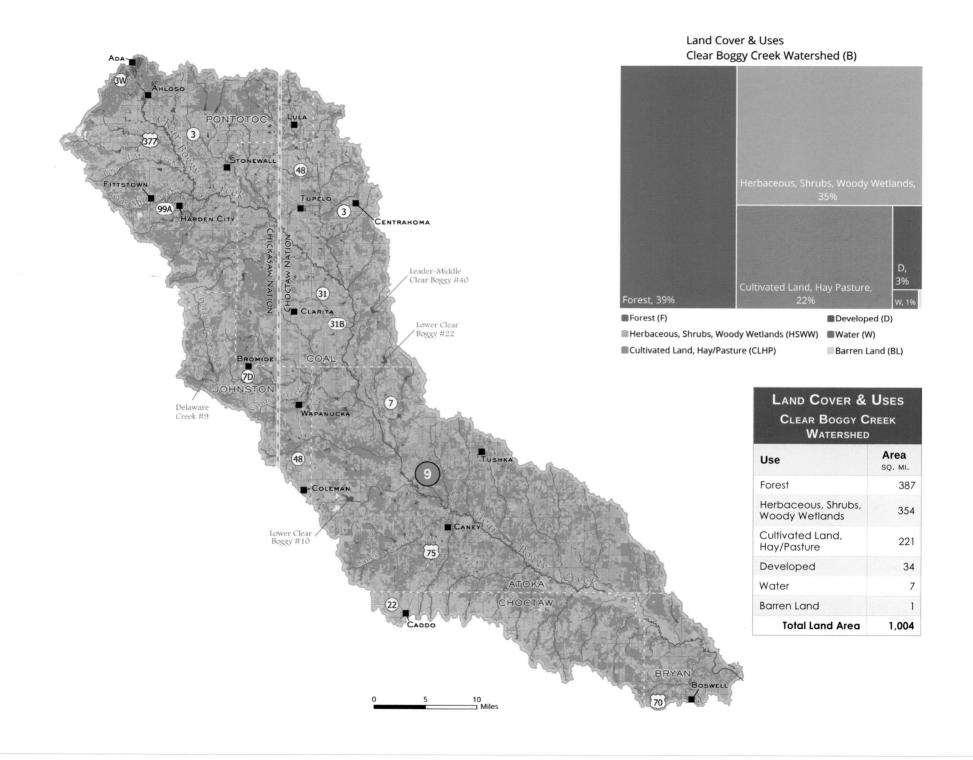

Land Cover & Uses
Clear Boggy Creek Watershed (B)

Forest, 39%

Herbaceous, Shrubs, Woody Wetlands, 35%

Cultivated Land, Hay Pasture, 22%

D, 3%

W, 1%

- Forest (F)
- Herbaceous, Shrubs, Woody Wetlands (HSWW)
- Cultivated Land, Hay/Pasture (CLHP)
- Developed (D)
- Water (W)
- Barren Land (BL)

LAND COVER & USES CLEAR BOGGY CREEK WATERSHED	
Use	**Area** SQ. MI.
Forest	387
Herbaceous, Shrubs, Woody Wetlands	354
Cultivated Land, Hay/Pasture	221
Developed	34
Water	7
Barren Land	1
Total Land Area	**1,004**

Groundwater

The Antlers aquifer is the dominant major ground-water basin underlying the Clear Boggy Creek watershed, primarily in the southern portion of Basin 9. An estimated 123 wells supply water for various purposes. A hydrologic study of the Antlers, formalized by the OWRB in February 1995, established an EPS of 2.1 ac-ft/acre. Four additional aquifers, including the Arbuckle-Simpson in the northwest portion of the watershed with a 0.2 ac-ft/acre EPS, lie within the watershed. The minor Pennsylvanian, Woodbine and Kiamichi groundwater basins have been assigned the default EPS of 2.0 ac-ft/acre until studies have been conducted and approved for each.

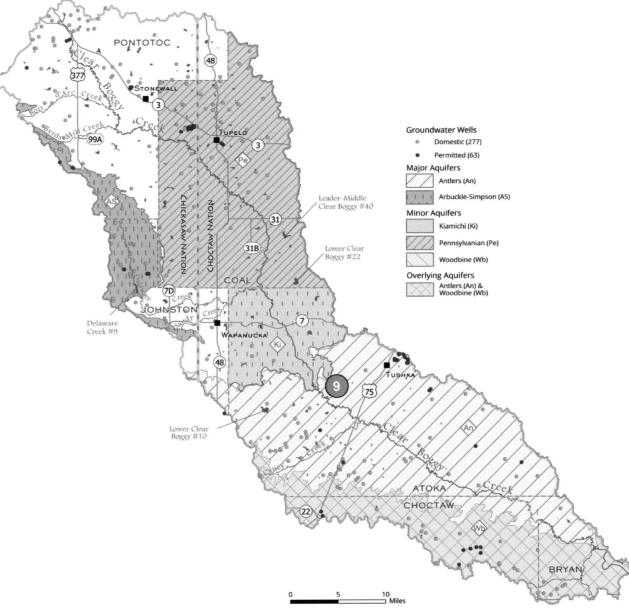

MAJOR & MINOR AQUIFERS BASIN 9			
Aquifer	**Area in Basin/ Watershed** SQUARE MILES	**EPS[1]** AC-FT/ACRE	**Number of Permitted & Domestic Wells in Basin/ Watershed[2]**
Antlers	417	2.1	123
Arbuckle-Simpson	52	0.2	37
Kiamichi	71	2.0	3
Pennsylvanian	221	2.0	60
Woodbine	128	2.0	38
Nondelineated Source Wells			79
Total Wells			**340**

[1]*Italic number signifies unstudied aquifers with a default temporary equal proportionate share (EPS) of 2.0 acre-feet per acre of land.*

[2]*Some wells are double-counted where one aquifer overlies another.*

NOTE: Significant color and shading variations may be apparent in areas where one aquifer overlies another. In some cases, for state administrative purposes, aquifer boundaries align directly with county lines or related political borders rather than geologic outcrop areas.

Permitted Water Use

Permitted surface water outpaces groundwater by a 61 (16,702 AFY) to 39 percent (10,575 AFY) margin in the Clear Boggy Creek watershed. The largest share of permitted water from sources in Basin 9 is assigned to public water supply (43 percent), primarily from surface water. Irrigation is a close second at 35 percent. Oil, gas and mining accounts for nine percent of permitted water; recreation, fish and wildlife purposes account for eight percent.

As the watershed's major water user, the City of Ada holds two large public water supply permits in the Clear Boggy Creek watershed, both diverting water from the same surface source: a regular permit for 5,340 AFY and a vested right from 1965 appropriating 3,360 AFY. Aside from several substantial irrigation permits, a private landowner holds a 2,346 AFY permit authorizing the use of groundwater for commercial, irrigation, and oil, gas and mining purposes. An individual water rights holder in Atoka County possesses a surface water permit for 1,564 AFY assigned to the recreation, fish and wildlife category.

Any application to appropriate water for use at a location outside of Basin 9 could be subject to conferral, depending upon the application amount, mean available flow and other relevant factors. See conditions associated with Class B Basins in the Tribal-State Water Settlement agreement in the *Oka Holisso* appendix.

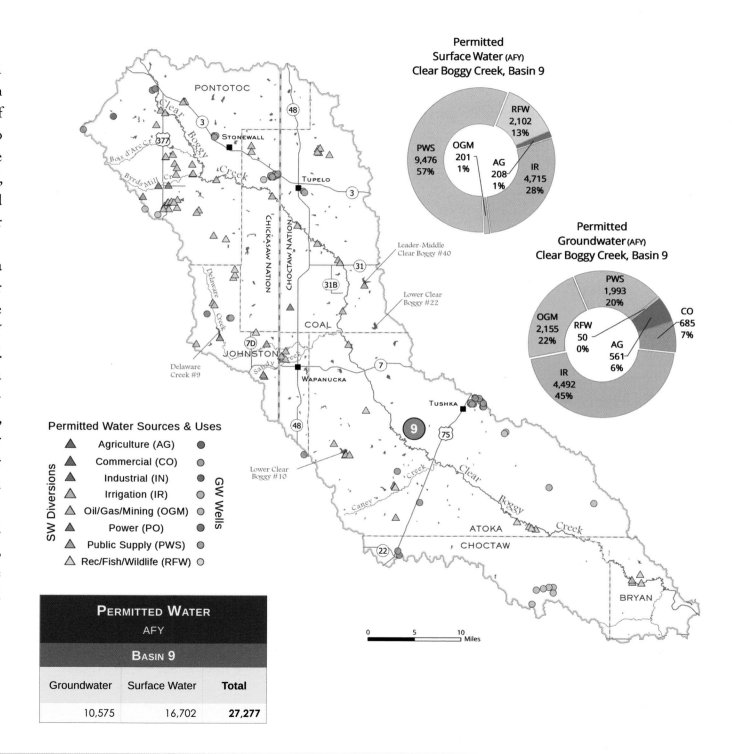

Permitted Surface Water (AFY) Clear Boggy Creek, Basin 9

PWS 9,476 57%
OGM 201 1%
AG 208 1%
IR 4,715 28%
RFW 2,102 13%

Permitted Groundwater (AFY) Clear Boggy Creek, Basin 9

PWS 1,993 20%
CO 685 7%
AG 561 6%
IR 4,492 45%
RFW 50 0%
OGM 2,155 22%

Permitted Water Sources & Uses

SW Diversions
- ▲ Agriculture (AG)
- ▲ Commercial (CO)
- ▲ Industrial (IN)
- ▲ Irrigation (IR)
- ▲ Oil/Gas/Mining (OGM)
- ▲ Power (PO)
- ▲ Public Supply (PWS)
- ▲ Rec/Fish/Wildlife (RFW)

GW Wells
- ● Agriculture (AG)
- ● Commercial (CO)
- ● Industrial (IN)
- ● Irrigation (IR)
- ● Oil/Gas/Mining (OGM)
- ● Power (PO)
- ● Public Supply (PWS)
- ○ Rec/Fish/Wildlife (RFW)

PERMITTED WATER		
AFY		
BASIN 9		
Groundwater	Surface Water	Total
10,575	16,702	**27,277**

Water Supply Systems

The Clear Boggy Creek watershed is characterized by a number of small and mid-sized water supply systems. However, a substantial portion of the 37,000 customers served by the City of Ada reside in Basin 9. Ada utilizes Byrds Mill Spring, near Fittstown, and several groundwater wells for its supply. The community sells water to four local RWDs. Only a small portion of Pontotoc Co. RWD #8, a large provider primarily serving the Lower Canadian (Class C) watershed, skirts the northern extent of the watershed. Another system of note is Atoka County Rural Water Sewer and Solid Waste Management District #4, a surface water supplier to 3,000 customers, as well as three water systems, in the watershed's southern region.

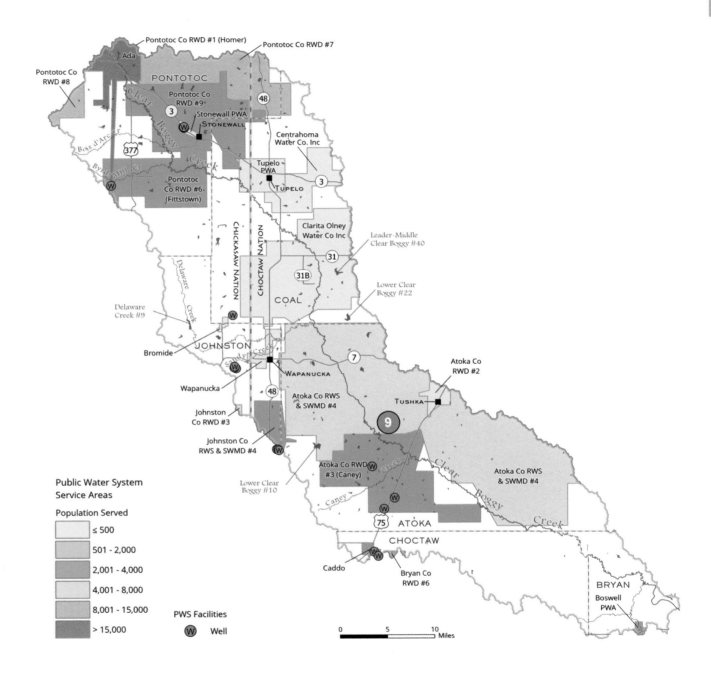

Public Water System Service Areas

Population Served

- ≤ 500
- 501 - 2,000
- 2,001 - 4,000
- 4,001 - 8,000
- 8,001 - 15,000
- > 15,000

PWS Facilities

(W) Well

0   5   10 Miles

System	Residential Customers Served[1]	Source(s) of Supply[2]	Water Sales	Water Purchases	Facilities[3]				
					Intake	Pump Facility	Storage	Treatment Plant	Well or Spring
Ada	37,000	GW	Pontotoc Co. #1, #6, #7, #9	—					1
Atoka Co. RWD #2	500	P (SW)	—	Atoka, Atoka Co. #4					
Atoka Co. RWD #3 (Caney)	1,500	GW	—	—					3
Atoka Co. RWS & SWMD #4	3,000	SW	Atoka Co. #2, Choctaw Co. #6, Stringtown PWA	—					
Boswell PWA	932	P (SW)	—	Choctaw Co. #6					1
Bromide	169	GW	—	—					
Bryan Co. RWD #6	990	GW	Kenefic	Caddo					
Caddo	944	GW	Bryan Co. #6	—					2
Centrahoma Water Co. Inc	150	P (SW)	—	Coalgate PWA					
Choctaw Co. RWSG & SWMD #6	850	P (SW)	Boswell PWA	Atoka Co. #4					
Clarita Olney Water Co. Inc	360	P (SW)	—	Coalgate PWA					
Johnston Co. RWD #3	2,783	GW	Milburn PWA, Ravia	—					
Johnston Co. RWS& SWMD #4	600	GW	—	—					3
Pontotoc Co. RWD #1 (Homer)	441	P (GW)	—	Ada					
Pontotoc Co. RWD #6 (Fittstown)	896	P (GW)	—	Ada					
Pontotoc Co. RWD #7	1,950	P (GW)	—	Ada					
Pontotoc Co. RWD #8	4,250	GW	Pontotoc Co. #9	Wingard Water Corp.					
Pontotoc Co. RWD #9	1,162	P (GW)	Tupelo PWA	Ada, Pontotoc Co. #8					
Stonewall PWA	465	GW	—	—					3
Tupelo PWA	377	P (GW)	—	Pontotoc Co. #9					
Wapanucka	198	GW	—	—					3

[1]Does not include wholesale customers served through water sales.

[2]GW = Groundwater; SW = Surface Water; P = Purchased.

[3]Includes both active and inactive (mostly wells) facilities in the watershed. Treatment plants include only those utilizing conventional water treatment and do not include chlorination stations associated with discrete source treatment.

Data: Oklahoma Department of Environmental Quality, Safe Drinking Water Information System, OWRB GIS and Arbuckle-Simpson Aquifer Drought Contingency Plan. Listed system facilities include those with service areas and/or facilities within relevant watershed.

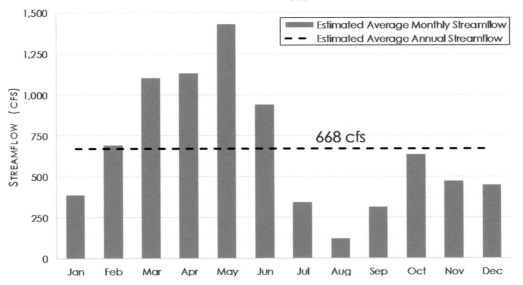

Estimated Streamflow, Clear Boggy Creek Watershed

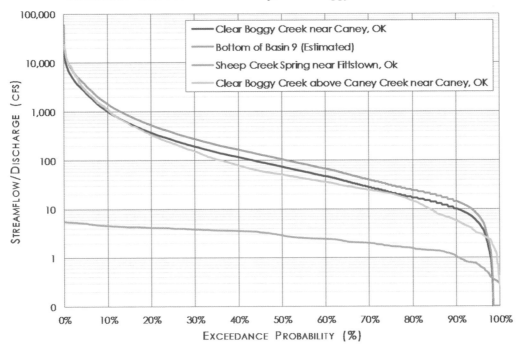

Streamflow Exceedance Probability, Clear Boggy Creek Watershed

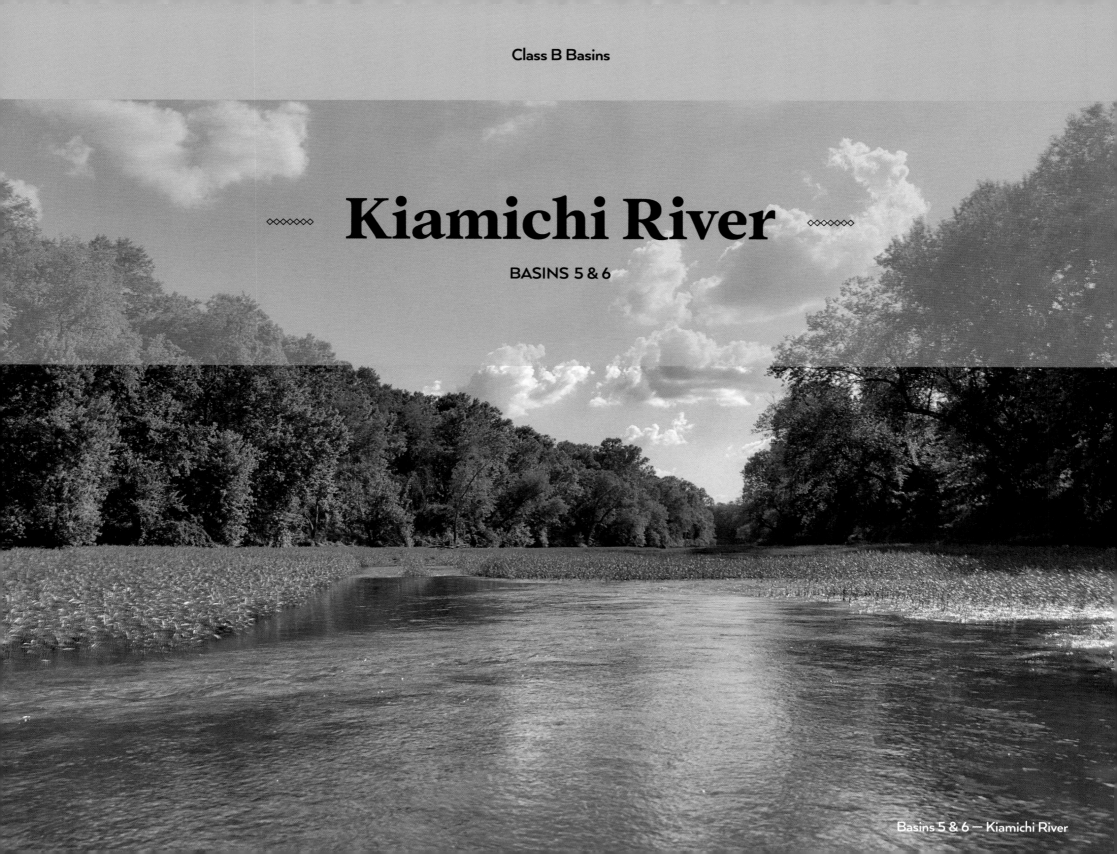

Kiamichi River

BASINS 5 & 6

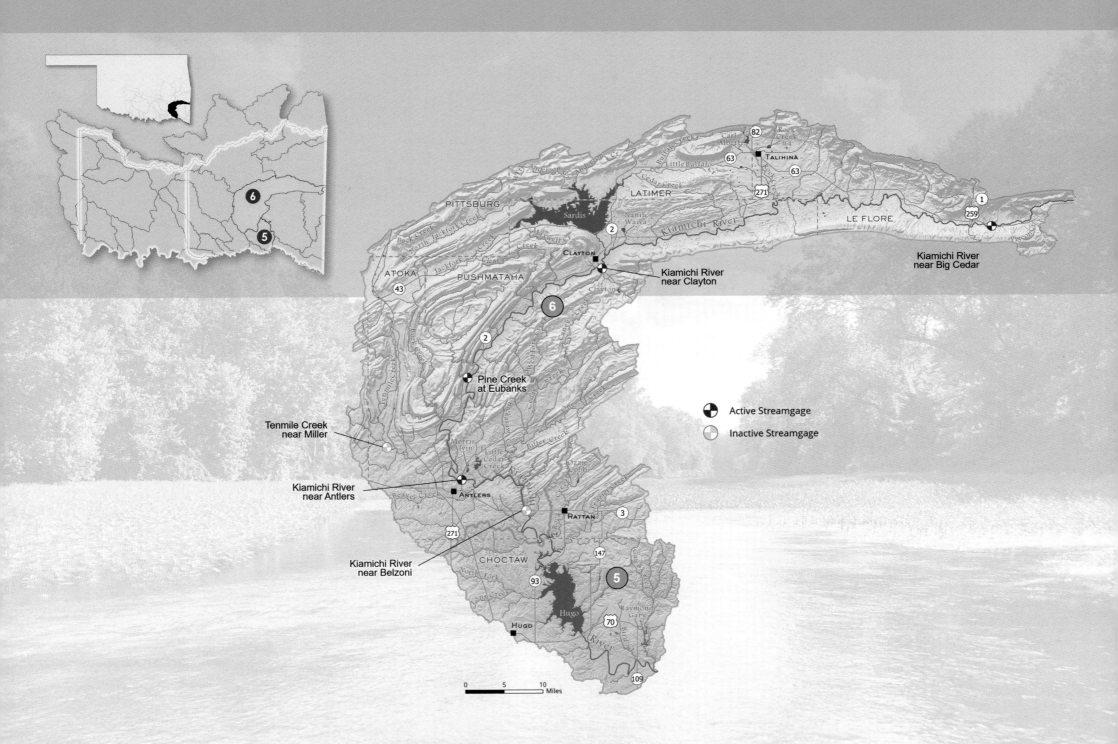

PITTSBURG

LATIMER

Sardis

Talihina

82

63

63

271

1

259

LE FLORE

Kiamichi River
near Big Cedar

CLAYTON

2

Kiamichi River
near Clayton

ATOKA

43

PUSHMATAHA

Clayton

6

2

Pine Creek
at Eubanks

Tenmile Creek
near Miller

Kiamichi River
near Antlers

Antlers

Kiamichi River
near Belzoni

Rattan

3

271

147

CHOCTAW

93

5

Raymond
Gary

70

Hugo

Hugo

109

6

5

Active Streamgage

Inactive Streamgage

0   5   10
Miles

The Kiamichi River watershed, represented by Basins 5 and 6, comprises 1,822 square miles of southeastern Oklahoma. The word "Kiamichi," of Caddo origin but adopted by the Choctaw people, means "old ones" or "ancient ones," primarily referring to the large trees that grew near the river and adjacent area. The Kiamichi River begins near Mena, Arkansas along the Oklahoma/Arkansas border, then flows westward near Big Cedar and through the Ouachita National Forest in LeFlore County. It meanders into Pushmataha County, beginning its turn to the southwest just south of Lake Nanih Waiya. East of Clayton, the Kiamichi River is joined by Jackfork Creek, which is impounded by Sardis Reservoir. It skirts a portion of the Pushmataha WMA, at some points mirroring the path of State Highway 2 as the river meanders to the south. North of Antlers, the Kiamichi River turns sharply to the east, then again to the south before entering Choctaw County and Basin 5, flowing through Hugo WMA and into the southern arm of Hugo Lake. South of the dam, the Kiamichi River meanders back east prior to entering the Red River. The average annual flow of the Kiamichi River, estimated at the bottom of Basin 5, is 2,466 cfs; this flow is available about 21 percent of the time. (The significant impacts of reservoir uses and operations at Hugo Lake, in Basin 5, necessitated utilization of upstream Basin 6 for streamflow exceedance estimations.)

According to the OWRB (August 2019), Sardis Lake contains 34,777 AFY of *available* yield. However, according to terms of the Settlement agreement, the release of this water is allowable only under specific hydrologic conditions. Hugo Lake has 2,568 AFY of its yield available for appropriation. According to the OWRB, Lake Carl Albert contains no firm yield, although the Talihina Public Works Authority holds a water supply permit from the OWRB.

The Kiamichi River watershed is home to diverse and unique flora and fauna, including 132 fish, 256 bird, fifty-five mammal and 1,067 plant species. The river and its tributaries also provide invaluable habitat for several protected mussels, which are sensitive to the river's specific seasonal flow regime as well as changes in temperature. Within Basins 5 and 6 are the Ouachita rock pocketbook, scaleshell mussel and winged mapleleaf, which are listed as endangered under the ESA. Also endangered are the harperella, Indiana bat, piping plover, red-cockaded woodpecker and whooping crane. Threatened species in the watershed include the American burying beetle, leopard darter, northern long-eared bat and red knot.

Water Quality

The Kiamichi River flows through the Ouachita Mountains to the South Central Plains ecoregion where streams have moderate to high gradients with gravel, cobble, boulder and bedrock bottoms and high ecological diversity. Jackfork Creek, including Sardis Reservoir, and Buffalo Creek are classified as sensitive public and private water supplies. Cedar Creek is designated as high quality waters. The Kiamichi is oligotrophic with extremely low nutrient and salinity levels. Nutrient concentrations increase downstream to Hugo Lake, which is eutrophic. Several lakes in the basin are impaired for fish consumption due to mercury, including Lake Carl Albert, Sardis Lake, Clayton Lake, Lake Ozzie Cobb, Schooler Lake and Hugo Lake. Lead, silver and zinc concentrations in the Kiamichi River are responsible for impairment of fish and wildlife propagation, fish consumption, and public and private water supply.

PRINCIPAL RIVERS & STREAMS BASINS 5 & 6	
River/Stream	**Length** MILES
Kiamichi River	172
Buck Creek	37
Tenmile Creek	36
Cedar Creek	35
Rock Creek	31
Jackfork Creek	30
North Jackfork Creek	25
Buffalo Creek	22
Gates Creek	20
One Creek	17
Frazier Creek	17
Caney Creek	14
Long Creek	12
Beaver Creek	12
West Fork Creek	12
Clear Creek	11

Minimum & Maximum Elevation (FT) Basins 5 & 6

Mean Slope 10.1%

2,662

363

PRINCIPAL LAKES									
BASINS 5 & 6									
Name	**Stream**	**Authority**	**Normal Elevation** FEET	**Normal Area** ACRES	**Normal Capacity** AC-FT	**Shoreline** MILES	**Purpose(s)[1]**	**Water Supply Storage** AC-FT	**Water Supply Yield** AC-FT/YR
Carl Albert[2]	Rock Creek	City of Talihina	761	180	2,739	3	WS. FC, R	—	—
Clayton	Peal Creek	State of Okla.	664	64	953	2.2	R	—	—
Hugo	Kiamichi River	USACE	404.5	12,340	163,349	102.4	FC, WS, WQ, R, FW	118,850	64,960
Little Cedar Creek	Kiamichi River TR	—	—	314	815	6.3	—	—	—
Morris (Alvin J.)	Kiamichi River TR	Gerald Wayne Flatt	—	60	581	1.6	—	—	—
Nanih Waiya	Kiamichi River TR	ODWC	594	105	1,064	2	R	—	—
Ozzie Cobb	Rock Creek	ODWC	513	62	833	2	R	—	—
Raymond Gary	Gates Creek	ODWC	401	273	1,681	9.3	R	—	—
Rock Creek #4	Rock Creek TR	SCS/Talihina CD	—	84	375	1.5	FC	—	—
Sardis	Jackfork Creek	USACE	599	13,530	274,310	91.3	FC, WS, R, FW	274,070	156,800

[1]WS=Water Supply, R=Recreation, HP=Hydroelectric Power, IR=Irrigation, WQ=Water Quality, FW=Fish & Wildlife, FC=Flood Control, LF=Low Flow Regulation, N=Navigation, C=Conservation, CW=Cooling Water

[2]A hydrographic survey and associated analysis conducted by the CCRWP Planning Team (specifically, Aqua Strategies Inc.) determined a firm yield of 2,465 AFY. However, due to infrastructure limitations, the estimated yield has been reduced to 2,430 AFY.

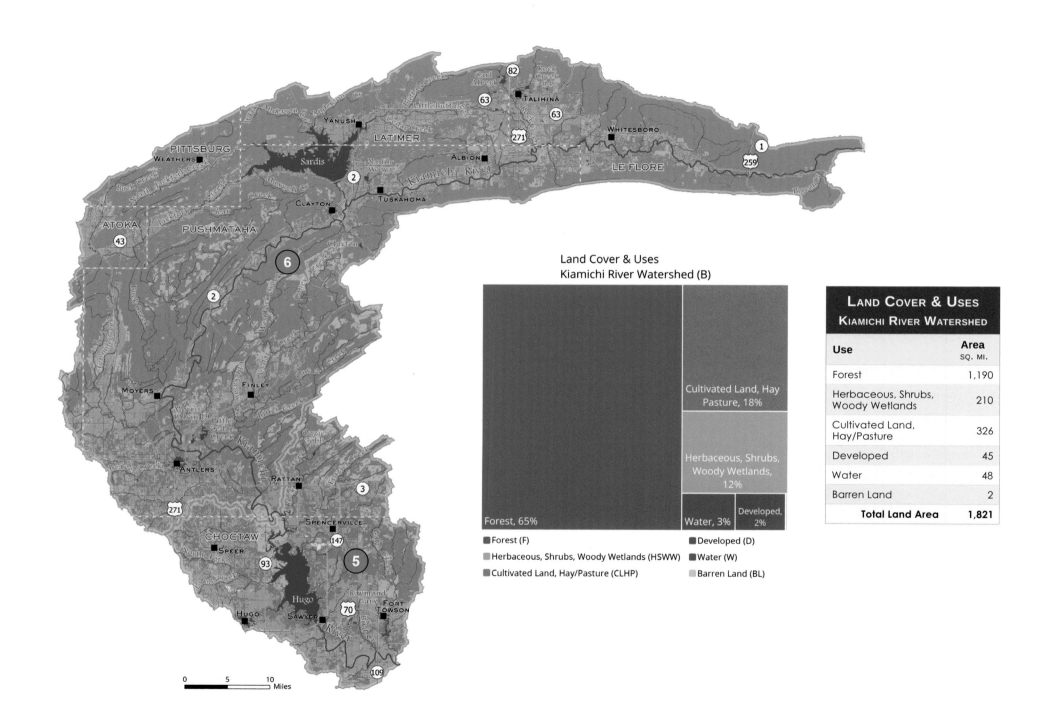

Land Cover & Uses
Kiamichi River Watershed (B)

Forest, 65%

Cultivated Land, Hay Pasture, 18%

Herbaceous, Shrubs, Woody Wetlands, 12%

Water, 3%

Developed, 2%

■ Forest (F)
■ Herbaceous, Shrubs, Woody Wetlands (HSWW)
■ Cultivated Land, Hay/Pasture (CLHP)
■ Developed (D)
■ Water (W)
■ Barren Land (BL)

LAND COVER & USES
KIAMICHI RIVER WATERSHED

Use	Area SQ. MI.
Forest	1,190
Herbaceous, Shrubs, Woody Wetlands	210
Cultivated Land, Hay/Pasture	326
Developed	45
Water	48
Barren Land	2
Total Land Area	**1,821**

Groundwater

As is the case with many Settlement Area watersheds encompassing southern areas of the state, the Antlers aquifer is a significant source of groundwater in the Kiamichi watershed. Along with the minor Woodbine aquifer (90 wells), the Antlers provides supply for some 258 permitted/domestic wells, primarily in Basin 5. Among the four minor groundwater basins underlying the watershed, the Kiamichi aquifer is the primary source with an estimated 206 water wells over its substantial 1,270-square-mile area.

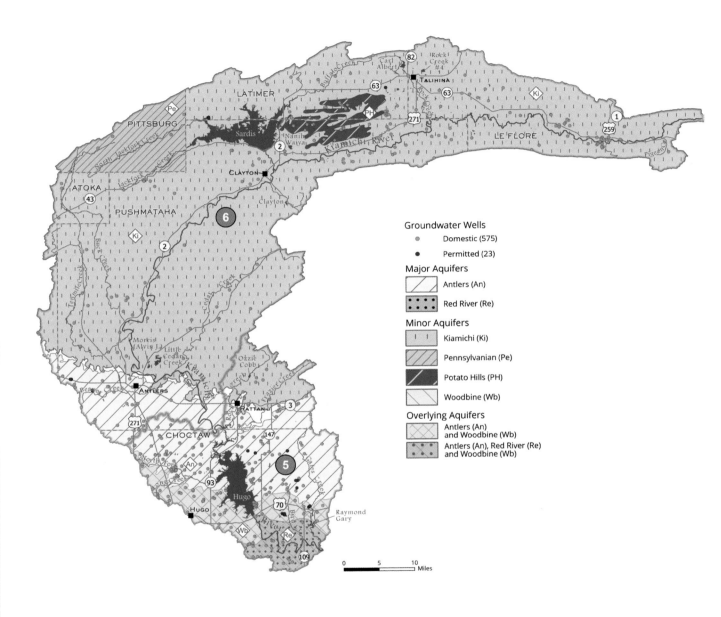

Aquifer	Area in Basin/ Watershed SQUARE MILES	EPS[1] AC-FT/ ACRE	Number of Permitted & Domestic Wells in Basin/Watershed[2]
MAJOR & MINOR AQUIFERS **BASINS 5 & 6**			
Antlers	419	2.1	258
Kiamichi	1,270	2.0	206
Pennsylvanian	84	2.0	6
Potato Hills	32	2.0	14
Red River	41	2.0	22
Woodbine	115	2.0	90
Nondelineated Source Wells			2
Total Wells			**598**

[1]*Italic number signifies unstudied aquifers with a default temporary equal proportionate share (EPS) of 2.0 acre-feet per acre of land.*

[2]*Some wells are double-counted where one aquifer overlies another.*

Groundwater Wells
- Domestic (575)
- Permitted (23)

Major Aquifers
- Antlers (An)
- Red River (Re)

Minor Aquifers
- Kiamichi (Ki)
- Pennsylvanian (Pe)
- Potato Hills (PH)
- Woodbine (Wb)

Overlying Aquifers
- Antlers (An) and Woodbine (Wb)
- Antlers (An), Red River (Re) and Woodbine (Wb)

NOTE: Significant color and shading variations may be apparent in areas where one aquifer overlies another. In some cases, for state administrative purposes, aquifer boundaries align directly with county lines or related political borders rather than geologic outcrop areas.

Surface water is the predominant source in the Kiamichi River watershed, accounting for 97 percent (192,292 AFY) of all permitted water. Approximately 79 percent of permitted water in Basins 5 and 6 is attributed to public supply, followed by power at 16 percent.

With a 115,000 AFY public supply appropriation approved by the OWRB in October 2017, the City of Oklahoma City is the largest water rights holder in the Kiamichi River watershed. The permit authorizes the diversion of water, supplemented by releases at Sardis Lake upstream, at a point on the river near Moyers, Oklahoma. Considering in-basin users, the Hugo Municipal Authority possesses two permits in Hugo Lake totaling 30,500 AFY while the Sardis Lake Water Authority holds a similar 6,000 AFY permit to take water from available lake storage. Western Farmers Electric Cooperative, a major power user in Choctaw County, holds water rights totaling 33,089 AFY for use at its Hugo facility.

Any application to appropriate water for use at a location outside of Basin 5 or 6 could be subject to conferral, depending upon the application amount, mean available flow and other relevant factors. See conditions associated with Class B Basins in the Tribal-State Water Settlement agreement in the *Oka Holisso* appendix.

PERMITTED WATER AFY		
BASIN 5		
Groundwater	Surface Water	Total
5,052	64,241	69,293
BASIN 6		
Groundwater	Surface Water	Total
428	128,051	128,479
WATERSHED TOTAL		
Groundwater	Surface Water	Total
5,479	192,292	197,771

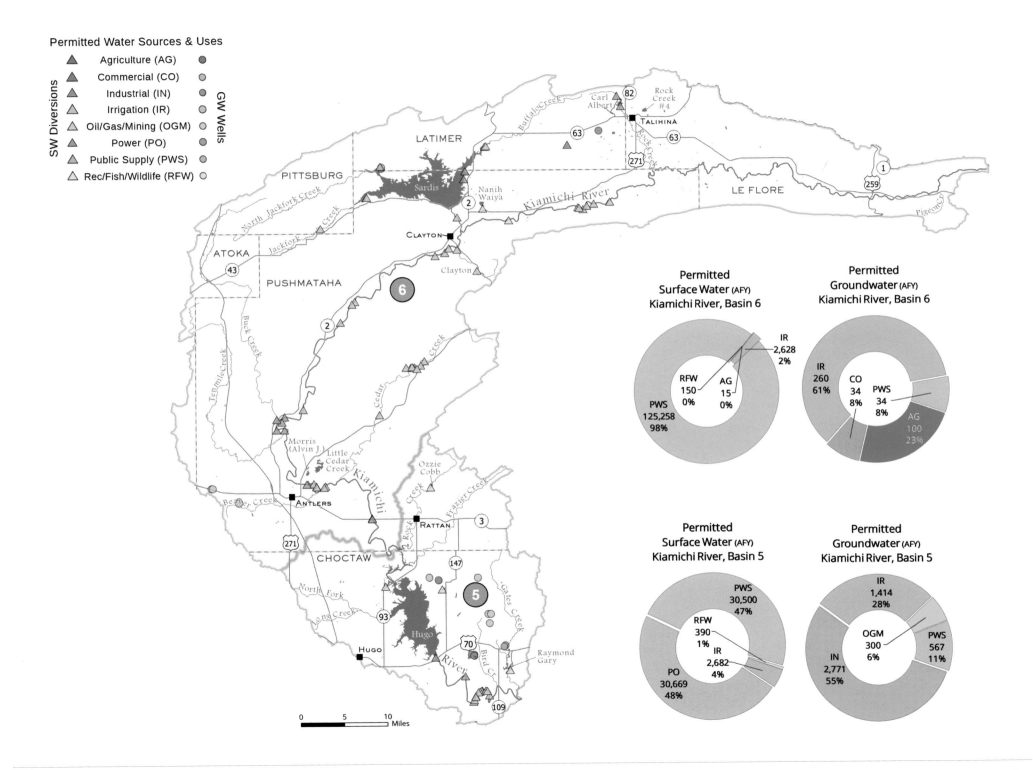

Permitted Water Sources & Uses

SW Diversions

- ▲ Agriculture (AG)
- ▲ Commercial (CO)
- ▲ Industrial (IN)
- ▲ Irrigation (IR)
- ▲ Oil/Gas/Mining (OGM)
- ▲ Power (PO)
- ▲ Public Supply (PWS)
- ▲ Rec/Fish/Wildlife (RFW)

GW Wells

- ● Agriculture (AG)
- ● Commercial (CO)
- ● Industrial (IN)
- ● Irrigation (IR)
- ● Oil/Gas/Mining (OGM)
- ● Power (PO)
- ● Public Supply (PWS)
- ○ Rec/Fish/Wildlife (RFW)

Permitted Surface Water (AFY) Kiamichi River, Basin 6

- IR 2,628 2%
- RFW 150 0%
- AG 15 0%
- PWS 125,258 98%

Permitted Groundwater (AFY) Kiamichi River, Basin 6

- IR 260 61%
- CO 34 8%
- PWS 34 8%
- AG 100 23%

Permitted Surface Water (AFY) Kiamichi River, Basin 5

- PWS 30,500 47%
- RFW 390 1%
- IR 2,682 4%
- PO 30,669 48%

Permitted Groundwater (AFY) Kiamichi River, Basin 5

- IR 1,414 28%
- OGM 300 6%
- PWS 567 11%
- IN 2,771 55%

0   5   10 Miles

All but one of the eleven water systems in the Kiamichi watershed that purchase water depend upon a single provider for their supply. Hugo Municipal Authority is the chief direct water provider in the watershed. In addition to its 5,536 residential customers, the Authority sells some of its appropriated supply from Hugo Lake to Choctaw County RWD #1 and Choctaw Co. Rural Water Sewer Gas and Solid Waste Management District #3.

Despite serving only 307 residential customers, Sardis Lake Water Authority is an important provider to the immediate region as it sells its supply from the lake to several nearby systems—Clayton PWA, Latimer Co. RWD #2, Pushmataha Co. RWD #1 and Pushmataha Co. RWD #5—increasing its reach by more than 4,000 customers. Talihina, also in the upper portion of Basin 6, serves 1,297 users and provides supply to thousands of members of four additional rural districts. Pushmataha Co. RWD #3, with a large service area occupying the middle portion of the watershed in both Basins 5 and 6, serves 4,825.

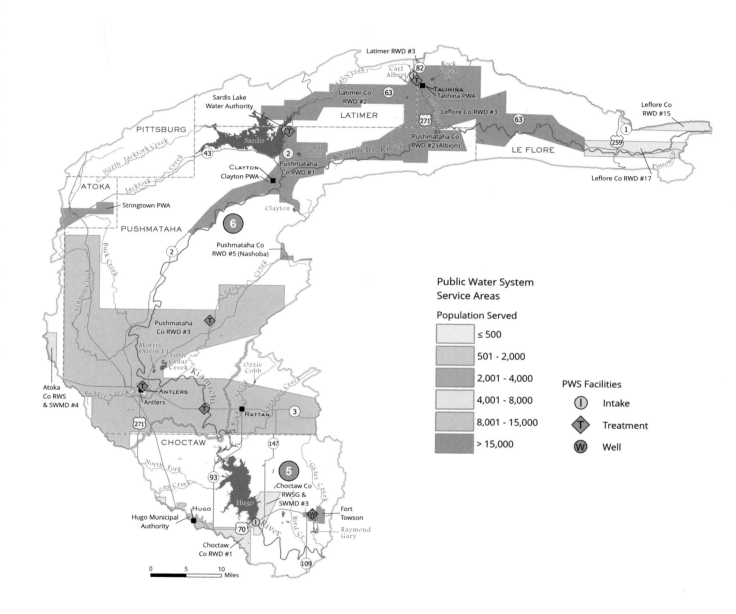

Public Water System Service Areas

Population Served

- ≤ 500
- 501 - 2,000
- 2,001 - 4,000
- 4,001 - 8,000
- 8,001 - 15,000
- > 15,000

PWS Facilities

- (I) Intake
- (T) Treatment
- (W) Well

PUBLIC WATER SUPPLY SYSTEMS
BASINS 5 & 6

System	Residential Customers Served[1]	Source(s) of Supply[2]	Water Sales	Water Purchases	Facilities[3]				
					Intake	Pump Facility	Storage	Treatment Plant	Well or Spring
Antlers	2,547	SW	—	—	1			2	
Atoka Co. RWS & SWMD #4	3,000	SW	Atoka Co. #2, Choctaw Co. #6, Stringtown PWA	—					
Choctaw Co. RWD #1	2,300	GW	—	Hugo MA					
Choctaw Co. RWSG & SWMD #3	235	P (SW)	—	Hugo MA					
Clayton PWA	719	P (SW)	—	Sardis Lake WA					
Fort Towson	611	GW	—	—				1	3
Hugo Municipal Authority	5,536	SW	Choctaw Co. #1, Choctaw Co. #3	—	1				
Latimer Co. RWD #2	1,500	P (SW)	—	Sardis Lake WA, Talihina PWA					
Latimer Co. RWD #3	175	P (SW)	—	Talihina PWA					
LeFlore Co. RWD #3	1,643	P (SW)	—	Talihina PWA					
LeFlore Co. RWD #15	425	P (SW)	—	Poteau Valley IA					
LeFlore Co. RWD #17	373	P (SW)	—	—					
Pushmataha Co. RWD #1	1,200	P (SW)	—	Sardis Lake WA					
Pushmataha Co. RWD #2 (Albion)	959	P (SW)	—	Talihina PWA					
Pushmataha Co. RWD #3	4,825	SW	Soper	—	1			1	
Pushmataha Co. RWD #5 (Nashoba)	725	P (SW)	—	Sardis Lake WA					
Sardis Lake Water Authority	307	SW	Clayton PWA, Latimer Co. #2, Pushmataha Co. #1, Pushmataha Co. #5	—	1			1	
Stringtown PWA	1,105	P (SW)	—	Atoka Co. #4					
Talihina PWA	1,297	SW	Latimer Co. #2, Latimer Co. #3, LeFlore Co. #3, Pushmataha Co. #2	—	1			1	

[1]Does not include wholesale customers served through water sales.

[2]GW = Groundwater; SW = Surface Water; P = Purchased.

[3]Includes both active and inactive (mostly wells) facilities in the watershed. Treatment plants include only those utilizing conventional water treatment and do not include chlorination stations associated with discrete source treatment.

Data: Oklahoma Department of Environmental Quality, Safe Drinking Water Information System, OWRB GIS and Arbuckle-Simpson Aquifer Drought Contingency Plan. Listed system facilities include those with service areas and/or facilities within relevant watershed.

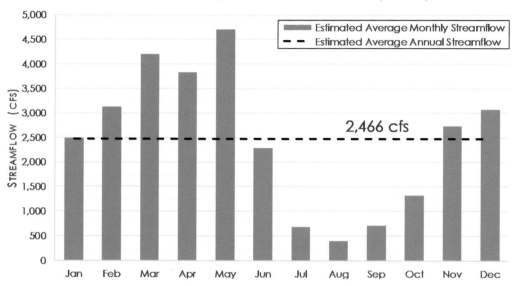

Estimated Streamflow, Kiamichi River Watershed (Basin 6)

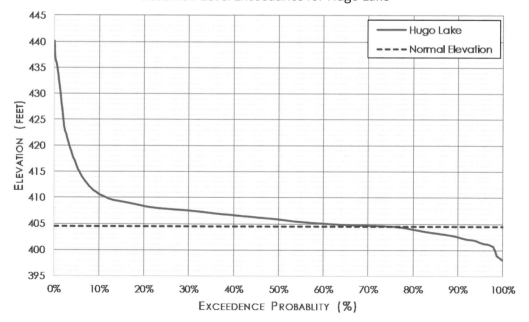

Reservoir Level Exceedance for Hugo Lake

Streamflow Exceedance Probability, Kiamichi River Watershed (Basin 6)

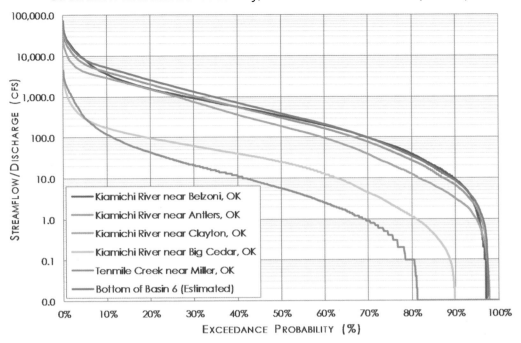

Reservoir Level Exceedance for Sardis Lake

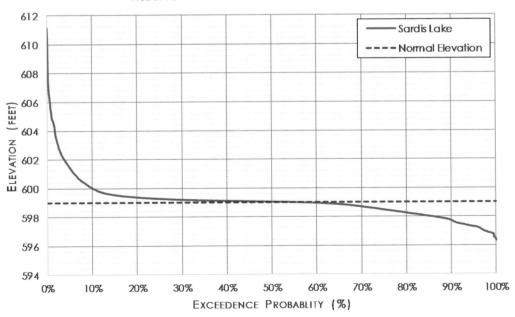

Lower Washita River

BASIN 14

Basin 14 — Travertine Creek, Chickasaw National Recreation Area

Washington Creek
near Pauls Valley

Rush Creek
at Purdy

Rush Creek
near Maysville

Washita River
near Pauls Valley

Peavine Creek #11

Peavine Creek #5

Byars

Peavine Creek #4

Peavine Creek #3

Peavine Creek #2

MCCLAIN

133

19

Pauls Valley

Peavine Cr.

Peavine Creek #1

RC Longmire

Cherokee Sandy #8

Cherokee Sandy #9

Outflow From Vendome Well at Sulphur

RUSH SPRINGS

81

Taylor

Rush Creek #10

GRADY

Rush Creek

Rush Creek #4

76

RushCreek

Red Br.

74

GARVIN

Elmore City

Sandy

WYNNEWOOD

Sandy Cr.

Rock Creek #14

29

PONTOTOC

Cherokee

MARLOW

Clear

Wildhorse Creek #23

29

Wildhorse Creek #25

Clear Creek

Wildhorse Creek #27

Fuqua

Wildhorse Creek #26

Wildhorse Creek #30

Humphreys

Wildhorse Creek #9

Fitzpatrick Creek

Duncan

Wildhorse

Creek

STEPHENS

76

Salt Creek

Black Bear Creek

West Sandy Creek

Wildhorse Creek

Wildhorse Creek near Hoover

Creek

35

Chigley Sandy Creek #6

177

SULPHUR

DAVIS

7

Antelope Spring at Sulphur

Rock Creek at Sulphur

VELMA

7

Wildhorse Creek #11

Wildhorse Creek #14

CARTER

14

Caddo Creek #2

Caddo Creek

Mountain

Willis Creek

Honey Creek

MURRAY

Washita River

Veterans

Arbuckle

110

177

Rock Creek at Dougherty

Honey Creek below Turner Falls near Davis

53

Caddo Creek #35

Jean Neustadt

SPRINGER

53

Caddo Creek #28

177

Caddo Creek #19

Caddo Creek #17

Rock Creek

Sandy Creek

Caddo Creek

Caddo Creek near Ardmore

199

Scott King

Ardmore

Ardmore City Lake

● Active Streamgage

◐ Inactive Streamgage

0   5   10
Miles

14

Water & Related Resources

The Lower Washita River watershed, represented by Basin 14, extends over some 1,870 square miles in southern Oklahoma's Chickasaw Nation. The Washita River enters Basin 14 in the north from Basin 15. It soon takes a predominantly eastern path north of Pauls Valley, then turns south, snaking parallel to Interstate 35 and eventually forming a portion of the Garvin/Murray County border. South of Davis, the Washita flows between Turner Falls State Park and the Chickasaw National Recreation Area in Sulphur. Later, the river forms the Carter/Murray County line, then jogs to the east and meanders south before it enters Basin 21 near its confluence with Caddo Creek. The average annual flow of the Washita River, estimated at the bottom of Basin 14, is 1,710 cfs; this flow is available less than 23 percent of the time.

Basin 14 is characterized by a number of significant lakes, which offer an abundance of water supply, recreation, flood control and other benefits. Principal among these is the Lake of the Arbuckles, near Sulphur, which was built by the Bureau of Reclamation in 1967. It is impounded by Rock Creek in Murray County. Adjacent to the lake in Sulphur, the Chickasaw National Recreation Area is a treasured resource that draws an estimated three million visitors each year.

Lakes Fuqua and Humphreys, both in Stephens County in the western portion of the Lower Washita watershed, serve as backup supplies for the City of Duncan. Some 2,182 AFY of Fuqua's 3,427 AFY yield is considered available for appropriation. Lake Jean Neustadt, on a tributary of Caddo Creek, provides water supply to the City of Ardmore; 883 AFY of its yield is considered available. In Garvin County, R.C. Longmire Lake, a supply for Pauls Valley, impounds water on Keel Sandy Creek.

The Lower Washita River watershed includes two endangered species: the piping plover and whooping crane. Threatened are the American burying beetle, Arkansas River shiner and red knot.

Water Quality

Basin 14 exists primarily in the Cross Timbers ecoregion, which includes the Level IV Arbuckle Uplift and Arbuckle Mountains, and also a portion of the Central Great Plains ecoregion. Stream salinity is high in the region and the Washita River is hypereutrophic. The basin consists of eight lake sub-watersheds—Rock Creek Reservoir, Arbuckle Reservoir, Pauls Valley Reservoir, Mountain Lake, Humphreys Lake, Fuqua Reservoir, Duncan Lake, and Clear Creek Lake—that are designated as sensitive water supplies (SWS). Most of the lakes in the basin are eutrophic. Taylor (Marlow) Lake, near Rush Springs, a hypereutrophic lake, is designated as a nutrient limited watershed (NLW). Honey Creek and Guy Sandy Creek are designated as high quality waters (HQW). TMDLs have been completed for bacteria on Caddo Creek, Wildhorse Creek, Kickapoo Sandy Creek, Chigley Sandy Creek and the Washita River itself.

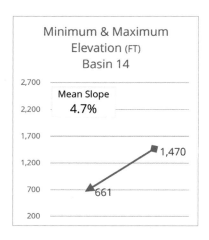

Minimum & Maximum Elevation (FT) Basin 14

Mean Slope 4.7%

1,470

661

PRINCIPAL RIVERS & STREAMS BASIN 14	
River/Stream	**Length** MILES
Washita River	76
Wildhorse Creek	64
Rush Creek	58
Caddo Creek	57
Rock Creek	47
Guy Sandy Creek	22
Black Bear Creek	21
Salt Creek	19
Sandy Creek	16
Cherokee Sandy Creek	14
Chigley Sandy Creek	14
Hickory Creek	14
Honey Creek	13
Clear Creek	12

PRINCIPAL LAKES
BASIN 14

Name	Stream	Authority	Normal Elevation FEET	Normal Area ACRES	Normal Capacity AC-FT	Shoreline MILES	Purpose(s)[1]	Water Supply Storage AC-FT	Water Supply Yield AC-FT/YR
Arbuckles	Rock Creek	BOR	872.2	2,430	72,400	34.7	WS, FC, FW, R	62,600	24,000
Ardmore	Caddo Creek TR	Lake Ardmore Club Assoc.	—	120	570	3.6	—	—	—
Ardmore City	Caddo Creek TR	City of Ardmore	818.5	144	600	4.5	R	—	—
Byars	Peavine Creek TR	Town of Byars	—	72	92	1.8	—	—	—
Caddo Creek #2	Caddo Creek TR	SCS/Arbuckle CD	—	61	166	1.6	FC	—	—
Caddo Creek #17	Caddo Creek TR	SCS/Arbuckle CD	—	47	217	1.6	FC	—	—
Caddo Creek #19	Caddo Creek TR	SCS/Arbuckle CD	—	41	123	2	FC	—	—
Caddo Creek #27	Caddo Creek TR	SCS/Arbuckle CD	—	45	300	1.6	FC	—	—
Caddo Creek #28	Washita River TR	SCS/Arbuckle CD	—	40	181	2.2	FC	—	—
Cherokee Sandy #8	Willow Sandy Creek TR	SCS/Garvin Co. CD	—	47	193	2.3	FC	—	—
Cherokee Sandy #9	Cherokee Sandy Creek	SCS/Garvin Co. CD	—	54	252	1.7	FC	—	—
Chigley Sandy Creek #6	Chigley Sandy Creek TR	SCS/Garvin Co. CD	—	51	346	1.3	FC	—	—
Clear Creek	Clear Creek	City of Duncan	1,150.3	697	7,710	9.5	WS, R	—	2,000
Duncan	Fitzpatrick Creek	City of Duncan	1,095.3	199	7,200	3.6	WS, R	—	—
Elmore City	Rock Creek TR	Garvin Co. CD	—	65	564	2.6	FC	—	77
Fuqua	Black Bear Creek	City of Duncan	1,076	986	21,100	13.9	WS. FC, R	21,100	3,427
Humphreys	Wildhorse Creek	City of Duncan	1,178	780	14,041	12.4	WS, FC, R	—	3,226
Jean Neustadt	Caddo Creek TR	City of Ardmore	809	397	6,106	8.3	R	—	2,150
Mountain	Hickory Creek	City of Ardmore	1,045.7	205	3,040	4.5	R	—	—
Pauls Valley	Washington Creek	City of Pauls Valley	900	507	8,730	7.7	WS, R	—	—
Peavine Creek #1	Peavine Creek	SCS/Garvin Co. CD	—	85	325	2.2	FC	—	—
Peavine Creek #2	Peavine Creek TR	SCS/Garvin Co. CD	—	70	358	2.2	FC	—	—
Peavine Creek #3	Peavine Creek TR	SCS/Garvin Co. CD	—	57	363	1.8	FC	—	—
Peavine Creek #4	Peavine Creek TR	SCS/Garvin Co. CD	—	55	326	1.5	FC	—	—
Peavine Creek #5	Peavine Creek TR	SCS/McClain Co. CD	—	53	319	1.5	FC	—	—

Name	Stream	Authority	Normal Elevation FEET	Normal Area ACRES	Normal Capacity AC-FT	Shoreline MILES	Purpose(s)[1]	Water Supply Storage AC-FT	Water Supply Yield AC-FT/YR
			PRINCIPAL LAKES **BASIN 14**						
Peavine Creek #11	Peavine Creek TR	SCS/McClain Co. CD	—	58	216	1.8	FC	—	—
R.C. Longmire	Keel Sandy Creek	SCS/City of Pauls Valley	979.2	919	14,424	12	WS, R	—	3,360
Rock Creek #14	Rock Creek	SCS/Pontotoc Co. CD	—	64	198	2.7	FC	—	—
Rush Creek #4	Rush Creek TR	SCS/Grady Co. CD	—	47	330	1.9	FC	—	—
Rush Creek #10	Rush Creek TR	SCS/Grady Co. CD	—	87	835	2.9	FC	—	—
Scott King	Rock Creek	City of Ardmore	808	221	3,588	4.8	R	—	1,220
Taylor	Rush Creek	City of Marlow (Leased)	1,255	195	1,877	4.1	WS, FC, R	—	—
Veterans	Rock Creek TR	City of Sulphur	965	66	600	2	R	—	—
Wildhorse Creek #11	Wildhorse Creek TR	SCS/Arbuckle CD	—	53	160	2.2	FC	—	—
Wildhorse Creek #14	Wildhorse Creek TR	SCS/Stephens Co. CD	—	80	639	1.7	FC	—	—
Wildhorse Creek #19	Fitzpatrick Creek	SCS/Stephens Co. CD	—	44	791	1.4	FC	—	—
Wildhorse Creek #23	Clear Creek	SCS/Stephens Co. CD	—	101	731	2.8	FC	—	—
Wildhorse Creek #25	Clear Creek TR	SCS/Stephens Co. CD	—	41	244	1.8	FC	—	—
Wildhorse Creek #26	Wildhorse Creek TR	SCS/Stephens Co. CD	—	87	646	1.9	FC	—	—
Wildhorse Creek #27	Wildhorse Creek TR	SCS/Stephens Co. CD	—	90	713	2.1	FC	—	—
Wildhorse Creek #30	Wildhorse Creek TR	SCS/Stephens Co. CD	—	43	286	1.7	FC	—	—

[1]WS=Water Supply, R=Recreation, HP=Hydroelectric Power, IR=Irrigation, WQ=Water Quality, FW=Fish & Wildlife, FC=Flood Control, LF=Low Flow Regulation, N=Navigation, C=Conservation, CW=Cooling Water

LAND COVER & USES
LOWER WASHITA RIVER WATERSHED

Use	Area SQ. MI.
Forest	452
Herbaceous, Shrubs, Woody Wetlands	1,057
Cultivated Land, Hay/Pasture	237
Developed	91
Water	29
Barren Land	3
Total Land Area	**1,869**

Land Cover & Uses
Lower Washita River Watershed (B)

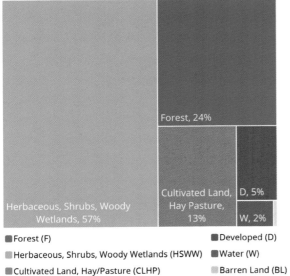

- Forest (F)
- Herbaceous, Shrubs, Woody Wetlands (HSWW)
- Cultivated Land, Hay/Pasture (CLHP)
- Developed (D)
- Water (W)
- Barren Land (BL)

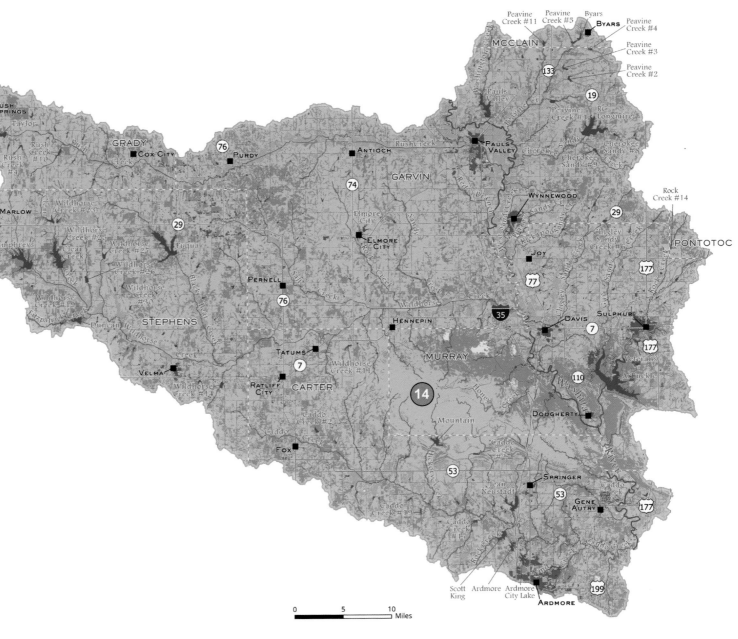

Groundwater

Several prolific groundwater basins underlie the Lower Washita River watershed. In the northwest portion of Basin 14, the major Rush Springs and minor El Reno aquifers are prolific sources of water with 199 and 190 existing wells, respectively. In the east, the Washita River, Arbuckle-Simpson and Gerty Sand, all major aquifers, provide largely reliable sources of groundwater for local users. A hydrologic study of the Rush Springs was completed in 2018; a recommended MAY is pending approval, but the temporary EPS of 2.0 ac-ft/acre is expected to be lowered. A study of the Washita River aquifer (Reaches 3 and 4) is ongoing.

While some 1,575 water wells have been drilled within the boundaries of Basin 14, almost two-thirds of these are completed in nondelineated groundwater sources, which supplement the watershed's already significant underground supplies.

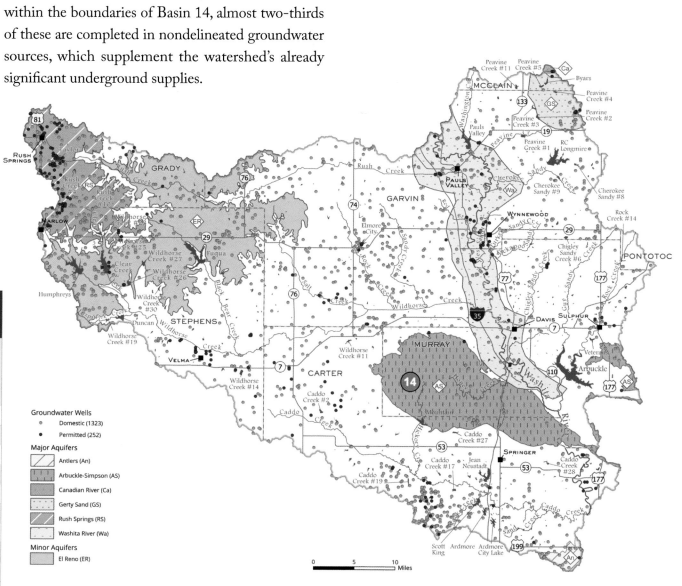

MAJOR & MINOR AQUIFERS BASIN 14			
Aquifer	Area in Basin/ Watershed SQUARE MILES	EPS[1] AC-FT/ACRE	Number of Permitted & Domestic Wells in Basin/ Watershed[2]
Antlers	7	2.1	23
Arbuckle-Simpson	133	0.2	35
Canadian River	1	2.0	4
El Reno	193	2.0	190
Gerty Sand	23	0.65	28
Rush Springs	82	2.0	199
Washita River	142	1.0 (Reach 4)	153
Nondelineated Source Wells			943
Total Wells			1,575

[1]Italic number signifies unstudied aquifers with a default temporary equal proportionate share (EPS) of 2.0 acre-feet per acre of land.

[2]Some wells are double-counted where one aquifer overlies another.

Groundwater Wells
- ○ Domestic (1323)
- ● Permitted (252)

Major Aquifers
- Antlers (An)
- Arbuckle-Simpson (AS)
- Canadian River (Ca)
- Gerty Sand (GS)
- Rush Springs (RS)
- Washita River (Wa)

Minor Aquifers
- El Reno (ER)

NOTE: Significant color and shading variations may be apparent in areas where one aquifer overlies another. In some cases, for state administrative purposes, aquifer boundaries align directly with county lines or related political borders rather than geologic outcrop areas.

The Lower Washita River watershed is characterized by varied and complex water supplies and uses. Surface water sources account for 64 percent (67,153 AFY) of all permitted water in Basin 14. Public supply is the predominant use for appropriated and allocated water at 53 percent, followed by irrigation (17 percent), industry (12 percent), and oil, gas and mining (9 percent). In addition, recreation, fish and wildlife uses account for a healthy eight percent share of overall uses. Agriculture is the only recognized water use category for which no permits are currently issued in Basin 14.

The largest and most influential public water supplier in the Lower Washita River watershed is the Arbuckle Master Conservancy District (MCD), which owns rights and storage in the Lake of the Arbuckles allowing for the distribution of up to 24,000 AFY among its many customers. The City of Duncan possesses a number of permits for public supply and recreation, fish and wildlife uses granting 9,670 AFY in surface water diversions, including from city-owned supplies at Lakes Humphreys and Fuqua in Stephens County. Other municipal providers in the watershed with relatively substantial water rights include Ardmore (6,092 AFY for public supply from multiple surface and groundwater sources) and Pauls Valley, including a 3,361 AFY public supply and industrial permit from Lake R.C. Longmire and a 1,993 AFY public supply and recreation, fish and wildlife right in Pauls Valley Lake. Also worth noting is the City of Davis, which possesses 3,025 AFY for public supply uses and a 1,600 AFY permit for recreation, fish and wildlife purposes associated with Turner Falls Park in Murray County.

The largest industrial user in Basin 14 is the Wynnewood Refinery in Garvin County, which has three prior rights allowing the use of 7,249 AFY of groundwater.

Any application to appropriate water for use at a location outside of Basin 14 could be subject to conferral, depending upon the application amount, mean available flow and other relevant factors. See conditions associated with Class B Basins in the Tribal-State Water Settlement agreement in the *Oka Holisso* appendix.

PERMITTED WATER AFY		
BASIN 14		
Groundwater	Surface Water	Total
38,585	67,153	105,738

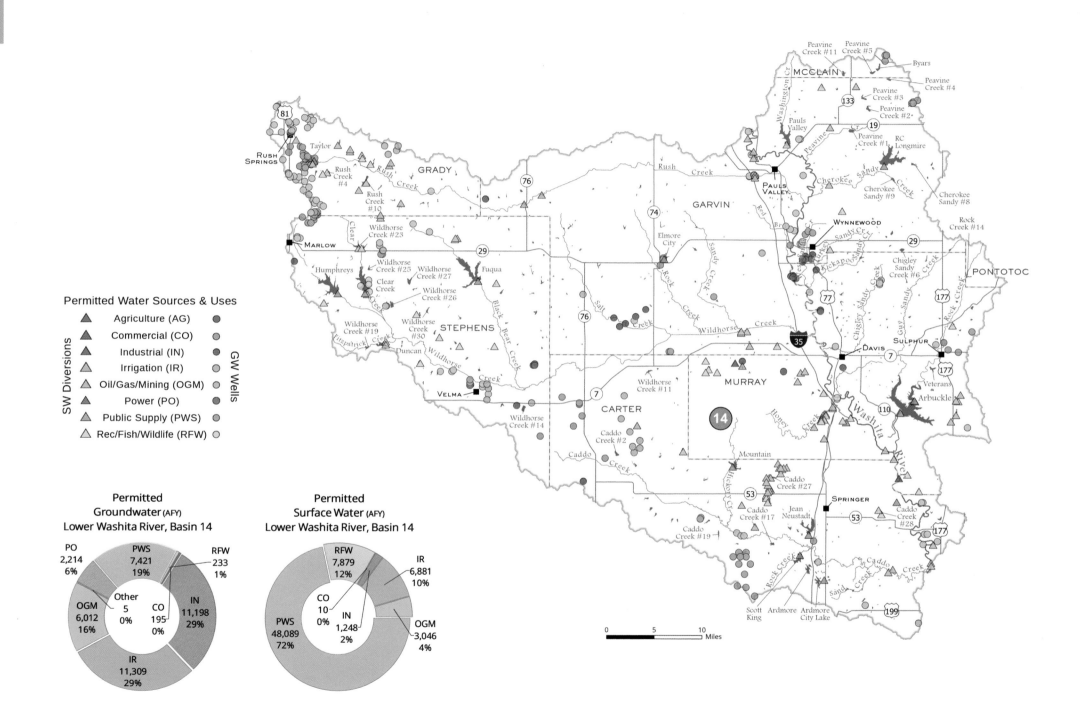

Permitted Water Sources & Uses

SW Diversions

▲ Agriculture (AG)　　● GW Wells
▲ Commercial (CO)　　●
▲ Industrial (IN)　　●
▲ Irrigation (IR)　　●
▲ Oil/Gas/Mining (OGM)　　●
▲ Power (PO)　　●
▲ Public Supply (PWS)　　●
▲ Rec/Fish/Wildlife (RFW)　　○

Permitted Groundwater (AFY)
Lower Washita River, Basin 14

PO 2,214 6%
PWS 7,421 19%
RFW 233 1%
Other 5 0%
CO 195 0%
IN 11,198 29%
IR 11,309 29%
OGM 6,012 16%

Permitted Surface Water (AFY)
Lower Washita River, Basin 14

RFW 7,879 12%
IR 6,881 10%
CO 10 0%
IN 1,248 2%
OGM 3,046 4%
PWS 48,089 72%

Water Supply Systems

The southern Lower Washita watershed includes a large portion of the area served by the City of Ardmore, the second largest (to the City of Ada) water provider in the Settlement Area with more than 25,000 residential customers. Ardmore is supplied by the Lake of the Arbuckles and smaller local reservoirs, including Jean Neustadt, Mountain Lake, Scott King (Rock Creek) and Ardmore City Lake. Water from Jean Neustadt, Mountain Lake and Scott King can be pumped to the city lake or directly to the municipal treatment plant. Ardmore has also developed a well field west of I-35 for use when required.

Ardmore maintains interconnections with Southern Oklahoma Water Corporation (SOWC, 14,000 customers), whose 600-square-mile service area surrounds the city. SOWC utilizes groundwater from nine active wells in the Oscar and Antlers aquifers. In addition, SOWC obtains 570 AFY from Lake Murray and approximately 1,120 AFY from Arbuckle Lake—the latter through a contract with Arbuckle MCD, which was originally established through the U.S. Bureau of Reclamation's Arbuckle project. The district operates and maintains Arbuckle Lake Dam and appurtenant water supply infrastructure, resulting in its position as the region's largest wholesale provider as it supplies

PUBLIC WATER SUPPLY SYSTEMS BASIN 14										
					Facilities[3]					
System	Residential Customers Served[1]	Source(s) of Supply[2]	Water Sales	Water Purchases	Intake	Pump Facility	Storage	Treatment Plant	Well or Spring
Ardmore	25,060	SW	Lone Grove, SOWC	Arbuckle Lake MCD, SOWC	1			1	
Buckhorn RWD #2	1,260	P (GW)	—	Murray Co. #1, Sulphur					
Byars	275	GW	—	—					5
Davis	2,610	SW	West Davis RWD, Western Carter Co. WC	Arbuckle Lake MCD	1			1	
Dougherty	224	P (GW)	—	Murray Co. #1	1			1	
Duncan PUA	23,000	SW	Jefferson Co. #1, Stephens Co. #5	—	2				
Elmore City	756	GW	Elmore City RW Corp.	Elmore City RWC					1
Elmore City RW Corp.	1,107	P (SW)	Elmore City	Elmore City, Pauls Valley					
Garvin Co. RWD #1	1,445	GW	—	—					
Garvin Co. RWD #2	1,570	GW	—	—					
Garvin Co. RWD #4	1,340	P (SW)	—	Pauls Valley					
Garvin Co. RWD #6 (SW Purchase)	862	P (SW)	—	Wynnewood W&L					
Garvin Co. RWD #6 (Wells)	2,762	GW	—	Wynnewood W&L					2
Grady Co. RWD #7 (Ninnekah)	2,425	GW	—	—					
Jefferson Co. RWD #1	8,276	GW	Healdton, Ringling, Ryan UA, Stephens Co. #4, Terral, Wilson MA	Comanche PWA, Duncan PUA, Stephens Co. #4, Waurika PWA, Wilson MA					
Lone Grove	4,863	GW	—	Ardmore					2
Marlow PWA	4,600	GW	—	—					28
McClain Co. RWD #8	1,897	GW	—	—					

water for an estimated 51,000 people. The MCD sells and delivers approximately 12,000 AFY of raw water supply (24,000 AFY is available) to Wynnewood, Davis and Ardmore, as well as the Wynnewood oil refinery and rural districts. The City of Sulphur, which currently utilizes groundwater from eleven wells in the Arbuckle-Simpson aquifer, has also contracted for 1,997 AFY of Arbuckle Lake water. A recent study was conducted to investigate a potential pipeline connection from the city to the lake.

Also deserving mention is Murray Co. RWD #1, serving a large area around and north of Sulphur. The district utilizes two Arbuckle-Simpson aquifer wells to supply 4,500 customers and is in the process of acquiring additional water rights to address the recent reduction in the aquifer's allocation limits.

Current growth in and around the city of Sulphur (5,000 customers, not including an agreement to provide emergency supply to Murray #1) presents considerable challenges due to currently insufficient supply (specifically water rights in the Arbuckle-Simpson) and infrastructure. This has prompted discussions with the nearby city of Davis, which is capable of expanding service to the community as well as Wynnewood and potentially other systems in the area. Up to an eight-mile pipeline would be required to connect Sulphur and Davis, which recently constructed a new treatment plant to serve its 2,610 customers and wholesale users of West Davis RWD and Western Carter County Water Corporation.

System	Residential Customers Served[1]	Source(s) of Supply[2]	Water Sales	Water Purchases	Intake	Pump Facility	Storage	Treatment Plant	Well or Spring
Murray Co. RWD #1	4,500	GW	Buckhorn #2, Dougherty	Sulphur					
Pauls Valley	6,256	SW	Elmore City RWC, Garvin Co. #4	—	1			1	
Ratliff City	131	P (SW)	—	Western Carter Co. WC					
Rush Springs	1,278	GW	—	—					3
Southern Oklahoma Water Corp.	14,000	SW/GW	Ardmore	Ardmore	1			1	4
Stephens Co. RW&SD #1	960	GW	—	—					5
Stephens Co. RWD #5	6,426	GW	—	Duncan PUA					
Sulphur	5,000	GW	Buckhorn #2, Murray Co. #1	—					10
West Davis RWD	492	GW	—	Davis, Western Carter Co. WC					
Western Carter Co. Water Corp.	658	GW	Ratliff City, West Davis RWD	Davis					2
Wynnewood Water & Light	2,307	SW	Garvin Co. #6, (Wells and SW Purchase)	Arbuckle Lake MCD	1			1	

PUBLIC WATER SUPPLY SYSTEMS — BASIN 14 (Facilities[3])

[1]Does not include wholesale customers served through water sales.

[2]GW = Groundwater; SW = Surface Water; P = Purchased.

[3]Includes both active and inactive (mostly wells) facilities in the watershed. Treatment plants include only those utilizing conventional water treatment and do not include chlorination stations associated with discrete source treatment.

Data: Oklahoma Department of Environmental Quality, Safe Drinking Water Information System, OWRB GIS and Arbuckle-Simpson Aquifer Drought Contingency Plan. Listed system facilities include those with service areas and/or facilities within relevant watershed.

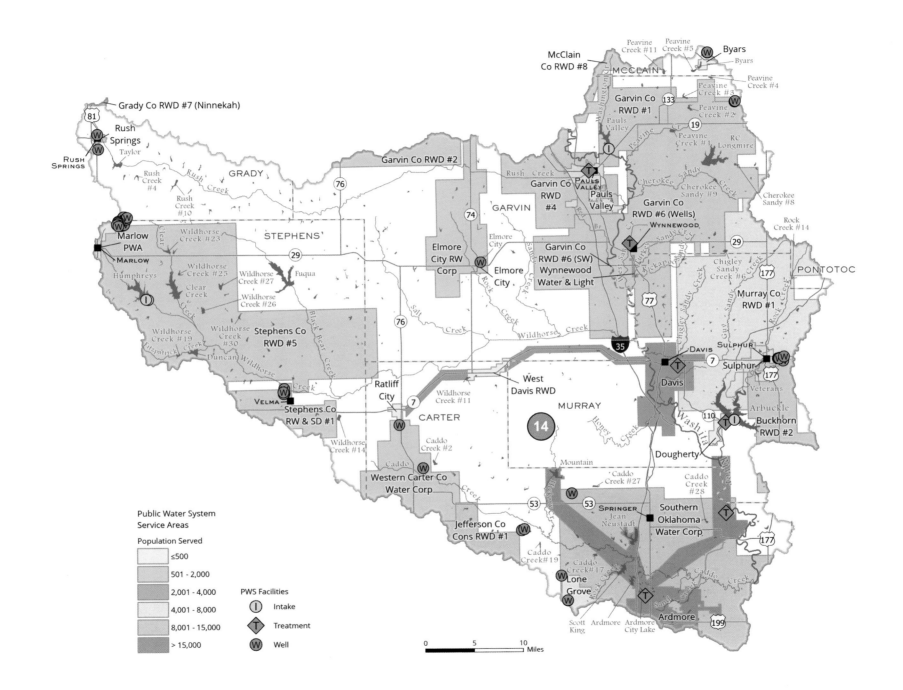

Public Water System Service Areas

Population Served

- ≤500
- 501 - 2,000
- 2,001 - 4,000
- 4,001 - 8,000
- 8,001 - 15,000
- > 15,000

PWS Facilities

- Ⓘ Intake
- ◆ T Treatment
- Ⓦ Well

0   5   10 Miles

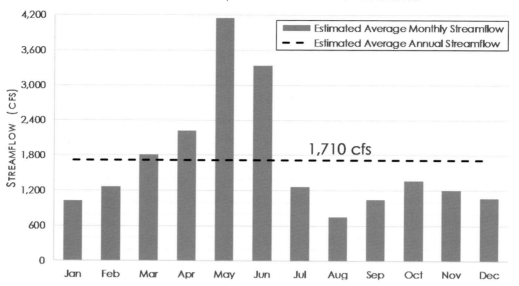

Estimated Streamflow, Lower Washita River Watershed

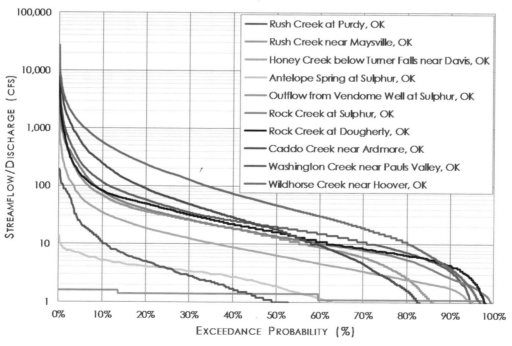

Streamflow Exceedance Probability, Lower Washita River Watershed

Reservoir Level Exceedance for Lake of The Arbuckles

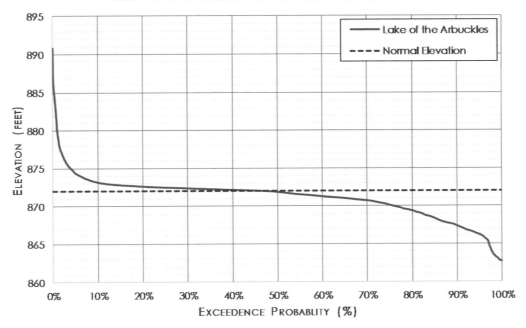

Streamflow Exceedance Probability, Lower Washita River Watershed

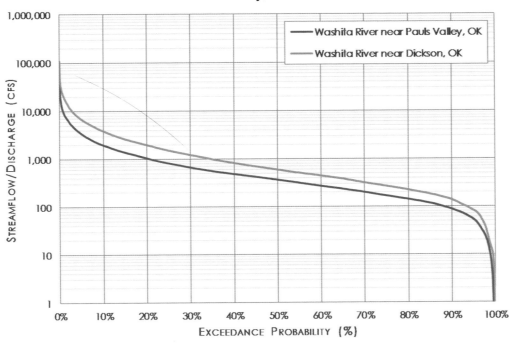

Mountain Fork River

BASIN 4

Basin 4 — Lower Mountain Fork River

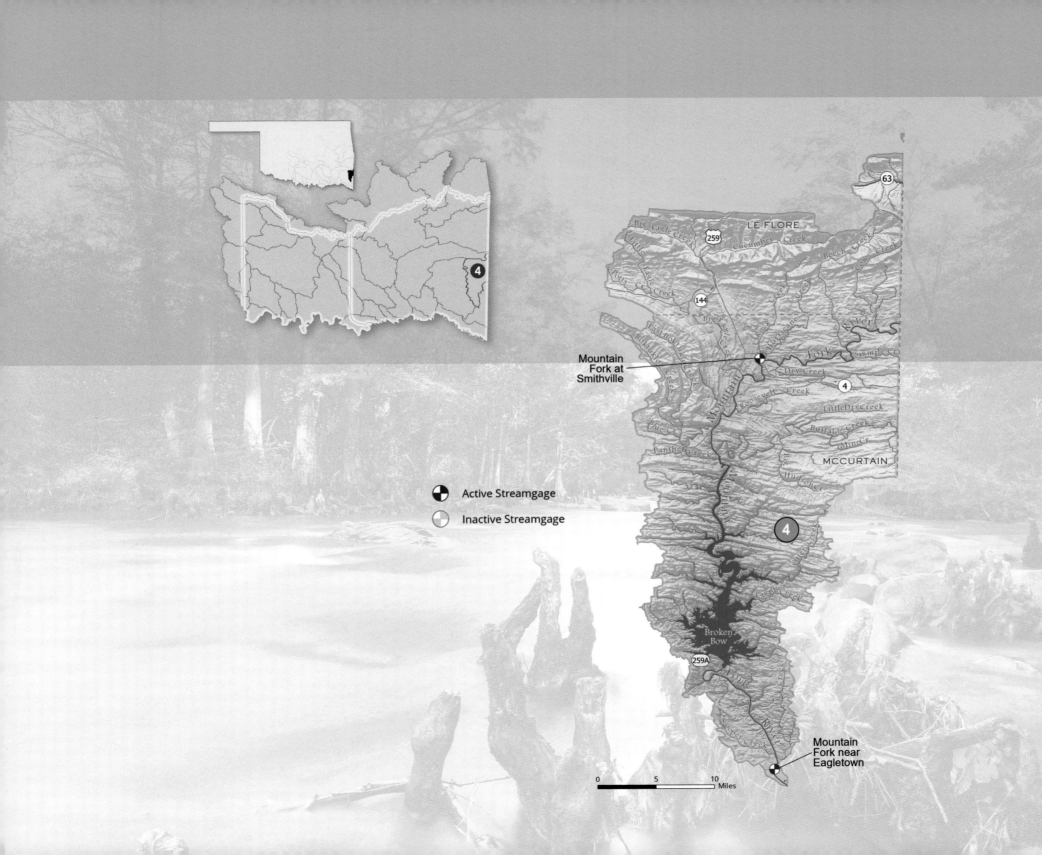

LE FLORE

259

259

144

63

Big Eagle Creek
Little Eagle Creek
Potts Cr
East Bokuklo Creek
Big Eagle Creek
Cucumber Creek
Creek
Beech Creek
Cow Creek

Mountain
Fork at
Smithville

Fork

River

Sixmile Cr

Dry Creek

4

Roosevelt Creek

LittleDryCreek

Buffalo Creek

MineCr

Placer Creek

PantherCreek

Mountain

HudsonCr

MCCURTAIN

⬤ Active Streamgage

◐ Inactive Streamgage

4

Broken
Bow

259A

Fork

River

Cooper Creek

Mountain
Fork near
Eagletown

0   5   10
                    Miles

The headwaters of the scenic Mountain Fork River originate in southwest Arkansas. In Oklahoma, the river resides entirely within McCurtain County. The Mountain Fork flows westward from the state line, then dips south as it enters the Ouachita National Forest, Broken Bow WMA, Ouachita WMA and McCurtain County Wilderness Area along Broken Bow Lake's northern arm. The Ouachita National Forest, which surrounds the lake, covers 1.8 million acres in central Arkansas and southeastern Oklahoma. The section of the river above the impoundment is noted for its high quality waters and has been designated as one of Oklahoma's six "scenic rivers," which are legislatively protected due to their unique free-flowing beauty and recreational value. Just downstream of Broken Bow Lake, the Mountain Fork meanders through Beavers Bend State Park, then

assumes a southeasterly path to its termination at the Little River and Basin 2.

Encompassing 555 square miles, Basin 4 is characterized by a considerable slope (relative to other watersheds) of more than 15 percent. The average annual flow of the Mountain Fork River, estimated at the bottom of Basin 4, is 1,353 cfs; this flow is available 26 percent of the time.

Broken Bow Lake is the sole large impoundment in Basin 4. Reallocation of the lake's water supply storage and associated yield has releases for downstream trout fishery. Beavers Bend State Park, encompassing almost 3,500 acres of land just downstream of the dam, including the site of an old Choctaw settlement, was named for John T. Beavers, a Choctaw intermarried citizen.

Basin 4 supports numerous exceptional plant and animal species, including the endangered harperella,

Indiana bat, piping plover, Ouachita rock pocketbook, red-cockaded woodpecker, Scaleshell mussel and Winged Mapleleaf. Threatened species in Basin 4 include the American burying beetle, leopard darter, northern long-eared bat, rabbitsfoot and red knot.

Water Quality

The Mountain Fork River watershed exists primarily in the Ouachita Mountains ecoregion (in the Athens Plateau and Central Mountain Ranges), where it is common for rocky stream substrates to be composed of gravel, cobbles, and boulders resulting in low turbidity during low flows. The entire basin area is defined by special source water protection designations. As mentioned, the Upper Mountain Fork River is a scenic river watershed. The Up-

PRINCIPAL RIVERS & STREAMS — BASIN 4

River/Stream	Length MILES
Mountain Fork River	68
Buffalo Creek	24
Big Eagle Creek	20
Boktuklo Creek	15
Rock Creek	14
Beech Creek	13
Cow Creek	11
Otter Creek	11
Cucumber Creek	11
Dry Creek	10

PRINCIPAL LAKES — BASINS 4

Name	Stream	Authority	Normal Elevation FEET	Normal Area ACRES	Normal Capacity AC-FT	Shoreline MILES	Purpose(s)[1]	Water Supply Storage AC-FT	Water Supply Yield[2] AC-FT/YR
Broken Bow[3]	Mountain Fork River	USACE	599.5	14,160	913,370	181.2	FC, HP, WS, R, FW	152,500	58,386

[1]WS=Water Supply, R=Recreation, HP=Hydroelectric Power, IR=Irrigation, WQ=Water Quality, FW=Fish & Wildlife, FC=Flood Control, LF=Low Flow Regulation, N=Navigation, C=Conservation, CW=Cooling Water
[2]107,000 AF of the lake's water supply storage (and corresponding yield) has been reallocated to facilitate releases for the downstream trout fishery and to mitigate fish loss, thus reducing the lake's total yield from 196,000 to 58,386 AFY.
[3]Reservoir utilizes seasonal operations plan.

per Mountain Fork River and Broken Bow Reservoir are also sensitive water supplies, as are Buffalo Creek, Otter Creek and Egypt Creek. Outstanding resource waters include Big Eagle Creek, Little Eagle Creek, Boktuklo Creek, Cow Creek, Beech Creek, Cucumber Creek, Blue Creek, and Panther Creek. The Little River downstream of Broken Bow Lake is designated as high quality waters. Broken Bow Lake is phosphorus-limited and mesotrophic exhibiting extremely low nutrient values. Fish consumption is not supported in Broken Bow Lake because of mercury levels; cadmium levels impair fish and wildlife propagation. The Mountain Fork River does not support Fish and Wildlife Propagation due to elevated lead and silver. TMDLs have been completed for pH on Buffalo Creek, Beech Creek and Cow Creek where acidic soils are common.

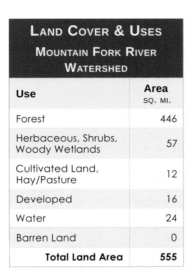

LAND COVER & USES MOUNTAIN FORK RIVER WATERSHED	
Use	**Area** SQ. MI.
Forest	446
Herbaceous, Shrubs, Woody Wetlands	57
Cultivated Land, Hay/Pasture	12
Developed	16
Water	24
Barren Land	0
Total Land Area	**555**

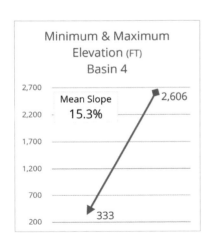

Minimum & Maximum Elevation (FT) Basin 4

Mean Slope 15.3%

2,606

333

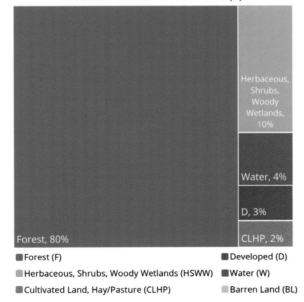

Land Cover & Uses
Mountain Fork River Watershed (B)

Forest, 80%
Herbaceous, Shrubs, Woody Wetlands, 10%
Water, 4%
D, 3%
CLHP, 2%

- ■ Forest (F)
- ■ Herbaceous, Shrubs, Woody Wetlands (HSWW)
- ■ Cultivated Land, Hay/Pasture (CLHP)
- ■ Developed (D)
- ■ Water (W)
- ■ Barren Land (BL)

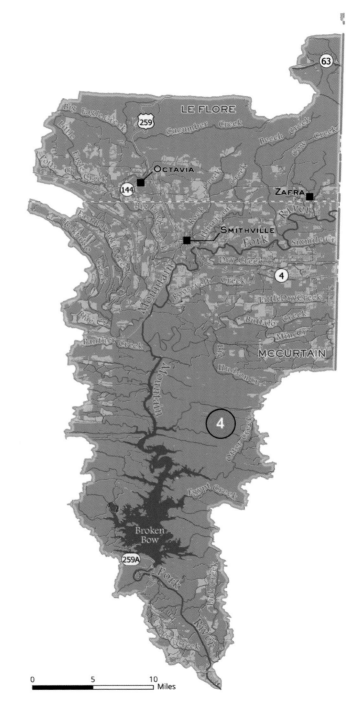

Groundwater

While groundwater usage is generally insignificant in Basin 4, the watershed is underlain by one major (albeit a minimal portion of the Antlers aquifer) and five minor groundwater basins. The Kiamichi aquifer is, by far, the most extensive and heavily utilized with 356 of the 372 wells completed within the watershed area.

MAJOR & MINOR AQUIFERS BASIN 4			
Aquifer	Area in Basin/ Watershed SQUARE MILES	EPS[1] AC-FT/ACRE	Number of Permitted & Domestic Wells in Basin/ Watershed[2]
Antlers	1	2.1	0
Broken Bow	100	2.0	13
Holly Creek	4	2.0	2
Kiamichi	431	2.0	356
Little River	2	1.0	1
Pine Mountain	22	2.0	0
Nondelineated Source Wells			0
		Total Wells	372

[1]Italic number signifies unstudied aquifers with a default temporary equal proportionate share (EPS) of 2.0 acre-feet per acre of land.
[2]Some wells are double-counted where one aquifer overlies another.

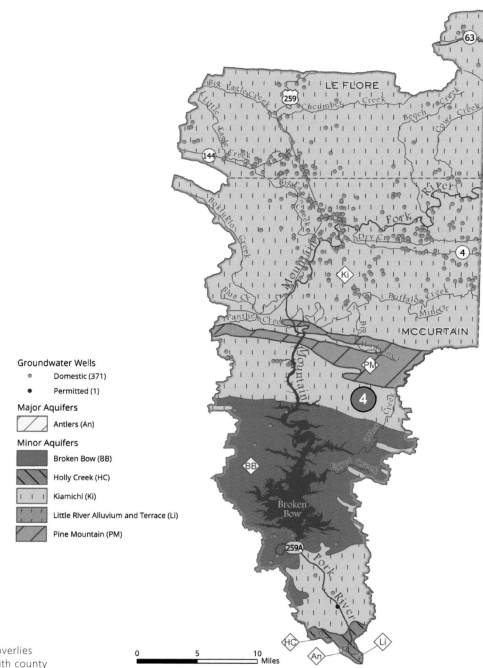

Groundwater Wells
- ○ Domestic (371)
- ● Permitted (1)

Major Aquifers
- Antlers (An)

Minor Aquifers
- Broken Bow (BB)
- Holly Creek (HC)
- Kiamichi (Ki)
- Little River Alluvium and Terrace (Li)
- Pine Mountain (PM)

NOTE: Significant color and shading variations may be apparent in areas where one aquifer overlies another. In some cases, for state administrative purposes, aquifer boundaries align directly with county lines or related political borders rather than geologic outcrop areas.

Permitted Water Use

Permitted groundwater use (aside from domestic wells) in the Mountain Fork River watershed is virtually nonexistent. Surface sources account for more than 99 percent of all permitted water in Basin 4.

Permitted uses basin-wide are almost exclusively confined to public water supply, which constitutes 99 percent of appropriations. Broken Bow Public Works Authority holds 10,660 AFY in rights while the Mountain Fork Water Supply Corporation maintains 1,711 AFY to serve its users. Two surface water rights account for all of the permitted irrigation in the Mountain Fork River watershed. The sole groundwater permit (two AFY) in the watershed is granted to the U.S. Army Corps of Engineers for recreation, fish and wildlife purposes.

Any application to appropriate water for use at a location outside of Basin 4 could be subject to conferral, depending upon the application amount, mean available flow and other relevant factors. See conditions associated with Class A Basins in the Tribal-State Water Settlement agreement in the *Oka Holisso* appendix.

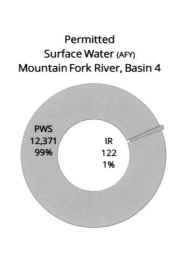

Permitted Surface Water (AFY)
Mountain Fork River, Basin 4

PWS 12,371 99%
IR 122 1%

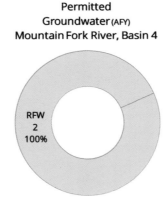

Permitted Groundwater (AFY)
Mountain Fork River, Basin 4

RFW 2 100%

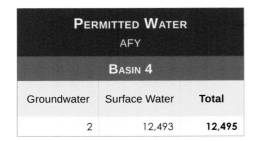

PERMITTED WATER		
AFY		
BASIN 4		
Groundwater	Surface Water	**Total**
2	12,493	**12,495**

Permitted Water Sources & Uses

SW Diversions / GW Wells

- ▲ Agriculture (AG) ●
- ▲ Commercial (CO) ◐
- ▲ Industrial (IN) ●
- △ Irrigation (IR) ◐
- △ Oil/Gas/Mining (OGM) ○
- ▲ Power (PO) ●
- ▲ Public Supply (PWS) ◐
- △ Rec/Fish/Wildlife (RFW) ○

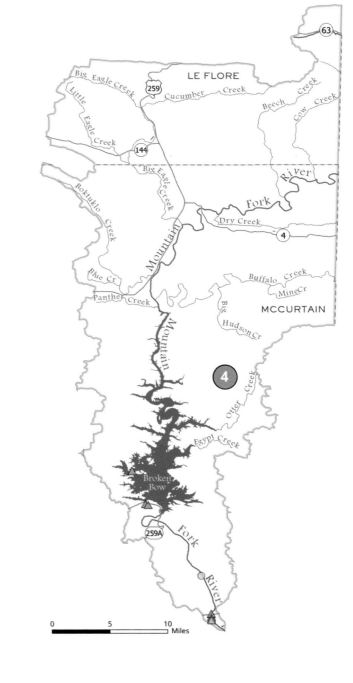

Water Supply Systems

The largely rural Mountain Fork watershed includes all or portions of only five water systems, all utilizing abundant surface supplies in the region. Chief among these is McCurtain Co. RWD #8 (Mountain Fork Water), which provides water from the river to 5,685 residential customers primarily residing south of Basin 4 in the adjacent Upper Little and Little River watersheds. Backup supply is provided by the Broken Bow PWA (in Basin 3). The authority and its high-quality water derived from Broken Bow Lake is the sole source for McCurtain Co. RWDs #5 and #6.

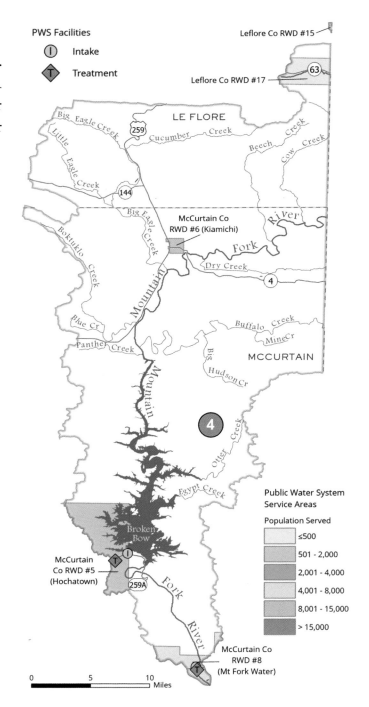

System	Residential Customers Served[1]	Source(s) of Supply[2]	Water Sales	Water Purchases	Intake	Pump Facility	Storage	Treatment Plant	Well or Spring
					Facilities[3]				
Broken Bow PWA	4,320	SW	Garvin, Haworth PWA, Idabel PWA, McCurtain Co. #1, McCurtain Co. #2, McCurtain Co. #5, McCurtain Co. #6, McCurtain Co. #7, McCurtain Co. #8, McCurtain Co. #9, Valliant PWA, Wright City PWA	—	1			1	
LeFlore Co. RWD #15	425	P (SW)	—	Poteau Valley Improvement Authority					
LeFlore Co. RWD #17	373	P (SW)	—	—					
McCurtain Co. RWD #5 (Hochatown)	1,614	P (SW)	—	Broken Bow PWA					
McCurtain Co. RWD #6 (Kiamichi)	600	P (SW)	—	Broken Bow PWA					
McCurtain Co. RWD #8 (Mt. Fork Water)	5,685	SW	—	Broken Bow PWA	1			1	

PUBLIC WATER SUPPLY SYSTEMS
BASIN 4

[1]Does not include wholesale customers served through water sales.

[2]GW = Groundwater; SW = Surface Water; P = Purchased.

[3]Includes both active and inactive (mostly wells) facilities in the watershed. Treatment plants include only those utilizing conventional water treatment and do not include chlorination stations associated with discrete source treatment.

Data: Oklahoma Department of Environmental Quality, Safe Drinking Water Information System, OWRB GIS and Arbuckle-Simpson Aquifer Drought Contingency Plan. Listed system facilities include those with service areas and/or facilities within relevant watershed.

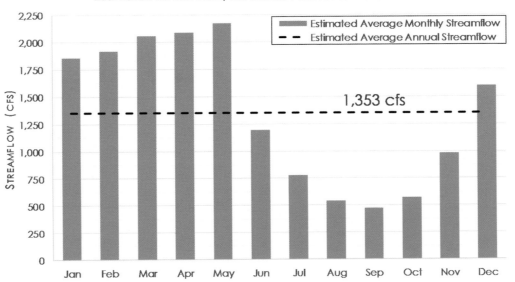

Estimated Streamflow, Mountain Fork River Watershed

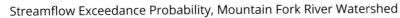

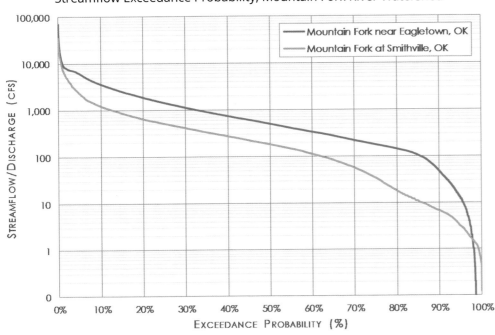

Streamflow Exceedance Probability, Mountain Fork River Watershed

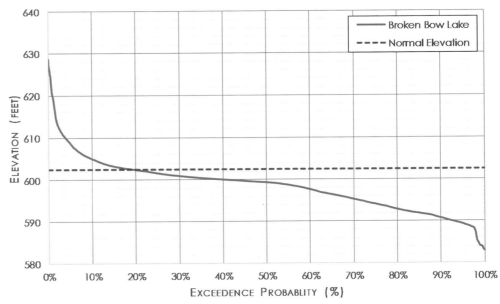

Reservoir Level Exceedance for Broken Bow Lake (Seasonal Operations)

Upper Little River

BASIN 3

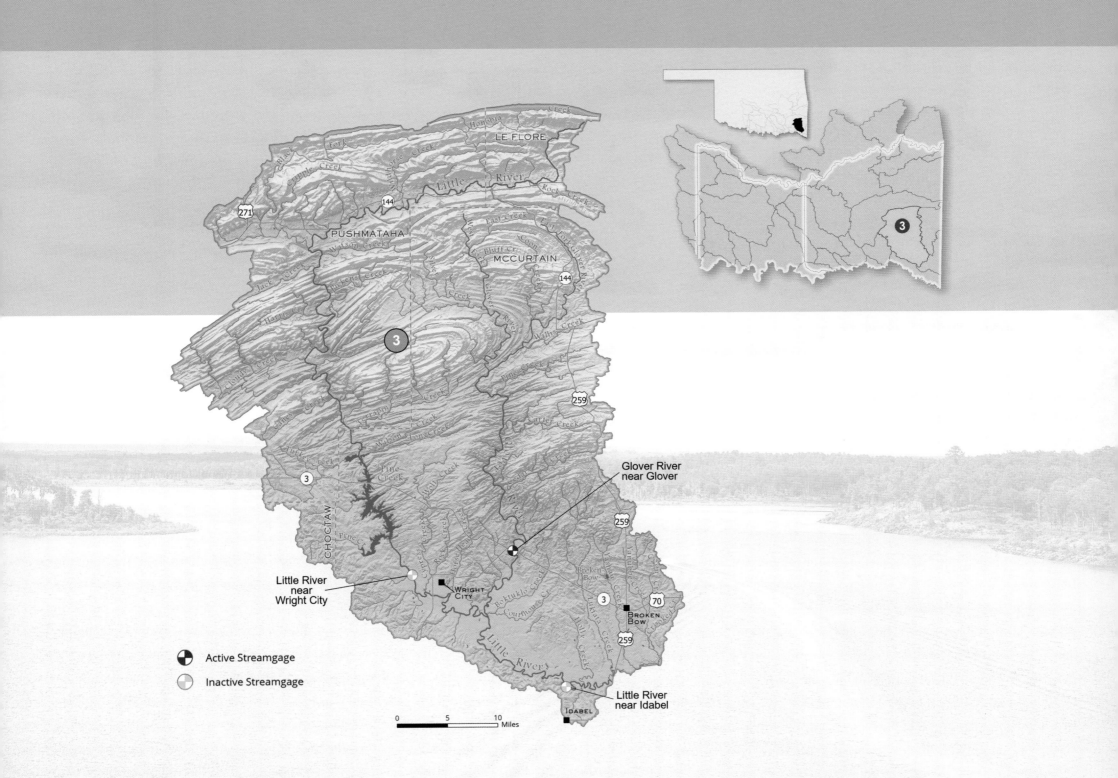

LE FLORE

PUSHMATAHA

MCCURTAIN

CHOCTAW

Glover River
near Glover

Little River
near
Wright City

WRIGHT
CITY

BROKEN
BOW

IDABEL

Little River
near Idabel

Active Streamgage

Inactive Streamgage

0   5   10
Miles

The Little River heads in southwestern LeFlore County, flowing southward, then westward, through a portion of the extensive Honobia Creek WMA just before crossing the Pushmataha County line. The river again encounters the WMA as it resumes a meandering southerly path before it enters the northern arm of Pine Creek Reservoir. Downstream of the dam in McCurtain County, the Little River makes a turn to the east and is joined by the Glover River, its largest tributary, southeast of Wright City. The Glover River, which contains an estimated 110 fish species and 22 mussel species, is one of only two free-flowing rivers in Oklahoma. At the confluence, the Little River flows primarily eastward through Little River National Wildlife Refuge, then enters Basin 2. Basin 3, which occupies a 1,294-square-mile area, is characterized by a considerable slope, relative to other watersheds, of 10.4 percent. The average annual flow of the Upper Little River, estimated at the bottom of Basin 3, is 1,851 cfs; this flow is available about 27 percent of the time.

Few lakes of note exist in Basin 3. However, Pine Creek Reservoir, on the Little River in McCurtain County, is an important water supply to the region. According to the OWRB, 60,475 AFY of the lake's yield remains available. Broken-Bow Lake, a relatively small reservoir, should not be confused with a similarly named, much larger, lake in Basin 4.

Due in part to its unique resources and habitat, Basin 3 contains many of Oklahoma's federally protected species. Endangered are the harperella, Indiana bat, Ouachita rock pocketbook, piping plover, red-cockaded woodpecker, scaleshell mussel and winged mapleleaf. Threatened species include the American burying beetle, leopard darter, northern long-eared bat, rabbitsfoot and red knot.

Water Quality

The Upper Little River watershed spans the Ouachita Mountains to the South Central Plains ecoregion where streams typically contain long, wide and deep pools occasionally interrupted by short, high gradient riffles with cobble and boulder substrates. Streams in Basin 3 are mesotrophic with low nutrient values and salinity, and excellent clarity. The entire basin, including Pine Creek Reservoir, is designated as high quality waters. The lake is phosphorus-limited and eutrophic, although water clarity is good. The lake does not support fish consumption due to elevated levels of mercury and lead. TMDLs have been completed for turbidity on the Little River and Cloudy Creek.

PRINCIPAL RIVERS & STREAMS BASIN 3	
River/Stream	Length MILES
Little River	121
Glover River	34
Black Fork	31
Cloudy Creek	26
East Fork Glover River	22
Holly Creek	21
Pine Creek	21
Cypress Creek	21
West Fork Glover River	21
Honobia Creek	21
Yashau Creek	20
Lukfata Creek	18
Rock Creek	18
Coon Creek	18
Cedar Creek	17
Long Creek	15

PRINCIPAL LAKES BASINS 3									
Name	Stream	Authority	Normal Elevation FEET	Normal Area ACRES	Normal Capacity AC-FT	Shoreline MILES	Purpose(s)[1]	Water Supply Storage AC-FT	Water Supply Yield AC-FT/YR
Broken-Bow	Yashau Creek	Gail Huffman Allen	—	51	240	1.4	—	—	—
Pine Creek	Little River	USACE	433	2,810	44,570	85	FC, WS, WQ, FW, R	49,400	94,080

[1]WS=Water Supply, R=Recreation, HP=Hydroelectric Power, IR=Irrigation, WQ=Water Quality, FW=Fish & Wildlife, FC=Flood Control, LF=Low Flow Regulation, N=Navigation, C=Conservation, CW=Cooling Water

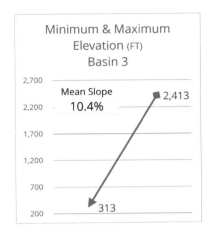

Minimum & Maximum Elevation (FT) Basin 3

Mean Slope **10.4%**

2,700
2,200
1,700
1,200
700
200

2,413
313

LAND COVER & USES
UPPER LITTLE RIVER WATERSHED

Use	Area SQ. MI.
Forest	876
Herbaceous, Shrubs, Woody Wetlands	235
Cultivated Land, Hay/Pasture	120
Developed	51
Water	11
Barren Land	1
Total Land Area	**1,294**

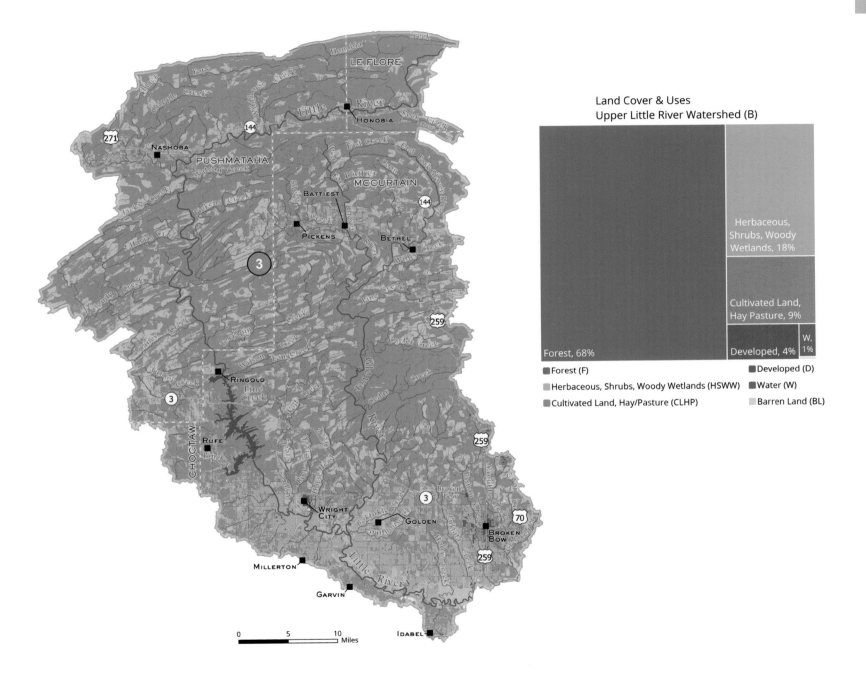

Land Cover & Uses
Upper Little River Watershed (B)

Forest, 68%

Herbaceous, Shrubs, Woody Wetlands, 18%

Cultivated Land, Hay Pasture, 9%

Developed, 4%

W, 1%

- Forest (F)
- Herbaceous, Shrubs, Woody Wetlands (HSWW)
- Cultivated Land, Hay/Pasture (CLHP)
- Developed (D)
- Water (W)
- Barren Land (BL)

Groundwater

The Antlers aquifer, in the far southern portion of Basin 3, is the sole major aquifer in the Upper Little watershed. According to OWRB data, 132 wells are drilled into the groundwater basin within the watershed's boundaries. As in surrounding watersheds/basins, the Kiamichi aquifer (395 wells) is the most frequent source of the region's quite limited groundwater use.

Aquifer	Area in Basin/ Watershed SQUARE MILES	EPS[1] AC-FT/ACRE	Number of Permitted & Domestic Wells in Basin/ Watershed[2]
Antlers	240	2.1	132
Broken Bow	124	2.0	71
Holly Creek	11	2.0	3
Kiamichi	918	2.0	395
Little River	80	1.0	43
Pine Mountain	<1	2.0	0
Woodbine	17	2.0	1
Nondelineated Source Wells			9
Total Wells			**654**

Table title: MAJOR & MINOR AQUIFERS BASIN 3

[1]*Italic number signifies unstudied aquifers with a default temporary equal proportionate share (EPS) of 2.0 acre-feet per acre of land.*
[2]*Some wells are double-counted where one aquifer overlies another.*

NOTE: Significant color and shading variations may be apparent in areas where one aquifer overlies another. In some cases, for state administrative purposes, aquifer boundaries align directly with county lines or related political borders rather than geologic outcrop areas.

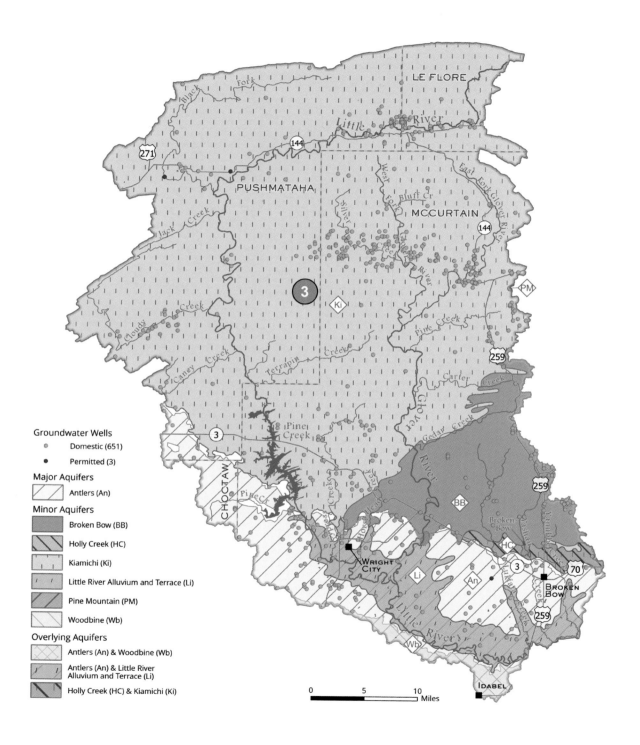

Groundwater Wells
- ○ Domestic (651)
- ● Permitted (3)

Major Aquifers
- Antlers (An)

Minor Aquifers
- Broken Bow (BB)
- Holly Creek (HC)
- Kiamichi (Ki)
- Little River Alluvium and Terrace (Li)
- Pine Mountain (PM)
- Woodbine (Wb)

Overlying Aquifers
- Antlers (An) & Woodbine (Wb)
- Antlers (An) & Little River Alluvium and Terrace (Li)
- Holly Creek (HC) & Kiamichi (Ki)

Permitted Water Use

Much like the Mountain Fork, in its neighboring watershed/basin, the Upper Little River watershed is defined by its surface supplies, which account for virtually all permitted sources. Uses are largely skewed toward industrial needs (81 percent), followed by public supply (17 percent).

Utilizing the region's abundant timber resources, International Paper Company, which is headquartered in Memphis, Tennessee, is far and away the largest permittee with 33,605 AFY of surface water rights that provide industrial needs at its facility in Valliant. The largest permitted public water supplier is the Idabel Public Works Authority, which has acquired 4,929 AFY of surface rights, including a 1,000 AFY vested right.

Any application to appropriate water for use at a location outside of Basin 3 could be subject to conferral, depending upon the application amount, mean available flow and other relevant factors. See conditions associated with Class B Basins in the Tribal-State Water Settlement agreement in the *Oka Holisso* appendix.

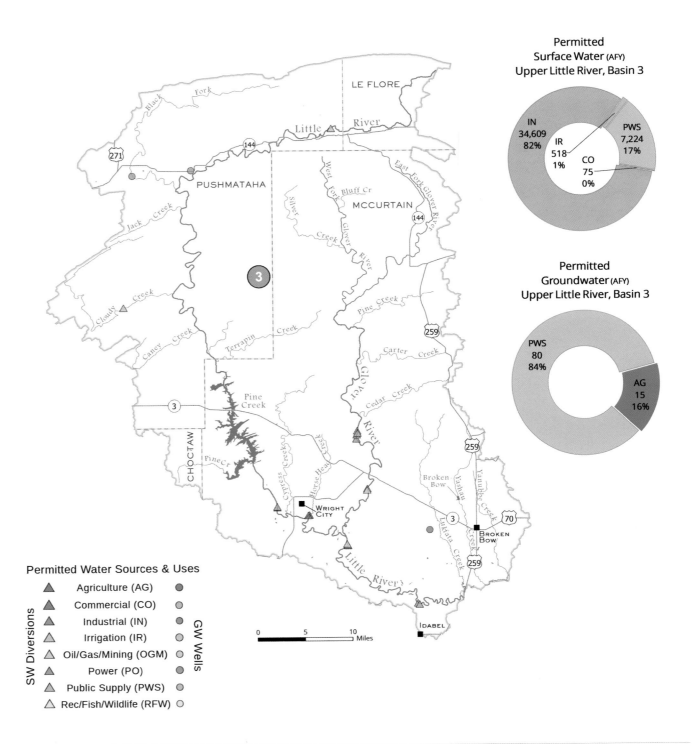

PERMITTED WATER		
AFY		
BASIN 3		
Groundwater	Surface Water	**Total**
95	42,426	**42,521**

Permitted
Surface Water (AFY)
Upper Little River, Basin 3

IN 34,609 82%
IR 518 1%
CO 75 0%
PWS 7,224 17%

Permitted
Groundwater (AFY)
Upper Little River, Basin 3

PWS 80 84%
AG 15 16%

Permitted Water Sources & Uses

SW Diversions / GW Wells

- ▲ Agriculture (AG) ⬤
- ▲ Commercial (CO) ⬤
- ▲ Industrial (IN) ⬤
- △ Irrigation (IR) ◐
- △ Oil/Gas/Mining (OGM) ◐
- △ Power (PO) ⬤
- △ Public Supply (PWS) ◐
- △ Rec/Fish/Wildlife (RFW) ○

0   5   10 Miles

Broken Bow PWA is the principal regional provider of water in the Upper Little River watershed. In addition to its 4,320 customers, the Authority sells water to a dozen water systems in southeast Oklahoma, including Idabel PWA and its approximately 7,000 customers. Of the watershed's fourteen water systems, ten depend entirely upon the Authority and Broken Bow Lake, in Basin 4, for their supply. In 2009, Broken Bow PWA's water treatment plant was expanded to a capacity of 10 million gallons per day.

A major system in Basin 3 that does not purchase water is Pushmataha County RWD #3, which serves a southwest portion of the watershed through permitted diversion of water from the Kiamichi River in that neighboring watershed. The district includes 4,825 total residential customers.

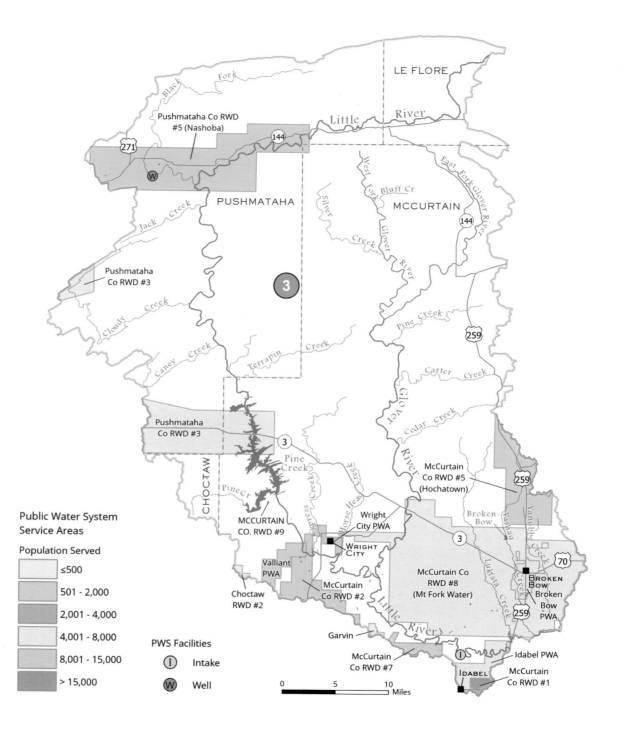

Public Water System Service Areas

Population Served

	≤500
	501 - 2,000
	2,001 - 4,000
	4,001 - 8,000
	8,001 - 15,000
	> 15,000

PWS Facilities

Ⓘ Intake

Ⓦ Well

0   5   10
Miles

Public Water Supply Systems
Basin 3

System	Residential Customers Served[1]	Source(s) of Supply[2]	Water Sales	Water Purchases	Facilities[3]				
					Intake	Pump Facility	Storage	Treatment Plant	Well or Spring
Broken Bow PWA	4,320	SW	Garvin, Haworth PWA, Idabel PWA, McCurtain Co. #1, McCurtain Co. #2, McCurtain Co. #5, McCurtain Co. #6, McCurtain Co. #7, McCurtain Co. #8, McCurtain Co. #9, Valliant PWA, Wright City PWA	—					
Choctaw Co. RWD #2	373	P (SW)	—	Valliant PWA					
Garvin	150	P (SW)	—	Broken Bow PWA, McCurtain Co. RWD #7					
Idabel PWA	6,952	SW	—	Broken Bow PWA	1				
McCurtain Co. RWD #1	3,842	P (SW)	Haworth PWA	Broken Bow PWA					
McCurtain Co. RWD #2	755	P (SW)	—	Broken Bow PWA					
McCurtain Co. RWD #5 (Hochatown)	1,614	P (SW)	—	Broken Bow PWA					
McCurtain Co. RWD #7	1,847	P (SW)	Garvin	Broken Bow PWA					
McCurtain Co. RWD #8 (Mt. Fork Water)	5,685	SW	—	Broken Bow PWA					
McCurtain Co. RWD #9	999	P (SW)	—	Broken Bow PWA					
Pushmataha Co. RWD #3	4,825	SW	Soper	—					
Pushmataha Co. RWD #5 (Nashoba)	725	P (SW)	—	Sardis Lake Water Authority					2
Valliant PWA	971	P (SW)	Choctaw Co. RWD #2	Broken Bow PWA					
Wright City PWA	792	P (SW)	—	Broken Bow PWA					

[1]Does not include wholesale customers served through water sales.

[2]GW = Groundwater; SW = Surface Water; P = Purchased.

[3]Includes both active and inactive (mostly wells) facilities in the watershed. Treatment plants include only those utilizing conventional water treatment and do not include chlorination stations associated with discrete source treatment.

Data: Oklahoma Department of Environmental Quality, Safe Drinking Water Information System, OWRB GIS and Arbuckle-Simpson Aquifer Drought Contingency Plan. Listed system facilities include those with service areas and/or facilities within relevant watershed.

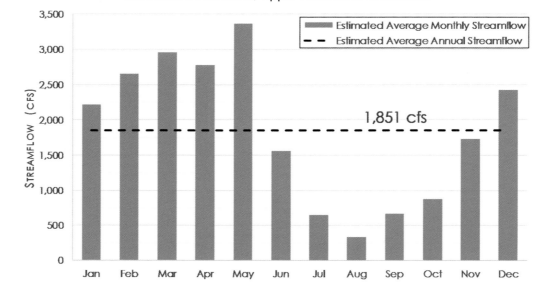

Estimated Streamflow, Upper Little River Watershed

1,851 cfs

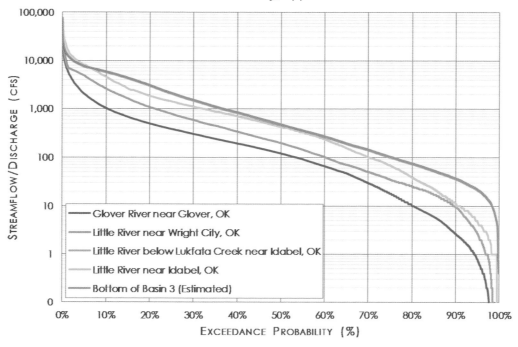

Streamflow Exceedance Probability, Upper Little River Watershed

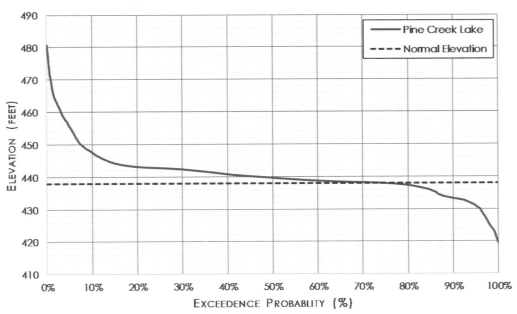

Reservoir Level Exceedance for Pine Creek Lake

Beaver Creek

BASINS 24, 25 & 26

Basins 24, 25 & 26 — Waurika Lake

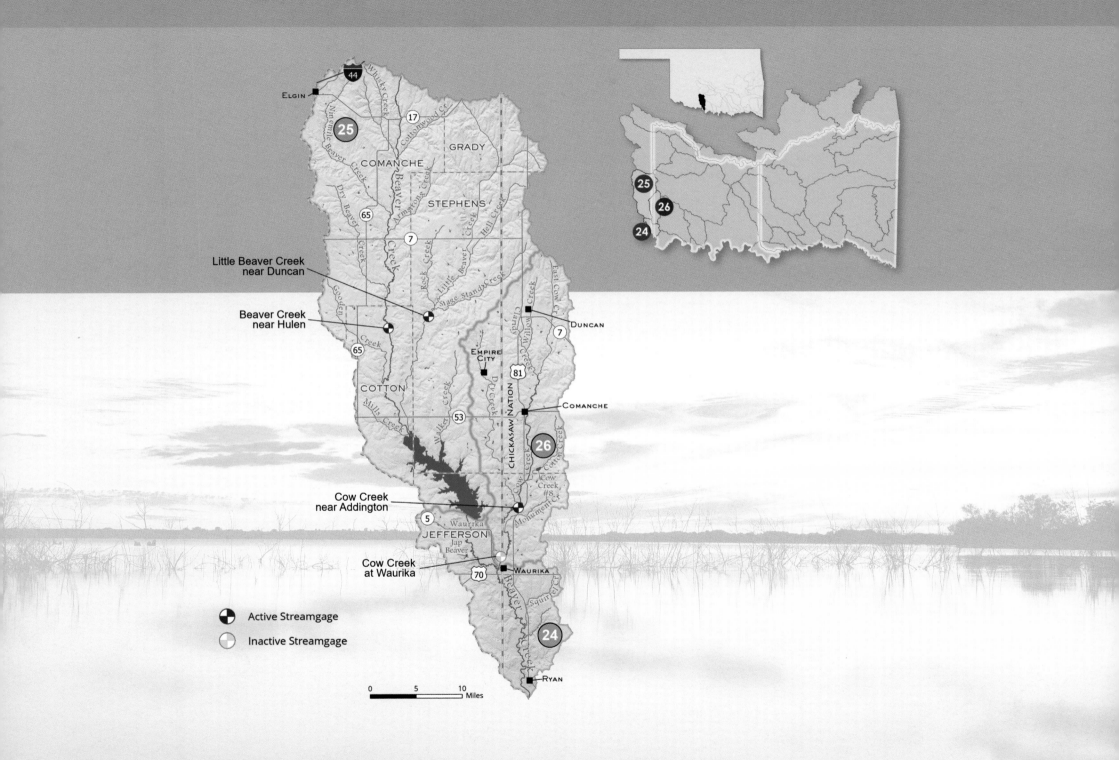

Little Beaver Creek
near Duncan

Beaver Creek
near Hulen

Cow Creek
near Addington

Cow Creek
at Waurika

⬒ Active Streamgage

◓ Inactive Streamgage

ELGIN

DUNCAN

EMPIRE
CITY

COMANCHE

WAURIKA

RYAN

GRADY

COMANCHE

STEPHENS

COTTON

JEFFERSON

CHICKASAW NATION

Whisky Creek

Ninemile Beaver Creek

Dry Beaver Creek

Cottonwood Cr

Armstrong Creek

Beaver Creek

Hell Creek

Little Beaver Creek

Rock Creek

Stage Stand Creek

East Cow Cr

Claret Creek

Wolf Creek

Dry Creek

Gooden Creek

Walker Creek

Mills Creek

Cow Creek

Cow Creek #8

Cotton Creek

Monument Cr

Waurika
Jap Beaver

Beaver Creek

Squirrel Cr

25

26

24

17

65

7

65

53

5

81

7

70

44

0   5   10
Miles

Water & Related Resources

Beaver Creek originates in Basin 25 north of Sterling in northeastern Comanche County. As it flows predominantly south through Comanche and Cotton Counties, the stream is joined by several tributaries before it encounters Waurika WMA. It is impounded by Waurika Lake in Jefferson County. Resuming its flow downstream of the lake in Basin 24, Beaver Creek is joined by Cow Creek, the predominant stream in adjacent Basin 26, at the town of Waurika. From there, Beaver Creek continues its southern path through Jefferson County before emptying into the mainstem of the Red River south of Ryan. The three basins constituting the Beaver Creek watershed occupy a combined land area of 864 square miles.

The average annual flow of Little Beaver Creek, estimated at the bottom of Basin 25, is 185 cfs; this flow is available about eight percent of the time. The annual flow of Cow Creek, estimated at the bottom of Basin 26, is approximately 37 cfs. (Due to the significant impacts of reservoir uses and operations at Lake Waurika in Basin 25, the Little Beaver Creek streamgage site, upstream of the lake, was used to estimate primary streamflow exceedance for the watershed.)

Existing just outside of Chickasaw Nation territorial lands in Basin 25, Waurika Lake is Oklahoma's fourteenth largest lake by volume. The lake was completed by the USACE in 1977. The only major water supply lake of note in the Beaver Creek watershed, none of the lake's considerable 40,549 AFY yield is currently available for appropriation.

Two federally listed endangered species occur in the Beaver Creek watershed: the piping plover and whooping crane. Also receiving protection is the red knot, a bird species that is threatened.

Water Quality

Beaver Creek flows through the Central Great Plains and Cross Timbers to the Great Red Plains ecoregions where stream substrates are loose sediments, such as sand and silt. Exhibiting typically high salinity, water clarity is poor to average with average turbidity. Lakes and streams are phosphorus-limited and moderately eutrophic, indicating higher than normal nutrient concentrations. Beaver Creek and its tributaries—including Little Beaver Creek, Hell Creek, Stage Sand Creek and Walker Creek—are designated sensitive water supplies. A TMDL has been completed for Lake Waurika, which is impaired due to high chlorophyll-a. TMDLs have also been completed for Little Beaver Creek and Cow Creek for bacteria and turbidity. TMDLs for bacteria have also been completed for Cottonwood Creek and Whisky Creek.

Principal Rivers & Streams — Basins 24, 25 & 26

River/Stream	Length MILES
Beaver Creek	83
Little Beaver Creek	40
Cow Creek	26
Dry Creek	21
Ninemile Beaver Creek	20
Gooden Creek	14
Dry Beaver Creek	14
Stage Stand Creek	13
Walker Creek	13
East Cow Creek	12
Whisky Creek	10

Principal Lakes — Basins 24, 25 & 26

Name	Stream	Authority	Normal Elevation FEET	Normal Area ACRES	Normal Capacity AC-FT	Shoreline MILES	Purpose(s)[1]	Water Supply Storage AC-FT	Water Supply Yield AC-FT/YR
Cow Creek #8	Cotton Creek	SCS/Stephens Co. CD	—	73	708	1.5	FC	—	—
Jap Beaver	Beaver Creek TR	ODWC	923	43	662	1.6	R	—	—
Waurika	Beaver Creek	USACE	951.4	9,926	190,044	72.6	FC, IR, WS, WQ, R, FW	151,400	40,549

[1]WS=Water Supply, R=Recreation, HP=Hydroelectric Power, IR=Irrigation, WQ=Water Quality, FW=Fish & Wildlife, FC=Flood Control, LF=Low Flow Regulation, N=Navigation, C=Conservation, CW=Cooling Water

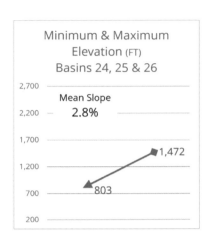

Minimum & Maximum Elevation (FT)
Basins 24, 25 & 26

Mean Slope
2.8%

2,700

2,200

1,700

1,200 ——————▲ 1,472

700 ◀———— 803

200

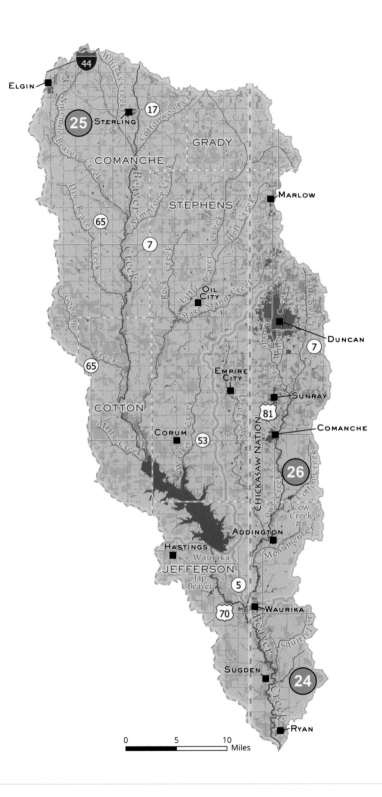

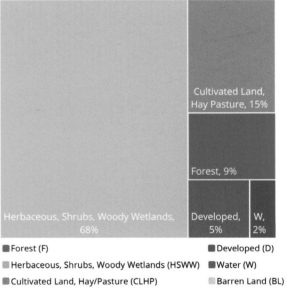

Land Cover & Uses
Beaver Creek Watershed (C)

Herbaceous, Shrubs, Woody Wetlands, 68%

Cultivated Land, Hay Pasture, 15%

Forest, 9%

Developed, 5%

W, 2%

- Forest (F)
- Herbaceous, Shrubs, Woody Wetlands (HSWW)
- Cultivated Land, Hay/Pasture (CLHP)
- Developed (D)
- Water (W)
- Barren Land (BL)

LAND COVER & USES
BEAVER CREEK WATERSHED

Use	Area SQ. MI.
Forest	77
Herbaceous, Shrubs, Woody Wetlands	589
Cultivated Land, Hay/Pasture	131
Developed	47
Water	20
Barren Land	0
Total Land Area	**864**

Groundwater

Some 985 wells, including 165 in the major Rush Springs aquifer, tap groundwater supplies in the Beaver Creek watershed. Small portions of two other major groundwater basins, the Red River and Arbuckle-Timbered Hills, also underlie Basins 24 and 25, respectively. The minor El Reno aquifer, in the watershed's northern area, is also a popular groundwater source for users in the region.

MAJOR & MINOR AQUIFERS BASINS 24, 25 & 26			
Aquifer	Area in Basin/ Watershed SQUARE MILES	EPS[1] AC-FT/ACRE	Number of Permitted & Domestic Wells in Basin/ Watershed[2]
Arbuckle-Timbered Hills	23	2.0	8
Beaver Creek	56	1.0	24
El Reno	54	2.0	166
Hennessey-Garber	216	1.6	68
Red River	25	2.0	12
Rush Springs	71	2.0	165
Nondelineated Source Wells			542
Total Wells			**985**

[1]*Italic number signifies unstudied aquifers with a default temporary equal proportionate share (EPS) of 2.0 acre-feet per acre of land.*
[2]*Some wells are double-counted where one aquifer overlies another.*

NOTE: Significant color and shading variations may be apparent in areas where one aquifer overlies another. In some cases, for state administrative purposes, aquifer boundaries align directly with county lines or related political borders rather than geologic outcrop areas.

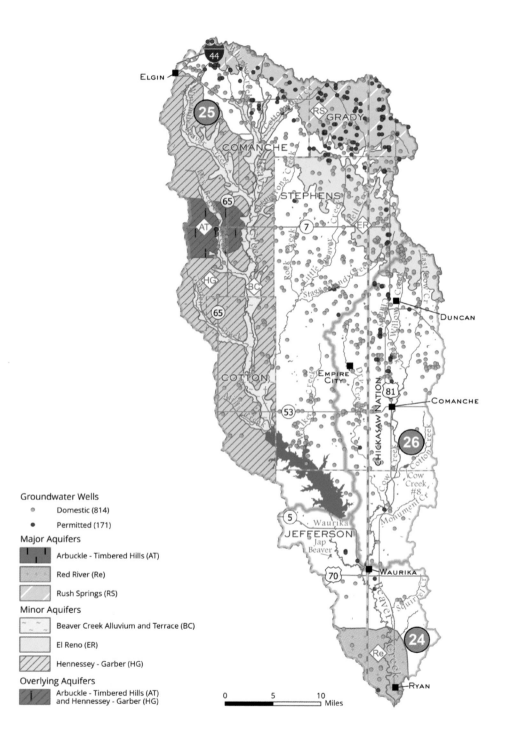

Groundwater Wells
- ○ Domestic (814)
- ● Permitted (171)

Major Aquifers
- Arbuckle - Timbered Hills (AT)
- Red River (Re)
- Rush Springs (RS)

Minor Aquifers
- Beaver Creek Alluvium and Terrace (BC)
- El Reno (ER)
- Hennessey - Garber (HG)

Overlying Aquifers
- Arbuckle - Timbered Hills (AT) and Hennessey - Garber (HG)

Surface water accounts for 63 percent (47,326 AFY) of permitted water sources within the three basins comprising the Beaver Creek watershed. However, in Basin 26, groundwater widely exceeds surface sources—by a 98 to 2 percent margin—in Basin 26. Public supply (74 percent) and irrigation (25 percent) are the two predominant uses of permitted water throughout Basins 24, 25 and 26.

Waurika Master Conservancy District, which operates and maintains Waurika Lake and its water supply facilities, is the largest permitted water user (44,806 AFY) in the Beaver Creek watershed. Other hold-ers of significant water rights associated with public water supply include: the City of Marlow with 1,674 AFY from a groundwater source in Grady County; City of Waurika (1,586 AFY, groundwater, Jefferson County); Jefferson County Conservation Rural Water and Sewer District #1 (1,371 AFY, groundwater, Grady and Stephens Counties); and Stephens County Rural Water District #3 (1,128 AFY, Stephens and Grady Counties). Numerous irrigation permits—including approximately 3,715 AFY utilized by a private landowner in Grady County—exist in the watershed, primarily from groundwater sources.

Any application to appropriate water for use at a location outside of Basin 24, 25 or 26 could be subject to conferral, depending upon the application amount, mean available flow and other relevant factors. See conditions associated with Class C Basins in the Tribal-State Water Settlement agreement in the *Oka Holisso* appendix.

PERMITTED WATER AFY		
BASIN 24		
Groundwater	Surface Water	Total
1,922	2,447	4,369
BASIN 25		
Groundwater	Surface Water	Total
21,353	47,288	68,641
BASIN 26		
Groundwater	Surface Water	Total
1,748	38	1,786
WATERSHED TOTAL		
Groundwater	Surface Water	Total
25,023	49,773	74,796

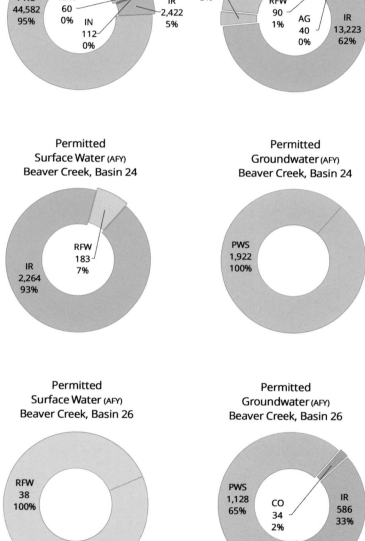

Permitted
Surface Water (AFY)
Beaver Creek, Basin 25

CO
112
0%

PWS
44,582
95%

RFW
60
0%

IN
112
0%

IR
2,422
5%

Permitted
Groundwater (AFY)
Beaver Creek, Basin 25

PWS
7,347
34%

OGM
653
3%

RFW
90
1%

AG
40
0%

IR
13,223
62%

Permitted
Surface Water (AFY)
Beaver Creek, Basin 24

RFW
183
7%

IR
2,264
93%

Permitted
Groundwater (AFY)
Beaver Creek, Basin 24

PWS
1,922
100%

Permitted
Surface Water (AFY)
Beaver Creek, Basin 26

RFW
38
100%

Permitted
Groundwater (AFY)
Beaver Creek, Basin 26

PWS
1,128
65%

CO
34
2%

IR
586
33%

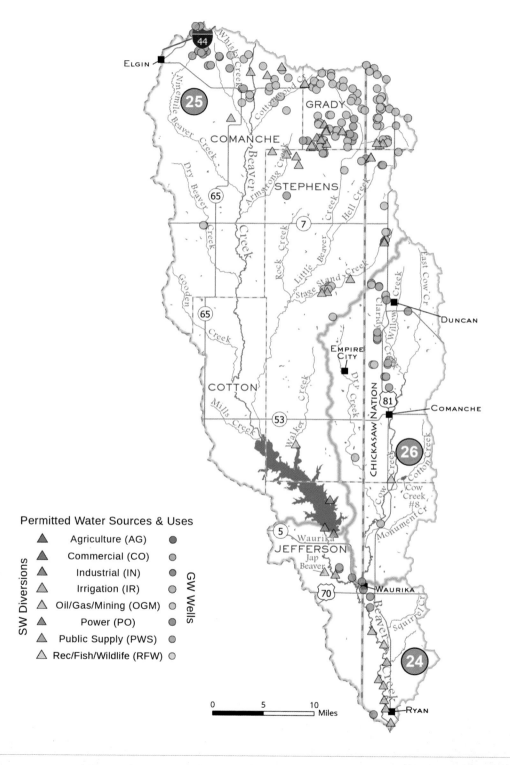

Permitted Water Sources & Uses

SW Diversions / GW Wells

▲ ● Agriculture (AG)
▲ ● Commercial (CO)
▲ ● Industrial (IN)
▲ ● Irrigation (IR)
▲ ● Oil/Gas/Mining (OGM)
▲ ● Power (PO)
▲ ● Public Supply (PWS)
△ ○ Rec/Fish/Wildlife (RFW)

0   5   10 Miles

Water Supply Systems

Duncan Public Utilities Authority, with the third largest customer base in the Settlement Area, is the dominant water system in the Beaver Creek watershed. In addition to its 23,000 base customers, Duncan sells water to Jefferson County RWD #1 and Stephens Co RWD #5. Its primary supply is from Waurika Lake (through Waurika Lake MCD), but the municipality uses nearby Lake Fuqua, Lake Humphreys, Clear Creek Lake and Duncan Lake as supplementary sources.

Jefferson Co. RWD #1 serves a large area in the south of the watershed. In addition to independent groundwater sources and water from Duncan, the district purchases supply from four additional providers in the region. Stephens Co. RWD #5, the other watershed provider of note, serves 6,426 residential customers.

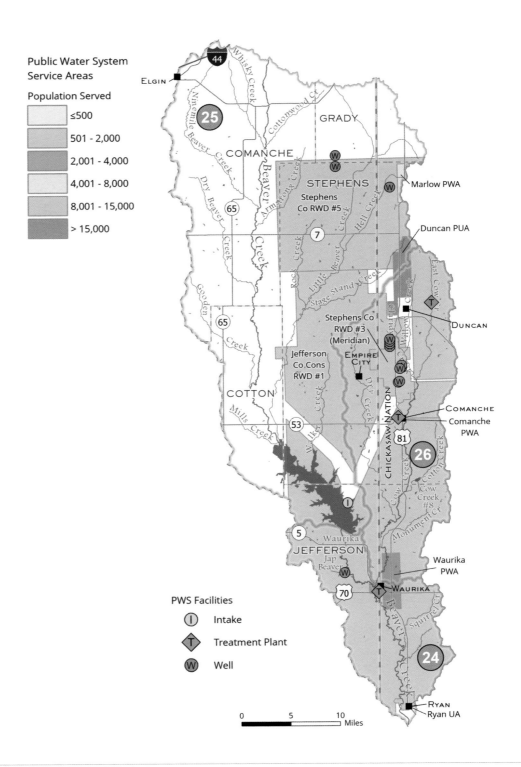

Public Water System Service Areas

Population Served

	≤500
	501 - 2,000
	2,001 - 4,000
	4,001 - 8,000
	8,001 - 15,000
	> 15,000

PWS Facilities

Ⓘ Intake

◇T Treatment Plant

Ⓦ Well

PUBLIC WATER SUPPLY SYSTEMS BASINS 24, 25 & 26										
						Facilities[3]				
System	Residential Customers Served[1]	Source(s) of Supply[2]	Water Sales	Water Purchases	Intake	Pump Facility	Storage	Treatment Plant	Well or Spring
Comanche PWA	1,649	SW	Jefferson Co. #1, Stephens Co. #3	—				1	
Duncan PUA	23,000	SW	Jefferson Co. #1, Stephens Co. #5	—				1	
Grady Co. RWD #7 (Ninnekah)	2,425	GW	—	—					1
Jefferson Co. RWD #1	8,276	GW	Healdton, Ringling, Ryan UA, Stephens Co. #4 (Loco), Terral, Wilson MA	Comanche PWA, Duncan PUA, Stephens Co. RWD #4 (Loco), Waurika PWA, Wilson MA					
Marlow PWA	4,600	GW	—	—					
Ryan UA	800	P (SW)	—	Jefferson Co. #1, Waurika PWA					
Stephens Co. RWD #3 (Meridian)	1,610	GW	—	Comanche PWA					9
Stephens Co. RWD #5	6,426	GW	—	Duncan PUA					2
Waurika PWA	2,100	SW	Jefferson Co. #1, Ryan UA	—				1	14

[1]Does not include wholesale customers served through water sales.

[2]GW = Groundwater; SW = Surface Water; P = Purchased.

[3]Includes both active and inactive (mostly wells) facilities in the watershed. Treatment plants include only those utilizing conventional water treatment and do not include chlorination stations associated with discrete source treatment.

Data: Oklahoma Department of Environmental Quality, Safe Drinking Water Information System, OWRB GIS and Arbuckle-Simpson Aquifer Drought Contingency Plan. Listed system facilities include those with service areas and/or facilities within relevant watershed.

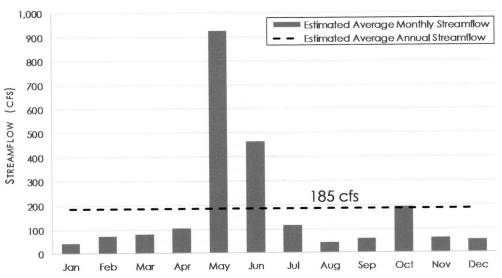

Estimated Streamflow, Beaver Creek Watershed (Basin 25)

185 cfs

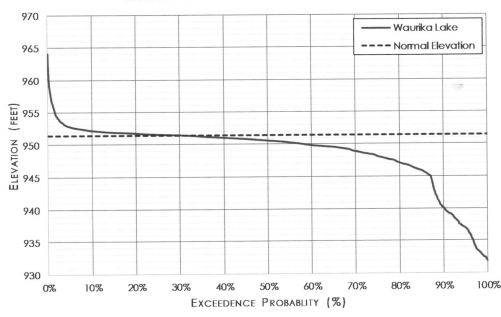

Reservoir Level Exceedance for Waurika Lake

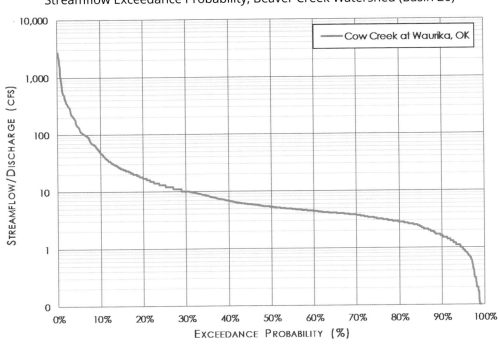

Streamflow Exceedance Probability, Beaver Creek Watershed (Basin 26)

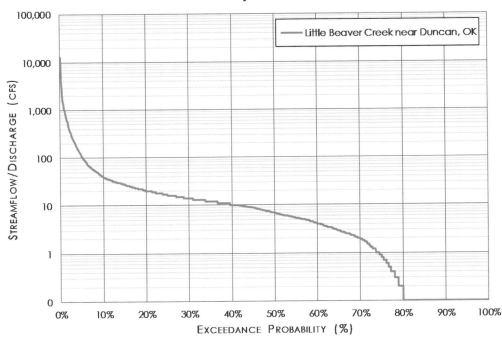

Streamflow Exceedance Probability, Beaver Creek Watershed (Basin 25)

Lower Arkansas River

BASINS 46 & 47

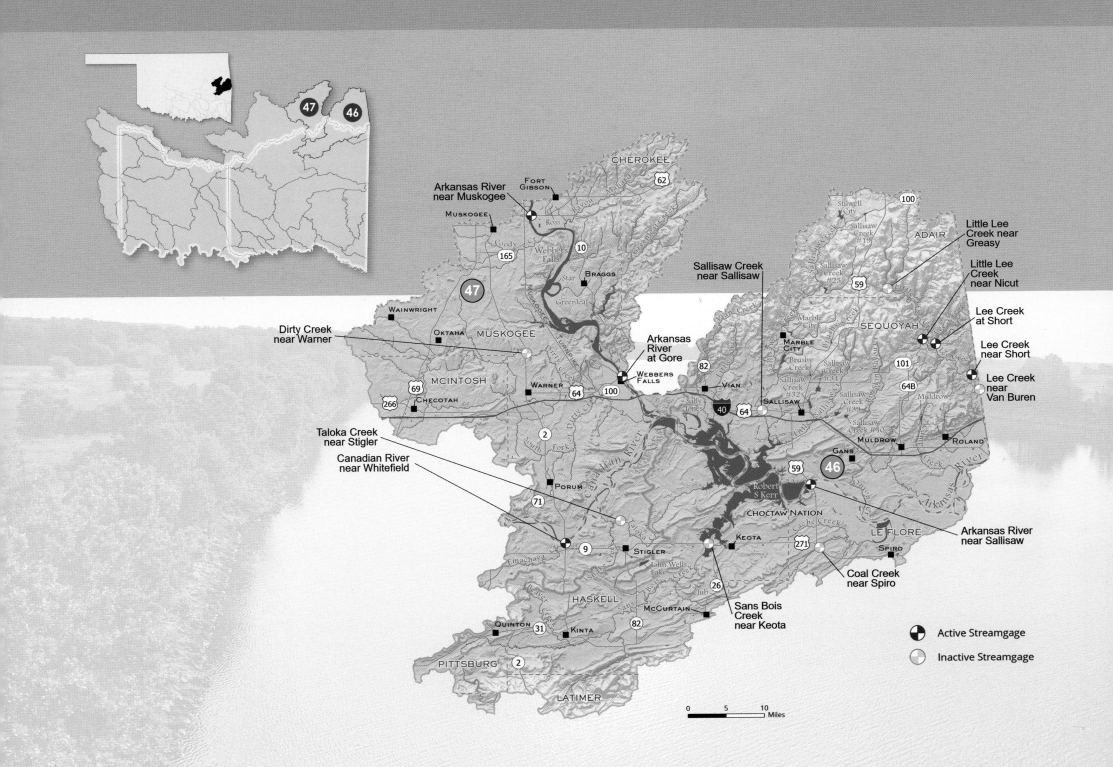

Arkansas River near Muskogee

Dirty Creek near Warner

Taloka Creek near Stigler

Canadian River near Whitefield

Arkansas River at Gore

Sallisaw Creek near Sallisaw

Little Lee Creek near Greasy

Little Lee Creek near Nicut

Lee Creek at Short

Lee Creek near Short

Lee Creek near Van Buren

Arkansas River near Sallisaw

Coal Creek near Spiro

Sans Bois Creek near Keota

CHEROKEE

MUSKOGEE

MCINTOSH

HASKELL

PITTSBURG

LATIMER

CHOCTAW NATION

SEQUOYAH

ADAIR

LE FLORE

47

46

WAINWRIGHT
OKTAHA
MUSKOGEE
CHECOTAH
WARNER
PORUM
QUINTON
KINTA
STIGLER
McCURTAIN
KEOTA
GANS
MULDROW
ROLAND
SPIRO
MARBLE CITY
SALLISAW
VIAN
WEBBERS FALLS
BRAGGS
FORT GIBSON
STILWELL CITY

● Active Streamgage
○ Inactive Streamgage

0   5   10 Miles

Water & Related Resources

Basins 46 and 47 occupy a prominent 2,411 square miles in eastern Oklahoma. The Arkansas River, which drains about two-thirds of Oklahoma's land area, enters Basin 47 near Fort Gibson as the southern arm of Webbers Falls Reservoir, an 11,600-acre lake located on the McClellan-Kerr Arkansas River Navigation System. In this region, including Muskogee County, the river and lake encounter the McClellan-Kerr WMA, nearby Greenleaf State Park (one of Oklahoma's seven original state parks) and Star Lake, an oxbow just off the Arkansas River channel west of Braggs. Adjacent to and immediately downstream of Webbers Falls Reservoir in Basin 46 is Robert S. Kerr Reservoir, yet another important component of the navigation system on the Haskell/Sequoyah County line. Kerr Reservoir, which also receives flows from the Canadian River, is entirely surrounded by the Sequoyah National Wildlife Refuge. Downstream of the dam, the Arkansas River meanders eastward constituting the border between LeFlore and Sequoyah Counties. Prior to leaving the state, the river passes close to Spiro Mound State Park, the location of a landmark prehistoric First American site about fifteen miles from Fort Smith, Arkansas. Lee's Creek and Little Lee's Creek, two far eastern tributaries of the Arkansas River in Sequoyah and Adair Counties, are each designated as Oklahoma "scenic rivers." The average annual flow of the Arkansas River, estimated at the bottom of Basin 46, is 30,105 cfs; supported by the upstream navigation system's locks and dams, this flow is available almost 27 percent of the time.

Neither Webbers Falls nor Kerr Reservoir has water supply included in their original project purposes, which are primarily associated with navigation, hydropower generation and recreation. John Wells (a water source for Stigler), Purcell and Stilwell City Lakes serve as sources of supply in the region. The Lower Arkansas River watershed also features Greenleaf Lake, a 920-acre recreational impoundment in Muskogee County. Constructed in 1939, the lake is leased by the State of Oklahoma.

The unique size and diversity of the Lower Arkansas River watershed has contributed to the presence of many protected animal species. Endangered are the gray bat, Indiana bat, Neosho mucket, Ozark big-eared bat, piping plover, scaleshell mussel, whooping crane and winged mapleleaf. Threatened species include the American burying beetle, northern long-eared bat, Rabbitsfoot and red knot.

Water Quality

The Lower Arkansas watershed spans four ecoregions: the Ozark Highlands, Boston Mountains, Central Irregular Plains and Arkansas Valley. Streams in Basins 46 and 47 are eutrophic with high salinity. Waterbodies designated as sensitive water supplies (SWS) include Greenleaf Creek to Greenleaf Lake, John Wells Reservoir and watershed, and Brushy Creek Reservoir and watershed. The segment of Sallisaw Creek upstream from U.S. Highway 64 is designated as high quality waters (HQW). Outstanding resource waters (ORW) designations have been applied to Jenkins Creek, Lee Creek and Briar (Bear) Creek. TMDLs have been completed for bacteria on Sallisaw Creek, Dirty Creek, Coody Creek, Sans Bois Creek, Shady Grove Creek and Butler Creek. Neither Kerr nor Webber Falls Reservoir fully supports fish and wildlife propagation due to elevated turbidity.

PRINCIPAL RIVERS & STREAMS BASINS 46 & 47	
River/Stream	Length MILES
Arkansas River	89
Sans Bois Creek	74
Dirty Creek	47
Sallisaw Creek	47
Big Skin Bayou Creek	29
Canadian River	28
Little Lee Creek	25
Greenleaf Creek	23
Little Sallisaw Creek	21
Vian Creek	20
Bayou Manard	19
Cache Creek	19
Lee Creek	18
Coody Creek	16
Taloka Creek	16
South Fork of Dirty Creek	16
Beaver Creek	15
Brushy Creek	15
Georges Fork	14
Camp Creek	14
Little Vian Creek	14
Emachaya Creek	14

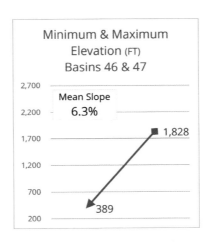

Minimum & Maximum Elevation (FT) Basins 46 & 47

Mean Slope 6.3%

1,828

389

		PRINCIPAL LAKES BASIN 46 & 47								
Name	Stream	Authority	Normal Elevation FEET	Normal Area ACRES	Normal Capacity AC-FT	Shoreline MILES	Purpose(s)[1]	Water Supply Storage AC-FT	Water Supply Yield AC-FT/YR
Brushy Creek	Brushy Creek	State of Okla.	633.9	225	3,258	3.9	FC, R	—	—
Club	Sans Bois Creek TR	McCurtain Club Lake	—	49	495	1.8	—	—	—
Greenleaf	Deep Branch	State of Okla. (Leased)	510	704	14,720	14.4	R	—	—
John Wells	Sans Bois Creek TR	City of Stigler	646.3	205	1,352	3.2	WS, R	—	—
Marble City	Dry Creek	Sequoyah Co. CD	—	58	255	1.6	FC	—	—
Muldrow	Camp Creek	City of Muldrow	—	76	887	1.8	—	—	—
Purcell	Walnut Creek TR	City of Purcell	1,068	144	2,600	3.1	WS, R	—	—
Robert S Kerr	Arkansas River	USACE	460	40,818	525,700	275.3	N, HP, R	—	—
Ross	Bayou Manard TR	—	—	67	—	3.8	—	—	—
Sallisaw Creek #19	Sallisaw Creek	SCS/Adair Co. CD	—	41	313	1.2	FC	—	—
Sallisaw Creek #25	Greasy Creek	SCS/Adair Co. CD	—	78	255	2	FC	—	—
Sallisaw Creek #32	Little Sallisaw Creek TR	SCS/Sequoyah Co. CD	—	149	218	3.2	FC	—	—
Sallisaw Creek #34	Little Sallisaw Creek TR	SCS/Sequoyah Co. CD	—	163	89	2.5	FC	—	—
Sallisaw Creek #39	Little Sallisaw Creek TR	SCS/Sequoyah Co. CD	—	119	85	2.1	FC	—	—
Sallisaw Creek #40	Little Sallisaw Creek TR	SCS/Sequoyah Co. CD	—	83	30	1.7	FC	—	—
Sally Jones	Lower Arkansas River TR	—	—	435	—	9.3	—	—	—
Star	Sand Creek	—	—	500	—	6.9	—	—	—
Stilwell City	Sallisaw Creek TR	City of Stilwell	947	197	3,110	4	WS, FC, R	—	—
Webbers Falls	Arkansas River	USACE	490	8,734	170,100	117.4	N, HP	—	—

[1]WS=Water Supply, R=Recreation, HP=Hydroelectric Power, IR=Irrigation, WQ=Water Quality, FW=Fish & Wildlife, FC=Flood Control, LF=Low Flow Regulation, N=Navigation, C=Conservation, CW=Cooling Water

Land Cover & Uses
Lower Arkansas River Watershed

Use	Area SQ. MI.
Forest	984
Herbaceous, Shrubs, Woody Wetlands	172
Cultivated Land, Hay/Pasture	1,031
Developed	117
Water	101
Barren Land	7
Total Land Area	**2,412**

Land Cover & Uses
Lower Arkansas River Watershed (C)

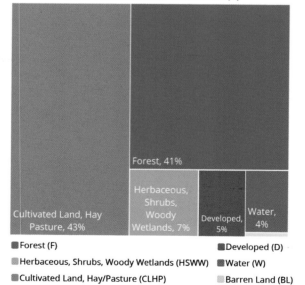

- Forest (F)
- Herbaceous, Shrubs, Woody Wetlands (HSWW)
- Cultivated Land, Hay/Pasture (CLHP)
- Developed (D)
- Water (W)
- Barren Land (BL)

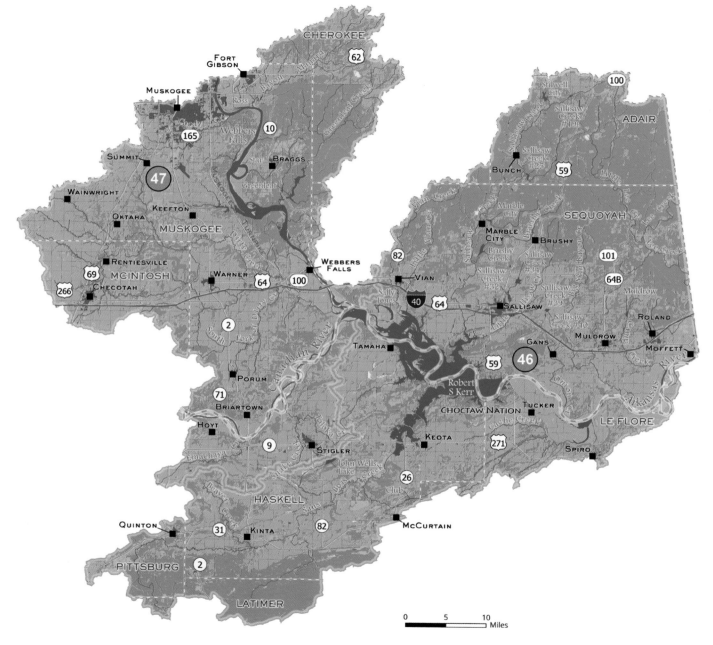

Groundwater

The Roubidoux, a major aquifer existing largely outside of the settlement area, is the largest—at more than 1,000 square miles—and most extensively utilized in the Lower Arkansas watershed with approximately 699 permitted and domestic wells. Two additional major alluvium and terrace aquifers, the Arkansas River and Canadian River, also underlie portions of Basins 46 and 47. Among four minor groundwater basins, the Pennsylvanian, Northeastern Oklahoma Pennsylvanian and Boone (overlying the Roubidoux along the northern edge of both basins) include a significant number of the watershed's 2,614 total wells.

MAJOR & MINOR AQUIFERS
BASINS 46 & 47

Aquifer	Area in Basin/ Watershed SQUARE MILES	EPS[1] AC-FT/ ACRE	Number of Permitted & Domestic Wells in Basin/ Watershed[2]
Arkansas River	259	2.0	203
Boone	255	2.0	329
Canadian River	127	2.0	74
Kiamichi	173	2.0	94
Northeastern Okla. Pennsylvanian	857	2.0	448
Pennsylvanian	588	2.0	611
Roubidoux	1,075	2.0	699
Nondelineated Source Wells			156
Total Wells			**2,614**

[1]*Italic number signifies unstudied aquifers with a default temporary equal proportionate share (EPS) of 2.0 acre-feet per acre of land.*
[2]*Some wells are double-counted where one aquifer overlies another.*

NOTE: Significant color and shading variations may be apparent in areas where one aquifer overlies another. In some cases, for state administrative purposes, aquifer boundaries align directly with county lines or related political borders rather than geologic outcrop areas.

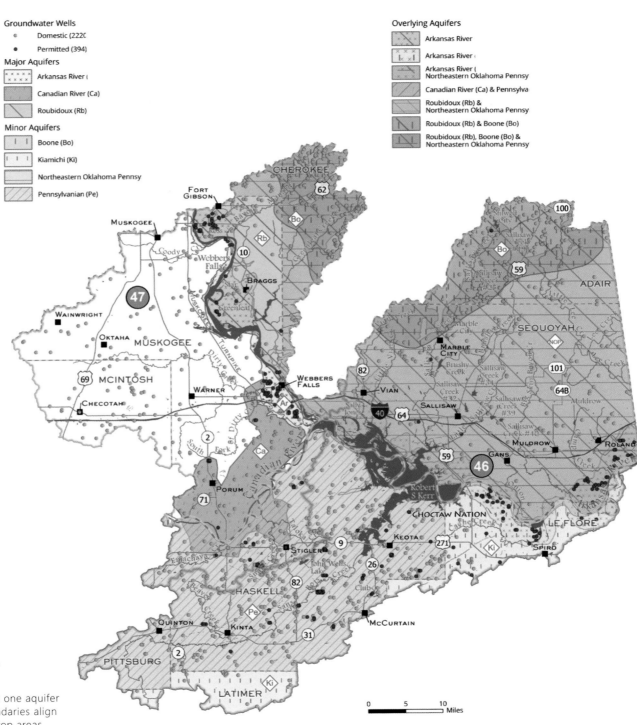

Groundwater Wells
- Domestic (2220
- Permitted (394)

Major Aquifers
- Arkansas River (
- Canadian River (Ca)
- Roubidoux (Rb)

Minor Aquifers
- Boone (Bo)
- Kiamichi (Ki)
- Northeastern Oklahoma Pennsy
- Pennsylvanian (Pe)

Overlying Aquifers
- Arkansas River
- Arkansas River (
- Arkansas River (Northeastern Oklahoma Pennsy
- Canadian River (Ca) & Pennsylva
- Roubidoux (Rb) & Northeastern Oklahoma Pennsy
- Roubidoux (Rb) & Boone (Bo)
- Roubidoux (Rb), Boone (Bo) & Northeastern Oklahoma Pennsy

Due to its large land area and prolific water resources, the Lower Arkansas River watershed contains the largest amount of permitted water of any Settlement Area watershed. Approximately 228,521 AFY (90 percent) of this water comes from surface sources.

At four percent, public supply comprises a relatively miniscule amount of the watershed's total permitted water. Instead, water appropriated and allocated for power purposes—some 150,790 AFY (59 percent), all derived from Basin 47—makes this watershed the largest user of water for power purposes. Irrigation and industry make up 21 and 14 percent, respectively, of permitted water in Basins 46 and 47.

Oklahoma Gas and Electric Company (150,790 AFY) is by far the largest individual water user in the watershed as it is the sole holder of permits for power uses, primarily from surface sources. This includes a

vested right of 98,598 AFY for power generation at the Riverbank Station near the Arkansas River in Muskogee. Georgia-Pacific, a manufacturer of paper and related products, possesses two large surface water permits: 19,593 and 15,842 AFY for industrial uses in Muskogee County. The City of Sallisaw holds the largest public supply permit in the watershed: 3,000 AFY from an SCS/NRCS site north of the city on Sallisaw Creek. A number of large irrigation permits are also utilized throughout the two basins.

Any application to appropriate water for use at a location outside of Basin 46 or 47 could be subject to conferral, depending upon the application amount, mean available flow and other relevant factors. See conditions associated with Class C Basins in the Tribal-State Water Settlement agreement in the *Oka Holisso* appendix.

PERMITTED WATER		
AFY		
BASIN 46		
Groundwater	Surface Water	Total
14,412	24,792	39,204
BASIN 47		
Groundwater	Surface Water	Total
10,554	203,729	214,283
WATERSHED TOTAL		
Groundwater	Surface Water	Total
24,965	228,521	253,487

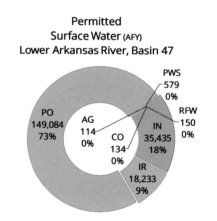

Permitted
Surface Water (AFY)
Lower Arkansas River, Basin 47

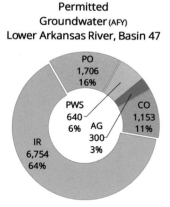

Permitted
Groundwater (AFY)
Lower Arkansas River, Basin 47

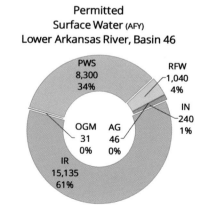

Permitted
Surface Water (AFY)
Lower Arkansas River, Basin 46

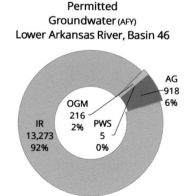

Permitted
Groundwater (AFY)
Lower Arkansas River, Basin 46

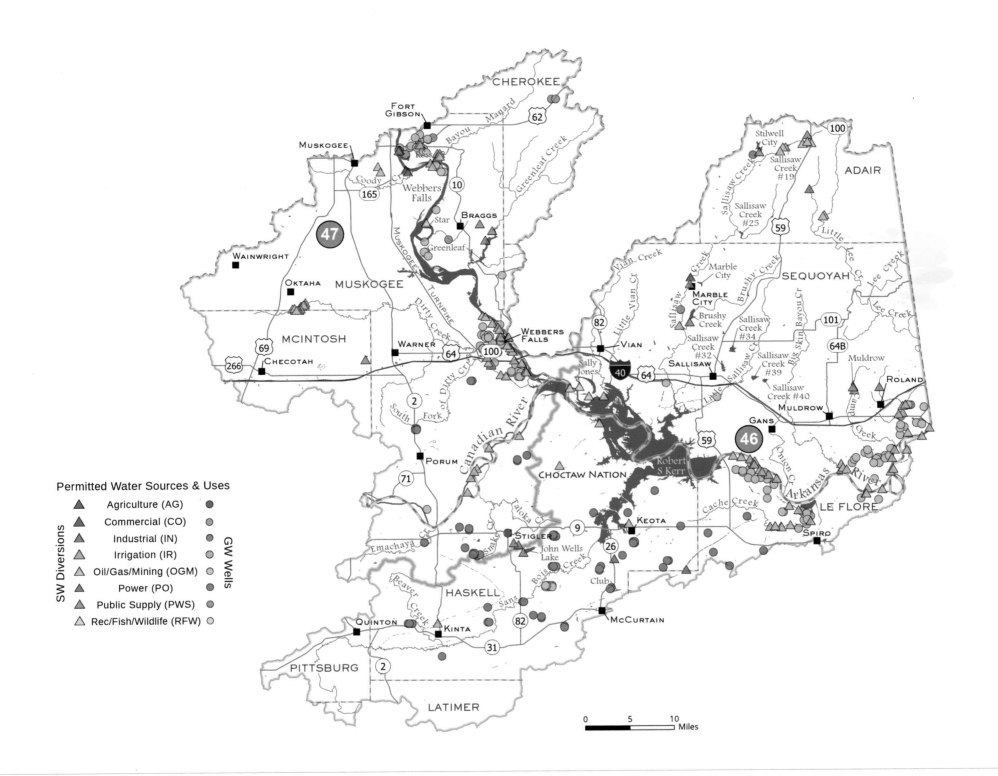

Permitted Water Sources & Uses

SW Diversions

- ▲ Agriculture (AG)
- ▲ Commercial (CO)
- ▲ Industrial (IN)
- ▲ Irrigation (IR)
- ▲ Oil/Gas/Mining (OGM)
- ▲ Power (PO)
- ▲ Public Supply (PWS)
- ▲ Rec/Fish/Wildlife (RFW)

GW Wells

- ● Agriculture (AG)
- ● Commercial (CO)
- ● Industrial (IN)
- ● Irrigation (IR)
- ● Oil/Gas/Mining (OGM)
- ● Power (PO)
- ● Public Supply (PWS)
- ● Rec/Fish/Wildlife (RFW)

Water Supply Systems

While primarily serving the two adjacent Poteau River basins, Poteau Valley Improvement Authority plays a vital role in the provision of water supply in the Lower Arkansas watershed. Five of the ten providers in Basins 46 and 47 purchase water from PVIA and three utilize the Authority as their sole water source. This includes LeFlore County RWD #14, the largest system in the watershed, and its 9,077 customers, many of whom reside in the Poteau watershed. In turn, LeFlore #14 sells supply to the City of Spiro. All providers utilize surface water sources.

Haskell Co. Water Company and the City of Stigler—two additional relatively large providers each with approximately 3,000 residential customers in overlapping service areas—maintain an agreement whereby the latter sells water to the former.

PUBLIC WATER SUPPLY SYSTEMS
BASINS 46 & 47

System	Residential Customers Served[1]	Source(s) of Supply[2]	Water Sales	Water Purchases	Facilities[3] Intake	Pump Facility	Storage	Treatment Plant	Well or Spring
Haskell Co. Water Company	3,000	SW	Keota PWA, Quinton	Stigler					
Keota PWA	564	P (SW)	—	Haskell Co. Water Comp., Poteau Valley Improvement Authority					
Latimer Co. RWD #4	412	SW	—	—					
LeFlore Co. RWD #14	9,077	P (SW)	Spiro	PVIA					
McCurtain MA	560	P (SW)	—	PVIA					
Pittsburg Co. RWD #14	1,680	SW	—	—					
Quinton	1,071	P (SW)	—	Haskell Co. Water Comp.					
Spiro	2,200	SW	—	LeFlore Co. #14, PVIA					
Spiro East Water Association	1,817	P (SW)	—	PVIA					
Stigler	2,731	SW	Haskell Co. Water Comp.	—			1		1

[1]Does not include wholesale customers served through water sales.

[2]GW = Groundwater; SW = Surface Water; P = Purchased.

[3]Includes both active and inactive (mostly wells) facilities in the watershed. Treatment plants include only those utilizing conventional water treatment and do not include chlorination stations associated with discrete source treatment.

Data: Oklahoma Department of Environmental Quality, Safe Drinking Water Information System, OWRB GIS and Arbuckle-Simpson Aquifer Drought Contingency Plan. Listed system facilities include those with service areas and/or facilities within relevant watershed.

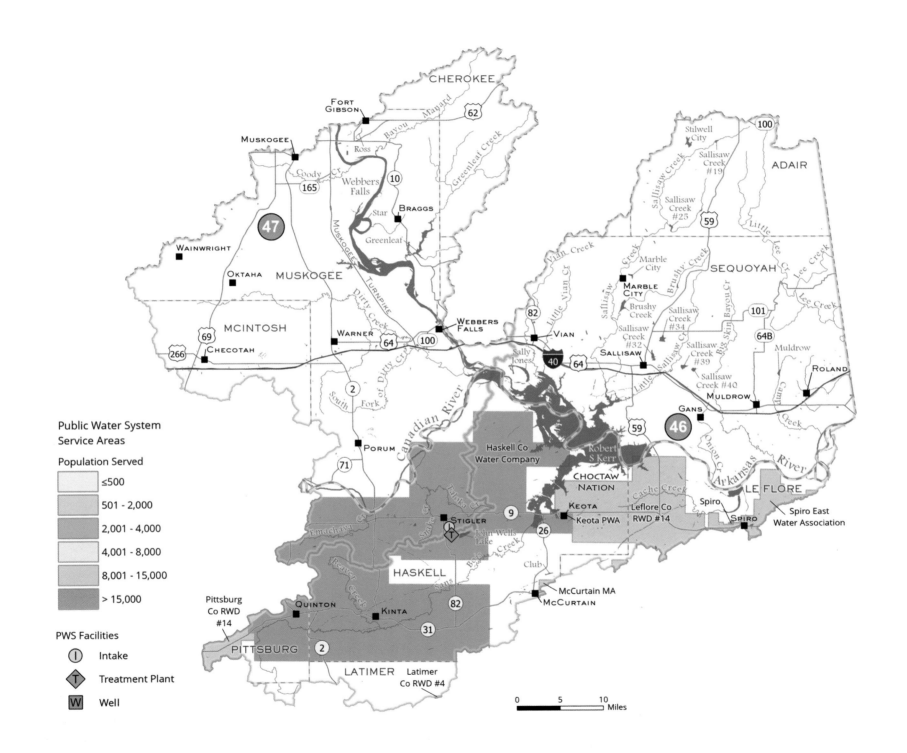

Public Water System Service Areas

Population Served

- ≤500
- 501 - 2,000
- 2,001 - 4,000
- 4,001 - 8,000
- 8,001 - 15,000
- > 15,000

PWS Facilities

- (I) Intake
- (T) Treatment Plant
- (W) Well

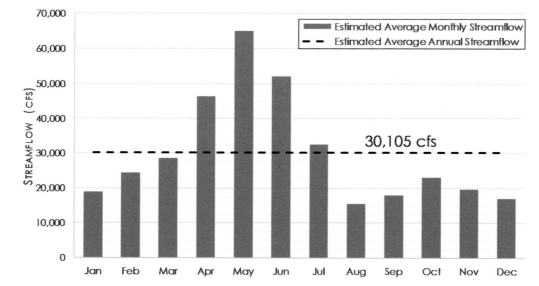

Estimated Streamflow, Lower Arkansas River Watershed

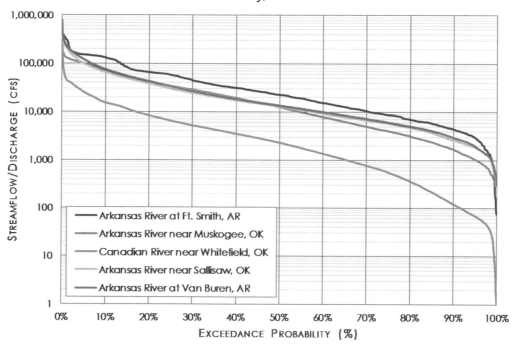

Streamflow Exceedance Probability, Lower Arkansas River Watershed

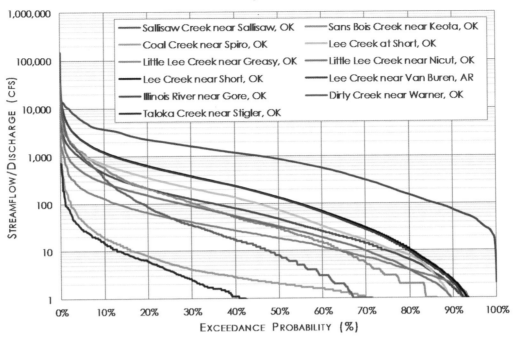

Streamflow Exceedance Probability, Lower Arkansas River Watershed

Lower Canadian River

BASINS 48 & 56

Basins 48 & 56 — Lake Eufaula dam (Credit: Leon Logan)

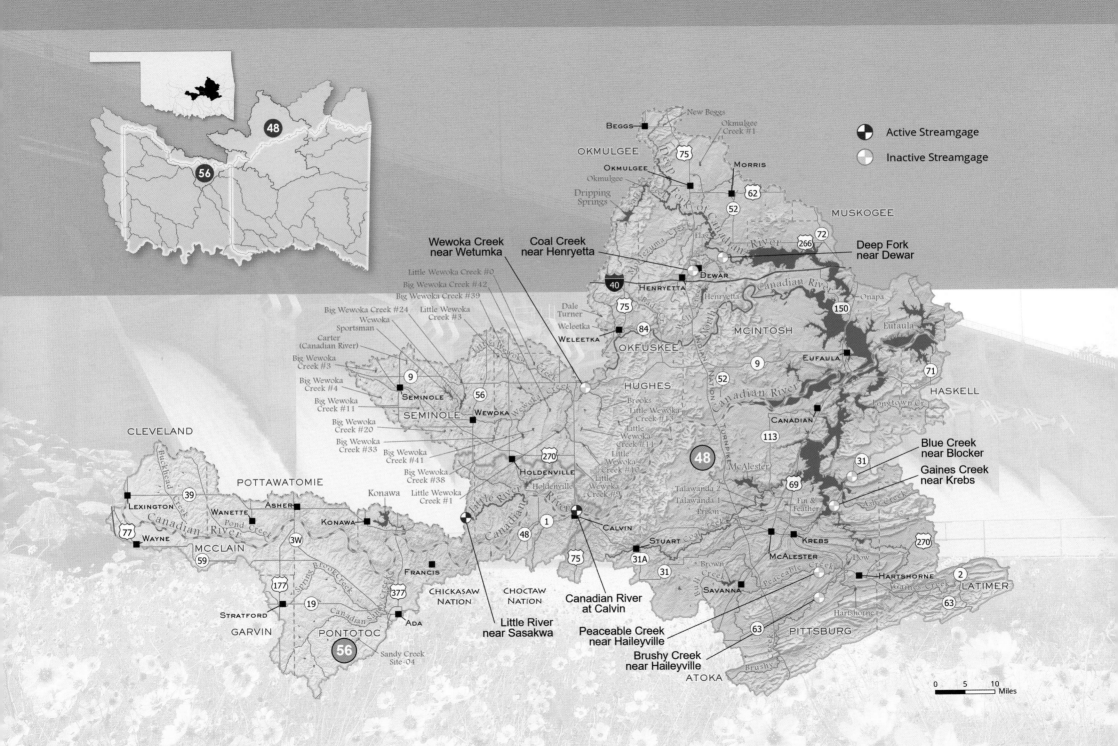

Active Streamgage

Inactive Streamgage

Wewoka Creek near Wetumka

Coal Creek near Henryetta

Deep Fork near Dewar

Little Wewoka Creek #0
Big Wewoka Creek #42
Big Wewoka Creek #39
Big Wewoka Creek #24   Little Wewoka Creek #3
Wewoka
Sportsman
Carter (Canadian River)
Big Wewoka Creek #3
Big Wewoka Creek #4
Big Wewoka Creek #11
Big Wewoka Creek #20
Big Wewoka Creek #33
Big Wewoka Creek #41
Big Wewoka Creek #38
Little Wewoka Creek #1

Blue Creek near Blocker

Gaines Creek near Krebs

Canadian River at Calvin

Little River near Sasakwa

Peaceable Creek near Haileyville

Brushy Creek near Haileyville

Brooks
Little Wewoka Creek #13
Little Wewoka Creek #11
Little Wewoka Creek #10
Little Wewoka Creek #9

New Beggs
BEGGS
Okmulgee Creek #1
OKMULGEE
OKMULGEE
MORRIS
Okmulgee
Dripping Springs
MUSKOGEE

Dale Turner
Weleetka
WELEETKA
OKFUSKEE
HUGHES
MCINTOSH
Onapa
Eufaula
EUFAULA
HASKELL

HENRYETTA
Henryetta
Dewar

Canadian River
CANADIAN
McALESTER
Talawanda 2
Talawanda 1
Frisco
Fin & Feather
KREBS
McALESTER
SAVANNA
Brown Creek
Dow
HARTSHORNE
Hartshorne 1
LATIMER
PITTSBURG
ATOKA
Brushy
Gaines Creek

CLEVELAND
POTTAWATOMIE
Konawa
Asher
Wanette
Pond Creek
Konawa
KONAWA
LEXINGTON
Lexington
WAYNE
Wayne
MCCLAIN
Buckhead Creek
Canadian River
SEMINOLE
SEMINOLE
WEWOKA
Wewoka
HOLDENVILLE
Holdenville
Holdenville
CALVIN
Calvin
STUART
Stuart

CHICKASAW NATION
CHOCTAW NATION

STRATFORD
Stratford
GARVIN
PONTOTOC
ADA
Ada
Sandy Creek Site-04
FRANCIS
Francis
Spring Brook Creek
Sandy Creek
Canadian River

0   5   10
Miles

Water & Related Resources

The Lower Canadian River watershed, which comprises an enormous land area of 4,167 miles in Basins 48 and 56, includes not only the Canadian River, but three major tributaries: the North Canadian and Deep Fork Rivers as well as the Little River (albeit a short 16-mile stretch prior to joining the Canadian in Hughes County). Entering Basin 56 from the bottom of Basin 58 (the Middle Canadian watershed), near Purcell, the Cana-

dian River flows eastward as it constitutes the border between Cleveland, McClain, Pottawatomie, Pontotoc and Seminole Counties as well as a portion of Hughes County. As the river jogs north in Hughes County, it is joined by the Little River (not to be confused with a river of the same name in the Red River Basin) north of Atwood and soon enters Basin 48 east of Calvin. At this point, the Canadian River assumes a general northeasterly path forming a portion of the Hughes, Pittsburg and McIntosh County lines. The river promptly enters the

west arm of Eufaula Lake, including Eufaula WMA, where it is joined by the waters of the North Canadian and Deep Fork Rivers as it proceeds into Basin 47. The average annual flow of the Lower Canadian River, estimated at the bottom of Basin 48, is 5,920 cfs; this flow is available less than 27 percent of the time.

A number of important lakes have been constructed in the watershed, including 42 occupying at least 40 surface acres. Most notable is Lake Eufaula, a vital source of water supply, hydropower and other uses. It is Oklahoma's largest

PRINCIPAL RIVERS & STREAMS
BASINS 48 & 56

River/Stream	Length MILES
Canadian River	171
Coal Creek	89
Deep Fork of Canadian River	72
North Canadian River	70
Wewoka Creek	59
Gaines Creek	58
Brushy Creek	44
Canadian Sandy Creek	38
Peaceable Creek	29
Spring Brook Creek	27
Longtown Creek	26
Pond Creek	25
Bull Creek	25
Mud Creek	23
Montezuma Creek	22
Salt Creek	22
Little Wewoka Creek	20
Ash Creek	20
Bad Creek	19
Wolf Creek	18

PRINCIPAL LAKES
BASINS 48 & 56

Name	Stream	Authority	Normal Elevation FEET	Normal Area ACRES	Normal Capacity AC-FT	Shoreline MILES	Purpose(s)[1]	Water Supply Storage AC-FT	Water Supply Yield AC-FT/YR
Big Wewoka Creek #3	Wewoka Creek TR	SCS/Seminole Co. CD	—	67	318	2.8	FC	—	—
Big Wewoka Creek #4	Wewoka Creek TR	SCS/Seminole Co. CD	—	46	279	2.2	FC	—	—
Big Wewoka Creek #11	Wewoka Creek TR	SCS/Seminole Co. CD	—	54	467	1.7	FC	—	—
Big Wewoka Creek #20	Wewoka Creek TR	SCS/Seminole Co. CD	—	40	280	1.4	FC	—	—
Big Wewoka Creek #24	Coon Creek	SCS/Seminole Co. CD	—	91	492	2	FC	—	—
Big Wewoka Creek #33	Wewoka Creek TR	SCS/Seminole Co. CD	—	122	614	4.6	FC	—	—
Big Wewoka Creek #38	Wewoka Creek TR	SCS/Hughes Co. CD	—	102	475	3.1	FC	—	—
Big Wewoka Creek #39	Wewoka Creek TR	SCS/Hughes Co. CD	—	124	587	4	FC	—	—
Big Wewoka Creek #41	Wewoka Creek TR	SCS/Hughes Co. CD	—	59	314	2	FC	—	—
Big Wewoka Creek #42	Wewoka Creek TR	SCS/Hughes Co. CD	—	54	278	1.7	FC	—	—
Brooks	Fish Creek	Hughes Co. CD	—	64	364	3.1	FC	—	—
Brown	Bull Creek	USDOD	—	553	4,525	8.1	—	—	—
Carter Lake	Wewoka Creek TR	Seminole Co. CD	—	65	332	3.5	FC	—	—
Dale Turner	Alabama Creek TR	—	—	49	—	1.1	—	—	—
Dow	Brushy Creek TR	—	—	92	—	2.1	—	—	—
Dripping Springs	Salt Creek	City of Okmulgee	741	1,118	16,200	18	WS, FC, R	—	7,214
Eufaula	Canadian River	USACE	585	93,544	2,194,857	829	FC, WS, HP, N, R	79,811	76,395
Fin & Feather	Gaines Creek TR	Fin and Feather Club	—	62	400	1.8	—	—	—
Flag	Deep Fork/Canadian River TR	—	—	75	—	2.9	—	—	—
Hartshorne	Blue Creek	—	—	90	—	2.2	—	—	—
Henryetta	Wolf Creek	City of Henryetta	660	505	6,660	9.4	WS, R	—	—
Holdenville	Bemore Creek	City of Holdenville	789	403	11,000	9.6	WS, R	11,000	—
Konawa	Jumper Creek	OG&E	924	1,321	23,000	16.6	CW	—	—

lake in area (93,544 acres) and second largest by volume (2,194,857 AF). According to the OWRB, 34,575 AFY of Eufaula's yield remains available for appropriation.

Lake McAlester, built in 1930, and Dripping Springs Lake, constructed by the City of Okmulgee in 1976, are two relatively large municipal impoundments. Lake Konawa provides cooling water for a nearby OG&E power generation facility.

Endangered species in the Lower Canadian River watershed include the gray bat, Ouachita rock pocket-book, piping plover and whooping crane. The American burying beetle, Arkansas River shiner, northern long-eared bat and red knot are listed as threatened.

Water Quality

The Lower Canadian watershed spans the Cross Timbers and Arkansas Valley ecoregions and portions of the Central Irregular and Central Great Plains ecoregions. Streams here are diverse and shallow, dominated by sand/silt/clay. The following waterbodies are designated as sensitive water supplies (SWS): Okmulgee Lake, Weleetka Lake, Henryetta Lake, Lake McAlester, Brown Lake, Holdenville Reservoir and Wewoka Lake. Fish consumption is impaired in Eufaula Lake due to elevated mercury levels. In Basins 48 and 56, TMDLs have been completed for bacteria on the Canadian River, Wewoka Creek, Brushy Creek, Peaceable Creek and a few small tributaries.

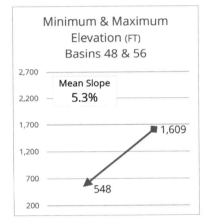

Minimum & Maximum Elevation (FT) Basins 48 & 56

Mean Slope 5.3%

1,609

548

PRINCIPAL LAKES BASINS 48 & 56									
Name	Stream	Authority	Normal Elevation FEET	Normal Area ACRES	Normal Capacity AC-FT	Shoreline MILES	Purpose(s)[1]	Water Supply Storage AC-FT	Water Supply Yield AC-FT/YR
Little Wewoka Creek #10	Graves Creek	SCS/Hughes Co. CD	—	84	522	2.7	FC	—	—
Little Wewoka Creek #11	Wewoka Creek TR	SCS/Hughes Co. CD	—	50	396	1.7	FC	—	—
Little Wewoka Creek #13	Wewoka Creek TR	SCS/Hughes Co. CD	—	65	343	2.5	FC	—	—
Little Wewoka Creek #3	Little Wewoka Creek TR	SCS/Hughes Co. CD	—	57	152	1.6	FC	—	—
Little Wewoka Creek #9	Graves Creek TR	SCS/Hughes Co. CD	—	41	259	1.8	FC	—	—
Little Wewoka Creek #0	Little Wewoka Creek TR	SCS/Hughes Co. CD	—	60	702	1.8	FC	—	—
Little Wewoka Creek #1	Graves Creek TR	SCS/Hughes Co. CD	—	111	691	3.5	FC	—	—
McAlester[2]	Bull Creek	City of McAlester	620	1,487	13,398	18.1	WS, R	16,900	9,200
New Beggs	Adams Creek TR	C. Brett & C. Ross	—	55	50	1.6	—	—	—
Okmulgee	Salt Creek	City of Okmulgee	690	629	14,170	13.8	WS, R	—	—
Okmulgee Creek #1	Deep Fork Canadian River TR	SCS/Okmulgee Co. CD	—	82	670	2.4	FC	—	—
Onapa	Deep Fork/ Canadian River TR	City of Checotah	—	67	1,137	2.7	—	—	—
Prison	Sandy Creek TR	State of Okla.	—	58	435	2.3	—	—	—
Sandy Creek #4	Canadian Sandy Creek TR	SCS/Pontotoc Co. CD	—	68	241	2.5	FC	—	—
Sportsman	Wewoka Creek TR	City of Seminole	868	365	5,349	12.9	FC, R	—	—
Talawanda 1	Coal Creek TR	City of McAlester	650	105	1,200	2.9	R	—	—
Talawanda 2	Coal Creek TR	City of McAlester	635	242	2,750	4.1	WS, R	—	—
Weleetka	Alabama Creek TR	City of Weleetka	743	58	385	1.6	WS, R	—	—
Wewoka	Coon Creek	City of Wewoka	826.66	357	3,301	9.5	WS, R	—	—

[1]WS=Water Supply, R=Recreation, HP=Hydroelectric Power, IR=Irrigation, WQ=Water Quality, FW=Fish & Wildlife, FC=Flood Control, LF=Low Flow Regulation, N=Navigation, C=Conservation, CW=Cooling Water

[2]A hydrographic survey and associated analysis conducted by the CCRWP Planning Team (specifically, Aqua Strategies Inc.) determined a firm yield of 8,970 AFY.

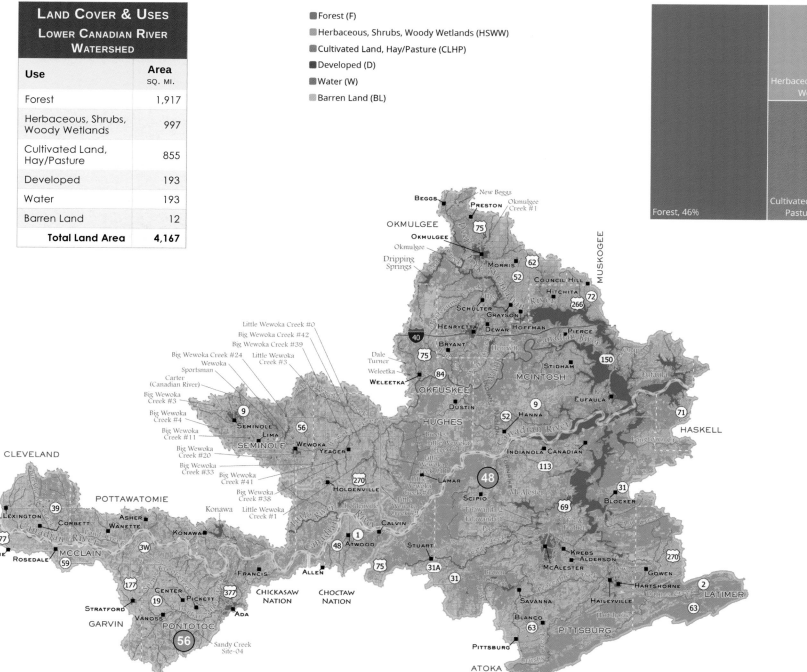

LAND COVER & USES
LOWER CANADIAN RIVER WATERSHED

Use	Area SQ. MI.
Forest	1,917
Herbaceous, Shrubs, Woody Wetlands	997
Cultivated Land, Hay/Pasture	855
Developed	193
Water	193
Barren Land	12
Total Land Area	**4,167**

- Forest (F)
- Herbaceous, Shrubs, Woody Wetlands (HSWW)
- Cultivated Land, Hay/Pasture (CLHP)
- Developed (D)
- Water (W)
- Barren Land (BL)

Land Cover & Uses
Lower Canadian River Watershed (C)

Forest, 46%
Herbaceous, Shrubs, Woody Wetlands, 24%
Cultivated Land, Hay Pasture, 21%
Developed, 5%
Water, 5%

Groundwater is a common source of supply throughout the Lower Canadian watershed, especially in Basin 56 and western portions of Basin 48 overlying the Canadian River (801 wells), Garber-Wellington (814), Ada-Vamoosa (427) and Gerty Sand (166) aquifers, all major groundwater basins. Among the four minor aquifers, the East-Central Oklahoma and Pennsylvanian formations, with around 500 wells each, are the most heavily utilized. Due to the large number and extent of groundwater sources in the watershed, detailed well logs are required to determine the exact number of wells penetrating each particular aquifer. An estimated 3,321 wells tap the region's groundwater supplies.

MAJOR & MINOR AQUIFERS BASINS 48 & 56			
Aquifer	Area in Basin/ Watershed SQUARE MILES	EPS[1] AC-FT/ACRE	Number of Permitted & Domestic Wells in Basin/ Watershed[2]
Ada-Vamoosa	175	2.0	427
Ashland	17	2.0	8
Canadian River	640	2.0	801
East-Central Okla.	949	2.0	510
Garber-Wellington	212	2.0	814
Gerty Sand	87	0.65	166
Kiamichi	209	2.0	23
North Canadian	159	1.3	74
Pennsylvanian	1,205	2.0	498
Nondelineated Source Wells			676
Total Wells			3,997

[1]Italic number signifies unstudied aquifers with a default temporary equal proportionate share (EPS) of 2.0 acre-feet per acre of land.
[2]Some wells are double-counted where one aquifer overlies another.

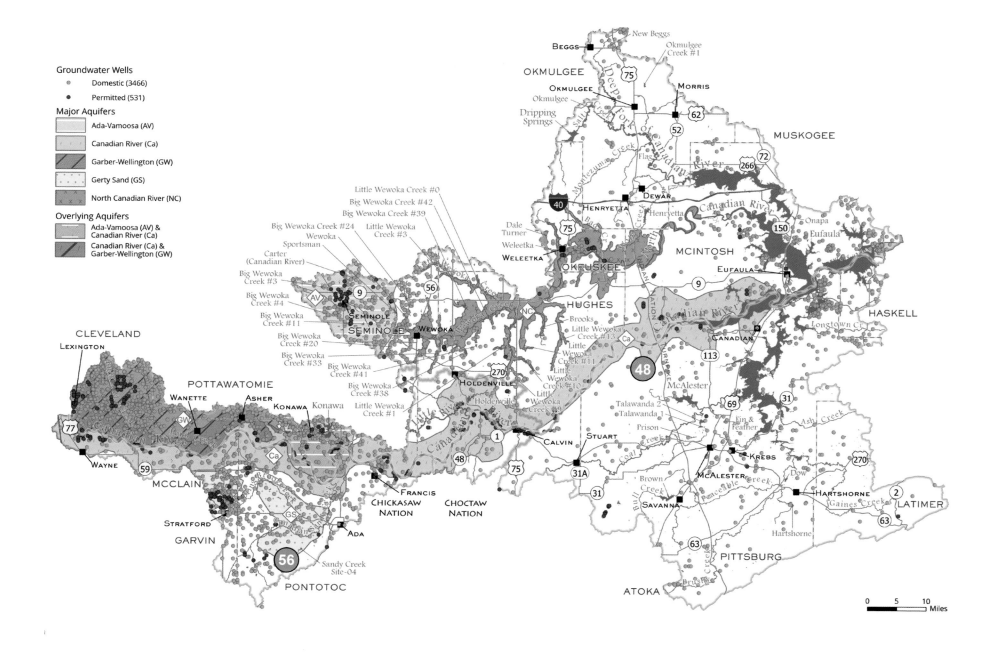

Groundwater Wells
- Domestic (3466)
- Permitted (531)

Major Aquifers
- Ada-Vamoosa (AV)
- Canadian River (Ca)
- Garber-Wellington (GW)
- Gerty Sand (GS)
- North Canadian River (NC)

Overlying Aquifers
- Ada-Vamoosa (AV) & Canadian River (Ca)
- Canadian River (Ca) & Garber-Wellington (GW)

NOTE: Significant color and shading variations may be apparent in areas where one aquifer overlies another. In some cases, for state administrative purposes, aquifer boundaries align directly with county lines or related political borders rather than geologic outcrop areas.

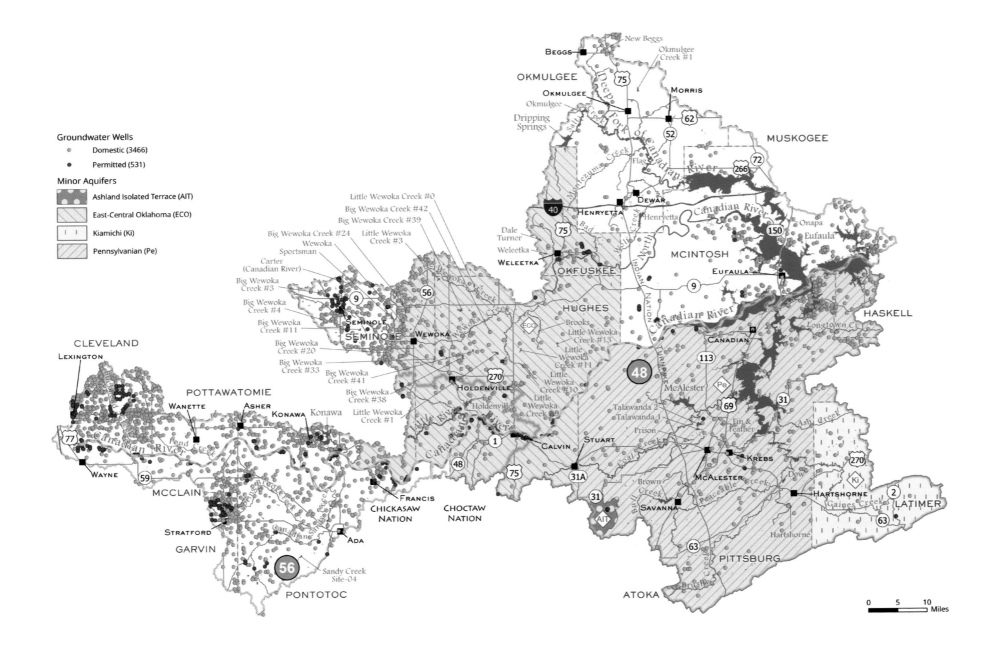

Groundwater Wells
- Domestic (3466)
- Permitted (531)

Minor Aquifers
- Ashland Isolated Terrace (AIT)
- East-Central Oklahoma (ECO)
- Kiamichi (Ki)
- Pennsylvanian (Pe)

NOTE: Significant color and shading variations may be apparent in areas where one aquifer overlies another. In some cases, for state administrative purposes, aquifer boundaries align directly with county lines or related political borders rather than geologic outcrop areas.

Groundwater is a common source for many users in the Lower Canadian River watershed, however, permitted surface water exceeds groundwater by 68 (149,826 AFY) to 32 percent (70,917 AFY). A total of 373 individual surface and groundwater permits, more than any other settlement area watershed, have been granted in Basins 48 and 56.

Public supply is the predominant use category in the Lower Canadian watershed, accounting for 46 percent of surface and groundwater permitted by the OWRB in this region. Most of this municipal use occurs in Basin 48. Power and irrigation comprise 23 and 22 percent, respectively, of the total share of appropriations and allocations.

Oklahoma Gas and Electric Company possesses the largest amount of water rights in the watershed, paced by a surface water permit of 27,000 AFY in Seminole County. In addition, Juniper Water Company utilizes 12,040 AFY for power purposes in Pittsburg County. From a municipal standpoint, the City of McAlester holds three public supply appropriations totaling 31,500 AFY from surface sources in Pittsburg County. The City of Okmulgee (11,484 AFY, surface water) and Purcell Public Works Authority (11,169 AFY, groundwater) are other significant holders of public supply rights. Okmulgee also possesses a 750 AFY permit for recreation, fish and wildlife use.

Any application to appropriate water for use at a location outside of Basin 48 or 56 could be subject to conferral, depending upon the application amount, mean available flow and other relevant factors. See conditions associated with Class C Basins in the Tribal-State Water Settlement agreement in the *Oka Holisso* appendix.

PERMITTED WATER AFY		
BASIN 48		
Groundwater	Surface Water	Total
14,185	101,675	115,860
BASIN 56		
Groundwater	Surface Water	Total
56,732	48,151	104,883
WATERSHED TOTAL		
Groundwater	Surface Water	Total
70,917	149,826	220,742

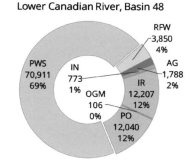

Permitted Surface Water (AFY)
Lower Canadian River, Basin 48

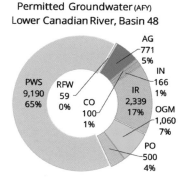

Permitted Groundwater (AFY)
Lower Canadian River, Basin 48

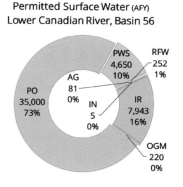

Permitted Surface Water (AFY)
Lower Canadian River, Basin 56

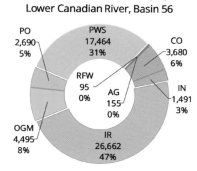

Permitted Groundwater (AFY)
Lower Canadian River, Basin 56

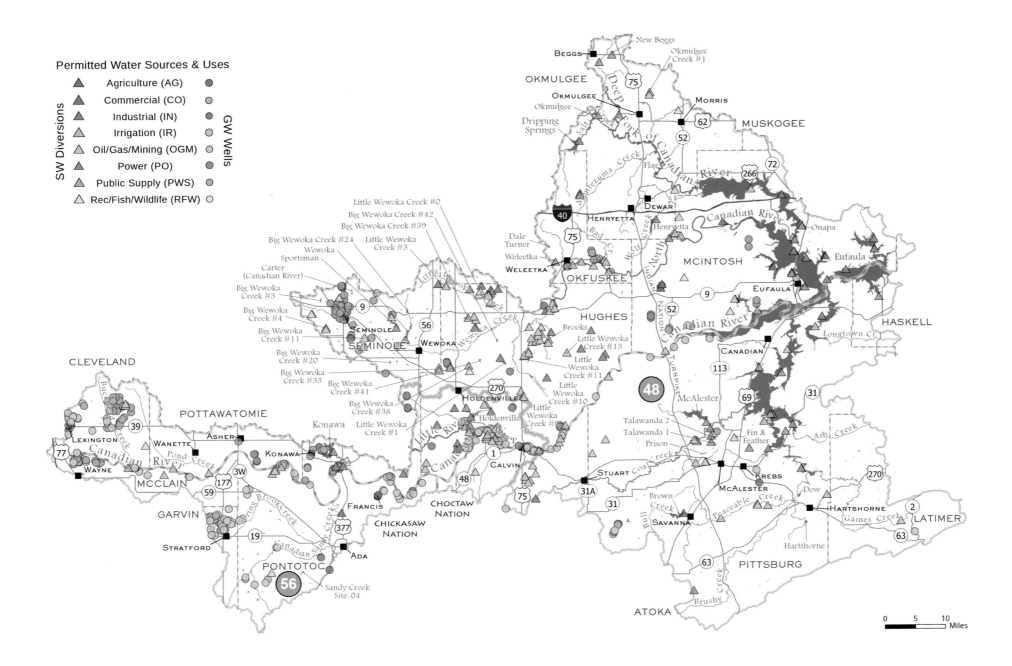

Permitted Water Sources & Uses

SW Diversions

▲ Agriculture (AG)
▲ Commercial (CO)
▲ Industrial (IN)
△ Irrigation (IR)
△ Oil/Gas/Mining (OGM)
▲ Power (PO)
△ Public Supply (PWS)
△ Rec/Fish/Wildlife (RFW)

GW Wells

● Agriculture (AG)
● Commercial (CO)
● Industrial (IN)
● Irrigation (IR)
● Oil/Gas/Mining (OGM)
● Power (PO)
○ Public Supply (PWS)
○ Rec/Fish/Wildlife (RFW)

OKA HOLISSO

Water Supply Systems

The uniquely large expanse of the Lower Canadian River watershed, as well as its many and varied surface and groundwater resources, lends itself to the existence of a number of water supply systems. The City of Ada, serving south-central Basin 56 with water from Byrds Mill Spring through two water lines and three supplemental wells when flows are low, is the largest water provider in the Settlement Area. Ada, which is the headquarters of the Chickasaw Nation, serves four rural water districts in Pontotoc County.

The City of McAlester, south of Lake Eufaula in Basin 48, is the fourth largest water provider in the Settlement Area as it serves 18,206 residential customers. McAlester PWA sells surface supply to five separate Pittsburg County rural water districts. Other systems worth mentioning include the City of Purcell, a groundwater supplier to 8,118 customers, albeit primarily in three adjacent watersheds; Longtown Rural Water and Sewer District #1 (5,444 residential customers), in the Lake Eufaula area; Pontotoc County RWD #8 (4,250), adjacent to Ada; Adamson RWD #8 (4,306), which purchases all of its surface supply and serves a large area in Basin 48; and Murray Co. RWD #1, near Sulphur, with a small portion of its service area in southern Basin 56.

System	Residential Customers Served[1]	Source(s) of Supply[2]	Water Sales	Water Purchases	Facilities[3]				
					Intake	Pump Facility	Storage	Treatment Plant	Well or Spring
Ada	37,000	GW	Pontotoc Co. #1, Pontotoc Co. #6, Pontotoc Co. #7, Pontotoc Co. #9	—					
Adamson RWD #8	4,306	P (SW)	—	Pittsburg Co. WA					
Allen PWA	937	GW	—	—					
Byars	275	GW	—	—					
Calvin	300	GW	—	—					4
Francis	390	GW	—	—					4
Garvin Co. RWD #1	1,445	GW	—	—					2
Garvin Co. RWD #6 (Wells)	2,762	GW	—	Wynnewood Water & Light					
Haileyville	889	P (SW)	—	Pittsburg Co. WA					
Hartshorne	2,300	P (SW)	—	Pittsburg Co. WA					
Haskell Co. Water Comp.	3,000	SW	Keota PWA, Quinton	Stigler	1			1	
Hughes Co. RWD #2	1,145	GW	—	—			1		
Hughes Co. RWD #4	800	P (GW)	—	Hughes Co. #6					
Hughes Co. RWD #6 (Gerty)	1,380	GW	Hughes Co. #4	—					
Indianola RWD #18	2,000	P (SW)	—	Pittsburg Co. PWA					
Krebs Utility Authority	2,051	SW	—	—	1			1	
Latimer Co. RWD #1	2,750	P (SW)	—	Wilburton					

Public Water Supply Systems
Basins 48 & 56

System	Residential Customers Served[1]	Source(s) of Supply[2]	Water Sales	Water Purchases	Facilities[3]				
					Intake	Pump Facility	Storage	Treatment Plant	Well or Spring
Longtown RW&SD #1 (Pittsburg Co.)	5,444	SW	Pittsburg Co. #20	—	1			1	
McAlester PWA	18,206	SW	Pittsburg Co. #5, Pittsburg Co. #6, Pittsburg Co. #7, Pittsburg Co. #9, Pittsburg Co. #16	—	1			1	
McClain Co. RWD #8	1,897	GW	—	—				1	3
Murray Co. RWD #1	4,500	GW	Buckhorn #2, Dougherty	Sulphur					
Pittsburg	280	SW	—	—	1			1	
Pittsburg Co. PWA (Crowder)	2,203	SW	Indianola #18	—	1			1	
Pittsburg Co. RWD #5	1,750	P (SW)	—	McAlester PWA					
Pittsburg Co. RWD #6 (Alderson)	300	P (SW)	—	McAlester PWA					
Pittsburg Co. RWD #7 (Arpelar)	1,900	P (SW)	—	McAlester PWA					
Pittsburg Co. RWD #9 (McAlester)	872	P (SW)	—	McAlester PWA					
Pittsburg Co. RWD #11 (Kiowa)	790	P (SW)	Atoka Co. #1	Kiowa					
Pittsburg Co. RWD #14	1,680	SW	—	—	1			1	
Pittsburg Co. RWD #16	1,268	P (SW)	—	McAlester PWA					
Pittsburg Co. RWD #20 (Carlton Landing)	38	P (SW)	—	Longtown #1					
Pittsburg Co. Water Authority	26	SW	Adamson #8, Haileyville, Hartshorne	—	1			1	
Pontotoc Co. RWD #1 (Homer)	441	P (GW)	—	Ada					
Pontotoc Co. RWD #7	1,950	P (GW)	—	Ada					
Pontotoc Co. RWD #8	4,250	GW	Pontotoc Co. #9	Wingard Water Corp.					
Purcell	8,118	GW	—	—					21
Savanna	800	P (SW)	—	—					
Stratford	1,575	GW	—	—					4
Wayne	688	GW	—	—					6
Wilburton	3,025	SW	Latimer Co. RWD #1	—					

[1]Does not include wholesale customers served through water sales.

[2]GW = Groundwater; SW = Surface Water; P = Purchased.

[3]Includes both active and inactive (mostly wells) facilities in the watershed. Treatment plants include only those utilizing conventional water treatment and do not include chlorination stations associated with discrete source treatment.

Data: Oklahoma Department of Environmental Quality, Safe Drinking Water Information System, OWRB GIS and Arbuckle-Simpson Aquifer Drought Contingency Plan. Listed system facilities include those with service areas and/or facilities within relevant watershed.

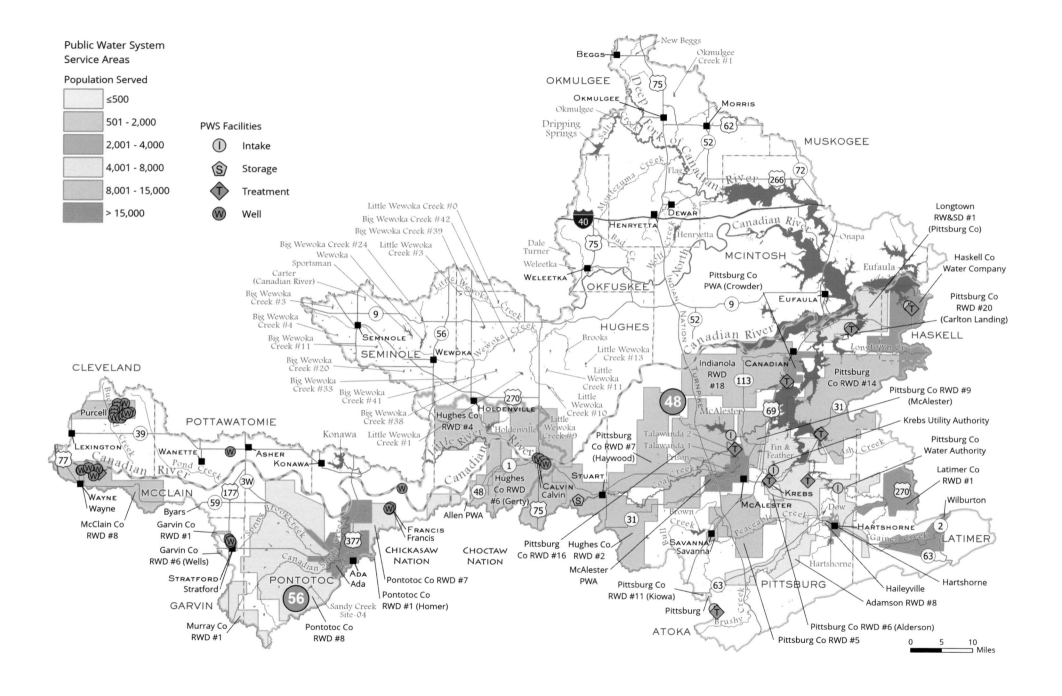

Public Water System Service Areas

Population Served

- ≤500
- 501 - 2,000
- 2,001 - 4,000
- 4,001 - 8,000
- 8,001 - 15,000
- > 15,000

PWS Facilities

- Ⓘ Intake
- Ⓢ Storage
- ⬦T Treatment
- Ⓦ Well

Estimated Streamflow, Lower Canadian River Watershed

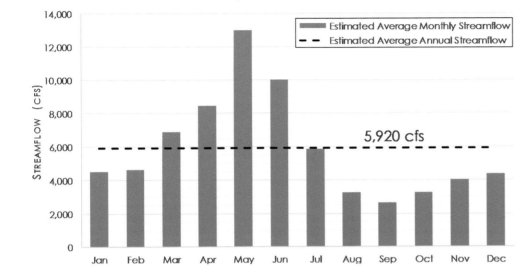

Reservoir Level Exceedance for Lake Eufaula

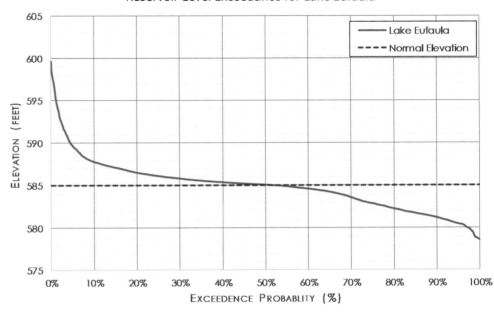

Streamflow Exceedance Probability, Lower Canadian River Watershed

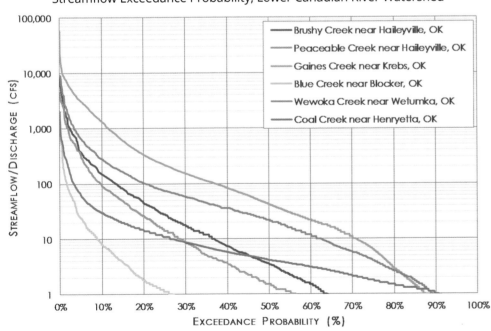

Streamflow Exceedance Probability, Lower Canadian River Watershed

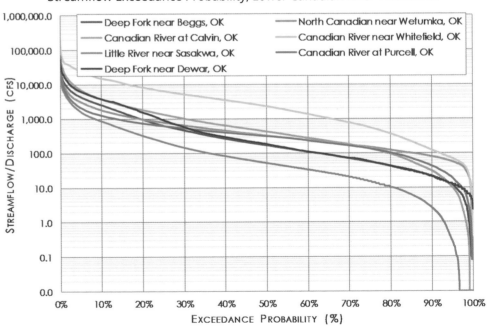

Middle Canadian River

BASIN 58

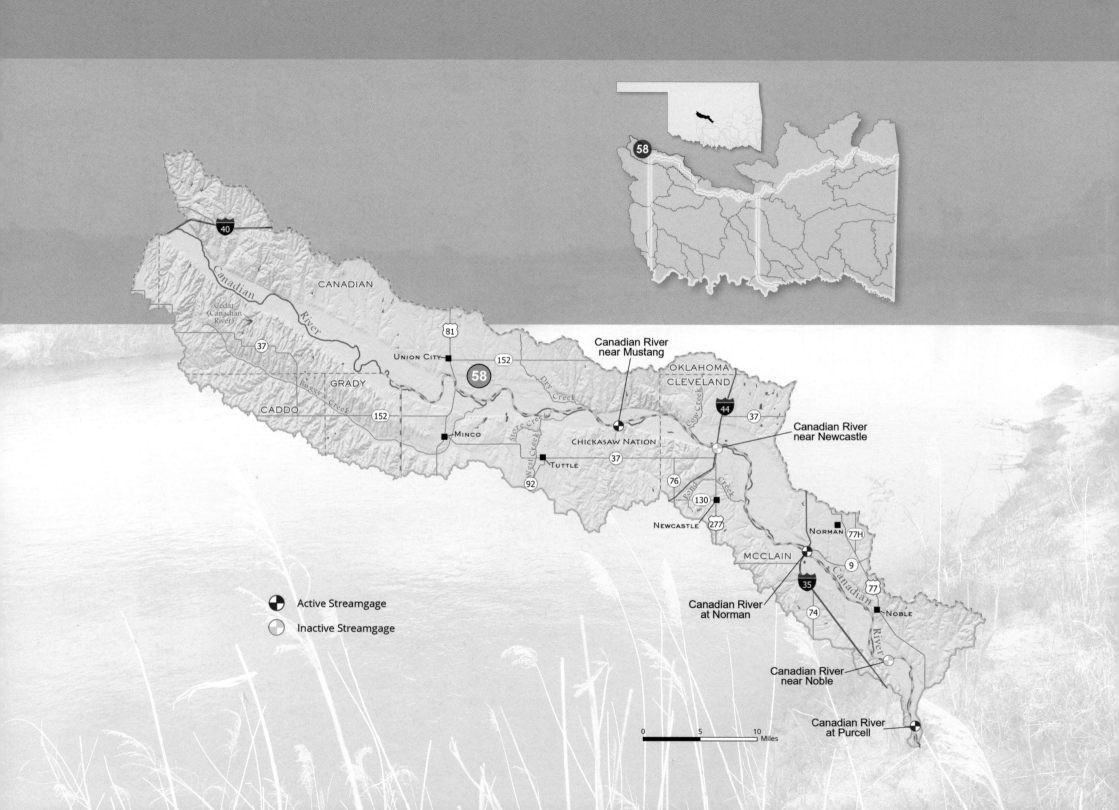

58

Canadian River
near Mustang

Canadian River
near Newcastle

Canadian River
at Norman

Canadian River
near Noble

Canadian River
at Purcell

CANADIAN

Cedar
(Canadian
River)

Canadian

River

GRADY

Bugget Creek

CADDO

Union City

Minco

Tuttle

Dry Creek

Shore Creek

West Creek

CHICKASAW NATION

Cow Creek

OKLAHOMA

CLEVELAND

Newcastle

Pond Creek

Norman

MCCLAIN

Noble

Canadian River

40

81

152

152

37

37

92

76

130

277

44

37

77H

9

77

74

35

Active Streamgage

Inactive Streamgage

0   5   10
                              Miles

Water & Related Resources

In Basin 58, the northern-most watershed intersecting the Chickasaw Nation, the Canadian River flows in a generally east-southeasterly direction as it forms the border of Canadian, Grady, Cleveland and McClain Counties. West of Slaughterville, the river plunges to the south and leaves Basin 58 near Purcell and Lexington. The Middle Canadian River watershed occupies 684 square miles. Its average annual flow, estimated at the bottom of Basin 58, is 677 cfs; this flow is available less than 23 percent of the time.

Cedar Lake, on a small Canadian River tributary in Canadian County, is the only notable lake of size in the watershed.

The whooping crane and piping plover are endangered species occurring in the watershed. Threatened species are the Arkansas River shiner and red knot.

Water Quality

The Middle Canadian River headwaters are in the Cross Timbers ecoregion, with the majority of the watershed in the Central Great Plains. This region is characterized by turbid, incised streams that have rocky or muddy substrates. Salinity and nutrients are high throughout Basin 58. TMDLs for bacteria have been completed on Buggy Creek and the Canadian River.

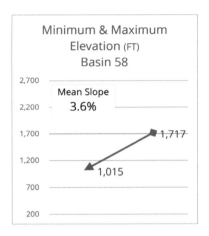

LAND COVER & USES MIDDLE CANADIAN RIVER WATERSHED	
Use	**Area** SQ. MI.
Forest	85
Herbaceous, Shrubs, Woody Wetlands	321
Cultivated Land, Hay/Pasture	188
Developed	80
Water	8
Barren Land	4
Total Land Area	**686**

PRINCIPAL RIVERS & STREAMS BASIN 58	
River/Stream	**Length** MILES
Canadian River	91
Buggy Creek	26

PRINCIPAL LAKES BASIN 58									
Name	**Stream**	**Authority**	**Normal Elevation** FEET	**Normal Area** ACRES	**Normal Capacity** AC-FT	**Shoreline** MILES	**Purpose(s)[1]**	**Water Supply Storage** AC-FT	**Water Supply Yield** AC-FT/YR
Cedar	Canadian River TR	Western Sportsman Club	—	53	1,125	2.2	—	—	—

[1]WS=Water Supply, R=Recreation, HP=Hydroelectric Power, IR=Irrigation, WQ=Water Quality, FW=Fish & Wildlife, FC=Flood Control, LF=Low Flow Regulation, N=Navigation, C=Conservation, CW=Cooling Water

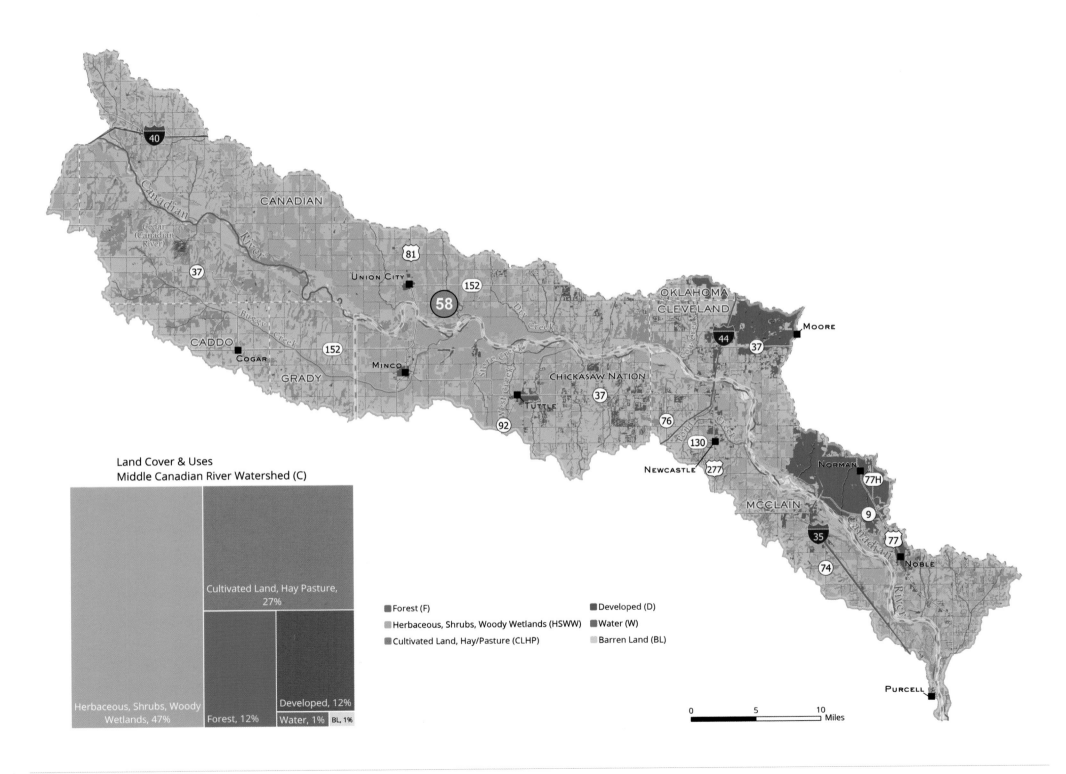

Land Cover & Uses
Middle Canadian River Watershed (C)

Cultivated Land, Hay Pasture, 27%

Herbaceous, Shrubs, Woody Wetlands, 47%

Forest, 12%

Developed, 12%

Water, 1% BL, 1%

■ Forest (F)
■ Herbaceous, Shrubs, Woody Wetlands (HSWW)
■ Cultivated Land, Hay/Pasture (CLHP)

■ Developed (D)
■ Water (W)
■ Barren Land (BL)

0   5   10 Miles

Groundwater

An estimated 5,550 wells, much more than in any other Settlement Area basin/watershed, tap the Middle Canadian River watershed. Recognizing that some wells are completed at depths sufficient to penetrate multiple groundwater formations, 2,118 and 1,235 permitted/domestic wells overlie the major Canadian River and Garber-Wellington aquifers in Basin 58. The minor El Reno aquifer includes 1,964 wells. All four groundwater basins in the watershed are assigned the default EPS of 2.0 ac-ft/acre. Hydrologic studies have been completed on the Garber-Wellington, Canadian River and Rush Springs (the third major aquifer in Basin 58), but none have yet received OWRB approval of a final EPS.

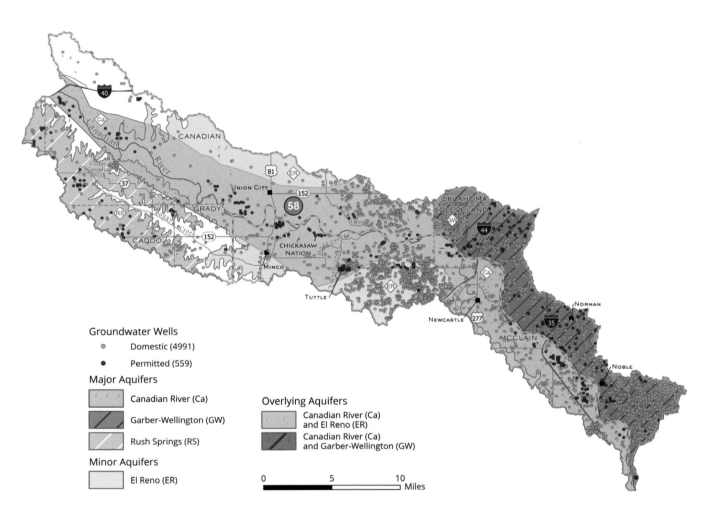

Groundwater Wells
- Domestic (4991)
- Permitted (559)

Major Aquifers
- Canadian River (Ca)
- Garber-Wellington (GW)
- Rush Springs (RS)

Minor Aquifers
- El Reno (ER)

Overlying Aquifers
- Canadian River (Ca) and El Reno (ER)
- Canadian River (Ca) and Garber-Wellington (GW)

0   5   10 Miles

MAJOR & MINOR AQUIFERS BASINS 58			
Aquifer	Area in Basin/ Watershed SQUARE MILES	EPS[1] AC-FT/ACRE	Number of Permitted & Domestic Wells in Basin/ Watershed[2]
Canadian River	393	2.0	2,118
El Reno	298	2.0	1,964
Garber-Wellington	131	2.0	1,235
Rush Springs	77	2.0	138
Nondelineated Source Wells			95
Total Wells			5,550

[1]Italic number signifies unstudied aquifers with a default temporary equal proportionate share (EPS) of 2.0 acre-feet per acre of land.
[2]Some wells are double-counted where one aquifer overlies another.

NOTE: Significant color and shading variations may be apparent in areas where one aquifer overlies another. In some cases, for state administrative purposes, aquifer boundaries align directly with county lines or related political borders rather than geologic outcrop areas.

Permitted Water Use

Typical of several basins/watersheds in the western portion of the Chickasaw Nation, permitted groundwater withdrawals in the Middle Canadian outnumber diversions from surface sources by a 68 to 32 percent margin, or 88,274 to 40,664 AFY. Water allocated and appropriated for irrigation in this largely rural area accounts for 45 percent of uses, followed by public supply (36 percent) and oil, gas and mining (12 percent).

WHB Cattle is the largest permittee in Basin 58 with 23,861 AFY in surface water diversions for both irrigation and agricultural uses in Grady and Canadian Counties. Similarly, Braum Family LP holds both surface and groundwater rights of 10,241 AFY for irrigation, agriculture and industrial uses in Grady County. Among a number of communities holding public supply rights in the watershed, the City of Norman possesses groundwater permits amounting to 19,372 AFY. The University of Oklahoma also has prior water rights authorizing the withdrawal of 3,279 AFY for commercial use at the school.

Any application to appropriate water for use at a location outside of Basin 58 could be subject to conferral, depending upon the application amount, mean available flow and other relevant factors. See conditions associated with Class C Basins in the Tribal-State Water Settlement agreement in the *Oka Holisso* appendix.

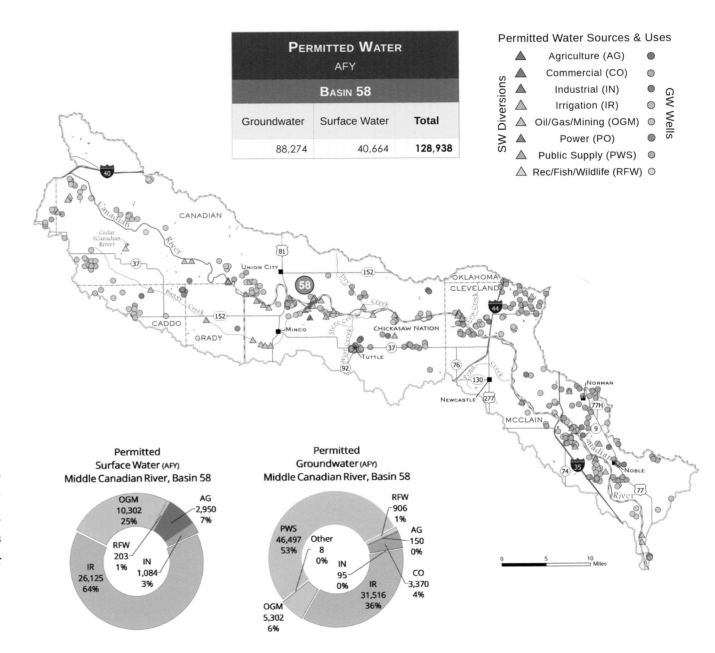

PERMITTED WATER AFY		
BASIN 58		
Groundwater	Surface Water	Total
88,274	40,664	128,938

Permitted Water Sources & Uses

SW Diversions / GW Wells
- Agriculture (AG)
- Commercial (CO)
- Industrial (IN)
- Irrigation (IR)
- Oil/Gas/Mining (OGM)
- Power (PO)
- Public Supply (PWS)
- Rec/Fish/Wildlife (RFW)

Permitted Surface Water (AFY)
Middle Canadian River, Basin 58

- OGM 10,302 25%
- AG 2,950 7%
- IN 1,084 3%
- IR 26,125 64%
- RFW 203 1%

Permitted Groundwater (AFY)
Middle Canadian River, Basin 58

- RFW 906 1%
- AG 150 0%
- CO 3,370 4%
- IR 31,516 36%
- OGM 5,302 6%
- IN 95 0%
- Other 8 0%
- PWS 46,497 53%

All six of the water supply systems in the Middle Canadian River watershed service the middle and lower end of Basin 58. Chief among these is the City of Newcastle with 7,900 residential customers. The community obtains its supply from groundwater in the alluvium of the Canadian River. Tuttle (4,500 customers) purchases some of its supply from Newcastle, as does Blanchard, which serves 4,500 customers between Newcastle and the far northern extent of Grady County RWD #6 (3,950 customers, primarily in the Middle Washita Class C watershed) service area. A small portion of Purcell's service area supplies users in the far southern extent of Basin 58.

					Facilities[3]				
System	**Residential Customers Served[1]**	**Source(s) of Supply[2]**	**Water Sales**	**Water Purchases**	Intake	Pump Facility	Storage	Treatment Plant	Well or Spring
Goldsby Water Authority Trust	2,000	GW	—	Newcastle					1
Grady Co. RWD #6	3,930	GW	Grady Co. #2	Chickasha MA, Tuttle					
Minco	1,632	GW	—	—				1	2
Newcastle	7,900	GW	Blanchard, Goldsby WA Trust, Tuttle	—				1	4
Purcell	8,118	GW	—	—					
Tuttle	4,500	GW	Blanchard, Grady Co. #6	Blanchard, Newcastle					2

PUBLIC WATER SUPPLY SYSTEMS
BASIN 58

[1]Does not include wholesale customers served through water sales.
[2]GW = Groundwater; SW = Surface Water; P = Purchased.
[3]Includes both active and inactive (mostly wells) facilities in the watershed. Treatment plants include only those utilizing conventional water treatment and do not include chlorination stations associated with discrete source treatment.
Data: Oklahoma Department of Environmental Quality, Safe Drinking Water Information System, OWRB GIS and Arbuckle-Simpson Aquifer Drought Contingency Plan. Listed system facilities include those with service areas and/or facilities within relevant watershed.

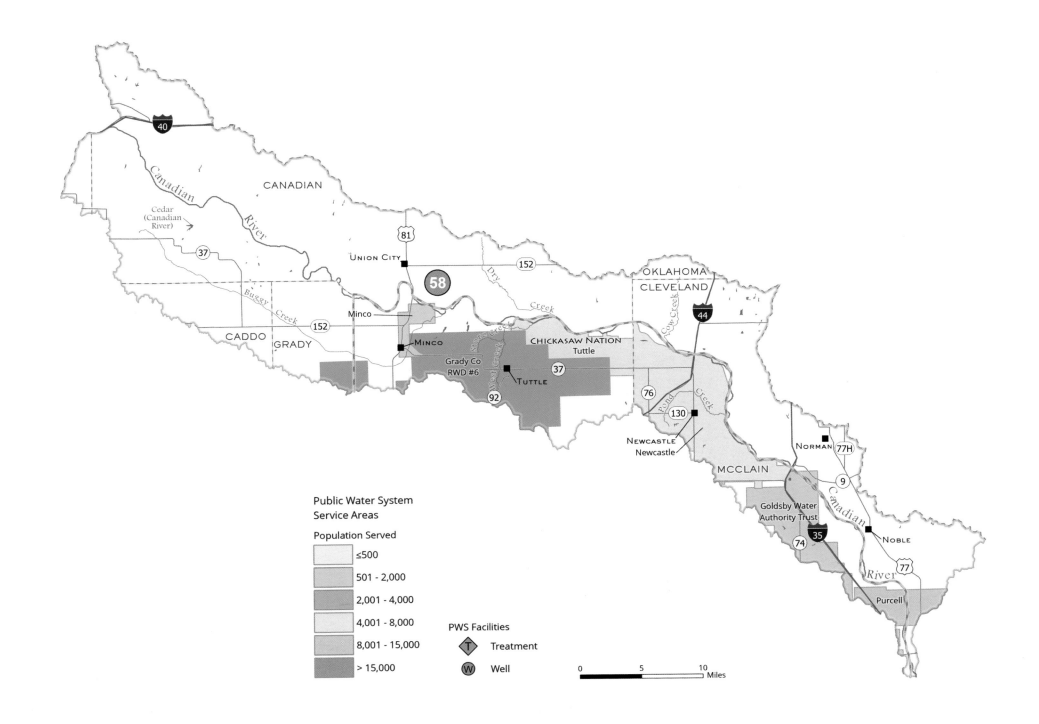

Public Water System
Service Areas

Population Served

	≤500
	501 - 2,000
	2,001 - 4,000
	4,001 - 8,000
	8,001 - 15,000
	> 15,000

PWS Facilities

Ⓣ Treatment

Ⓦ Well

0   5   10
Miles

Estimated Streamflow, Middle Canadian River Watershed

677 cfs

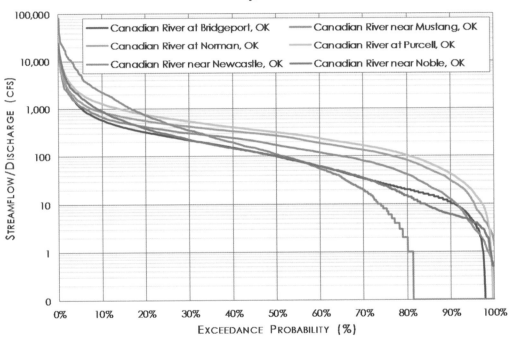

Streamflow Exceedance Probability, Middle Canadian River Watershed

Middle Washita River

BASIN 16

Basin 16 — The Washita River near Chickasha

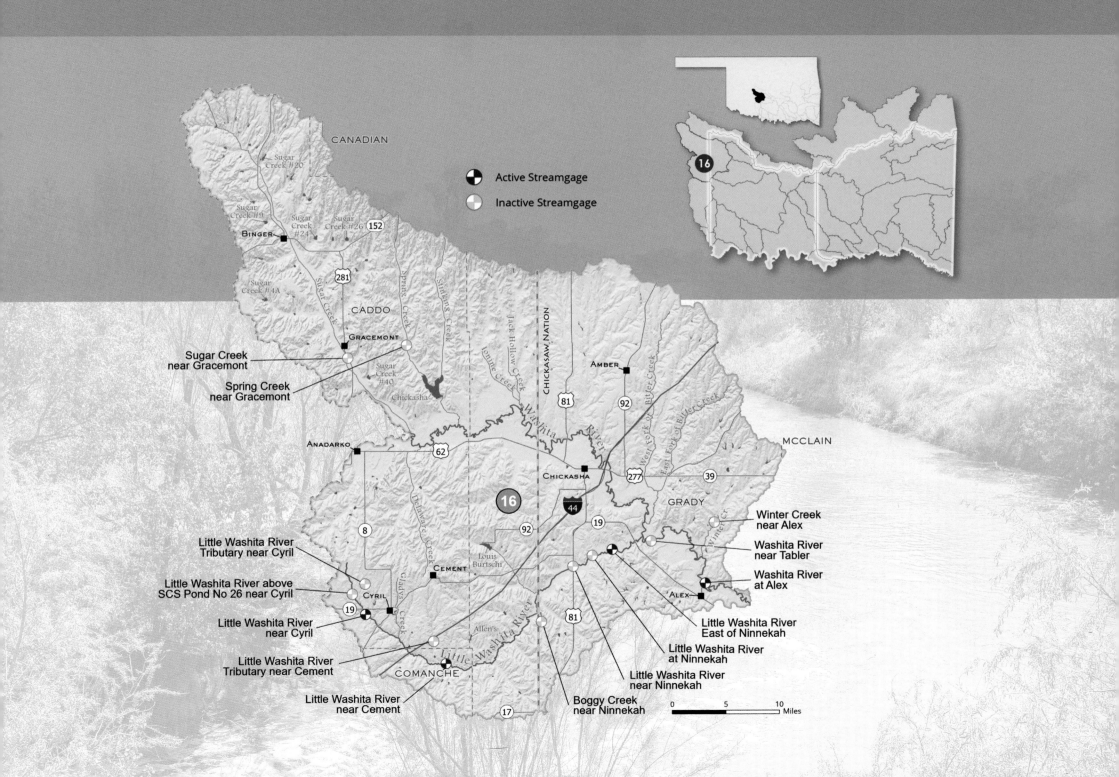

Active Streamgage

Inactive Streamgage

CANADIAN

Sugar Creek #20

Sugar Creek #9

Sugar Creek #24   Sugar Creek #26   152

BINGER

281

Sugar Creek #4A

CADDO

Sugar Creek #40

GRACEMONT

Sugar Creek
near Gracemont

Spring Creek
near Gracemont

Chickasha

Jack Hollow Creek

CHICKASAW NATION

Amber

West Fork of Bitter Creek

East Fork of Bitter Creek

MCCLAIN

ANADARKO

62

Washita River

CHICKASHA

277   39

81

92

GRADY

16

44

8

92

19

Winter Creek
near Alex

Winter Cr.

Washita River
near Tabler

Little Washita River
Tributary near Cyril

Delaware Creek

CEMENT

Louis
Burtschi

Washita River
at Alex

Little Washita River above
SCS Pond No 26 near Cyril

CYRIL

Gladys Creek

Little Washita River
near Cyril

19

Little Washita River
East of Ninnekah

Little Washita River
Tributary near Cement

Allen's

Little Washita River

Little Washita River
at Ninnekah

Little Washita River
near Cement

COMANCHE

81

Little Washita River
near Ninnekah

17

Boggy Creek
near Ninnekah

ALEX

0   5   10
Miles

The Washita River, a robust watercourse characterized by numerous and sudden twists and turns, enters Basin 16 in central Caddo County. It meanders to the east near Verden, then turns to the southeast at Chickasha in Grady County where it is joined from the south by the Little Washita River, which heads northwest of Cyril in southern Caddo County. At the confluence, the Washita River continues its southeasterly path as it enters downstream Basin 15 (the Class A Middle Washita watershed) east of Alex. Basin 16 is 1,125 square miles in size. The average annual flow of the Class C Middle Washita River, estimated at the bottom of Basin 16, is 665 cfs; this flow is available 25 percent of the time.

Lakes Chickasha, constructed by the city in 1958, and Louis Burtschi, built by the ODWC in 1954, are the two principal lakes of note in the Middle Washita River watershed. Both lakes primarily serve local recreational needs.

Basin 16 is inhabited by two endangered species: the piping plover and whooping crane. Threatened species are the Arkansas River shiner and red knot.

The Middle Washita River watershed crosses both the Central Great Plains and Cross Timbers ecoregions where streams are morphologically diverse and shallow with sandy soils or gravel/cobble bottoms in deep pools and riffles. Clarity is poor and salinity is very high in Basin 16. The Spring Creek and Lake Chickasha watersheds are designated as nutrient limited watersheds (NLW). Lake Chikasha is phosphorus-limited and hyper-eutrophic. TMDLs have been completed for bacteria on Spring Creek and Bitter Creek as well as on the Little Washita and Washita Rivers.

PRINCIPAL RIVERS & STREAMS BASIN 16	
River/Stream	**Length** MILES
Washita River	74
Little Washita River	38
Sugar Creek	32
Spring Creek	19
West Fork of Bitter Creek	17
East Fork of Bitter Creek	13
Stinking Creek	13
Delaware Creek	12

PRINCIPAL LAKES BASIN 16									
Name	**Stream**	**Authority**	**Normal Elevation** FEET	**Normal Area** ACRES	**Normal Capacity** AC-FT	**Shoreline** MILES	**Purpose(s)**[1]	**Water Supply Storage** AC-FT	**Water Supply Yield** AC-FT/YR
Allen's	Little Washita River TR	Grady Co. CD	—	43	318	1.6	FC	—	—
Chickasha	Spring Creek	City of Chickasha	1,170	839	41,080	8.4	WS, R	—	—
Louis Burtschi	East Bills Creek	ODWC	1,207	138	2,140	2.6	R	—	—
Sugar Creek #4A	Sugar Creek TR	SCS/South Caddo CD	—	47	266	1.5	FC	—	—
Sugar Creek #9	Sugar Creek TR	SCS/South Caddo CD	—	41	254	1.1	FC	—	—
Sugar Creek #20	Sugar Creek TR	SCS/North Caddo CD	—	50	312	1.4	FC	—	—
Sugar Creek #24	Sugar Creek TR	SCS/South Caddo CD	—	47	272	1.2	FC	—	—
Sugar Creek #26	Sugar Creek TR	SCS/South Caddo CD	—	46	238	1.1	FC	—	—
Sugar Creek #40	Sugar Creek TR	SCS/South Caddo CD	—	42	211	1	FC	—	—

[1]WS=Water Supply, R=Recreation, HP=Hydroelectric Power, IR=Irrigation, WQ=Water Quality, FW=Fish & Wildlife, FC=Flood Control, LF=Low Flow Regulation, N=Navigation, C=Conservation, CW=Cooling Water

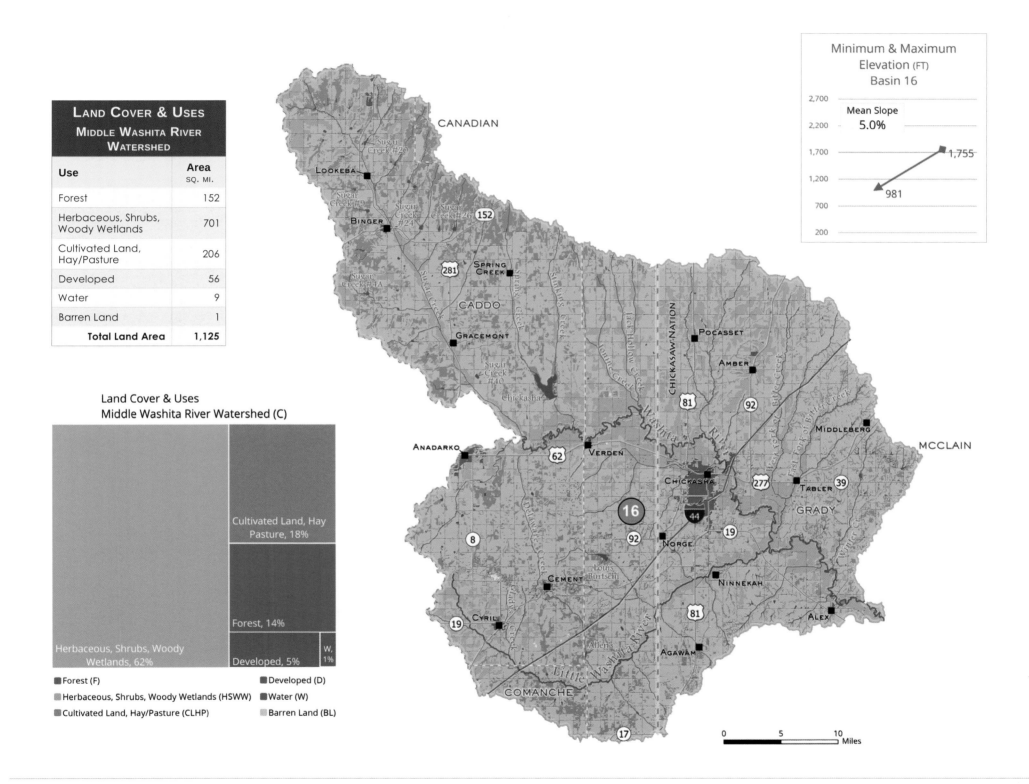

LAND COVER & USES
MIDDLE WASHITA RIVER WATERSHED

Use	Area SQ. MI.
Forest	152
Herbaceous, Shrubs, Woody Wetlands	701
Cultivated Land, Hay/Pasture	206
Developed	56
Water	9
Barren Land	1
Total Land Area	**1,125**

Land Cover & Uses
Middle Washita River Watershed (C)

Cultivated Land, Hay Pasture, 18%

Forest, 14%

Herbaceous, Shrubs, Woody Wetlands, 62%

Developed, 5%

W, 1%

■ Forest (F)
■ Herbaceous, Shrubs, Woody Wetlands (HSWW)
■ Cultivated Land, Hay/Pasture (CLHP)
■ Developed (D)
■ Water (W)
■ Barren Land (BL)

Minimum & Maximum Elevation (FT) Basin 16

Mean Slope
5.0%

1,755

981

Groundwater

As in the adjacent Middle Canadian watershed, abundant groundwater resources supply users in the Middle Washita River watershed area. The major Rush Springs aquifer, in the western portion of Basin 16, supplies an estimated 722 wells. The Washita River aquifer, a major groundwater basin with 273 overlying wells in Basin 16, includes two separate units for study/management purposes. Reach 3 and Reach 4 have been assigned EPS of 1.5 and 1.0 acre-feet/acre, respectively. The El Reno bedrock aquifer, the sole minor groundwater basin which outcrops in the eastern portion of the watershed, is the source for 679 permitted and domestic wells. An additional 115 wells are completed in nondelineated groundwater areas.

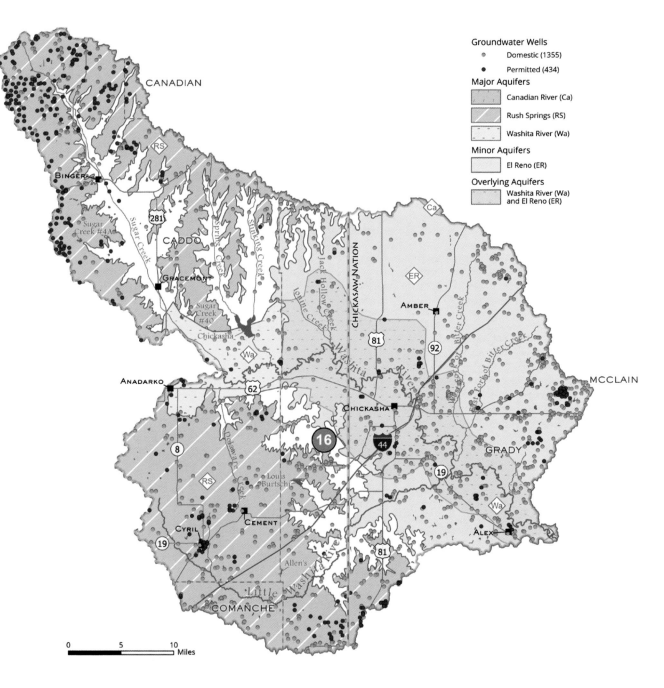

MAJOR & MINOR AQUIFERS BASINS 16			
Aquifer	Area in Basin/ Watershed SQUARE MILES	EPS[1] AC-FT/ACRE	Number of Permitted & Domestic Wells in Basin/ Watershed[2]
Canadian River	1	2.0	0
El Reno	451	2.0	679
Rush Springs	447	2.0	722
Washita River	229	1.5 (Reach 3) 1.0 (Reach 4)	273
Nondelineated Source Wells			115
Total Wells			1,789

[1]Italic number signifies unstudied aquifers with a default temporary equal proportionate share (EPS) of 2.0 acre-feet per acre of land.
[2]Some wells are double-counted where one aquifer overlies another.

NOTE: Significant color and shading variations may be apparent in areas where one aquifer overlies another. In some cases, for state administrative purposes, aquifer boundaries align directly with county lines or related political borders rather than geologic outcrop areas.

Permitted Water Use

Like adjacent Basin 58 (Middle Canadian), the Middle Washita River watershed is characterized by considerable groundwater use. Permitted groundwater in Basin 16 exceeds surface water by 64 (45,592 AFY) to 36 percent (25,940 AFY). OWRB records indicate 256 total active groundwater permits in the watershed.

Irrigation far outpaces other uses as it accounts for 64 percent of permitted water uses. Seventeen percent of allocations and appropriations are attributed to the public supply use followed by oil, gas and mining at 10 percent.

The City of Lindsay (and Lindsay PWA) is the largest permittee in Basin 16 with four public water supply permits totaling 2,168 AFY mostly from groundwater sources in Garvin County. Two energy companies, Continental Resources and Select Energy Services, possess oil, gas and mining permits of 1,624 and 1,400 AFY, respectively, accessed through surface water diversions in Grady and Garvin Counties.

Any application to appropriate water for use at a location outside of Basin 16 could be subject to conferral, depending upon the application amount, mean available flow and other relevant factors. See conditions associated with Class C Basins in the Tribal-State Water Settlement agreement in the *Oka Holisso* appendix.

PERMITTED WATER		
AFY		
BASIN 16		
Groundwater	Surface Water	Total
45,592	25,940	71,532

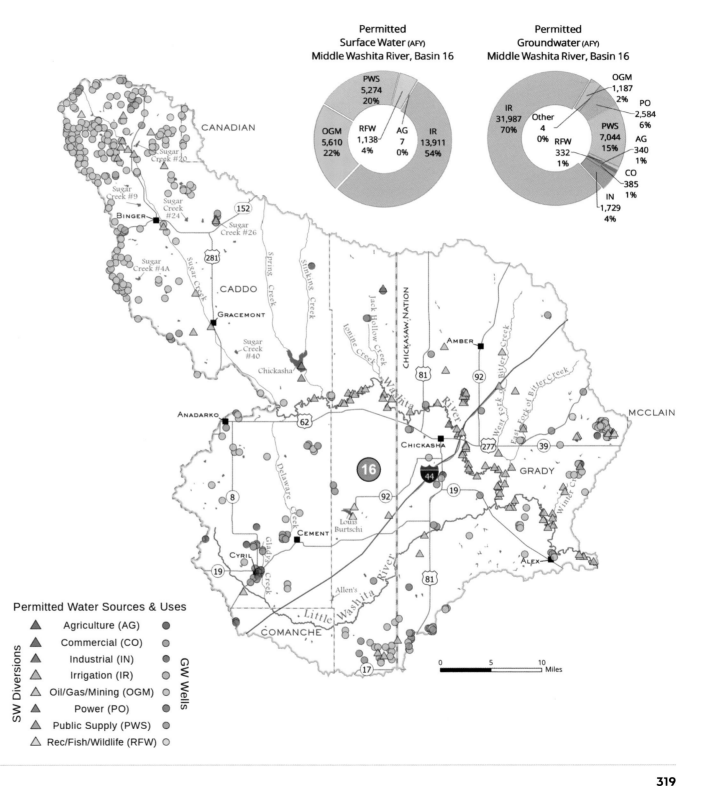

Permitted Surface Water (AFY)
Middle Washita River, Basin 16

PWS 5,274 20%
OGM 5,610 22%
RFW 1,138 4%
AG 7 0%
IR 13,911 54%

Permitted Groundwater (AFY)
Middle Washita River, Basin 16

OGM 1,187 2%
PO 2,584 6%
IR 31,987 70%
Other 4 0%
PWS 7,044 15%
RFW 332 1%
AG 340 1%
CO 385 1%
IN 1,729 4%

Permitted Water Sources & Uses

SW Diversions / GW Wells

- ▲ ● Agriculture (AG)
- ▲ ◐ Commercial (CO)
- ▲ ● Industrial (IN)
- ▲ ◐ Irrigation (IR)
- △ ◯ Oil/Gas/Mining (OGM)
- ▲ ● Power (PO)
- ▲ ◐ Public Supply (PWS)
- △ ◯ Rec/Fish/Wildlife (RFW)

Water Supply Systems

The City of Chickasha is the predominant water provider for users in the Middle Washita watershed. More than 16,000 residents, as well as some of the 3,930 customers of Grady County RWD #6 and 890 customers of Norge Water Company, depend upon the Municipal Authority for supply. Chickasha obtains its primary supply from Fort Cobb Reservoir (west of the settlement area) and utilizes Lake Chickasha as a secondary source.

Grady Co. RWD #6, with a relatively large service area extending throughout the middle portion of Basin 16, provides only groundwater supply to its customers. The district also sells water to adjacent Grady Co. RWD #2.

PUBLIC WATER SUPPLY SYSTEMS BASIN 16					Facilities[3]				
System	Residential Customers Served[1]	Source(s) of Supply[2]	Water Sales	Water Purchases	Intake	Pump Facility	Storage	Treatment Plant	Well or Spring
Alex	635	GW	—	—					3
Chickasha MA	16,036	SW	Grady Co. #6, Norge Water Comp.	—				1	
Dibble	550	P (SW)	—	Blanchard					
Grady Co. RWD #1	300	GW	—	—					7
Grady Co. RWD #2	455	GW	—	Grady Co. RWD #6					3
Grady Co. RWD #6	3,930	GW	Grady Co. RWD #2	Chickasha MA, Tuttle					
Grady Co. RWD #7 (Ninnekah)	2,425	GW	—	—					7
Norge Water Company	890	P (SW)	—	Chickasha MA					

[1]Does not include wholesale customers served through water sales.

[2]GW = Groundwater; SW = Surface Water; P = Purchased.

[3]Includes both active and inactive (mostly wells) facilities in the watershed. Treatment plants include only those utilizing conventional water treatment and do not include chlorination stations associated with discrete source treatment.

Data: Oklahoma Department of Environmental Quality, Safe Drinking Water Information System, OWRB GIS and Arbuckle-Simpson Aquifer Drought Contingency Plan. Listed system facilities include those with service areas and/or facilities within relevant watershed.

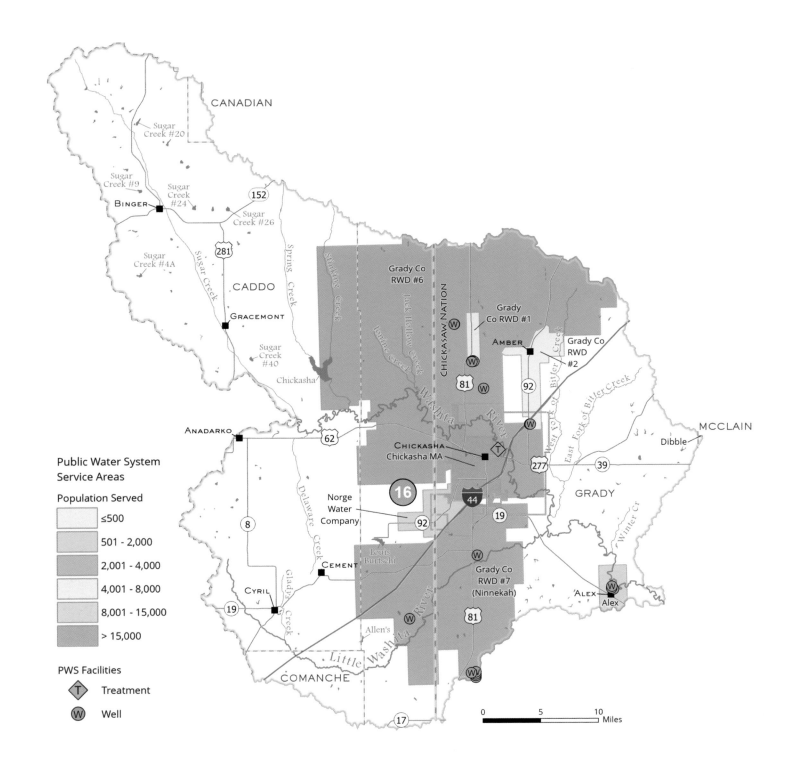

Public Water System
Service Areas

Population Served

	≤500
	501 - 2,000
	2,001 - 4,000
	4,001 - 8,000
	8,001 - 15,000
	> 15,000

PWS Facilities

T — Treatment

W — Well

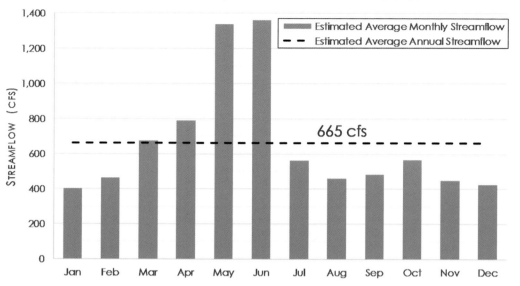

Estimated Streamflow, Middle Washita River Watershed

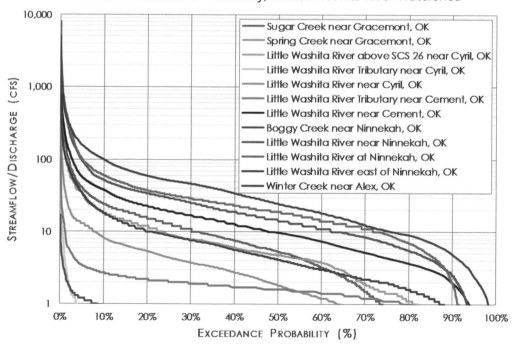

Streamflow Exceedance Probability, Middle Washita River Watershed

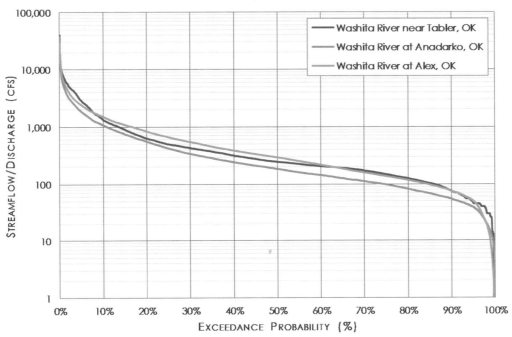

Streamflow Exceedance Probability, Middle Washita River Watershed

Appendix

Glossary

Acre-foot. The volume of water that would cover one acre of land to a depth of one foot; equivalent to 43,560 cubic feet or 325,851 gallons.

Alkalinity. Measurement of the water's ability to neutralize acids. High alkalinity usually indicates the presence of carbonate, bicarbonates, or hydroxides. Waters that have high alkalinity values are often considered undesirable because of excessive hardness and high concentrations of sodium salts. Waters with low alkalinity have little capacity to buffer acidic inputs and are susceptible to acidification (low pH).

Alluvial aquifer. Aquifer with porous media consisting of loose, unconsolidated sediments deposited by fluvial (river) or aeolian (wind) processes, typical of river beds, floodplains, dunes and terraces.

Alluvium. Sediments of clay, silt, gravel, or other unconsolidated material deposited over time by a flowing stream on its floodplain or delta; frequently associated with higher-lying terrace deposits of groundwater.

Appendix B areas. Waters of the state into which discharges may be limited and that are located within the boundaries of areas listed in Appendix B of OWRB rules Chapter 45 on Oklahoma's water quality standards (OWQS); including but not limited to national and state parks, forests, wilderness areas, wildlife management areas, and wildlife refuges. Appendix B may include areas inhabited by federally listed threatened or endangered species and other appropriate areas.

Appropriation. Acquisition of a water right under the procedure provided by law to take a specific quantity of water by direct diversion from a stream, an impoundment or a playa lake, and to apply such water to a specific beneficial use or uses.

Aquifer. Geologic unit or formation that contains sufficient saturated, permeable material to yield economically significant quantities of water to wells and springs. (Also see "groundwater basin".)

Basin. Geographic area drained by a single stream system. Related to implementation of the Tribal-State Settlement agreement, the Chickasaw and Choctaw Nation territories have been divided into thirty surface water planning basins.

Basin outlet. The farthest downstream geographic point in a surface water basin.

Bedrock aquifer. Aquifer with porous media consisting of lithified (semi-consolidated or consolidated) sediments, such as limestone, sandstone, siltstone, or fractured crystalline rock.

Bedrock groundwater. Water found in a bedrock aquifer.

Beneficial use. (1) The use of stream or groundwater when reasonable intelligence and diligence are exercised in its application for a lawful purpose and as is economically necessary for that purpose. Beneficial uses include but are not limited to municipal, industrial, agricultural, irrigation, recreation, fish and wildlife, etc., as defined in OWRB rules, Chapter 20 on stream water use and Chapter 30 on groundwater use.

(2) A classification in Oklahoma water quality standards of the waters of the state, according to their best uses in the interest of the public set forth in OWRB rules, Chapter 45.

Chlorophyll-a. Primary photosynthetic plant pigment used in water quality analysis as a measure of algae growth.

Conductivity. A measure of the ability of water to pass electrical current. High specific conductance indicates high concentrations of dissolved solids.

Conservation. Protection from loss and waste. Conservation of water may mean to save or store water for later use or to use water more efficiently.

Conservation pool. Reservoir storage of water for the project's authorized purpose other than flood control.

Consumptive use. A use of water that diverts it from a water supply.

Dam. Any artificial barrier, together with appurtenant works, which does or may impound or divert water.

Degradation. Any condition caused by the activities of humans resulting in the prolonged impairment of any constituent of an aquatic environment.

Demand. Amount of water required to meet the needs of people, communities, industry, agriculture and other users.

Demand management. Adjusting use of water through temporary or permanent conservation measures to meet the water needs of a basin or region.

Dissolved oxygen. Amount of oxygen gas dissolved in a given volume of water at a particular temperature and pressure, often expressed as a concentration in parts of oxygen per million parts of water. Low levels of dissolved oxygen facilitate the release of nutrients from sediments.

Diversion. To take water from a stream or waterbody into a pipe, canal, or other conduit, either by pumping or gravity flow.

Domestic use. In relation to OWRB water use permitting, the use of water by a natural individual or by a family or household for household purposes, for farm and domestic animals up to the normal grazing capacity of the land whether or not the animals are actually owned by such natural individual or family, and for the irrigation of land not exceeding a total of three acres in area for the growing of gardens, orchards, and lawns.

Domestic use also includes: (1) the use of water for agriculture purposes by natural individuals, (2) use of water for fire protection, and (3) use of water by non-household entities for drinking water purposes, restroom use, and the watering of lawns, provided that the amount of water used for any such purposes does not exceed five acre-feet per year.

Drainage area. Total area above the discharge point drained by a receiving stream.

Ecoregion (ecological region). An ecologically and geographically defined area.

Effluent. Any fluid emitted by a source to a stream, reservoir, or basin, including a partially or completely treated waste fluid that is produced by and flows out of an industrial or wastewater treatment plant or sewer.

Elevation. Elevation in feet in relation to mean sea level (MSL).

Equal proportionate share (EPS). Portion of the maximum annual yield of water from a groundwater basin that is allocated to each acre of land overlying the basin or subbasin.

Eutrophic. A water quality characterization, or "trophic status," that indicates abundant nutrients and high rates of productivity in a lake, frequently resulting in oxygen depletion.

Eutrophication. The process whereby the condition of a waterbody changes from one of low biologic productivity and clear water to one of high productivity and water made turbid by the accelerated growth of algae.

Flood control pool. Reservoir storage of excess runoff above the conservation pool storage capacity that is discharged at a regulated rate to reduce potential downstream flood damage.

Floodplain. The land adjacent to a body of water which has been or may be covered by flooding, including, but not limited to, the 100-year flood (the flood expected to be equaled or exceeded every 100 years on average).

Fresh water. Water that has less than five thousand (5,000) parts per million total dissolved solids.

Gap. An anticipated shortage of water supply due to a deficiency of physical water or the inability or failure to obtain necessary water rights.

Groundwater. Fresh water under the surface of the earth regardless of the geologic structure in which it is standing or moving outside the cut bank of a definite stream.

Groundwater basin. A distinct underground body of water overlain by contiguous land having substantially the same geological and hydrological characteristics and yield capabilities, commonly associated with an aquifer. The area of a major or minor basin, as determined by the OWRB, can be specified by political boundaries, geological, hydrological, or other reasonable physical boundaries. In Oklahoma, such groundwater basin delineations facilitate the OWRB's reasonable regulation and allocation of those waters based on the results of hydrologic surveys.

Groundwater recharge. *see Recharge*

Hardness. A measure of the mineral content of water. Water containing high concentrations (usually greater than 60 ppm) of iron, calcium, magnesium, and hydrogen ions is usually considered "hard" water.

High Quality Waters (HQW). A designation in the Oklahoma Water Quality Standards referring to waters that exhibit water quality exceeding levels necessary to support the propagation of fishes, shellfishes, wildlife, and recreation in and on the water. This designation prohibits any new point source discharge or additional load or increased concentration of specified pollutants.

Hydraulic conductivity. The capacity of rock to transmit groundwater under pressure.

Hydrologic unit code (HUC). A numerical designation recognized by the United States Geologic Survey and other federal and state agencies as a way of identifying all drainage basins in the U.S. in a nested arrangement from largest to smallest, consisting of a multi-digit code that identifies each of the levels of classification within two-digit fields.

Hypereutrophic. A surface water quality characterization, or "trophic status," that indicates excessive primary productivity and excessive nutrient levels in a lake.

Impaired water. Waterbody in which the quality fails to meet specific standards prescribed for its beneficial uses.

Impoundment. Body of water, such as a pond or lake, confined by a dam, dike, floodgate or other barrier established to collect and store water.

Infiltration. The gradual downward flow of water from the surface of the earth into the subsurface.

Instream (environmental) flow. A quantity of water set aside in a stream or river to ensure that downstream environmental, social and economic benefits are met.

Levee. A man-made structure, usually an earthen embankment, designed and constructed to contain, control or divert the flow of water so as to provide protection from temporary flooding.

Major groundwater basin. A distinct underground body of water overlain by contiguous land and having essentially the same geological and hydrological characteristics and from which groundwater wells yield at least 50 gallons per minute on the average basin-wide if from a bedrock aquifer, and at least 150 gallons per minute on the average basin-wide if from an alluvium and terrace aquifer, or as otherwise designated by the OWRB.

Marginal quality water. Waters that have been historically unusable due to technological or economic issues associated with diversion, treatment or conveyance.

Maximum annual yield (MAY). Determination by the OWRB of the total amount of fresh groundwater that can be produced from each basin or subbasin allowing a minimum twenty-year life of such basin or subbasin.

Mesotrophic. A surface water quality characterization, or "trophic status," describing those lakes with moderate primary productivity and moderate nutrient levels.

Million gallons per day (MGD). A rate of flow equal to 1.54723 cubic feet per second or 3.0689 acre-feet per day.

Minor groundwater basin. A distinct underground body of water overlain by contiguous land and having substantially the same geological and hydrological characteristics and which is not a major groundwater basin.

Narrative criteria. Statements or other qualitative expressions of chemical, physical or biological parameters that are assigned to protect a beneficial use of a waterbody.

Non-consumptive use. Use of water in a manner that does not reduce the amount of supply, such as navigation, hydropower production, protection of habitat for hunting, maintaining water levels for boating recreation, or maintaining flow, level and/or temperature for fishing, swimming, habitat, etc.

Non-delineated groundwater source. An area where no major or minor aquifer has been studied that may or may not supply a well yield; also referred to as a "non-delineated minor aquifer."

Nonpoint source (NPS). A source of pollution without a well-defined point of origin. Nonpoint source pollution is commonly caused by sediment, nutrients, and organic or toxic substances originating from land use activities. It occurs when the rate of material entering a waterbody exceeds its natural level.

Normal pool elevation. The target lake elevation at which a reservoir was designed to impound water to create a dependable water supply; sometimes referred to as the top of the conservation pool.

Normal pool storage. The volume of water held in a reservoir when it is at normal pool elevation.

Numerical criteria. Concentrations or other quantitative measures of chemical, physical or biological parameters that are assigned to protect the beneficial use of a waterbody.

Nutrients. Elements or compounds essential as raw materials for an organism's growth and development; these include carbon, oxygen, nitrogen and phosphorus.

Oklahoma Water Quality Standards (OWQS). Rules promulgated by the OWRB in Oklahoma Administrative Code Title 785, Chapter 45, which establish classifications of uses of waters of the state, criteria to maintain and protect such classifications, and other standards or policies pertaining to the quality of such waters.

Oligotrophic. A surface water quality characterization, or "trophic status," describing those lakes with low primary productivity and/or low nutrient levels.

pH. The measurement of the hydrogen-ion concentration in water. A pH below 7 is acidic (the lower the number, the more acidic the water, with a decrease of one full unit representing an increase in acidity of ten times) and a pH above 7 (to a maximum of 14) is basic (the higher the number, the more basic the water). In Oklahoma, fresh waters typically exhibit a pH range from 5.5 in the southeast to almost 9.0 in central areas.

Phosphorus-limited. In reference to water chemistry, where growth or amount of primary producers (e.g., algae) is restricted in a waterbody due in large part to the amount of available phosphorus.

Point source. Any discernible, confined and discrete conveyance, including any pipe, ditch, channel, tunnel, well, discrete fissure, container, rolling stock or concentrated animal feeding operation from which pollutants are or may be discharged. This term does not include return flows from irrigation agriculture.

Potable. Describing water suitable for drinking.

Primary Body Contact Recreation (PBCR). A classification in OWQS of a waterbody's use; involves direct body contact with the water where a possibility of ingestion exists. In these cases, the water shall not contain chemical, physical or biological substances in concentrations that irritate the skin or sense organs or are toxic or cause illness upon ingestion by human beings.

Primary productivity. The production of chemical energy in organic compounds by living organisms. In lakes and streams, this is essentially the lowest denominator of the food chain (phytoplankton) bringing energy into the system via photosynthesis.

Prior right. Comparable to a permit, a right to use groundwater recognized by the OWRB as having been established by compliance with state groundwater laws in effect prior to 1973.

Provider. Private or public entity — for purposes of the *Oka Holisso*, non-profit, local governmental municipal or community water systems and rural water districts — that supplies water to end users or other providers.

Recharge. The inflow of water to an alluvial or bedrock aquifer.

Reservoir. A surface depression containing water impounded by a dam.

Return water or return flow. The portion of water diverted from a water supply that returns to a watercourse.

Reverse osmosis. A process that removes salts and other substances from water. Pressure is placed on the stronger of two unequal concentrations separated by a semi-permeable membrane; a common method of desalination.

Riparian. Relating to or situated on the banks of a river. A riparian water right provides an owner of land adjoining a stream or watercourse with permission to use water from that stream for reasonable purposes.

Riverine. Relating to, formed by, or resembling a river (including tributaries), stream, etc.

Salinity. The concentration of salt in water measured in milligrams per liter (mg/L) or parts per million (ppm).

Salt water. Any water containing more than five thousand (5,000) parts per million total dissolved solids.

Saturated thickness. Thickness below the zone of the water table in which the interstices are filled with groundwater.

Scenic rivers. Streams in "scenic river" areas designated by the Oklahoma Legislature that possess unique natural scenic beauty, water conservation, fish, wildlife and outdoor recreational values. These areas are listed and described in Title 82 of Oklahoma Statutes, Section 1451.

Sediment. Particles transported and deposited by water deriving from rocks, soil or biological material.

Sensitive sole source groundwater basin or subbasin. A major groundwater basin or subbasin, all or a portion of which has been designated by the U.S. Environmental Protection Agency (EPA) as a "sole source aquifer" and serves as a mechanism to protect drinking water supplies in areas with limited water supply alternatives. It includes any portion of a contiguous aquifer located within five miles of the known areal extent of the surface outcrop of the designated groundwater basin or subbasin.

Sensitive Water Supplies (SWS). Designation that applies to public and private water supplies possessing conditions that make them more susceptible to pollution events. This designation restricts point source discharges in the watershed and institutes a 10 μg/L (micrograms per liter) chlorophyll-a criterion to protect against taste and odor problems and reduce water treatment costs.

Settlement Area. That area lying between the South Canadian River and the Oklahoma and Texas state line, the Oklahoma and Arkansas state line, and the 98th Meridian, which generally includes the following counties, or portions thereof: Atoka, Bryan, Carter, Choctaw, Coal, Garvin, Grady, McClain, Murray, Haskell, Hughes, Jefferson, Johnston, Latimer, LeFlore, Love, Marshall, McCurtain, Pittsburgh, Pontotoc, Pushmataha and Stephens.

Settlement Area Hydrologic Basin(s). Hydrologic basins, as delineated in the 2012 Update of the Oklahoma Comprehensive Water Plan, occurring within or partially within the Settlement Area utilized to implement and enforce provisions of the Tribal-State Settlement agreement.

Slope. In relation to a surface water basin or watershed, the steepness or total elevation change from the main channel's headwaters to its outlet, expressed as a percentage.

Stormwater. Runoff, such as that generated from rain and snowmelt events, that flows over land or impervious surfaces, such as paved streets, parking lots and building rooftops, and does not soak into the ground.

Stream system. Drainage area of a watercourse or series of watercourses that converges in a large watercourse with defined boundaries.

Stream water. Water in a definite stream that includes water in ponds, lakes, reservoirs, and playa lakes.

Streamflow. The rate of water discharged from a source indicated in volume with respect to time.

Surface water. Water in streams and waterbodies as well as diffused over the land surface.

Surface water basin. *see Basin*

Temporary permit. For groundwater basins or subbasins for which a maximum annual yield has not been determined,

temporary permits are granted to users allocating two acre-feet of water per acre of land per year. Temporary permits are for one-year terms that can be revalidated annually by the permittee. When the maximum annual yield and equal proportionate share are approved by the OWRB, all temporary permits overlying the studied basin are converted to regular permits at the new approved allocation amount.

Terrace deposits. Fluvial or wind-blown deposits occurring along the margin and above the level of a body of water and representing the former floodplain of a stream or river.

Total dissolved solids (TDS). A measure of the amount of dissolved material in the water column, reported in mg/L, with values in fresh water naturally ranging from 0–1000 mg/L. High concentrations of TDS limit the suitability of water as a drinking and livestock watering source as well as irrigation supply.

Total maximum daily load (TMDL). Sum of individual wasteload allocations for point sources, safety reserves, and loads from nonpoint source and natural backgrounds.

Total phosphorus. For water quality analysis, a measure of all forms of phosphorus, often used as an indicator of eutrophication and excessive productivity.

Transmissivity. Measure of how much water can be transmitted horizontally through an aquifer. Transmissivity is the product of hydraulic conductivity of the rock and saturated thickness of the aquifer.

Tributary. Stream or other body of water, surface or underground, that contributes to another larger stream or body of water.

Trophic status. A lake's trophic state, essentially a measure of its biological productivity. The various trophic status levels (oligotrophic, mesotrophic, eutrophic, and hypereutrophic) provide a relative measure of overall water quality conditions in a lake.

Turbidity. A combination of suspended and colloidal materials (e.g., silt, clay, or plankton) that reduce the transmission of light through scattering or absorption. Turbidity values are generally reported in nephelometric turbidity units (NTUs).

Vested stream water right (vested right). Comparable to a permit, a right to use stream water recognized by the OWRB as having been established by compliance with state stream water laws in effect prior to 1963.

Water quality. Physical, chemical and biological characteristics of water that determine diversity, stability and productivity of the climax biotic community or affect human health.

Water right. Right to the use of stream or groundwater for beneficial use reflected by permits or vested rights for stream water or permits or prior rights for groundwater.

Wastewater reuse. Treated municipal and industrial wastewater captured and reused commonly for non-potable irrigation and industrial applications to reduce demand upon potable water systems.

Watershed. The boundaries of a drainage area of a watercourse or series of watercourses that diverge above a designated location or diversion point.

Water supply. A body of water, whether static or moving on or under the surface of the ground, or in a man-made reservoir, available for beneficial use on a dependable basis.

Water supply yield. The maximum amount of water a reservoir can dependably supply from storage during a drought of record. Also referred to as firm yield.

Water table. The upper surface of a zone of saturation; the upper surface of the groundwater.

Waterbody. Any specified segment or body of waters of the state, including but not limited to an entire stream or lake or a portion thereof.

Watercourse. The channel or area that conveys a flow of water.

Well. Any type of excavation for the purpose of obtaining groundwater or to monitor or observe conditions under the surface of the earth; does not include oil and gas wells.

Well yield. Amount of water that a water supply well can produce (usually in gallons per minute), which generally depends on the geologic formation and well construction.

Wholesale. For purposes of the *Oka Holisso*, water sold from one public water provider to another.

Water Quantity Conversion

Initial Unit	Desired Unit				
	CFS	**GPM**	**MGD**	**AFY**	**AFD**
CFS	—	450	.646	724	1.98
GPM	.00222	—	.00144	1.61	.00442
MGD	1.55	695	—	1120	3.07
AFY	.0014	.62	.00089	—	.00274
AFD	.504	226	.326	365	—

CFS: cubic feet per second
GPM: gallons per minute
MGD: million gallons per day
AFY: acre-feet per year
AFD: acre-feet per day
1 acre-foot = 325,851 gallons

Acronyms

AF: acre-foot or acre-feet

AFY: acre-feet per year

BIA: Bureau of Indian Affairs

BHI: Basin of Heightened Interest

BMPs: best management practices

BOD: biochemical oxygen demand

BOR: U.S. Bureau of Reclamation

CD: climate division

CE: Common Era

cfs: cubic feet per second

CCRWP: Chickasaw-Choctaw Regional Water Plan

CNRA: Chickasaw National Recreation Area

CWAC: Cool Water Aquatic Community

DBP: disinfection by-product

DBPR: disinfection byproducts rule

DO: dissolved oxygen

EPA: U.S. Environmental Protection Agency

EPS: equal proportionate share

ESA: Endangered Species Act

GCM: global climate model

GIS: Geographic Information System

GPM: gallons per minute

HQW: high quality waters

HUC: hydrologic unit code

MCD: Master Conservancy District

MAY: maximum annual yield

MGD: million gallons per day

mg/L: milligrams per liter

MRLC: Multi-Resolution Land Characteristics

NHD: National Hydrography Dataset

NLCD: National Land Cover Database

NLW: nutrient-limited watershed

NPS: nonpoint source

NRCS: Natural Resources Conservation Service

NRI: Noble Research Institute

NWR: National Wildlife Refuge

OCS: Oklahoma Climatological Survey

OCWP: Oklahoma Comprehensive Water Plan

ODEQ: Oklahoma Department of Environmental Quality

ODTR: Oklahoma Department of Tourism and Recreation

ODWC: Oklahoma Department of Wildlife Conservation

O&G: oil and gas

ORW: outstanding resource water

OWQS: Oklahoma Water Quality Standards

OWRB: Oklahoma Water Resources Board

PAST: Planning Assistance to States and Tribes

PBCR: primary body contact recreation

PDSI: Palmer Drought Severity Index

pH: hydrogen ion activity

PT: provisional temporary

PVIA: Poteau Valley Improvement Authority

PWA: Public Works Authority

PWS: public water system

RD: rural development

RWD: rural water district

SBCR: secondary body contact recreation

SCCASC: South Central Climate Adaptation Science Center

SCOOP: South Central Oklahoma Oil Province

SCS: Soil Conservation Service

SDWIS: Safe Drinking Water Information System

SOWC: Southern Oklahoma Water Corporation

SWP: source water protection

SWS: sensitive water supply

TAP: Technical Assistance Program

TDS: total dissolved solids

THM: trihalomethane

TMDL: total maximum daily load

TOC: total organic carbon

USACE: United States Army Corps of Engineers

USEPA: United States Environmental Protection Agency

USGS: United States Geological Survey

WBP: watershed based plan

WHAT: web-based hydrograph analysis tool

WMA: wildlife management area

STATE OF OKLAHOMA, CHOCTAW NATION OF OKLAHOMA,

CHICKASAW NATION, CITY OF OKLAHOMA CITY WATER SETTLEMENT

PREAMBLE

WHEREAS, the State of Oklahoma is a state of the United States of America possessing the sovereign powers and rights of a state;

WHEREAS, the Chickasaw Nation is a federally recognized American Indian Tribe possessing sovereign powers and rights to self-government under federal law;

WHEREAS, the Choctaw Nation of Oklahoma is a federally recognized American Indian Tribe possessing sovereign powers and rights to self-government under federal law;

WHEREAS, the City of Oklahoma City is an Oklahoma municipal corporation and a charter city organized and existing pursuant to the Oklahoma State Constitution;

WHEREAS, unresolved questions of law relating to tribal water rights and jurisdictional authorities relating thereto have precipitated long-running conflicts in the Settlement Area, in particular within the Kiamichi Basin and with regard to Sardis Lake, which conflicts most recently included *Chickasaw Nation and Choctaw Nation of Oklahoma v. Fallin, et al.*, and *Oklahoma Water Resources Board v. United States, et al.*;

WHEREAS, for purposes of satisfying Pub. Law 114-322, § 3608(i)(1)(A), 130 Stat. 1628, 1810, the parties signatory hereto have met, conferred, and amended the agreement deemed effective August 22, 2016, so that it conforms with the federal legislation enacted to approve, ratify, and confirm the settlement they have negotiated;

WHEREAS, this Settlement Agreement, which the parties signatory hereto now execute, supersedes and replaces the agreement deemed effective August 22, 2016, in satisfaction of the requirement of Pub. Law 114-322, § 3608(i)(1)(B), 130 Stat. 1628, 1810; and

WHEREAS, by entering into the Settlement Agreement, the State, the Nations, and the City resolve disputes relating to Sardis Lake and the Chickasaw Nation's and Choctaw Nation of Oklahoma's claims to water and to water rights and agree to proceed as set forth herein.

NOW, THEREFORE, the parties signatory hereto ("Parties" or, when singular, "Party") agree and bind themselves as follows:

1. **DEFINITIONS**

   1.1 **1974 Storage Contract** – means the contract approved by the Secretary of the Army on April 9, 1974, between the Secretary of the Army and the Water Conservation Storage Commission of the State of Oklahoma pursuant to section 301 of the Water Supply Act of 1958, and other applicable federal law.

   1.2 **2010 Agreement** – means the agreement entered into among the OWRB and the Trust, dated June 15, 2010, relating to the assignment by the State of the 1974 Storage Contract and transfer of rights, title, interests, and obligations under that contract to the Trust, including the interests of the State in the Conservation Storage Capacity and associated repayment obligations to the United States.

   1.3 **Adequate Hydrological Model** – means a hydrologic model that satisfies the requirements of Section 5.3.1.2.2.

   1.4 **Administrative Set-Aside** – means thirty-seven thousand nine hundred eight (37,908) AF of Conservation Storage Capacity for the twenty thousand (20,000) AFY set-aside for use in southeastern Oklahoma, inclusive of the subcontract between the Oklahoma Water

1   Resources Board and the Sardis Lake Water Authority dated October 22, 1999, as specified in

2   OAC § 785:20-5-5(b)(3), as such rule exists as of the Execution Date.

3   **1.5**   **Advanced Drought Conditions** – means those conditions when: (i) the cumulative

4   amount of stored water in the City Reservoirs is between sixty-five percent (65%) and fifty

5   percent (50%) of the cumulative amount of Live Storage Capacity for the City Reservoirs and

6   (ii) the amounts of water stored in Hefner Reservoir and Draper Reservoir are between sixty-five

7   percent (65%) and fifty percent (50%) of each reservoir's respective Live Storage Capacity.

8   **1.6**   **AF** – means acre-feet.

9   **1.7**   **AFY** – means acre-feet per year.

10   **1.8**   **Allotment** – means the land within the Settlement Area held by an Allottee subject to

11   a statutory restriction on alienation or held by the United States in trust for the benefit of an

12   Allottee.

13   **1.9**   **Allottee** – means an enrolled member of the Choctaw Nation or citizen of the

14   Chickasaw Nation who, or whose estate, holds an interest in an Allotment.

15   **1.10**   **Amended Permit Application** – means the permit application of the City to the

16   OWRB, No. 2007-017, as amended pursuant to Section 6.1.

17   **1.11**   **Amended Storage Contract Transfer Agreement; Amended Storage Contract** –

18   means the 2010 Agreement between the City, the Trust, and the OWRB, as amended, as

19   provided by the Settlement Agreement and the Settlement Act, and included as Exhibit 4.

20   **1.12**   **Atoka and Sardis Conservation Projects Fund** – means the Atoka and Sardis

21   Conservation Projects Fund established, funded, and managed in accordance with Section

22   6.5.2.1.2.

1   **1.13**   **Atoka and Sardis Conservation Projects Board** – means the body formed pursuant

2   to Section 6.5.2.1.1.

3   **1.14**   **Atoka Reservoir** – means the reservoir located approximately four (4) miles

4   northeast of the City of Atoka, whose dam is in Section 30, Township 1 South, Range 12 East of

5   the Indian Meridian in Atoka County, Oklahoma.

6   **1.15**   **Baseline Lake Levels** – means those Sardis Lake surface elevations specified at

7   Section 6.1.8.1.

8   **1.16**   **Bypass Requirement** – means fifty (50) cfs of the three hundred (300) cfs flow rate,

9   specified at Section 6.1.5.2 for the City Permit, as measured within reasonable operational

10   constraints, which shall be bypassed at the Point of Diversion when the City is diverting water at

11   the Point of Diversion.

12   **1.17**   **Canton Reservoir** – means the reservoir located on the North Canadian River at river

13   mile 394.3, about two (2) miles north of the Town of Canton in Blaine County, Oklahoma.

14   **1.18**   **cfs** – means cubic-feet per second.

15   **1.19**   **Chickasaw Nation** – means the Chickasaw Nation, a federally recognized American

16   Indian Tribe organized by a Constitution its citizens ratified in 1856 and subsequently modified

17   and re-ratified in 1983 and subsequently amended.

18   **1.20**   **Choctaw Nation** – means the Choctaw Nation of Oklahoma, a federally recognized

19   American Indian Tribe organized by a Constitution its citizens ratified in 1830 and subsequently

20   modified and re-ratified in 1983.

21   **1.21**   **City** – means the City of Oklahoma City, or the City and the Trust acting jointly, as

22   applicable.

23   **1.22**   **City Diversion Rate** – means the diversion rate specified at Section 6.1.5.1.

1.23 **City Permit** – means any permit issued to the City by the OWRB pursuant to the Amended Permit Application and consistent with the Settlement Agreement and the Settlement Act.

1.24 **City Reservoirs** – means Atoka Reservoir, Canton Reservoir, Draper Reservoir, Hefner Reservoir, McGee Creek Reservoir, and Overholser Reservoir; individually, "City Reservoir."

1.25 **City Sardis Storage** – means the Conservation Storage Capacity the City will receive pursuant to the Amended Storage Contract Transfer Agreement and use and maintain in accord with Section 6.

1.26 **Conservation Storage Capacity** – means the total storage space as stated in the 1974 Storage Contract in Sardis Lake between elevations five hundred ninety-nine (599) feet above MSL and five hundred forty-two (542) feet above MSL, which is estimated to contain two hundred ninety-seven thousand two hundred (297,200) AF of water after adjustment for sediment deposits, and which may be used for municipal and industrial water supply, fish and wildlife, and recreation.

1.27 **Draper Reservoir ("Lake Stanley Draper")** – means the reservoir whose dam is located in Section 24, Township 10 North, Range 2 West of the Indian Meridian in Cleveland County, Oklahoma.

1.28 **Drought Conditions** – means Moderate Drought Conditions, Advanced Drought Conditions, or Extreme Drought Conditions.

1.29 **Enactment Date** – means December 16, 2016, which date is when the Settlement Act became a federal public law.

1.30 **Enforceability Date** – means the date on which the Secretary of the Interior publishes in the Federal Register a notice certifying that the conditions of Section 4.1 and subsection (i) of the Settlement Act have been satisfied.

1.31 **Execution Date** – means the date on which the State (including the OWRB), Chickasaw Nation, Choctaw Nation, City, and Trust shall have signed the Settlement Agreement, which shall be deemed August 22, 2016, once the Settlement Agreement has been executed by the State (including the OWRB), the Chickasaw Nation, the Choctaw Nation, the City, and the Trust.

1.32 **Expiration Date** – means September 30, 2020, unless extended as allowed by Section 4.4.

1.33 **Extreme Drought Conditions** – means those conditions when: (i) the cumulative amount of stored water in the City Reservoirs is less than fifty percent (50%) of the cumulative amount of Live Storage Capacity for the City Reservoirs and (ii) the amounts of water in Hefner Reservoir and Draper Reservoir are less than fifty percent (50%) of each reservoir's respective Live Storage Capacity.

1.34 **Hefner Reservoir** – means the reservoir whose dam is located in Section 23, Township 13 North, Range 4 West of the Indian Meridian in Oklahoma County, Oklahoma.

1.35 **Kiamichi Basin Hydrologic Model** – means the surface water hydrologic model for the Kiamichi Basin, inclusive of tributaries thereto, that the State, the Chickasaw Nation, the Choctaw Nation, and the City developed for purposes of the Settlement Agreement and as referenced in Sections 5.3.1.2.5.6, 5.3.1.2.5.7, and 6.2.1. Documentation of the Kiamichi Basin Hydrologic Model will be available at OWRB offices in Oklahoma City, as provided in Section 4.1.8. A summary technical memorandum describing the model is included as Exhibit 3.

1 **1.36 Kiamichi Basin** – means that hydrologic basin designated by the OWRB in the 2012

2 Update to the Oklahoma Comprehensive Water Plan as subbasins 5 and 6, and generally

3 depicted in Exhibit 10.

4 **1.37 Live Storage Capacity** – means the amount of storage capacity in a City Reservoir,

5 as calculated and measured pursuant to Section 6.1.8.3.

6 **1.38 McGee Creek Reservoir** – means the reservoir whose dam is located in Section 7,

7 Township 3 South, Range 14 East of the Indian Meridian in Atoka County, Oklahoma.

8 **1.39 Mean Annual Flow** – means the average annual runoff for a Settlement Area

9 Hydrologic Basin modeled at, or in close proximity to, the basin outflow point utilizing primarily

10 stream flow data from USGS gaging stations.

11 **1.40 Mean Available Flow** – means the Mean Annual Flow of a Settlement Area

12 Hydrologic Basin that remains after subtracting that portion of such flows as are necessary to

13 satisfy permitted appropriative uses, any surface water right developed by either Nation pursuant

14 to Section 7.7, domestic use set aside calculated based on six (6) AFY per one hundred sixty

15 (160) acres within the basin, prior vested rights, any surface water right recognized pursuant to

16 Section 8 (to the extent not already subtracted), pending applications, reservoir yields, and other

17 designated purposes in the Settlement Area Hydrologic Basin, including but not limited to

18 apportionment provisions of interstate stream compacts to which the State is a party as calculated

19 by any rules developed by any applicable compact commission.

20 **1.41 mgd** – means million-gallons per day.

21 **1.42 MSL** – means mean sea level.

22 **1.43 Moderate Drought Conditions** – means those conditions when: (i) the cumulative

23 amount of stored water in the City Reservoirs is between seventy-five percent (75%) and sixty-

1 five percent (65%) of the cumulative amount of Live Storage Capacity for the City Reservoirs

2 and (ii) the amounts of water stored in Hefner Reservoir and Draper Reservoir are between

3 seventy-five percent (75%) and sixty-five percent (65%) of each reservoir's respective Live

4 Storage Capacity.

5 **1.44 Nations** – means collectively the Choctaw Nation and the Chickasaw Nation.

6 **1.45 Non-Trust Land** – means land within the State held by either the Chickasaw Nation

7 or Choctaw Nation in fee and in which the United States holds no interest as trustee.

8 **1.46 Oklahoma City Water Utilities Trust ("Trust")** – means the Oklahoma City Water

9 Utilities Trust, formerly known as the Oklahoma City Municipal Improvement Authority, a

10 public trust established pursuant to state law with the City as the beneficiary. A reference in the

11 Settlement Agreement or the Settlement Act to "Oklahoma City Water Utilities Trust" or "Trust"

12 refers to the Oklahoma City Water Utilities Trust, acting severally.

13 **1.47 Out-of-State Use of Settlement Area Waters** – means any use of water or the

14 transfer of any right to use water, including by forbearance agreement, diverted or taken from a

15 location within the Settlement Area for use at a location outside the exterior boundaries of the

16 State.

17 **1.48 Overholser Reservoir** – means the reservoir whose dam is located in Section 30,

18 Township 12 North, Range 4 West of the Indian Meridian in Oklahoma County, Oklahoma.

19 **1.49 OWRB** – means the Oklahoma Water Resources Board, and its successor entities, if

20 any.

21 **1.50 Parallel City Pipeline** – means the second pipeline the City contemplates

22 constructing between Lake Atoka in Atoka County, Oklahoma, and Lake Stanley Draper in

23 Cleveland County, Oklahoma, approximately ninety-six (96) miles in length whose route is

identified as generally following an existing pipeline constructed for the same purposes and placed in operation in 1962, and which includes a water diversion structure, pumping station, and pipeline beginning at a point on the Kiamichi River near Moyer's Crossing and following road rights of way, purchased, or existing easements to a terminus point at Lake Atoka in Atoka County, Oklahoma.

1.51 **Parties** – means the State (including the OWRB), Chickasaw Nation, Choctaw Nation, City, and Trust as of the Execution Date; and the United States, State (including the OWRB), Chickasaw Nation, Choctaw Nation, City, and Trust as of the Post-Enactment Execution Date.

1.52 **Point of Diversion** – means the point of diversion for the City Permit, as defined at Section 6.1.3.

1.53 **Post-Enactment Execution Date** – means the date after the Enactment Date on which the Chickasaw Nation and Choctaw Nation, the Secretary of the Interior on behalf of the United States, the State, the City, and the Trust have all executed the Settlement Agreement.

1.54 **Sardis Lake** – means the reservoir, formerly known as Clayton Lake, whose dam is located in Section 19, Township 2 North, Range 19 East of the Indian Meridian, Pushmataha County, Oklahoma, the construction, operation, and maintenance of which was authorized by section 203 of the Flood Control Act of 1962 (Public Law 87-874; 76 Stat. 1187).

1.55 **Sardis Lake Release Restrictions** – means those limitations on the City's ability to release water from City Sardis Storage specified at Section 6.1.8.

1.56 **Settlement Act** – means Pub. Law 114-322, § 3608, 130 Stat. 1628, 1796-1814, included as Exhibit 2.

1.57 **Settlement Agreement** – means the settlement agreement as approved by the Nations, the State, the City, and the Trust effective August 22, 2016, as revised to conform with the Settlement Act, as applicable.

1.58 **Settlement Area** – means –

1.58.1 the area lying between -

1.58.1.1 the South Canadian River and Arkansas River to the north;

1.58.1.2 the Oklahoma-Texas state line to the south;

1.58.1.3 the Oklahoma-Arkansas state line to the east; and

1.58.1.4 the 98th Meridian to the west; and

1.58.2 the area depicted in Exhibit 1 (dated August 2016) and generally including the following counties, or portions of, in the State:

1.58.2.1 Atoka.

1.58.2.2 Bryan.

1.58.2.3 Carter.

1.58.2.4 Choctaw.

1.58.2.5 Coal.

1.58.2.6 Garvin.

1.58.2.7 Grady.

1.58.2.8 McClain.

1.58.2.9 Murray.

1.58.2.10 Haskell.

1.58.2.11 Hughes.

1.58.2.12 Jefferson.

1 **1.58.2.13** Johnston.

2 **1.58.2.14** Latimer.

3 **1.58.2.15** LeFlore.

4 **1.58.2.16** Love.

5 **1.58.2.17** Marshall.

6 **1.58.2.18** McCurtain.

7 **1.58.2.19** Pittsburgh.

8 **1.58.2.20** Pontotoc.

9 **1.58.2.21** Pushmataha.

10 **1.58.2.22** Stephens.

11 **1.59** **Settlement Area Hydrologic Basin(s)** – basins depicted in Exhibit 10 (dated August

12 2016), including any of the following basins as denominated in the 2012 Update of the

13 Oklahoma Comprehensive Water Plan:

14 **1.59.1** Beaver Creek (24, 25, and 26).

15 **1.59.2** Blue (11 and 12).

16 **1.59.3** Clear Boggy (9).

17 **1.59.4** Kiamichi (5 and 6).

18 **1.59.5** Little (2).

19 **1.59.6** Lower Arkansas (46 and 47).

20 **1.59.7** Lower Canadian (48, 56, and 57).

21 **1.59.8** Lower Washita (14).

22 **1.59.9** Middle Canadian (58).

23 **1.59.10** Mountain Fork (4).

1 **1.59.11** Middle Washita (15 and 16).

2 **1.59.12** Mud Creek (23).

3 **1.59.13** Muddy Boggy (7 and 8).

4 **1.59.14** Poteau (44 and 45).

5 **1.59.15** Red River Mainstem (1, 10, 13, and 21).

6 **1.59.16** Upper Little (3).

7 **1.59.17** Walnut Bayou (22).

8 **1.60** **Settlement Area Waters** – Means

9 **1.60.1** Groundwater located within the Settlement Area; and

10 **1.60.2** Surface waters located within both—

11 **1.60.2.1** a Settlement Area Hydrologic Basin, and

12 **1.60.2.2** the Settlement Area.

13 **1.61** **Settlement Commission** – means the body established in accord with Section 5.3.3.2

14 and subsection (g) of the Settlement Act.

15 **1.62** **State** – means the State of Oklahoma, inclusive of its subsidiary agencies (including

16 the OWRB).

17 **1.63** **Technical Committee** – means that committee formed pursuant to Section 5.3.1.2.1.

18 **1.64** **Title 82** – means Title 82 of the Oklahoma Statutes or any recodification thereof.

19 **1.65** **Trust Land** – means allotted or unallotted land held by the United States in trust for

20 the benefit of either the Chickasaw Nation or the Choctaw Nation.

21 **1.66** **United States** – means the United States of America acting in its capacity as trustee

22 for the Nations, their respective members, citizens, and Allottees, or as specifically stated or

APPENDIX

limited in any given reference herein, in which case it means the United States of America acting in the capacity as set forth in said reference.

2. WAIVERS AND RELEASES OF CLAIMS AND OBJECTIONS

2.1 **Waiver and Release of Claims by the Nations and the United States as Trustee for the Nations** – Subject to the retention of rights and claims provided in Section 2.5 and paragraph (h)(3) of the Settlement Act, and except to the extent that rights are recognized in the Settlement Agreement or Settlement Act, the Nations, each in its own right and on behalf of itself and its respective citizens and members (but not individuals in their capacities as Allottees), and the United States, acting as trustee for the Nations (but not individuals in their capacities as Allottees), waive and release:

2.1.1 all of the following claims asserted or which could have been asserted in any proceeding filed or that could have been filed during the period ending on the Enforceability Date, including *Chickasaw Nation, Choctaw Nation v. Fallin et al.,* CIV 11-927 (W.D. Ok.), *OWRB v. United States, et al.* CIV 12-275 (W.D. Ok.), or any general stream adjudication, relating to:

2.1.1.1 claims to the ownership of water in the State;

2.1.1.2 claims to water rights and rights to use water diverted or taken from a location within the State;

2.1.1.3 claims to authority over the allocation and management of water and administration of water rights, including authority over third-party ownership of or rights to use water diverted or taken from a location within the State and ownership or use of water on Allotments by Allottees or any other person using water on an Allotment with the permission of an Allottee;

2.1.1.4 claims that the State lacks authority over the allocation and management of water and administration of water rights, including authority over the ownership of or rights to use water diverted or taken from a location within the State;

2.1.1.5 any other claim relating to the ownership of water, regulation of water, or authorized diversion, storage, or use of water diverted or taken from a location within the State, which claim is based on the Chickasaw Nation's or the Choctaw Nation's unique sovereign status and rights as defined by federal law and alleged to arise from treaties to which they are signatories, including but not limited to the Treaty of Dancing Rabbit Creek, Act of Sept. 30, 1830, 7 Stat. 333, Treaty of Doaksville, Act of Jan. 17, 1837, 11 Stat. 573, and the related March 23, 1842, patent to the Choctaw Nation; and

2.1.1.6 claims or defenses asserted or which could have been asserted in *Chickasaw Nation, Choctaw Nation v. Fallin et al.,* CIV 11-927 (W.D. Ok.), *OWRB v. United States, et al.* CIV 12-275 (W.D. Ok.), or any general stream adjudication;

2.1.2 all claims for damages, losses or injuries to water rights or water, or claims of interference with, diversion, storage, taking, or use of water (including claims for injury to land resulting from the damages, losses, injuries, interference with, diversion, storage, taking, or use of water) attributable to any action by the State, the OWRB, or any water user authorized pursuant to state law to take or use water in the State, including the City, that accrued during the period ending on the Enforceability Date;

2.1.3 all claims and objections relating to the Amended Permit Application and the City Permit, including:

2.1.3.1 all claims regarding regulatory control over or OWRB jurisdiction relating to the permit application and permit; and

2.1.3.2   all claims for damages, losses or injuries to water rights or rights to use water, or claims of interference with, diversion, storage, taking, or use of water (including claims for injury to land resulting from the damages, losses, injuries, interference with, diversion, storage, taking, or use of water) attributable to the issuance and lawful exercise of the City Permit;

2.1.4   all claims to regulatory control over the Permit Numbers P80-48 and 54-613 of the City for water rights from the Muddy Boggy River for Atoka Reservoir and P73-282D for water rights from the Muddy Boggy River, including McGee Creek, for the McGee Creek Reservoir;

2.1.5   all claims that the State lacks regulatory authority over or OWRB jurisdiction relating to Permit Numbers P80-48 and 54-613 for water rights from the Muddy Boggy River for Atoka Reservoir and P73-282D for water rights from the Muddy Boggy River, including McGee Creek, for the McGee Creek Reservoir;

2.1.6   all claims to damages, losses or injuries to water rights or water, or claims of interference with, diversion, storage, taking, or use of water (including claims for injury to land resulting from such damages, losses, injuries, interference with, diversion, storage, taking, or use of water) attributable to the lawful exercise of Permit Numbers P80-48 and 54-613 for water rights from the Muddy Boggy River for Atoka Reservoir and P73-282D for water rights from the Muddy Boggy River, including McGee Creek, for the McGee Creek Reservoir, that accrued during the period ending on the Enforceability Date;

2.1.7   all claims and objections relating to the approval by the Secretary of the Army of the assignment of the 1974 Storage Contract pursuant to the Amended Storage Contract; and

2.1.8   all claims for damages, losses, or injuries to water rights or water, or claims of interference with, diversion, storage, taking, or use of water (including claims for injury to land resulting from such damages, losses, injuries, interference with, diversion, storage, taking, or use of water) attributable to the lawful exercise of rights pursuant to the Amended Storage Contract.

2.2   **Waivers and Releases of Claims by the Nations Against the United States** – Subject to the retention of rights and claims provided in Section 2.5 and paragraph (h)(3) of the Settlement Act, and except to the extent that rights are recognized in the Settlement Agreement or the Settlement Act, the Nations waive and release all claims against the United States (including any agency or employee of the United States) relating to:

2.2.1   all of the following claims asserted or which could have been asserted in any proceeding filed or that could have been filed by the United States as a trustee during the period ending on the Enforceability Date, including *Chickasaw Nation, Choctaw Nation v. Fallin et al.,* CIV 11-927 (W.D. Ok.) or *OWRB v. United States, et al.* CIV 12-275 (W.D. Ok.), or any general stream adjudication relating to:

2.2.1.1   claims to the ownership of water in the State;

2.2.1.2   claims to water rights and rights to use water diverted or taken from a location within the State;

2.2.1.3   claims to authority over the allocation and management of water and administration of water rights, including authority over third-party ownership of or rights to use water diverted or taken from a location within the State and ownership or use of water on Allotments by Allottees or any other person using water on an Allotment with the permission of an Allottee;

2.2.1.4   claims that the State lacks authority over the allocation and management of water and administration of water rights, including authority over the ownership of or rights to use water diverted or taken from a location within the State;

2.2.1.5   any other claim relating to the ownership of water, regulation of water, or authorized diversion, storage, or use of water diverted or taken from a location within the State, which claim is based on the Chickasaw Nation's or the Choctaw Nation's unique sovereign status and rights as defined by federal law and alleged to arise from treaties to which they are signatories, including but not limited to the Treaty of Dancing Rabbit Creek, Act of Sept. 30, 1830, 7 Stat. 333, Treaty of Doaksville, Act of Jan. 17, 1837, 11 Stat. 573, and the related March 23, 1842, patent to the Choctaw Nation; and

2.2.1.6   claims or defenses asserted or which could have been asserted in *Chickasaw Nation, Choctaw Nation v. Fallin et al.,* CIV 11-927 (W.D. Ok.), *OWRB v. United States, et al.* CIV 12-275 (W.D. Ok.), or any general stream adjudication;

2.2.2   all claims for damages, losses or injuries to water rights or water, or claims of interference with, diversion, storage, taking, or use of water (including claims for injury to land resulting from the damages, losses, injuries, interference with, diversion, storage, taking, or use of water) attributable to any action by the State, the OWRB, or any water user authorized pursuant to state law to take or use water in the State, including but not limited to the City, that accrued during the period ending on the Enforceability Date;

2.2.3   all claims and objections relating to the Amended Permit Application, and the City Permit, including:

2.2.3.1   all claims regarding regulatory control over or OWRB jurisdiction relating to the permit application and permit; and

2.2.3.2   all claims for damages, losses or injuries to water rights or rights to use water, or claims of interference with, diversion, storage, taking, or use of water (including claims for injury to land resulting from the damages, losses, injuries, interference with, diversion, storage, taking, or use of water) attributable to the issuance and lawful exercise of the City Permit;

2.2.4   all claims to regulatory control over the Permit Numbers P80-48 and 54-613 for water rights from the Muddy Boggy River for Atoka Reservoir and P73-282D for water rights from the Muddy Boggy River, including McGee Creek, for the McGee Creek Reservoir;

2.2.5   all claims that the State lacks regulatory authority over or OWRB jurisdiction relating to Permit Numbers P80-48 and 54-613 for water rights from the Muddy Boggy River for Atoka Reservoir and P73-282D for water rights from the Muddy Boggy River, including McGee Creek, for the McGee Creek Reservoir;

2.2.6   all claims to damages, losses or injuries to water rights or water, or claims of interference with, diversion, storage, taking, or use of water (including claims for injury to land resulting from the damages, losses, injuries, interference with, diversion, storage, taking, or use of water) attributable to the lawful exercise of Permit Numbers P80-48 and 54-613 for water rights from the Muddy Boggy River for Atoka Reservoir and P73-282D for water rights from the Muddy Boggy River, including McGee Creek, for the McGee Creek Reservoir, that accrued during the period ending on the Enforceability Date;

2.2.7   all claims and objections relating to the approval by the Secretary of the Army of the assignment of the 1974 Storage Contract pursuant to the Amended Storage Contract;

2.2.8 all claims relating to litigation by the United States, prior to the Enforceability Date, of the water rights of the Nations in the State of Oklahoma; and

2.2.9 all claims relating to the negotiation, execution, or adoption of the Settlement Agreement (including exhibits) or the Settlement Act.

2.3 Tolling of Claims - Each applicable period of limitation and time-based equitable defense relating to a claim described in Section 2.1 and 2.2 and subsection (h) of the Settlement Act shall be tolled during the period beginning on the Enactment Date and ending on the earlier of the Enforceability Date or the Expiration Date under paragraph (i)(2) of the Settlement Act.

2.4 Effectiveness of Waivers and Releases - The waivers and releases under Sections 2.1 and 2.2 and subsection (h) of the Settlement Act take effect on the Enforceability Date.

2.5 Retention and Reservation of Claims by the Nations and the United States– Notwithstanding the waiver and releases of claims in Section 2.1 and 2.2 and paragraphs (h)(1) and (h)(2) of the Settlement Act, the Nations and the United States, acting as trustee, retain:

2.5.1 all claims for enforcement of the Settlement Agreement and the Settlement Act;

2.5.2 all rights to use and protect any water right of the Nations recognized by or established pursuant to the Settlement Agreement, including the right to assert claims for injuries relating to the rights and the right to participate in any general stream adjudication, including any *inter se* proceeding;

2.5.3 all claims under:

2.5.3.1 the Comprehensive Environmental Response, Compensation, and Liability Act of 1980 (42 U.S.C. § 9601 *et seq.*), including for damages to natural resources;

2.5.3.2 the Safe Drinking Water Act (42 U.S.C. § 300f *et seq.*);

2.5.3.3 the Federal Water Pollution Control Act (33 U.S.C. § 1251 *et seq.*); and

2.5.3.4 any regulations implementing the Acts described in Sections 2.5.3.1 through 2.5.3.3 and subclauses (h)(3)(A)(iii)(I) through (III) of the Settlement Act;

2.5.4 all claims relating to damage, loss, or injury resulting from an unauthorized diversion, use, or storage of water, including damages, losses, or injuries to land or nonwater natural resources associated with any hunting, fishing, gathering, or cultural right; and

2.5.5 all rights, remedies, privileges, immunities, and powers not specifically waived and released pursuant to the Settlement Act or the Settlement Agreement.

2.6 Nations' Non-Objection to Amended Permit Application – In return for the bargained-for exchange of benefits in the Settlement Agreement and upon the Enactment Date, the Nations:

2.6.1 Shall not object to the OWRB's proceeding, in accord with state law and subject to the Settlement Agreement, with public notice and hearing on the City's Amended Permit Application;

2.6.2 Shall not seek or support the imposition by the OWRB of any terms and conditions on the storage, release from storage, diversion, and use of water under the City Permit other than terms and conditions consistent with the provisions of Section 6.1; and

2.6.3 Shall not object to the OWRB's issuance of the City Permit, in accord with state law and subject to the Settlement Agreement, that contains terms and conditions consistent with the provisions of Section 6.1.

2.7 Nations' Non-Objection in Other Proceedings – In return for the bargained-for exchange of benefits in the Settlement Agreement and upon the Enforceability Date, the Nations:

2.7.1   Shall not object to local, state, or federal agencies proceeding, in accord with applicable law and subject to the Settlement Agreement, with any public notice, hearing or procedure for any permits or approvals for the storage, release from storage, diversion, and use of water, including the Parallel Pipeline, that are necessary for the City's beneficial use and delivery of water to its customers consistent with the provisions of Section 6;

2.7.2   Shall not seek or support the imposition by local, state, or federal agencies of any terms and conditions on any permits or approvals for the storage, release from storage, diversion, and use of water, including the Parallel Pipeline, that are necessary for the City's beneficial use and delivery of water consistent with the provisions of Section 6 other than terms and conditions consistent with the Settlement Agreement; and

2.7.3   Shall not object to issuance of any local, state, or federal agency permits or approvals, in accord with applicable law and subject to the Settlement Agreement, for the storage, release from storage, diversion, and use of water, including the Parallel Pipeline, that are necessary for the City's beneficial use and delivery of water consistent with the provisions of Section 6.

3.   JURISDICTION, WAIVERS OF SOVEREIGN IMMUNITY FOR INTERPRETATION AND ENFORCEMENT

3.1   Jurisdiction –

3.1.1   In General. –

3.1.1.1   Exclusive Jurisdiction - The United States District Court for the Western District of Oklahoma shall have exclusive jurisdiction for all purposes and for all causes of action relating to the interpretation and enforcement of the Settlement Agreement, the Amended Storage Contract, or interpretation or enforcement of the Settlement Act, including all actions filed by an Allottee pursuant to subparagraph (e)(6)(B) of the Settlement Act.

3.1.1.2   Right to Bring Action – The Choctaw Nation, the Chickasaw Nation, the State, the City, the Trust, and the United States shall each have the right to bring an action pursuant to the Settlement Act.

3.1.1.3   No Action in Other Courts; No Exhaustion – No action may be brought in any other Federal, Tribal, or State court or administrative forum for any purpose relating to the Settlement Agreement, Amended Storage Contract, or the Settlement Act. Each Party further waives and shall not invoke inconvenient forum or any exhaustion doctrine, including the doctrines of tribal exhaustion, or exhaustion of administrative remedies, as a prerequisite for any Party's bringing an action under this Section 3.

3.1.1.4   No Monetary Judgment – Nothing in this Section 3 or the Settlement Act authorizes any money judgment or otherwise allows the payment of funds by the United States, the Nations, the State (including the OWRB), the City, or the Trust.

3.1.1.5   Limitation - Neither the Settlement Commission established by the Settlement Act in accord with Section 5.3.3.2 nor the Atoka and Sardis Conservation Projects Board established pursuant to Section 6.5.2.1.1 may sue or be sued, and neither shall be considered a proper or necessary party for any purpose in any action, including actions to interpret or enforce the terms of the Settlement Agreement, the Amended Storage Contract, or the Settlement Act.

3.1.2   Notice and Conference – Any entity seeking to interpret or enforce the Settlement Agreement shall comply with the following:

3.1.2.1 Any party asserting noncompliance or seeking interpretation of the Settlement Agreement or the Settlement Act shall first serve written notice on the Party alleged to be in breach of the Settlement Agreement or violation of the Settlement Act.

3.1.2.2 The notice under 3.1.2.1 and clause (j)(1)(B)(i) of the Settlement Act shall identify the specific provision of the Settlement Agreement or the Settlement Act alleged to have been violated or in dispute and shall specify in detail the contention of the Party asserting the claim and any factual basis for the claim.

3.1.2.3 Representatives of the Party alleging a breach or violation and the Party alleged to be in breach or violation shall meet not later than thirty (30) days after receipt of notice under 3.1.2.1 and clause (j)(1)(B)(i) of the Settlement Act in an effort to resolve the dispute.

3.1.2.4 If the matter is not resolved to the satisfaction of the Party alleging breach not later than ninety (90) days after the original notice under 3.1.2.1 and clause (j)(1)(B)(i) of the Settlement Act, the Party may take any appropriate enforcement action consistent with the Settlement Agreement and subsection (j) of the Settlement Act.

3.2   Limited Waivers of Sovereign Immunity – Effective upon and after the Enforceability Date, in the case of any action to interpret or enforce the Settlement Agreement or Settlement Act:

3.2.1   United States Immunity. – Pursuant to subparagraph (j)(2)(B) of the Settlement Act, any claim by the United States to sovereign immunity from suit is irrevocably waived for any action brought by the State, the Chickasaw Nation, the Choctaw Nation, the City, or the Trust in the United States District Court for the Western District of Oklahoma relating to interpretation or enforcement of the Settlement Agreement or the Settlement Act,

including of the appellate jurisdiction of the United States Court of Appeals for the Tenth Circuit and the Supreme Court of the United States.

3.2.2   Chickasaw Nation Immunity. – For the exclusive benefit of the State (including the OWRB), the City, the Trust, the Choctaw Nation, and the United States, and in addition to the waiver in § 3680(j)(2)(C) of the Settlement Act, the Chickasaw Nation expressly and irrevocably consents to suit and waives sovereign immunity from suit solely for any action brought in the United States District Court for the Western District of Oklahoma relating to interpretation or enforcement of the Settlement Agreement or the Settlement Act, if the action is brought by the State, the OWRB, the City, the Trust, the Choctaw Nation, or the United States, including the appellate jurisdiction of the United States Court of Appeals for the Tenth Circuit and the Supreme Court of the United States.

3.2.3   Choctaw Nation Immunity. – For the exclusive benefit of the State (including the OWRB), the City, the Trust, the Chickasaw Nation, and the United States, the Choctaw Nation expressly and irrevocably consents to suit and waives sovereign immunity from suit solely for any action brought in the United States District Court for the Western District of Oklahoma relating to interpretation or enforcement of the Settlement Agreement or the Settlement Act, if the action is brought by the State, the OWRB, the City, the Trust, the Chickasaw Nation, or the United States, including the appellate jurisdiction of the United States Court of Appeals for the Tenth Circuit and the Supreme Court of the United States.

3.2.4   State Immunity. – For the exclusive benefit of the City, the Trust, the Choctaw Nation, the Chickasaw Nation, and the United States, the State (including the OWRB) expressly and irrevocably consents to suit, waives its sovereign immunity from suit, and agrees not to raise the Eleventh Amendment to the United States Constitution or comparable defense to the validity of such consent or waiver solely for any action of any kind brought in the United States District Court for the Western District of Oklahoma relating to interpretation or enforcement of the Settlement Agreement or Settlement Act, which action is brought by the Chickasaw Nation, the Choctaw Nation, the City, the Trust, or the United States, including the appellate jurisdiction of the United States Court of Appeals for the Tenth Circuit and the Supreme Court of the United States.

3.2.5 OWRB Immunity. – Exclusively for the benefit of an Allottee who files an action pursuant to Sections 8.4 or 8.5 in the United States District Court for the Western District of Oklahoma, the OWRB expressly and irrevocably consents to suit, waives its sovereign immunity from suit, and agrees not to raise the Eleventh Amendment to the United States Constitution or comparable defense to the validity of such consent or waiver, including the appellate jurisdiction of the United States Court of Appeals for the Tenth Circuit and the Supreme Court of the United States.

4. ENFORCEABILITY DATE

4.1 In General – The Settlement Agreement shall take effect and be enforceable on the date on which the Secretary of the Interior publishes in the Federal Register a certification that:

4.1.1 Conformance of Settlement Agreement – to the extent the Settlement Agreement conflicts with the Settlement Act, the Settlement Agreement has been amended to conform with the Settlement Act;

4.1.2 Execution of Settlement Agreement – the Settlement Agreement, as amended, has been executed by the Secretary of the Interior, the Nations, the Governor and the Attorney General of the State, the OWRB, the City, and the Trust;

4.1.3 Execution of Waivers and Releases of Claims – the United States and the Chickasaw Nation have executed the waivers of claims stated in Exhibit 5, and the United States and the Choctaw Nation have executed the waivers of claims stated in Exhibit 6;

4.1.4 Conformance of Amended Storage Contract – to the extent the Amended Storage Contract conflicts with the Settlement Act, the Amended Storage Contract has been amended to conform with the Settlement Act;

4.1.5 Execution and Approval of Amended Storage Contract – the Amended Storage Contract, as amended to conform with the Settlement Act, has been—

4.1.5.1 executed by the State, the City, and the Trust; and

4.1.5.2 approved by the Secretary of the Army;

4.1.6 Modification of September 11, 2009, Court Order – an order has been entered in *United States v. Oklahoma Water Resources Board*, CIV 98-C-521-E (N.D. Ok.), with any modifications to the order dated September 11, 2009, as necessary to conform the order to the Amended Storage Contract, the Settlement Agreement, and the Settlement Act, and as provided in the Settlement Agreement and the Settlement Act; the motion and proposed form of order for these purposes is included as Exhibit 7;

4.1.7 City Permit – the OWRB has issued the City Permit;

4.1.8 Model Documentation – the final documentation of the Kiamichi Basin Hydrologic Model is on file at the Oklahoma City offices of the OWRB;

4.1.9 Atoka and Sardis Conservation Projects Fund – the Atoka and Sardis Conservation Projects Fund has been funded as provided in Section 6.5.2.1.2; and

4.1.10 Orders of Dismissal –orders of dismissal have been entered in *Chickasaw Nation, Choctaw Nation v. Fallin, et al.*, CIV. 11-927 (W.D. Ok.), and *OWRB v. United*

1 *States, et al.* CIV 12-275 (W.D. Ok.), as provided in the Settlement Agreement; the proposed

2 forms of orders for these purposes are included as Exhibit 8 and Exhibit 9, respectively.

3 **4.2   Expiration Date**—If the Secretary of the Interior fails to publish a statement of

4 findings under 4.1 and paragraph (i)(1) of the Settlement Act by not later than September 30,

5 2020, or such alternative later date as is agreed to by the Secretary of the Interior, the Nations,

6 the State, the City, and the Trust under 4.4 and paragraph (i)(4) of the Settlement Act, the

7 following shall apply:

8   **4.2.1** The Settlement Act, except for subsection (i) of the Settlement Act and any

9 provisions of the Settlement Act that are necessary to carry out subsection (i) of the

10 Settlement Act (but only for purposes of carrying out subsection (i) of the Settlement Act), are

11 not effective beginning on September 30, 2020, or the alternative date.

12   **4.2.2** The waivers and releases of claims, and the limited waivers of sovereign

13 immunity, shall not become effective.

14   **4.2.3** The Settlement Agreement shall be null and void, except for this Section 4.2

15 and any provisions of the Settlement Agreement that are necessary to carry out this Section

16 4.2 and paragraph (i)(2) of the Settlement Act.

17   **4.2.4** Except with respect to this Section 4.2 and paragraph (i)(2) of the Settlement

18 Act, the State, the Nations, the City, the Trust, and the United States shall not be bound by any

19 obligations or benefit from any rights recognized under the Settlement Agreement.

20   **4.2.5** If the City Permit has been issued, the permit shall be null and void, except that

21 the City may resubmit to the OWRB, and the OWRB shall be considered to have accepted,

22 OWRB Permit Application No. 2007-017 without having waived the original application

23 priority date and appropriative quantities.

1   **4.2.6** If the Amended Storage Contract has been executed or approved, the Contract

2 shall be null and void, and the 2010 Agreement shall be considered to be in force and effect as

3 between the State and the Trust.

4   **4.2.7** If the Atoka and Sardis Conservation Projects Fund has been established and

5 funded, the funds shall be returned to the respective funding Parties with any accrued interest.

6 **4.3   No Prejudice**--The occurrence of the Expiration Date under 4.2 and paragraph

7 (i)(2) of the Settlement Act shall not in any way prejudice:

8   **4.3.1** any argument or suit that the Nations may bring to contest—

9   **4.3.1.1**   the pursuit by the City of OWRB Permit Application No. 2007-017, or a

10 modified version; or

11   **4.3.1.2**   the 2010 Agreement;

12   **4.3.2** any argument, defense, or suit the State may bring or assert with regard to the

13 claims of the Nations to water or over water in the Settlement Area; or

14   **4.3.3** any argument, defense or suit the City may bring or assert—

15   **4.3.3.1**   with regard to the claims of the Nations to water or over water in the

16 Settlement Area relating to OWRB Permit Application No. 2007-017, or a modified version; or

17   **4.3.3.2**   to contest the 2010 Agreement.

18 **4.4   Extension**--The Expiration Date under 4.2 and paragraph (i)(2) of the Settlement Act

19 may be extended in writing if the Nations, the State, the OWRB, the United States, and the City

20 agree that an extension is warranted.

21 **4.5   Notice of Satisfaction of Conditions Precedent** – The State, City, and Nations shall

22 jointly notify the Secretary of the Interior when the conditions specified in Sections 4.1.1 through

1 4.1.10 have been satisfied, which notification shall include documentation sufficient for purposes

2 of certification pursuant to Section 4.1.

3 **5.   GENERAL PROVISIONS**

4   **5.1   State Jurisdiction** – The State has and shall exercise, through the OWRB,

5 jurisdiction over the permitting and administration of water and rights to water within the

6 Settlement Area.

7   **5.1.1**   By entering the Settlement Agreement, the United States does not concede that

8 the State and the OWRB had jurisdiction over water or rights on Trust Lands or Allotments

9 prior to the Enactment Date.

10   **5.1.2**   Beginning on the Enforceability Date, Settlement Area Waters shall be

11 permitted, allocated, and administered by the OWRB in accordance with this Settlement

12 Agreement and the Settlement Act.

13   **5.2   Future OWRB Rulemakings** – If the OWRB proposes a new rule or an amendment

14 to a rule in effect as of the Execution Date that affects the permitting or administration of

15 Settlement Area Waters, the Nations or either Nation may review and comment on the proposed

16 rule or amendment to the OWRB, which comment the Nations or either Nation shall submit in

17 the form and through the process provided by state law. Prior to the OWRB's finalization of the

18 proposed rule or amendment, the OWRB shall provide the commenting Nation or Nations

19 opportunity to meet and confer with OWRB staff regarding any comments submitted by a Nation

20 or the Nations. Nothing herein expands or limits the rights any Party has for the interpretation or

21 enforcement of the Settlement Agreement pursuant to Section 3 and the Settlement Act.

1   **5.3   Permitting, Allocation, and Administration**

2   **5.3.1   In General** – The OWRB shall process all applications submitted to it for

3 permits to appropriate surface water from a Settlement Area Hydrologic Basin filed on or after

4 the Enforceability Date pursuant to state law, consistent with the Settlement Agreement and

5 the Settlement Act. The OWRB shall process the Amended Permit Application pursuant to

6 Section 6.2.

7   **5.3.1.1   Basin Classification and Conferral Threshold**

8   **5.3.1.1.1   Water Basin Classifications**

9   **5.3.1.1.1.1   Class A Basins** – For purposes of the Settlement Agreement,

10 Class A Basins are the following Settlement Area Hydrologic Basins, as depicted in Exhibit 10:

11 Basin 23 (commonly referred to as the Mud Creek), Basins 7 and 8 (commonly referred to as the

12 Muddy Boggy), Basins 44 and 45 (commonly referred to as the Poteau), Basins 1, 10, 13, and 21

13 (commonly referred as the Red River Mainstem), Basin 2 (commonly referred to as the Little),

14 Basin 15 (commonly referred to as the Middle Washita), Basin 22 (commonly referred to as the

15 Walnut Bayou), and Basin 57 (commonly referred to as the Lower Canadian).

16   **5.3.1.1.1.2   Class B Basins** – For purposes of the Settlement Agreement,

17 Class B Basins are those Settlement Area Hydrologic Basins that contain surface streams of

18 significant cultural, ecological or recreational values within the Settlement Area, which are the

19 following Settlement Area Hydrologic Basins, as depicted in Exhibit 10: Basins 11 and 12

20 (commonly referred to as the Blue), Basin 9 (commonly referred to as the Clear Boggy), Basins

21 5 and 6 (commonly referred to as the Kiamichi), Basin 14 (commonly referred to as the Lower

22 Washita), Basin 4 (commonly referred to as the Mountain Fork), and Basin 3 (commonly

23 referred to as the Upper Little).

5.3.1.1.1.3   **Class C Basins** – Class C Basins are those Settlement Area Hydrologic Basins that lie partially within the Settlement Area, which are the following Settlement Area Hydrologic Basins, as depicted in Exhibit 10: Basins 24, 25, and 26 (commonly referred to as the Beaver Creek), Basins 46 and 47 (commonly referred to as the Lower Arkansas), Basins 48 and 56 (commonly referred to as the Lower Canadian), Basin 58 (commonly referred to as the Middle Canadian), and Basin 16 (commonly referred to as the Middle Washita).

5.3.1.1.2   **Conferral Threshold** – The process specified at Section 5.3.1.2 shall be a precondition to OWRB consideration of those applications that satisfy the following conditions:

5.3.1.1.2.1   **Class A Basin** – An application to appropriate water for use at a location outside of the Settlement Area in an amount that is five percent (5%) or more of the Mean Available Flow in a Class A Basin. Applications filed for an appropriation from the same point of diversion for use outside of the Settlement Area filed within any twelve (12) month period which collectively equal or exceed five percent (5%) of the Mean Available Flow shall be subject to the conferral threshold even if individually each application would not exceed five percent (5%) of the Mean Available Flow.

5.3.1.1.2.2   **Class B Basin** – An application to appropriate water for use at a location outside of the source basin in an amount that is more than either twenty thousand (20,000) AFY or three percent (3%) of the Mean Available Flow, whichever is less, in a Class B Basin. Applications filed for an appropriation from the same point of diversion for use outside of the source basin filed within any twenty-four (24) month period which collectively equal or exceed twenty thousand (20,000) AFY or three percent (3%) of the Mean Available Flow,

whichever is less, shall be subject to the conferral threshold even if individually each application would not exceed twenty thousand (20,000) AFY or three percent (3%) of the Mean Available Flow, whichever is less.

5.3.1.1.2.3   **Class C Basin** – An application to appropriate water for use at a location outside of the source basin and the Settlement Area in an amount that is ten percent (10%) or more of the Mean Available Flow in a Class C Basin. Applications filed for an appropriation from the same point of diversion for use outside of the Settlement Area filed within any twelve (12) month period which collectively equal or exceed ten percent (10%) of the Mean Available Flow shall be subject to the conferral threshold even if individually each application would not exceed ten percent (10%) of the Mean Available Flow.

5.3.1.1.2.4   **No Avoidance** – In processing applications to appropriate water from a Settlement Area Hydrologic Basin, the OWRB shall evaluate and determine whether any applicant has or applicants have structured and submitted an application or applications in a manner to attempt to avoid a conferral threshold specified in Sections 5.3.1.1.2.1, 5.3.1.1.2.2, or 5.3.1.1.2.3. If the OWRB determines an application has or applications have been structured and submitted to avoid a conferral threshold, the OWRB shall process the application or applications in such a manner as having satisfied the relevant conferral threshold, even if individually each application would not have done so.

5.3.1.2   **Conferral and Modeling**

5.3.1.2.1   **Technical Committee** – No later than ninety (90) days from the Enactment Date, the State and the Nations shall establish the Technical Committee. The Technical Committee shall be comprised of two (2) members, one (1) member for the Nations and one (1) member for the State. The City may also appoint one (1) member to the Technical

1 Committee with respect to any work performed pursuant to Section 5.3.1.2 relating to the

2 Kiamichi Basin.

3   **5.3.1.2.1.1**   **Appointment of Members** – Technical Committee members

4 shall be appointed and serve at the discretion of the appointing entities and must have expertise

5 relevant to the purposes of the Technical Committee. Each appointing entity shall provide notice

6 to the other entities as to who shall serve as its member; for purposes of this Section 5.3.1.2.1.1,

7 the Nations and the City shall provide notice to the OWRB.

8   **5.3.1.2.1.1.1**   Failure of any Party to appoint a Technical Committee

9 Member shall not constitute a breach of the Settlement Agreement.

10   **5.3.1.2.1.1.2**   Any Party's failure to appoint a Technical Committee

11 Member shall not preclude or excuse the OWRB from performing its functions under Section

12 5.3.1.2 or 5.3.1.3.

13   **5.3.1.2.1.2**   **Performance of Modeling Work**

14   **5.3.1.2.1.2.1**   Each Party shall support its respective Technical

15 Committee member with such resources and expertise as are necessary and appropriate for the

16 completion of the Technical Committee's work. Members shall endeavor to achieve consensus

17 regarding work to be performed. Any documentation of the Technical Committee's work shall be

18 maintained in electronic format at the OWRB as a public record.

19   **5.3.1.2.1.2.2**   The OWRB shall provide all members of the Technical

20 Committee full and equal access to any model (including all information relevant to its proper

21 use) that is subject to evaluation, refinement, or development under Section 5.3.1.2.

1   **5.3.1.2.1.2.3**   The OWRB and the Technical Committee may use all

2 resources available to them for purposes of evaluating, refining, or developing a model,

3 including but not limited to information from the applicant.

4   **5.3.1.2.2**   **Adequate Model** – The OWRB may determine a model is

5 adequate for purposes of Sections 5.3.1.2.2, 5.3.1.2.5, and 5.3.1.3 if it includes, at a minimum,

6 the model inputs identified at Section 5.3.1.2.3 and the model has been calibrated for purposes of

7 evaluating the following:

8   **5.3.1.2.2.1**   Whether water is available at the proposed point of diversion

9 based on the Mean Available Flow and what may be required for projected beneficial use within

10 the basin and, to the extent applicable pursuant to Section 5.3.1.1.2.2, any water quality,

11 ecological, and recreational needs evaluated in a manner consistent with OAC § 785:20-5-5(e);

12 and

13   **5.3.1.2.2.2**   Whether a proposed use would interfere with existing

14 beneficial uses of water.

15   **5.3.1.2.3**   **Model Inputs** – An Adequate Hydrologic Model shall include, at a

16 minimum, the following inputs:

17   **5.3.1.2.3.1**   Existing water rights in the basin as of the date of the

18 application, including permitted appropriative uses, vested rights, any surface water uses

19 developed by either Nation pursuant to Section 7.7, domestic use set aside calculated based on

20 the OWRB numerical assumption of six (6) AFY per one hundred sixty (160) acres within the

21 basin upstream of the proposed point of diversion and twenty-four (24) AFY for each linear mile

22 downstream of the proposed point of diversion, any surface water right recognized pursuant to

23 Section 8, and any pending application;

1   **5.3.1.2.3.2**   Quantity of flow necessary to fulfill obligations under

2 apportionment provisions of interstate stream compacts to which the State is a party as calculated

3 by any rules developed by any applicable compact commission;

4   **5.3.1.2.3.3**   For those applications that satisfy the conferral threshold

5 provided at Section 5.3.1.1.2.2, the quantity of flow sufficient to satisfy water quality, ecological,

6 and recreational needs evaluated in a manner consistent with OAC § 785:20-5-5(e) using the

7 United States Geological Survey's seven (7) day average low flow of the stream with a fifty

8 percent (50%) occurrence probability (seven day, two-year low flow or 7Q2) for the entire

9 period of record and any other basin-specific data.

10   **5.3.1.2.3.4**   Projected total in-basin demands using a minimum fifty (50)

11 year time frame and calculated for:

12   **5.3.1.2.3.4.1**   Population-based demands using the methodology

13 relied on in the latest update to the Oklahoma Comprehensive Water Plan or a standard

14 methodology that is widely accepted for demographic planning purposes and which is

15 appropriate based on all local considerations regarding water that may be required for in-basin

16 beneficial uses; and

17   **5.3.1.2.3.4.2**   Non-population-based demands using information

18 included in and methodology relied on in the latest update to the Oklahoma Comprehensive

19 Water Plan or a standard methodology that is widely accepted for planning purposes and which

20 is appropriate based on all local considerations regarding water that may be required for in-basin

21 beneficial uses.

22   **5.3.1.2.3.5**   Measured or synthesized data sufficient to simulate basin

23 hydrology, including reservoir characteristics (*e.g.*, yield, area-capacity, normal storage,

1 authorized purposes, date of construction, evaporation, sedimentation, release schedules and

2 other operational requirements) and seasonal flow variability, using the entire period of record,

3 except for those data which diminish statistical confidence.

4   **5.3.1.2.4**   **Notice** – Prior to approving a proposed publication notice for a

5 permit application that satisfies any of the conferral thresholds set forth in Section 5.3.1.1.2, the

6 OWRB shall:

7   **5.3.1.2.4.1**   notify the Nations and each Technical Committee member in

8 writing of such application, which notice will include a complete copy of the application and a

9 description of any model for the relevant basin that the OWRB previously determined to be an

10 Adequate Hydrologic Model under Section 5.3.1.2.5 and describing updates, if any, to such

11 model since it was determined to be an Adequate Hydrologic Model; and

12   **5.3.1.2.4.2**   confer with the Technical Committee regarding any

13 information provided pursuant to Section 5.3.1.2.4.1 and inform the Technical Committee of the

14 OWRB's preliminary assessment of any available hydrologic models.

15   **5.3.1.2.5**   **Determination** – The OWRB shall determine whether an

16 Adequate Hydrologic Model is available to it, including models that have been refined or

17 developed under Section 5.3.1.2.5.4. In making such determination, the OWRB shall:

18   **5.3.1.2.5.1**   Assess models that the OWRB has access to for the basin from

19 which the waters are proposed to be appropriated, including any model previously determined to

20 be an Adequate Hydrologic Model and any updates thereto.

21   **5.3.1.2.5.2**   If the OWRB determines an Adequate Hydrologic Model is

22 available to it, it shall notify the Technical Committee of such determination and then process the

23 application pursuant to Section 5.3.1.3.

5.3.1.2.5.3 If the OWRB determines that an Adequate Hydrologic Model is not available to it, it shall proceed in accord with Section 5.3.1.2.5.4.

5.3.1.2.5.4 If the OWRB determines an Adequate Hydrologic Model is not available to it, the OWRB shall notify the Technical Committee of such determination and direct the Technical Committee either refine an existing hydrologic model or develop a new model so that it is an Adequate Hydrologic Model. The Technical Committee shall complete its model refinement or development work within one hundred and eighty (180) days of the notification pursuant to Section 5.3.1.2.5.2, after which the OWRB may either: (i) give the Technical Committee additional time or (ii) complete the model refinement or development. Once work on the model is completed, the OWRB shall proceed with its determination under Section 5.3.1.2.5.

5.3.1.2.5.5 The OWRB shall exercise its discretion in making determinations under Section 5.3.1.2.5. In making its determinations, OWRB must ensure that a model satisfies the criteria provided at Section 5.3.1.2.2. The OWRB shall provide the Technical Committee with written documentation of its determination.

5.3.1.2.5.6 Subsequent to the Enforceability Date, if the conferral threshold of Section 5.3.1.1.2.2 is satisfied with respect to an application to appropriate water from the Kiamichi Basin, the Kiamichi Basin Hydrologic Model shall be the starting point for OWRB's determination under Section 5.3.1.2.5.

5.3.1.2.5.7 Once a model is determined adequate under Section 5.3.1.2.5, the OWRB shall use it for purposes of allocation of water and administration of water rights within the relevant basin. The Kiamichi Basin Hydrologic Model, including any updates, shall be used for the allocation of water and administration of water rights in the Kiamichi Basin.

5.3.1.3 **Permit Application Processing**

5.3.1.3.1 **Hydrologic Findings** – In reliance on an Adequate Hydrologic Model, the OWRB will process an application subject to Section 5.3.1.3 under Title 82 and OWRB rules and regulations and make written findings on the following as part of its final decision:

5.3.1.3.1.1 That the applicant's proposed diversions of water would not interfere with existing water rights in the source basin;

5.3.1.3.1.2 That the applicant's proposed diversion of water would not interfere with projected future consumptive-use water needs within the source basin; and

5.3.1.3.1.3 For those applications that satisfy the conferral threshold provided at Section 5.3.1.1.2.2 or which have satisfied the requirements of Section 5.3.3, that existing water quality, ecological, and recreational needs evaluated in a manner consistent with OAC § 785:20-5-5(e) would be protected in approving the applicant's proposed diversion of water.

5.3.1.3.2 **Applicant's Use and Demand Findings** – Using the evidence tendered in administrative proceedings on the application in addition to relevant data included in the most recent update to the Oklahoma Comprehensive Water Plan, OWRB will process the application under Title 82 and OWRB rules and regulations and make written findings on the following as part of its final decision:

5.3.1.3.2.1 That the applicant has demonstrated it has a need for the water requested for appropriation within a reasonable period of time but not longer than seven (7) years or as set forth in a schedule of use that is supported by any findings required by state law; and

1   **5.3.1.3.2.2**   That the applicant has demonstrated the works intended for the

2   delivery of the water are feasible and capable of efficient delivery of the water requested for

3   appropriation without committing waste.

4   **5.3.1.3.3**   **Permit Issuance** – The OWRB may issue a permit if it has made

5   affirmative conclusions supported by the record on each of the findings specified in Sections

6   5.3.1.3.1 and 5.3.1.3.2.

7   **5.3.1.4**   **No Modification of Rights** – Nothing herein modifies in any way the

8   rights available to any person pursuant to state law to participate in OWRB proceedings and to

9   appeal from decisions based thereon.

10   **5.3.2**   **Arbuckle-Simpson Groundwater Basin**

11   **5.3.2.1**   **In General** – The Arbuckle-Simpson Groundwater Basin is located in a

12   region of significant historic, cultural, economic and environmental value to the State and the

13   Nations and has been the subject of substantive engagement and cooperative efforts among the

14   Nations and the OWRB. The Arbuckle-Simpson Groundwater Basin is classified as a sensitive

15   sole-source aquifer, and 82 O.S. § 1020.9A requires consideration and protection of the natural

16   flow of springs and streams emanating from the Arbuckle-Simpson Groundwater Basin. OWRB

17   shall administer the Arbuckle-Simpson Groundwater Basin in accord with 82 O.S. §§ 1020.9 and

18   1020.9A, the Settlement Agreement, and the Settlement Act.

19   **5.3.2.2**   **Maximum Annual Yield and Administration** – The OWRB shall

20   consider all applications for the Arbuckle-Simpson Groundwater Basin pursuant to 82 O.S.

21   §§ 1020.9A and 1020.9 in accord with Section 5.3.2. In accord with Title 82, the OWRB has

22   developed a maximum annual yield ("MAY") for the Arbuckle-Simpson Groundwater Basin, *see*

23   Maximum Annual Yield for the Arbuckle-Simpson Groundwater Basin, OWRB (Findings of

1   Fact, Conclusions of Law, and Board Order, Oct. 23, 2013) ("2013 Order"). OWRB shall

2   administer the Arbuckle-Simpson Groundwater Basin in accord with Title 82 and the 2013

3   Order; *provided that* if a court of competent jurisdiction modifies or otherwise determines the

4   2013 Order is invalid, OWRB shall develop a new MAY and either issue a new MAY order or

5   modify the 2013 Order in conformance with 82 O.S. §§ 1020.9 and 1020.9A and any applicable

6   court order ("MAY Order"), and administer the Arbuckle-Simpson Groundwater Basin pursuant

7   to such MAY Order. Any order establishing a MAY for the Arbuckle-Simpson Groundwater

8   Basin and OWRB administration thereunder shall ensure that any groundwater permit issued by

9   the OWRB will not reduce the natural flow of water from springs or streams emanating from the

10   Arbuckle-Simpson Groundwater Basin.

11   **5.3.2.3**   **Applications for Groundwater** – The OWRB shall evaluate any

12   regular permit to use groundwater from the Arbuckle-Simpson Groundwater Basin in accord

13   with the MAY Order and shall approve the permit if it finds that:

14   **5.3.2.3.1**   The lands owned or leased by the applicant overlie the Arbuckle-

15   Simpson Groundwater Basin;

16   **5.3.2.3.2**   The use to which the applicant intends to put the water is

17   beneficial;

18   **5.3.2.3.3**   The proposed use does not constitute waste as defined in 82 O.S.

19   § 1020.15; and

20   **5.3.2.3.4**   The proposed use is not likely to degrade or interfere with springs

21   or streams emanating in whole or in part from water originating from the Arbuckle-Simpson

22   Groundwater Basin.

5.3.3 Out-of-State Use of Settlement Area Waters

5.3.3.1 **In General** – The Parties recognize and agree that, as of the Execution Date, state law prohibits any Out-of-State Use of Settlement Area Waters. Nothing in the Settlement Agreement changes such state law or otherwise permits or authorizes such use. Any Out-of-State Use of Settlement Area Waters shall be in accord with the Settlement Agreement, the Settlement Act, and any state law not inconsistent herewith.

5.3.3.2 **Settlement Commission**

5.3.3.2.1 **Establishment** – The Settlement Act established the Settlement Commission, the duties and authority of which are defined and limited by the Settlement Agreement and the Settlement Act.

5.3.3.2.2 **Members** –

5.3.3.2.2.1 **In General** – The Settlement Commission shall be comprised of five (5) members, appointed as follows:

5.3.3.2.2.1.1 One (1) by the Governor of the State.

5.3.3.2.2.1.2 One (1) by the Attorney General of the State.

5.3.3.2.2.1.3 One (1) by the Chief of the Choctaw Nation.

5.3.3.2.2.1.4 One (1) by the Governor of the Chickasaw Nation.

5.3.3.2.2.1.5 One (1) by agreement of the members described in 5.3.3.2.2.1.1 through 5.3.3.2.2.1.4 and clauses (g)(2)(A)(i) through (g)(2)(A)(iv) of the Settlement Act.

5.3.3.2.2.2 **Jointly Appointed Member** – If the members described in Sections 5.3.3.2.2.1.1 through 5.3.3.2.2.1.4 and clauses (g)(2)(A)(i) through (g)(2)(A)(iv) of the Settlement Act do not agree on a member appointed pursuant to Section 5.3.3.2.2.1.5 and clause (g)(2)(A)(v) of the Settlement Act:

5.3.3.2.2.2.1 the members shall submit to the Chief Judge for the United States District Court for the Eastern District of Oklahoma, a list of not less than three (3) persons; and

5.3.3.2.2.2.2 from the list under Section 5.3.3.2.2.2.1 and clause (g)(2)(B)(i) of the Settlement Act, the Chief Judge shall make the appointment.

5.3.3.2.2.3 **Initial Appointments** – The initial appointments to the Settlement Commission shall be made not later than ninety (90) days after the Enforceability Date.

5.3.3.2.3 **Member Terms** –

5.3.3.2.3.1 **In General** – Each Settlement Commission member shall serve at the pleasure of the appointing authority.

5.3.3.2.3.2 **Compensation** – A member of the Settlement Commission shall serve without compensation, but an appointing authority may reimburse the member appointed by the entity for costs associated with service on the Settlement Commission. The fifth member shall have their costs associated with service on the Settlement Commission reimbursed by the State and the Nations.

5.3.3.2.3.3 **Vacancies** – If a member of the Settlement Commission is removed or resigns, the appointing authority shall appoint the replacement member.

5.3.3.2.3.4 **Jointly Appointed Member** – The member of the Settlement Commission described in Section 5.3.3.2.2.1.5 and clause (g)(2)(A)(v) of the Settlement Act may

1 be removed or replaced by a majority vote of the Settlement Commission based on a failure of

2 the member to carry out the duties of the member.

3   **5.3.3.2.4**   **Duties** – The Settlement Commission's duties shall be as follows:

4   **5.3.3.2.4.1**   **Evaluation** – to evaluate any proposed Out-of-State Use of

5 Settlement Area Waters in accord with Section 5.3.3.3.2;

6   **5.3.3.2.4.2**   **Report** – to prepare, finalize, and submit a report in accord

7 with Section 5.3.3.3.3, which report shall document the Settlement Commission's evaluation of

8 those matters indicated in Section 5.3.3.3.2 and such other relevant issues presented by the

9 proposed Out-of-State Use of Settlement Area Waters;

10   **5.3.3.2.4.3**   **Appeals from Denials of Funding for Settlement Area**

11 **Projects** – to hear and decide appeals submitted to it pursuant to Section 5.3.3.5.2.5; and

12   **5.3.3.2.4.4**   **Internal Procedures** – to establish such procedures as are

13 necessary for purposes of the Settlement Commission's operation and performance of the duties

14 set forth in Section 5.3.3.

15   **5.3.3.2.4.5**   **Limitation** – The Settlement Commission shall not possess or

16 exercise any duty or authority not stated in the Settlement Agreement.

17   **5.3.3.3**   **Proposal Evaluation; Report**

18   **5.3.3.3.1**   **Proposal** – Any person proposing an Out-of-State Use of

19 Settlement Area Waters shall submit a proposal to the Settlement Commission for evaluation, a

20 copy of which the Settlement Commission shall provide to the OWRB.

21   **5.3.3.3.2**   **Evaluation** – In performing its evaluation of a proposal, the

22 Settlement Commission may consider all available information, including, at a minimum: (i) the

23 use to which the water will be placed; (ii) the feasibility of the works proposed for delivering

1 water; (iii) the effect of the proposed use on water availability in the source basin and throughout

2 Oklahoma; (iv) the likely environmental and economic impact of the proposed use on the source

3 basin and Oklahoma; and (v) the appropriate valuation to be imposed as a condition of the

4 proposed Out-of-State Use of Settlement Area Waters. To support the Settlement Commission's

5 performance of its duties under Section 5.3.3, the OWRB shall provide to the Settlement

6 Commission a preliminary technical evaluation of the availability of water in the source basin,

7 including permitted uses, any pending applications, and any other known, projected, or proposed

8 water uses; *provided*, that such preliminary evaluation shall not prejudge or otherwise control

9 any subsequent administrative processing of the proposed Out-of-State Use of Settlement Area

10 Waters by the OWRB.

11   **5.3.3.3.3**   **Report; Legislative Action** – The Settlement Commission's

12 evaluation shall be contained in a report that the Settlement Commission shall submit to the

13 Speaker of the Oklahoma House of Representatives and the President *Pro Tem* of the Oklahoma

14 Senate. The Oklahoma Legislature may consider and act on the Settlement Commission's report

15 as the Legislature deems appropriate.

16   **5.3.3.3.4**   **Administrative Fees and Costs** – Any person proposing an Out-

17 of-State Use of Settlement Area Waters shall pay those fees and costs associated with the

18 Settlement Commission's evaluation and preparation of its report. The Nations and State will

19 coordinate to provide additional reasonable administrative support, including funding, to allow

20 the Settlement Commission to fulfill its duties.

21   **5.3.3.4**   **Applications for a Proposed Out-of-State Use of Settlement Area**

22 **Waters** – No Out-of-State Use of Settlement Area Waters shall be lawful unless and until such

23 use is made pursuant to a validly issued OWRB permit. Once a proposed Out-of-State Use of

Settlement Area Waters has been evaluated by the Settlement Commission and authorized by the Oklahoma Legislature, the person proposing such use shall submit to the OWRB an application for a water use permit, which application the OWRB shall process in accord with Section 5.3.1, including Sections 5.3.1.2 and 5.3.1.3, without regard to the amount proposed for appropriation and use. Any Out-of-State Use of Settlement Area Waters permitted by the OWRB shall be subject to State jurisdiction and administered by the OWRB in accord with the permit issued, state law, the Settlement Agreement, and the Settlement Act.

5.3.3.5 Water Preservation Infrastructure Fund

5.3.3.5.1 Created – Any monies paid relating to an Out-of-State Use of Settlement Area Waters shall be deposited into the Water Preservation Infrastructure Fund, hereby created. The purpose of the Water Preservation Infrastructure Fund, inclusive of all monies deposited therein, shall be solely and exclusively to provide grants for the construction and maintenance of public water infrastructure throughout Oklahoma, including but not limited to public infrastructure for municipal and rural water supply, irrigation supply, and wastewater projects.

5.3.3.5.2 Administration of Water Preservation Infrastructure Fund

5.3.3.5.2.1 Allocation and Disbursement – Monies deposited pursuant to Section 5.3.3.5.1 may only be allocated and disbursed in accord with the Settlement Agreement and the Settlement Act.

5.3.3.5.2.2 Administration of Fund – The OWRB shall administer the Water Preservation Infrastructure Fund in accord with Section 5.3.3.5, the Settlement Act, and state law.

5.3.3.5.2.3 Consideration of Applications – The OWRB shall consider applications for funding in the order in which such requests are received, with the exception of applications for funding for public water infrastructure projects located within or serving the Settlement Area which shall be considered prior to all others. In considering such applications for funding from the Water Preservation Infrastructure Fund, the OWRB shall apply the point system and procedures set forth in Exhibit 11.

5.3.3.5.2.4 Settlement Area Projects Priority – As provided in Section 2 of Exhibit 11, applications for funding for public water infrastructure projects located within or serving the Settlement Area shall receive an additional ten (10) points.

5.3.3.5.2.5 Appeal of Denial of Funding for Settlement Area Projects – If the OWRB denies an application for funding for a public water infrastructure project located within or serving the Settlement Area, the aggrieved applicant may, within thirty (30) days, appeal the OWRB's decision to the Settlement Commission, which shall determine whether the OWRB correctly applied the criteria of Section 5.3.3.5 (inclusive of Exhibit 11) including preferences for Settlement Area projects. If the Settlement Commission determines that the OWRB properly applied the criteria, the decision of the OWRB shall stand and be final, subject to the applicant's right to reapply to the OWRB consistent with Exhibit 11. If the Settlement Commission determines the OWRB did not correctly apply the criteria of Section 5.3.3.5 (inclusive of Exhibit 11), the application shall be remanded to the OWRB for reconsideration.

6. PROVISIONS RELATING TO PENDING OWRB APPLICATION NO. 2007-017 – As provided in this Section 6, the Parties have agreed to provisions to enhance water availability for use within the Settlement Area, to support recreation, fish and wildlife needs, and to resolve the Nations' objections to the OWRB's consideration of the City's Amended Permit Application.

1   These provisions include Sardis Lake Release Restrictions, Bypass Flow Requirements, and City

2   water conservation requirements to protect Sardis Lake recreation, fish and wildlife benefits; a

3   set-aside of Conservation Storage Capacity for local use of the Administrative Set-Aside; and the

4   Atoka and Sardis Conservation Projects Board.

5   **6.1**   **Amended Permit Application** – To facilitate the implementation of provisions

6   referenced above, the City will file with the OWRB within one hundred twenty (120) days after

7   the Execution Date the Amended Permit Application, which shall include the terms and

8   conditions set forth in this Section 6.1:

9   **6.1.1**   **Scope** – that the permit provide a right: (i) to store Kiamichi Basin water in

10   Sardis Lake consistent with the Amended Storage Contract; (ii) to release water from Sardis

11   Lake for delivery to the Point of Diversion; and (iii) to divert and beneficially use water from

12   the Kiamichi Basin.

13   **6.1.2**   **Amount of Appropriation** – that the permit provide a right to appropriate one

14   hundred fifteen thousand (115,000) AFY and specify that water bypassed in accord with

15   Section 6.1.5.2 shall not be counted against the City's one hundred fifteen thousand (115,000)

16   AFY appropriation; *provided*, that the City's compliance with the Bypass Requirement of

17   Section 6.1.5.2 shall not be grounds for finding any forfeiture of such appropriation.

18   **6.1.3**   **Point of Diversion** – that the permit specify a point of diversion from the

19   Kiamichi River in the general vicinity of Moyers Crossing in Pushmataha County, Oklahoma.

20   **6.1.4**   **Sources** – that the permit provide that the sources of water shall be stream

21   water from the Kiamichi River, water released from City Sardis Storage, or any combination

22   thereof.

1   **6.1.5**   **City Diversion Rate, Bypass Requirement, and Flow Rate** – that the permit

2   provide for:

3   **6.1.5.1**   a diversion rate of two hundred fifty (250) cfs;

4   **6.1.5.2**   a requirement that the City bypass fifty (50) cfs at the Point of Diversion

5   as a precondition to diverting water; and

6   **6.1.5.3**   a flow rate of three hundred (300) cfs, which is the combined amount of

7   the City Diversion Rate and the Bypass Requirement.

8   **6.1.6**   **Exercise of City Diversion Rate, Bypass Requirement, and Flow Rate** –

9   that the permit provide:

10   **6.1.6.1**   that regardless of hydrological conditions, the City may divert water

11   under the City Permit only when the full amount of the Bypass Requirement flows past the Point

12   of Diversion;

13   **6.1.6.2**   that the City may divert natural flow to the extent the natural flow

14   exceeds the Bypass Requirement at the Point of Diversion;

15   **6.1.6.3**   that the City may divert flows that result from City Sardis Storage

16   releases to the extent that such releases in combination with any natural flow exceed the Bypass

17   Requirement at the Point of Diversion; and

18   **6.1.6.4**   that the City provide to the OWRB an accounting of its releases from

19   City Sardis Storage and measurement of its diversions and bypasses at the Point of Diversion.

20   **6.1.7**   **Purposes** – that the permit provide that the purposes for which water may be

21   beneficially used shall be municipal use by the City, the City's current and future wholesale

22   and retail water customers and other public water supply entities in Oklahoma, and incidental

purposes in Sardis Lake for recreation, fish and wildlife benefits as necessary to exercise the City's one hundred fifteen thousand (115,000) AFY appropriation.

6.1.8   Sardis Lake Release Restrictions – that the permit provide that the City may not have water released from City Sardis Storage except in conformance with the terms and conditions of this Section 6.1.8, which terms and conditions shall be deemed to satisfy the requirements of OAC § 785:20-5-5(b)(3)(iv) for a lake level management plan; *provided*, that such release restrictions shall not restrict the City's right to divert natural flow from the Kiamichi Basin when the natural flow at the Point of Diversion exceeds fifty (50) cfs.

6.1.8.1   Baseline Lake Levels – Regardless of whether Drought Conditions exist and notwithstanding any other condition herein, the City, subject to the rights reserved to the United States under Article 1(c) of the 1974 Contract, shall be entitled to have water released from City Sardis Storage as follows:

6.1.8.1.1   From April 1 through August 31, the City may have water released from City Sardis Storage whenever the Sardis Lake surface elevation is at or above 599' MSL; and

6.1.8.1.2   From September 1 through March 31, the City may have water released from City Sardis Storage whenever the Sardis Lake surface elevation is at or above 595' MSL.

6.1.8.2   Drought Withdrawals – During Drought Conditions, the City may have water released from City Sardis Storage in amounts that cause the Sardis Lake surface elevation to drop below the Baseline Lake Levels in Section 6.1.8.1 only if it is implementing and enforcing the water conservation measures described in Exhibit 12 for all of its retail and wholesale customers, inside and outside of the City's municipal boundaries. The City Reservoir

storage level triggers contained in Exhibit 12 are distinct from and intended to operate independently of the City Reservoir storage level triggers that are contained in the Settlement Agreement's definitions of Moderate Drought Conditions, Advanced Drought Conditions, and Extreme Drought Conditions. The City may modify the water conservation measures described in Exhibit 12 with the prior written consent of the Nations, which consent shall not be unreasonably withheld, for: (i) procedural modifications that do not increase water use and (ii) changes in irrigation technology that enable different patterns of use without increasing annual irrigation demand. Nothing herein shall preclude the City from implementing water conservation measures more restrictive than those described in Exhibit 12; *provided*, that the Nations shall be given written notice of such measures prior to their implementation.

6.1.8.2.1   Moderate Drought Withdrawals – When Moderate Drought Conditions exist, the City may have water released from City Sardis Storage from July 5 through August 31 and lower the Sardis Lake surface elevation below the Baseline Lake Levels in Section 6.1.8.1 to the lake level of 597' MSL.

6.1.8.2.2   Advanced Drought Withdrawals – When Advanced Drought Conditions exist, the City may have water released from City Sardis Storage and lower the Sardis Lake surface elevation below the Baseline Lake Levels in Section 6.1.8.1 to the lake level of 592' MSL.

6.1.8.2.3   Extreme Drought Withdrawals – When Extreme Drought Conditions exist, the City may have water released from City Sardis Storage and lower the Sardis Lake surface elevation below the Baseline Lake Levels in Section 6.1.8.1 to the lake level of 589' MSL.

1   **6.1.8.2.4**   **Meet and Confer** – At least thirty (30) days prior to commencing

2 Advanced Drought Withdrawals or Extreme Drought Withdrawals, the City shall provide notice

3 to and offer to meet and confer with OWRB staff and the Nations. If either the OWRB or the

4 Nations desire to meet, then as part of the conferral process: (i) the City will demonstrate that

5 Advanced Drought Conditions or Extreme Drought Conditions exist, as applicable, and the

6 appropriate water conservation measures in Exhibit 12 and water conservation program

7 established pursuant to Section 6.5.1 are in effect; and (ii) the City and OWRB staff and the

8 Nations will consider whether to commence discussions under Section 6.5.7.

9   **6.1.8.3**   **Calculations and Measurement** – For purposes of Section 6.1.8 and

10 determinations of relative Drought Conditions, as defined in Sections 1.5, 1.33, and 1.43, Live

11 Storage Capacity shall be calculated follows:

12   **6.1.8.3.1**   **Live Storage Capacity Calculation** – Live Storage Capacity shall

13 be calculated as the volume of City Reservoir storage space between the top of the conservation

14 pool and the specified lower elevation using the elevation-capacity relationship documented in

15 Exhibit 13, as set forth in Table 1, unless otherwise agreed pursuant to Section 6.5.7. The

16 cumulative amount of Live Storage Capacity for the City Reservoirs resulting from this

17 calculation is four hundred seven thousand one hundred five (407,105) AF.

18

Table 1: City Reservoir Live Storage Capacity and Lake Elevations

City Reservoir	Top Elev. (MSL)	Lower Elev. (MSL)	Max. Live Stor. Cap. (AF)	75% (MSL)	65% (MSL)	50% (MSL)
Atoka	590.0	550.0	107,940	n/a	n/a	n/a
Canton	1,615.4	1,596.5	68,023	n/a	n/a	n/a
Draper	1,191.0	1,145.0	72,195	1,183.10	1,179.50	1,173.70
Hefner	1,199.0	1,165.0	57,593	1,193.10	1,190.40	1,186.10
McGee	577.1	533.0	88,445	n/a	n/a	n/a
Overholser	1,241.5	1,231.8	12,909	n/a	n/a	n/a
Total			407,105			

1   **6.1.8.3.2**   **Lake Elevation Measurement** – All lake elevations shall be

2 determined in reference to official United States Army Corps of Engineer or United States

3 Geological Survey measurements.

4   **6.1.8.3.3**   **Accounting** – Accounting for the City Permit shall be in accord

5 with the accounting memorandum included as Exhibit 13.

6   **6.1.9**   **Schedule of Use** – that the permit provide a schedule of use as set forth in

7 Exhibit 14.

8   **6.1.10 Exercise of City Permit** – that the permit provide that the City's exercise of

9 the City Permit shall be in accord with the City Permit terms, the Settlement Agreement, and

10 the Settlement Act.

11   **6.2**   **OWRB Review of Amended Permit Application**

12   **6.2.1**   **Evaluation of Application** – The OWRB shall evaluate the evidence

13 submitted by the City and otherwise tendered by any interested party in the administrative

14 proceeding held on the Amended Permit Application and use the Kiamichi Basin Hydrologic

15 Model, as it exists as of the Execution Date, to determine pursuant to the applicable provisions

16 of Title 785 of the Oklahoma Administrative Code and Title 82 whether the City Permit shall

17 be issued. No permit may be issued that does not include those terms and conditions stated in

18 Section 6.1.

19   **6.2.2**   **Timing**

20   **6.2.2.1**   **Commencement of OWRB Process; Issuance of Notice** – No later

21 than thirty (30) days from the Enactment Date, the OWRB staff shall issue to the City a notice

22 for publication ("Notice") of the Amended Permit Application, which the City shall cause to be

23 published in accord with Section 6.2.2 and OAC § 785:20-5-1.

6.2.2.2   **Contents of Notice; Timing and Schedule for Hearing** – In addition to any requirements of state law, the Notice shall set a schedule for consideration of the Amended Permit Application. The schedule shall provide that: (i) any protest to the Amended Permit Application must be filed within thirty (30) days of the date of last publication of Notice; and (ii) in the event the Amended Permit Application is protested, a hearing shall be conducted and concluded no later than one hundred eighty (180) days from the date of last publication of Notice.

6.2.2.3   **Conduct of Hearing; Protests** – The hearing shall be conducted by a hearing examiner. Pursuant to state law, protests shall be limited to the elements of OAC § 785:20-5-4 and the applicable factors of OAC § 785:20-5-5.

6.2.2.4   **Hearing Examiner Proposed Final Order; Presentation; Exceptions** – The hearing examiner shall prepare a proposed Final Order which shall be presented to the Board within forty-five (45) days of the conclusion of the hearing if the Amended Permit Application is protested. In the event the Amended Permit Application is not protested, the OWRB staff shall present a proposed Final Order to the Board within forty-five (45) days of the date of last publication of Notice. The proposed Final Order shall be presented and any exceptions to the proposed Final Order filed in accord with OAC § 785:4-9-1.

6.2.2.5   **Final Order of OWRB** – The Board shall consider the proposed Final Order and any exceptions thereto and issue a Final Order within thirty (30) days of the filing of any exceptions in the manner prescribed by OAC § 785:4-9-2. Appeals from the OWRB's Final Order shall be in accord with state law. The Parties may agree in writing that the condition of Section 4.1.7 and subparagraph (i)(1)(G) of the Settlement Act, shall be deemed satisfied, notwithstanding such appeal. If the Parties agree that the condition of Section 4.1.7 and

subparagraph (i)(1)(G) of the Settlement Act, shall be deemed satisfied, then each will be deemed to have waived any right it may have under Section 6.2.3.

6.2.2.6   **Timelines Not to Be Extended** – Unless the State, the Nations, and the City agree or it is otherwise ordered by a court of competent jurisdiction, the timelines set forth in Section 6.2.2 shall not be subject to extension and the State shall allocate sufficient resources to allow all time requirements to be met.

6.2.2.7   **Effective Only on Enforceability Date** – No permit the OWRB may issue to the City based on the Amended Permit Application will have any force or effect and the City shall exercise no rights thereunder prior to the Enforceability Date, and any permit the OWRB may issue to the City based on the Amended Permit Application shall include a condition implementing this limitation.

6.2.3   **Permit Conformance**

6.2.3.1   **Process for Addressing Non-Conformance** – If the OWRB issues a final permit and the City or either Nation asserts the final permit does not conform with the terms and conditions of Section 6.1, then the Party or Parties asserting such non-conformance shall: (i) within ten (10) days of the issuance of the final permit, provide notice to the other Parties of such assertion and (ii) seek to convene a meeting of the Parties to discuss such assertion and seek to resolve any disagreements relating to non-conformance and/or necessary modifications to the final permit in order to ensure conformance.

6.2.3.2   **Remedy for Non-Conformance** – In the event the Parties can neither agree that the final permit conforms to Section 6.1 nor to modifications thereto that would resolve assertions of non-conformance, then: (i) the Parties will be unable to satisfy the condition precedent specified at Section 4.1.7, which circumstance will automatically activate the Expiration Date; and (ii) the City at its sole discretion may resubmit to the OWRB, and the OWRB shall be deemed to have accepted, OWRB Permit Application No. 2007-017 without the City's having waived the priority date and proposed appropriative amounts of its initial permit application (Application No. 2007-017).

6.2.3.3 **Final Permit** – For purposes of Section 6.2.3, a permit shall be considered final and not subject to further appeal if: (i) any and all appeals from the OWRB's issuance of the permit have been exhausted or (ii) the time has expired for any person to seek appellate review of the permit issued by the OWRB.

6.3 **Surrender** – Notwithstanding the possible cancellation or reduction in the future of the City Permit that could result by operation of state law, the City Permit shall be deemed surrendered in accord with 82 O.S. § 105.19 and OAC § 785:20-9-3(H) without any further action by the OWRB or City if the City by 2043 does not construct the Parallel City Pipeline and divert under the City Permit an amount equal to what the schedule of use specifies for 2040, *see* Exhibit 14; *provided*, that this deadline shall be tolled and extended for the duration of: (i) any court injunction that delays or halts the City's construction of the Parallel City Pipeline, which injunction is entered as part of any litigation challenging the issuance of environmental permits, rights of way, or easements necessary for the Parallel City Pipeline; or (ii) any delay in excess of three (3) years from the City's initiation of legal action(s) to secure any Bureau of Indian Affairs' approval necessary for the purpose of acquiring easements or rights-of-way for the Parallel City Pipeline; *provided*, that the City shall diligently initiate and pursue such legal action(s). Regardless of any surrender, cancellation, or reduction of the City Permit pursuant to this Section 6.3, any use of Conservation Storage Capacity transferred to the City pursuant to the Amended

Storage Contract Transfer Agreement, except for the storage for the Administrative Set-Aside, shall remain subject to the Sardis Lake Release Restrictions set forth at Section 6.1.8.

6.4 **Administration of City Permit**

6.4.1 Water released from City Sardis Storage for delivery to the Point of Diversion will not be considered or administered as part of the natural flow of Jack Fork Creek or the Kiamichi River subject to or available for diversion or appropriation by others. The City shall not be obligated to release water from City Sardis Storage to maintain the Bypass Requirement when it is not diverting water at the Point of Diversion. The City shall bear any and all conveyance losses from the Sardis Lake outlet structure to the Point of Diversion.

6.4.2 The City shall have independent standing to bring a judicial action to enforce the provisions of Section 6.4.1 as against third party water users, regardless of whether prior administrative relief was sought from the OWRB and regardless of whether the OWRB is a party to or consents to said judicial proceeding.

6.5 **Additional Provisions**

6.5.1 **Water Conservation Program** – Within three (3) years of the Enforceability Date, the City will administratively approve a water conservation program appropriate for its water utility that generally follows American Water Works Association Water Conservation Standards. Following the approval, the City will periodically review and, as appropriate for its water utility, update its water conservation program to conform with changes in American Water Works Association Water Conservation Standards. The City and the Trust will implement the conservation program as approved and thereafter updated by the City.

6.5.2   Atoka and Sardis Conservation Projects Board and Fund

2   **6.5.2.1   Establishment**

3   **6.5.2.1.1   Projects Board** – No later than ninety (90) days from the

4   Enactment Date, the State, the Chickasaw Nation, the Choctaw Nation, and the City shall each

5   appoint a representative to the Atoka and Sardis Conservation Projects Board. Each member

6   shall serve at the pleasure of its appointing entity. Failure to appoint a member shall not

7   constitute a breach of the Settlement Agreement nor shall it preclude the Board from performing

8   its duties, as specified herein. Each appointing entity may reimburse from its own funds its

9   respective appointed member for costs associated with their service, but each member shall

10 otherwise serve without compensation.

11   **6.5.2.1.2   Projects Fund**

12   **6.5.2.1.2.1   Contributions** – Upon the Enactment Date and subject to an

13 escrow agreement implementing the requirements of Section 6.5.2.1.2, the State, Nations, and

14 City shall each contribute to a ten million dollar ($10,000,000) fund, with: (i) the City

15 contributing five million dollars ($5,000,000), of which two million five hundred thousand

16 dollars ($2,500,000) would have been monies otherwise due to the State under the terms of the

17 Storage Contract Transfer Agreement; and (ii) the Nations contributing five million dollars

18 ($5,000,000), with the Choctaw Nation paying seventy-five percent (75%) and the Chickasaw

19 Nation paying twenty-five percent (25%) of such amount. The Atoka and Sardis Conservation

20 Projects Board shall authorize expenditures from the Atoka and Sardis Conservation Projects

21 Fund solely for purposes of scoping, designing, implementing, operating, and maintaining

22 projects to enhance recreational use or habitat for fish and wildlife at Atoka or Sardis Lake

23 and/or to mitigate environmental impacts at Atoka or Sardis Lake.

1   **6.5.2.1.2.2   Interest-Bearing Account; Administration by Oklahoma**

2   **City Water Utilities Trust** – Subject to a fiduciary obligation owed to each of the Parties

3   represented on the Atoka and Sardis Conservation Projects Board, the Trust shall deposit the

4   monies specified in Section 6.5.2.1.2.1 into a restricted interest-bearing account in accord with

5   the procedures and contracts applicable to other similarly held Trust funds, with five million

6   ($5,000,000) allocated to Atoka Lake conservation projects and five million ($5,000,000)

7   allocated to Sardis Lake conservation projects, and it shall cause allocation of any interest earned

8   on principal to be made in proportion to the balance of unexpended monies allocated to projects

9   for the two lakes. The Trust will be responsible to each of the Parties represented on the Atoka

10 and Sardis Conservation Projects Board for the proper administration, accounting, and

11 expenditure of all monies in this account. The Trust will provide to the Atoka and Sardis

12 Conservation Projects Board a quarterly report of all claims, receipts, and expenditures from this

13 account.

14   **6.5.2.1.2.3   Grants and Donations** – Subject to the same conditions that

15 otherwise apply pursuant to Section 6.5.2.1, the Trust may accept grants and donations of monies

16 for deposit in the fund described in Section 6.5.2.1.2.2 and may, further, accept donations of

17 goods or services for the benefit of any project authorized by the Atoka and Sardis Conservation

18 Projects Board. Any such grant or donation will be in addition to the contributions specified in

19 Section 6.5.2.1.2.1 and not in lieu thereof.

20   **6.5.2.1.2.4   Withdrawal, Expenditure, and Obligation of Account** – The

21 Oklahoma City Water Utilities Trust may make no withdrawal or expenditure from or otherwise

22 obligate any monies in the account described in Section 6.5.2.1.2.2 unless and until directed to

23 do so by a resolution of the Atoka and Sardis Conservation Projects Board that has been

1 approved by consensus of its members, and the Atoka and Sardis Conservation Projects Board

2 shall authorize expenditures from the Atoka and Sardis Conservation Projects Fund solely for

3 purposes of scoping, designing, implementing, operating, and maintaining projects to enhance

4 recreational use or habitat for fish and wildlife at Atoka or Sardis Lake and/or to mitigate

5 environmental impacts at Atoka or Sardis Lake.

6   **6.5.2.2**   **Duties** – The Atoka and Sardis Conservation Projects Board's duties

7 shall be as follows:

8   **6.5.2.2.1**   **Identification and Analysis of Need** – direct and supervise the

9 identification and analysis of conservation needs and projects appropriate to the purposes

10 described in Section 6.5.2.1.2.4;

11   **6.5.2.2.2**   **Project Directions** – direct the scoping, design, and

12 implementation of projects appropriate to the purposes described in Section 6.5.2.1.2.4; and

13   **6.5.2.2.3**   **Internal Procedures** – to establish such procedures as are

14 necessary for purposes of the Atoka and Sardis Conservation Project Board's operation and

15 performance of the duties set forth in Section 6.5.2.

16   **6.5.2.3**   **Public Comment** – When developing project designs or

17 implementation, operation, and maintenance plans, the Atoka and Sardis Conservation Projects

18 Board will:

19   **6.5.2.3.1**   early in its project or plan development process, hold a public

20 meeting in Atoka or Pushmataha County for purposes of presenting proposed project or plan

21 goals and soliciting public input thereon;

1   **6.5.2.3.2**   prior to finalizing any proposed design or plan, publish details of

2 developed proposals online for a period not less than forty-five (45) days and thereafter receive

3 and consider public comments submitted during that period; and

4   **6.5.2.3.3**   not sooner than forty-five (45) days after the close of the comment

5 period, finalize and publish details of finalized designs and plans online.

6   **6.5.2.4**   **Project Administration** – Subject to availability of funds in the account

7 described in Section 6.5.2.1.2.2 and the Atoka and Sardis Conservation Projects Board's

8 beneficial interest therein, the Oklahoma City Water Utilities Trust shall administer all projects

9 (including project operation, maintenance, and repair throughout the useful life of the project)

10 that the Atoka and Sardis Conservation Projects Board authorizes and approves, entering into

11 such contracts as are necessary and appropriate for such purposes. The Atoka and Sardis

12 Conservation Projects Board's authorization and approval of projects shall be in the same

13 manner and subject to the same restrictions specified in Section 6.5.2.1.2.4. The Oklahoma City

14 Water Utilities Trust will provide to the Atoka and Sardis Conservation Projects Board a

15 quarterly report of all project work, including incurred and anticipated costs.

16   **6.5.3**   **Scope of Sardis Lake Release Restrictions** – The effect of the Sardis Lake

17 Release Restrictions imposed on the City Permit by Section 6.1.8 is to limit to an estimated

18 one hundred thousand sixteen six hundred sixteen (116,616) AF the amount of Conservation

19 Storage Capacity the City may store water in and release water from for purposes of diverting

20 up to one hundred fifteen thousand (115,000) AFY at the Point of Diversion. The Sardis Lake

21 Release Restrictions shall not apply to the use of the estimated thirty-seven thousand nine

22 hundred eight (37,908) AF of Conservation Storage Capacity reserved for purposes of the

23 twenty thousand (20,000) AFY set aside by OAC § 785:20-5-5(b)(3). The estimated

1 remaining one hundred forty-two thousand six hundred seventy-six (142,676) AF of

2 Conservation Storage Capacity shall be limited to maintenance of lake levels in support of

3 recreation, fish and wildlife benefits, and no yield from Sardis Lake in excess of the City's

4 one hundred fifteen thousand (115,000) AFY and the twenty thousand (20,000) AFY set aside

5 by OAC § 785:20-5-5(b)(3) will be available for contract or appropriation by any person.

6 Table 2: Effect and Scope of Sardis Lake Release Restrictions on Conservation Storage Capacity

Storage	Estimated Conservation Storage Capacity (AF)	Conservation Storage Capacity (Percent of Total)	Subject to Sardis Release Restrictions
Lake Level Maintenance (Recreation, Fish and Wildlife)	142,676	48%	n/a
Administrative Set-Aside	37,908	13%	No
City Use	116,616	39%	Yes
Total	297,200	100%	n/a

7

8 **6.5.4   Infrastructure Corridor** – The City shall reserve capacity in the Parallel City

9 Pipeline for use by the Chickasaw Nation or its assignee. The reserve capacity shall be

10 sufficient to convey five thousand (5,000) AFY with an average demand of six (6) mgd and a

11 maximum future peak demand of twelve (12) mgd. Water conveyed through such reserve

12 capacity shall be supported by a water use permit obtained from the OWRB pursuant to state

13 law. The Chickasaw Nation or its assignee may negotiate and contract with the City on

14 appropriate and reasonable terms for the use of such reserve capacity, but the City shall not

15 require the payment of anything more than capital repayment and the operation, maintenance,

16 and replacement costs in proportion to actual use of such reserve capacity under such contract.

17 Nothing herein precludes the City from agreeing to negotiate and contract for the use of

18 additional amounts of water transmission infrastructure capacity.

1 **6.5.5   Right-of-Way** –

2 **6.5.5.1   In General** –The Chickasaw Nation agrees to convey an easement to the

3 City, which easement shall be as described and depicted in Exhibit 15.

4 **6.5.5.2   Application** - The Chickasaw Nation and the City shall cooperate and

5 coordinate on the submission of an application for approval by the Secretary of the Interior of

6 the conveyance under Section 6.5.5.1 and clause (h)(3)(B)(i) of the Settlement Act, in

7 accordance with applicable federal law.

8 **6.5.5.3   Recording** - On approval by the Secretary of the Interior of the

9 conveyance of the easement under 6.5.5.1 and clause (h)(3)(B)(i) of the Settlement Act, the

10 City shall record the easement.

11 **6.5.5.4   Consideration** - In exchange for conveyance of the easement under

12 Section 6.5.5.1 and clause (h)(3)(B)(i) of the Settlement Act, the City shall pay to the

13 Chickasaw Nation the value of past unauthorized use and consideration for future use of the

14 land burdened by the easement, based on an appraisal secured by the City and Nations and

15 approved by the Secretary of the Interior.

16 **6.5.6   Unused Permit or Storage Rights** – For purposes of ensuring reasonable

17 availability to Settlement Area users of water under the City Permit or storage from City

18 Sardis Storage, and exclusive of the storage rights available to users in southeastern

19 Oklahoma pursuant to the Administrative Set-Aside, the Parties agree as follows:

20 **6.5.6.1**   The City may subcontract its rights to City Sardis Storage, but any

21 subcontracted right, inclusive of direct diversions from Sardis Lake, shall be subject to the Sardis

22 Lake Release Restrictions of Section 6.1.8.

6.5.6.2 In the event that: (i) prior to the later of 2043 or the date that is tolled and extended as provided in Section 6.3, the City has not yet constructed the Parallel City Pipeline or has not yet diverted water under the City Permit in an amount equal to what the schedule of use specifies for 2040, *see* Exhibit 14; or (ii) the City's Permit has been surrendered pursuant to Section 6.3, the City shall not, subject to Section 6.5.6.4, unreasonably deny water users within the Settlement Area access to unexercised City Sardis Storage, pursuant to short-term contracts of no more than ten (10) years. The City shall charge for such access to City Sardis Storage no more than a *pro rata* reimbursement of its own storage contract costs.

6.5.6.3 In the event the City has timely constructed the Parallel City Pipeline and diverted water under the City Permit in an amount equal to what the schedule of use specifies for 2040, *see* Exhibit 14, then the City shall not, subject to Section 6.5.6.4, unreasonably deny water users within the Settlement Area access to the City's unexercised City Sardis Storage and/or the City's unexercised right to use water under the City Permit, if any, pursuant to short-term contracts of no more than ten (10) years. The City shall charge for such access and/or use, including any implicated City infrastructure, no more than a *pro rata* share of costs associated with the acquisition, impoundment, transportation, and storage, which amounts shall be calculated in accord with the cost of service and rate design principles published by the American Water Works Association and Water Research Foundation or comparable successor entity.

6.5.6.4 The City may require short-term contracts entered pursuant to Sections 6.5.6.2 or 6.5.6.3 to specify how the water user will avoid long-term reliance on City Sardis Storage and/or the City Permit.

6.5.6.5 Any person or entity that enters a short-term contract with the City pursuant to Section 6.5.6.2 for the use of City Sardis Storage must obtain a water use permit from the OWRB prior to the commencement of any use of water in conjunction with such storage.

6.5.6.6 Any person or entity that enters a short-term contract with the City pursuant to Sections 6.5.6.3 for the use of water under the City Permit must obtain a water use permit from the OWRB prior to the commencement of such use if such use would involve a purpose of use, place of use, or point of diversion not authorized by the City Permit.

6.5.7 Future Technical Discussions – In order to equitably preserve the mutual benefits of Section 6.1 or otherwise pursuant to Section 6.1.8.2.4, the Nations, City, and OWRB may negotiate technical mechanisms to:

6.5.7.1 allow for flexibility in the measurement, accounting, and timing of water stored or available for storage in the City Reservoirs under Sections 1.5, 1.33, and 1.43; and

6.5.7.2 take into account potential benefits to the City and Nations from use of reclaimed water by the City and/or adjustments to water quality mixing zones in the City Reservoirs due to increased sedimentation.

7. NATIONS USE OF WATER – Beginning on the Enforceability Date, the Nations shall have the right to use and to develop the right to use Settlement Area Waters only in accordance with this Settlement Agreement and the Settlement Act.

7.1 In General – Nothing herein precludes either Nation from obtaining a permit to use water pursuant to and in accord with state law, and neither Nation shall have any less right under the Settlement Agreement and the Settlement Act than what any person has pursuant to state law

1 with respect to the use of water without a permit, including the drilling and use of wells for

2 domestic purposes.

3   **7.2   Existing Uses by Permit** – The Nations shall possess and may exercise all existing

4 uses by permit identified in this Section 7.2, which uses shall be in accord with state law and the

5 identified permits. Administration and enforcement of these identified permitted uses shall be in

6 accord with state law.

7   **7.2.1   Chickasaw Nation** – The Chickasaw Nation's existing uses by permit are

8 identified in Table 3.

9

Table 3: Chickasaw Nation – Existing Water Use by Permit

Permit No.	Property	Location	Land Status	County	Amount (AFY)	No. of Wells	Depth	Source	Purpose of Use
2005-554	WinStar (CTUA)	Use Location: Public water supply system Well Locations: Three in SW NW NW of Sec. 29, T9S, R2EI	Trust	Love	680.4	3	750	Antlers	Public supply
2005-553	WinStar (CTUA)	Use Location: Public water supply system Well Locations: Two in NW NE SE of Sec. 19, T9S, R2EI, and one in SW NE SE of Sec. 19, T9S, R2EI	Trust	Love	464.1	3	750	Antlers	Public supply
2005-520	WinStar (golf course)	Use Location: N NW SW of Sec. 29, T9S, R2EI and EE of Sec. 30, T9S, R2EI Well Locations: Two in the NW SW NW, one in the SW SW NW, and one in the SE SW NW of Sec. 29, T9S, R2EI	Non-Trust	Love	440.0	4	50	Alluvium and terrace deposits of the Red River	Irrigation
1989-544	Chickasaw Nation Medical Center (G.O. Philpot, prior owner)	Use and Well Locations: One in the NW NW SW and one in the SW SE NW	Trust	Pontotoc	509.0	2	Unknown	Boggy Formation, Wewoka Formation, Holdenville	Agriculture

Permit No.	Property	Location	Land Status	County	Amount (AFY)	No. of Wells	Depth	Source	Purpose of Use
		of Sec. 14, T3N, R6EI						Shale, Delaware Shale	
1984-623	Chickasaw Children's Village and Texoma Gaming Center (W.E. Culbertson, prior owner)	Use and Well Locations: One in the SE NE SW of Sec. 28, T6S, R6EI, one in the SW SW NW and one in the SE SW SW of Sec. 27, T6S, R6EI	Trust	Marshall	1176.0	3	One at 628', one at 168', and one unknown	Antlers	Public supply

1

2   **7.2.2   Choctaw Nation** – The Choctaw Nation's existing uses by permit are identified

3 in Table 4.

4

Table 4: Choctaw Nation – Existing Water Use by Permit

Permit No.	Property	Location	Land Status	County	Amount (AFY)	No. of Wells	Depth	Source	Purpose of Use
1999-21	Silverado Golf Course	Diversion Location: SE NW NW, Sec. 3, T6S, R9EI Use Location: Sec.4, T6S, R9EI	Non-Trust	Bryan	250.0	n/a	n/a	Blue River	Irrigation
1952-450	Tom Ranch	Well and Use Locations: SW, Sec. 9, T10S, R26EI	Non-Trust	McCurtain	158.0	1	Unknown	Alluvium and terrace deposits of the Red River	Irrigation

5

6   **7.3   Changes to Existing Uses by Permit** – Any changes to an existing use by permit

7 shall be made pursuant to state law.

8   **7.4   Existing Uses Without Permit** – Each Nation shall have the right to the uses of

9 water without permit for so long as such uses are limited to the amounts, well location, places of

10 use, and purposes of use identified in Sections 7.4.1 or 7.4.2, respectively, or otherwise in accord

11 with Section 7.

7.4.1 **Chickasaw Nation** – The Chickasaw Nation's existing uses without permit are identified in Table 5.

Table 5: Chickasaw Nation – Existing Uses Without Permit

Use No. (Well Id.)	Property	Location	Land Status	County	Amount (AFY)	No. of Wells	Depth	Source	Purpose of Use
CN-1[1] (77354, 77898, 84381, and 122089)	WinStar (CTUA)	Use Location: Public Water Supply system / Well locations: E SE SW of Sec. 19, T9S, R2EI	Trust	Love	750.0	4	Three at 750' and one at 690'	Antlers	Public supply
CN-2[2] (n/a)	WinStar (golf course)	Use Location: N NW SW of Sec. 29, T9S, R2EI and E E of Sec. 30, T9S, R2EI and S S of Sec. 20, T9S, R2EI / Well Locations: W W NW of Sec. 29, T9S, R2EI	Non-Trust	Love	330.0	4	All at 50' or less	Alluvium and terrace of the Red River	Irrigation
CN-3 (non-irr. ag. 122341; others n/a)	Chickasaw Farms	Use Location: N NW of Sec. 7, T1S, R2RI and N N of Sec. 12, T1S, R2EI / Well Locations: NE SW of Sec. 6, T1S, R2EI and NE NE of Sec 12, T1S, R2EI	Non-Trust	Murray	260.0	9	One at 40' and eight unknown	Washita	One for non-irrigation agriculture and eight for irrigation
CN-4 (n/a)	Chickasaw Nation Dry Cleaning	Use and Well Location: NE of Sec. 9, T1N, R1EI	Trust	Garvin	10.0	1	Unknown	Washita	Commercial
CN-5 (n/a)	Golden Tract	Use and Well Locations: NE SW of Sec. 3, T4S, R6EI	Non-Trust	Johnston	Domestic	1	Unknown	Antlers	Domestic
CN-6 (136049)	Connerville Senior Site	Use and Well Location: SW SW NW of Sec. 25, T1S, R6EI	Trust	Johnston	Domestic	1	260'	Arbuckle-Simpson	Domestic
CN-7 (n/a)	Johnston White House	Use and Well Location: NW SW; S SW NW of Sec. 14, T4S, R7EI	Trust	Johnston	Domestic	1	Unknown	Antlers	Domestic
CN-8 (n/a)	Burney Institute	Use and Well Location: NE SW NE of Sec. 4, T7S, R4EI	Trust	Marshall	Domestic	1	Unknown	Antlers	Domestic
CN-9 (103638 and 103650)	Artesian Hotel	Use and Well Locations: SE SE SE of Sec. 34, T1N, R3EI	Trust	Murray	Domestic	2	One at 850' and one at 595'	Arbuckle-Simpson	Domestic
CN-10 (n/a)	Chigley Mansion	Use and Well Locations: S SE SW of Sec. 32, T1N, R2EI	Trust	Murray	Domestic	2	Unknown	Washita	Domestic
CN-11 (13541)	Chickasaw Farms	Use and Well Location: SW NE NE of Sec. 1, T1S, R1EI	Non-Trust	Murray	Domestic	1	215'	Washita	Domestic
CN-12	Red Springs Cemetery	Use and Well Location: NE SE SE of Sec. 17, T3N, R8EI	Trust	Pontotoc	Domestic	1	47.5'	Unidentified	Domestic

[1] To the extent the uses of CN-1 are redundant of uses pursuant to OWRB Permits Nos. 2005-554 or 2005-553, the permits will govern.

[2] To the extent the uses of CN-2 are redundant of uses pursuant to OWRB Permit No. 2005-520, the permit will govern.

7.4.2 **Choctaw Nation** – The Choctaw Nation's existing uses without permit are identified in Table 6.

Table 6: Choctaw Nation – Existing Water Uses Without Permit

Use No. (Well Id.)	Property	Location	Land Status	County	Amount (AFY)	No. of Wells	Depth	Source	Purpose of Use
CNO-1	Lickskillet Ranch (named Idabel Ranch as of 2020)	Well Locations: One, in the NW SW of Sec. 21, one in the NE SE of Sec. 29; one in the SW SW of Sec. 29, one in the NE NE of Sec. 29, one in the NW NE of Sec. 30, and one in the E1/2 NW SE and W1/2 NE SE of Sec. 19, all in T8S, R23EI. Use Locations: Secs. 19-21, 28 to 32 of T8S, R23EI; and Secs. 24 and 25 of T8S, R22EI	Non-Trust	McCurtain	300.0	6	All at 400'	Woodbine bedrock	Irrigation, stock

Use No. (Well Id.)	Property	Location	Land Status	County	Amount (AFY)	No. of Wells	Depth	Source	Purpose of Use
CNO-2 (32877)	4 Star Ranch (named Tuskahoma Ranch East as of 2020)	Well Locations: In T2N, R20EI, one in the SW-SW of Sec. 7, and one in the SW- NW of Sec. 18. Use Location: Sec. 7, 17, and 18 of T2N, R20EI; and Sec. 13 of T2N R19EI.	Non-Trust	Pushmataha	15.0	2	125'	Kiamichi bedrock	Irrigation, stock
CNO-3	Sawyer Ranch	Well Locations: One in the NE SW of Sec. 31, T6S, R19EI. In T7S, R19EI, one in the NE NW of Sec.7 and one in the SE NW of Sec. 6. Use locations: Secs. 5 and 6 of T7S, R19EI, and Sec. 31 of, T6S, R19EI.	Non-Trust	McCurtain	150.0	3	All at 275'	Woodbine bedrock	Irrigation, stock
CNO-4[3]	Tom Ranch	Well Location: NW SE of Section 8 in T10S, R26EI. Use Locations: Secs. 3, 5, 6, 8-10, 15, and 16, T10S, R26EI; Sec. 15 of T10S, R25EI	Non-Trust	McCurtain	250.0	1	Unknown	Woodbine bedrock	Irrigation, stock
CNO-5	Grant Tract (named Harris Ranch as of 2020)	Well Location: The NE SE of Sec. 3 in T10S, R25EI. Use Locations: Secs. 3 and 10 of T10S R25EI.	Non-Trust	McCurtain	25.0	1	Unknown	Woodbine bedrock	Irrigation, stock

1

---

[3] To the extent the uses of CN0-4 are redundant of uses pursuant to OWRB Permit No. 1952-450, the permit will govern.

7.5   **Changes to Existing Uses Without Permit**

    7.5.1   Non-Trust Land – Any change in the amount of water, well location, place of use, or purpose of use for any right to use water that is recognized under Section 7.4 as located on Non-Trust Land shall be applied for, evaluated, and processed pursuant to state law and shall thereafter be administered and enforced in accord with state law.

    7.5.2   Trust Land – With respect to any right to use water recognized under Section 7.4 which is located on Trust Land, either Nation may change the well location, place of use, or purpose of use of such right so long as the new well location and/or new place of use is also located on Trust Land and over the same source aquifer. No less than sixty (60) days prior to making such change, the Nation taking such action will provide the OWRB with written notice that identifies the use number and location of the subject right, a legal description of the new well location and/or new place of use, and/or a description of the new purpose of use, as applicable. Any change of a right recognized under Section 7.4 from Trust Lands to Non-Trust Lands must be applied for, evaluated, and processed pursuant to state law and shall thereafter be administered and enforced in accord with state law. Any increase in the amount of water used on Trust Land beyond what is recognized under Section 7.4 shall be made in accord with Section 7.6.2.

7.6   **Future Development of Groundwater Use**

    7.6.1   Non-Trust Land – Any additional taking of groundwater underlying Non-Trust Land by either Nation, other than what is identified in Sections 7.2 or 7.4 or otherwise provided for in Section 7.1, must be applied for, evaluated, and processed pursuant to state law and shall thereafter be administered and enforced in accord with state law.

7.6.2   Trust Land Non-Domestic Use Wells – Subject to Section 7.6 and in accord with the Settlement Agreement and the Settlement Act, the Nations have the right to take and use groundwater underlying any Trust Lands within the Settlement Area in an amount not to exceed the equal proportionate share established pursuant to state law for the underlying source aquifer; *provided*, that acreage dedicated to a use of groundwater under Section 7.6 shall not be used for purposes of any state law permit or existing use recognized pursuant to Section 7 to take and use groundwater from the same source aquifer. The Nation proposing to take and use groundwater shall:

7.6.2.1   Employ a state-licensed water well driller and require such driller to comply with state well drilling and construction rules, including the filing of a completion report with the OWRB;

7.6.2.2   Locate the well(s) in accord with state well spacing requirements and/or spring or stream setbacks;

7.6.2.3   Provide the following information to the OWRB at least sixty (60) days prior to commencing any drilling for such purpose: (i) the well location; (ii) the acreage overlying the source aquifer that is dedicated to such use; (iii) the amounts annually to be withdrawn from such well(s); (iv) the location at which such water is to be placed in use; and (v) the use to which the withdrawn water is to be placed.

7.6.3   Trust Land Domestic Wells – Subject to Section 7.6 and in accord with the Settlement Agreement and the Settlement Act, the Nations shall have no less right to take groundwater from Trust Land for domestic use than what any person has pursuant to state law. In drilling any such well, the Nations will employ a state-licensed water well driller,

require such driller to comply with state well drilling and construction rules, and within thirty (30) days of drilling such well, cause a well completion report to be filed with the OWRB.

7.7   Future Development of Surface Water Uses

7.7.1   Non-Trust Land – Any appropriation of surface water from a point of diversion on Non-Trust Land by either Nation must be applied for, evaluated, and processed pursuant to state law and shall thereafter be administered and enforced in accord with state law.

7.7.2   Trust Land – Subject to Section 7.7 and in accord with the Settlement Agreement and the Settlement Act, each Nation has the right to appropriate surface water within the Settlement Area for use on Trust Lands, which lands would constitute riparian land under state law. The maximum amount of water which either Nation may appropriate for use on riparian Trust Lands under Section 7.7 in any individual Settlement Area Hydrologic Basin shall be five hundred (500) AFY.

7.7.3   In the event either Nation intends to develop surface water on Trust Lands pursuant to Section 7.7, that Nation shall provide notice to the OWRB of the intent to appropriate water. The notice shall be in writing and specify: (i) the location and acreage of the riparian Trust Lands where the water will be used; (ii) the amount of water subject to the appropriation; (iii) the basin and stream from which the water would be appropriated; (iv) the use to which the water will be placed; and (v) the point of diversion.

7.7.4   Following notice to the OWRB and in advance of any appropriation, the Nation intending to appropriate the water and the OWRB shall meet and, using the model then available for the source basin, evaluate whether: (i) water is available at the point of diversion based on an evaluation of Mean Available Flow and, to the extent applicable, any water

quality, ecological, and recreational needs evaluated in a manner consistent with OAC §
785:20-5-5(e); and (ii) the intended use would interfere with existing beneficial uses of water.

     7.7.4.1   If following the evaluation the OWRB and the Nations agree that water is available for the appropriation from the stream, the Nation may proceed with the appropriation as noticed or as modified by agreement as between the Nation and OWRB. The priority date for the water developed under Section 7.7 shall be the date of the notice of intent to appropriate. The Nation shall provide notice to the OWRB when the works related to the appropriation are complete and when beneficial use of the water has commenced. In the event the Nation does not develop the works or place any water to beneficial use within seven (7) years of a notice of intent to appropriate provided pursuant to Section 7.7.3, any unused water shall revert to the public and the Nation's right to develop the water pursuant to the notice shall terminate, subject to the right to refile a notice of intent to appropriate. The Nation's appropriation and use of water shall remain subject to the OWRB's right to file an action pursuant to Section 3 to enforce the prohibition against waste or interference in Section 7.8.2 and to administer the right in priority, if necessary.

     7.7.4.2   If the Nation and OWRB agree that water is not available for the appropriation from the stream, the Nation shall not proceed with the noticed appropriation.

     7.7.4.3   If the Nation and OWRB disagree as to water availability, the Nation may proceed with its noticed appropriation subject to the OWRB's right to file an action pursuant to Section 3 to seek a determination of availability and/or enforce the prohibition against waste or interference in Section 7.8.2.

     7.7.5   A Nation making an appropriation pursuant to Section 7.7 may make changes to the place and purpose or point of diversion of the appropriation, but only within the tract of

riparian Trust Land for which the appropriation was originally made and only after written notice to the OWRB at least sixty (60) days prior to such changes. No appropriation made under Section 7.7 may be transferred for purposes of use on another parcel of land without a permit from the OWRB. No increase in the amount of water appropriated shall occur without first satisfying the requirements of Sections 7.7.3 and 7.7.4.

     7.7.6 Choctaw Nation Development of Impoundment – In addition to the Choctaw Nation's right to appropriate surface water pursuant to Sections 7.7.1 and 7.7.2, the Choctaw Nation may develop an impoundment consistent with the Oklahoma Scenic Rivers Act, 82 O.S. § 896.1, *et seq.* This single impoundment may be located on lands within the Settlement Area and held or controlled by the Choctaw Nation within one of the following Settlement Area Hydrologic Basins: Muddy Boggy, Lower Canadian, Lower Arkansas, Poteau, Kiamichi, Upper Little, or Mountain Fork. The Choctaw Impoundment shall be subject to the following limitations:

     7.7.6.1   The Choctaw Impoundment shall not exceed one hundred fifty (150) acres in surface extent nor impound more than one thousand five hundred (1,500) AF.

     7.7.6.2   Subject to a water availability determination made consistent with Section 7.7.4, the right to develop the impoundment shall include an initial right to divert up to one thousand five hundred (1,500) AF to fill the impoundment and the right thereafter to offset the evaporative losses in an amount not to exceed five hundred (500) AFY.

     7.7.6.3   If the Choctaw Nation chooses to develop the Choctaw Impoundment, it shall provide notice to the OWRB one hundred eighty (180) days prior to commencing construction of the impoundment, which notice shall include plan and design specifications prepared by a registered engineer relating to the design, performance, and safety standards of the

1 dam, which shall, at a minimum, conform to the design, performance and safety standards of

2 OAC § 785 Chapter 25, or updates thereto.

3 **7.8 General Conditions**

4   **7.8.1 Annual Reporting** – Each Nation shall, by March 15 of each year, provide a

5 report to the OWRB indicating the amount of groundwater taken or surface water

6 appropriated and placed to beneficial use in the preceding calendar year, the well location or

7 point of diversion, the purpose of use, and the acreage on which the use occurred.

8   **7.8.2 Prohibition Against Waste and Interference** – No right recognized and

9 provided for herein, nor any change in such the use of such right, authorizes either Nation to

10 appropriate water in a manner that would commit waste or interfere with existing water rights.

11 Determinations of waste or interference shall be based on state law.

12   **7.8.3 OWRB Verification** – Upon reasonable notice, the Nations shall provide the

13 OWRB with access to Non-Trust Lands, Trust Lands, and the lands on which the Choctaw

14 Impoundment is constructed for purposes of OWRB's verification of appropriations, uses, and

15 dam safety requirements for purposes of ensuring compliance with Section 7. The Nations

16 shall have the opportunity to be represented during any on-site verification.

17 **8. ALLOTTEE RIGHTS**

18   **8.1 In General** – Pursuant to the Atoka Agreement as ratified by section 29 of the Act of

19 June 28, 1898 (30 Stat. 505, chapter 517) (as modified by the Act of July 1, 1902 (32 Stat. 641,

20 chapter 1362)), the Nations issued patents to their respective tribal members and citizens and

21 thereby conveyed to individual Choctaws and Chickasaws all right, title, and interest in and to

22 land that was possessed by the Nations, other than certain mineral rights.

1   **8.1.1 No Regulatory Authority** – When title passed from the Nations to their

2 respective tribal members and citizens, the Nations did not convey and those individuals did

3 not receive any right of regulatory or sovereign authority, including with respect to water.

4   **8.1.2 Waiver and Delegation by Nations** – In addition to the waivers under

5 subsection (h) of the Settlement Act and Sections 2.1.1.3 and 2.1.1.4, the Nations, on their

6 own behalf, permanently delegate to the State any regulatory authority each Nation may

7 possess over water rights on Allotments, which the State shall exercise in accordance with this

8 Section 8 and subsection (e) of the Settlement Act.

9   **8.2 Allottee Rights to Use of Water on an Allotment** – An Allottee may use water on

10 an Allotment in accordance with Section 8 and subsection (e) of the Settlement Act.

11   **8.2.1 Surface Water Use** –

12   **8.2.1.1 In General** – An Allottee may divert and use, on the Allotment of the

13 Allottee, six (6) AFY of surface water per one hundred sixty (160) acres, to be used solely for

14 domestic uses on an Allotment that constitutes riparian land under applicable state law as of the

15 Enactment Date.

16   **8.2.1.2 Effect of State Law** – The use of surface water described in this Section

17 8.2.1 and clause (e)(5)(B)(i) of the Settlement Act shall be subject to all rights and protections

18 of state law, as of the Enactment Date, including all protections against loss for non-use.

19   **8.2.1.3 No Permit Required** – An Allottee may divert water under this Section

20 8.2.1 and paragraph (e)(5) of the Settlement Act without a permit or any other authorization

21 from the OWRB.

8.2.2 Groundwater Use –

8.2.2.1 In General – An Allottee may drill wells on the Allotment of the Allottee to take and use for domestic uses the greater of—

8.2.2.1.1 five (5) AFY; or

8.2.2.1.2 any greater quantity allowed under state law.

8.2.2.2 Effect of State Law – The groundwater use described in this Section 8.2.2 and clause (e)(5)(C)(i) of the Settlement Act shall be subject to all rights and protections of state law, as of the Enactment Date, including all protections against loss for non-use.

8.2.2.3 No Permit Required – An Allottee may drill wells and use water under this Section 8.2.2 and subparagraph (e)(5)(C) of the Settlement Act without a permit or any other authorization from the OWRB.

8.2.3 Future Changes in State Law –

8.2.3.1 In General – If state law changes to limit use of water to a quantity that is less than the applicable quantity specified in Section 8.2.1 or 8.2.2 and subparagraph (e)(5)(B) or (e)(5)(C) of the Settlement Act, as applicable, an Allottee shall retain the right to use water in accord with those Sections and subparagraphs, subject to Section 8.4.4 and clause (e)(6)(B)(iv) and paragraph (e)(7) of the Settlement Act.

8.2.3.2 Opportunity to be heard – Prior to taking any action to limit the use of water by an individual, the OWRB shall provide to the individual an opportunity to demonstrate that the individual is:

8.2.3.2.1 an Allottee; and

8.2.3.2.2 using water on the Allotment pursuant to and in accordance with the Settlement Agreement and the Settlement Act.

8.3 Allottee Options for Additional Water –

8.3.1 In General – To use a quantity of water in excess of the quantities provided under Section 8.2 and paragraph (e)(5) of the Settlement Act, an Allottee shall—

8.3.1.1 file an action under Section 8.4 and subparagraph (e)(6)(B) of the Settlement Act; or

8.3.1.2 apply to the OWRB for a permit pursuant to, and in accordance with, state law.

8.4 Determination in Federal District Court

8.4.1.1 In General – In lieu of applying to OWRB for a permit to use more water than is allowed under Section 8.2 and paragraph (e)(5) of the Settlement Act, an Allottee may file an action in the United States District Court for the Western District of Oklahoma for determination of the right to water of the Allottee. At least ninety (90) days prior to filing such an action, the Allottee shall provide written notice of the suit to the United States and the OWRB. For the United States, notice shall be provided to the Solicitor's Office, Department of the Interior, Washington, D.C., and to the Office of the Regional Director of the Muskogee Region, Bureau of Indian Affairs, Department of the Interior.

8.4.2 Jurisdiction – For purposes of this Section 8.4 and subparagraph (e)(6)(B) of the Settlement Act:

8.4.2.1 the United States District Court for the Western District of Oklahoma shall have jurisdiction; and

8.4.2.2 as part of the complaint, the Allottee shall include certification of the pre-filing notice to the United States and OWRB required by Section 8.4.1.1 and clause (e)(6)(B)(i) of the Settlement Act. If such certification is not included with the complaint, the

1 complaint will be deemed filed ninety (90) days after such certification is complete and filed

2 with the court. Within sixty (60) days after the complaint is filed or deemed filed or within

3 such extended time as the District Court in its discretion may permit, the United States may

4 appear or intervene. After such appearance, intervention or the expiration of the said sixty (60)

5 days or any extension thereof, the proceedings and judgment in such action shall bind the

6 United States and the parties thereto without regard to whether the United States elects to

7 appear or intervene in such action.

8 **8.4.3 Requirements** – An Allottee filing an action pursuant to this Section and

9 subparagraph (e)(6)(B) of the Settlement Act shall:

10 **8.4.3.1** join the OWRB as a party; and

11 **8.4.3.2** publish notice in a newspaper of general circulation within the

12 Settlement Area Hydrologic Basin in which the Allotment is located for two (2) consecutive

13 weeks, with the first publication appearing not later than thirty (30) days after the date on

14 which the action is filed.

15 **8.4.4 Determination Final** –

16 **8.4.4.1 In General** – Subject to Section 8.4.2.4.2 and subclause (e)(6)(B)(ii)(II)

17 of the Settlement Act, if an Allottee elects to have the rights of the Allottee determined

18 pursuant to Section 8.4 and subparagraph (e)(6)(B) of the Settlement Act, the determination

19 shall be final as to any rights under federal law and in lieu of any rights to use water on an

20 Allotment as provided in Section 8.2 and paragraph (e)(5) of the Settlement Act.

21 **8.4.4.2 Reservation of Rights** – Section 8.4.4 and subclause (e)(6)(B)(iv)(I) of

22 the Settlement Act shall not preclude an Allottee from:

23 **8.4.4.2.1** applying to the OWRB for water rights pursuant to state law; or

1 **8.4.4.2.2** using any rights allowed by state law that do not require a permit

2 from the OWRB.

3 **8.5 OWRB Administration and Enforcement** –

4 **8.5.1 In General** – If an Allottee exercises any right under Section 8.2 and

5 paragraph (e)(5) of the Settlement Act or has rights determined under Section 8.4 and

6 subparagraph (e)(6)(B) of the Settlement Act, the OWRB shall have jurisdiction to administer

7 those rights.

8 **8.5.2 Challenges** – An Allottee may challenge OWRB administration of rights

9 determined under Section 8.4 and subparagraph (e)(6)(B) of the Settlement Act in the United

10 States District Court for the Western District of Oklahoma.

11 **8.6 Prior Existing State-Law Rights** – Water rights held by an Allottee as of the

12 Enforceability Date pursuant to a permit issued by the OWRB shall be governed by the terms of

13 that permit and applicable state law (including regulations).

14 **9. WATER PLANNING IN SETTLEMENT AREA**

15 **9.1 In General**

16 **9.1.1 Oklahoma Comprehensive Water Plan** – In addition to the OWRB's other

17 regulatory and administrative responsibilities under state law, 82 O.S. § 1086.2 authorizes,

18 empowers, and directs the OWRB to serve as the State's lead water planning agency, to

19 conduct technical studies in support of ongoing water planning work, and to prepare and

20 publish an update to the Oklahoma Comprehensive Water Plan each decade.

21 **9.1.2 Common Interest** – The State and Nations have a common interest in the

22 long-term sustainability of Settlement Area Waters and supporting water planning with sound

23 science, best available information, and stakeholder input. The State and Nations recognize

the value inherent in communicating and coordinating on technical studies and other planning efforts related to Settlement Area Waters. Nothing in Section 9 creates any enforcement right under Section 3.

9.2   Communication and Coordination

9.2.1   Annual Planning Meeting – For purposes of supporting the effective coordination of planning efforts relating to the management, protection, conservation, development, and utilization of Settlement Area Waters, OWRB staff and representatives of the Nations will meet annually for:

9.2.1.1   Presentations regarding work the State and each Nation has conducted the prior year relating to technical studies and other water planning efforts within the Settlement Area and discussions of ongoing efforts to update the Oklahoma Comprehensive Water Plan;

9.2.1.2   Presentations regarding work plans and goals the State and each Nation has for the coming year or years relating to technical studies and other water planning efforts within the Settlement Area, including any anticipated federal funding sources for such efforts;

9.2.1.3   Discussion of opportunities for coordination in the interests of efficiency and effectiveness in: (i) water planning efforts and (ii) the application for and use of federal funding; and

9.2.1.4   Designation of appropriate staff-level lines of communication for the coming year.

9.2.2   Notification – To facilitate effective communication, coordination, and efficient use of resources between annual planning meetings, the Nations will provide timely notice to the OWRB of any additional plans to undertake specific studies, other planning efforts, or federal funding applications, and OWRB staff and representatives of the Nations may meet to discuss potential coordination of efforts in accord with the prior annual planning meeting.

10.   GENERAL COMMITMENTS

10.1   The State, the Nations, and the City shall take any and all actions necessary to support all terms and conditions of the Settlement Agreement, take all necessary actions to satisfy all conditions precedent to the enforceability of the Settlement Agreement, and undertake all actions necessary to fulfill all obligations set forth herein, whether those obligations arise prior to or after the Enforceability Date. Such support and actions include but are not limited to the following:

10.1.1 Nations' non-objection consistent with Section 2.6 to the conditions relating to the City's Amended Permit as set forth in Section 6; and

10.1.2 OWRB staff support for the conditions relating to the City's Amended Permit as set forth in Section 6.

10.1.3 To the extent the OWRB may be required to take action prior to the Enforceability Date which implicates the Settlement Agreement, the OWRB shall work with the Nations and the City to ensure that the integrity of the Settlement Agreement and the benefits it secures to the Parties are maintained and secured from the Execution Date through the Enforceability Date and thereafter.

10.2   Binding Effect – Execution of the Settlement Agreement by all Parties signifies that all provisions of the Settlement Agreement have been approved by each signatory Party, that each person signing had the lawful authority to do so on behalf of the Party designated, and that each Party is bound by all provisions of the Settlement Agreement according to its terms and the Settlement Act.

11. NOTICE

11.1   Unless otherwise specified by any Party in writing sent to all other Parties, all notice

required to be given under the Settlement Agreement shall be written and given as follows:

   11.1.1 To the State

      The Governor of the State of Oklahoma
      2300 N. Lincoln Boulevard, Room 212
      Oklahoma City, Oklahoma 73105

      The Attorney General of the State of Oklahoma
      313 NE 21st Street
      Oklahoma City, Oklahoma 73105

   11.1.2 To the Choctaw Nation

      The Chief of the Choctaw Nation of Oklahoma
      P.O. Box 1210
      Durant, Oklahoma 74702

      The General Counsel of the Choctaw Nation of Oklahoma
      P.O. Box 1210
      Durant, Oklahoma 74702

   11.1.3 To the Chickasaw Nation

      The Governor of the Chickasaw Nation
      P.O. Box 1548
      Ada, Oklahoma 74821

      The General Counsel of the Chickasaw Nation
      P.O. Box 1548
      Ada, Oklahoma 74821

   11.1.4 To the OWRB

      The Executive Director of the Oklahoma Water Resources Board
      3800 N. Classen Boulevard
      Oklahoma City, Oklahoma 73118

      The General Counsel for the Oklahoma Water Resources Board
      3800 N. Classen Boulevard
      Oklahoma City, Oklahoma 73118

   11.1.5 To the City

      The Mayor of the City of Oklahoma City
      200 N. Walker Avenue
      Oklahoma City, Oklahoma 73102

      The City Manager of the City of Oklahoma City
      200 N. Walker Avenue
      Oklahoma City, Oklahoma 73102

      The Municipal Counselor for the City of Oklahoma City
      200 N. Walker Avenue
      Oklahoma City, Oklahoma 73102

   11.1.6 To the Trust

      The General Manager of the Oklahoma City Water Utilities Trust
      420 W. Main Street, Suite 500
      Oklahoma City, Oklahoma 73102

   11.1.7 To the United States

      The Secretary of the United States Department of the Interior
      1849 C Street NW
      Washington, DC 20240

12. DISCLAIMER

12.1   **No Precedent** – The Settlement Agreement applies only to the claims and rights of

the Nations, and nothing in the Settlement Act or the Settlement Agreement shall be construed in

any way to quantify, establish, or serve as precedent regarding the land and water rights, claims,

or entitlements to water of any American Indian Tribe other than the Nations, including any

other American Indian Tribe in the State.

12.2   **Limitation** – Nothing in the Settlement Agreement or Settlement Act:

   12.2.1 affects the ability of the United States, acting as sovereign, to take actions

authorized by law, including any laws relating to health, safety, or the environment, including:

12.2.1.1 the Comprehensive Environmental Response, Compensation, and Liability Act of 1980 (42 U.S.C. § 9601 *et seq.*);

12.2.1.2 the Safe Drinking Water Act (42 U.S.C. § 300f *et seq.*);

12.2.1.3 the Federal Water Pollution Control Act (33 U.S.C. § 1251 *et seq.*); and

12.2.1.4 any regulations implementing the Acts described in Section 12.2.1 and paragraph (k)(3) of the Settlement Act;

12.2.2 affects the ability of the United States to raise defenses based on 43 U.S.C. § 666(a);

12.2.3 affects any rights, claims, or defenses the United States may have with respect to the use of water on federal lands in the Settlement Area that are not Trust Lands or Allotments; and

12.2.4 affects the authority of each respective Nation to manage and regulate the exercise, on Trust Land consistent with the Settlement Agreement and the Settlement Act, of its water rights recognized by or established pursuant to Section 7.

13. **EFFECT OF SETTLEMENT AGREEMENT** - The Settlement Agreement shall bind the United States as trustee for the Nations, the State (including the OWRB), and the Nations as to the claims and rights of the Nations in any general stream adjudication that may in the future be filed in the State of Oklahoma.

14. **EXECUTION OF AGREEMENT; COUNTERPARTS**

14.1 The Parties may execute the Settlement Agreement in several counterparts, each of which shall be deemed an original and all of which shall constitute one and the same instrument and shall not become effective unless and until counterparts have been signed by all of the Parties and delivered to the other Parties; it being understood that all Parties need not sign the same counterparts.

14.2 The exchange of copies of the Settlement Agreement and of signature pages by transmission of electronic facsimile, regardless of format, shall constitute effective execution and delivery of the Settlement Agreement as to the Parties and may be used in lieu of the original Settlement Agreement for all purposes. Signatures of the Parties transmitted by facsimile or electronic record shall be deemed to be their original signatures for all purposes.

15. SIGNATURES

UNITED STATES OF AMERICA

Date: 1/15/21

David L. Bernhardt, Secretary
United States Department of the Interior

STATE OF OKLAHOMA

Date: 12/15/20

Kevin Stitt, Governor

Date: 12/15/2020

Mike J. Hunter, Attorney General

CHICKASAW NATION

Date: December 16, 2020

Bill Anoatubby, Governor

CHOCTAW NATION OF OKLAHOMA

Date: December 22, 2020

Gary Batton, Chief

OKLAHOMA WATER RESOURCES BOARD

Date: 12/17/20

Robert L. Stallings, Jr., Chair

Attestation

Date: 12-19-2020

Bob Drake, Secretary

CITY OF OKLAHOMA CITY

Date: 12-16-2020

David Holt, Mayor

City Clerk

Reviewed for form and legality.

Assistant Municipal Counselor

OKLAHOMA CITY WATER UTILITIES TRUST

Date: 12-16-2020

James D Couch, Chairman

Secretary

130 STAT. 1796   PUBLIC LAW 114–322—DEC. 16, 2016

PUBLIC LAW 114–322—DEC. 16, 2016

WATER INFRASTRUCTURE IMPROVEMENTS
FOR THE NATION ACT

SEC. 3608. CHOCTAW NATION OF OKLAHOMA AND THE CHICKASAW NATION WATER SETTLEMENT.

(a) PURPOSES.—The purposes of this section are—

(1) to permanently resolve and settle those claims to Settlement Area Waters of the Choctaw Nation of Oklahoma and the Chickasaw Nation as set forth in the Settlement Agreement and this section, including all claims or defenses in and to Chickasaw Nation, Choctaw Nation v. Fallin et al., CIV 11–927 (W.D. Ok.), OWRB v. United States, et al. CIV 12–275 (W.D. Ok.), or any future stream adjudication;

(2) to approve, ratify, and confirm the Settlement Agreement;

(3) to authorize and direct the Secretary of the Interior to execute the Settlement Agreement and to perform all obligations of the Secretary of the Interior under the Settlement Agreement and this section;

(4) to approve, ratify, and confirm the amended storage contract among the State, the City and the Trust;

(5) to authorize and direct the Secretary to approve the amended storage contract for the Corps of Engineers to perform all obligations under the 1974 storage contract, the amended storage contract, and this section; and

(6) to authorize all actions necessary for the United States to meet its obligations under the Settlement Agreement, the amended storage contract, and this section.

(b) DEFINITIONS.—In this section:

(1) 1974 STORAGE CONTRACT.—The term "1974 storage contract" means the contract approved by the Secretary on April 9, 1974, between the Secretary and the Water Conservation Storage Commission of the State of Oklahoma pursuant to section 301 of the Water Supply Act of 1958, and other applicable Federal law.

(2) 2010 AGREEMENT.—The term "2010 agreement" means the agreement entered into among the OWRB and the Trust, dated June 15, 2010, relating to the assignment by the State of the 1974 storage contract and transfer of rights, title, interests, and obligations under that contract to the Trust, including the interests of the State in the conservation storage capacity and associated repayment obligations to the United States.

(3) ADMINISTRATIVE SET-ASIDE SUBCONTRACTS.—The term "administrative set-aside subcontracts" means the subcontracts the City shall issue for the use of Conservation Storage Capacity in Sardis Lake as provided by section 4 of the amended storage contract.

(4) ALLOTMENT.—The term "allotment" means the land within the Settlement Area held by an allottee subject to a statutory restriction on alienation or held by the United States in trust for the benefit of an allottee.

(5) ALLOTTEE.—The term "allottee" means an enrolled member of the Choctaw Nation or citizen of the Chickasaw Nation who, or whose estate, holds an interest in an allotment.

(6) AMENDED PERMIT APPLICATION.—The term "amended permit application" means the permit application of the City to the OWRB, No. 2007–17, as amended as provided by the Settlement Agreement.

(7) AMENDED STORAGE CONTRACT TRANSFER AGREEMENT; AMENDED STORAGE CONTRACT.—The terms "amended storage contract transfer agreement" and "amended storage contract" mean the 2010 Agreement between the City, the Trust, and the OWRB, as amended, as provided by the Settlement Agreement and this section.

(8) ATOKA AND SARDIS CONSERVATION PROJECTS FUND.—The term "Atoka and Sardis Conservation Projects Fund" means the Atoka and Sardis Conservation Projects Fund established, funded, and managed in accordance with the Settlement Agreement.

(9) CITY.—The term "City" means the City of Oklahoma City, or the City and the Trust acting jointly, as applicable.

(10) CITY PERMIT.—The term "City permit" means any permit issued to the City by the OWRB pursuant to the amended permit application and consistent with the Settlement Agreement.

(11) CONSERVATION STORAGE CAPACITY.—The term "conservation storage capacity" means the total storage space as stated in the 1974 storage contract in Sardis Lake between elevations 599.0 feet above mean sea level and 542.0 feet above mean sea level, which is estimated to contain 297,200 acre-feet of water after adjustment for sediment deposits, and which may be used for municipal and industrial water supply, fish and wildlife, and recreation.

(12) ENFORCEABILITY DATE.—The term "enforceability date" means the date on which the Secretary of the Interior publishes in the Federal Register a notice certifying that the conditions of subsection (i) have been satisfied.

(13) FUTURE USE STORAGE.—The term "future use storage" means that portion of the conservation storage capacity that was designated by the 1974 Contract to be utilized for future water use storage and was estimated to contain 155,500 acre feet of water after adjustment for sediment deposits, or 52.322 percent of the conservation storage capacity.

(14) NATIONS.—The term "Nations" means, collectively, the Choctaw Nation of Oklahoma ("Choctaw Nation") and the Chickasaw Nation.

(15) OWRB.—The term "OWRB" means the Oklahoma Water Resources Board.

(16) SARDIS LAKE.—The term "Sardis Lake" means the reservoir, formerly known as Clayton Lake, whose dam is located in Section 19, Township 2 North, Range 19 East of the Indian Meridian, Pushmataha County, Oklahoma, the construction, operation, and maintenance of which was authorized by section 203 of the Flood Control Act of 1962 (Public Law 87–874; 76 Stat. 1187).

(17) SETTLEMENT AGREEMENT.—The term "Settlement Agreement" means the settlement agreement as approved by the Nations, the State, the City, and the Trust effective August 22, 2016, as revised to conform with this section, as applicable.

(18) SETTLEMENT AREA.—The term "settlement area" means—

(A) the area lying between—

(i) the South Canadian River and Arkansas River to the north;

(ii) the Oklahoma–Texas State line to the south;

(iii) the Oklahoma–Arkansas State line to the east; and

(iv) the 98th Meridian to the west; and

(B) the area depicted in Exhibit 1 to the Settlement Agreement and generally including the following counties, or portions of, in the State:

(i) Atoka.
(ii) Bryan.
(iii) Carter.
(iv) Choctaw.
(v) Coal.
(vi) Garvin.
(vii) Grady.

(viii) McClain.
(ix) Murray.
(x) Haskell.
(xi) Hughes.
(xii) Jefferson.
(xiii) Johnston.
(xiv) Latimer.
(xv) LeFlore.
(xvi) Love.
(xvii) Marshall.
(xviii) McCurtain.
(xix) Pittsburgh.
(xx) Pontotoc.
(xxi) Pushmataha.
(xxii) Stephens.

(19) SETTLEMENT AREA WATERS.—The term "settlement area waters" means the waters located—

(A) within the settlement area; and
(B) within a basin depicted in Exhibit 10 to the Settlement Agreement, including any of the following basins as denominated in the 2012 Update of the Oklahoma Comprehensive Water Plan:

(i) Beaver Creek (24, 25, and 26).
(ii) Blue (11 and 12).
(iii) Clear Boggy (9).
(iv) Kiamichi (5 and 6).
(v) Lower Arkansas (46 and 47).
(vi) Lower Canadian (48, 56, 57, and 58).
(vii) Lower Little (2).
(viii) Lower Washita (14).
(ix) Mountain Fork (4).
(x) Middle Washita (15 and 16).
(xi) Mud Creek (23).
(xii) Muddy Boggy (7 and 8).
(xiii) Poteau (44 and 45).
(xiv) Red River Mainstem (1, 10, 13, and 21).
(xv) Upper Little (3).
(xvi) Walnut Bayou (22).

(20) STATE.—The term "State" means the State of Oklahoma.

(21) TRUST.—

(A) IN GENERAL.—The term "Trust" means the Oklahoma City Water Utilities Trust, formerly known as the Oklahoma City Municipal Improvement Authority, a public trust established pursuant to State law with the City as the beneficiary.

(B) REFERENCES.—A reference in this section to "Trust" refers to the Oklahoma City Water Utilities Trust, acting severally.

(22) UNITED STATES.—The term "United States" means the United States of America acting in its capacity as trustee for the Nations, their respective members, citizens, and allottees, or as specifically stated or limited in any given reference herein, in which case it means the United States of America acting in the capacity as set forth in said reference.

(c) APPROVAL OF THE SETTLEMENT AGREEMENT.—

(1) RATIFICATION.—

(A) IN GENERAL.—Except as modified by this section, and to the extent the Settlement Agreement does not conflict with this section, the Settlement Agreement is authorized, ratified, and confirmed.

(B) AMENDMENTS.—If an amendment is executed to make the Settlement Agreement consistent with this section, the amendment is also authorized, ratified and confirmed to the extent the amendment is consistent with this section.

(2) EXECUTION OF SETTLEMENT AGREEMENT.—

(A) IN GENERAL.—To the extent the Settlement Agreement does not conflict with this section, the Secretary of the Interior shall promptly execute the Settlement Agreement, including all exhibits to or parts of the Settlement Agreement requiring the signature of the Secretary of the Interior and any amendments necessary to make the Settlement Agreement consistent with this section.

(B) NOT A MAJOR FEDERAL ACTION.—Execution of the Settlement Agreement by the Secretary of the Interior under this subsection shall not constitute a major Federal action under the National Environmental Policy Act of 1969 (42 U.S.C. 4321 et seq.).

(d) APPROVAL OF THE AMENDED STORAGE CONTRACT AND 1974 STORAGE CONTRACT.—

(1) RATIFICATION.—

(A) IN GENERAL.—Except to the extent any provision of the amended storage contract conflicts with any provision of this section, the amended storage contract is authorized, ratified, and confirmed.

(B) 1974 STORAGE CONTRACT.—To the extent the amended storage contract, as authorized, ratified, and confirmed, modifies or amends the 1974 storage contract, the modification or amendment to the 1974 storage contract is authorized, ratified, and confirmed.

(C) AMENDMENTS.—To the extent an amendment is executed to make the amended storage contract consistent with this section, the amendment is authorized, ratified, and confirmed.

(2) APPROVAL BY THE SECRETARY.—After the State and the City execute the amended storage contract, the Secretary shall approve the amended storage contract.

(3) MODIFICATION OF SEPTEMBER 11, 2009, ORDER IN UNITED STATES V. OKLAHOMA WATER RESOURCES BOARD, CIV 98–00521 (N.D. OK).—The Secretary, through counsel, shall cooperate and work with the State to file any motion and proposed order to modify or amend the order of the United States District Court for the Northern District of Oklahoma dated September 11, 2009, necessary to conform the order to the amended storage contract transfer agreement, the Settlement Agreement, and this section.

(4) CONSERVATION STORAGE CAPACITY.—The allocation of the use of the conservation storage capacity in Sardis Lake for administrative set-aside subcontracts, City water supply, and fish and wildlife and recreation as provided by the amended storage contract is authorized, ratified and approved.

(5) ACTIVATION; WAIVER.—

(A) FINDINGS.—Congress finds that—

(i) the earliest possible activation of any increment of future use storage in Sardis Lake will not occur until after 2050; and

(ii) the obligation to make annual payments for the Sardis future use storage operation, maintenance and replacement costs, capital costs, or interest attributable to Sardis future use storage only arises if, and only to the extent, that an increment of Sardis future use storage is activated by withdrawal or release of water from the future use storage that is authorized by the user for a consumptive use of water.

(B) WAIVER OF OBLIGATIONS FOR STORAGE THAT IS NOT ACTIVATED.—Notwithstanding section 301 of the Water Supply Act of 1958 (43 U.S.C. 390b), section 203 of the Flood Control Act of 1962 (Public Law 87–874; 76 Stat. 1187), the 1974 storage contract, or any other provision of law, effective as of January 1, 2050—

(i) the entirety of any repayment obligations (including interest), relating to that portion of conservation storage capacity allocated by the 1974 storage contract to future use storage in Sardis Lake is waived and shall be considered nonreimbursable; and

(ii) any obligation of the State and, on execution and approval of the amended storage contract, of the City and the Trust, under the 1974 storage contract regarding capital costs and any operation, maintenance, and replacement costs and interest otherwise attributable to future use storage in Sardis Lake is waived and shall be nonreimbursable, if by January 1, 2050, the right to future use storage is not activated by the withdrawal or release of water from future use storage for an authorized consumptive use of water.

(6) CONSISTENT WITH AUTHORIZED PURPOSES; NO MAJOR OPERATIONAL CHANGE.—

(A) CONSISTENT WITH AUTHORIZED PURPOSE.—The amended storage contract, the approval of the Secretary of the amended storage contract, and the waiver of future use storage under paragraph (5)—

(i) are deemed consistent with the authorized purposes for Sardis Lake as described in section 203 of the Flood Control Act of 1962 (Public Law 87–874; 76 Stat. 1187) and do not affect the authorized purposes for which the project was authorized, surveyed, planned, and constructed; and

(ii) shall not constitute a reallocation of storage.

(B) NO MAJOR OPERATIONAL CHANGE.—The amended storage contract, the approval of the Secretary of the amended storage contract, and the waiver of future use storage under paragraph (5) shall not constitute a major operational change under section 301(e) of the Water Supply Act of 1958 (43 U.S.C. 390b(e)).

(7) NO FURTHER AUTHORIZATION REQUIRED.—This section shall be considered sufficient and complete authorization, without further study or analysis, for—

(A) the Secretary to approve the amended storage contract; and

(B) after approval under subparagraph (A), the Corps of Engineers to manage storage in Sardis Lake pursuant to and in accordance with the 1974 storage contract, the amended storage contract, and the Settlement Agreement.

(e) SETTLEMENT AREA WATERS.—

(1) FINDINGS.—Congress finds that—

(A) pursuant to the Atoka Agreement as ratified by section 29 of the Act of June 28, 1898 (30 Stat. 505, chapter 517) (as modified by the Act of July 1, 1902 (32 Stat. 641, chapter 1362)), the Nations issued patents to their respective tribal members and citizens and thereby conveyed to individual Choctaws and Chickasaws, all right, title, and interest in and to land that was possessed by the Nations, other than certain mineral rights; and

(B) when title passed from the Nations to their respective tribal members and citizens, the Nations did not convey and those individuals did not receive any right of regulatory or sovereign authority, including with respect to water.

(2) PERMITTING, ALLOCATION, AND ADMINISTRATION OF SETTLEMENT AREA WATERS PURSUANT TO THE SETTLEMENT AGREEMENT.—Beginning on the enforceability date, settlement area waters shall be permitted, allocated, and administered by the OWRB in accordance with the Settlement Agreement and this section.

(3) CHOCTAW NATION AND CHICKASAW NATION.—Beginning on the enforceability date, the Nations shall have the right to use and to develop the right to use settlement area waters only in accordance with the Settlement Agreement and this section.

(4) WAIVER AND DELEGATION BY NATIONS.—In addition to the waivers under subsection (h), the Nations, on their own behalf, shall permanently delegate to the State any regulatory authority each Nation may possess over water rights on allotments, which the State shall exercise in accordance with the Settlement Agreement and this subsection.

(5) RIGHT TO USE WATER.—

(A) IN GENERAL.—An allottee may use water on an allotment in accordance with the Settlement Agreement and this subsection.

(B) SURFACE WATER USE.—

(i) IN GENERAL.—An allottee may divert and use, on the allotment of the allottee, 6 acre-feet per year of surface water per 160 acres, to be used solely for domestic uses on an allotment that constitutes riparian land under applicable State law as of the date of enactment of this Act.

(ii) EFFECT OF STATE LAW.—The use of surface water described in clause (i) shall be subject to all rights and protections of State law, as of the date of enactment of this Act, including all protections against loss for nonuse.

(iii) NO PERMIT REQUIRED.—An allottee may divert water under this subsection without a permit or any other authorization from the OWRB.

(C) GROUNDWATER USE.—

(i) IN GENERAL.—An allottee may drill wells on the allotment of the allottee to take and use for domestic uses the greater of—

(I) 5 acre-feet per year; or

(II) any greater quantity allowed under State law.

(ii) EFFECT OF STATE LAW.—The groundwater use described in clause (i) shall be subject to all rights and protections of State law, as of the date of enactment of this Act, including all protections against loss for nonuse.

(iii) NO PERMIT REQUIRED.—An allottee may drill wells and use water under this subsection without a permit or any other authorization from the OWRB.

(D) FUTURE CHANGES IN STATE LAW.—

(i) IN GENERAL.—If State law changes to limit use of water to a quantity that is less than the applicable quantity specified in subparagraph (B) or (C), as applicable, an allottee shall retain the right to use water in accord with those subparagraphs, subject to paragraphs (6)(B)(iv) and (7).

(ii) OPPORTUNITY TO BE HEARD.—Prior to taking any action to limit the use of water by an individual, the OWRB shall provide to the individual an opportunity to demonstrate that the individual is—

(I) an allottee; and

(II) using water on the allotment pursuant to and in accordance with the Settlement Agreement and this section.

(6) ALLOTTEE OPTIONS FOR ADDITIONAL WATER.—

(A) IN GENERAL.—To use a quantity of water in excess of the quantities provided under paragraph (5), an allottee shall—

(i) file an action under subparagraph (B); or

(ii) apply to the OWRB for a permit pursuant to, and in accordance with, State law.

(B) DETERMINATION IN FEDERAL DISTRICT COURT.—

(i) IN GENERAL.—In lieu of applying to the OWRB for a permit to use more water than is allowed under paragraph (5), an allottee may file an action in the United States District Court for the Western District of Oklahoma for determination of the right to water of the allottee. At least 90 days prior to filing such an action, the allottee shall provide written notice of the suit to the United States and the OWRB. For the United States, notice shall be provided to the Solicitor's Office, Department of the Interior, Washington D.C., and to the Office of the Regional Director of the Muskogee Region, Bureau of Indian Affairs, Department of the Interior.

(ii) JURISDICTION.—For purposes of this subsection—

(I) the United States District Court for the Western District of Oklahoma shall have jurisdiction; and

(II) as part of the complaint, the allottee shall include certification of the pre-filing notice to the

United States and OWRB required by subparagraph (B)(i). If such certification is not included with the complaint, the complaint will be deemed filed 90 days after such certification is complete and filed with the court. Within 60 days after the complaint is filed or deemed filed or within such extended time as the District Court in its discretion may permit, the United States may appear or intervene. After such appearance, intervention or the expiration of the said 60 days or any extension thereof, the proceedings and judgment in such action shall bind the United States and the parties thereto without regard to whether the United States elects to appear or intervene in such action.

(iii) REQUIREMENTS.—An allottee filing an action pursuant to this subparagraph shall—

(I) join the OWRB as a party; and

(II) publish notice in a newspaper of general circulation within the Settlement Area Hydrologic Basin for 2 consecutive weeks, with the first publication appearing not later than 30 days after the date on which the action is filed.

(iv) DETERMINATION FINAL.—

(I) IN GENERAL.—Subject to subclause (II), if an allottee elects to have the rights of the allottee determined pursuant to this subparagraph, the determination shall be final as to any rights under Federal law and in lieu of any rights to use water on an allotment as provided in paragraph (5).

(II) RESERVATION OF RIGHTS.—Subclause (I) shall not preclude an allottee from—

(aa) applying to the OWRB for water rights pursuant to State law; or

(bb) using any rights allowed by State law that do not require a permit from the OWRB.

(7) OWRB ADMINISTRATION AND ENFORCEMENT.—

(A) IN GENERAL.—If an allottee exercises any right under paragraph (5) or has rights determined under paragraph (6)(B), the OWRB shall have jurisdiction to administer those rights.

(B) CHALLENGES.—An allottee may challenge OWRB administration of rights determined under this paragraph, in the United States District Court for the Western District of Oklahoma.

(8) PRIOR EXISTING STATE LAW RIGHTS.—Water rights held by an allottee as of the enforceability date pursuant to a permit issued by the OWRB shall be governed by the terms of that permit and applicable State law (including regulations).

(f) CITY PERMIT FOR APPROPRIATION OF STREAM WATER FROM THE KIAMICHI RIVER.—The City permit shall be processed, evaluated, issued, and administered consistent with and in accordance with the Settlement Agreement and this section.

(g) SETTLEMENT COMMISSION.—

(1) ESTABLISHMENT.—There is established a Settlement Commission.

(2) MEMBERS.—

(A) IN GENERAL.—The Settlement Commission shall be comprised of 5 members, appointed as follows:

(i) 1 by the Governor of the State.

(ii) 1 by the Attorney General of the State.

(iii) 1 by the Chief of the Choctaw Nation.

(iv) 1 by the Governor of the Chickasaw Nation.

(v) 1 by agreement of the members described in clauses (i) through (iv).

(B) JOINTLY APPOINTED MEMBER.—If the members described in clauses (i) through (iv) of subparagraph (A) do not agree on a member appointed pursuant to subparagraph (A)(v)—

(i) the members shall submit to the Chief Judge for the United States District Court for the Eastern District of Oklahoma, a list of not less than 3 persons; and

(ii) from the list under clause (i), the Chief Judge shall make the appointment.

(C) INITIAL APPOINTMENTS.—The initial appointments to the Settlement Commission shall be made not later than 90 days after the enforceability date.

(3) MEMBER TERMS.—

(A) IN GENERAL.—Each Settlement Commission member shall serve at the pleasure of appointing authority.

(B) COMPENSATION.—A member of the Settlement Commission shall serve without compensation, but an appointing authority may reimburse the member appointed by the entity for costs associated with service on the Settlement Commission.

(C) VACANCIES.—If a member of the Settlement Commission is removed or resigns, the appointing authority shall appoint the replacement member.

(D) JOINTLY APPOINTED MEMBER.—The member of the Settlement Commission described in paragraph (2)(A)(v) may be removed or replaced by a majority vote of the Settlement Commission based on a failure of the member to carry out the duties of the member.

(4) DUTIES.—The duties and authority of the Settlement Commission shall be set forth in the Settlement Agreement, and the Settlement Commission shall not possess or exercise any duty or authority not stated in the Settlement Agreement.

(h) WAIVERS AND RELEASES OF CLAIMS.—

(1) CLAIMS BY THE NATIONS AND THE UNITED STATES AS TRUSTEE FOR THE NATIONS.—Subject to the retention of rights and claims provided in paragraph (3) and except to the extent that rights are recognized in the Settlement Agreement or this section, the Nations, each in its own right and on behalf of itself and its respective citizens and members (but not individuals in their capacities as allottees), and the United States, acting as a trustee for the Nations (but not individuals in their capacities as allottees), shall execute a waiver and release of—

(A) all of the following claims asserted or which could have been asserted in any proceeding filed or that could have been filed during the period ending on the enforceability date, including Chickasaw Nation, Choctaw Nation v. Fallin et al., CIV 11–927 (W.D. Ok.), OWRB v. United States, et al. CIV 12–275 (W.D. Ok.), or any general stream adjudication, relating to—

(i) claims to the ownership of water in the State;

(ii) claims to water rights and rights to use water diverted or taken from a location within the State;

(iii) claims to authority over the allocation and management of water and administration of water rights, including authority over third-party ownership of or rights to use water diverted or taken from a location within the State and ownership or use of water on allotments by allottees or any other person using water on an allotment with the permission of an allottee;

(iv) claims that the State lacks authority over the allocation and management of water and administration of water rights, including authority over the ownership of or rights to use water diverted or taken from a location within the State;

(v) any other claim relating to the ownership of water, regulation of water, or authorized diversion, storage, or use of water diverted or taken from a location within the State, which claim is based on the status of the Chickasaw Nation's or the Choctaw Nation's unique sovereign status and rights as defined by Federal law and alleged to arise from treaties to which they are signatories, including but not limited to the Treaty of Dancing Rabbit Creek, Act of Sept. 30, 1830, 7 Stat. 333, Treaty of Doaksville, Act of Jan. 17, 1837, 11 Stat. 573, and the related March 23, 1842, patent to the Choctaw Nation; and

(vi) claims or defenses asserted or which could have been asserted in Chickasaw Nation, Choctaw Nation v. Fallin et al., CIV 11–927 (W.D. Ok.), OWRB v. United States, et al. CIV 12–275 (W.D. Ok.), or any general stream adjudication;

(B) all claims for damages, losses or injuries to water rights or water, or claims of interference with, diversion, storage, taking, or use of water (including claims for injury to land resulting from the damages, losses, injuries, interference with, diversion, storage, taking, or use of water) attributable to any action by the State, the OWRB, or any water user authorized pursuant to State law to take or use water in the State, including the City, that accrued during the period ending on the enforceability date;

(C) all claims and objections relating to the amended permit application, and the City permit, including—

(i) all claims regarding regulatory control over or OWRB jurisdiction relating to the permit application and permit; and

(ii) all claims for damages, losses or injuries to water rights or rights to use water, or claims of interference with, diversion, storage, taking, or use of water (including claims for injury to land resulting from the damages, losses, injuries, interference with, diversion, storage, taking, or use of water) attributable to the issuance and lawful exercise of the City permit;

(D) all claims to regulatory control over the Permit Numbers P80–48 and 54–613 of the City for water rights from the Muddy Boggy River for Atoka Reservoir and P73–282D for water rights from the Muddy Boggy River, including McGee Creek, for the McGee Creek Reservoir;

(E) all claims that the State lacks regulatory authority over or OWRB jurisdiction relating to Permit Numbers P80–48 and 54–613 for water rights from the Muddy Boggy River for Atoka Reservoir and P73–282D for water rights from the Muddy Boggy River, including McGee Creek, for the McGee Creek Reservoir;

(F) all claims to damages, losses or injuries to water rights or water, or claims of interference with, diversion, storage, taking, or use of water (including claims for injury to land resulting from such damages, losses, injuries, interference with, diversion, storage, taking, or use of water) attributable to the lawful exercise of Permit Numbers P80–48 and 54–613 for water rights from the Muddy Boggy River for Atoka Reservoir and P73–282D for water rights from the Muddy Boggy River, including McGee Creek, for the McGee Creek Reservoir, that accrued during the period ending on the enforceability date;

(G) all claims and objections relating to the approval by the Secretary of the assignment of the 1974 storage contract pursuant to the amended storage contract; and

(H) all claims for damages, losses, or injuries to water rights or water, or claims of interference with, diversion, storage, taking, or use of water (including claims for injury to land resulting from such damages, losses, injuries, interference with, diversion, storage, taking, or use of water) attributable to the lawful exercise of rights pursuant to the amended storage contract.

(2) WAIVERS AND RELEASES OF CLAIMS BY THE NATIONS AGAINST THE UNITED STATES.—Subject to the retention of rights and claims provided in paragraph (3) and except to the extent that rights are recognized in the Settlement Agreement or this section, the Nations are authorized to execute a waiver and release of all claims against the United States (including any agency or employee of the United States) relating to—

(A) all of the following claims asserted or which could have been asserted in any proceeding filed or that could have been filed by the United States as a trustee during the period ending on the enforceability date, including Chickasaw Nation, Choctaw Nation v. Fallin et al., CIV 11–927 (W.D. Ok.) or OWRB v. United States, et al. CIV 12–275 (W.D. Ok.), or any general stream adjudication, relating to—

(i) claims to the ownership of water in the State;

(ii) claims to water rights and rights to use water diverted or taken from a location within the State;

(iii) claims to authority over the allocation and management of water and administration of water rights, including authority over third-party ownership of or rights to use water diverted or taken from a location within the State and ownership or use of water on allotments by allottees or any other person using

water on an allotment with the permission of an allottee;

(iv) claims that the State lacks authority over the allocation and management of water and administration of water rights, including authority over the ownership of or rights to use water diverted or taken from a location within the State;

(v) any other claim relating to the ownership of water, regulation of water, or authorized diversion, storage, or use of water diverted or taken from a location within the State, which claim is based on the status of the Chickasaw Nation's or the Choctaw Nation's unique sovereign status and rights as defined by Federal law and alleged to arise from treaties to which they are signatories, including but not limited to the Treaty of Dancing Rabbit Creek, Act of Sept. 30, 1830, 7 Stat. 333, Treaty of Doaksville, Act of Jan. 17, 1837, 11 Stat. 573, and the related March 23, 1842, patent to the Choctaw Nation; and

(vi) claims or defenses asserted or which could have been asserted in Chickasaw Nation, Choctaw Nation v. Fallin et al., CIV 11–927 (W.D. Ok.), OWRB v. United States, et al. CIV 12–275 (W.D. Ok.), or any general stream adjudication;

(B) all claims for damages, losses or injuries to water rights or water, or claims of interference with, diversion, storage, taking, or use of water (including claims for injury to land resulting from the damages, losses, injuries, interference with, diversion, storage, taking, or use of water) attributable to any action by the State, the OWRB, or any water user authorized pursuant to State law to take or use water in the State, including the City, that accrued during the period ending on the enforceability date;

(C) all claims and objections relating to the amended permit application, and the City permit, including—

(i) all claims regarding regulatory control over or OWRB jurisdiction relating to the permit application and permit; and

(ii) all claims for damages, losses or injuries to water rights or rights to use water, or claims of interference with, diversion, storage, taking, or use of water (including claims for injury to land resulting from the damages, losses, injuries, interference with, diversion, storage, taking, or use of water) attributable to the issuance and lawful exercise of the City permit;

(D) all claims to regulatory control over the Permit Numbers P80–48 and 54–613 for water rights from the Muddy Boggy River for Atoka Reservoir and P73–282D for water rights from the Muddy Boggy River, including McGee Creek, for the McGee Creek Reservoir;

(E) all claims that the State lacks regulatory authority over or OWRB jurisdiction relating to Permit Numbers P80–48 and 54–613 for water rights from the Muddy Boggy River for Atoka Reservoir and P73–282D for water rights from the Muddy Boggy River, including McGee Creek, for the McGee Creek Reservoir;

(F) all claims to damages, losses or injuries to water rights or water, or claims of interference with, diversion, storage, taking, or use of water (including claims for injury to land resulting from the damages, losses, injuries, interference with, diversion, storage, taking, or use of water) attributable to the lawful exercise of Permit Numbers P80–48 and 54–613 for water rights from the Muddy Boggy River for Atoka Reservoir and P73–282D for water rights from the Muddy Boggy River, including McGee Creek, for the McGee Creek Reservoir, that accrued during the period ending on the enforceability date;

(G) all claims and objections relating to the approval by the Secretary of the assignment of the 1974 storage contract pursuant to the amended storage contract;

(H) all claims relating to litigation brought by the United States prior to the enforceability date of the water rights of the Nations in the State; and

(I) all claims relating to the negotiation, execution, or adoption of the Settlement Agreement (including exhibits) or this section.

(3) RETENTION AND RESERVATION OF CLAIMS BY NATIONS AND THE UNITED STATES.—

(A) IN GENERAL.—Notwithstanding the waiver and releases of claims authorized under paragraphs (1) and (2), the Nations and the United States, acting as trustee, shall retain—

(i) all claims for enforcement of the Settlement Agreement and this section;

(ii) all rights to use and protect any water right of the Nations recognized by or established pursuant to the Settlement Agreement, including the right to assert claims for injuries relating to the rights and the right to participate in any general stream adjudication, including any inter se proceeding;

(iii) all claims under—

(I) the Comprehensive Environmental Response, Compensation, and Liability Act of 1980 (42 U.S.C. 9601 et seq.), including for damages to natural resources;

(II) the Safe Drinking Water Act (42 U.S.C. 300f et seq.);

(III) the Federal Water Pollution Control Act (33 U.S.C. 1251 et seq.); and

(IV) any regulations implementing the Acts described in items (I) through (III);

(iv) all claims relating to damage, loss, or injury resulting from an unauthorized diversion, use, or storage of water, including damages, losses, or injuries to land or nonwater natural resources associated with any hunting, fishing, gathering, or cultural right; and

(v) all rights, remedies, privileges, immunities, and powers not specifically waived and released pursuant to this section or the Settlement Agreement.

(B) AGREEMENT.—

(i) IN GENERAL.—As provided in the Settlement Agreement, the Chickasaw Nation shall convey an easement to the City, which easement shall be as described and depicted in Exhibit 15 to the Settlement Agreement.

(ii) APPLICATION.—The Chickasaw Nation and the City shall cooperate and coordinate on the submission of an application for approval by the Secretary of the Interior of the conveyance under clause (i), in accordance with applicable Federal law.

(iii) RECORDING.—On approval by the Secretary of the Interior of the conveyance of the easement under this clause, the City shall record the easement.

(iv) CONSIDERATION.—In exchange for conveyance of the easement under clause (i), the City shall pay to the Chickasaw Nation the value of past unauthorized use and consideration for future use of the land burdened by the easement, based on an appraisal secured by the City and Nations and approved by the Secretary of the Interior.

(4) EFFECTIVE DATE OF WAIVER AND RELEASES.—The waivers and releases under this subsection take effect on the enforceability date.

(5) TOLLING OF CLAIMS.—Each applicable period of limitation and time-based equitable defense relating to a claim described in this subsection shall be tolled during the period beginning on the date of enactment of this Act and ending on the earlier of the enforceability date or the expiration date under subsection (i)(2).

(i) ENFORCEABILITY DATE.—

(1) IN GENERAL.—The Settlement Agreement shall take effect and be enforceable on the date on which the Secretary of the Interior publishes in the Federal Register a certification that—

(A) to the extent the Settlement Agreement conflicts with this section, the Settlement Agreement has been amended to conform with this section;

(B) the Settlement Agreement, as amended, has been executed by the Secretary of the Interior, the Nations, the Governor of the State, the OWRB, the City, and the Trust;

(C) to the extent the amended storage contract conflicts with this section, the amended storage contract has been amended to conform with this section;

(D) the amended storage contract, as amended to conform with this section, has been—

(i) executed by the State, the City, and the Trust; and

(ii) approved by the Secretary;

(E) an order has been entered in United States v. Oklahoma Water Resources Board, Civ. 98–C–521–E with any modifications to the order dated September 11, 2009, as provided in the Settlement Agreement;

(F) orders of dismissal have been entered in Chickasaw Nation, Choctaw Nation v. Fallin et al., Civ 11–297 (W.D. Ok.) and OWRB v. United States, et al. Civ 12–275 (W.D. Ok.) as provided in the Settlement Agreement;

(G) the OWRB has issued the City Permit;

(H) the final documentation of the Kiamichi Basin hydrologic model is on file at the Oklahoma City offices of the OWRB; and

(I) the Atoka and Sardis Conservation Projects Fund has been funded as provided in the Settlement Agreement.

(2) EXPIRATION DATE.—If the Secretary of the Interior fails to publish a statement of findings under paragraph (1) by not later than September 30, 2020, or such alternative later date as is agreed to by the Secretary of the Interior, the Nations, the State, the City, and the Trust under paragraph (4), the following shall apply:

(A) This section, except for this subsection and any provisions of this section that are necessary to carry out this subsection (but only for purposes of carrying out this subsection) are not effective beginning on September 30, 2020, or the alternative date.

(B) The waivers and release of claims, and the limited waivers of sovereign immunity, shall not become effective.

(C) The Settlement Agreement shall be null and void, except for this paragraph and any provisions of the Settlement Agreement that are necessary to carry out this paragraph.

(D) Except with respect to this paragraph, the State, the Nations, the City, the Trust, and the United States shall not be bound by any obligations or benefit from any rights recognized under the Settlement Agreement.

(E) If the City permit has been issued, the permit shall be null and void, except that the City may resubmit to the OWRB, and the OWRB shall be considered to have accepted, OWRB permit application No. 2007–017 without having waived the original application priority date and appropriative quantities.

(F) If the amended storage contract has been executed or approved, the contract shall be null and void, and the 2010 agreement shall be considered to be in force and effect as between the State and the Trust.

(G) If the Atoka and Sardis Conservation Projects Fund has been established and funded, the funds shall be returned to the respective funding parties with any accrued interest.

(3) NO PREJUDICE.—The occurrence of the expiration date under paragraph (2) shall not in any way prejudice—

(A) any argument or suit that the Nations may bring to contest—

(i) the pursuit by the City of OWRB permit application No. 2007–017, or a modified version; or

(ii) the 2010 agreement;

(B) any argument, defense, or suit the State may bring or assert with regard to the claims of the Nations to water or over water in the settlement area; or

(C) any argument, defense or suit the City may bring or assert—

(i) with regard to the claims of the Nations to water or over water in the settlement area relating to OWRB permit application No. 2007–017, or a modified version; or

(ii) to contest the 2010 agreement.

(4) EXTENSION.—The expiration date under paragraph (2) may be extended in writing if the Nations, the State, the OWRB, the United States, and the City agree that an extension is warranted.

(j) JURISDICTION, WAIVERS OF IMMUNITY FOR INTERPRETATION AND ENFORCEMENT.—

(1) JURISDICTION.—

(A) IN GENERAL.—

(i) EXCLUSIVE JURISDICTION.—The United States District Court for the Western District of Oklahoma shall have exclusive jurisdiction for all purposes and for all causes of action relating to the interpretation and enforcement of the Settlement Agreement, the amended storage contract, or interpretation or enforcement of this section, including all actions filed by an allottee pursuant to subsection (e)(6)(B).

(ii) RIGHT TO BRING ACTION.—The Choctaw Nation, the Chickasaw Nation, the State, the City, the Trust, and the United States shall each have the right to bring an action pursuant to this section.

(iii) NO ACTION IN OTHER COURTS.—No action may be brought in any other Federal, Tribal, or State court or administrative forum for any purpose relating to the Settlement Agreement, amended storage contract, or this section.

(iv) NO MONETARY JUDGMENT.—Nothing in this section authorizes any money judgment or otherwise allows the payment of funds by the United States, the Nations, the State (including the OWRB), the City, or the Trust.

(B) NOTICE AND CONFERENCE.—An entity seeking to interpret or enforce the Settlement Agreement shall comply with the following:

(i) Any party asserting noncompliance or seeking interpretation of the Settlement Agreement or this section shall first serve written notice on the party alleged to be in breach of the Settlement Agreement or violation of this section.

(ii) The notice under clause (i) shall identify the specific provision of the Settlement Agreement or this section alleged to have been violated or in dispute and shall specify in detail the contention of the party asserting the claim and any factual basis for the claim.

(iii) Representatives of the party alleging a breach or violation and the party alleged to be in breach or violation shall meet not later than 30 days after receipt of notice under clause (i) in an effort to resolve the dispute.

(iv) If the matter is not resolved to the satisfaction of the party alleging breach not later than 90 days after the original notice under clause (i), the party may take any appropriate enforcement action consistent with the Settlement Agreement and this subsection.

(2) LIMITED WAIVERS OF SOVEREIGN IMMUNITY.—

(A) IN GENERAL.—The United States and the Nations may be joined in an action filed in the United States District Court for the Western District of Oklahoma.

(B) UNITED STATES IMMUNITY.—Any claim by the United States to sovereign immunity from suit is irrevocably waived for any action brought by the State, the Chickasaw Nation, the Choctaw Nation, the City, or the Trust in the Western District of Oklahoma relating to interpretation or enforcement of the Settlement Agreement or this section, including of the appellate jurisdiction of the United States Court of Appeals for the Tenth Circuit and the Supreme Court of the United States.

(C) CHICKASAW NATION IMMUNITY.—For the exclusive benefit of the State (including the OWRB), the City, the Trust, the Choctaw Nation, and the United States, the sovereign immunity of the Chickasaw Nation from suit is waived solely for any action brought in the Western District of Oklahoma relating to interpretation or enforcement of the Settlement Agreement or this section, if the action is brought by the State or the OWRB, the City, the Trust, the Choctaw Nation, or the United States, including the appellate jurisdiction of the United States Court of Appeals for the Tenth Circuit and the Supreme Court of the United States.

(D) CHOCTAW NATION IMMUNITY.—For the exclusive benefit of the State (including of the OWRB), the City, the Trust, the Chickasaw Nation, and the United States, the Choctaw Nation shall expressly and irrevocably consent to a suit and waive sovereign immunity from a suit solely for any action brought in the Western District of Oklahoma relating to interpretation or enforcement of the Settlement Agreement or this section, if the action is brought by the State, the OWRB, the City, the Trust, the Chickasaw Nation, or the United States, including the appellate jurisdiction of the United States Court of Appeals for the Tenth Circuit and the Supreme Court of the United States.

(k) DISCLAIMER.—

(1) IN GENERAL.—The Settlement Agreement applies only to the claims and rights of the Nations.

(2) NO PRECEDENT.—Nothing in this section or the Settlement Agreement shall be construed in any way to quantify, establish, or serve as precedent regarding the land and water rights, claims, or entitlements to water of any American Indian Tribe other than the Nations, including any other American Indian Tribe in the State.

(3) LIMITATION.—Nothing in the Settlement Agreement—

(A) affects the ability of the United States, acting as sovereign, to take actions authorized by law, including any laws related to health, safety, or the environment, including—

(i) the Comprehensive Environmental Response, Compensation, and Liability Act of 1980 (42 U.S.C. 9601 et seq.);

(ii) the Safe Drinking Water Act (42 U.S.C. 300f et seq.);

(iii) the Federal Water Pollution Control Act (33 U.S.C. 1251 et seq.); and

(iv) any regulations implementing the Acts described in this section;

(B) affects the ability of the United States to raise defenses based on 43 U.S.C. 666(a); and

(C) affects any rights, claims, or defenses the United States may have with respect to the use of water on Federal lands in the Settlement Area that are not trust lands or Allotments.

CHICKASAW NATION TRIBAL LEGISLATURE
General Resolution Number 33-052
Approval of the Water Settlement agreement among the Chickasaw Nation, the Choctaw Nation of Oklahoma, the State of Oklahoma, the Oklahoma Water Resources Board, the City of Oklahoma City, and the Oklahoma City Water Utilities Trust

WHEREAS, in accordance with Article VII, Sections 4 and 7 of the Constitution of the Chickasaw Nation, the Chickasaw Tribal Legislature shall enact rules and regulations pertaining to the acquisition, leasing, disposition and management of real property, subject to federal law, and

WHEREAS, in accordance with Article XI, Section 1 of the Constitution of the Chickasaw Nation, the Governor shall perform all duties appertaining to the office of Chief Executive and shall sign official papers on behalf of the Chickasaw Nation, and

WHEREAS, the Chickasaw Nation, with the Choctaw Nation of Oklahoma, filed a federal court lawsuit ("Water Lawsuit") in 2011 against Governor Fallin, the Oklahoma Water Resources Board, the City of Oklahoma City, and the Oklahoma City Water Utilities Trust, which lawsuit sought declaratory and injunctive relief from ongoing State efforts to exercise unilateral and exclusive state-law authority over and control of water resources throughout the Chickasaw and Choctaw Nations' historic treaty territory, with particular relation to the waters of the Kiamichi Basin and Sardis Lake, which efforts the Chickasaw and Choctaw Nations argued violated tribal rights secured by treaty and other federal law, and

WHEREAS, the State of Oklahoma filed a state court lawsuit ("Stream Adjudication") in 2012 naming all claimants to water rights in the Kiamichi, the Clear Boggy, and the Muddy Boggy stream basins and specifically including the United States as trustee for the Chickasaw and Choctaw Nations and individual allottees of both Nations, which lawsuit sought an adjudication of all property rights to water within the three identified basins, and

WHEREAS, Governor Bill Anoatubby, working closely with Choctaw Nation Chief Gary Batton and the joint tribal legal team, has negotiated terms with the State of Oklahoma, the Oklahoma Water Resources Board, the City of Oklahoma City, and the Oklahoma City Water Utilities Trust ("Water Settlement") for a final and comprehensive resolution of claims associated with the Water Lawsuit and the Stream Adjudication, as specifically set forth in the Water Settlement, which terms establish a sovereign-to-sovereign framework for the Chickasaw and Choctaw Nations, enforceable under federal law and in federal court, to engage with the State on significant water resources matters relating to the historic treaty territory, with particular relation to Oklahoma City's use of waters from the Kiamichi, the Clear Boggy, and the Muddy Boggy stream basins, and

WHEREAS, given its relation to the Chickasaw Nation's claims to real property rights and interests, finalization of the Water Settlement will require approval by the Chickasaw Nation Tribal Legislature, and

WHEREAS, given its relation to Chickasaw Nation trust assets and interests, finalization of the Water Settlement will require congressional action and approval by the United States Department of the Interior, and

WHEREAS, given the Water Lawsuit and the Stream Adjudication, finalization of the Water Settlement will require the entry of appropriate court orders, and

WHEREAS, approval of the Water Settlement by the Chickasaw Nation, the Choctaw Nation of Oklahoma, the State of Oklahoma, the Oklahoma Water Resources Board, the City of Oklahoma City, and the Oklahoma City Water Utilities Trust must occur before congressional action, United States Department of the Interior approval, and entry of appropriate court orders can occur, and

WHEREAS, approval of the Water Settlement would be in the best interests of the Chickasaw Nation and its citizens.

NOW, THEREFORE BE IT RESOLVED, that the Chickasaw Nation Tribal Legislature, having been fully apprised of the terms of the Water Settlement, hereby expresses its approval of those terms and support for Governor Bill Anoatubby's execution thereof, inclusive of the stated waivers of claims and limited waivers of sovereign immunity set forth therein, on behalf of the Chickasaw Nation and his taking such other steps as necessary to finalize and effectuate it in full.

Executed in regular session of the Chickasaw Tribal Legislature, meeting at Ada, Oklahoma, on August 15, 2016, by a vote of 13 ayes, 0 nays, 0 abstentions.

_____   _____
Chairperson   Secretary
Chickasaw Tribal Legislature   Chickasaw Tribal Legislature

Concur: _____ Date: _____
Bill Anoatubby, Governor
The Chickasaw Nation

CHICKASAW NATION TRIBAL LEGISLATURE
General Resolution Number 33-052
Approval of the Water Settlement agreement among the Chickasaw Nation, the Choctaw Nation of Oklahoma, the State of Oklahoma, the Oklahoma Water Resources Board, the City of Oklahoma City, and the Oklahoma City Water Utilities Trust

Explanation: This resolution approves the terms of the described Water Settlement and support for Governor Bill Anoatubby's execution thereof and taking such steps as necessary to finalize and effectuate it in full.

Presented by: Legislative Committee

CB - 138 - 16

TO APPROVE A WATER SETTLEMENT AGREEMENT

IN THE TRIBAL COUNCIL OF THE CHOCTAW NATION

ANTHONY DILLARD INTRODUCED THE FOLLOWING COUNCIL BILL

A COUNCIL BILL

TO APPROVE a Water Settlement Agreement.

WHEREAS, in accordance with Article IX, Sections 4 and 6 of the Constitution of the Choctaw Nation of Oklahoma ("Choctaw Nation"), the Tribal Council shall enact legislation, rules and regulations not inconsistent with this Constitution for the general good of the Choctaw Nation and for the administration and regulation of the affairs of the Choctaw Nation; the Tribal Council shall make decisions pertaining to the acquisition, leasing, disposition and management of tribal property, and

WHEREAS, in accordance with Article VI, Section 1 of the Constitution of the Choctaw Nation, the supreme executive power of this Nation shall be vested in a chief magistrate, who shall be styled "The Chief of the Choctaw Nation"; and in accordance with Article VII, Sections 1 and 6 of the Constitution of the Choctaw Nation, the

WHEREAS, the Choctaw Nation is a plaintiff in an action entitled *Chickasaw Nation, Choctaw Nation v. Fallin et al.*, CIV 11-927 (W.D. Ok.), this "Nations' Lawsuit" was jointly filed with the Chickasaw Nation;

WHEREAS, in 2012, the Nations, State, and Oklahoma City began a mediation to resolve the Nations' Lawsuit as well as a parallel action filed by the OWRB against the United States in its capacity as trustee for the Chickasaw Nation and Choctaw Nation entitled *OWRB v. United States*, et al. CIV 12-275 (W.D. Ok.) (collectively with the Nations' Litigation "Water Litigation"); and

WHEREAS, the negotiations between the parties, and with the participation from the United States Department of Justice and the United States Department of the Interior, has produced a Water Settlement Agreement that constitutes a comprehensive resolution of immediate and foreseeable conflicts over water rights administration, including the dismissal of the Water Litigation; and

WHEREAS, the Settlement Agreement approval through a Federal law enacted by the United States Congress; and

WHEREAS, the Federal law will provide for enforcement the Settlement Agreement in the United States District Court for the Western District of Oklahoma; and

WHEREAS, reciprocal waivers of sovereign immunity, including from Choctaw Nation are limited and conditional; and

WHEREAS, The Chief of the Choctaw Nation and the Tribal Council have reviewed the terms and conditions of the proposed Settlement Agreement and the Tribal Council finds the terms and conditions of the proposed Settlement Agreement acceptable

THEREFORE BE IT ENACTED, by the Tribal Council of the Choctaw Nation that the Chief of the Choctaw Nation, Gary Batton, or his designee will execute and take all actions necessary required for approval of the Settlement Agreement and any conditions for its enforceability.

CERTIFICATION

I, the undersigned, as speaker of the Tribal Council of the Choctaw Nation of Oklahoma, do hereby certify that the Tribal Council is composed of twelve (12) seats. Eight (8) members must be present to constitute a quorum. I further certify that ___eleven___ *(11) members answered roll call and that a quorum was present at the Regular Session of the Tribal Council at Tuskahoma, Oklahoma on* ___August 13, 2016___ *. I further certify that the foregoing Council Bill CB-* 138 *-16 was adopted at such meeting by the affirmative vote of* ___eleven___ *(11) members,* ___zero___ *(0) negative votes, and* ___one___ *(1) abstaining.*

Thomas Williston, Speaker
Choctaw Nation Tribal Council

Anthony Dillard, Secretary
Choctaw Nation Tribal Council

Gary Batton, Chief
Choctaw Nation of Oklahoma

Date ___8-17-16___

Selected USGS Streamgages

Watershed (Basin Class)	Basin	Streamgage Number	Streamgage Name	Status	Period of Record			Notes
					Mean Annual Streamflow (cfs)	Start Date	End Date	
Little River (A)	2	07340000	Little River near Horatio, AR	Active	3,923	4/1/1931	Present	
		07338500	Little River below Lukfata Creek, near Idabel	Active	1,754	10/1/1946	Present	
Lower Canadian River (A)	57	07229300	Walnut Creek at Purcell	Active	83	10/1/1965	Present	
Middle Washita River (A)	15	07328500	Washita River near Pauls Valley	Active	885	10/1/1937	Present	
		07328100	Washita River at Alex	Active	661	10/1/1964	Present	
		07328180	North Criner Creek near Criner	Active	2	10/1/1989	Present	
Mud Creek (A)	23	07315700	Mud Creek near Courtney	Active	183	10/1/1960	Present	
Muddy Boggy Creek (A)	7	07335300	Muddy Boggy Creek near Unger	Active	1,891	8/25/1982	Present	
	8	07334000	Muddy Boggy Creek near Farris	Active	886	10/1/1937	Present	
		07332950	Muddy Boggy Creek at Atoka	Inactive	182	10/1/1978	9/30/1981	Limited period of record
		07333910	McGee Creek near Farris	Inactive	132	10/1/1977	5/31/1982	
		07333000	North Boggy Creek near Stringtown	Inactive	122	10/1/1955	5/31/1959	Limited period of record
		07333800	McGee Creek near Stringtown	Inactive	87	4/1/1956	9/29/1968	
		07333500	Chickasaw Creek near Stringtown	Inactive	30	10/1/1955	9/29/1968	
		07332900	Coal Creek near Lehigh	Inactive	3	10/1/1977	9/29/1981	

Selected USGS Streamgages

Watershed (Basin Class)	Basin	Streamgage Number	Streamgage Name	Status	Mean Annual Streamflow (cfs)	Start Date	End Date	Notes
Poteau River (A)	44	07249413	Poteau River near Panama	Active	2,147	10/1/1989	Present	
		07249422	Holi-tuska Creek near Panama	Inactive	3	7/1/1978	9/29/1981	Limited period of record
	45	07248500	Poteau River near Wister	Inactive	1,111	4/2/1938	9/29/1984	
		07247015	Poteau River at Loving	Active	316	4/1/1992	Present	
		07247250	Black Fork below Big Creek near Page	Active	168	3/1/1992	Present	
		07247500	Fourche Maline near Red Oak	Active	135	10/1/1938	Present	
		07248600	Caston Creek at Wister	Inactive	75	10/1/1978	9/29/1982	
		07249080	Brazil Creek near Walls	Inactive	73	10/1/1978	9/29/1985	
		07248700	Sugarloaf Creek near Monroe	Inactive	60	10/1/1978	9/29/1981	Limited period of record
		07247450	Fourche Maline near Wilburton	Inactive	38	7/1/1978	9/29/1981	Limited period of record
		07249100	Owl Creek near McCurtain	Inactive	26	7/1/1978	9/29/1981	Limited period of record
		07248620	Morris Creek at Howe	Inactive	19	10/1/1978	9/29/1981	Limited period of record
		07247550	Red Oak Creek near Red Oak	Inactive	13	7/1/1978	9/29/1982	
Red River (A)	1	07336820	Red River near De Kalb, TX	Active	9,953	10/1/2004	Present	
	10	07335500	Red River at Arthur City, TX	Active	8,977	10/1/1905	Present	
	13	07332000	Red River near Colbert	Inactive	5,244	10/1/1923	9/29/1959	
		07331600	Red River at Denison Dam near Denison, TX	Active	4,897	1/1/1924	Present	
	21	07316000	Red River near Gainesville, TX	Active	3,112	10/1/1936	Present	
		07315500	Red River near Terral	Active	2,363	4/1/1938	Present	
		07331000	Washita River near Dickson	Active	1,713	10/1/1928	Present	
		07331383	Pennington Creek at Capitol Ave at Tishomingo	Active	136	12/6/2012	Present	
		07331250	Mill Creek near Ravia	Inactive	47	10/1/1968	9/29/1971	Limited period of record
		07331300	Pennington Creek near Reagan	Active	47	10/1/2003	Present	
		07331200	Mill Creek near Mill Creek	Active	26	9/7/2006	Present	
		07331295	Pennington Creek East of Mill Creek	Inactive	20	9/9/2006	5/31/2011	
		07315650	Red River near Courtney	Active		6/6/2017	Present	Currently no flow data; gage height data only
		07331290	Washita River near Tishomingo	Active		9/8/2016	Present	Currently no flow data; gage height data only
Walnut Bayou (A)	22	07315900	Walnut Bayou near Burneyville	Inactive	37	10/1/1960	9/29/1971	

Selected USGS Streamgages

Watershed (Basin Class)	Basin	Streamgage Number	Streamgage Name	Status	Mean Annual Streamflow (cfs)	Start Date	End Date	Notes
Blue River (B)	11	07332500	Blue River near Blue	Active	318	6/1/1936	Present	
	12	07332400	Blue River at Milburn	Inactive	142	10/1/1965	6/30/1987	
		07332390	Blue River near Connerville	Active	105	10/1/1976	Present	
Clear Boggy Creek (B)	9	07334800	Clear Boggy Creek above Caney Creek near Caney	Active	556	5/16/2012	Present	
		07335000	Clear Boggy Creek near Caney	Inactive	476	10/1/1942	6/7/2012	
		07334238	Sheep Creek Spring near Fittstown	Active	3	8/14/2014	Present	Limited period of record
Kiamichi River (B)	6	07336500	Kiamichi River near Belzoni	Inactive	1,699	10/1/1925	9/29/1972	
		07336200	Kiamichi River near Antlers	Active	1,530	10/1/1972	Present	
		07335790	Kiamichi River near Clayton	Active	996	11/20/1980	Present	
		07335700	Kiamichi River near Big Cedar	Active	84	10/1/1965	Present	
		07336000	Tenmile Creek near Miller	Inactive	76	10/1/1955	9/29/1970	
		07335840	Pine Creek at Eubanks	Active		3/28/2017	Present	Currently no flow data; gage height data only
Lower Washita (B)	14	07331000	Washita River near Dickson	Active	1,713	10/1/1928	Present	
		07328500	Washita River near Pauls Valley	Active	885	10/1/1937	Present	
		07329700	Wildhorse Creek near Hoover	Active	271	10/1/1969	Present	Historic flow data; gage height data only
		07330500	Caddo Creek near Ardmore	Inactive	152	10/1/1936	12/31/1997	
		07329000	Rush Creek at Purdy	Inactive	80	10/1/1939	9/30/1994	
		07329900	Rock Creek at Dougherty	Inactive	60	10/1/1956	6/30/1967	
		07329500	Rush Creek near Maysville	Inactive	52	10/1/1954	9/29/1976	
		07329852	Rock Creek at Sulphur	Active	49	10/1/1989	Present	
		07329780	Honey Creek below Turner Falls near Davis	Active	20	10/1/2004	Present	
		07328550	Washington Creek near Pauls Valley	Inactive	6	6/27/1991	3/31/1994	Limited period of record
		07329849	Antelope Spring at Sulphur	Active	2	11/20/1985	Present	Spring flow data
		07329851	Outflow from Vendome Well at Sulphur	Inactive	1	11/20/1985	9/29/1989	Limited period of record; spring flow data
Mountain Fork River (B)	4	07339000	Mountain Fork near Eagletown	Active	1,350	4/1/1924	Present	
		07338750	Mountain Fork at Smithville	Active	590	10/1/1991	Present	
Upper Little River (B)	3	07338500	Little River below Lukfata Creek, near Idabel	Active	1,754	10/1/1946	Present	
		07338000	Little River near Idabel	Inactive	1,631	10/1/1929	9/29/1946	
		07337500	Little River near Wright City	Inactive	911	10/2/1929	9/29/1989	
		07337900	Glover River near Glover	Active	492	10/1/1961	Present	

Selected USGS Streamgages

Watershed (Basin Class)	Basin	Streamgage Number	Streamgage Name	Status	Period of Record — Mean Annual Streamflow (cfs)	Period of Record — Start Date	Period of Record — End Date	Notes
Beaver Creek (C)	25	07313000	Little Beaver Creek near Duncan	Active	51	10/1/1948	12/31/1963	Currently no flow data; gage height data only
		07312920	Beaver Creek near Hulen	Active		10/6/2016	Present	Currently no flow data; gage height data only
	26	07313600	Cow Creek at Waurika	Inactive	38	3/1/1966	9/29/1970	
		07313585	Cow Creek near Addington	Active		10/16/2016	Present	Currently no flow data; gage height data only
Lower Arkansas River (C)	46	07249455	Arkansas River at Fort Smith, AR	Active	42,619	9/29/2014	Present	Limited period of record
		07246500	Arkansas River near Sallisaw	Active	26,073	10/1/1947	Present	Historic flow data; gage height data only
		07249985	Lee Creek near Short	Active	549	10/1/1930	Present	
		07250000	Lee Creek near Van Buren, AR	Inactive	541	10/1/1930	11/22/1992	
		07249800	Lee Creek at Short	Active	315	9/16/1999	Present	
		07246000	Sans Bois Creek near Keota	Inactive	240	10/1/1938	9/29/1942	
		07245500	Sallisaw Creek near Sallisaw	Inactive	202	10/1/1942	9/29/1976	
		07249920	Little Lee Creek near Nicut	Active	124	10/1/2000	Present	
		07249870	Little Lee Creek near Greasy	Inactive	59	10/1/2000	9/29/2005	
		07246615	Coal Creek near Spiro	Inactive	13	10/1/1978	9/29/1982	
	47	07194500	Arkansas River near Muskogee	Active	24,980	7/25/2003	Present	
		07198000	Illinois River near Gore	Active	1,601	3/25/1924	Present	
		07198500	Dirty Creek near Warner	Inactive	224	10/1/1939	9/29/1946	
		07245030	Taloka Creek near Stigler	Inactive	8	10/1/1978	9/29/1981	Limited period of record
		07194555	Arkansas River at Gore	Active		10/16/2016	Present	Currently no flow data; gage height data only
Lower Canadian River (C)	48	07245000	Canadian River near Whitefield	Active	5,948	10/1/1938	Present	
		07231500	Canadian River at Calvin	Active	1,721	7/1/1905	Present	
		07244000	Deep Fork near Dewar	Inactive	1,337	10/1/1937	9/29/1950	
		07243500	Deep Fork near Beggs	Active	919	9/2/1938	Present	
		07242000	North Canadian River near Wetumka	Active	825	10/1/1937	Present	
		07232000	Gaines Creek near Krebs	Inactive	564	10/1/1942	9/29/1963	
		07242100	Wewoka Creek near Wetumka	Inactive	172	10/1/1959	9/29/1967	
		07231975	Brushy Creek near Haileyville	Inactive	107	7/1/1978	1/6/1983	
		07231990	Peaceable Creek near Haileyville	Inactive	74	7/1/1978	1/6/1983	
		07244100	Coal Creek near Henryetta	Inactive	20	3/20/1996	9/29/2004	
		07232010	Blue Creek near Blocker	Inactive	10	1/29/1976	1/6/1983	
	56	07229200	Canadian River at Purcell	Active	688	10/1/1959	Present	
		07231000	Little River near Sasakwa	Active	373	10/1/1942	Present	

Selected USGS Streamgages

Watershed (Basin Class)	Basin	Streamgage Number	Streamgage Name	Status	Mean Annual Streamflow (cfs)	Start Date	End Date	Notes
					Period of Record			
Middle Canadian River (C)	58	07229000	Canadian River near Newcastle	Inactive	1,135	10/1/1938	9/29/1945	
		07229200	Canadian River at Purcell	Active	688	10/1/1959	Present	
		07229050	Canadian River at Norman	Active	481	2/1/1996	Present	
		07229100	Canadian River near Noble	Inactive	431	10/1/1959	9/29/1975	
		07228940	Canadian River near Mustang	Active	378	5/1/2006	Present	
		07228500	Canadian River at Bridgeport	Active	350	10/1/1944	Present	
Middle Washita River (C)	16	07328000	Washita River near Tabler	Inactive	670	10/1/1939	9/29/1952	
		07328100	Washita River at Alex	Active	661	10/1/1964	Present	
		07326500	Washita River at Anadarko	Active	486	1/1/1903	Present	
		07327550	Little Washita River East of Ninnekah	Active	53	2/1/1992	Present	
		07327500	Little Washita River at Ninnekah	Inactive	44	10/1/1951	9/29/1963	
		07327490	Little Washita River near Ninnekah	Inactive	35	10/1/1963	12/31/1985	
		07327447	Little Washita River near Cement	Active	21	2/1/1992	Present	
		07327000	Sugar Creek near Gracemont	Inactive	15	10/1/1955	9/29/1974	
		07328070	Winter Creek near Alex	Inactive	11	10/1/1964	5/14/1987	
		07327050	Spring Creek near Gracemont	Inactive	10	6/25/1991	9/30/1994	Limited period of record
		07327442	Little Washita River near Cyril	Active	5	10/1/1992	Present	
		073274458	Little Washita River Tributary near Cement	Inactive	2	6/1/1995	9/29/2004	
		073274406	Little Washita River above SCS Pond #26 near Cyril	Inactive	2	2/24/1995	9/29/2013	
		07327483	Boggy Creek near Ninnekah	Inactive	0	4/1/1996	9/29/2004	
		073274408	Little Washita River Tributary near Cyril	Inactive	0	2/24/1995	9/29/2004	

Data: U.S. Geological Survey (September 2017)

Principal Lakes of 40 Acres or More

Lake Name	Watershed/Basin Name & Class	Stream	Authority	Normal Elevation	Normal Area	Normal Capacity	Shoreline	Purpose(s)[1]	Water Supply Storage	Water Supply Yield
				FEET	ACRES	ACRE-FEET	MILES		ACRE-FEET	AC-FT/YR
1908 Cutt-off	Red River (A)	Red River Tributary	—	—	56	—	3	—	—	—
Allen's	Middle Washita River (C)	Little Washita River Tributary	Grady Co. CD	—	43	318	1.6	FC	—	—
Arbuckle	Lower Washita (B)	Rock Creek	BOR	872.2	2,430	72,400	34.7	WS, FC, FW, R	62,600	24,000
Ardmore	Lower Washita (B)	Caddo Creek Tributary	Lake Ardmore Club Association	—	120	570	3.6	—	—	—
Ardmore City	Lower Washita (B)	Caddo Creek Tributary	City of Ardmore	818.5	144	600	4.5	R	—	—
Atoka	Muddy Boggy Creek (A)	North Boggy Creek	City of Okla. City	590	5,420	105,195	51.2	WS, R	123,500	92,067
Banks (W.J.)	Walnut Bayou (A)	Walnut Bayou Tributary	Phillip E & Carol Green	—	66	110	1.6	—	—	—
Big Wewoka Creek #11	Lower Canadian River (C)	Wewoka Creek Tributary	SCS/Seminole Co. CD	—	54	467	1.7	FC	—	—
Big Wewoka Creek #20	Lower Canadian River (C)	Wewoka Creek Tributary	SCS/Seminole Co. CD	—	40	280	1.4	FC	—	—
Big Wewoka Creek #24	Lower Canadian River (C)	Coon Creek	SCS/Seminole Co. CD	—	91	492	2	FC	—	—
Big Wewoka Creek #3	Lower Canadian River (C)	Wewoka Creek Tributary	SCS/Seminole Co. CD	—	67	318	2.8	FC	—	—
Big Wewoka Creek #33	Lower Canadian River (C)	Wewoka Creek Tributary	SCS/Seminole Co. CD	—	122	614	4.6	FC	—	—
Big Wewoka Creek #38	Lower Canadian River (C)	Wewoka Creek Tributary	SCS/Hughes Co. CD	—	102	475	3.1	FC	—	—
Big Wewoka Creek #39	Lower Canadian River (C)	Wewoka Creek Tributary	SCS/Hughes Co. CD	—	124	587	4	FC	—	—
Big Wewoka Creek #4	Lower Canadian River (C)	Wewoka Creek Tributary	SCS/Seminole Co. CD	—	46	279	2.2	FC	—	—
Big Wewoka Creek #41	Lower Canadian River (C)	Wewoka Creek Tributary	SCS/Hughes Co. CD	—	59	314	2	FC	—	—
Big Wewoka Creek #42	Lower Canadian River (C)	Wewoka Creek Tributary	SCS/Hughes Co. CD	—	54	278	1.7	FC	—	—
Bluestem	Muddy Boggy Creek (A)	Elm Creek	State of Okla.	—	97	840	2.3	—	—	—
Boggy Cutoff	Muddy Boggy Creek (A)	Muddy Boggy Creek Tributary	—	—	69	—	8	—	—	—
Broken Bow[2]	Mountain Fork River (B)	Mountain Fork River	USACE	599.5	14,160	913,370	181.2	FC, HP, WS, R, FW	152,500	58,386
Broken-Bow	Upper Little River (B)	Yashau Creek	Gail Huffman Allen	—	51	240	1.4	—	—	—
Brooks	Lower Canadian River (C)	Fish Creek	Hughes Co. CD	—	64	364	3.1	FC	—	—
Brown	Lower Canadian River (C)	Bull Creek	USDOD	—	553	4,525	8.1	—	—	—
Brushy Creek	Lower Arkansas River (C)	Brushy Creek	State of Okla.	633.86	225	3,258	3.9	FC, R	—	—
Bryarly	Red River (A)	Red River Tributary	—	—	56	—	2.6	—	—	—
Byars	Lower Washita (B)	Peavine Creek Tributary	Town of Byars	—	72	92	1.8	—	—	—
Caddo Creek #17	Lower Washita (B)	Caddo Creek Tributary	SCS/Arbuckle CD	—	47	217	1.6	FC	—	—
Caddo Creek #19	Lower Washita (B)	Caddo Creek Tributary	SCS/Arbuckle CD	—	41	123	2	FC	—	—
Caddo Creek #2	Lower Washita (B)	Caddo Creek Tributary	SCS/Arbuckle CD	—	61	166	1.6	FC	—	—
Caddo Creek #27	Lower Washita (B)	Caddo Creek Tributary	SCS/Arbuckle CD	—	45	300	1.6	FC	—	—
Caddo Creek #28	Lower Washita (B)	Washita River Tributary	SCS/Arbuckle CD	—	40	181	2.2	FC	—	—

Principal Lakes of 40 Acres or More

Lake Name	Watershed/Basin Name & Class	Stream	Authority	Normal Elevation	Normal Area	Normal Capacity	Shoreline	Purpose(s)[1]	Water Supply Storage	Water Supply Yield
				FEET	ACRES	ACRE-FEET	MILES		ACRE-FEET	AC-FT/YR
Caney Coon Creek #1	Muddy Boggy Creek (A)	Caney Creek	SCS/Coal Co. CD	—	122	398	3.3	FC	—	—
Caney Creek #12	Clear Boggy Creek (B)	Caney Creek Tributary	SCS/Atoka Co. CD	—	53	206	1.6	FC	—	—
Caney Creek #13	Clear Boggy Creek (B)	Caney Creek Tributary	SCS/Atoka Co. CD	—	44	77	1.6	FC	—	—
Carl Albert	Kiamichi River (B)	Rock Creek	City of Talihina	761	180	2,739	3	WS. FC, R	—	—
Carlton	Poteau River (A)	Fourche Maline Creek	State of Okla.	714	42	552	1.5	R	—	—
Carter	Red River (A)	Glasses Creek	City of Madill	831	108	990	3	WS, R	—	—
Carter (Canadian River)	Lower Canadian River (C)	Wewoka Creek Tributary	Seminole Co. CD	—	65	332	3.5	FC	—	—
Caston Mountain Creek #3	Poteau River (A)	Caston Creek Tributary	SCS/LeFlore Co. CD	—	51	295	1.2	FC	—	—
Cedar	Poteau River (A)	Cedar Creek	USDA	718	92	1,000	2.5	R	—	—
Cedar (Canadian River)	Middle Canadian River (C)	Canadian River Tributary	Western Sportsman Club	—	53	1,125	2.2	—	—	—
Charles	Red River (A)	Red River Tributary	—	—	88	—	2.4	—	—	—
Cherokee Sandy #8	Lower Washita (B)	Willow Sandy Creek Tributary	SCS/Garvin Co. CD	—	47	193	2.3	FC	—	—
Cherokee Sandy #9	Lower Washita (B)	Cherokee Sandy Creek	SCS/Garvin Co. CD	—	54	252	1.7	FC	—	—
Chickasha	Middle Washita River (C)	Spring Creek	City of Chickasha	1170	839	41,080	8.4	WS, R	—	—
Chigley Sandy Creek #6	Lower Washita (B)	Chigley Sandy Creek Tributary	SCS/Garvin Co. CD	—	51	346	1.3	FC	—	—
Clayton	Kiamichi River (B)	Peal Creek	State of Okla.	664	64	953	2.2	R	—	—
Clear 1	Red River (A)	Red River Tributary	—	—	84	—	3.2	—	—	—
Clear 2	Red River (A)	Red River Tributary	—	—	84	—	3.7	—	—	—
Clear Creek	Lower Washita (B)	Clear Creek	City of Duncan	1150.335	697	7,710	9.5	WS, R	—	2,000
Club	Lower Arkansas River (C)	Sans Bois Creek Tributary	McCurtain Club Lake	—	49	495	1.8	—	—	—
Coalgate	Muddy Boggy Creek (A)	Coon Creek	City of Coalgate	619	393	3,466	7.9	WS, FC, R	—	—
Colbert	Red River (A)	Red River Tributary	—	—	51	—	2	—	—	—
Comanche	Mud Creek (A)	Deer Creek Tributary	City of Comanche	1045	186	2,500	4.6	WS, R	—	—
Conoco	Mud Creek (A)	Willow Branch	Lowery Farms LLC	—	60	168	1.8	—	—	—
Country Club	Muddy Boggy Creek (A)	Buck Creek Tributary	Town of Kiowa	—	133	700	2.8	—	—	—
Cow Creek #8	Beaver Creek (C)	Cotton Creek	SCS/Stephens Co. CD	—	73	708	1.5	FC	—	—
Criner Creek #1	Middle Washita River (A)	Criner Creek	SCS/McClain Co. CD	—	52	321	2.1	FC	—	—
Criner Creek #13	Middle Washita River (A)	Criner Creek Tributary	SCS/McClain Co. CD	—	61	258	2.5	FC	—	—
Dale Turner	Lower Canadian River (C)	Alabama Creek Tributary	—	—	49	—	1.1	—	—	—
Delaware Creek #10	Clear Boggy Creek (B)	Delaware Creek Tributary	SCS/Johnston Co. CD	—	65	143	1.7	FC	—	—
Delaware Creek #9	Clear Boggy Creek (B)	Delaware Creek	SCS/Johnston Co. CD	—	102	620	2.6	FC	—	—

Principal Lakes of 40 Acres or More

Lake Name	Watershed/Basin Name & Class	Stream	Authority	Normal Elevation	Normal Area	Normal Capacity	Shoreline	Purpose(s)[1]	Water Supply Storage	Water Supply Yield
				FEET	ACRES	ACRE-FEET	MILES		ACRE-FEET	AC-FT/YR
Diamondhead Corp.	Walnut Bayou (A)	Walnut Bayou Tributary	Falconhead POA	—	84	40	1.5	—	—	—
Dow	Lower Canadian River (C)	Brushy Creek Tributary	—	—	92	—	2.1	—	—	—
Dripping Springs	Lower Canadian River (C)	Salt Creek	City of Okmulgee	741	1,118	16,200	18	WS, FC, R	—	7,214
Duncan	Lower Washita (B)	Fitzpatrick Creek	City of Duncan	1095.299	199	7,200	3.6	WS, R	—	—
Durant	Blue River (B)	Blue River Tributary	City of Durant	624	288	4,121	6	—	—	—
Elmore City	Lower Washita (B)	Rock Creek Tributary	Garvin Co. CD	—	65	564	2.6	FC	—	77
Eufaula	Lower Canadian River (C)	Canadian River	USACE	585	93,544	2,194,857	829	FC, WS, HP, N, R	79,811	76,395
Fin & Feather	Lower Canadian River (C)	Gaines Creek Tributary	Fin and Feather Club	—	62	400	1.8	—	—	—
Finn Creek #22	Middle Washita River (A)	Finn Creek Tributary	SCS/McClain Co. CD	—	43	114	1.8	FC	—	—
Fish Pond	Red River (A)	Red River Tributary	—	—	75	—	3.5	—	—	—
Flag	Lower Canadian River (C)	Deep Fork of Canadian River Tributary	—	—	75	—	2.9	—	—	—
Forty One Cutt-off	Red River (A)	Red River Tributary	—	—	247	—	7.9	—	—	—
Fourche Maline #1	Poteau River (A)	Little Fourche Maline Creek	SCS/Latimer Co. CD	—	40	239	1.9	FC	—	—
Fourche Maline #3	Poteau River (A)	Fourche Maline Creek Tributary	SCS/Latimer Co. CD	—	41	219	1.3	FC	—	—
Fourche Maline #6	Poteau River (A)	Bandy Creek	SCS/Latimer Co. CD	—	103	430	2.1	FC	—	—
Fourche Maline #7	Poteau River (A)	Fourche Maline Creek Tributary	SCS/Latimer Co. CD	—	50	397	1.6	FC	—	—
Fourche Maline #8	Poteau River (A)	Pigeon Creek	SCS/Latimer Co. CD	—	42	232	1.2	FC	—	—
Fourche Maline #9	Poteau River (A)	Long Creek	SCS/Latimer Co. CD	—	42	471	1	FC	—	—
Fuqua	Lower Washita (B)	Black Bear Creek	City of Duncan	1076	986	21,100	13.9	WS. FC, R	21,100	3,427
Goddard (C.B.)	Red River (A)	Oil Creek	CB Goddard	—	91	184	2.3	—	—	—
Grassy 1	Red River (A)	Red River Tributary	—	—	59	—	2.2	—	—	—
Greenleaf	Lower Arkansas River (C)	Deep Branch	State of Okla., Leased	510	704	14,720	14.4	R	—	—
Hartshorne	Lower Canadian River (C)	Blue Creek	—	—	90	—	2.2	—	—	—
Healdton	Walnut Bayou (A)	Walnut Creek	City of Healdton	889	407	3,766	7.6	WS, FC, R	—	3,000
Henryetta	Lower Canadian River (C)	Wolf Creek	City of Henryetta	660	505	6,660	9.4	WS, R	—	—
Holdenville	Lower Canadian River (C)	Bemore Creek	City of Holdenville	789	403	11,000	9.6	WS, R	11,000	—
Hugo	Kiamichi River (B)	Kiamichi River	USACE	404.5	12,340	163,349	102.4	FC, WS, WQ, R, FW	118,850	64,960
Humphreys	Lower Washita (B)	Wildhorse Creek	City of Duncan	1178	780	14,041	12.4	WS, FC, R	—	3,226
Jap Beaver	Beaver Creek (C)	Beaver Creek Tributary	ODWC	923	43	662	1.6	R	—	—
Jean Neustadt	Lower Washita (B)	Caddo Creek Tributary	City of Ardmore	809	397	6,106	8.3	R	—	2,150

Principal Lakes of 40 Acres or More

Lake Name	Watershed/Basin Name & Class	Stream	Authority	Normal Elevation	Normal Area	Normal Capacity	Shoreline	Purpose(s)[1]	Water Supply Storage	Water Supply Yield
				FEET	ACRES	ACRE-FEET	MILES		ACRE-FEET	AC-FT/YR
John Wells	Lower Arkansas River (C)	Sans Bois Creek Tributary	City of Stigler	646.3	205	1,352	3.2	WS, R	—	—
Konawa	Lower Canadian River (C)	Jumper Creek	OG&E	924	1,321	23,000	16.6	CW	—	—
Leader-Middle Clear Boggy #23	Clear Boggy Creek (B)	Clear Boggy Creek Tributary	SCS/Pontotoc Co. CD	—	44	95	1.1	FC	—	—
Leader-Middle Clear Boggy #40	Clear Boggy Creek (B)	Clear Boggy Creek Tributary	SCS/Coal Co. CD	—	111	133	2.7	FC	—	—
Leeper 1	Red River (A)	Red River Tributary	—	—	168	—	2.7	—	—	—
Little Cedar Creek	Kiamichi River (B)	Kiamichi River Tributary	—	—	314	815	6.3	—	—	—
Little Wewoka Creek #0	Lower Canadian River (C)	Little Wewoka Creek Tributary	SCS/Hughes Co. CD	—	60	702	1.8	FC	—	—
Little Wewoka Creek #1	Lower Canadian River (C)	Graves Creek Tributary	SCS/Hughes Co. CD	—	111	691	3.5	FC	—	—
Little Wewoka Creek #10	Lower Canadian River (C)	Graves Creek	SCS/Hughes Co. CD	—	84	522	2.7	FC	—	—
Little Wewoka Creek #11	Lower Canadian River (C)	Wewoka Creek Tributary	SCS/Hughes Co. CD	—	50	396	1.7	FC	—	—
Little Wewoka Creek #13	Lower Canadian River (C)	Wewoka Creek Tributary	SCS/Hughes Co. CD	—	65	343	2.5	FC	—	—
Little Wewoka Creek #3	Lower Canadian River (C)	Little Wewoka Creek Tributary	SCS/Hughes Co. CD	—	57	152	1.6	FC	—	—
Little Wewoka Creek #9	Lower Canadian River (C)	Graves Creek Tributary	SCS/Hughes Co. CD	—	41	259	1.8	FC	—	—
Lloyd Church	Poteau River (A)	Bandy Creek Tributary	City of Wilburton	755	171	3,025	3.5	WS, FC, R	—	1,523
Louis Burtschi	Middle Washita River (C)	East Bills Creek	ODWC	1207	138	2,140	2.6	R	—	—
Lower Clear Boggy #10	Clear Boggy Creek (B)	Clear Boggy Creek Tributary	SCS/Atoka Co. CD	—	151	281	2.7	FC	—	—
Lower Clear Boggy #14	Clear Boggy Creek (B)	Clear Boggy Creek Tributary	SCS/Atoka Co. CD	—	41	136	2.2	FC	—	—
Lower Clear Boggy #20	Clear Boggy Creek (B)	Clear Boggy Creek Tributary	SCS/Atoka Co. CD	—	57	73	1.5	FC	—	—
Lower Clear Boggy #22	Clear Boggy Creek (B)	Clear Boggy Creek Tributary	SCS/Coal Co. CD	—	109	135	2.3	FC	—	—
Lower Clear Boggy #24	Clear Boggy Creek (B)	Clear Boggy Creek Tributary	SCS/Atoka Co. CD	—	60	152	1.3	FC	—	—
Lower Clear Boggy #25	Clear Boggy Creek (B)	Clear Boggy Creek Tributary	SCS/Atoka Co. CD	—	59	179	1.5	FC	—	—
Madill	Red River (A)	Red River Tributary	City of Madill	—	218	3,000	3.7	—	—	—
Marble City	Lower Arkansas River (C)	Dry Creek	Sequoyah Co. CD	—	58	255	1.6	FC	—	—
McAlester	Lower Canadian River (C)	Bull Creek	City of McAlester	620	1,487	13,398	18.1	WS, R	16,900	9,200
McGee Creek	Muddy Boggy Creek (A)	McGee Creek	BOR	577.1	5,116	113,930	94.7	WS, WQ, FC, R, FW	109,800	71,800
Mintubbe	Red River (A)	Red River Tributary	—	—	45	—	1.8	—	—	—
Morris (Alvin J.)	Kiamichi River (B)	Kiamichi River Tributary	Gerald Wayne Flatt	—	60	581	1.6	—	—	—
Mountain	Lower Washita (B)	Hickory Creek	City of Ardmore	1045.7	205	3,040	4.5	R	—	—
Muldrow	Lower Arkansas River (C)	Camp Creek	City of Muldrow	—	76	887	1.8	—	—	—

Principal Lakes of 40 Acres or More

Lake Name	Watershed/Basin Name & Class	Stream	Authority	Normal Elevation	Normal Area	Normal Capacity	Shoreline	Purpose(s)[1]	Water Supply Storage	Water Supply Yield
				FEET	ACRES	ACRE-FEET	MILES		ACRE-FEET	AC-FT/YR
Murray	Red River (A)	Anadarche Creek	State of Okla.	750	5,458	153,250	80.8	R	111,921	1,008
Nanih Waiya	Kiamichi River (B)	Kiamichi River Tributary	ODWC	594	105	1,064	2	R	—	—
New Beggs	Lower Canadian River (C)	Adams Creek Tributary	Charles Brett & Crystal Ross	—	55	50	1.6	—	—	—
New Spiro	Poteau River (A)	Holi-Tuska Creek	City of Spiro	426	261	2,160	5.2	WS, R	—	—
OK Noname	Mud Creek (A)	West Mud Creek Tributary	Berry Wendel	—	43	502	1.4	—	—	—
Okmulgee	Lower Canadian River (C)	Salt Creek	City of Okmulgee	690	629	14,170	13.8	WS, R	—	—
Okmulgee Creek #1	Lower Canadian River (C)	Deep Fork of Canadian River Tributary	SCS/Okmulgee Co. CD	—	82	670	2.4	FC	—	—
Onapa	Lower Canadian River (C)	Deep Fork of Canadian River Tributary	City of Checotah	—	67	1,137	2.7	—	—	—
Oteka	Red River (A)	Washita River Tributary	Dan V & Prudence Little	—	54	380	2.3	—	—	—
Ozzie Cobb	Kiamichi River (B)	Rock Creek	ODWC	513	62	833	2	R	—	—
Pauls Valley	Lower Washita (B)	Washington Creek	City of Pauls Valley	900	507	8,730	7.7	WS, R	—	—
Peavine Creek #1	Lower Washita (B)	Peavine Creek	SCS/Garvin Co. CD	—	85	325	2.2	FC	—	—
Peavine Creek #11	Lower Washita (B)	Peavine Creek Tributary	SCS/McClain Co. CD	—	58	216	1.8	FC	—	—
Peavine Creek #2	Lower Washita (B)	Peavine Creek Tributary	SCS/Garvin Co. CD	—	70	358	2.2	FC	—	—
Peavine Creek #3	Lower Washita (B)	Peavine Creek Tributary	SCS/Garvin Co. CD	—	57	363	1.8	FC	—	—
Peavine Creek #4	Lower Washita (B)	Peavine Creek Tributary	SCS/Garvin Co. CD	—	55	326	1.5	FC	—	—
Peavine Creek #5	Lower Washita (B)	Peavine Creek Tributary	SCS/McClain Co. CD	—	53	319	1.5	FC	—	—
Pine Creek	Upper Little River (B)	Little River	USACE	433	2,810	44,570	85	FC, WS, WQ, FW, R	49,400	94,080
Prison	Lower Canadian River (C)	Sandy Creek Tributary	State of Okla.	—	58	435	2.3	—	—	—
Purcell	Lower Canadian River (A)	Walnut Creek Tributary	City of Purcell	1068	144	2,600	3.1	WS, R	—	—
Raymond Gary	Kiamichi River (B)	Gates Creek	ODWC	401	273	1,681	9.3	R	—	—
RC Longmire	Lower Washita (B)	Keel Sandy Creek	SCS/City of Pauls Valley	979.2	919	14,424	12	WS, R	—	3,360
Red	Red River (A)	Red River Tributary	—	—	65	—	2.5	—	—	—
Roaring Creek #9	Middle Washita River (A)	Roaring Creek	SCS/Grady Co. CD	—	48	227	2.5	FC	—	—
Robert S Kerr	Lower Arkansas River (C)	Arkansas River	USACE	460	40,818	525,700	275.3	N, HP, R	—	—
Rock Creek #14	Lower Washita (B)	Rock Creek	SCS/Pontotoc Co. CD	—	64	198	2.7	FC	—	—
Rock Creek #4	Kiamichi River (B)	Rock Creek Tributary	SCS/Talihina CD	—	84	375	1.5	FC	—	—
Roebuck	Red River (A)	Red River Tributary	—	—	139	—	5	—	—	—
Ross	Lower Arkansas River (C)	Bayou Manard Tributary	—	—	67	—	3.8	—	—	—
Round Creek #6	Middle Washita River (A)	Washita River Tributary	SCS/Grady Co. CD	—	42	245	1.2	FC	—	—

Principal Lakes of 40 Acres or More

Lake Name	Watershed/Basin Name & Class	Stream	Authority	Normal Elevation	Normal Area	Normal Capacity	Shoreline	Purpose(s)[1]	Water Supply Storage	Water Supply Yield
				FEET	ACRES	ACRE-FEET	MILES		ACRE-FEET	AC-FT/YR
Rush Creek #10	Lower Washita (B)	Rush Creek Tributary	SCS/Grady Co. CD	—	87	835	2.9	FC	—	—
Rush Creek #4	Lower Washita (B)	Rush Creek Tributary	SCS/Grady Co. CD	—	47	330	1.9	FC	—	—
Sallisaw Creek #19	Lower Arkansas River (C)	Sallisaw Creek	SCS/Adair Co. CD	—	41	313	1.2	FC	—	—
Sallisaw Creek #25	Lower Arkansas River (C)	Greasy Creek	SCS/Adair Co. CD	—	78	255	2	FC	—	—
Sallisaw Creek #32	Lower Arkansas River (C)	Little Sallisaw Creek Tributary	SCS/Sequoyah Co. CD	—	149	218	3.2	FC	—	—
Sallisaw Creek #34	Lower Arkansas River (C)	Little Sallisaw Creek Tributary	SCS/Sequoyah Co. CD	—	163	89	2.5	FC	—	—
Sallisaw Creek #39	Lower Arkansas River (C)	Little Sallisaw Creek Tributary	SCS/Sequoyah Co. CD	—	119	85	2.1	FC	—	—
Sallisaw Creek #40	Lower Arkansas River (C)	Little Sallisaw Creek Tributary	SCS/Sequoyah Co. CD	—	83	30	1.7	FC	—	—
Sally Jones	Lower Arkansas River (C)	Lower Arkansas River Tributary	—	—	435	—	9.3	—	—	—
Sandy Creek #4	Lower Canadian River (C)	Canadian Sandy Creek Tributary	SCS/Pontotoc Co. CD	—	68	241	2.5	FC	—	—
Sardis	Kiamichi River (B)	Jackfork Creek	USACE	599	13,530	274,310	91.3	FC, WS, R, FW	274,070	156,800
Scott King	Lower Washita (B)	Rock Creek	City of Ardmore	808	221	3,588	4.8	R	—	1,220
Shadwick	Poteau River (A)	Coal Creek	Justin Decker	—	123	330	2.4	—	—	—
Sportsman	Lower Canadian River (C)	Wewoka Creek Tributary	City of Seminole	868	365	5,349	12.9	FC, R	—	—
Star	Lower Arkansas River (C)	Sand Creek	—	—	500	—	6.9	—	—	—
Stilwell City	Lower Arkansas River (C)	Sallisaw Creek Tributary	City of Stilwell	947	197	3,110	4	WS, FC, R	0	—
Stonewall	Clear Boggy Creek (B)	Clear Boggy Creek Tributary	Michael J. & Joe D. Williams	—	46	180	1.5	—	—	—
Sugar Creek #20	Middle Washita River (C)	Sugar Creek Tributary	SCS/North Caddo CD	—	50	312	1.4	FC	—	—
Sugar Creek #24	Middle Washita River (C)	Sugar Creek Tributary	SCS/South Caddo CD	—	47	272	1.2	FC	—	—
Sugar Creek #26	Middle Washita River (C)	Sugar Creek Tributary	SCS/South Caddo CD	—	46	238	1.1	FC	—	—
Sugar Creek #40	Middle Washita River (C)	Sugar Creek Tributary	SCS/South Caddo CD	—	42	211	1	FC	—	—
Sugar Creek #4A	Middle Washita River (C)	Sugar Creek Tributary	SCS/South Caddo CD	—	47	266	1.5	FC	—	—
Sugar Creek #9	Middle Washita River (C)	Sugar Creek Tributary	SCS/South Caddo CD	—	41	254	1.1	FC	—	—
Talawanda 1	Lower Canadian River (C)	Coal Creek Tributary	City of McAlester	650	105	1,200	2.9	R	—	—
Talawanda 2	Lower Canadian River (C)	Coal Creek Tributary	City of McAlester	635	242	2,750	4.1	WS, R	—	—
Taylor	Lower Washita (B)	Rush Creek	City of Marlow, Leased	1255	195	1,877	4.1	WS, FC, R	—	—
Texoma[2]	Red River (A)	Red River	USACE	617	74,686	2,516,232	495.4	FC, WS, HP, LF, R	150,000	168,000
Upper Clear Boggy #23	Clear Boggy Creek (B)	Clear Boggy Creek Tributary	SCS/Pontotoc Co. CD	—	70	140	3.3	FC	—	—
Upper Clear Boggy #25	Clear Boggy Creek (B)	Clear Boggy Creek Tributary	SCS/Pontotoc Co. CD	—	42	168	1.4	FC	—	—
Upper Clear Boggy #30	Clear Boggy Creek (B)	Bois d'Arc Creek Tributary	SCS/Pontotoc Co. CD	—	52	87	1.3	FC	—	—
Upper Clear Boggy #31	Clear Boggy Creek (B)	Bois d'Arc Creek	SCS/Pontotoc Co. CD	—	46	190	1.3	FC	—	—

Principal Lakes of 40 Acres or More

Lake Name	Watershed/Basin Name & Class	Stream	Authority	Normal Elevation	Normal Area	Normal Capacity	Shoreline	Purpose(s)[1]	Water Supply Storage	Water Supply Yield
				FEET	ACRES	ACRE-FEET	MILES		ACRE-FEET	AC-FT/YR
Upper Clear Boggy #32	Clear Boggy Creek (B)	Clear Boggy Creek Tributary	SCS/Pontotoc Co. CD	—	48	200	1.7	FC	—	—
Upper Clear Boggy #42	Clear Boggy Creek (B)	Clear Boggy Creek Tributary	SCS/Pontotoc Co. CD	—	58	151	1.5	FC	—	—
Upper Clear Boggy #46	Clear Boggy Creek (B)	Clear Boggy Creek Tributary	SCS/Pontotoc Co. CD	—	60	233	1.5	FC	—	—
Upper Clear Boggy #47	Clear Boggy Creek (B)	Clear Boggy Creek Tributary	SCS/Pontotoc Co. CD	—	57	145	1.5	FC	—	—
Upper Clear Boggy #7	Clear Boggy Creek (B)	Clear Boggy Creek Tributary	SCS/Coal Co. CD	—	49	92	2.4	FC	—	—
Upper Clear Boggy #9	Clear Boggy Creek (B)	Clear Boggy Creek Tributary	SCS/Coal Co. CD		94	172	2.7	FC	—	—
Upper Muddy Boggy #20	Muddy Boggy Creek (A)	Caney Boggy Creek Tributary	SCS/Coal Co. CD	—	84	644	4.2	FC	—	—
Van Sickle Bros. 1	Red River (A)	Red River Tributary	JD Vansickle	—	75	247	2.9	—	—	—
Veterans	Lower Washita (B)	Rock Creek Tributary	City of Sulphur	965	66	600	2	R	—	—
Wapanucka City	Clear Boggy Creek (B)	Sandy Creek Tributary	Johnston Co. CD	—	73	107	2.4	FC	—	—
Ward	Red River (A)	Norwood Creek Tributary	—	—	331	—	4.3	—	—	—
Waurika	Beaver Creek (C)	Beaver Creek	USACE	951.4	9,926	190,044	72.6	FC, IR, WS, WQ, R, FW	151,400	40,549
Wayne Creek #1	Middle Washita River (A)	Washita River Tributary	SCS/McClain Co. CD	—	51	279	2.2	FC	—	—
Wayne Wallace	Poteau River (A)	Fourche Maline Creek	State of Okla.	797	111	1,746	3.4	R, FC	—	—
Webbers Falls	Lower Arkansas River (C)	Arkansas River	USACE	490	8,734	170,100	117.4	N, HP	—	—
Weleetka	Lower Canadian River (C)	Alabama Creek Tributary	City of Weleetka	743	58	385	1.6	WS, R	—	—
Wewoka	Lower Canadian River (C)	Coon Creek	City of Wewoka	826.66	357	3,301	9.5	WS, R	—	—
Whitegrass-Waterhole Creek #6	Red River (A)	Waterhole Creek	SCS/Goolsby Ranch Inc.	—	56	302	1.5	FC	—	—
Wildhorse Creek #11	Lower Washita (B)	Wildhorse Creek Tributary	SCS/Arbuckle CD	—	53	160	2.2	FC	—	—
Wildhorse Creek #14	Lower Washita (B)	Wildhorse Creek Tributary	SCS/Stephens Co. CD	—	80	639	1.7	FC	—	—
Wildhorse Creek #19	Lower Washita (B)	Fitzpatrick Creek	SCS/Stephens Co. CD	—	44	791	1.4	FC	—	—
Wildhorse Creek #23	Lower Washita (B)	Clear Creek	SCS/Stephens Co. CD	—	101	731	2.8	FC	—	—
Wildhorse Creek #25	Lower Washita (B)	Clear Creek Tributary	SCS/Stephens Co. CD	—	41	244	1.8	FC	—	—
Wildhorse Creek #26	Lower Washita (B)	Wildhorse Creek Tributary	SCS/Stephens Co. CD	—	87	646	1.9	FC	—	—
Wildhorse Creek #27	Lower Washita (B)	Wildhorse Creek Tributary	SCS/Stephens Co. CD	—	90	713	2.1	FC	—	—
Wildhorse Creek #30	Lower Washita (B)	Wildhorse Creek Tributary	SCS/Stephens Co. CD	—	43	286	1.7	FC	—	—
Wiley Post Memorial	Middle Washita River (A)	Washita River Tributary	City of Maysville	965	239	2,082	4.7	WS, FC, R	0	538
Winter Creek #20	Middle Washita River (A)	Laflin Creek Tributary	SCS/Grady Co. CD	—	61	169	2.5	FC	—	—
Wister	Poteau River (A)	Poteau River	USACE	478	6,078	53,359	91.3	FC, WS, LF, C	14,000	31,364

[1]WS=Water Supply, R=Recreation, HP=Hydroelectric Power, IR=Irrigation, WQ=Water Quality, FW=Fish & Wildlife, FC=Flood Control, LF=Low Flow Regulation, N=Navigation, C=Conservation, CW=Cooling Water. Data: Oklahoma Water Resources Board/Oklahoma Inventory of Dams and USACE (2012).

[2]Reservoir utilizes seasonal operations plan.

Federally Listed Endangered & Threatened Species

Common Name	Status	Basin																													
		1	2	3	4	5	6	7	8	9	10	11	12	13	14	15	16	21	22	23	24	25	26	44	45	46	47	48	56	57	58
American burying beetle	Threatened	X	X	X	X	X	X	X	X	X	X	X	X	X	X		X	X						X	X	X	X	X			
Arkansas River shiner (fish)	Threatened							X	X	X		X	X		X	X	X							X	X	X	X		X	X	X
Gray bat	Endangered																							X	X	X	X		X	X	X
Harperella (plant)	Endangered		X	X	X	X																				X			X	X	X
Indiana bat	Endangered			X	X				X	X																X			X	X	X
Leopard darter (fish)	Threatened	X	X	X	X	X					X			X	X			X						X	X	X	X		X	X	X
Neosho mucket (mussel)	Endangered	X	X	X	X	X	X	X	X	X	X	X	X	X	X	X	X							X	X		X		X	X	X
Northern long-eared bat	Threatened	X	X	X	X	X	X	X	X	X	X	X	X	X	X	X	X							X	X	X	X		X	X	X
Ouachita rock pocketbook (mussel)	Endangered	X	X	X	X	X	X	X	X	X		X	X	X	X	X	X							X	X		X		X	X	X
Ozark big-eared bat	Endangered																							X	X	X	X		X	X	X
Piping plover (bird)	Endangered	X	X	X	X	X	X	X	X	X	X	X	X	X	X	X	X	X	X	X	X	X	X	X	X	X	X	X	X	X	X
Rabbitsfoot (mussel)	Threatened	X	X	X	X				X	X	X	X	X			X	X							X	X	X	X		X	X	X
Red-cockaded woodpecker	Endangered	X	X	X	X	X	X	X	X		X	X	X	X	X	X	X							X	X	X	X		X	X	X
Red knot (bird)	Threatened	X	X	X	X	X	X	X	X	X	X	X	X	X	X	X	X	X	X	X	X	X	X	X	X	X	X	X	X	X	X
Scaleshell mussel	Endangered	X	X	X	X	X	X	X	X	X		X	X	X	X	X	X							X	X	X	X		X	X	X
Whooping crane (bird)	Endangered	X				X	X	X	X	X	X	X	X	X	X	X	X	X	X	X	X	X	X	X		X	X	X	X	X	X
Winged mapleleaf (mussel)	Endangered	X	X	X	X	X	X	X	X	X		X	X	X	X	X	X							X	X	X	X		X	X	X

Data: U.S. Fish and Wildlife Service (March 2021)

Land Cover and Uses

Basin Class/Watershed	Forest		Herbaceous, Shrubs, Woody Wetlands		Cultivated Land, Hay/Pasture		Developed		Water		Barren Land		Total Land Area
	SQUARE MILES	%	SQUARE MILES	%	SQUARE MILES	%	SQUARE MILES	%	SQUARE MILES	%	SQUARE MILES	%	SQUARE MILES
Class A													
Little River	197	56%	80	23%	59	17%	15	4%	2	1%	0	0%	353
Lower Canadian River	37	18%	121	60%	28	14%	16	8%	1	0%	0	0%	203
Middle Washita River	80	15%	309	59%	105	20%	22	4%	6	1%	0	0%	522
Mud Creek	94	15%	449	69%	88	14%	14	2%	3	0%	0	0%	648
Muddy Boggy Creek	706	49%	329	23%	334	23%	43	3%	22	2%	1	0.1%	1,435
Poteau River	806	60%	98	7%	373	28%	52	4%	18	1%	2	0.1%	1,349
Red River	721	27%	960	36%	695	26%	108	4%	148	6%	19	0.7%	2,651
Walnut Bayou	112	34%	163	49%	41	12%	16	5%	2	1%	0	0%	334
Class B													
Blue River	186	27%	299	44%	167	24%	29	4%	4	1%	0	0%	685
Clear Boggy Creek	387	39%	354	35%	221	22%	34	3%	7	1%	1	0.1%	1,004
Kiamichi River	1,190	65%	210	12%	326	18%	45	2%	48	3%	2	0.1%	1,821
Lower Washita River	452	24%	1,057	57%	237	13%	91	5%	29	2%	3	0.2%	1,869
Mountain Fork River	446	80%	57	10%	12	2%	16	3%	24	4%	0	0%	555
Upper Little River	876	68%	235	18%	120	9%	51	4%	11	1%	1	0.1%	1,294
Class C													
Beaver Creek	77	9%	589	68%	131	15%	47	5%	20	2%	0	0%	864
Lower Arkansas River	984	41%	172	7%	1,031	43%	117	5%	101	4%	7	0.3%	2,412
Lower Canadian River	1,917	46%	997	24%	855	21%	193	5%	193	5%	12	0.3%	4,167
Middle Canadian River	85	12%	321	47%	188	27%	80	12%	8	1%	4	0.6%	686
Middle Washita River	152	14%	701	62%	206	18%	56	5%	9	1%	1	0.1%	1,125

Data: USGS National Land Cover Database (2011)

Aquifers Within or Intersecting Basins

Aquifer Name	Type	Watershed & Basin Class	Area in Settlement Area Basins (SQUARE MILES)	Equal Proportionate Share (ACRE-FEET PER ACRE)	Hydraulic Conductivity (FEET PER DAY)	Transmissivity (GALLONS PER DAY PER FOOT)	Recharge Rate (INCHES PER YEAR)	Specific Capacity (GALLONS PER MINUTE PER FOOT)	Specific Yield	Storage Coefficient	Number of Wells
Major Aquifers											
Ada-Vamoosa	Bedrock	Lower Canadian (C)	175	2.0	3.0	—	1.52	—	—	—	427
Antlers	Bedrock	Blue (B) Clear Boggy (B) Kiamichi (B) Little (A) Lower Washita (B) Mountain Fork (B) Mud (A) Muddy Boggy (A) Red (A) Upper Little (B) Walnut Bayou (A)	4,276	2.1	0.10 to 12.97	112 to 19,149	0.3 to 1.7	3.2 to 11.1	—	0.0004 to 0.0010 dimensionless	2,592
Arbuckle-Simpson	Bedrock	Blue (B) Clear Boggy (B) Lower Washita (B) Lower Washita (B) Red (A)	530	0.2	0.39 (Simpson) 3.3 (Arbuckle)	1,324 (Simpson) 83,028 (Arbuckle)	5.58	—	—	—	416
Arbuckle-Timbered Hills	Bedrock	Beaver (C)	23	2.0	0.5	1,720	< 0.6	0.25 to 0.88	—	1.2 x 10⁻⁵	8
Arkansas River	Alluvium & Terrace	Lower Arkansas (C) Poteau (A)	270	2.0	—	50,000 to 109,000	9.0	—	—	0.004 to 0.2	203
Canadian River	Alluvium & Terrace	Lower Arkansas (C) Lower Canadian (A) Lower Canadian (C) Lower Washita (B) Middle Canadian (C) Middle Washita (A) Middle Washita (C) Muddy Boggy (A)	1,254	2.0	0.1 to 100 (39 ft/day average)	—	2.0	—	—	—	3,996
Garber-Wellington	Bedrock	Lower Canadian (C) Middle Canadian (C)	343	2.0	3.3 (fine sandstone) 0.33 (silty claystone)	—	1.84	—	—	0.0013	2,049
Gerty Sand	Alluvium & Terrace	Lower Canadian (C) Lower Washita (B)	110	0.65	—	12,000 to 27,000	0.9 to 1.0	—	—	—	360
North Canadian River	Alluvium & Terrace	Lower Canadian (C)	159	0.8 (Phase 3a) 1.3 (Phase 3b)	310	—	3.3	—	—	0.15	74

Aquifers Within or Intersecting Basins

Aquifer Name	Type	Watershed & Basin Class	Area in Settlement Area Basins (Square Miles)	Equal Proportionate Share (Acre-Feet Per Acre)	Hydraulic Conductivity (Feet Per Day)	Transmissivity (Gallons Per Day Per Foot)	Recharge Rate (Inches Per Year)	Specific Capacity (Gallons Per Minute Per Foot)	Specific Yield	Storage Coefficient	Number of Wells
Red River	Alluvium & Terrace	Beaver (C) Blue (B) Kiamichi (B) Little (A) Mud (A) Muddy Boggy (A) Red (A) Walnut Bayou (A)	1,240	2.0	—	—	2.5 to 5.0	—	—	—	3,281
Roubidoux	Bedrock	Lower Arkansas (C) Poteau (A)	1,076	2.0	2.3 to 4.0	2,992 to 5,236	—	0.29 to 18.50	—	1×10^{-6}	699
Rush Springs	Bedrock	Beaver (C) Lower Washita (B) Middle Canadian (C) Middle Washita (A) Middle Washita (C)	687	2.0	—	5,012 to 13,988	1.8	—	0.13 to 0.34	—	1,246
Washita River	Alluvium & Terrace	Lower Washita (B) Middle Washita (A) Middle Washita (C)	515	1.5 (Reach 3) 1.0 (Reach 4)	—	—	2.65 to 4.41	—	—	—	1,047
MINOR AQUIFERS											
Ashland Isolated Terrace	Alluvium & Terrace	Lower Canadian (C) Muddy Boggy (A)	24	2.0	104 to 125	19,488	3.9	—	0.2	—	13
Beaver Creek	Alluvium & Terrace	Beaver Creek (C)	56	1.0	132	15,840	3.45	—	0.17	—	24
Boone	Bedrock	Lower Arkansas (C)	255	2.0	22	32,912	10.0	—	0.07	—	329
Broken Bow	Bedrock	Little (A) Mountain Fork (B) Upper Little (B)	234	2.0	0.5	1,047	1.2	—	0.005	10^{-3} to 10^{-5}	85
East-Central Oklahoma	Bedrock	Lower Canadian (C) Muddy Boggy (A)	1,069	2.0	1.25	252	2.8	—	0.005 (shales) 0.125 (sands)	—	568
El Reno	Bedrock	Beaver (C) Lower Canadian (A) Lower Washita (B) Middle Canadian (C) Middle Washita (A) Middle Washita (C) Mud Creek (A)	1,379	2.0	1.0	1,571	0.75	—	0.01 (shale) 0.05 (sandstone)	—	4,797
Haworth Isolated Terrace	Alluvium & Terrace	Little (A) Red (A)	25	1.0	50	6,358	4.8	—	0.15	—	—
Hennessey-Garber	Bedrock	Beaver (C)	216	1.6	2.7	16,000	4.1	—	0.02	—	68

Aquifers Within or Intersecting Basins

Aquifer Name	Type	Watershed & Basin Class	Area in Settlement Area Basins (Square Miles)	Equal Proportionate Share (Acre-Feet per Acre)	Hydraulic Conductivity (Feet per Day)	Transmissivity (Gallons per Day per Foot)	Recharge Rate (Inches per Year)	Specific Capacity (Gallons per Minute per Foot)	Specific Yield	Storage Coefficient	Number of Wells
Holly Creek	Bedrock	Little (A) Mountain Fork (B) Upper Little (B)	30	2.0	10	2,244	1.2	—	0.1	—	9
Kiamichi	Bedrock	Clear Boggy (B) Kiamichi (B) Little (A) Lower Arkansas (C) Lower Canadian (C) Mountain Fork (B) Muddy Boggy (A) Poteau (A) Upper Little (B)	4,951	2.0	0.055	94	1.1	—	0.005	—	1,594
Little River	Alluvium & Terrace	Little (A) Mountain Fork (B) Upper Little (B)	144	1.0	40	4,488	4.8	—	0.15	—	60
Marietta	Bedrock	Red (A) Walnut Bayou (A)	156	2.0	0.5	374	1.6	—	0.05	—	93
Northeastern OK Pennsylvanian	Bedrock	Lower Arkansas (C) Poteau (A)	857	2.0	0.003	3.74	2.1	—	0.01	—	448
Pennsylvanian	Bedrock	Clear Boggy (B) Kiamichi (B) Lower Arkansas (C) Lower Canadian (C) Muddy Boggy (A) Poteau (A)	2,524	2.0	1.25 (sandstone) 0.0001 (fractured shale or siltstone)	980 (sandstone) 2 (shale)	1.1	—	0.125 (sandstone) 0.005 (shale, unconfined portion)	0.001 (confined portion)	1,243
Pine Mountain	Bedrock	Little (A) Mountain Fork (B) Upper Little (B)	30	2.0	0.5	1,047	1.2	—	0.005	10^{-3} to 10^{-5}	0
Potato Hills	Bedrock	Kiamichi (B)	32	2.0	0.5	1,403	1.15	—	0.005	—	14
Texoma	Bedrock	Red (A)	25	2.0	0.5	374	1.8	—	0.05	—	56
Woodbine	Bedrock	Blue (B) Clear Boggy (B) Kiamichi (B) Little (A) Muddy Boggy (A) Red (A) Upper Little (B)	2,255	2.0	0.5	935 to 1,219	2.28	—	0.06 (loose unconsolidated sandstone) 0.02 (clay and limestone)	0.001 (confined sandstone) 0.00001 (confined clay and limestone)	1,234

[1]Italic number signifies unstudied aquifers with a default temporary equal proportionate share (EPS) of 2.0 acre-feet per acre of land.

Data: OWRB and Chickasaw Nation (2017)

Distribution of Permitted/Domestic Wells Among Aquifers & Watersheds

Class	Aquifer Name	Type	Little	Lower Canadian	Middle Washita	Mud	Muddy Boggy	Poteau	Red	Walnut Bayou	Blue	Clear Boggy	Kiamichi	Lower Washita	Mountain Fork	Upper Little	Beaver	Lower Arkansas	Lower Canadian	Middle Canadian	Middle Washita
MAJOR	Ada-Vamoosa	Bedrock																		427	
	Antlers	Bedrock	36			1	155		1,454	136	274	123	258	23	0	132					
	Arbuckle-Simpson	Bedrock							96			213	37	35							
	Arbuckle-Timbered Hills	Bedrock															8				
	Arkansas River	Alluvium & Terrace						0										203			
	Canadian River	Alluvium & Terrace		192	5		1							4				74	801	2,118	0
	Garber-Wellington	Bedrock																	814	1,235	
	Gerty Sand	Alluvium & Terrace												28				166			
	North Canadian River	Alluvium & Terrace																74			
	Red River	Alluvium & Terrace	0			24	18		627	64	6			22			12				
	Roubidoux	Bedrock						0										699			
	Rush Springs	Bedrock			22									199				165		138	722
	Washita River	Alluvium & Terrace			174									153							273
MINOR	Ashland Isolated Terrace	Alluvium & Terrace					5													8	
	Beaver Creek	Alluvium & Terrace															24				
	Boone	Bedrock															329				
	Broken Bow	Bedrock	1												13	71					
	East-Central Oklahoma	Bedrock					58											510			
	El Reno	Bedrock		1,386	412	0								190				166		1,964	679
	Haworth Isolated Terrace	Alluvium & Terrace	0						0												
	Hennessey - Garber	Bedrock															68				
	Holly Creek	Bedrock	4												2	3					
	Kiamichi	Bedrock	14				29	474				3	206		356	395			94	23	
	Little River	Alluvium & Terrace	16												1	43					
	Marietta	Bedrock							91	2											
	Northeastern Oklahoma Pennsylvanian	Bedrock						0										448			
	Pennsylvanian	Bedrock					64	4				60	6					611	498		
	Pine Mountain	Bedrock	0												0	0					
	Potato Hills	Bedrock												14							
	Texoma	Bedrock							56												
	Woodbine	Bedrock	15				99		758			233	38	90			1				
	Nondelineated Wells			5	102	224	38		202	283	25	79	2	943		9	542	156	676	95	115
	Total Wells		**86**	**1,583**	**715**	**249**	**467**	**478**	**3,284**	**485**	**751**	**340**	**598**	**1,575**	**372**	**654**	**985**	**2,614**	**3,997**	**5,550**	**1,789**

Data: OWRB (February 2020)

Permitted Water by Source

Watershed (Basin Class)	Basin/Source	Number of Permits	Permitted Amount (AFY)	%
Little River (A)	**Basin 2**			
	Groundwater	2	93	4%
	Surface Water	3	2,125	96%
	WATERSHED TOTAL	5	2,218	
Lower Canadian River (A)	**Basin 57**			
	Groundwater	22	3,949	28%
	Surface Water	15	10,232	72%
	WATERSHED TOTAL	37	14,181	
Middle Washita River (A)	**Basin 15**			
	Groundwater	55	14,750	60%
	Surface Water	26	9,813	40%
	WATERSHED TOTAL	81	24,563	
Mud Creek (A)	**Basin 23**			
	Groundwater	13	5,884	93%
	Surface Water	3	466	7%
	WATERSHED TOTAL	16	6,349	
Muddy Boggy Creek (A)	**Basin 7**			
	Groundwater	11	2,661	37%
	Surface Water	11	4,526	63%
	BASIN TOTAL / % WATERSHED	22	7,187	4%
	Basin 8			
	Groundwater	31	4,531	3%
	Surface Water	42	167,540	97%
	BASIN TOTAL / % WATERSHED	73	172,071	96%
	WATERSHED TOTAL GROUNDWATER	42	7,192	4%
	WATERSHED TOTAL SURFACE WATER	53	172,066	96%
	WATERSHED TOTAL	95	179,258	
Poteau River (A)	**Basin 44**			
	Groundwater	4	61	3%
	Surface Water	9	2,091	97%
	BASIN TOTAL / % WATERSHED	13	2,152	4%
	Basin 45			
	Groundwater	18	2,280	5%
	Surface Water	37	43,866	95%
	BASIN TOTAL / % WATERSHED	55	46,146	96%
	WATERSHED TOTAL GROUNDWATER	22	2,341	5%
	WATERSHED TOTAL SURFACE WATER	46	45,957	95%
	WATERSHED TOTAL	68	48,298	
Red River (A)	**Basin 1**			
	Groundwater	14	7,836	71%
	Surface Water	7	3,227	29%
	BASIN TOTAL / % WATERSHED	21	11,062	7%
	Basin 10			
	Groundwater	6	5,592	44%
	Surface Water	8	7,184	56%
	BASIN TOTAL / % WATERSHED	14	12,776	8%
	Basin 13			
	Groundwater	38	10,264	31%
	Surface Water	52	22,889	69%
	BASIN TOTAL / % WATERSHED	90	33,153	21%
	Basin 21			
	Groundwater	142	36,810	38%
	Surface Water	103	61,261	62%
	BASIN TOTAL / % WATERSHED	245	98,071	63%
	WATERSHED TOTAL GROUNDWATER	200	60,502	39%
	WATERSHED TOTAL SURFACE WATER	170	94,561	61%
	WATERSHED TOTAL	370	155,063	
Walnut Bayou (A)	**Basin 22**			
	Groundwater	29	15,128	90%
	Surface Water	5	1,628	10%
	WATERSHED TOTAL	34	16,756	
Blue River (B)	**Basin 11**			
	Groundwater	3	2,077	25%
	Surface Water	9	6,329	75%
	BASIN TOTAL / % WATERSHED	12	8,406	20%
	Basin 12			
	Groundwater	45	10,364	31%
	Surface Water	25	23,541	69%
	BASIN TOTAL / % WATERSHED	70	33,905	80%
	WATERSHED TOTAL GROUNDWATER	48	12,441	29%
	WATERSHED TOTAL SURFACE WATER	34	29,870	71%
	WATERSHED TOTAL	82	42,311	
Clear Boggy Creek (B)	**Basin 9**			
	Groundwater	22	10,575	39%
	Surface Water	47	16,702	61%
	WATERSHED TOTAL	69	27,277	

Permitted Water by Source

WATERSHED (BASIN CLASS)	BASIN/SOURCE	NUMBER OF PERMITS	PERMITTED AMOUNT (AFY)	
Kiamichi River (B)	**Basin 5**			
	Groundwater	9	5,052	7%
	Surface Water	10	64,241	93%
	BASIN TOTAL / % WATERSHED	19	69,293	35%
	Basin 6			
	Groundwater	4	428	0%
	Surface Water	30	128,051	100%
	BASIN TOTAL / % WATERSHED	34	128,479	65%
	WATERSHED TOTAL GROUNDWATER	13	5,480	3%
	WATERSHED TOTAL SURFACE WATER	40	192,292	97%
	WATERSHED TOTAL	53	197,771	
Lower Washita (B)	**Basin 14**			
	Groundwater	134	38,585	36%
	Surface Water	93	67,153	64%
	WATERSHED TOTAL	227	105,738	
Mountain Fork River (B)	**Basin 4**			
	Groundwater	1	2	0%
	Surface Water	6	12,493	100%
	WATERSHED TOTAL	7	12,495	
Upper Little River (B)	**Basin 3**			
	Groundwater	2	95	0%
	Surface Water	12	42,426	100%
	WATERSHED TOTAL	14	42,521	
Beaver Creek (C)	**Basin 24**			
	Groundwater	3	1,922	44%
	Surface Water	8	2,447	56%
	BASIN TOTAL / % WATERSHED	11	4,369	6%
	Basin 25			
	Groundwater	82	21,353	31%
	Surface Water	26	47,288	69%
	BASIN TOTAL / % WATERSHED	108	68,641	92%
	Basin 26			
	Groundwater	15	1,748	98%
	Surface Water	1	38	2%
	BASIN TOTAL / % WATERSHED	16	1,786	2%
	WATERSHED TOTAL GROUNDWATER	97	23,101	31%
	WATERSHED TOTAL SURFACE WATER	27	47,326	63%
	WATERSHED TOTAL	135	74,796	
Lower Arkansas River (C)	**Basin 46**			
	Groundwater	67	14,412	37%
	Surface Water	60	24,792	63%
	BASIN TOTAL / % WATERSHED	127	39,204	15%
	Basin 47			
	Groundwater	50	10,554	5%
	Surface Water	52	203,729	95%
	BASIN TOTAL / % WATERSHED	102	214,283	85%
	WATERSHED TOTAL GROUNDWATER	117	24,966	10%
	WATERSHED TOTAL SURFACE WATER	112	228,521	90%
	WATERSHED TOTAL	229	253,487	
Lower Canadian River (C)	**Basin 48**			
	Groundwater	54	14,185	12%
	Surface Water	150	101,675	88%
	BASIN TOTAL / % WATERSHED	204	115,860	52%
	Basin 56			
	Groundwater	140	56,732	54%
	Surface Water	29	48,151	46%
	BASIN TOTAL / % WATERSHED	169	104,883	48%
	WATERSHED TOTAL GROUNDWATER	194	70,917	32%
	WATERSHED TOTAL SURFACE WATER	179	149,826	68%
	WATERSHED TOTAL	373	220,742	
Middle Canadian River (C)	**Basin 58**			
	Groundwater	181	88,274	68%
	Surface Water	35	40,664	32%
	WATERSHED TOTAL	216	128,937	
Middle Washita River (C)	**Basin 16**			
	Groundwater	256	45,592	64%
	Surface Water	85	25,940	36%
	WATERSHED TOTAL	341	71,532	
	SETTLEMENT AREA TOTAL	2,452	1,624,292	

Data: OWRB (September 2019)

Water Use Permits of 1,000 AFY or More

Watershed (Basin Class)	Basin	Permit #	Entity Name	Source	Amount (AFY)	Permit Type[1]	Primary Purpose[2]	County	Date Filed	Date Issued	Facility
Little River (A)	2	19660337	McCurtain Co RWD #1	SW	2,000.0	Regular	PWS	McCurtain	06/22/1966	10/11/1966	
Lower Canadian River (A)	57	20180085	Bluefin Water Solutions LLC	SW	3,093.4	Term	OGM	McClain	09/27/2018	04/16/2019	
	57	20190008	Bluefin Water Solutions LLC	SW	3,093.4	Term	OGM	McClain	01/24/2019	05/21/2019	
	57	20150002	Purcell PWA	SW	1,495.0	Regular	IR	McClain	01/06/2015	12/02/2015	
	57	19900536	Blanchard, City of	GW	1,200.0	Temporary	PWS	McClain	06/14/1990	11/13/1990	
Middle Washita River (A)	15	20140002	Continental Resources Inc	SW	1,624.0	Regular	OGM	Grady	01/22/2014	04/15/2014	
	15	20060572	Arthur Farms	GW	1,528.0	Regular	PWS	Garvin	08/01/2006	02/13/2007	
	15	20130053	Select Energy Services	SW	1,400.0	Term	OGM	Garvin	12/23/2013	04/15/2014	
	15	19810620	Green, Allen and Kimberly and Wayne	GW	1,395.0	Temporary	IR	Garvin	04/08/1981	09/08/1981	
	15	19980023	Sandy Creek Farms, Inc.	SW	1,357.0	Regular	IR	Grady	07/15/1998	10/13/1998	
	15	19810956	Winham, Allan	GW	1,230.0	Temporary	IR	Grady	12/28/1981	05/11/1982	
	15	19550129	Lindsay, City of	GW	1,129.0	Prior Right	PWS	Garvin	01/13/1955	05/10/1983	
	15	20140051	Crescent Services LLC	SW	1,056.0	Term	OGM	Grady	09/03/2014	04/21/2015	
Mud Creek (A)	23	19810514D	Crews, Kenneth S	GW	2,260.0	Temporary	IR	Carter	02/03/1981	02/09/1982	
Muddy Boggy Creek (A)	8	19800048	Oklahoma City, City of	SW	60,300.0	Regular	PWS	Atoka	03/27/1980	10/14/1980	
	8	19730282D	Oklahoma City, City of	SW	40,000.0	Regular	PWS	Atoka	07/19/1973	01/08/1974	
	8	19540613	Oklahoma City, City of	SW	31,367.0	Vested	PWS	Atoka	09/11/1954	03/09/1965	
	8	19730282B	County Commissioners of Atoka Co,	SW	8,000.0	Regular	IN	Atoka	07/19/1973	01/08/1974	
	8	19730282A	Atoka, City of	SW	8,000.0	Regular	PWS	Atoka	07/19/1973	01/08/1974	
	8	20040009	Coalgate, City of	SW	4,608.0	Regular	PWS	Atoka	04/19/2004	07/10/2007	
	8	19730282C	Southern Oklahoma Development Trust	SW	4,000.0	Regular	IN	Atoka	07/19/1973	01/08/1974	
	8	19800078	Coalgate PWA	SW	3,000.0	Regular	PWS	Coal	06/20/1980	09/09/1980	
	8	19910049	Atoka, City of	SW	2,000.0	Regular	PWS	Atoka	09/03/1991	06/14/1994	
	8	20080001	WACCAW Development LLC	SW	1,851.0	Term	OGM	Coal	01/16/2008	05/14/2008	
	7	19980049	BC Wetlands LTD	SW	1,100.0	Regular	RFW	Choctaw	10/26/1998	09/12/1999	
	7	20020014	Wilhelm, Gerald F and Gay Lynn	SW	1,012.0	Regular	IR	Choctaw	03/18/2002	09/10/2002	
Poteau River (A)	45	19850043	OG&E Energy Corp	SW	11,600.0	Regular	PO	LeFlore	08/08/1985	01/14/1986	
	45	20090020	Poteau Valley Improvement Authority	SW	7,053.0	Regular	PWS	LeFlore	08/13/2009	12/08/2009	
	45	20090010	Poteau Valley Improvement Authority	SW	7,053.0	Regular	PWS	LeFlore	04/17/2009	12/08/2009	
	45	19660268	Poteau Valley Improvement Authority	SW	3,400.0	Regular	PWS	LeFlore	05/27/1966	05/27/1966	
	45	19940038	Heavener Utilities Authority	SW	3,075.0	Regular	PWS	LeFlore	06/09/1994	01/10/1995	
	45	19780045	Poteau Valley Improvement Authority	SW	2,700.0	Regular	PWS	LeFlore	04/24/1978	07/11/1978	
	45	20060511	Thumbs Up Ranch, LLC	GW	1,282.0	Temporary	IR	LeFlore	02/08/2006	07/11/2006	
	45	19620084	Wilburton, City of	SW	1,185.0	Regular	PWS	Latimer	06/04/1962	06/13/1969	

Water Use Permits of 1,000 AFY or More

Watershed (Basin Class)	Basin	Permit #	Entity Name	Source	Amount (AFY)	Permit Type[1]	Primary Purpose[2]	County	Date Filed	Date Issued	Facility
Red River (A)	21	19770165	Tourism & Recreation, Dept of	SW	12,620.0	Regular	RFW	Carter	11/14/1977	03/14/1978	
	21	20160023	Tishomingo, City of	SW	7,000.0	Regular	PWS	Johnston	10/11/2016	02/21/2017	
	13	20040007	Ritchey Materials Co LC, Alan	SW	4,839.0	Regular	OGM	Bryan	02/23/2004	06/08/2004	
	21	20130022	Redi-Mix, LLC	SW	4,787.0	Regular	OGM	Love	04/30/2013	08/20/2013	
	21	20080025	Lattimore Materials Corporation	SW	4,023.0	Regular	OGM	Love	09/08/2008	12/09/2008	
	13	20080012	K D Holdings, LP	SW	3,950.0	Regular	IR	Bryan	04/11/2008	08/12/2008	
	1	20110633	I P Eat Four LLC	GW	3,554.7	Regular	IN	McCurtain	09/20/2011	11/08/2011	
	21	20150600	Burns Family Limited Partnership	GW	3,140.9	Regular	IR	Carter	11/05/2015	02/16/2016	
	10	20110666	Schulz, Curtis & Brenda	GW	2,927.8	Regular	IR	Choctaw	11/21/2011	03/13/2012	
	10	20160035	R B Q, L.P.	SW	2,800.0	Regular	OGM	Choctaw	12/21/2016	05/16/2017	
	21	19790114	Madill PWA	SW	2,500.0	Regular	PWS	Marshall	09/17/1979	12/11/1979	
	13	19930602	K D Holdings, LP	GW	2,465.0	Temporary	IR	Bryan	10/28/1993	06/14/1994	
	21	20170543	Oklahoma Sand LLC	GW	2,450.4	Regular	IN	Love	06/23/2017	12/19/2017	
	13	20080006	K D Holdings, LP	GW	2,275.0	Regular	IR	Bryan	03/04/2008	07/08/2008	
	21	20050014	Hanson Aggregates LLC	SW	2,116.0	Regular	OGM	Love	05/11/2005	12/13/2005	
	13	20180010	Weger, Lacey	SW	1,968.9	Regular	IR	Bryan	02/09/2018	01/15/2019	
	10	20170009	Harrington, George	SW	1,820.0	Regular	IR	Choctaw	02/13/2017	11/01/2017	
	21	19310018	US Fish & Wildlife Service	SW	1,813.0	Vested	RFW	Johnston	05/15/1931	08/12/1969	
	21	19720356	Marietta PWA	GW	1,780.0	Prior Right	PWS	Love	08/09/1972	12/11/1984	
	21	19970004	Marshall County Water Corporation	SW	1,616.0	Regular	PWS	Marshall	02/26/1997	06/10/1997	
	21	19580298	Chapman, Fred A	SW	1,600.0	Vested	IR	Johnston	09/04/1958	08/12/1969	
	21	20140070	XTO Energy	SW	1,500.0	Regular	OGM	Love	11/13/2014	04/21/2015	
	10	20150514	Bradshaw, Jack and Jennifer	GW	1,486.0	Temporary	IR	Choctaw	02/03/2015	08/18/2015	
	21	20010025	Meridian Aggregates Company	SW	1,485.0	Regular	OGM	Johnston	09/13/2001	01/13/2004	Troy Quarry
	21	20040033	Vulcan Construction Materials LLC	SW	1,425.0	Regular	OGM	Johnston	10/26/2004	12/14/2004	
	21	20130562	Sheffield, Oryn Treadwaye & Cynthia Rene	GW	1,380.0	Temporary	IR	Love	03/27/2013	07/16/2013	
	21	20150553	Keith R. Gray Trust	GW	1,276.0	Regular	PWS	Johnston	04/09/2015	04/19/2016	
	21	19800670	Kingston Municipal Authority	GW	1,250.0	Regular	PWS	Marshall	10/14/1980	12/09/1980	
	21	20190005	Ashby Investments LLC	SW	1,200.0	Regular	OGM	Johnston	01/18/2019	08/20/2019	Blue Sky Quarry
	1	20170002	Sylte Real Estate Ltd Partnerships, Chris	SW	1,100.0	Regular	IR	McCurtain	01/19/2017	12/19/2017	
	21	19780541	Conrad, Jimmie L	GW	1,085.0	Regular	IR	Marshall	03/16/1978	07/11/1978	
	10	20020023	Wilhelm, Gerald F and Gay Lynn	SW	1,012.0	Regular	IR	Choctaw	04/22/2002	11/12/2002	
	21	20050551	Huebsch, George F & Clara	GW	1,008.0	Regular	PWS	Marshall	07/26/2005	11/01/2005	
	21	20110003	Tishomingo National Wildlife Refuge	SW	1,000.0	Regular	RFW	Johnston	01/12/2011	04/12/2011	

Water Use Permits of 1,000 AFY or More

Watershed (Basin Class)	Basin	Permit #	Entity Name	Source	Amount (AFY)	Permit Type[1]	Primary Purpose[2]	County	Date Filed	Date Issued	Facility
Walnut Bayou (A)	22	19750784	Noble Research Institute LLC	GW	3,640.0	Regular	IR	Love	08/19/1975	11/18/1975	
	22	20140568	Davenport, John Kelly	GW	1,590.1	Regular	IR	Love	05/16/2014	04/21/2015	
	22	19740481	Healdton, City of	SW	1,473.0	Regular	PWS	Carter	12/05/1974	05/13/1975	SCS Site #10
	22	19800515	Gray, Zane and Sherry	GW	1,344.0	Regular	IR	Carter	01/24/1980	05/13/1980	
	22	20020506	Thomas, Dan E	GW	1,079.4	Regular	IR	Love	01/10/2002	07/09/2002	
	22	20180604	Southern Oklahoma Water Corporation	GW	1,050.0	Regular	PWS	Love	10/25/2018	04/16/2019	
Blue River (B)	12	19360076	Wildlife Conservation, Dept of	SW	6,445.0	Vested	RFW	Bryan	10/15/1936	04/13/1965	
	12	19780140	Durant, City of	SW	6,000.0	Regular	PWS	Bryan	10/06/1978	01/09/1979	
	11	20040005	Green Acre Sod Farms Inc, Robert Cook's	SW	5,350.0	Regular	IR	Bryan	02/19/2004	06/08/2004	
	12	19710554	Durant, City of	SW	4,500.0	Regular	PWS	Bryan	12/31/1971	04/11/1972	
	12	19400050	Durant, City of	SW	1,842.0	Vested	PWS	Bryan	06/03/1940	04/13/1965	
	12	19840646C	Roos Ranch Inc	GW	1,817.3	Regular	PWS	Pontotoc	09/21/1984	05/14/1985	
	12	20060561	Lively, Mel & Beverly	GW	1,500.0	Regular	OGM	Johnston	06/29/2006	11/13/2006	
	12	19880556	Ada, City of	GW	1,404.6	Regular	PWS	Pontotoc	07/29/1988	05/09/1989	
	11	19750749	Caddo Public Works Auth	GW	1,337.0	Regular	PWS	Bryan	07/15/1975	11/18/1975	
	12	19840645	Jacobs Ranch LLC	GW	1,271.0	Regular	PWS	Pontotoc	09/24/1984	05/14/1985	
Clear Boggy Creek (B)	9	19800107	Ada, City of	SW	5,340.0	Regular	PWS	Pontotoc	08/21/1980	05/12/1981	
	9	19590157	Ada, City of	SW	3,360.0	Vested	PWS	Pontotoc	05/19/1959	03/09/1965	
	9	20070566	G Hump Ltd,	GW	3,220.0	Regular	IR	Bryan	10/01/2007	10/14/2008	
	9	20010578	Mobbs, Roy & Shirley	GW	2,345.7	Regular	OGM	Atoka	10/30/2001	04/08/2003	
	9	20090547	Mungle Corporation	GW	1,980.1	Regular	PWS	Atoka	08/19/2009	07/13/2010	
	9	20140038	Phillhower, Tim & Linda	SW	1,564.0	Regular	RFW	Atoka	06/10/2014	03/11/2015	
	9	20020004	Reinauer, Robert M and Susan E	SW	1,000.0	Regular	IR	Pontotoc	02/04/2002	10/08/2002	
Kiamichi River (B)	6	20070017	Oklahoma City, City of	SW	115,000.0	Regular	PWS	Pushmataha	03/13/2007	10/10/2017	
	5	19770160	Western Farmers Electric Coop	SW	30,669.0	Regular	PO	Choctaw	12/14/1977	04/11/1978	Hugo Plant
	5	19720048	Hugo Municipal Authority	SW	28,800.0	Regular	PWS	Choctaw	02/28/1972	04/11/1972	
	6	19910054	Sardis Lake Water Authority	SW	6,000.0	Regular	PWS	Pushmataha	09/26/1991	12/17/1991	
	5	19770876	Western Farmers Electric Coop	GW	2,420.0	Regular	IN	Choctaw	12/14/1977	04/11/1978	Hugo Plant
	5	20160024	Harrington, GM & EJ	SW	2,090.0	Regular	IR	Choctaw	10/20/2016	04/18/2017	
	5	19540795	Hugo Municipal Authority	SW	1,700.0	Vested	PWS	Choctaw	10/07/1954	01/12/1965	Hugo Water Plant
	6	19680415	Talihina PWA	SW	1,500.0	Regular	PWS	Latimer	11/15/1968	03/11/1969	
	5	19740127B	MENS Ranch	GW	1,098.0	Regular	IR	Choctaw	03/27/1974	06/11/1974	
	6	19880022	Latimer Co RWD #2	SW	1,000.0	Regular	PWS	Pushmataha	07/14/1988	10/11/1988	

Water Use Permits of 1,000 AFY or More

Watershed (Basin Class)	Basin	Permit #	Entity Name	Source	Amount (AFY)	Permit Type[1]	Primary Purpose[2]	County	Date Filed	Date Issued	Facility
Lower Washita (B)	14	19820009	Arbuckle Master Conservancy District	SW	20,873.0	Regular	PWS	Murray	01/21/1982	05/11/1982	
	14	19770152	Davis, City of	SW	5,600.0	Regular	RFW	Murray	11/02/1977	03/14/1978	
	14	20150601	SEA Cattle Company LLC	GW	3,956.8	Temporary	IR	Carter	11/05/2015	05/17/2016	
	14	19840064	Pauls Valley, City of	SW	3,361.0	Regular	PWS	Garvin	10/05/1984	02/12/1985	RC Longmire
	14	19890003	Duncan, City of	SW	3,240.0	Regular	PWS	Stephens	12/23/1988	12/13/1994	Lakes Humphreys/ Fuqua
	14	19570516	Arbuckle Master Conservancy District	SW	3,127.0	Vested	PWS	Murray	05/14/1957	08/12/1969	
	14	19680400	Wynnewood Refining Co LLC	GW	3,000.0	Prior Right	IN	Garvin	10/28/1968	05/10/1983	
	14	19680402	Wynnewood Refining Co LLC	GW	3,000.0	Prior Right	IN	Garvin	10/28/1968	05/10/1983	
	14	20180046	Newfield Exploration - Mid Cont Inc.	SW	2,700.0	Term	OGM	Garvin	05/15/2018	01/15/2019	
	14	19030002	Ardmore, City of	SW	2,668.0	Vested	PWS	Carter	10/06/1903	08/12/1969	SCS Site #13 & #18
	14	19510039	Oklahoma Gas & Electric Company	GW	2,214.0	Prior Right	PO	Murray	04/07/1951	04/30/1951	
	14	19550061	Duncan, City of	SW	2,168.0	Vested	PWS	Stephens	01/07/1955	08/12/1969	
	14	19530524	Pauls Valley, City of	SW	1,993.0	Vested	RFW	Garvin	06/22/1953	08/12/1969	
	14	19690101	Marlow, City of	SW	1,877.0	Regular	PWS	Grady	02/17/1969	07/13/1971	
	14	20140609	Parker, Klint	GW	1,760.0	Temporary	OGM	Grady	09/02/2014	02/17/2015	
	14	19551265	Kerr-McGee Corp	GW	1,629.0	Prior Right	IN	Garvin	06/08/1955	05/10/1983	
	14	19530815B	Kerr-McGee Corp	GW	1,613.0	Prior Right	IN	Garvin	12/28/1953	05/10/1983	
	14	20140076	Duncan, City of	SW	1,600.0	Regular	PWS	Stephens	12/16/2014	04/21/2015	
	14	19730427	Citation Oil and Gas Corp	GW	1,280.0	Temporary	OGM	Carter	10/19/1973	01/08/1974	
	14	19650046	Ardmore, City of	SW	1,267.0	Regular	PWS	Carter	01/18/1965	04/14/1970	
	14	19650047	Ardmore, City of	SW	1,267.0	Regular	PWS	Carter	01/18/1965	04/14/1970	Jean Neustadt Lake
	14	19480007	Wynnewood Refining Co LLC	GW	1,249.0	Prior Right	IN	Garvin	02/02/1948	05/10/1983	
	14	19620028	Duncan, City of	SW	1,245.0	Vested	PWS	Stephens	02/02/1962	08/12/1969	Lake Fuqua
	14	19560906	Sulphur, City of	GW	1,120.0	Prior Right	PWS	Murray	12/10/1956	01/10/1957	
	14	19570146	Marlow, City of	GW	1,107.0	Prior Right	PWS	Stephens	02/14/1957	12/11/1984	
	14	19770832	Marlow, City of	GW	1,056.0	Temporary	PWS	Grady	10/05/1977	12/18/1977	
	14	20090017	Baptist General Convention of OK	SW	1,008.0	Regular	PWS	Murray	07/13/2009	10/13/2009	
	14	20110030	Wisian, Joel & Amy	SW	1,000.0	Regular	IR	Carter	06/13/2011	02/13/2012	
Mountain Fork River (B)	4	19860015	Broken Bow PWA	SW	9,720.0	Regular	PWS	McCurtain	03/27/1986	07/09/1986	
	4	19800098	Mountain Fork Water Supply Corp	SW	1,173.0	Regular	PWS	McCurtain	08/07/1980	12/09/1980	
Upper Little River (B)	3	19670560	International Paper Company	SW	33,605.0	Regular	IN	McCurtain	06/12/1967	06/10/1969	Valliant Plant
	3	19820137	Idabel PWA	SW	3,929.0	Regular	PWS	McCurtain	12/22/1982	11/08/1983	
	3	20020016	Smith, Bryant & Mavis	SW	1,900.0	Regular	PWS	McCurtain	03/26/2002	06/11/2002	
	3	19550764	Idabel PWA	SW	1,000.0	Vested	PWS	McCurtain	03/08/1955	02/09/1965	

Water Use Permits of 1,000 AFY or More

Watershed (Basin Class)	Basin	Permit #	Entity Name	Source	Amount (AFY)	Permit Type[1]	Primary Purpose[2]	County	Date Filed	Date Issued	Facility
Beaver Creek (C)	25	19650363	Waurika Master Conservancy District	SW	44,022.0	Regular	PWS	Jefferson	06/07/1965	07/13/1965	
	25	20010520	Nunley, William E & Shirley J	GW	2,043.8	Temporary	IR	Grady	02/27/2001	04/12/2005	
	25	20020595	Marlow, City of	GW	1,674.0	Temporary	PWS	Grady	10/16/2002	02/11/2003	
	24	20100023	Nitschke, Gary & Lauren	SW	1,547.0	Term	IR	Jefferson	08/25/2010	12/14/2010	
	24	19540988	Waurika, City of	GW	1,288.0	Prior Right	PWS	Jefferson	11/15/1954	01/08/1985	
Lower Arkansas River (C)	47	19500186	Oklahoma Gas & Electric Company	SW	98,598.0	Vested	PO	Muskogee	07/19/1950	08/10/1965	Riverbank Station
	47	19720375	Oklahoma Gas & Electric Company	SW	30,000.0	Regular	PO	Muskogee	08/21/1972	11/14/1972	
	47	20060046	Georgia-Pacific Consumer Operations	SW	19,593.0	Regular	IN	Muskogee	08/17/2006	02/13/2007	
	47	19750026	Georgia-Pacific Consumer Operations	SW	15,842.0	Regular	IN	Muskogee	04/14/1975	06/10/1975	
	47	19720376	Oklahoma Gas & Electric Company	SW	13,221.0	Regular	PO	Muskogee	08/21/1972	11/14/1972	
	47	19770163	Oklahoma Gas & Electric Company	SW	7,265.0	Regular	PO	Muskogee	12/22/1977	07/11/1978	
	46	19630010	Sallisaw, City of	SW	3,000.0	Regular	PWS	Sequoyah	01/18/1963	10/12/1965	SCS Site #29
	47	20030011	JRC Ranch LLC	SW	2,622.0	Regular	IR	Muskogee	03/27/2003	07/08/2003	
	47	20020056	Williams, Daniel B & Cyanne R	SW	2,190.0	Regular	IR	Haskell	12/23/2002	03/11/2003	
	47	20120066	Ford, Richard A & Sonja G	SW	2,034.0	Regular	IR	Haskell	11/14/2012	03/19/2013	
	46	19620152	Stilwell Area Development Authority	SW	2,000.0	Regular	PWS	Adair	10/31/1962	04/12/1966	Stilwell City Lake
	47	20030582	Oklahoma Gas & Electric Company	GW	1,646.4	Temporary	PO	Muskogee	09/16/2003	03/09/2004	Muskogee Station
	46	20140045	Johnson Jr, Foster S & Lawana	SW	1,338.8	Regular	IR	LeFlore	07/28/2014	02/17/2015	
	46	19850654B	Werschky, Carl & Sue, dba C W Farms	GW	1,280.3	Temporary	IR	LeFlore	11/06/1985	04/08/1986	
	46	20070037	Synar, John & Barbara	SW	1,200.0	Regular	IR	Sequoyah	07/12/2007	10/09/2007	
	47	20040547	Whitlock Packaging Corporation	GW	1,153.4	Regular	CO	Muskogee	05/13/2004	03/08/2005	
	46	19860526	Rose Real Estate Partnership	GW	1,020.0	Temporary	IR	LeFlore	03/24/1986	06/10/1986	
	46	20150029	Smith, Evelyn	SW	1,001.0	Regular	IR	LeFlore	07/23/2015	08/12/2016	
	46	20140014	Stigler, City of	SW	1,000.0	Regular	PWS	Haskell	03/14/2014	10/23/2014	
	47	20180038	Williams, Daniel Bryan	SW	1,000.0	Regular	IR	Muskogee	04/30/2018	04/16/2019	
	46	19770814	Hawkins Family Farms LLC	GW	1,000.0	Temporary	IR	Sequoyah	08/22/1977	11/08/1977	
	46	19900034	U.S. Fish & Wildlife Service, Sequoyah NWR	SW	1,000.0	Regular	RFW	Sequoyah	11/06/1990	11/06/1990	

Water Use Permits of 1,000 AFY or More

Watershed (Basin Class)	Basin	Permit #	Entity Name	Source	Amount (AFY)	Permit Type[1]	Primary Purpose[2]	County	Date Filed	Date Issued	Facility
Lower Canadian River (C)	56	19670592	Oklahoma Gas & Electric Company	SW	27,000.0	Regular	PO	Seminole	07/03/1967	09/12/1967	
	48	19790093	McAlester, City of	SW	16,000.0	Regular	PWS	Pittsburg	07/13/1979	12/11/1979	
	48	19790128	McAlester, City of	SW	12,500.0	Regular	PWS	Pittsburg	11/26/1979	02/12/1980	
	56	19840658	Purcell PWA	GW	10,849.0	Temporary	PWS	Cleveland	10/16/1984	12/03/1985	
	56	19670593	Oklahoma Gas & Electric Company	SW	8,000.0	Regular	PO	Seminole	07/03/1967	09/12/1967	
	48	19710443	Okmulgee, City of	SW	7,800.0	Regular	PWS	Okmulgee	08/11/1971	03/14/1972	
	56	20160551	Karges Revocable Trust, Brock	GW	6,608.0	Temporary	OGM	Cleveland	07/15/2016	10/12/2016	
	48	20000018	Juniper Water Company LLC	SW	6,020.0	Regular	PO	Pittsburg	06/07/2000	09/12/2000	
	48	20000040	Juniper Water Company LLC	SW	6,020.0	Regular	PO	Pittsburg	10/20/2000	05/08/2001	
	56	20060001	Karges Revocable Trust, Brock Robert	SW	4,626.0	Regular	IR	Cleveland	01/05/2006	03/14/2006	
	48	19390059	Okmulgee, City of	SW	4,434.0	Vested	PWS	Okmulgee	10/26/1939	12/12/1967	
	48	19880001	Hilseweck Partnership	SW	4,328.0	Regular	IR	Pittsburg	01/19/1988	05/12/1988	
	56	19760796	Lexington Assessment & Reception Center	GW	3,680.0	Temporary	CO	Cleveland	09/20/1976	03/08/1977	
	56	19760011	Holdenville, City of	SW	3,150.0	Regular	PWS	Hughes	02/05/1976	10/12/1976	
	48	19670151	Seminole, City of	SW	3,000.0	Regular	PWS	Seminole	02/27/1967	04/11/1967	
	48	19790116	McAlester, City of	SW	3,000.0	Regular	PWS	Pittsburg	09/19/1979	02/12/1980	
	48	19870025	Henryetta Municipal Authority	SW	2,874.0	Regular	PWS	Okmulgee	06/16/1987	10/13/1987	Henryetta Lake
	56	19690410	Oklahoma Gas & Electric Company	GW	2,600.0	Prior Right	PO	Pontotoc	09/29/1969	05/08/1984	Seminole Station
	56	19950579	HP Land & Cattle Co LLC	GW	2,440.0	Temporary	IR	Cleveland	07/07/1995	09/12/1995	
	56	19830575	Sherry Brothers,	GW	2,360.0	Temporary	IR	Hughes	04/21/1983	08/09/1983	
	48	20020055	Pittsburg County Water Authority	SW	2,000.0	Regular	PWS	Pittsburg	12/13/2002	05/13/2003	
	56	20160554	Cleveland Co RWSG&SWM #1	GW	1,920.0	Temporary	PWS	Cleveland	08/11/2016	11/15/2016	
	48	20080011	Henryetta Municipal Authority	SW	1,814.0	Regular	PWS	Okmulgee	04/02/2008	08/11/2009	
	48	19770795	Seminole, City of	GW	1,730.0	Regular	PWS	Seminole	08/16/1977	04/11/1978	
	48	19660568	Haskell County Water Corporation	SW	1,713.0	Regular	PWS	Haskell	08/30/1966	11/08/1966	
	48	19390058	Henryetta Municipal Authority	SW	1,653.0	Vested	PWS	Okmulgee	10/26/1939	12/12/1967	Henryetta Lake
	56	19810515	Braum Family, LP, W.H.	GW	1,500.0	Temporary	IR	Pontotoc	02/03/1981	04/14/1981	
	56	19810021	Holdenville, City of	SW	1,500.0	Regular	PWS	Hughes	02/02/1981	05/12/1981	
	48	19930613	Seminole, City of	GW	1,446.0	Regular	PWS	Seminole	12/15/1993	04/12/1994	
	48	19780522	Tri-County RWD #2	GW	1,395.0	Regular	PWS	Seminole	02/10/1978	05/09/1978	
	48	19810098	Checotah, City of	SW	1,353.0	Regular	PWS	McIntosh	04/10/1981	10/12/1982	
	48	19560845	Seminole, City of	GW	1,074.0	Prior Right	PWS	Seminole	11/07/1956	11/08/1983	
	48	20060057	Checotah, City of	SW	1,051.0	Regular	PWS	McIntosh	09/22/2006	07/10/2007	
	48	20090005	Harbin, Mark and Pam	SW	1,017.0	Regular	AG	Hughes	03/11/2009	07/14/2009	
	48	19950039	RWS & SW Mgt Dist #2, McIntosh Co	SW	1,000.0	Regular	PWS	McIntosh	09/08/1995	12/12/1995	Eufaula Lake
	48	19830050	Longtown Rural Water & Sewer Dist 1	SW	1,000.0	Regular	PWS	Pittsburg	08/22/1983	12/13/1983	

Water Use Permits of 1,000 AFY or More

Watershed (Basin Class)	Basin	Permit #	Entity Name	Source	Amount (AFY)	Permit Type[1]	Primary Purpose[2]	County	Date Filed	Date Issued	Facility
Middle Canadian River (C)	58	20060034	WHB Cattle LP	SW	10,080.0	Regular	IR	Grady	07/18/2006	02/13/2007	
	58	19780503A	Norman, City of	GW	8,073.0	Temporary	PWS	Cleveland	01/09/1978	06/13/1978	
	58	19780503B	Norman, City of	GW	6,334.0	Temporary	PWS	Cleveland	01/09/1978	06/13/1978	
	58	19840655	Braum Family, LP, W H	GW	5,935.0	Temporary	IR	Grady	10/03/1984	01/08/1985	
	58	19810687	Norman, City of	GW	3,562.0	Temporary	PWS	Cleveland	06/08/1981	11/10/1981	
	58	19800641A	Mustang, City of	GW	3,408.0	Temporary	PWS	Cleveland	09/08/1980	12/09/1980	
	58	20180040	Bluefin Water Solutions LLC Matthan	SW	3,096.0	Term	OGM	McClain	05/04/2018	12/06/2018	
	58	19960052	WHB Cattle LP	SW	3,000.0	Regular	AG	Grady	08/26/1996	11/05/1996	
	58	19790770	Moore, City of	GW	2,880.0	Temporary	PWS	Cleveland	11/28/1979	07/08/1980	
	58	19980574	Tuttle, City of	GW	2,611.3	Temporary	PWS	Grady	06/30/1998	09/29/1998	
	58	20180003	Southwind Hills Land & Development	SW	2,578.0	Regular	OGM	McClain	01/23/2018	08/21/2018	
	58	19840656	Braum Family, LP, W H	GW	2,444.0	Temporary	IR	Grady	09/21/1984	01/08/1985	
	58	20130567	Schieber, John Jay & Jenny Lee	GW	2,370.0	Temporary	IR	Canadian	04/04/2013	08/20/2013	
	58	20030036	WHB Cattle LP	SW	2,200.0	Regular	IR	Grady	10/16/2003	05/11/2004	
	58	20030037	WHB Cattle LP	SW	2,200.0	Regular	IR	Canadian	10/16/2003	05/11/2004	
	58	20110607A	Goldsby Water Authority	GW	2,190.8	Temporary	PWS	McClain	08/01/2011	03/13/2012	
	58	20020018	McComas, Chris & Christy	SW	1,985.0	Regular	IR	Grady	03/29/2002	07/09/2002	
	58	20060560	Carpenter Living Trusts, Ray and Evelyn	GW	1,923.2	Temporary	PWS	Canadian	06/29/2006	09/12/2006	
	58	20060035	WHB Cattle LP	SW	1,775.0	Regular	IR	Grady	07/18/2006	01/09/2007	
	58	20030038	WHB Cattle LP	SW	1,600.0	Regular	IR	Grady	10/16/2003	05/11/2004	
	58	20040581	Dolese Bros Co	GW	1,556.0	Temporary	OGM	Canadian	09/24/2004	04/12/2005	Mustang Sand Plant
	58	19930578	Wright, Danny M & Donna K	GW	1,510.0	Temporary	IR	Canadian	07/29/1993	11/16/1993	
	58	19840062	WHB Cattle LP	SW	1,500.0	Regular	IR	Grady	10/03/1984	01/08/1985	
	58	20040527	Scripsick, John & Jan	GW	1,500.0	Temporary	IR	McClain	03/09/2004	06/14/2005	
	58	20000579	KMA Holding Company Inc.	GW	1,500.0	Temporary	IR	Canadian	09/28/2000	02/13/2001	
	58	20130004	WHB Cattle LP	SW	1,482.0	Regular	IR	Grady	01/18/2013	06/18/2013	
	58	20070012	McComas, Chris	SW	1,418.0	Regular	IR	Grady	02/28/2007	06/12/2007	
	58	19530112	University of Oklahoma	GW	1,379.0	Prior Right	CO	Cleveland	01/20/1953	12/09/1980	
	58	19800623	Smith, Hattie June	GW	1,280.0	Temporary	IR	Cleveland	08/07/1980	01/13/1981	
	58	20120667	Gilleran Children's Trust, John B & Mary Ann	GW	1,280.0	Temporary	OGM	Canadian	10/04/2012	02/19/2013	
	58	20180004	Russell, Jason	SW	1,280.0	Regular	OGM	Canadian	01/25/2018	02/19/2019	
	58	19551482	Norman, City of	GW	1,219.0	Prior Right	PWS	Cleveland	10/01/1955	12/09/1980	
	58	19910045	Braum Family, LP, W H	SW	1,200.0	Regular	AG	Grady	08/15/1991	03/10/1992	
	58	19990581	Noble, City of	GW	1,198.0	Temporary	PWS	Cleveland	10/26/1999	01/09/2001	
	58	20170070	Cimarex Energy Company	SW	1,000.0	Regular	OGM	Canadian	11/17/2017	08/21/2018	
	58	20160019	R J C Resources LLC	SW	1,000.0	Regular	OGM	Canadian	08/09/2016	12/20/2016	

Water Use Permits of 1,000 AFY or More

Watershed (Basin Class)	Basin	Permit #	Entity Name	Source	Amount (AFY)	Permit Type[1]	Primary Purpose[2]	County	Date Filed	Date Issued	Facility
Middle Washita River (C)	16	19551469	Chickasha, City of	SW	5,200.0	Vested	PWS	Caddo	09/23/1955	08/12/1969	Chickasha Lake
	16	20180095	Aquahawk Energy LLC	SW	4,168.0	Term	OGM	Grady	12/10/2018	05/21/2019	
	16	19510071	Western Farmers Electric Coop	GW	2,534.0	Prior Right	PO	Caddo	07/30/1951	11/08/1983	
	16	19950639	Winter Creek Golf & Country Club	GW	1,117.0	Temporary	IR	Grady	11/28/1995	03/19/1996	
	16	20040014	Jantz, Raymond & Jason	SW	1,083.0	Regular	IR	Grady	05/10/2004	08/10/2004	
	16	20180067	Bluefin Water Solutions LLC	SW	1,072.0	Regular	OGM	Grady	08/14/2018	02/19/2019	
	16	20040545	Jantz, Raymond & Jason	GW	1,040.0	Temporary	IR	Grady	05/10/2004	11/09/2004	

[1]Includes Prior Right, Regular, Temporary, Term or Vested.

[2]Some permits include more than one use: Agriculture (AG); Commercial (CO); Industrial (IN); Irrigation (IR);
Oil, Gas & Mining (OGM); Power (PO); Public Water Supply (PWS); Recreation, Fish & Wildlife (RFW).

Data: OWRB (September 2019)

Water Systems

System	PWSID	Watershed(s)	Residential Customers Served[1]	Source(s) of Supply[2]	Water Sales	Water Purchases
Achille	OK2000707	Red	506	GW	—	—
Ada	OK2006201	Blue, Clear Boggy, Lower Canadian, Muddy Boggy	37,000	GW	Pontotoc Co. RWD # 1 (Homer), Pontotoc Co. RWD # 6 (Fittstown), Pontotoc Co. RWD # 7, Pontotoc Co. RWD # 9	—
Adamson RWD #8	OK3006112	Lower Canadian	4,306	P (SW)	—	Pittsburg Co. Water Authority
Alex	OK2002603	Middle Washita, Middle Washita	635	GW	—	—
Allen PWA	OK2006202	Lower Canadian, Muddy Boggy	937	GW	—	—
Antlers	OK1010302	Kiamichi	2,547	SW	—	—
Ardmore	OK1010814	Lower Washita, Red	25,060	SW	Lone Grove, Southern Okla. Water Corp.	Arbuckle Lake MCD, Southern Okla. Water Corp.
Arkoma	OK3004013	Poteau	2,180	P (SW)	—	—
Atoka	OK1010401	Muddy Boggy	2,988	SW	Atoka Co. RWD #2	—
Atoka Co. RWD #1 (Wardville)	OK3000305	Muddy Boggy	125	P (SW)	—	Pittsburg Co. RWD #11 (Kiowa)
Atoka Co. RWD #2	OK3000306	Clear Boggy, Muddy Boggy	500	P (SW)	—	Atoka, Atoka Co. RWS & SWMD #4
Atoka Co. RWD #3 (Caney)	OK2000302	Clear Boggy	1,500	GW	—	—
Atoka Co. RWS & SWMD #4	OK1010412	Clear Boggy, Kiamichi, Muddy Boggy	3,000	SW	Atoka Co. RWD #2, Choctaw Co. RWSG & SWMD #6, Stringtown PWA	—
Blanchard	OK3004710	Lower Canadian	2,966	P (SW)	Cole, Dibble, Tuttle	Newcastle, Tuttle
Bokchito	OK2000704	Blue	564	GW	—	Bryan Co. RW&SD #5
Bokoshe PWA	OK3004012	Poteau	450	P (SW)	—	PVIA
Boswell Public Works Authority	OK2001205	Clear Boggy, Muddy Boggy	932	P (SW)	—	Choctaw Co. RWSG & SWMD #6
Broken Bow PWA	OK1010214	Little, Upper Little	4,320	SW	Garvin, Haworth PWA, Idabel PWA, McCurtain Co. RWD #1, McCurtain Co. RWD #2, McCurtain Co. RWD #5 (Hochatown), McCurtain Co. RWD #6 (Kiamichi), McCurtain Co. RWD #7, McCurtain Co. RWD #8 (Mt. Fork Water), McCurtain Co. RWD #9, Valliant PWA, Wright City PWA	—
Bromide	OK2003517	Clear Boggy	169	GW	—	—
Bryan Co. RWS & SWMD #2	OK1010604	Blue, Red	9,055	SW/GW	Bryan Co. RW&SD #5	Durant Utilities Authority
Bryan Co. RW&SD #5	OK3000704	Blue, Red	8,250	GW	Bokchito, Bryan Co. RWD #7, Calera PWA, Colbert PUA	Bryan Co. RWS & SWMD #2, Durant Utilities Authority
Bryan Co. RWD #6	OK3000725	Blue, Clear Boggy	990	GW	Kenefic	Caddo
Bryan Co. RWD #7	OK2000705	Blue, Red	302	GW	—	Bryan Co. RW&SD #5
Bryan Co. RWD #9	OK2000713	Red	820	GW	—	—
Buckhorn RWD #2	OK3005002	Lower Washita, Red	1,260	P (GW)	—	Murray Co. RWD # 1, Sulphur
Byars	OK2004709	Lower Canadian, Lower Washita	275	GW	—	—
Caddo	OK2000703	Blue, Clear Boggy	944	GW	Bryan Co. RWD #6	—

Water Systems

System	PWSID	Watershed(s)	Residential Customers Served[1]	Source(s) of Supply[2]	Water Sales	Water Purchases
Calera PWA	OK2000702	Red	2,164	GW	—	Bryan Co. RW&SD #5
Calvin	OK2003201	Lower Canadian	300	GW	—	—
Cameron PWA	OK3004011	Poteau	302	P (SW)	—	PVIA
Centrahoma Water Co. Inc	OK3001502	Clear Boggy, Muddy Boggy	150	P (SW)	—	Coalgate PWA
Chickasha Municipal Authority	OK1010821	Middle Washita	16,036	SW	Grady Co. RWD #6, Norge Water Co	—
Choctaw Co. RWD #1	OK2001204	Kiamichi, Muddy Boggy, Red	2,300	GW	—	Hugo Municipal Authority
Choctaw Co. RWD #2	OK3001203	Red, Upper Little	373	P (SW)	—	Valliant PWA
Choctaw Co. RWSG & SWMD #3	OK3001209	Kiamichi	235	P (SW)	—	Hugo Municipal Authority
Choctaw Co. RWSG & SWMD #6	OK3001214	Clear Boggy, Muddy Boggy	850	P (SW)	Boswell PWA	Atoka Co. RWS & SWMD #4
Clarita Olney Water Co. Inc	OK3001501	Clear Boggy, Muddy Boggy	360	P (SW)	—	Coalgate PWA
Clayton PWA	OK3006408	Kiamichi	719	P (SW)	—	Sardis Lake Water Authority
Coal Co. RWD #5	OK3001505	Muddy Boggy	366	P (SW)	—	Coalgate PWA
Coalgate PWA	OK1010402	Muddy Boggy	2,005	GW/SW	Centrahoma Water Co. Inc, Clarita Olney Water Co. Inc, Coal Co. RWD #5, Phillips RWD #1, Roundhill RWD #4	—
Colbert PUA	OK2000716	Red	2,312	GW	—	Bryan Co. RW&SD #5
Cole	OK3004708	Lower Canadian	473	P (SW)	—	Blanchard
Comanche Public Works Authority	OK1011101	Beaver, Mud	1,649	SW	Jefferson Co. RWD #1, Stephens Co. RWD #3 (Meridian)	—
Cornish	OK3003404	Mud	41	P (GW)	—	Ringling
Davis	OK1010822	Lower Washita	2,610	SW	West Davis RWD, Western Carter Co. Water Corp.	Arbuckle Lake MCD
Dibble	OK3004709	Lower Canadian, Middle Washita, Middle Washita	550	P (SW)	—	Blanchard
Dougherty	OK1010824	Lower Washita	224	P (GW)	—	Murray Co. RWD # 1
Duncan Public Utilities Authority	OK1010809	Beaver	23,000	SW	Jefferson Co. RWD #1, Stephens Co. RWD #5	—
Durant Utilities Authority	OK1010601	Blue	15,545	SW	Bryan Co. RW&SD #5, Bryan Co. RWS & SWMD #2	—
Elmore City	OK2002521	Lower Washita	756	GW	Elmore City RW Corp.	Elmore City RW Corp.
Elmore City RW Corp.	OK3002505	Lower Washita, Middle Washita	1,107	P (SW)	Elmore City	Elmore City, Pauls Valley
Fort Towson	OK2001207	Kiamichi	611	GW	—	—
Francis	OK2006205	Lower Canadian	390	GW	—	—
Garvin	OK3004809	Red, Upper Little	150	P (SW)	—	Broken Bow PWA, McCurtain Co. RWD #7
Garvin Co. RWD #1	OK2002516	Lower Canadian, Lower Washita, Middle Washita	1,445	GW	—	—
Garvin Co. RWD #2	OK2002514	Lower Washita, Middle Washita	1,570	GW	—	—

Water Systems

System	PWSID	Watershed(s)	Residential Customers Served[1]	Source(s) of Supply[2]	Water Sales	Water Purchases
Garvin Co. RWD #4	OK3002503	Lower Washita, Middle Washita	1,340	P (SW)	—	Pauls Valley
Garvin Co. RWD #6 (SW Purchase)	OK3002515	Lower Washita	862	P (SW)	—	Wynnewood Water & Light
Garvin Co. RWD # 6 (Wells)	OK2002511	Lower Canadian, Lower Washita	2,762	GW	—	Wynnewood Water & Light
Goldsby Water Authority Trust	OK2004707	Lower Canadian, Middle Canadian	2,000	GW	—	Newcastle
Grady Co. RWD #1	OK2002604	Middle Washita	300	GW	—	—
Grady Co. RWD #2	OK2002605	Middle Washita	455	GW	—	Grady Co. RWD #6
Grady Co. RWD #3	OK2002607	Middle Washita	80	GW	—	—
Grady Co. RWD #6	OK3002603	Middle Canadian, Middle Washita	3,930	GW	Grady Co. RWD #2	Chickasha Municipal Authority, Tuttle
Grady Co. RWD #7 (Ninnekah)	OK2002633	Lower Washita, Middle Washita, Middle Washita	2,425	GW	—	—
Haileyville	OK3006111	Lower Canadian	889	P (SW)	—	Pittsburg Co. Water Authority
Hartshorne	OK3006101	Lower Canadian	2,300	P (SW)	—	Pittsburg Co. Water Authority
Haskell Co. Water Company	OK1020301	Lower Arkansas, Lower Canadian, Poteau	3,000	SW	Keota PWA, Quinton	Stigler
Haworth PWA	OK3004810	Red	354	P (SW)	—	Broken Bow PWA, McCurtain Co. RWD #1
Healdton	OK1011102	Mud, Walnut Bayou	2,785	GW/SW	—	Jefferson Co. RWD #1
Heavener Utility Auth/PSG	OK1020101	Poteau	3,300	SW	—	PVIA
Hughes Co. RWD #2	OK1010414	Lower Canadian, Muddy Boggy	1,145	GW	—	—
Hughes Co. RWD #4	OK3003203	Lower Canadian	800	P (GW)	—	Hughes Co. RWD #6 (Gerty)
Hughes Co. RWD #6 (Gerty)	OK2003224	Lower Canadian, Muddy Boggy	1,380	GW	Hughes Co. RWD #4	—
Hugo Municipal Authority	OK1010314	Kiamichi, Red	5,536	SW	Choctaw Co. RWD #1, Choctaw Co. RWSG & SWMD #3	—
Idabel PWA	OK1010203	Little, Red, Upper Little	6,952	SW	—	Broken Bow PWA
Indianola RWD #18	OK3006110	Lower Canadian	2,000	P (SW)	—	Pittsburg Co. PWA (Crowder)
Jefferson Co. RWD #1	OK3003401	Beaver, Lower Washita, Mud, Red, Walnut Bayou	8,276	GW	Healdton, Ringling, Ryan Utilities Authority, Stephens Co. RWD #4 (Loco), Terral, Wilson Municipal Authority	Comanche PWA, Duncan Public Utilities Authority, Stephens Co. RWD #4 (Loco), Waurika PWA, Wilson Municipal Authority
Johnston Co. RWD #3	OK2003511	Blue, Clear Boggy, Red	2,783	GW	Milburn PWA, Ravia	—
Johnston Co. RWS& SWMD #4	OK2003503	Blue, Clear Boggy	600	GW	—	—
Kenefic	OK2000701	Blue	165	GW	—	Bryan Co. RWD #6
Keota PWA	OK3003112	Lower Arkansas	564	P (SW)	—	Haskell Co. Water Company, PVIA
Kingston PWA	OK2004501	Red	1,600	GW	—	Marshall County Water Corp.
Kiowa	OK1020611	Muddy Boggy	731	SW	Pittsburg Co. RWD #11 (Kiowa)	—
Krebs Utility Authority	OK1020606	Lower Canadian	2,051	SW	—	—

Water Systems

System	PWSID	Watershed(s)	Residential Customers Served[1]	Source(s) of Supply[2]	Water Sales	Water Purchases
Latimer Co. RWD #1	OK3003904	Lower Canadian, Poteau	2,750	P (SW)	—	Wilburton
Latimer Co. RWD #2	OK3003903	Kiamichi	1,500	P (SW)	—	Sardis Lake Water Authority, Talihina PWA
Latimer Co. RWD #3	OK3003908	Kiamichi, Poteau	175	P (SW)	—	Talihina PWA
Latimer Co. RWD #4	OK1020110	Lower Arkansas, Poteau	412	SW	—	—
LeFlore Co. Consolidated RWD #1	OK3004040	Poteau	1,800	P (SW)	—	PVIA
LeFlore Co. RWD #1	OK3004003	Poteau	1,758	P (SW)	—	PVIA
LeFlore Co. RWD #2	OK3004007	Poteau	4,700	P (SW)	—	PVIA
LeFlore Co. RWD #3	OK3004006	Kiamichi	1,643	P (SW)	—	Talihina PWA
LeFlore Co. RWD #5	OK3004010	Poteau	1,593	P (SW)	—	PVIA
LeFlore Co. RWD #14	OK3004001	Lower Arkansas, Poteau	9,077	P (SW)	Spiro	PVIA
LeFlore Co. RWD #15	OK3004046	Kiamichi, Mountain Fork, Poteau	425	P (SW)	—	PVIA
LeFlore Co. RWD #17	OK3004048	Kiamichi, Mountain Fork	373	P (SW)	—	—
Lehigh	OK2001501	Muddy Boggy	396	GW	—	—
Leon RWD #1 (Love County)	OK2004302	Red	300	GW	—	—
Lindsay PWA	OK2002501	Middle Washita	2,850	GW	—	—
Lone Grove	OK2001007	Lower Washita, Red, Walnut Bayou	4,863	GW	—	Ardmore
Longtown RW&SD #1 (Pittsburg Co.)	OK1020623	Lower Canadian	5,444	SW	Pittsburg Co. RWD #20 (Carlton Landing)	—
Madill	OK1010820	Red	3,410	SW	Marshall County Water Corp., Oakland PWA	Marshall County Water Corp.
Mannsville Public Works Authority	OK2003505	Red	587	GW	—	Marshall County Water Corp.
Marietta PWA	OK2004301	Red	2,626	GW	—	—
Marlow PWA	OK2006907	Beaver, Lower Washita	4,600	GW	—	—
Marshall County Water Corp.	OK1010848	Red	14,717	SW	Kingston PWA, Madill, Mannsville PWA	Madill
Maysville	OK1010807	Middle Washita	1,212	SW	—	—
McAlester PWA	OK1020609	Lower Canadian	18,206	SW	Pittsburg Co. RWD #16, Pittsburg Co. RWD #5, Pittsburg Co. RWD #6 (Alderson), Pittsburg Co. RWD #7 (Arpelar), Pittsburg Co. RWD #9 (McAlester)	—
McClain Co. RWD # 8	OK2004711	Lower Canadian, Lower Washita, Middle Washita	1,897	GW	—	—
McCurtain Co. RWD #1	OK3004806	Little, Red, Upper Little	3,842	P (SW)	Haworth PWA	Broken Bow PWA
McCurtain Co. RWD #2	OK3004814	Red, Upper Little	755	P (SW)	—	Broken Bow PWA
McCurtain Co. RWD #5 (Hochatown)	OK3004804	Mountain Fork, Upper Little	1,614	P (SW)	—	Broken Bow PWA
McCurtain Co. RWD #6 (Kiamichi)	OK3004817	Mountain Fork	600	P (SW)	—	Broken Bow PWA
McCurtain Co. RWD #7	OK3004801	Little, Red, Upper Little	1,847	P (SW)	Garvin	Broken Bow PWA
McCurtain Co. RWD #8 (Mt. Fork Water)	OK1010207	Little, Mountain Fork, Upper Little	5,685	SW	—	Broken Bow PWA

Water Systems

System	PWSID	Watershed(s)	Residential Customers Served[1]	Source(s) of Supply[2]	Water Sales	Water Purchases
McCurtain Co. RWD #9	OK3004820	Upper Little	999	P (SW)	—	Broken Bow PWA
McCurtain Municipal Authority	OK3003101	Lower Arkansas, Poteau	560	P (SW)	—	PVIA
Milburn Public Works Authority	OK2003520	Blue, Red	317	P (GW)	—	Johnston Co. RWD #3
Mill Creek	OK2003501	Red	310	GW	—	—
Minco	OK2002610	Middle Canadian	1,632	GW	—	—
Murray Co. RWD # 1	OK2005012	Blue, Lower Canadian, Lower Washita, Red	4,500	GW	Buckhorn RWD #2, Dougherty	Sulphur
Newcastle	OK2004704	Lower Canadian, Middle Canadian	7,900	GW	Blanchard, Goldsby Water Auth., Tuttle	—
Norge Water Co	OK3002601	Middle Washita	890	P (SW)	—	Chickasha Municipal Authority
Oakland PWA	OK3004513	Red	1,050	P (SW)	—	Madill
PVIA	OK1020104	Poteau	6,500	SW	Bokoshe PWA, Cameron PWA, Heavener Utility Auth./PSG, Keota PWA, LeFlore Co. Consolidated RWD #1, LeFlore Co. RWD #1, LeFlore Co. RWD #14, LeFlore Co. RWD #15, LeFlore Co. RWD #2, LeFlore Co. RWD #5, McCurtain Municipal Authority, Panama PWA, Poteau PWA, Spiro, Spiro East Water Association, Water Distributors, Inc., Wister	—
Panama PWA	OK3004016	Poteau	1,400	P (SW)	—	PVIA
Paoli	OK2002502	Middle Washita	610	GW	—	—
Pauls Valley	OK1010808	Lower Washita	6,256	SW	Elmore City RW Corp., Garvin Co. RWD #4	—
Phillips RWD #1	OK3001503	Muddy Boggy	140	P (SW)	—	Coalgate PWA
Pittsburg	OK1020604	Lower Canadian	280	SW	—	—
Pittsburg Co. PWA (Crowder)	OK1020603	Lower Canadian	2,203	SW	Indianola RWD #18	—
Pittsburg Co. RWD #5	OK3006115	Lower Canadian	1,750	P (SW)	—	McAlester PWA
Pittsburg Co. RWD #6 (Alderson)	OK3006109	Lower Canadian	300	P (SW)	—	McAlester PWA
Pittsburg Co. RWD #7 (Arpelar)	OK3006108	Lower Canadian	1,900	P (SW)	—	McAlester PWA
Pittsburg Co. RWD #9 (McAlester)	OK3006107	Lower Canadian	872	P (SW)	—	McAlester PWA
Pittsburg Co. RWD #11 (Kiowa)	OK3006105	Lower Canadian	790	P (SW)	Atoka Co. RWD #1 (Wardville)	Kiowa
Pittsburg Co. RWD #14	OK1020625	Lower Arkansas, Lower Canadian	1,680	SW	—	—
Pittsburg Co. RWD #16	OK3006106	Lower Canadian	1,268	P (SW)	—	McAlester PWA
Pittsburg Co. RWD #20 (Carlton Landing)	OK3006139	Lower Canadian	38	P (SW)	—	Longtown RW&SD #1 (Pittsburg Co.)
Pittsburg Co. Water Authority	OK1020616	Lower Canadian	26	SW	Adamson RWD #8, Haileyville, Hartshorne	—
Pontotoc Co. RWD # 1 (Homer)	OK3006205	Clear Boggy, Lower Canadian, Muddy Boggy	441	P (GW)	—	Ada
Pontotoc Co. RWD # 6 (Fittstown)	OK3006222	Blue, Clear Boggy	896	P (GW)	—	Ada

Water Systems

System	PWSID	Watershed(s)	Residential Customers Served[1]	Source(s) of Supply[2]	Water Sales	Water Purchases
Pontotoc Co. RWD # 7	OK3006215	Clear Boggy, Lower Canadian, Muddy Boggy	1,950	P (GW)	—	Ada
Pontotoc Co. RWD # 8	OK2006215	Blue, Clear Boggy, Lower Canadian	4,250	GW	Pontotoc Co. RWD # 9	Wingard Water Corp.
Pontotoc Co. RWD # 9	OK3006218	Clear Boggy	1,162	P (GW)	Tupelo PWA	Ada, Pontotoc Co. RWD # 8
Poteau PWA	OK3004015	Poteau	7,939	P (SW)	—	PVIA
Purcell	OK2004701	Lower Canadian, Lower Canadian, Middle Canadian, Middle Washita	8,118	GW	—	—
Pushmataha Co. RWD #1	OK3006403	Kiamichi	1,200	P (SW)	—	Sardis Lake Water Authority
Pushmataha Co. RWD #2 (Albion)	OK3006402	Kiamichi	959	P (SW)	—	Talihina PWA
Pushmataha Co. RWD #3	OK1010318	Kiamichi, Muddy Boggy, Upper Little	4,825	SW	Soper	—
Pushmataha Co. RWD #5 (Nashoba)	OK3006410	Kiamichi, Upper Little	725	P (SW)	—	Sardis Lake Water Authority
Quinton	OK3006123	Lower Arkansas	1,071	P (SW)	—	Haskell Co. Water Company
Ratliff City	OK3001004	Lower Washita	131	P (SW)	—	Western Carter Co. Water Corp.
Ravia	OK2003504	Red	459	GW	—	Johnston Co. RWD #3
Red Oak PWA	OK1020105	Poteau	581	SW	Water Distributors, Inc.	—
Ringling	OK2003404	Mud	1,200	GW	Cornish	Jefferson Co. RWD #1
Roff	OK2006206	Blue	850	GW	—	—
Roundhill RWD #4	OK3001504	Muddy Boggy	219	P (SW)	—	Coalgate PWA
Rush Springs	OK2002609	Lower Washita	1,278	GW	—	—
Ryan Utilities Authority	OK3003405	Beaver, Red	800	P (SW)	—	Jefferson Co. RWD #1, Waurika PWA
Sardis Lake Water Authority	OK1010319	Kiamichi	307	SW	Clayton PWA, Latimer Co. RWD #2, Pushmataha Co. RWD #1, Pushmataha Co. RWD #5 (Nashoba)	—
Savanna	OK3006104	Lower Canadian	800	P (SW)	—	—
Soper	OK2001201	Muddy Boggy	300	GW	—	Pushmataha Co. RWD #3
Southern Okla. Water Corp.	OK1010830	Lower Washita, Red, Walnut Bayou	14,000	SW/GW	Ardmore	Ardmore
Spiro	OK1020106	Lower Arkansas, Poteau	2,200	SW	—	LeFlore Co. RWD #14, PVIA
Spiro East Water Association	OK3004005	Lower Arkansas, Poteau	1,817	P (SW)	—	PVIA
Stephens Co. RW&SD #1	OK2006906	Lower Washita, Mud	960	GW	—	—
Stephens Co. RWD #3 (Meridian)	OK2006905	Beaver	1,610	GW	—	Comanche PWA
Stephens Co. RWD #4 (Loco)	OK2006904	Mud	122	GW	Jefferson Co. RWD #1	Jefferson Co. RWD #1
Stephens Co. RWD #5	OK2006969	Beaver, Lower Washita, Mud	6,426	GW	—	Duncan Public Utilities Authority
Stigler	OK1020303	Lower Arkansas	2,731	SW	Haskell Co. Water Company	—
Stonewall PWA	OK2006203	Clear Boggy	465	GW	—	—
Stratford	OK2002503	Lower Canadian	1,575	GW	—	—

Water Systems

System	PWSID	Watershed(s)	Residential Customers Served[1]	Source(s) of Supply[2]	Water Sales	Water Purchases
Stringtown PWA	OK3000303	Kiamichi, Muddy Boggy	1,105	P (SW)	—	Atoka Co. RWS & SWMD #4
Sulphur	OK2005001	Lower Washita	5,000	GW	Buckhorn RWD #2, Murray Co. RWD # 1	—
Talihina PWA	OK1010304	Kiamichi	1,297	SW	Latimer Co. RWD #2, Latimer Co. RWD #3, LeFlore Co. RWD #3, Pushmataha Co. RWD #2 (Albion)	—
Terral	OK2003405	Red	386	GW	—	Jefferson Co. RWD #1
Thackerville	OK2004303	Red	2,000	GW	—	—
Tishomingo Municipal Authority	OK1010815	Red	3,100	SW	—	—
Tupelo PWA	OK3001506	Clear Boggy	377	P (GW)	—	Pontotoc Co. RWD # 9
Tuttle	OK2002608	Middle Canadian	4,500	GW	Blanchard, Grady Co. RWD #6	Blanchard, Newcastle
Valliant PWA	OK3004812	Red, Upper Little	971	P (SW)	Choctaw Co. RWD #2	Broken Bow PWA
Wapanucka	OK2003518	Clear Boggy	198	GW	—	—
Washington	OK2004703	Lower Canadian	600	GW	—	—
Water Distributors, Inc.	OK3004009	Poteau	3,875	P (SW)	—	PVIA, Red Oak PWA
Waurika Public Works Authority	OK1011201	Beaver	2,100	SW	Jefferson Co. RWD #1, Ryan Utilities Authority	—
Wayne	OK2004702	Lower Canadian, Middle Washita	688	GW	—	—
West Davis RWD	OK3005004	Lower Washita	492	GW	—	Davis, Western Carter Co. Water Corp.
Western Carter Co. Water Corp.	OK2001003	Lower Washita, Mud, Walnut Bayou	658	GW	Ratliff City, West Davis RWD	Davis
Wilburton	OK1020103	Lower Canadian, Poteau	3,025	SW	Latimer Co. RWD #1	—
Wilson Municipal Authority	OK2001001	Walnut Bayou	1,600	GW	Jefferson Co. RWD #1	Jefferson Co. RWD #1
Wister	OK3004014	Poteau	1,002	P (SW)	—	PVIA
Wright City PWA	OK3004811	Upper Little	792	P (SW)	—	Broken Bow PWA
Wynnewood Water & Light	OK1010812	Lower Washita	2,307	SW	Garvin Co. RWD # 6 (Wells), Garvin Co. RWD #6 (SW Purchase)	Arbuckle Lake MCD

[1]Does not include wholesale customers served through water sales.

[2]GW = Groundwater; SW = Surface Water; P = Purchased.

Data: Oklahoma Department of Environmental Quality/Safe Drinking Water Information System (December 2019), OWRB GIS (2012) and Arbuckle-Simpson Aquifer Drought Contingency Plan (November 2017)

Bibliography

Source Materials

Interviews & Manuscript Material

Manuscript Collections

"Coleman Cole Collection." Western History Collection, Choctaw Nation' Manuscript Collections at the University of Oklahoma Libraries, Norman, Oklahoma.

Interviews

Culbertson, Charline M. *Interview with William T. Culbertson*. University of Oklahoma: Western History Collections – Indian Pioneer Collection (30 April 1937). https://digital.libraries.ou.edu/WHC/pioneer.

Official Documents

Chickasaw & Choctaw Documents

Acts of the Choctaw Nation: October and November 1883, October 1892, October 1893, and October 1894.

Chickasaw Nation and Davis A. Homer. *Constitution and Laws of the Chickasaw Nation: Together with the Treaties of 1832, 1833, 1834, 1837, 1852, 1855 and 1866*. Parsons, Kansas: The Foley Railway Printing Company (1899).

Choctaw Nation of Oklahoma. *Acts and Resolutions of the General Council of the Choctaw Nation Passed at its Regular Session, 1898, and its Special Session, 1899*. Caddo Indian Territory: The Herald Press (1899).

———. *The Constitution and Laws of the Choctaw Nation*. Park Hill, Cherokee Nation: Mission Press (Edwin Archer, printer) (1847).

Choctaw Nation of Oklahoma and A.R. Durant, ed. *Constitution and Laws of the Choctaw Nation: Together with the Treaties of 1837, 1855, 1865 and 1866*. Dallas, Texas: John F. Worley (1894).

"Wapanucka Academy." Binders, Local Histories, Narratives and Articles. Holisso Research Center at the Chickasaw Cultural Center, Sulphur, Oklahoma.

Federal Documents

U.S. Office of Indian Affairs. "Annual Report of the Commissioner of Indian Affairs for the Year 1884." Government Publishing Office (1884).

Senate Document No. 145: "Report on Hugo Reservoir, Kiamichi River, Oklahoma." 87th Congress, 2nd Session (1962).

Secondary Materials

Books, Journals, Pamphlets & Articles

Akers, Donna L. *Living in the Land of Death: The Choctaw Nation, 1830 – 1860*. Michigan State University Press (2004).

Aldridge, Reginald. *Ranch Notes in Kansas, Colorado, the Indian Territory and Northern Texas*. London: Longmans, Green, and Co. (1884).

Benson, Henry Clark. *Life Among the Choctaw Indians*. Cincinnati, Ohio: L. Swormstedt and A. Poe (1860).

Brown, Opal Hartsell. Murray County, Oklahoma: *In the Heart of Eden*. Wichita Falls, Texas: Nortex Press (1977).

Brown, Opal Hartsell and Richard G. Garrity. *City of Many Facets*. Oklahoma City, Oklahoma: Western Heritage Books (1981).

Burris, George W. "Reminiscences of Old Stonewall." *The Chronicles of Oklahoma* 20(2): 152–158 (June 1942).

Cobb-Greetham, Amanda J. *Listening to Our Grandmothers' Stories: The Bloomfield Academy for Chickasaw Females, 1852 –1949*. University of Nebraska Press (2007).

Cushman, Horatio B. *History of the Choctaw, Chickasaw and Natchez Indians*. Greenville, Texas: Headlight Printing House (1899).

Dary, David. *Stories of Old-Time Oklahoma*. University of Oklahoma Press (2013).

Debo, Angie. *And Still the Waters Run: The Betrayal of the Five Civilized Tribes*. Princeton University Press (1973).

———. *The Rise and Fall of the Choctaw Republic*. University of Oklahoma Press (1961).

Driscoll, Fletcher G. *Groundwater and Wells*, 2nd ed. New Brighton, Minnesota: Johnson Screens (1986).

Faiman-Silva, Sandra. *Choctaws at the Crossroads: The Political Economy of Class and Culture in the Oklahoma Timber Region*. University of Nebraska Press (1997).

Faulk, Odie B., Kenny A. Franks, and Paul F. Lambert, eds. *Early Military Forts and Posts in Oklahoma*. Oklahoma City, Oklahoma: Oklahoma Historical Society (1978).

Goins, Charles R. and Danney Goble. *The Historic Atlas of Oklahoma*, 4th ed. University of Oklahoma Press (2006).

Hoyt, Anne Kelley. *Bibliography of the Chickasaw*. Lanham, Maryland: Scarecrow Press (1987).

Kerr, Robert S. *Land, Wood, and Water*. New York: Fleet Publishing Corporation (1960).

Kidwell, Clara Sue. *The Choctaws in Oklahoma: From Tribe to Nation, 1855–1970*. University of Oklahoma Press (2007).

Kidwell, Clara Sue and Charles Roberts. *The Choctaws: A Critical Bibliography*. Indiana University Press (1980).

Lambert, Valerie. *Choctaw Nation: A Story of American Indian Resurgence*. University of Nebraska Press (2007).

Lewis, Anna. "Nunih Waiya." *The Chronicles of Oklahoma* 16(2): 214-21 (June 1938).

Littleheart, Oleta. *The Lure of the Indian Country and a Romance of Its Great Resort*. Sulphur, Oklahoma: A. Abbott (1908).

Mann, Charles C. *1491: New Revelations of the Americas Before Columbus*. New York: Alfred A. Knopf (2005).

Marcy, Randolph B. *The Prairie Traveler: A Hand-Book for Overland Expeditions*. New York: Cosimo Classics (2007) (originally published 1857).

Marcy, Randolph B., George B. McClellan, and ed. Grant Foreman. *Adventure on Red River: Report on the Exploration of the Headwaters of the Red River*. University of Oklahoma Press (1937).

Miles, Dennis B. "'Educate or We Perish: The Armstrong Academy's History as Part of the Choctaw Educational System." *The Chronicles of Oklahoma* 89(3): 312-37 (Fall 2011).

Miner, H. Craig. *The Corporation and the Indian: Tribal Sovereignty and Industrial Civilization in Indian Territory, 1865–1907*. University of Oklahoma Press. (1989).

Mitchell, Marshal D. *Bromide Oklahoma Centennial: From Boastown to Ghostown. Our Hometown*. Fort Worth, Texas: M.D. Mitchell (2007).

Morris, John W. *Ghost Towns of Oklahoma*. University of Oklahoma Press (1978).

Morrison, James D., and ed. Joy Culbreath and Kathy Carpenter. *Schools for the Choctaws*. Durant, Oklahoma: Ameba Publishing (2016).

Morrison, James D., and eds. James C. Milligan and L. David Norris. *The Social History of the Choctaw Nation, 1865–1907*. Durant, Oklahoma: Creative Informatics (1987).

Nuttall, Thomas. *A Journal of Travels into the Arkansas Territory During the Year 1819*. Philadelphia: Thos. H. Palmer (1821).

Ormsby, Waterman L. *The Butterfield Overland Mail*. San Marino, California: Huntington Library Press (2007).

Parent, Laurence. *Chickasaw National Recreation Area*. Tucson, Arizona: Western National Parks Association (1993).

Shirk, George H. "The Site of Old Camp Arbuckle." *The Chronicles of Oklahoma* 27(3): 313-315 (Autumn 1949).

Workers of the Writers' Program of the Work Projects Administration in the State of Oklahoma. *Oklahoma: A Guide to the Sooner State*. University of Oklahoma Press (1941).

Wright, Muriel H. "The Butterfield Overland Mail One Hundred Years Ago." *The Chronicles of Oklahoma* 35(1): 55-71 (January 1957).

——. "Initial Point and Fort Arbuckle." Oklahoma Club Woman. Oklahoma State Archives, Vertical Files (originally published March 1937).

——. *A Guide to the Indian Tribes of Oklahoma*. University of Oklahoma Press (1986).

——. "Historic Spots in the Vicinity of Tuskahoma." *The Chronicles of Oklahoma* 9(1): 27-42 (March 1931).

——. "Wapanucka Academy, Chickasaw Nation," *The Chronicles of Oklahoma* 12(4): 402-431 (December 1934).

Wright, Muriel H., and LeRoy H. Fischer. "Civil War Sites in Oklahoma." *The Chronicles of Oklahoma* 44(2): 158-215 (Summer 1966).

——. "1963 Wright and Fischer Pictorial Map of Oklahoma Civil War Sites." Created for the Oklahoma Civil War Centennial Commission. Oklahoma State Highway Commission (1963).

Wright, Muriel H., George H. Shirk, and Kenny A. Franks. *Mark of Heritage*. Oklahoma City, Oklahoma: Oklahoma Historical Society (1976).

Wright, Muriel H., and George H. Shirk. *Oklahoma Place Names*. University of Oklahoma Press (1965).

Periodicals

Antle, H. R. "The Story of Kali Homma." *Harlow's Weekly* 39, No. 27: 4-5 (1932).

Burge, Steve. "Blue River Public Hunting and Fishing Area." *Outdoor Oklahoma* (January/February 2007).

"Chickasaw Emphasis on Education Inspired Burney Institute." *The Chickasaw Times*, Vol. XXXXI No. 1 (January 2006).

"Five Civilized Nations." *American Bar Association Journal* Vol. 53, No. 4: 342–343 (April 1967) (editorial).

Lambert, Valerie. "Political Protest, Conflict, and Tribal Nationalism: The Oklahoma Choctaws and the Termination Crisis of 1959 – 1970." *American Indian Quarterly* 31, No. 2: 283-309 (2007).

Leeds, Stacy L. "Defeat or Mixed Blessing: Tribal Sovereignty and the State of Sequoyah." *Tulsa Law Review* 43, No. 1: 5-16 (2007).

Mittlestet, Aaron R., Michael D. Smolen, Garey A. Fox, and Damian C. Adams. "Comparison of Aquifer Sustainability Under Groundwater Administration in Oklahoma and Texas." *Journal of American Water Resource Association* (JAWRA) 47(2): 424-431 (March 2011).

"Tribe to Acquire Historic Burney Institute." *The Chickasaw Times* Vol. XXXXI No. 1 (January 2006).

Online Sources

Adkins-Rochette, Patricia. "Bourland in North Texas and Indian Territory During the Civil War: Fort Cobb, Fort Arbuckle & the Wichita Mountains." Bourland Civil War (24 May 2017). bourlandcivilwar.com/.

"America's Mussels: Silent Sentinels." *U.S. Fish and Wildlife Service* (updated 29 May 2019). fws.gov/midwest/endangered/clams/mussels.html.

"An Insider's Guide to McCurtain County." *Visit McCurtain County* (24 March 2017). visitmccurtaincounty.com/insiders-guide-mccurtain-county.

"Arrowhead State Park." *Oklahoma State Parks*. stateparks.com/arrowhead_state_park_in_oklahoma.html.

Bamburg, Maxine. "Tishomingo." *The Encyclopedia of Oklahoma History and Culture*. okhistory.org/publications/enc.php?entry=TI008.

"Beavers Bend State Resort Park." *Visit McCurtain County* (accessed 25 April 2020). visitmccurtaincounty.com/parks/parks-rivers-lakes/beavers-bend-state-park.

"Blanchard Consumer Confidence Report – 2019 (Covering Calendar Year 2018)." *City of Blanchard*. cityofblanchard.us/sites/g/files/vyhlif2821/f/uploads/2018_ccr.pdf.

"Blue River Public Fishing and Hunting Area – Tishomingo, Oklahoma USA." *Waymarking* (15 October 2017). waymarking.com/waymarks/WMWV5X_Blue_River_public_fishing_and_hunting_area_Tishomingo_Oklahoma_USA.

"Broken Bow Public Works Authority." *City of Broken Bow* (May 2020). cityofbrokenbow.com/public-works-authority/.

"Camp Leavenworth – Kingston, OK." *Waymarking* (20 May 2016). waymarking.com/waymarks/WMR74Q_Camp_Leavenworth_Kingston_OK.

Cathey, Michael. "Before McAlester, There Was Perryville." *McAlester News-Capital* (15 March 2019). mcalesternews.com/opinion/column-before-mcalester-there-was-perryville/article_0784e6ef-13db-5bfa-804e-700174c4ddba.html.

———. "Nanih Waiya: 'Mother Mound' and First Capital of the Choctaw Nation of Oklahoma." *McAlester News-Capital* (15 November 2019). mcalesternews.com/news/local_news/cathey-nanih-waiya-mother-mound-and-first-capital-of-the/article_beccbf98-619f-5da7-bc49-45169d4fdfbc.html.

"Chickasaw Children's Village." *The Chickasaw Nation* (accessed 11 January 2019). chickasaw.net/childrensvillage.

"Chickasaw Cultural Center – The Heartbeat of a Nation." *Chickasaw Cultural Center*. chickasawculturalcenter.com/about-us.

"Chickasaw National Capitol." *The Chickasaw Nation*. chickasaw.net/Services/Culture/Chickasaw-National-Capitol.aspx.

"Chickasaw White House." *The Chickasaw Nation* (accessed 3 November 2019). chickasaw.net/whitehouse.

Chickasaw.TV. "Arrival in Indian Territory – Fort Washita." *The Chickasaw Nation*, Chickasaw TV: Video Network (accessed 5 February 2020). chickasaw.tv/episodes/winter-fire-season-1-episode-4-arrival-in-indian-territory-fort-washita.

———. "Kullihoma: A Traditional Community." *The Chickasaw Nation*, Chickasaw TV: Video Network (accessed 19 January 2019). chickasaw.tv/videos/kullihoma-a-traditional-community.

Choctaw Nation Historic Preservation Department. "Traditional Uses of Freshwater Mussels." *The Biskinik* (February 2013).

choctawnation.com/sites/default/files/2015/10/14/2013.2_Traditional_uses_of_freshwater_mussels.pdf.

Clift, John. "Woman's Home Is All That's Left of Institute." *The Oklahoman* (24 February 1985). Oklahoman.com/article/2099434/womans-home-is-all-thats-left-of-institute.

"Climate of Oklahoma." *Oklahoma Climatological Survey*. climate.ok.gov/index.php/site/page/climate_of_oklahoma.

Cobb-Greetham, Amanda J. "Chickasaw Schools." *The Encyclopedia of Oklahoma History and Culture* (accessed 27 September 2018). okhistory.org/publications/enc/entry.php?entry=CH034.

Davis, Kendall. "A Tribute and Educational Reminder: The Burney Institute." *Lake Texoma* (accessed 23 September 2018). laketexoma.com/entertainment-a-tribute-and-educational-reminder-the-burney-institute/5159.

"Durant State Fish Hatchery – Durant, Oklahoma." *Waymarking* (18 August 2009). waymarking.com/waymarks/WM71H7_Durant_State_Fish_Hatchery_Durant_Oklahoma.

Elkin, Kimberly. "Protecting Oklahoma Watersheds." *The Nature Conservancy* (4 May 2020). nature.org/en-us/about-us/where-we-work/united-states/oklahoma/stories-in-oklahoma/protecting-watersheds/.

"Endangered Species Act – Overview." *U.S. Fish and Wildlife Service* (accessed February 2021). fws.gov/endangered/laws-policies/.

"Eufaula WMA, Oklahoma." *Outdoors Oklahoma*. outdoorsok.com/oklahoma/eufaulawma/.

"Fort Washita." *The Chickasaw Nation* (accessed 17 August 2019). chickasaw.net/fortwashita.

"Freshwater Springs – Chickasaw National Recreation Area." *U.S. National Park Service* (24 February 2015). nps.gov/chic/learn/nature/freshwatersprings.htm.

Godfrey, Ed. "Wildlife Department Continues to Add More Public Hunting Land." *The Oklahoman* (23 September 2017). oklahoman.com/article/5565218/wildlife-department-continues-to-add-more-public-hunting-land.

"Good Springs – Tishomingo, Oklahoma." *Waymarking* (2 December 2017). waymarking.com/waymarks/WMX5ZP_Good_Springs_Tishomingo_OK%20(January%202,%202019).

"Heavener Runestone Park." *Travel Oklahoma* – Oklahoma Tourism and Recreation Department. travelok.com/listings/view.profile/id.3398.

"History & Culture." *Chickasaw Country* (accessed 25 March 2020). chickasawcountry.com/history-culture.

"Indian Removal Act (May 28, 1830 CE)." *National Geographic* – This Day in Geographic History. nationalgeographic.org/thisday/may28/indian-removal-act/.

Indians at the Post Office, Native Themes in New Deal-Era Murals, Signing of the Treaty of Dancing Rabbit Creek. Smithsonian National Postal Museum. https://postalmuseum.si.edu/indiansatthepostoffice/mural22.html.

"John Taylor Beavers (1850–1936)." *Find A Grave* (accessed 25 April 2020). findagrave.com/memorial/39256627/john-taylor-beavers.

"Find a State Park" (See: Lake Murray State Park, Robbers Cave State Park, Lake Wister State Park). Travel Oklahoma – Oklahoma Tourism and Recreation Department. https://www.travelok.com/state-parks/search.

Layden, Logan. "Tribes Save Boggy Depot Park After State Spending Cuts." *StateImpact Oklahoma* (29 September 2011). stateimpact.npr.org/oklahoma/2011/09/29/tribes-save-boggy-depot-park-after-state-spending-cuts/.

"Little River National Wildlife Refuge." *Visit McCurtain County* (accessed 8 April 2020). visitmccurtaincounty.com/directory/little-river-national-wildlife-management-area/.

May, Jon D. "Fort McCulloch." *The Encyclopedia of Oklahoma History and Culture* (accessed 4 January 2020). okhistory.org/publications/enc/entry.php?entry=FO036.

———. "Black Beaver." *The Encyclopedia of Oklahoma History and Culture* (accessed 3 July 2020). okhistory.org/publications/enc/entry.php?entry=BL001.

———. "Nunih Waya." *The Encyclopedia of Oklahoma History and Culture* (accessed 29 March 2020). okhistory.org/publications/enc/entry.php?entry=NU002.

———. "Perryville." *The Encyclopedia of Oklahoma History and Culture* (accessed 14 December 2018). okhistory.org/publications/enc/entry.php?entry=PE020.

"McCurtain County Wilderness Area." *Visit McCurtain County* (accessed 25 April 2020). visitmccurtaincounty.com/parks/forests-wetlands/mccurtain-county-wilderness-area.

"Measuring Drought." *National Drought Mitigation Center* – The University of Nebraska-Lincoln (accessed 02 January 2021). drought.unl.edu/ranchplan/DroughtBasics/Weatherand-Drought/MeasuringDrought.aspx.

Miles, Dennis B. "Choctaw Schools." *The Encyclopedia of Oklahoma History and Culture* (accessed 27 March 2020). okhistory.org/publications/enc/entry.php?entry=CH049.

Moss, Bret. "OU Students Learn How Water Has Shaped Choctaw Culture, Past and Present." *The Choctaw Nation*, News and Events. choctawnation.com/news-events/press-media/ou-students-learn-how-water-has-shaped-choctaw-culture-past-and-present.

"Moundville Archaeological Park – Ancient Site." *Moundville Archaeological Park*, University of Alabama. moundville.museums.ua.edu/ancient-site/.

Rodden, Kirk A. "Murray State College." *The Encyclopedia of Oklahoma History and Culture* (accessed 20 Nov. 2020). okhistory.org/publications/enc/entry.php?entry=MU012.

"National Register of Historic Places – Index." *U.S. National Park Service* (updated 14 September 2020). nps.gov/subjects/nationalregister/index.htm.

"Nature Conservancy Acquires More than 3,000 Acres in the Arbuckle Plains." *The Daily Ardmoreite* (20 August 2016). ardmoreite.com/news/20160830/nature-conservancy-acquires-more-than-3000-acres-in-arbuckle-plains.

Noble Research Institute. "Cross Timbers Prescribed Fire Field Day" (meeting announcement). *Oklahoma Prescribed Burn Association* (February 2020). ok-pba.org/events/2020/2/6/cross-timbers-prescribed-fire-field-day.

Norris, L. David. "Colleges and Universities, Normal." *The Encyclopedia of Oklahoma History and Culture*. okhistory.org/publications/enc/entry.php?entry=CO027.

O'Dell, Larry. "Colbert's Ferry." *The Encyclopedia of Oklahoma History and Culture* (accessed 4 March 2018). Fokhistory.org/publications/enc/entry.php?entry=CO018.

———. "Little River National Wildlife Refuge." *The Encyclopedia of Oklahoma History and Culture* (accessed 17 April 2020). okhistory.org/publications/enc/entry.php?entry=LI016.

———. "Tishomingo National Wildlife Refuge." *The Encyclopedia of Oklahoma History and Culture*. okhistory.org/publications/enc/entry.php?entry=TI009.

"Oka Yanahli Preserve – Places We Protect." *The Nature Conservancy* (accessed 18 April 2018). nature.org/en-us/get-involved/how-to-help/places-we-protect/okayanahli-preserve.

Oklahoma Department of Wildlife Conservation. "Where to Fish: Blue River." *Oklahoma Department of Wildlife Conservation* (accessed April 2020). wildlifedepartment.com/fishing/wheretofish/southeast/blue-river.

Oklahoma Department of Wildlife Conservation. "Wildlife Management Areas: Alphabetical List." *Oklahoma Department of Wildlife Conservation.* (See: Atoka, Arbuckle Springs, Broken Bow, Cross Timbers, Fobb Bottom, Gary Sherrer, Grady County, Grassy Slough, Hickory Creek, Honobia Creek, Hugo, James Collins, Love Valley, McCurtain County Wilderness Area, McGee Creek, Ouachita Leflore Unit, Ouachita McCurtain Unit, Pine Creek, Pushmataha, Robbers Cave, Stringtown, Three Rivers, Whitegrass Flats, Wister, Yourman) (access dates: April 2020). wildlifedepartment.com/hunting/wma/all.

Otwell, Bob. "Groundwater – Invisible but Precious." *FLOW* (For Love of Water) (4 January 2017). flowforwater.org/groundwater-invisible-precious/.

"Ouachita National Forest." *Visit McCurtain County* (accessed 25 April 2020). visitmccurtaincounty.com/parks/forests-wetlands/ouachita-national-forest/.

Peterson, Dennis A. "Fort Coffee." *The Encyclopedia of Oklahoma History and Culture.* okhistory.org/publications/enc/entry.php?entry=FO058.

———. "Spiro Mounds." *The Encyclopedia of Oklahoma History and Culture.* okhistory.org/publications/enc/entry.php?entry=SP012.

"Pontotoc Ridge Preserve – Places We Protect." *The Nature Conservancy* (accessed 5 March 2020). nature.org/en-us/get-involved/how-to-help/places-we-protect/pontotoc-ridge-preserve/.

"Poteau Valley Improvement Authority – About PVIA." *Poteau Valley Improvement Authority* (23 June 2012). pvia.org/about/.

"Quickfacts Oklahoma – Census Bureau." *U.S. Census Bureau* (accessed 20 June 2020). https://www.census.gov/quickfacts/ok.

"Red Slough WMA." *Ducks Unlimited* (accessed 8 April 2020). ducks.org/oklahoma/oklahoma-conservation-projects/red-slough-wma.

Ruth, Kent. "Ferry on Red River Served State's Pioneering Traffic." *The Oklahoman* (5 January 1986). oklahoman.com/article/2133283/ferry-on-red-river-served-states-pioneering-traffic.

Sager, Cliff. "Florida Largemouth Bass Program." *Durant State Fish Hatchery* (presentation). rrva.org/08282017/Durant%20State%20Fish%20Hatchery.pdf.

"Sardis Lake Recreation." *U.S. Army Corps of Engineers* – Tulsa District Website (accessed 29 April 2020). swt.usace.army.mil/Locations/Tulsa-District-Lakes/Oklahoma/Sardis-Lake/Sardis-Lake-Recreation/.

"Searching for the Wild River Cane." *The Creative-Native Project* (28 May 2011). creativenativeproject.blogspot.com/2011/05/searching-for-wild-river-cane.html.

Standridge, Eric. "Fort Coffee: How an Old Fort Helped Shape Southeastern Oklahoma." *Owlcation* (2 October 2017). owlcation.com/humanities/Fort-Coffee-How-an-Old-Fort-Helped-Shape-Southeastern-Oklahoma.

———. "Skullyville, Oklahoma: Gold, Choctaws, and Covered Wagons." *Owlcation* (18 December 2017). owlcation.com/humanities/SkullyvilleOklahoma.

"Tishomingo National Fish Hatchery." *U.S. Fish and Wildlife Service* (accessed 13 November 2018). fws.gov/southwest/fisheries/tishomingo/.

Turner, Alvin O. "East Central University." *The Encyclopedia of Oklahoma History and Culture* (accessed 13 February 2019). okhistory.org/publications/enc/entry.php?entry=EA005.

"Wapanucka Institute – Chickasaw Rock Academy." *The Gateway to Oklahoma History* – The Oklahoma Historical Society (12 November 2013). gateway.okhistory.org/ark:/67531/metadc228604/.

Weiser-Alexander, Kathy. "Fort McCulloch, Oklahoma." *Legends of America* (February 2020). legendsofamerica.com/fort-mcculloch-oklahoma/.

"Welcome to Hugo Lake." *United States Army Corp of Engineers* – Tulsa District Website (accessed 29 April 2020). swt.usace.army.mil/Locations/Tulsa-District-Lakes/Oklahoma/Hugo-Lake/.

Wertz, Joe. "The Five Most Expensive State Parks in Oklahoma." *StateImpact Oklahoma* (15 September 2011). stateimpact.npr.org/oklahoma/2011/09/15/the-five-most-expensive-state-parks-in-oklahoma/.

"Wheelock Academy Historic Site." *Choctaw Nation of Oklahoma Cultural Services* (accessed 27 March 2020). choctawnation-culture.com/wheelock/wheelock-academy-historic-site.aspx.

Whitecotton, Karen. "Lake Murray State Park." *The Encyclopedia of Oklahoma History and Culture.* okhistory.org/publications/enc/entry.php?entry=LA008.

"Wildlife Commission Tours Durant State Fish Hatchery." *The Tulsa World* (13 September 2013) (updated 31 August 2020). tulsaworld.com/communities/skiatook/news/wildlife-commission-tours-durant-state-fish-hatchery/article_e41ca114-c514-5ab3-b348-9564004bcdbf.html.

"Wildlife Sanctuary Offers Unique View of the Chickasaw Nation." *The Chickasaw Nation* (accessed 10 October 2018). chickasaw.net/News/Press-Releases/Release/Wildlife-sanctuary-offers-unique-view-of-the-Chick-1503.aspx

Water Planning & Related Studies (including online sources)

Aqua Strategies, Inc. "Regional Asset Management System Infrastructure Summary." Choctaw and Chickasaw Regional Water Plan (September 2015).

Becker, Mark F. and Runkle, Donna L. "Hydrogeology, Water Quality & Geochemistry of the Rush Springs Aquifer, Western Oklahoma." U.S. Geological Survey, Water-Resources Investigation Report 98-4081 (1998).

Belden, Mark. "Hydrogeologic Report of the El Reno, Fairview, Isabella, and Loyal Minor Groundwater Basins in Central Oklahoma." Oklahoma Water Resources Board Technical Report 2000-1 (March 2000).

Bingham, Roy H. and Robert L. Moore. "Hydrologic Atlas 4: Reconnaissance of the Water Resources of the Oklahoma City Quadrangle, Central Oklahoma." U.S. Geological Survey, Oklahoma Geological Survey (1975; reprinted 2004).

Bingham, Roy H., and DeRoy L. Bergman. "Hydrologic Atlas 7: Reconnaissance of the Water Resources of the Enid Quadrangle North Central Oklahoma." U.S. Geological Survey, Oklahoma Geological Survey (1980).

Castro, Antonio J. et al. "Social Perception and Supply of Ecosystem Services: A Watershed Approach for Carbon Related Ecosystem Services." *Biodiversity in Ecosystems – Linking Structure and Function.* Universidad Publica de Navarra, Spain (2015).

Chickasaw Nation and Choctaw Nation of Oklahoma. "Essentials 2.0." Produced for use by Chickasaw Nation and Choctaw Nation of Oklahoma (2017) (unpublished).

Christenson, Scott C., David L. Parkhurst, and Roy W. Fairchild. "Geohydrology and Water Quality of the Roubidoux Aquifer, Northeastern Oklahoma." Oklahoma Geological Survey, Open-File Report 90-570 (1990).

Christenson, Scott C., Noel I. Osborn, Christopher R. Neel, Jason R. Faith, Charles D. Blome, James Puckette, and Michael P. Pantea. "Hydrogeology and Simulation of Groundwater Flow in the Arbuckle Simpson Aquifer, Southcentral Oklahoma." U.S. Geological Survey, Scientific Investigation Report 2011-5029 (2011).

Chickasaw and Choctaw Nations, Duane Smith & Associates, and AquaStrategies, Inc. "Arbuckle-Simpson Aquifer Drought Contingency Plan." (November 2017).

Dean, Kyle D. "Estimating the Oklahoma Economic Impact of the Chickasaw Nation." Steven C. Agee Economic Research & Policy Institute (2012).

———. "The Statewide Impacts of Oklahoma Tribes." Steven C Agee Economic Research & Policy Institute (2012)

D'Lugosz, Joseph L., Roger G. McClaflin, and Melvin V. Marcher. "Geohydrology of the Vamoosa-Ada Aquifer East Central Oklahoma." Oklahoma Geological Survey, Circular 87 (1986).

Ellis, John, H., Shana L. Mashburn, Grant M. Graves, Steven M. Peterson, S. Jerrod Smith, Lelend T. Fuhrig, Derrick L. Wagner, and Jon E. Sanford. "Hydrogeology and Simulation of Groundwater Flow and Analysis of Projected Water Use for the Canadian River Alluvial Aquifer, Western and Central Oklahoma." U.S. Geological Survey, Scientific Investigation Report 2016-5180 (March 2017).

Evans, R.E and Associates. "A Study of the Impact of the Hugo Reservoir on Choctaw and Pushmataha Counties: A View Four Years After Completion." Institute for Water Research, Research Report 80-R1 (April 1980).

Greeley, Benjamin Betke. "Groundwater Resources of Southern Comanche County, Southwestern Oklahoma" (MS Thesis). Oklahoma State University (1986).

Hanson, Ronald L. and Steven W. Cates. "Hydrogeology of the Chickasaw National Recreation Area, Murray County, Oklahoma." U.S. Geological Survey, Water-Resources Investigations Report 94-4102 (1994).

Hart, Donald L. and Robert E. Davis. "Geohydrology of the Antlers Aquifer (Cretaceous), Southern Oklahoma." Oklahoma Geological Survey, Circular 81 (1981).

Havens, John S. "Reconnaissance of Ground Water in Vicinity of Wichita Mountains Southwestern Oklahoma." Oklahoma Geological Survey, Circular 85 (1983).

———. "Reconnaissance of the Water Resources of the Lawton Quadrangle, Southwestern Oklahoma." U.S. Geological Survey, Open-File Report 96-376, Hydrologic Atlas 6 (1996).

Johnson, William K. and Richard J. DiBuono. "Authorized and Operating Purposes of Corps of Engineers Reservoirs." U.S. Army Corps of Engineers, Washington D.C. (July 1992) (revised November 1994).

Kent, Douglas C. and Lester Duckwitz. "Evaluation of Aquifer Performance and Water Supply Capabilities of the Isolated Terrace (Gerty Sand) in Garvin, McClain and Pontotoc Counties." Oklahoma Water Resources Board in partnership with Oklahoma State University (April 1987).

Kottek, M., J. Grieser, C. Beck, B. Rudolf, and F. Rubel. "World Map of the Köppen-Geiger Climate Classification Updated." Meteorol. Z., Vol. 15, No. 3, 259-263 (June 2006).

"Lindsay Public Works Authority – Consumer Confidence Report, 2019 (Covering Calendar Year 2018)." City of Lindsay, Oklahoma (1 November 2019).

Manandhar, Sharmina. "Boggy Depot State Park operations unchanged under Chickasaw Nation management." The Chickasaw Nation. https://www.chickasaw.net/News/Press-Releases/Release/Boggy-Depot-State-Park-operations-unchanged-under-1187.aspx. (September 12, 2011).

Mashburn, Shana L. and Jessica S. Magers. "Water Levels in the Garber Wellington (Central Oklahoma) Aquifer, 1986–87 to 2009." U.S. Geological Survey Presentation at the Oklahoma Governor's Water Conference (November 2009).

Mashburn, Shana L., Derek W. Ryter, Christopher R. Neel, S. Jerrod Smith and Jessica S. Magers. "Hydrogeology and Simulation of Groundwater Flow in the Central Oklahoma (Garber-Wellington) Aquifer, Oklahoma, 1987–2009 and Simulation of Available Water in Storage, 2010–2059." U.S. Geological Survey, Scientific Report 2013-5219 (2014).

Mogg, Joe L., Stuart L. Schoff, and E.W. Reed. "Groundwater Resources of Canadian County, Oklahoma." Oklahoma Geological Survey, Bulletin 87 (1960).

Oklahoma Department of Environmental Quality (ODEQ). "Water Quality in Oklahoma: 2016 Integrated Report." ODEQ (2016).

Oklahoma Water Resources Board (OWRB). "2012 Oklahoma Comprehensive Water Plan Executive Report." OWRB, University of Oklahoma Printing Services (February 2012).

———. "2015 Oklahoma Lakes Report: Beneficial Use Monitoring Program." OWRB (2015).

———. "2015 Oklahoma Streams Report: Beneficial Use Monitoring Program." OWRB (2015).

———. "2016 Oklahoma Lakes Report: Beneficial Use Monitoring Program." OWRB (2016).

———. "2016 Oklahoma Streams Report: Beneficial Use Monitoring Program." OWRB (2016).

———. "Chapter 45: Oklahoma's Water Quality Standards." OWRB (unofficial publication 2017).

———. "Hydrographic Survey: North Boggy Creek Stream System, Oklahoma." OWRB (1958).

———. "Oklahoma's Water Atlas." OWRB, Publication No. 120 (November 1984).

Oklahoma Water Resources Board and Oklahoma Department of Wildlife Conservation. "Lakes of Oklahoma," Second and Third Editions. OWRB (2012/2015).

Oliver, Wade, Jevon Harding, and Daniel Lupton. "Development of a Groundwater Model for the Antlers Aquifer in Southeastern Oklahoma." Prepared for the Chickasaw and Choctaw Nations as part of the Choctaw and Chickasaw Regional Water Plan. Intera Inc. (2013).

Osborn, Alan J. and Ralph J. Hartley. Archeological Survey within the Chickasaw National Recreation Area, Murray County, Oklahoma." National Park Service (Midwest Archeological Center), Technical Report No. 108 (2008).

Osborn, Noel I. "Hydrogeologic Investigation Report of the Boone Groundwater Basin, Northeastern Oklahoma." Oklahoma Water Resources Board, Technical Report GW 2001-2 (July 2001).

Osborn, Noel I., and Ray H. Hardy. "Statewide Groundwater Vulnerability Map of Oklahoma." Oklahoma Water Resources Board, Technical Report 99-1 (January 1999).

Ryder, Paul D. "Ground Water Atlas of the United States – Oklahoma, Texas – Alluvial Aquifers Along Major Streams." U.S. Geological Survey, HA 730-E: 11-16 (1996).

———. "Ground Water Atlas of the United States – Oklahoma, Texas – Aquifers of Paleozoic Rocks." U.S. Geological Survey, HA 730-E: 117-129 (1996).

Southern Climate Impact Planning Program (SCIPP). "Simple Planning Tool for Oklahoma Climate Hazards." L. T. Kos and R. E. Riley, eds. SCIPP (2018).

Smith, Jerrod S., Staley T. Paxton, Scott Christenson, Robert W. Puls, and James R. Greer. "Flow Contribution and Water Quality with Depth in a Test Hole and Public Supply Wells: Implications for Arsenic Remediation through Well Modification, Norman, Oklahoma 2003–2006." U.S. Environmental Protection Agency, Washington D.C., EPA/600/R-09/036 (October 2009).

U.S. Department of Interior, U.S. Bureau of Reclamation, and Intera Incorporated. "Technical Report: Chickasaw and Choctaw Nations Disinfection By-Product Study." (April 2016).

Vaughn, Caryn C., Jason P. Julian, Carla L. Atkinson, and Kiza Gates. "Environmental Flow Considerations for Freshwater Mussels: Droughts, Dams, Timing, and Temperature" (presentation). U.S. Fish and Wildlife Service.

"Water Quality Report (2017 Consumer Confidence Report)." Jefferson Rural Water District #1 (2017).

Wilkins, Kent. "Hydrologic Investigation Report of the Kiamichi, Potato Hills, Broken Bow, Pine Mountain and Holly Creek Minor Bedrock Groundwater Basins in Southeast Oklahoma." Oklahoma Water Resources Board (January 2001).

———. "Hydrologic Report of the East-Central Oklahoma Minor Bedrock and Groundwater Basin in Seminole,

Hughes and Okfuskee Counties." Oklahoma Water Resources Board, Technical Report 97-2 (January 1997).

———. "Hydrologic Report of the Marietta Minor, Texoma Minor and the Woodbine Minor Bedrock Groundwater Aquifers." Oklahoma Water Resources Board (February 2014).

———. "Hydrogeologic Report of the Northeastern Oklahoma Minor Groundwater Basin and the Neosho River Minor Groundwater Basin." Oklahoma Water Resources Board, Technical Report 97-3 (June 1997).

———. "Hydrogeologic Report of the Pennsylvanian Minor Groundwater Basin and the Ashland Isolated Terrace Groundwater Basin in Coal, Pittsburg and Haskell Counties." Oklahoma Water Resources Board (January 1997).

———. "Hydrologic Report of the Woodbine, Marietta and Texoma Minor Bedrock Groundwater Basins and the Haworth Terrace and Little River Alluvial and Terrace Minor Groundwater Basins." Oklahoma Water Resources Board, Technical Report 99-2 (July 1998).

Wood, P.R., and L.C. Burton. "Ground-Water Resources Cleveland and Oklahoma Counties." Oklahoma Geological Survey, Circular 71 (1968).

Miscellaneous

Addington, Donna, ed. *The Sardis Lake History*. (unpublished 1998).

Barker, Steve and Oklahoma Department of Commerce. "2012 Demographic State of the State Report: Oklahoma State and County Population Projections Through 2075." *Oklahoma Department of Commerce* (2012).

Fortney, Jeffrey Lee. *Robert M. Jones and the Choctaw Nation: Indigenous Nationalism in the American South, 1820–1877* (PhD Dissertation). University of Oklahoma (2014).

Matthews, William J. and Edie Marsh-Matthews. "Fishes of Concern in the Upper Blue River, Johnston County, Oklahoma, and Suggestions for Conservation Actions." University of Oklahoma (unsolicited report to the Oklahoma Department of Wildlife Conservation) (15 January 2018).

U.S. Army Corps of Engineers – Tulsa District: Aimee Jordan, Water Supply Specialist, Technical Services Section (email correspondence re: water supply storage and yield of USACE Oklahoma projects) (August 2019 and June 2021).

U.S. Geological Survey. "Digital Datasets that Describe Aquifer Characteristics of Selected Aquifers in Oklahoma." U.S. Geological Survey, Open File Reports 96-443 through 96-454.

Watkins, Bradley W. *Reconstructing the Choctaw Nation of Oklahoma, 1894–1898: Landscape Settlement on the Eve of Allotment* (PhD Thesis). Oklahoma State University (2007).

Wray, Jacilee and Alexandra J. Roberts. *An Ethnohistory of the Relationship between the Community of Sulphur, Oklahoma and Chickasaw National Recreation Area*. U.S. Department of the Interior, National Park Service (July 2004).

Woods, A.J., J.M. Omernik, D.R. Butler, J.G. Ford, J.E. Henley, B.W. Hoagland, D.S. Arndt, and B.C. Moran. "Ecoregions of Oklahoma" (color poster with map, descriptive text, summary tables, and photographs). *U.S. Geological Survey*, Reston, Virginia (2005) (map scale 1:1,250,000).